1999

Strategy Synthesis
Resolving Strategy
Paradoxes to Create
Competitive Advantage

If you are interested in keeping up with the latest developments in strategy visit:
http://www.dewit-meyer.com

Strategy Synthesis
Resolving Strategy Paradoxes to Create Competitive Advantage

Bob de Wit

Maastricht School of Management
The Netherlands

Ron Meyer

Rotterdam School of Management
Erasmus University
The Netherlands

INTERNATIONAL THOMSON BUSINESS PRESS
I(T)P® An International Thomson Publishing Company

London • Bonn • Johannesburg • Madrid • Melbourne • Mexico City • New York • Paris
Singapore • Tokyo • Toronto • Albany, NY • Belmont, CA • Cincinnati, OH • Detroit, MI

Strategy Synthesis: Resolving Strategy Paradoxes to Create Competitive Advantage

Copyright © 1999 Bob de Wit and Ron Meyer

I(T)P A division of International Thomson Publishing
       The ITP logo is a trademark under licence

British Library Cataloguing-in-Publication Data
A catalogue record for this book is available from the British Library

First published 1999 by International Thomson Business Press

Typeset by J&L Composition Ltd, Filey, North Yorkshire
Printed by TJ International, Padstow, Cornwall

Paperback ISBN 1–86152–317–3
Hardback ISBN 1–86152–518–4

International Thomson Business Press
Berkshire House
168–173 High Holborn
London WC1V 7AA
UK

http://www.itbp.com
http://www.dewit-meyer.com

General Table of Contents

Contents

3   Strategy Formation   96

4   Strategic Change   140

SECTION III
Strategy Content   189

5   Business Level Strategy   191

6   Corporate Level Strategy   235

7   Network Level Strategy   280

SECTION IV
Strategy Context   329

8   The Industry Context   331

9   The Organizational Context   364

10   The International Context   395

Acknowledgements

This book is somewhat unusual. Most books, both fiction and non-fiction, tell a story. Readers are taken on a journey by an author who is trying to make a point. In this book, however, there is not one story-line being conveyed by one narrator. Here, readers are introduced to ten key debates among strategists. Our role in this book is to act as chairmen of these debates. As chairmen, we have seen it as our responsibility to let others bring forward their views. It has been our intention to bring together the ideas of the leading thinkers on the topic of strategy and to let them clash with one another. We have attempted to faithfully represent the variety of opinions on each central strategy theme, without taking a partisan position in any of the debates. In our view, readers are better served by a structured and balanced debate among conflicting perspectives, than by yet another grand solution to their strategic problems. Readers must shape their own opinions, based on the informed discussion in the pages of this book. As chairmen, it is our task to present a stimulating and even-handed debate, but to leave the drawing of conclusions up to each individual.

However, a stimulating debate depends not only on the chairmen, but also on the quality of the discussants, whose writings we have incorporated into this book. We are much indebted to these writers, and to their publishers, and greatly appreciate their goodwill and cooperative spirit. Without their collaboration we would not have been able to create the structure of the book as we had envisioned.

The strategy debates, as they are presented in this book, have also been conducted 'live', in the many classes, workshops and conferences that we have participated in during the last few years. The valuable inputs that we received during these sessions have greatly contributed to the quality of our book. In this context, we would like to express our special appreciation to our students and workshop participants at the Maastricht School of Management and at the Rotterdam School of

Management, who have been eager debaters and our willing guinea pigs for many years now.

We have also debated the various strategy perspectives with business people and consultants, to gain further depth and to ensure practical relevance. In this context we are greatly indebted to the clients of De Wit & Meyer Strategy Works, who have provided an important 'reality check' for the conceptual development of this book. We also would like to greatly thank Mascha Brouwer and Dafir Kramer of De Wit & Meyer Strategy Works for their critical and enthusiastic contribution to this work.

Furthermore, we wish to thank the many people who have provided feedback on the 'textbook' version of this work, *Strategy – Process, Content, Context: An International Perspective*[1]. Without the very useful comments and ideas brought forward by our many book users and colleagues from around the world, this book would never be as it is today.

Turning a 'live' debate into a book also requires a publisher, who is willing to try something innovative. In this case, International Thomson Publishing has played the important role of helping us to realize our intentions. In particular, we would like to thank David Godden, who was our great supporter during the initial phases, and Nicholas Edwards, who has done well managing two Dutchmen intent on debating everything.

Last, but not least, we would like to express our appreciation to a number of individuals who closely helped us during the writing process. First, we would like to thank Marc Huygens, who was our assistant for two years during the development of the first textbook edition, and was again, now as a colleague, of great help. Furthermore, thanks are due to Melbert Visscher, for keeping us, and the growing mountain of files, organized. But most of all, we would like to thank our assistant of the past two years, Pursey Heugens, for helping us with the process, the content and the context of this book project.

[1] De Wit, B., and R.J.H. Meyer, *Strategy – Process, Content, Context: An International Perspective*, 2nd edition, International Thomson Publishing, London, 1998, 1250 pages.

Preface

Woe be to him who reads but one book.

(George Herbert 1593–1632; English Poet)

Core competencies, business process reengineering, transnational management, strategic alliances, learning organizations, chaos theory, total quality management, virtual organizations, shareholder value – as wave after wave of new management concepts have washed over the business community, many managers have been left behind in bewilderment. Some managers bravely struggle to keep up with the newest management fashions, hoping that by riding the next wave they will achieve a competitive edge. Others feel they are drowning, unable to keep afloat amongst the frequent waves of new business ideas. What all managers share is the impression that our knowledge of strategy and management is fragmented, unstructured, inconsistent and even self-contradictory.

We agree. In the field of strategy there is a startling variety of theories, approaches and philosophies, that all profess to offer fundamental insights into successful business management. A dynamic market place for ideas exists, with a confusing array of suppliers presenting their wares. Year after year the supply of strategy concepts swells, making it increasingly difficult to oversee the subject area. To make things worse, many of the strategy theories put forward are in conflict with one another – sometimes actually prescribing the exact opposite approach for dealing with strategic issues. There seem to be few generally accepted strategy principles, while scientific research has not been able to resolve which theories are most valid. No wonder that many managers are sympathetic to management gurus offering clear-cut strategy recipes. No wonder that other managers are skeptical about the value of strategy concepts altogether, opting instead for a 'common sense' approach to business.

Yet, managers should not shield themselves from the on-going debate with regard to the best approach to strategy. Ignoring the profound differences between the various schools of thought does not enhance a manager's capacity for strategic thinking. Rather, managers should seek exposure to the wide range of strategy concepts available. The mind of the strategist is sharpened by critically comparing rival perspectives and determining their advantages and limitations. Strategic thinking is all about questioning basic assumptions and being able to see things from a variety of angles. Only where there is knowledge of the various points of view can strategists truly see the spectrum of options open to them.

It was this conviction, that managers would profit from understanding the major conflicting approaches to strategy, that formed the point of departure for writing this book. It has resulted in a work that offers a broad overview of the various strategy perspectives, reflecting the richness of the current debate among academics and practitioners in the field of strategic management.

Providing managers with a structured and balanced overview of the strategic management field is a valuable goal in itself, but in our view it is not enough. Arguably, presenting managers with an overwhelming variety of strategy theories could actually lead to overload, confusion, and paralysis. Managers not only need to understand the broad spectrum of strategy approaches, but they also need to find a way to choose between them, or integrate them, to be practically effective. In other words, the various strategy perspectives need to be critically compared with one another, to give managers the insights needed to select the most suitable approach or to allow them to creatively combine elements from various approaches.

To structure the comparison of strategy approaches, the most important conflicting strategy perspectives have been clustered together around ten central strategy issues, each of which is dealt with in a separate chapter. These ten strategy issues represent the key questions confronting strategists in practice. Only the theories having a direct bearing on how to approach a particular strategy issue are discussed and compared in each chapter.

To further streamline the enormous diversity of strategy approaches, each chapter has subsequently been structured by contrasting the two most extreme ways of dealing with each strategy issue. This makes each chapter a debate between two positions that are largely each other's opposites. These two opposite positions act as the *thesis* and the *antithesis* of the debate, challenging the reader to search for an appropriate *synthesis* somewhere between the two extremes. Both positions are presented in an even-handed way to create a real sense of debate, after which we purposely do not lead the reader to a synthesis of our own making. As we will argue in Chapter 1, it is our view that there is no ultimate strategy synthesis that is the best approach under all circumstances. Consequently, it is the intention of this book to help readers to form their own opinions and to encourage them to pragmatically bridge the conflicting perspectives to shape their own synthesis, which is best suited to their own unique circumstances.

The basic structure of this book is therefore that of a *dialectical debate* (thesis-antithesis-synthesis). This format has been selected for a number of reasons:

- *Range of ideas*. By presenting the two opposite poles in each debate, readers can quickly acquire an understanding of the full range of ideas on the strategy issue. These two extreme positions sometimes do not represent the most widely held views, but they do clarify for the reader how diverse the thinking actually is on each strategy issue. We refer to this as the *book-end function* of presenting the two opposite perspectives – they 'frame' the full set of views that exist on the topic.

- *Points of contention*. Usually there is not across-the-board disagreement between the various approaches to each strategy issue, but opinions tend to diverge on a number of critical points. By presenting the two opposite poles in each debate, readers can rapidly gain insight into these major points of contention. We refer to this as the *contrast function* of presenting the two opposite perspectives – they bring the key points of contention into sharper focus.

- *Stimulus for bridging*. As the two opposite poles in each debate are presented, readers will be struck by the fact that neither position can be easily dismissed. Both extreme strategy perspectives make a strong case for a particular approach and readers will experience difficulty in simply choosing one over the other. With each extreme position offering certain advantages, readers will feel challenged to incorporate aspects of both into a more sophisticated synthesis. We refer to this as the *integrative function* of presenting the two opposite perspectives – they stimulate readers to seek a way of getting the best of both worlds.

- *Stimulus for creativity*. Nothing is more creativity evoking than a challenging paradox, whereby two opposites seem to be true at the same time. By presenting the two opposite poles of each debate, which both make a realistic claim to being valid, readers are challenged to creatively tackle this paradoxical situation. We refer to this as the *generative function* of presenting the two opposite perspectives – they stimulate readers to generate innovative ways of 'resolving' the strategy paradoxes.

Each chapter starts with the most traditional pole as the 'thesis', which is then contrasted with the less established opposite pole as the 'antithesis'. After this introduction, the two extreme positions are compared on a number of important points. To give the reader an authentic flavor of the actual intellectual debate, we then introduce two classic readings, representing the two opposite positions. These works, by influential theorists from each camp, offer the reader a first-hand account of the key ideas, concepts and theories that are central to these two perspectives on strategy. They are our 'discussants', making the strategy debates more tangible and allowing the reader to judge the arguments of the two extreme positions without our 'interpretive filter'.

In total there are 22 readings in this book – 2 per chapter – which together represent a broad overview of the strategic management field. Most of these readings are classics, that are generally accepted as belonging on the 'must read' list of any manager. The other readings are classics-in-the-making, putting forward less well-known points of view, that are essential for a broad and balanced understanding of strategic management. To keep the size of the book within acceptable limits, most readings have been reduced in length, while extensive footnotes and references have been dropped. At all times this editing has been guided by the principle that the author's key ideas and arguments should be preserved in tact.

If these 22 readings do not yet satisfy your craving for strategy classics, the 'references' section at the end of the book will point towards stimulating further readings. The true 'glutton for punishment' can also turn to our 1250 page textbook, *Strategy – Process, Content, Context: An International Perspective*, which includes 55 key readings. We also invite you to visit our website **http://www.dewit-meyer.com** if you are interested in keeping abreast of developments in the field of strategy. We also value your feedback and would enjoy hearing your comments and questions about this book – it is your opportunity to turn the 'virtual' debate in the pages of the book into one which is 'live'.

To our children,
Liza and Suzanne, Thomas and Simone,
our ultimate works of synthesis.

Section I

Strategy

Introduction

*Men like the opinions to which they have
become accustomed from youth; this
prevents them from finding the truth, for
they cling to the opinions of habit.*

(Moses Maimonides 1135–1204; Egyptian physician and philosopher)

*Where there is much desire to learn, there
of necessity will be much arguing, much
writing, many opinions; for opinion in
good men is but knowledge in the making.*

(John Milton 1608–1674; English poet)

The Nature of Strategy

In a book entitled *Strategy Synthesis*, it would seem reasonable to expect
Chapter 1 to begin with a clear definition of strategy, that would be
employed with consistence in all subsequent chapters. An early and
precise definition would help to avoid conflicting interpretations of
what should be considered strategy and, by extension, what should be
understood by the term 'strategic management'. However, any such
sharp definition of strategy here would actually be misleading. It would
suggest that there is widespread agreement among practitioners,
researchers and theorists as to the precise nature of strategy. The impression would be given that the fundamental concepts in the area of strategy
are generally accepted and hardly questioned. Yet, even a quick glance

through current writings on the topic indicates otherwise. There are strongly differing opinions on most of the key issues. The disagreements run so deep that even a common definition of the term strategy is illusive.

This is bad news for those who prefer simplicity and certainty. It means that strategy cannot be reduced to a set of accepted definitions, laws and formulas, fit for memorization and mechanistic application. The variety of partially conflicting views means that learning about strategy cannot be simply a matter of practicing to fill in 2×2 matrices or flow diagrams. If the fundamental differences of opinion are not swept under the carpet, the consequence is that a book on strategy cannot be like an instruction manual that takes you through the steps of how something should be done. On the contrary, a strategy book should acknowledge the disagreements and encourage thinking about the value of each of the different points of view. That is the intention of this book.

The philosophy embraced here is that an understanding of the topic of strategy can only be gained by grappling with the diversity of insights presented by so many prominent thinkers and by coming to terms with the fact that there is no simple answer to the question of what strategy is. Readers who prefer the certainty of reading only one opinion, as opposed to the intellectual stimulation of being confronted with a wide variety, should read no further – there are plenty of alternatives available. Those who wish to proceed should lay aside their 'opinions of habit,' and open their minds to the many other opinions presented, for in these pages there is 'knowledge in the making.'

Identifying the Strategy Issues

If the only tool you have is a hammer, you treat everything like a nail.
(Abraham Maslow 1908–1970; American psychologist)

As should be clear by now, the approach taken in this book is in line with the moral of Maslow's remark. To avoid hammering strategy issues with only one theory, a variety of ways of viewing strategic questions will be presented. But there are two different ways of presenting a broad spectrum of theoretical lenses. This point can be made clear by extending Maslow's hammer-and-nail analogy. To become a good carpenter, who wisely uses a variety of tools depending on what is being crafted, an apprentice carpenter will need to learn about these different instruments. One way is for the apprentice to study the characteristics and functioning of all tools individually, and only then to apply each where appropriate. Another possibility is for the apprentice to first learn about what must be crafted, getting a feel for the materials and the problems that must be solved, and only then to turn to the study of the necessary tools. The first approach to learning can be called *tools-oriented* – understanding each tool comes first, while combining them to solve real problems comes later. The second approach can be labelled *problem-oriented* – understanding problems comes first, while searching for the appropriate tools is based on the type of problem.

Both options can also be used for the 'apprentice' strategist. In a tools-oriented approach to learning about strategy, all major theories can first be understood separately, to be compared or combined later when using them in practice. A logical structure for a book aiming at this mode of learning would be to allot one chapter to each of the major theories or schools of thought. The advantage of such a *theory-based* book structure would be that each chapter would focus on giving the reader a clear and cohesive overview of one major theory within the field of strategy. For readers with an interest in grasping the essence of each theory individually, this would probably be the ideal book format. However, the principal disadvantage of a theory-by-theory summary of the field of strategy would be that the reader would not have a clear picture of how the various theories relate to one another. The apprentice strategist would be left with important questions such as: Where do the theories agree and where do they differ? Which strategy phenomena does each theory claim to explain and which phenomena are left unaccounted for? Can various theories be successfully combined or are they based on mutually exclusive assumptions? And which strategy is right, or at least most appropriate under particular circumstances? Not knowing the answers to these questions, how could the apprentice strategist try to apply these new theoretical tools to practice?

This book is based on the assumption that the reader wants to be able to actively solve strategic problems. Understanding the broad spectrum of theories is not an end in itself, but a means for more effective strategizing. Therefore, the problem-oriented approach to learning about strategy has been adopted. In this approach, key strategy issues are first identified and then each looked at from the perspective of the most appropriate theories. This has resulted in an *issue-based* book structure, in which each chapter deals with a particular set of strategy issues. In each chapter, only the theories that shed some light on the issues under discussion are brought forward and compared to one another. Of course, some theories are relevant to more than one set of issues and therefore appear in various chapters.

In total, ten sets of strategy issues have been identified, that together largely cover the entire field of strategic management. These ten will be the subjects of the remaining ten chapters of this book. How the various strategy issues have been divided into these ten sets is explained in the following paragraphs.

Strategy Dimensions: Process, Content, and Context

The most fundamental distinction made in this book is between strategy process, strategy content and strategy context (see Figure 1.1). These are the three *dimensions of strategy* that can be recognized in every real-life strategic problem situation. They can be generally defined as follows:

- *Strategy Process.* The manner in which strategies come about is referred to as the strategy process. Stated in terms of a number of questions, strategy process is concerned with the *how, who* and *when* of strategy – how is, and should, strategy be made, analyzed, dreamt-up, formulated, implemented, changed and controlled; who is involved; and when do the necessary activities take place?

- *Strategy Content.* The product of a strategy process is referred to as the strategy content. Stated in terms of a question, strategy content is concerned with the *what* of strategy – what is, and should be, the strategy for the company and each of its constituent units?

- *Strategy Context.* The set of circumstances under which both the strategy process and the strategy content are determined is referred to as the strategy context. Stated in terms of a question, strategy context is concerned with the *where* of strategy – where, that is in which firm and which environment, are the strategy process and strategy content embedded?

It cannot be emphasized enough that strategy process, content and context are not different parts of strategy, but are distinguishable *dimensions*. Just as it is misguided to speak of the length, width and height parts of a

FIGURE 1.1
Dimensions of strategy

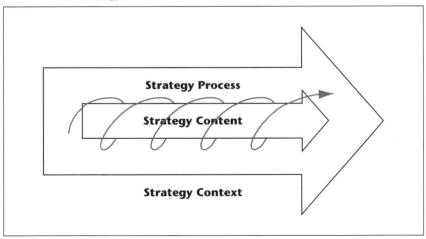

box, one cannot speak of the three parts of strategy either. Each strategic problem situation is by its nature three dimensional, possessing process, content and context characteristics, and only the understanding of all three dimensions will give the strategist real *depth* of comprehension. In particular, it must be acknowledged that the three dimensions interact[1]. For instance, the manner in which the strategy process is organized will have a significant impact on the resulting strategy content, while, likewise, the content of the current strategy will strongly influence the way in which the strategy process will be conducted in future. If these linkages are ignored, the strategist will have a *flat*, instead of a *three-dimensional*, view of strategy. A useful analytical distinction for temporarily unravelling a strategic problem situation will have turned into permanent means for fragmenting reality.

However, it is possible to concentrate on one of the strategy dimensions, if the other two are kept in mind. In fact, to have a focused discussion, it is even necessary to look at one dimension at a time. The alternative is a debate in which all topics on all three dimensions would be discussed simultaneously – such a cacophony of opinions would be lively, but most likely less than fruitful. Therefore, the process–content–context distinction will cautiously be used as the main structuring principle of this book, splitting the text into three major sections.

This structure also fits closely with the situation within the academic field of strategic management. To a large extent, strategy literature is divided along these lines. Most strategy research, by its very nature, is more analytic than synthetic – focusing on just a few variables at once. Consequently, most writings on strategy, including most of the theories discussed in this book, tend to favor just one, or at most two, strategy dimensions, which is usually complex enough, given the need to remain comprehensible. Especially the divide between strategy process and strategy content has been quite pronounced – to the extent of worrying some scholars about whether the connections between the two are being sufficiently recognized[2]. Although sharing this concern, use of the process–content–context distinction here reflects the reality of the current state of the debate within the field of strategic management.

Strategy Process: Thinking, Forming, and Changing

Section II of this book will deal with the strategy process. Traditionally, most books have portrayed the strategy process as a basically linear progression through a number of distinct steps. Usually a split is made between the *strategy analysis* stage, the *strategy formulation* stage and the *strategy implementation* stage. In the analysis stage, strategists identify the opportunities and threats in the environment, as well as the strengths and weaknesses of the organization. Next, in the formulation stage, strategists determine which strategic options are available to them, evaluate each and choose one. Finally, in the implementation stage the selected strategic option is translated into a number of concrete activities that are then carried out. It is commonly presumed that this process is not only *linear*, but also largely *rational* – strategists identify, determine, evaluate, choose, translate and carry out, based on rigorous logic and extensive knowledge of all important factors. Furthermore, the assumption is frequently made that the strategy process is *comprehensive* – strategy is made for the entire organization and everything can be radically changed all at once.

All of these beliefs have been challenged. For instance, many authors have criticized the strong emphasis on rationality in these traditional views of the strategy process. Some writers have even argued that the true nature of strategic thinking is more intuitive and creative than rational. In their opinion, strategizing is about perceiving strengths and weaknesses, envisioning opportunities and threats, and creating the future, for which imagination and judgement are more important than analysis and logic. This constitutes quite a fundamental disagreement about the cognitive processes of the strategist. These issues surrounding the nature of *strategic thinking* will be discussed in Chapter 2.

The division of the strategy process into a number of sequential phases has also drawn heavy criticism from authors who believe that in reality no such identifiable stages exist. They dismiss the linear analysis–formulation–implementation distinction as an unwarranted simplification, arguing that the strategy process is more messy, with analysis, formulation and implementation activities going on all the time, thoroughly intertwined with one another. In their view, organizations do not first make strategic plans and then execute them as intended. Rather, strategies are usually formed incrementally, as organizations think and act in small iterative steps, letting strategies emerge as they go along. This represents quite a difference of opinion on how strategies are conceived within organizations. These issues surrounding the nature of *strategy formation* will be discussed in Chapter 3.

The third major assumption of the traditional view, comprehensiveness, has also been challenged. Many authors have pointed out that it is unrealistic to suppose that a company can be boldly redesigned. They argue that it is terribly difficult to orchestrate an overarching strategy for the entire organization, especially when this entails a significant departure from the current course of action. It is virtually impossible to get various aspects of an organization all lined up to go through a change at the same time, certainly if a radical change is intended. In practice, different aspects of an organization will be under different pressures, on different timetables and have different abilities to change, leading to a differentiated approach to change. Moreover, the rate and direction of change will be seriously limited by the cultural, political and cognitive inheritance of the firm. Hence, it is argued, strategic change is usually more gradual and fragmented, than radical and co-ordinated. The issues surrounding this difference of opinion on the nature of *strategic change* will be discussed in Chapter 4.

These three chapter topics – strategic thinking, strategy formation, and strategic change – do not constitute entirely separate subjects. Let it be clear that they are not phases, stages or elements of the strategy process, that can be understood in isolation. Strategic thinking, strategy formation and strategic change are different aspects of the strategy process, that are strongly linked and partially overlapping. They have been selected because they are sets of issues on which there is significant debate within the field of strategy. As will become clear, having a particular opinion on one of these aspects will have a consequence for views held on all other aspects as well.

Strategy Content: Business, Corporate and Network Levels

Section III of this book will deal with the strategy content. Strategies come in all shapes and sizes, and almost all strategy writers, researchers and practitioners agree that each strategy is essentially unique. There is widespread disagreement, however, about the principles to which strategies should adhere. The debates are numerous, but there are three fundamental sets of issues around which most conflicts generally center. These three topics can be clarified by distinguishing the *level of strategy* at which each is most relevant.

Strategies can be made for different groups of people and/or activities within an organization. The lowest level of aggregation is one person or task, while the highest level of aggregation encompasses all people and/or activities within an organization. The most common distinction between aggregation levels made in strategic management literature is between the functional, business and corporate levels (see Figure 1.2). Strategy issues at the *functional level* refer to questions regarding specific functional aspects of a company (operations strategy, marketing strategy, financial strategy, etc.). Strategy at the *business level* requires the integration of functional level strategies for a distinct set of products and/or services, that are intended for a specific group of customers. Often companies only operate in one such business, so that this is the highest level of aggregation within the firm. However, there are also many companies that are in two or more businesses. In such companies, a multibusiness or *corporate level* strategy is required, that aligns the various business level strategies.

A logical extension of the functional–business–corporate distinction is to explicitly recognize the level of aggregation higher than the individual organization. Firms often cluster together into groups of two or more organizations. This level is referred to as the multi-company or

FIGURE 1.2
Levels of strategy

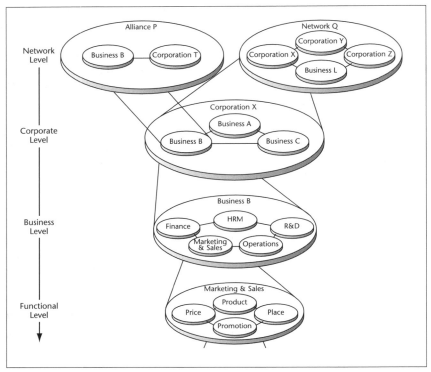

network level. Most multi-company groups consist of only a few parties, as is the case in strategic alliances, joint ventures and value-adding partnerships. However, networks can also have dozens, even hundreds, of participants. In some circumstances, the corporation as a whole might be a member of a group, while in other situations only a part of the firm joins forces with other organizations. In all cases, when a strategy is developed for a group of firms, this is called a network level strategy.

In line with the generally accepted boundaries of the strategic management field, this book will focus on the business, corporate and network levels of strategy, although this will often demand consideration of strategy issues at the functional level as well. In Section II, on the strategy process, this level distinction will not be emphasized yet, but in Section III, on the strategy content, the different strategy issues encountered at the different levels of strategy will be explored. And at each level of strategy, the focus will be on the fundamental differences of opinion that divide strategy theorists.

Chapter 5 will deal with strategy issues at the business level. Here the fundamental debate is whether firms are, and should be, primarily market-driven or resource-driven. Some authors argue that firms should be strongly externally-oriented, engaged in a game of positioning *vis-à-vis* customers, competitors, suppliers and other parties in the environment, and should adapt the firm to the demands of the game. In other words, companies should think outside-in. Yet, other authors strongly disagree, stressing the need for companies to exploit and expand their strengths. They recommend a more inside-out view, whereby companies search for those environments and positions that best fit with their resource base.

Chapter 6 is concerned with strategy issues at the corporate level. The fundamental debate in this chapter is whether corporations are, and should be, run as federations of autonomous business units or as highly integrated organizations. Some authors argue that corporate strategists should view themselves as investors, with financial stakes in a portfolio of business units. As a shrewd investor, the corporate center should buy up cheap companies, divest underperforming business units, and put money into its business units with the highest profit potential, independent of what industry they are in. Each business unit should be judged on its own merits and given a large measure of autonomy, to be optimally responsive to the specific conditions in its industry. However, other authors are at odds with this view, pointing to the enormous potential for synergy that is left untapped. They argue that corporations should be tightly-knit groupings of closely-related business units, that share resources and align their strategies with one another. The ensuing synergies, it is forecast, will provide an important source of competitive advantage.

Chapter 7 focuses on the strategy issues at the network level. The fundamental debate in this chapter revolves around the question whether firms should develop long-term collaborative relationships with other firms or should remain essentially independent. Some authors believe that competition between organizations is sometimes more destructive than beneficial, and argue that building up durable partnerships with other organizations can often be mutually advantageous. Participation in joint ventures, alliances and broader networks requires a higher level of interorganizational trust and interdependence, but can pay off handsomely. It is therefore recommended to selectively engage in joint – that is, multi-company – strategy development. Other authors, however, are thoroughly skeptical about the virtues of interdependence. They prefer independence, pointing to the dangers of opportunistic partners and creeping dependence on the other. Therefore, they recommend avoiding multi-company level strategy development and only to use alliances as a tactical measure.

Again, it must be emphasized that the analytical distinction employed here should not be interpreted as an absolute means for isolating issues. In reality, these three levels of strategy do not exist as tidy categories, but are strongly interrelated and partially overlapping. As a consequence, the three sets of strategy issues identified above are also linked to one another. In Section III, it will become clear that taking a stand in one debate will affect the position that one can take in others as well.

Strategy Context: Organizational, Industry, International

Section IV in this book is devoted to the strategy context. While Sections II and III discuss strategy process and strategy content issues in general, Section IV explicitly acknowledges that process and content are embedded in a particular strategy context. Strategy researchers, writers and practitioners largely agree that every strategy context is unique. Moreover, they are almost unanimous that it is usually wise for strategists to adapt the strategy process and strategy content to the specific circumstances prevalent in the strategy context. However, disagreement arises as soon as the discussion turns to the actual level of influence that the strategy context has. Some people argue or assume that the strategy context fully determines the strategy process and the strategy content. These *determinists* believe that strategists do not really have much liberty to make their own choices. Rather, process and content are largely the result of circumstances that strategists do not control. On the other hand, people with a *voluntarist* perspective believe that strategists are not driven by the context, but have a large measure of freedom to set their own course of action. Frequently it is argued that strategists can, and should, create their own circumstances, instead of being enslaved by the circumstances they find. In short, the strategy context can be determined, instead of letting it determine.

In Section IV, the same difference of opinion on the power of the context to determine strategy surfaces when discussing the various aspects of the strategy context. The section has been split into three chapters, each focusing on a different aspect of the strategy context. Two distinctions have been used to arrive at the division into three chapters. The first dichotomy employed is that between the organization and its industry environment. The *industry context* will be the subject of Chapter 8. In this chapter, the strategic issues revolve around the question whether the industry circumstances set the rules to which companies must comply, or whether companies have the freedom to choose their own strategy and even change the industry conditions. The *organizational context* will be dealt with in Chapter 9. Here, the key strategic issues have to do with the question of whether the organizational circumstances largely determine the strategy process and strategy content followed, or whether the strategist has a significant amount of control over the course of action adopted.

The second dichotomy employed is that between the domestic and the international strategy context. The domestic context does not raise any additional strategic issues, but the international context clearly does. Strategists must deal with the question whether adaptation to the diversity of the international context is strictly required or companies have considerable freedom to choose their strategy process and content irrespective of the international context. The difference of opinion between writers on the international context actually goes even one step further. Some authors predict that the diversity of the international context will decline over time and that companies can encourage this process. If global convergence takes place, it is argued, adaptation to the international context will become a non-issue. Other authors, however, disagree that international diversity is declining and therefore argue that the international context will remain an issue that strategists must attempt to deal with. This debate on the future of the international context is conducted in Chapter 10.

Organizational Purpose

While there are many different opinions about what strategy is, it is clear to all that strategies are used to achieve something. Making strategy is not an end in itself, but a means for reaching particular objectives. Organizations exist to fulfill a purpose and strategies are employed to ensure that the organizational purpose is realized.

Oddly enough, most authors write about strategy without any reference to the organizational purpose being pursued. It is generally assumed that all organizations exist for the same basic reasons, and that this is widely accepted. However, in reality, there is extensive disagreement about what the current purposes of organizations are, and especially about what their purpose should be. Some people argue that it is the business of business to make money. In their view, firms are owned by shareholders and therefore should pursue shareholders' interests. And it is the primary interest of shareholders to see the value of their stocks increase. On the other hand, many other people believe that companies exist to serve the interests of multiple stakeholders. In their opinion, having a financial stake in a firm should not give shareholders a dominant position *vis-à-vis* other groups that also have an interest in what the organization does. Other stakeholders usually include the employees, customers, suppliers and bankers, but could also include the local community, the industry and even the natural environment.

This is a very fundamental debate, with broader societal implications than any of the other strategy issues. Given the important role played by business organizations in modern times, the purposes they attempt to fulfill will have a significant impact on the functioning of society. It is not surprising, therefore, to see that organizational purpose is also discussed by others than strategy theorists and practitioners. The role of firms and the interests they should pursue are widely debated by members of political parties, unions, political action groups, environmental conservation groups, the media, and the general public.

Arguably, in a book on strategy, organizational purpose should be discussed before moving on to the subject of strategy itself. In principle this is true, but the 'issue of existence' is not an easy topic with which to begin a book – it would be quite a hefty appetizer to start a strategy meal. Therefore, to avoid intellectual indigestion, the topic of purpose will be saved for dessert. Chapter 11 will be devoted to the issues surrounding purpose.

Structuring the Strategy Debates

> *For every complex problem there is a simple solution that is wrong.*
> (George Bernard Shaw 1856–1950; Irish playwright and critic)

Every real-life strategic problem is complex. Most of the strategic issues outlined above will be present in every strategic problem, making the prospect of a simple solution an illusion. Yet, even if each set of strategy issues is looked at independently, it seems that strategy theorists cannot agree on the right way to approach them. On each of the topics, there is widespread disagreement, indicating that no simple solution can be expected here either.

Why is it that theorists cannot agree on how to solve strategic problems? Might it be that some theorists are right, while others are just plain wrong? In that case, it would be wise for problem-solvers to select the valid theory and discard the false ones. While this might be true in some cases, it seems unlikely that false theories would stay around long enough to keep a lively debate going. Eventually, the right (i.e. unfalsified) theory would prevail and disagreements would disappear. Yet, this does not seem to be happening in the field of strategic management.

Could it be that each theorist only emphasizes one aspect of an issue – only takes one cut of a multifaceted reality? In that case, it would be wise for problem-solvers to combine the various theories that each look at the problem from a different angle. However, if this were true, one would expect the different theories to be largely complementary. Each theory would simply be a piece in the bigger puzzle of strategic management. Yet, this does not explain why there is so much disagreement, and even contradiction, within the field of strategy.

It could also be that strategy theorists start from divergent assumptions about the nature of each strategy issue and therefore logically arrive at a different perspective on how to solve strategic problems. In that case, it would be wise for problem-solvers to uncover the assumptions on which each theory is built and to decide which assumptions seem most appropriate.

All three possibilities for explaining the existing theoretical disagreements should be kept open. However, entertaining the thought that divergent positions are rooted in fundamentally different assumptions about strategy issues is by far the most fruitful to the strategist confronted with complex problems. It is too simple to hope that one can deal with the contradictory opinions within the field of strategy by discovering which strategy theories are right and which are wrong. But it is also not particularly practical to accept all divergent theories as valid depictions of different aspects of reality – if two theories suggest a different approach to the same problem, the strategist will have to sort out this contradiction. Therefore, in this book the emphasis will be on surfacing the basic assumptions underlying the major theoretical perspectives on strategy, and to debate whether, or under which circumstances, these assumptions are appropriate.

Assumptions about Strategy Tensions

At the heart of every set of strategy issues, a fundamental tension between apparent opposites can be identified. For instance, in Chapter 7 on network level strategy, the issues revolve around the fundamental tension between competition and cooperation. In Chapter 8 on the industry context, the fundamental tension between the opposites of compliance and choice lies at the center of the subject (see Table 1.1). Each pair of opposites creates a tension, as they seem to be inconsistent, or even incompatible, with one another – it seems as if both elements cannot be fully true at the same time. If firms are competing, they are not cooperating. If firms must comply to the industry context, they have no choice. Yet, although these opposites confront strategists with conflicting pressures, strategists must somehow deal with them simultaneously. Strategists are caught in a bind, trying to cope with contradictory forces at the same time.

The challenge of strategic management is to wrestle with these tricky strategy tensions. Consequently, all strategy theories make assumptions, explicitly or implicitly, about the nature of these tensions and the way in which to deal with them. However, their assumptions differ significantly, giving rise to a wide variety of positions. In fact, many of the major disagreements within the field of strategic management are rooted in the different assumptions made about coping with strategy tensions. For this reason, the theoretical debate in each chapter will be centered around the different perspectives on dealing with a particular strategy tension.

TABLE 1.1
The 10 strategy tensions

Chapter	Strategy Tension	Strategy Perspectives
2. Strategic Thinking	Logic vs. Creativity	Rational Thinking vs. Generative Thinking
3. Strategy Formation	Deliberateness vs. Emergentness	Planning vs. Incrementalism
4. Strategic Change	Revolution vs. Evolution	Discontinuous Change vs. Continuous Change
5. Business Level Strategy	Markets vs. Resources	Outside-in vs. Inside-out
6. Corporate Level Strategy	Responsiveness vs. Synergy	Portfolio vs. Core Competence
7. Network Level Strategy	Competition vs. Cooperation	Discrete Organization vs. Embedded Organization
8. The Industry Context	Compliance vs. Choice	Industry Evolution vs. Industry Creation
9. The Organizational Context	Control vs. Chaos	Organizational Leadership vs. Organizational Dynamics
10. The International Context	Globalization vs. Localization	Global Convergence vs. International Diversity
11. Organizational Purpose	Profitability vs. Responsibility	Shareholder Value vs. Stakeholder Values

Identifying Strategy Perspectives

The strategy issues in each chapter can be viewed from many perspectives. On each topic there are many different theories and hundreds of books and articles. While very interesting, a comparison or debate between all of these would probably be very chaotic, unfocused and incomprehensible. Therefore, in each chapter the debate has been condensed into its most powerful form – two diametrically opposed perspectives are confronted with one another. These two poles of each debate are not always the most widely held perspectives on the particular set of strategy issues, but they do expose the major points of contention within the topic area.

In every chapter, the two strategy perspectives selected for debate each emphasize one side of a strategy tension over the other. For instance, in Chapter 7 the discrete organization perspective stresses competition over cooperation, while the embedded organization perspective does the opposite. In Chapter 8, the industry evolution perspective accentuates compliance over choice, while the industry creation perspective does the opposite (see Table 1.1). In other words, the two perspectives represent the two extreme ways of dealing with a strategy tension – emphasizing one side or emphasizing the other.

In the first pages of each chapter, the strategic issues and the underlying strategy tension will be explained. Also, the two strategy perspectives will be outlined and compared. However, such a measured overview of the perspectives lacks color, depth and vigor. Reading the summary of a debate does not do it justice. Therefore, to give a firsthand impression of the debate, theorists representing both sides will be given an opportunity to state their own case by means of a reading. Each chapter will contain two classic readings that forcefully put forward the arguments of the two poles of each debate. All of these contributions will be accompanied by a short introduction, to clarify their pertinence to the debate at hand. The only thing that will not be done – and cannot be done – is to give readers the outcome of the debate. This is what readers will have to decide for themselves.

Viewing Strategy Tensions as Strategy Paradoxes

So, what should readers be getting out of each debate? With both strategy perspectives emphasizing the importance of one side of a strategy tension over the other, how should readers deal with these opposites? Of course, after hearing the arguments, it is up to readers to judge for themselves how the strategy tensions should be handled. Still, there are four general ways of approaching them:

- *As a puzzle.* A puzzle is a challenging problem with an *optimal solution*. Think of a crossword puzzle as an example. Puzzles can be quite complex and extremely difficult to analyze, but there is a best way of solving them. Some of the most devious puzzles are those with seemingly contradictory premises. Strategy tensions can also be viewed as puzzles. While the pair of opposites seem to be incompatible with one another, this is only because the puzzle is not yet well understood. In reality, there is one best way of relieving the tension, but the strategist must unravel the problem first. Some writers seem to suggest that there are optimal ways of dealing with strategy tensions under all circumstances, but others argue that the optimal solution is situation dependent.

■ *As a dilemma.* A dilemma is a vexing problem with *two possible solutions*, neither of which is logically the best. Think of the famous prisoner's dilemma as an example. Dilemmas confront problem-solvers with difficult *either-or* choices, each with its own advantages and disadvantages, but neither clearly superior to the other. The uneasy feeling this gives the decision-maker is reflected in the often used expression 'horns of a dilemma' – neither choice is particularly comfortable. Strategy tensions can also be viewed as dilemmas. If this approach is taken, the incompatibility of the opposites is accepted, and the strategist is forced to make a choice for either one or the other. For instance, the strategist must choose to either compete or cooperate. Which of the two the strategist judges to be most appropriate will usually depend on the specific circumstances.

■ *As a trade-off.* A trade-off is a problem situation in which there are *many possible solutions*, each striking a different balance between two conflicting pressures. Think of the trade-off between work and leisure time as an example – more of one will necessarily mean less of the other. In a trade-off, many different combinations between the two opposites can be found, each with its own pros and cons, but none of the many solutions is inherently superior to the others. Strategy tensions can also be viewed as trade-offs. If this approach is taken, the conflict between the two opposites is accepted, and the strategist will constantly strive to find the most appropriate balance between them. For instance, the strategist will attempt to balance the pressures for competition and cooperation, depending on the circumstances encountered.

■ *As a paradox.* A paradox is a situation in which two seeming contradictory, or even mutually exclusive, factors appear to be true at the same time[3]. A problem that is a paradox has *no definitive solution*, as there is no way to logically integrate the two opposites into an internally consistent understanding of the problem. As opposed to the either-or nature of the dilemma, the paradox can be characterized as a *both-and* problem – one factor is true and a contradictory factor is simultaneously true[4]. Hence, the problem-owner must resolve a paradox by trying to find a way to reconcile the opposites in the most productive manner. Strategy tensions can also be viewed as paradoxes. If this approach is taken, the conflict between the two opposites is accepted, but the strategist will strive to accommodate both factors at the same time. The strategist will search for new ways of reconciling the opposites in an attempt to get the 'best of both worlds'. To take the same example as above, the strategist faced with the tension between competition and cooperation will strive to combine the two as much as possible with the intention of reaping the benefits of both.

Most people are used to solving puzzles, tackling dilemmas and making trade-offs. These ways of understanding and dealing with opposite demands are common in daily life. They are based on the assumption that, by analysis, one or a number of fixed solutions can be identified. It might require a sharp mind and considerable effort, but the definitive answers can be found.

However, most people are not used to, or inclined to, think of a problem as a paradox. A paradox has no fixed answer or set of answers – it can only be coped with as best as possible. Faced with a paradox, one can try to find novel ways of resolving the tension between the opposites, but will know that none of these creative reconciliations will ever be *the* answer. Paradoxes will always remain surrounded by uncertainty and disagreements on how to get the best of both worlds.

So, should strategy tensions be seen as puzzles, dilemmas, trade-offs or paradoxes? Arguments can be made for all, but viewing strategy tensions as strategy paradoxes is the ultimate intellectual challenge. Looking at the tensions as paradoxes will help strategists to avoid 'jumping to solutions' and will encourage them to use their creativity to find ways of benefiting from both sides of a tension at the same time. Hence, throughout the book, the strategy tensions will be presented as strategy paradoxes, and readers will be invited to view them as such.

Striving towards Strategy Synthesis

By now it should be clear that the two diametrically opposed perspectives are the *thesis* and *antithesis* of each debate. In other words, they are the poles between which the debate takes place. Both sides have a valid contribution to make, but neither side can fully explain the issues being discussed. The challenge for strategists is to bridge the gap between the conflicting perspectives. Aspects of both poles will need to be combined into a *synthesis*, that is better suited to deal with the strategy paradox being confronted.

Such a strategy synthesis, that blends the insights of both perspectives, will necessarily be situation dependent. As strategy paradoxes have no fixed set of answers, every synthesis of perspectives will be a unique hybrid, fitted to the circumstances encountered. Strategists will need to reconcile the two sides of the debate, in order to find an approach that is best suited to the company, industry and country they are in. In short, strategy synthesis cannot be the end product of this book, but must be the creation of each individual strategist each time again.

Developing an International Perspective

Every man takes the limits of his own field of vision for the limits of the world.
                    (Arthur Schopenhauer 1788–1860; German philosopher)

In a highly integrated world economy, in which many firms operate across national boundaries, strategy is by nature an international affair. Some theorists view the international arena as irrelevant, uninteresting or too complex, but most theorists, particularly those interested in strategy content, acknowledge the importance of the international context and write extensively on international competition and global strategy. In this book, there has been a strong preference to include those authors who explicitly place their arguments within an international setting. Gaining an international perspective is greatly enhanced by reading works that do not take a domestic arena as their default assumption.

To further accentuate the international angle in this book, the international context has been singled out for a closer look in Chapter 10. In this chapter, the conflicting views about the developments in the international context will be debated. This, too, should challenge readers to take an international perspective.

However, despite all this attention paid to the international competitive arena, internationalizing companies, cross-border strategies, and global products, few authors explicitly question whether their own strategy theories can be globally standardized. Most fail to wonder whether their theories are equally applicable in a variety of national settings. It is seldom asked whether they base themselves on universally valid assumptions, or whether they have been severely limited by their domestic 'field of vision'. Yet, there is a very real danger that theories are based on local assumptions that are not true or appropriate in other nations – a threat that could be called 'think local, generalize global.'

Developing an international perspective requires that strategists guard against the indiscriminate export of domestically-generated strategy theories across international borders. For international strategists it is important to question whether theories 'travel' as well as the companies they describe. Unfortunately, at the moment, strategists have little to base themselves on. There has been only a modest amount of international comparative research done in the field of strategy. National differences in strategic management practices and preferences have occasionally been identified, but in general the topic has received little attention. In practice, the international validity of locally-formulated strategy theories has gone largely unquestioned in international journals and forums.

Although there is still so little published material to go on, in this book readers will be encouraged to question the international limitations of strategy theories. Furthermore, readers will be challenged to question whether certain strategy perspectives are more popular and/or appropriate in some countries than in others. To point readers in the right direction, at the end of each chapter a paragraph will be presented that places the strategy topic being debated in an international perspective. In these paragraphs, it will be argued that the strategy paradoxes identified in this book are fundamentally the same around the world, but that there might be international differences in how each paradox is coped with. Strategy perspectives and theories might be more predominant in particular countries because they are based on certain assumptions about dealing with the strategy paradoxes that are more suitable to the national context. In each 'international perspective' paragraph, a number of factors will be discussed that might cause national differences in strategy styles.

EXHIBIT 1.1
MTV case

MTV NETWORKS: BETWEEN ROCK AND A HARD PLACE?

Back in the 1980s, Mark Knopfler of Dire Straits sang 'I want my MTV,' and since then 280 million households in 76 countries have been granted this request. Launched in the United States in 1981, MTV was the first 24-hour music television network in the world, and has been leading internationally ever since. It was the first network with a presence on all five continents and currently broadcasts a number of geographically customized versions of the American original around the globe. For instance, MTV Latino is the Spanish-language affiliate broadcasting two region-specific versions of MTV for the Latin American market, while MTV Europe produces three English-language variations for different parts of Europe. Back home, MTV reaches more than 62 million households across the United States, either via cable or by satellite.

MTV is part of MTV Networks, that also operates a number of other TV channels, including VH-1 (music), Nickelodeon (children), Nick at Nite (classic sitcoms), Showtime (films) and Showtime Event Television. Of these, only VH-1 has followed MTV abroad, recently starting in Germany and the UK. Just like MTV, VH-1 is a 24-hour a day music channel, but while MTV is directed at the age group 15–35, VH-1 aims at the 25–40 year-olds. MTV Networks is in turn owned by media giant Viacom, which also owns Paramount Pictures, various television and radio stations and a number of cable systems.

A large part of MTV's success is attributable to the network's ability to understand, follow and even shape the volatile audience of teens and twenty-somethings in a way that suit-and-tie wearing executives at stodgier networks have found difficult to imitate. In many countries young people have been a poorly served segment, opening the door for MTV's entrance into the market. However, in broadcasting much more is needed to be successful than merely a good channel format and a receptive target audience. Success depends on a network's ability to manage relationships with a number of key external stakeholders. First, a channel needs suppliers – someone must provide MTV with videos. At this moment, the record companies produce these highly expensive videos as promotional devices to sell their CDs and supply them free of cost to music channels. But while both sides benefit from this relationship, it places the record companies in a relatively dependent position. If MTV decides not to broadcast a new video, the record company has few alternatives. Unsurprisingly, the record companies would be happy if MTV had more competitors. Writing on the wall for MTV is that its leading challenger in Germany, VIVA, was initiated by the record companies PolyGram, EMI Music, Sony Music and Warner Music.

Second, to survive as a TV channel, advertisers are essential. Most commercial broadcasters do not rely on viewers to pay for the programs watched (either by subscription or pay-per-view), but largely finance operations out of advertising revenues. This is also true for MTV, which is heavily dependent on attracting enough advertisers interested in the 15–35 year old age segment. Some advertisers have become whole-hearted partners of MTV. For instance, PepsiCo has a long-term relationship with MTV, with the intention of co-promoting both brands and reinforcing each others' positions world-wide. However, there are not very many companies that want the internationally standardized advertising that MTV is so good at offering outside of the US. Furthermore, many advertisers in the US wouldn't mind a bit of competition for MTV, to keep advertising prices down.

A third success factor for TV channels is distribution – programs need to reach viewers' TV sets, either by satellite or by cable. Transmitting via satellite is relatively simple. Satellite 'slots' can be rented from third parties and viewers can receive transmissions with a dish. However, in most countries the number of households with a dish is quite low, given the high initial cost, varying from $1000 to $3000. Therefore, most commercial channels prefer distribution via cable systems, which have a high level of penetration in most developed economies. Yet getting cable operators to carry a channel often proves to be an arduous task. Most cable operators have small regional monopolies and need to be convinced of the need to make extra costs to carry an additional channel. Many cable systems are technically limited to a fixed number of channels and therefore need to drop an existing broadcaster before a new channel can be accommodated. This gives cable companies quite a bit of power, leading operators in some countries to demand that commercial channels pay for a slot on the cable.

Although MTV has been at the top of the charts for more than 15 years, other channels have been steadily rising in the ratings, challenging

MTV's virtual ownership of the youth market. In the US, real competition has only recently emerged. The Canadian network MuchMusic launched a channel in the US in 1994 and by 1997 was also present in Mexico, Argentina and Finland. The Box, a channel that allows viewers to call in and select the videos to be played, has been doing moderately well, expanding from the US to the UK, the Netherlands, Argentina, Peru and Chile. MOR Music Television is a music shopping network that combines videos with merchandising breaks. Besides these general music channels, MTV is facing a number of competitors focusing on only one type of music. BET on Jazz, Black Entertainment Television, The Nashville Network, Country Music Television, The Gospel Network and Z Music (Christian) may all draw viewers away from MTV.

Outside its home base, competition varies per country, but is becoming fierce in a number of mature markets. For instance, in Germany MTV's position is under siege by VIVA, which employs German-speaking VJs and mixes international and local music. The same is true in the Netherlands, where MTV is being battered by the local player TMF, and in the UK, where Kiss TV and BBC Radio One channel have launched an assault. In all these cases the competitive advantage of MTV's new rivals is their ability to tailor programming to the demands of the local market. The success of the local upstarts has led many commentators to question whether 'the new generation' is really as globally similar as once thought.

Taken together, these developments form a rather wicked strategic problem for MTV. Its competitive formula as the globally standardized youth channel is being attacked from a variety of angles, which seems to demand some type of response. Yet, any move by MTV will need to acknowledge the web of interdependency relationships with the record companies, advertisers and cable operators, in which the company is embedded.

Until now, MTV has not initiated any radical strategic changes, but is actively searching for ways to gradually adapt to the new competitive circumstances. One idea that emerged and was implemented within a few months, was the launch of M2 in the US market in August 1996. M2 is an all-video channel that closely resembles the early free-form MTV, before it began running more long-form non-music programs. Industry analysts remark that even if M2 does not break even, it might block the way for new competitors and should satisfy record companies' complaints that MTV does not offer enough airtime to new acts.

Outside the US, MTV is expanding to new markets, such as India, largely according to plan. However, MTV's head of international activities, Bill Roedy, seems to have seriously altered his views on the international context. Instead of sticking to a globally standardized product, based on a belief in global convergence, Roedy has acknowledged the need to go local – he wants to adapt MTV's programming to meet national tastes. Roedy is contemplating partially autonomous regional channels in the local language, to counter MTV's crumbling marketshare. Yet, reaping the advantages of localization, while not losing too many of the benefits of globalization, is proving to be an interesting paradox.

But there are many more strategy paradoxes confronting MTV. As a former rule-breaker within the broadcasting industry, MTV must ask to what extent it can still set, or must follow, the industry rules – a paradox of compliance and choice. Should they primarily be driven by market considerations or should they focus more on perfecting and leveraging their unique resources – a paradox of markets and resources. Should their relationships with advertisers, cable operators and record companies be arm's length and tough, or close and collaborative – a paradox of competition and cooperation. MTV must also work out whether there is added value to working with other parts of its parent, Viacom, or whether MTV should remain largely autonomous – a paradox of responsiveness and synergy. In answering all of these questions, MTV can adopt a strategic thinking style that is either more analytical or more imaginative – a paradox of logic and creativity. It can develop strategic plans or let strategies form more incrementally over time – a paradox of deliberateness and emergentness. And the strategic changes realized can come about more gradually or more radically – a paradox of evolution and revolution. In short, MTV has some difficult nuts to crack – which is not exactly getting 'your money for nothing and your chicks for free.'

Sources: *Financial Times*, February 20 1997; *Broadcasting & Cable*, September 2 1996; *The Economist*, February 25 1995.

The Readings

> *Unless a variety of opinions are laid before us, we have no opportunity of selection, but are bound of necessity to adopt the particular view which may have been brought forward. The purity of gold cannot be ascertained by a single specimen; but when we have carefully compared it with others, we are able to fix upon the finest ore.*
>
> (Herodotus, Fifth century BC; Greek historian)

In the following ten chapters the readings will represent the two opposite points of view in the debate and will 'lay the variety of opinions before us.' However, in this chapter there is no central debate. Yet, two contributions have been selected that provide an interesting introduction to the topic of strategy, and reinforce some of the arguments made in the preceding pages. Here, both readings will be shortly introduced and the relevance for the discussion at hand will be underlined.

The opening reading, 'Complexity: The Nature of Real World Problems,' is the first chapter of Richard Mason and Ian Mitroff's classic book, *Challenging Strategic Planning Assumptions*[5]. In this thought-provoking contribution, Mason and Mitroff argue that most strategic problems facing organizations are not *tame* – that is, they are not simple problems that can be separated and reduced to a few variables and relationships, and then quickly solved. Strategic problems are usually *wicked*. Strategists are faced with a situation of organized complexity in which problems are complicated and interconnected, there is much uncertainty and ambiguity, and they must deal with conflicting views and interests. Therefore, strategic problems have no clearly identifiable correct solutions, but must be tackled by debating the alternatives and selecting the most promising option. Mason and Mitroff call on strategists to systematically doubt the value of all available solutions and to employ *dialectics* – a method of argumentation that contrasts two diametrically opposed positions, the thesis and the antithesis, to arrive at a better understanding of the subject. As stated before, this is in fact the approach adopted in this book. The presentation of two diametrically opposed positions in each chapter is used as a means for gaining a richer understanding of the complex strategy issues under discussion.

The second reading, 'Cultural Constraints in Management Theories' by Geert Hofstede[6], has been selected to sow further doubt about the universal validity of strategic management theories. Hofstede is one of the most prominent cross-cultural researchers in the field of management and is known, in particular, for his five dimensions for measuring cultural traits. In this article he briefly describes the major characteristics of management in Germany, Japan, France, Holland, South-East Asia, Africa, Russia and China, contrasting them all to the US, to drive home his point that management practices differ from country to country, depending on the local culture. Each national style is based on cultural characteristics, that differ sharply around the world. Hofstede argues that theories are formulated within these national cultural contexts, and thus reflect the local demands and predispositions. Therefore, he concludes that universal management theories do not exist – each theory is culturally constrained. If Hofstede is right, this reemphasizes the necessity to view strategic management and strategy theories from an international perspective. In the following chapters, Hofstede's arguments will be revisited and the question will be raised whether the debate is influenced by cultural differences. If so, readers will have to judge which strategy approach is best suited to the national circumstances with which they are confronted.

Reading 1   Complexity: The Nature of Real World Problems

By Richard Mason and Ian Mitroff[†]

Try a little experiment. Make a short list of the major problems or issues facing policymakers in the world today. Now take your list and arrange it as a matrix like the one in Figure 1.3. For each element in the matrix ask yourself the following question: Is the solution to one problem (the row problem) in any way related to the solution of the other problem (the column problem)? If the answer is yes, place a check mark at the point where the row and column intersect; otherwise leave it blank. When you

FIGURE 1.3
Problem interaction matrix

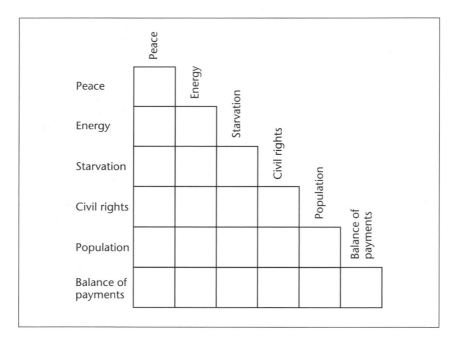

[†] Source: This article was adapted with permission from chapter 1 of *Challenging Strategic Planning Assumptions*, Wiley, New York, 1981.

have completed the process, review the matrix and count the number of blanks. Are there any?

'No fair!' you may say. 'There were a lot of check marks in my matrix because many of these world problems are linked together.' World problems involve all nations. One would not expect to get the same result if the focus was, say, on one's company, city, family, or personal life. Really? Try it and see. Recently, several managers at a major corporation tried this little experiment as part of a strategic planning effort. Among the issues and problem areas they identified were the following:

■   Satisfy stockholder dividend and risk requirements.

■   Acquire adequate funds for expansion from the capital markets.

■   Insure a stable supply of energy at reasonable prices.

■   Train a corps of middle managers to assume more responsibility.

■   Develop a marketing force capable of handling new product lines.

The managers found that all of these problems and issues were related to each other. Some were only related weakly, but most were related quite strongly. Repeated attempts in other contexts give the same result: *basically, every real world policy problem is related to every other real world problem*. This is an important finding. It means that every time a policymaker attempts to solve a particular policy problem he or she must consider its potential relationship with all other problems. To do this one must have both a comprehensive set of concepts for dealing with any policy and a rich set of tools for acquiring the holistic information needed to guide policy making.

Characteristics of Complexity

There are several characteristics of policy making that the foregoing little experiment is intended to illustrate:

■   Any policy-making situation comprises many problems and issues.

■   These problems and issues tend to be highly interrelated. Consequently, the solution to one problem requires a solution to all the other problems. At the same time, each solution creates additional dimensions to be incorporated in the solutions to other problems.

■   Few, if any, problems can be isolated effectively for separate treatment.

These are the characteristics of complexity. Complexity literally means the condition of being tightly woven or twined together. Most policymakers find that the problems they face today are complex in this sense.

Moreover, almost all of today's problems seem to be getting more plentiful and complex.

There is an especially vexing aspect of complexity as it presents itself to policymakers. It is organized. As we have seen in the little experiment, there tends to be an illusive structure underlying problems that gives pattern and organization to the whole. Organization is usually considered the route to the solution of a complex problem. In reality, however, organization in complexity can become an insurmountable barrier to the solution of a problem. This is the major challenge to real world problem solving because we have very few intellectual tools for coping with 'organized complexity.'

The tools we have available seem to work best on simple problems, those that can be separated and reduced to relatively few variables and relationships. These problems of simplicity usually have a one-dimensional value system or goal structure that guides the solution. Three factors – separability, reducibility, and one-dimensional goal structure – mean that simple problems can be bounded, managed, and, as Horst Rittel[7] puts it, 'tamed.'

Ironically, problems of the utmost complexity can also be tamed as long as the complexity is 'disorganized.' That is, whenever the number of variables is very large and the variables are relatively disconnected, the problem can be tamed with the elegant simplicity of statistical mechanics. For example, there is no known way of predicting how a given individual will vote on a political candidate. However, using polling procedures and statistical techniques it is possible to predict with a fair degree of confidence how an entire population of voters will vote. Similarly, it is difficult to predict whether a given customer will purchase a new product or not. However, using market research methods, a fairly good estimate can be made of a new product's potential market share.

Perhaps one of the greatest insights of the twentieth century is the discovery that when a problem situation meets the condition for random sampling – many individual elements exhibiting independent, probabilistic behavior – there is a potential statistical solution to the problem. In short, disorganized complexity can generally be tamed by statistical means.

One place where the assumption of disorganized complexity has proven invaluable in the past is in the actuarial sciences. Today, however, the insurance industry is discovering that many of the risks once assumed to be reasonably independent and hence analyzable according to standard actuarial methods are no longer so. People, organizations, and facilities have become more tightly woven together over wider geographical areas. Consequently, the probabilities of death, accident, fire, or disaster on which the risks and premiums are based are no longer as straightforward as they once were. The result is that the statistical methods that applied under conditions of disorganized complexity have become less reliable as the system has become more organized.

The great difficulty with connected systems of organized complexity is that deviations in one element can be transmitted to other elements. In turn, these deviations can be magnified, modified, and reverberated so that the system takes on a kind of unpredictable life of its own. Emery and Trist[8] refer to this condition as 'environmental connectedness' and have labeled this type of environment the 'turbulent' environment.

Emery and Trist cite an interesting case to illustrate the nature of environmental connectedness and the great difficulties it presents to policy makers. In Great Britain after World War II, a large food canning company began to expand. Its main product was a canned vegetable – a staple in the English diet. As part of the expansion plan, the company decided to build a new, automated factory, requiring an investment of several million pounds sterling. For over a decade the company had enjoyed a 65 percent market share for their product line and saw no reason for this strong market position to deteriorate. Given this large volume, the new plant offered the 'experience curve' advantages of economies to scale and made possible the long production runs required to meet the demand from the traditional market.

After ground was broken, but well before the factory was completed, a series of seemingly detached and isolated socioeconomic events occurred. These relatively insignificant events were to change the destiny of the company. Taken collectively, they rendered the factory economically obsolete and threw the corporate board of directors into a state of turmoil. The scenario of events went something like this. Due to the release of wartime controls on steel strip and tin, a number of new small firms that could economically can imported fruit sprang up. Initially, they in no way competed directly with the large vegetable canner. However, since their business was seasonal, they began to look for ways to keep their machinery and labor employed during the winter. Their answer came from a surprising source – the US quick-frozen food industry. The quick-freezing process requires a substantial degree of consistency in the crop. This consistency is very difficult to achieve. However, it turned out that large crops of the vegetable were grown in the United States and a substantial portion of US crops was unsuitable for quick freezing (a big industry in the United States) but quite suitable for canning. Furthermore, American farmers had been selling this surplus crop at a very low price for animal feed and were only too happy to make it available at an attractive price to the small canners in the United Kingdom. The canners jumped at the opportunity and imported the crop. Using off-season production capacity they began to offer a low-cost product in the large canner's market. The small canners' position was further strengthened as underdeveloped countries began to vie with the

United States in an effort to become the cheapest source of supply for the crop.

These untimely events in the large canner's supply market were compounded by events in its product market. Prior to the introduction of quick-freezing, the company featured a high quality, higher price premier brand that dominated the market. This market advantage, however, was diminished by the cascading effect of several more unpredictable events. As the scenario unfolded the quick-frozen product captured the high-quality strata of the market, a growing dimension due to increased affluence. The smaller canners stripped off the lower price layers of the market, aided in part by another seemingly unrelated development in retailing – the advent of supermarkets. As supermarkets and large grocery chains developed, they sought to improve their position by establishing their own in-house brand names and by buying in bulk. The small canner filled this need for the supermarket chains. Small canners could undercut the price of the manufacturer's brand product because they had low production costs and almost no marketing expenses. Soon supermarket house brands (which had accounted for less than 1 percent of the market prior to the war) became the source of 50 percent of the market sales. The smaller canners were the benefactors of almost all of this growth.

As a result, the company's fancy new automated factory was totally inappropriate for the current market situation. The company's management had failed to appreciate that a number of outside events were becoming connected with each other in a way that was leading up to an inevitable general change. They tried desperately to defend their traditional product lines, but, in the end, this was to no avail. After a series of financial setbacks, the company had to change its mission. It reemerged several years later with a new product mix and a new identity. Management had learned the hard way that their strategy problems were neither problems of simplicity nor problems of disorganized complexity. They were problems of organized complexity.

Many corporate policy planning and strategy issues exhibit this property of organized complexity. The vegetable canning company's automated plant decision clearly was made under conditions of organized complexity. Pricing problems also frequently display this characteristic. Recently, a large pharmaceutical firm addressed the seemingly simple problem of setting a price for its primary drug line. The company's management soon learned, however, that there was an intricate web of corporate relationships woven around this one decision. Below the surface there was a structure of complex relationships between the firm's drug pricing policy and physicians, pharmacists, patients, competitors, suppliers, the FDA, and other parties. These relationships organized the complexity of the firm's pricing decision problem. Purely analytical or statistical methods were rendered inappropriate.

'Wicked' Problems

Today, few of the pressing problems are truly problems of simplicity or of disorganized complexity. They are more like the problems described in the illustrative cases above and the ones we uncovered in our little experiment – problems of organized complexity. These problems simply cannot be tamed in the same way that other problems can. For this reason Rittel refers to these problems of organized complexity as 'wicked' problems. Wicked problems are not necessarily wicked in the perverse sense of being evil. Rather, they are wicked like the head of a hydra. They are an ensnarled web of tentacles. The more you attempt to tame them, the more complicated they become.

Rittel has identified several characteristic properties of wicked problems that distinguish them from tame problems. These properties are:

1   *Ability to formulate the problem*

   (a) Tame problems can be exhaustively formulated and written down on a piece of paper.

   (b) Wicked problems have no definitive formulation.

2   *Relationship between problem and solution*

   (a) Tame problems can be formulated separately from any notion of what their solution might be.

   (b) Every formulation of a wicked problem corresponds to a statement of solution and vice versa. Understanding the problem is synonymous with solving it.

3   *Testability*

   (a) The solution to a tame problem can be tested. Either it is correct or it is false. Mistakes and errors can be pinpointed.

   (b) There is no single criteria system or rule that determines whether the solution to a wicked problem is correct or false. Solutions can only be good or bad relative to one another.

4   *Finality*

   (a) Tame problems have closure – a clear solution and ending point. The end can be determined by means of a test.

   (b) There is no stopping rule for wicked problems. Like a Faustian bargain, they require eternal vigilance. There is always room for improvement. Moreover, since there is neither an immediate nor ultimate test for the solution to the problem, one never knows when one's work is done. As a result, the potential consequences of the problem are played out indefinitely.

5   *Tractability*

    (a) There is an exhaustive list of permissible operations that can be used to solve a tame problem.

    (b) There is no exhaustive, enumerable list of permissible operations to be used for solving a wicked problem.

6   *Explanatory characteristics*

    (a) A tame problem may be stated as a 'gap' between what 'is' and what 'ought' to be and there is a clear explanation for every gap.

    (b) Wicked problems have many possible explanations for the same discrepancy. Depending on which explanation one chooses, the solution takes on a different form.

7   *Level of analysis*

    (a) Every tame problem has an identifiable, certain, natural form; there is no need to argue about the level of the problem. The proper level of generality can be found for bounding the problem and identifying its root cause.

    (b) Every wicked problem can be considered as a symptom of another problem. It has no identifiable root cause; since curing symptoms does not cure problems, one is never sure the problem is being attacked at the proper level.

8   *Reproducibility*

    (a) A tame problem can be abstracted from the real world, and attempts can be made to solve it over and over again until the correct solution is found.

    (b) Each wicked problem is a one-shot operation. Once a solution is attempted, you can never undo what you have already done. There is no trial and error.

9   *Replicability*

    (a) The same tame problem may repeat itself many times.

    (b) Every wicked problem is essentially unique.

10   *Responsibility*

    (a) No one can be blamed for failing to solve a tame problem, although solving a tame problem may bring someone acclaim.

    (b) The wicked problem solver has 'no right to be wrong.' He is morally responsible for what he is doing and must share the blame when things go wrong. However, since there is no way of knowing when a wicked problem is solved, very few people are praised for grappling with them.

Characteristics of wicked problems   Most policy planning and strategy problems are wicked problems of organized complexity. These complex wicked problems also exhibit the following characteristics:

1   *Interconnectedness.* Strong connections link each problem to other problems. As a result, these connections sometimes circle back to form feedback loops. 'Solutions' aimed at the problem seem inevitably to have important opportunity costs and side effects. How they work out depends on events beyond the scope of any one problem.

2   *Complicatedness.* Wicked problems have numerous important elements with relationships among them, including important 'feedback loops' through which a change tends to multiply itself or perhaps even cancel itself out. Generally, there are various leverage points where analysis and ideas for intervention might focus, as well as many possible approaches and plausible programs of action. There is also a likelihood that different programs should be combined to deal with a given problem.

3   *Uncertainty.* Wicked problems exist in a dynamic and largely uncertain environment, which creates a need to accept risk, perhaps incalculable risk. Contingency planning and also the flexibility to respond to unimagined and perhaps unimaginable contingencies are both necessary.

4   *Ambiguity.* The problem can be seen in quite different ways, depending on the viewer's personal characteristics, loyalties, past experiences, and even on accidental circumstances of involvement. There is no single 'correct view' of the problem.

5   *Conflict.* Because of competing claims, there is often a need to trade off 'goods' against 'bads' within the same value system. Conflicts of interest among persons or organizations with different or even antagonistic value systems are to be expected. How things will work out may depend on interaction among powerful interests that are unlikely to enter into fully cooperative arrangements.

6   *Societal Constraints.* Social, organizational, and political constraints and capabilities, as well as technological ones, are central both to the feasibility and the desirability of solutions.

These characteristics spell difficulty for the policymaker who seeks to serve a social system by changing it for the better. Policymakers must choose the means for securing improvement for the people they serve. They must design, steer, and maintain a stable social system in the context of a complex environment. To do this, they require new methods of real world problem solving to guide their policy-making activities. Otherwise, they run the risk of setting their social systems adrift.

Implications for policy making The wicked problems of organized complexity have two major implications for designing processes for making policy:

1   There must be a broader participation of affected parties, directly and indirectly, in the policy-making process.

2   Policy making must be based on a wider spectrum of information gathered from a larger number of diverse sources.

Let us consider each of these implications in turn. The first implication indicates that policy making is increasingly becoming a political process, political in the sense that it involves individuals forming into groups to pursue common interests. Turn again to the results of the little experiment conducted at the outset of this chapter. You will find that in almost every case there are a variety of individual interests at stake in each problem area cited. Furthermore, one of the major factors creating the linkages between problem areas – organizing their complexity – is the number of diverse individual interests that cut across problem areas. Individuals are part of the problem and hence must be part of the solution.

This means that the raw material for forging solutions to wicked problems is not concentrated in a single head, but rather is widely dispersed among the various parties at stake. For any given wicked problem there is a variety of classes of expertise. Every affected party is an expert on some aspect of the problem and its solution. Furthermore, the disparate parties are bound together in a common venture. Thus some form of collective risk sharing is needed in order to deal effectively with the consequences of wicked problems. This suggests the need for a substantial degree of involvement in the policy-making process by those potentially affected by a policy in its formulation process. Effective policy is made *with*, or if adequate representation is present, *for*, but *not at* people. At least those involved should be able to voice their opinion on the relative goodness or badness of proposed solutions.

The diversity of parties at stake is related to the second implication. Since much of the necessary information for coping with wicked problems resides in the heads of several individuals, methods are needed to obtain this information from them and to communicate it to others. This means that as many of the different sources of information as possible must be identified. The relevant information must be obtained from each and stated in an explicit manner.

Contained in the minds of each participant in a wicked problem are powerful notions as to what is, what ought to be, why things are the way they are, how they can be changed, and how to think about their complexity. This represents a much broader class of information than is commonly used to solve problems of simplicity or of disorganized complexity. Also, this participant-based information is less likely to have been stated and recorded in a communicable form. Consequently, this information must be 'objectified' – explicitly, articulated – so that the basis for each party's judgments may be exchanged with others. Objectification has the advantages of being explicit, providing a memory, controlling the delegation of judgments, and raising pertinent issues that might have been ignored otherwise. It also stimulates *doubt*.

To be in doubt about a piece of information is to withhold assent to it. Given the range of diverse information that characterizes a wicked problem, participants in the policy-making process are well advised to develop a healthy respect for the method of doubt. In dealing with problems of organized complexity one should start with Descartes' rule: 'The first precept was never to accept a thing as true until I knew it was such without a single doubt.' This does not mean that one should be a 'nay sayer' or a permanent skeptic. To do so would impede responsible action that must be taken. What it does imply is that one should withhold judgment on things until they have been tested.

All problem-solving methods presuppose some form of guarantor for the correctness of their solutions. Problems of simplicity can be tested and solutions guaranteed by means of repeated solving, just as a theorem is proven in mathematics. This is because simple problems can be stated in closed form. The solutions to problems of disorganized complexity can be guaranteed within some stated confidence interval or degree of risk because the problems are statistical in nature. However, since there are no clearly identifiable correct solutions to problems of organized complexity, neither analytic nor statistical proofs can guarantee results. For solutions to wicked problems, the method of doubt is the best guarantor available.

Dialectics and argumentation are methods of *systematizing* doubt. They entail the processes of

1   making information and its underlying assumptions explicit;

2   raising questions and issues toward which different positions can be taken;

3   gathering evidence and building arguments for and against each position;

4   attempting to arrive at some final conclusion.

Being fundamentally an argumentative process, these four processes are inherent to policy making. For every policy decision there are always at least two alternative choices that can be made. There is an argument for and against each alternative. It is by weighing the pros and cons of each argument that an informed decision can be reached. In policy making these processes of dialectics and argumentation are inescapable.

In addition to the need for participation by a variety of parties and the existence of diverse information sources, two other characteristics of wicked problems should be noted. One is that they must be dealt with in a holistic or synthetic way as well as in an analytic way. Two processes are necessary: to subdivide a complex problem into its elements and to determine the nature of the linkages that give organization to its complexity – the task of analysis; and to understand the problem as a *whole* – the task of synthesis. A critical dimension of wicked problems of organized complexity is that they must ultimately be dealt with in their totality. This calls for holistic thinking. Analysis is only an aid toward reaching a synthesis.

A second characteristic of these problems is that there is some form of latent structure within them. They are organized to some extent. Organization is not an all or nothing phenomenon. Consequently, systems thinking and methods can be used to gain better insight into the structural aspects of wicked problems.

Quest for new methods The nature and implications of organized complexity suggest some new criteria for the design of real world problem-solving methods. These criteria are:

1   *Participative.* Since the relevant knowledge necessary to solve a complex problem and also the relevant resources necessary to implement the solution are distributed among many individuals, the methods must incorporate the active involvement of groups of people.

2   *Adversarial.* We believe that the best judgment on the assumptions in a complex problem is rendered in the context of opposition. Doubt is the guarantor.

3   *Integrative.* A unified set of assumptions and a coherent plan of action are needed to guide effective policy planning and strategy making. Participation and the adversarial process tend to differentiate and expand the knowledge base. Something else is needed to bring this diverse but relevant knowledge together in the form of a total picture.

4   *Managerial Mind Supporting.* Most problem-solving methods and computer aids focus on 'decision support systems,' that is, on systems that provide guidance for choosing a particular course of action to solve a particular decision problem. Problems of organized complexity, as we have seen, are ongoing, ill structured, and generally 'wicked.' The choice of individual courses of action is only a part of the manager's or policymaker's need. More important is the need to achieve insight into the nature of the complexity and to formulate concepts and world views for coping with it. It is the policymaker's thinking process and his or her mind that needs to be supported.

Reading 2   Cultural Constraints in Management Theories

By Geert Hofstede[†]

Lewis Carroll's *Alice in Wonderland* contains the famous story of Alice's croquet game with the Queen of Hearts. Alice thought she had never seen such a curious croquet-ground in all her life; it was all ridges and furrows; the balls were live hedgehogs, the mallets live flamingoes, and the soldiers had to double themselves up and to stand on their hands and feet to make the arches. You probably know how the story goes: Alice's flamingo mallet turns its head whenever she wants to strike with it; her hedgehog ball runs away; and the doubled-up soldier arches walk around all the time. The only rule seems to be that the Queen of Hearts always wins.

Alice's croquet playing problems are good analogies to attempts to build culture-free theories of management. Concepts available for this purpose are themselves alive with culture, having been developed within a particular cultural context. They have a tendency to guide our thinking toward our desired conclusion. As the same reasoning may also be applied to the arguments in this reading, I better tell you my conclusion before I continue – so that the rules of my game are understood. In this reading we take a trip around the world to demonstrate that there are no such things as universal management theories.

Diversity in management *practices* as we go around the world has been recognized in US management literature for more than 30 years. The term 'comparative management' has been used since the 1960s. However, it has taken much longer for the US academic community to accept that not only practices but also the validity of theories may stop at national borders, and I wonder whether even today everybody would agree with this statement.

The idea that the validity of a theory is constrained by national borders is more obvious in Europe, with all its borders, than in a huge borderless country like the US. Already in the sixteenth century Michel de Montaigne, a Frenchman, wrote a statement which was made famous by Blaise Pascal about a century later; '*Vérite en-deça des Pyrenées, erreur au-delà*' – 'There are truths on this side of the Pyrenées which are falsehoods on the other.'

[†] Source: This article was adapted with permission from Cultural Constraints in Management Theories, *Academy of Management Executive*, vol. 7 No. 1, 1993.

From Don Armado's Love to Taylor's Science

According to the comprehensive ten-volume Oxford English Dictionary, the words 'manage,' 'management,' and 'manager' appeared in the English language in the sixteenth century. The oldest recorded use of the word 'manager' is in Shakespeare's *Love's Labour's Lost*, dating from 1588, in which Don Adriano de Armado, 'a fantastical Spaniard,' exclaims (Act I scene ii. 188): 'Adieu, valour! rust, rapier! be still, drum! for your manager is in love; yea, he loveth'.

The linguistic origin of the word is from Latin *manus*, hand, via the Italian *maneggiare*, which is the training of horses in the manege; subsequently its meaning was extended to skillful handling in general, like of arms and musical instruments, as Don Armado illustrates. However, the word also became associated with the French *menage*, household, as an equivalent of 'husbandry' in its sense of the art of running a household. The theater of present-day management contains elements of both *manege* and *menage* and different managers and cultures may use different accents.

The founder of the science of economics, the Scot Adam Smith, in his 1776 book *The Wealth of Nations*, used 'manage,' 'management' (even 'bad management') and 'manager' when dealing with the process and the persons involved in operating joint stock companies. British economist John Stuart Mill (1806–1873) followed Smith in this use and clearly expressed his distrust of such hired people who were not driven by ownership. Since the 1880s the word 'management' appeared occasionally in writings by American engineers, until it was canonized as a modern science by Frederick W. Taylor in *Shop Management* in 1903 and in *The Principles of Scientific Management* in 1911.

While Smith and Mill used 'management' to describe a process and 'managers' for the persons involved, 'management' in the American sense – which has since been taken back by the British – refers not only to the process but also to the managers as a class of people. This class (1) does not own a business but sells its skills to act on behalf of the owners and (2) does not produce personally but is indispensable for making others produce, through motivation. Members of this class carry a high status and many American boys and girls aspire to the role. In the US, the manager is a cultural hero.

Let us now turn to other parts of the world. We will look at management in its context in other successful modern economies: Germany, Japan, France, Holland, and among the Overseas Chinese. Then we will examine management in the much larger part of the world that is still poor, especially South-East Asia and Africa, ·and in the new political configurations of Eastern Europe, and Russia in particular. We will then return to the US via mainland China.

Germany

The manager is not a cultural hero in Germany. If anybody, it is the engineer who fills the hero role. Frederick Taylor's scientific management was conceived in a society of immigrants – where a large number of workers with diverse backgrounds and skills had to work together. In Germany this heterogeneity never existed.

Elements of the mediaeval guild system have survived in historical continuity in Germany until the present day. In particular, a very effective apprenticeship system exists both on the shop floor and in the office, which alternates practical work and classroom courses. At the end of the apprenticeship the worker receives a certificate, the *Facharbeiterbrief*, which is recognized throughout the country. About two thirds of the German worker population holds such a certificate and a corresponding occupational pride. In fact, quite a few German company presidents have worked their way up from the ranks through an apprenticeship. In comparison, two thirds of the worker population in Britain have no occupational qualification at all.

The highly skilled and responsible German workers do not necessarily need a manager, American-style, to 'motivate' them. They expect their boss or Meister to assign their tasks and to be the expert in resolving technical problems. Comparisons of similar German, British, and French organizations show the Germans as having the highest rate of personnel in productive roles and the lowest both in leadership and staff roles.

Japan

The American type of manager is also missing in Japan. In the United States, the core of the enterprise is the managerial class. The core of the Japanese enterprise is the permanent worker group; workers who for all practical purposes are tenured and who aspire at life-long employment. They are distinct from the non-permanent employees – most women and subcontracted teams led by gang bosses, to be laid off in slack periods. University graduates in Japan first join the permanent worker group and subsequently fill various positions, moving from line to staff as the need occurs while paid according to seniority rather than position. They take part in Japanese-style group consultation sessions for important decisions, which extend the decision-making period but guarantee fast implementation afterwards. Japanese are to a large extent controlled by their peer group rather than by their manager.

American theories of leadership are ill-suited for the Japanese group-controlled situation. During the past two decades, the Japanese have developed their own 'PM' theory of leadership, in which P stands for performance and M for maintenance. The latter is less a concern for individual employees than for maintaining social stability. In view of the amazing success of the Japanese economy in the past 30 years, many Americans have sought for the secrets of Japanese management, hoping to copy them.

France

The manager, US style, does not exist in France either. The French researcher Philippe d'Iribarne (1990) identifies three kinds of basic principles (*logiques*) of management. In the USA, the principle is the *fair contract* between employer and employee, which gives the manager considerable prerogatives, but within its limits. This is really a labor market in which the worker sells his or her labor for a price. In France, the principle is the *honor* of each class in a society which has always been and remains extremely stratified, in which superiors behave as superior beings and subordinates accept and expect this, conscious of their own lower level in the national hierarchy but also of the honor of their own class. The French do not think in terms of managers versus nonmanagers but in terms of *cadres* versus *non-cadres*; one becomes cadre by attending the proper schools and one remains it forever; regardless of their actual task, cadres have the privileges of a higher social class, and it is very rare for a non-cadre to cross the ranks.

The conflict between French and American theories of management became apparent in the beginning of the twentieth century, in a criticism by the great French management pioneer Henri Fayol (1841–1925) on his US colleague and contemporary Frederick W. Taylor (1856–1915). Fayol was a French engineer whose career as a cadre supérieur culminated in the position of *Président-Directeur-Général* of a mining company. After his retirement he formulated his experiences in a pathbreaking text on organization: *Administration industrielle et générale*, in which he focused on the sources of authority. Taylor was an American engineer who started his career in industry as a worker and attained his academic qualifications through evening studies. From chief engineer in a steel company he became one of the first management consultants. Taylor was not really concerned with the issue of authority at all; his focus was on efficiency. He proposed to split the task of the first-line boss into eight specialisms, each exercised by a different person; an idea which eventually led to the idea of a matrix organization.

Taylor's work appeared in a French translation in 1913, and Fayol read it and showed himself generally impressed but shocked by Taylor's 'denial of the principle of the Unity of Command' in the case of the eight-boss-system. Seventy years later André Laurent, another of Fayol's compatriots, found that French managers in a survey reacted very strongly against a suggestion that one employee could report to two different bosses, while US managers in the same survey showed fewer misgivings. Matrix organization has never become popular in France as it has in the United States.

Holland

In my own country, Holland or as it is officially called, the Netherlands, the study by Philippe d'Iribarne found the management principle to be a need for consensus among all parties, neither predetermined by a contractual relationship nor by class distinctions, but based on an open-ended exchange of views and a balancing of interests. In terms of the different origins of the word 'manager,' the organization in Holland is more menage (household) while in the United States it is more manege (horse drill).

At my university, the University of Limburg at Maastricht, we asked both the Americans and a matched group of Dutch students to describe their ideal job after graduation, using a list of 22 job characteristics. The Americans attached significantly more importance than the Dutch to earnings, advancement, benefits, a good working relationship with their boss, and security of employment. The Dutch attached more importance to freedom to adopt their own approach to the job, being consulted by their boss in his or her decisions, training opportunities, contributing to the success of their organization, fully using their skills and abilities, and helping others. This list confirms d'Iribarne's findings of a contractual employment relationship in the United States, based on earnings and career opportunities, against a consensual relationship in Holland. The latter has centuries-old roots, the Netherlands were the first republic in Western Europe (1609–1810), and a model for the American republic. The country has been and still is governed by a careful balancing of interests in a multi-party system.

In terms of management theories, both motivation and leadership in Holland are different from what they are in the United States. Leadership in Holland presupposes modesty, as opposed to assertiveness in the United States. No US leadership theory has room for that. Working in Holland is not a constant feast, however. There is a built-in premium on mediocrity and jealousy, as well as time-consuming ritual consultations to maintain the appearance of consensus and the pretense of modesty. There is unfortunately another side to every coin.

The Overseas Chinese

Among the champions of economic development in the past 30 years we find three countries mainly populated by Chinese living outside the Chinese mainland: Taiwan, Hong Kong and Singapore. Moreover, overseas Chinese play a very important role in the economies of Indonesia, Malaysia, the Philippines and Thailand, where they form an ethnic minority. If anything, the little dragons – Taiwan, Hong Kong and Singapore – have been more economically successful than Japan, moving from rags to riches and now counted among the world's wealthy industrial countries. Yet very little attention has been paid to the way in which their enterprises have been managed.

Overseas Chinese enterprises lack almost all characteristics of modern management. They tend to be small, cooperating for essential functions with other small organizations through networks based on personal relations. They are family-owned, without the separation between ownership and management typical in the West, or even in Japan and Korea. They normally focus on one product or market, with growth by opportunistic diversification; in this, they are extremely flexible. Decision making is centralized in the hands of one dominant family member, but other family members may be given new ventures to try their skills on. They are low-profile and extremely cost-conscious, applying Confucian virtues of thrift and persistence. Their size is kept small by the assumed lack of loyalty of non-family employees, who, if they are any good, will just wait and save until they can start their own family business.

Overseas Chinese prefer economic activities in which great gains can be made with little manpower, like commodity trading and real estate. They employ few professional managers, except their sons and sometimes daughters who have been sent to prestigious business schools abroad, but who upon return continue to run the family business the Chinese way.

The origin of this system, or – in the Western view – this lack of system, is found in the history of Chinese society, in which there were no formal laws, only formal networks of powerful people guided by general principles of Confucian virtue. The favors of the authorities could change daily, so nobody could be trusted except one's kinfolk – of whom, fortunately, there used to be many, in an extended family structure. The overseas Chinese way of doing business is also very well adapted to their position in the countries in which they form ethnic minorities, often envied and threatened by ethnic violence.

Overseas Chinese businesses following this unprofessional approach command a collective gross national product of some 200 to 300 billion US dollars, exceeding the GNP of Australia. There is no denying that it works.

Management Transfer to Poor Countries

Four-fifths of the world population live in countries that are not rich but poor. After World War II and decolonization, the stated purpose of the

United Nations and the World Bank has been to promote the development of all the world's countries in a war on poverty. After 40 years it
looks very much like we are losing this war. If one thing has become clear,
it is that the export of Western – mostly American – management practices and theories to poor countries has contributed little to nothing to
their development. There has been no lack of effort and money spent for
this purpose: students from poor countries have been trained in this
country, and teachers and Peace Corps workers have been sent to the
poor countries. If nothing else, the general lack of success in economic
development of other countries should be sufficient argument to doubt
the validity of Western management theories in non-Western environments.

    If we examine different parts of the world, the development pic-
ture is not equally bleak, and history is often a better predictor than
economic factors for what happens today. There is a broad regional
pecking order with East Asia leading. The little dragons have passed
into the camp of the wealthy: then follow South-East Asia (with its
overseas Chinese minorities), Latin America (in spite of the debt crisis),
South Asia, and Africa always trails behind. Several African countries
have only become poorer since decolonization.

Russia and China

The crumbling of the former Eastern bloc has left us with a scattering of
states and would-be states of which the political and economic future is
extremely uncertain. The best predictions are those based on a knowledge of history, because historical trends have taken revenge on the
arrogance of the Soviet rulers who believed they could turn them around
by brute power. One obvious fact is that the former bloc is extremely
heterogeneous, including countries traditionally closely linked with the
West by trade and travel, like the Czech Republic, Hungary, Slovenia, and
the Baltic states, as well as others with a Byzantine or Turkish past: some
having been prosperous, others always extremely poor.

    Let me limit myself to the Russian republic, a huge territory with
some 140 million inhabitants, mainly Russians. We know quite a bit
about the Russians as their country was a world power for several hundreds of years before communism, and in the nineteenth century it has
produced some of the greatest writers in world literature. If I want to
understand the Russians – including how they could so long support the
Soviet regime – I tend to re-read Lev Nikolayevich Tolstoy. In his most
famous novel *Anna Karenina* one of the main characters is a landowner,
Levin, whom Tolstoy uses to express his own views and convictions
about his people. Russian peasants used to be serfs; serfdom had been
abolished in 1861, but the peasants, now tenants, remained as passive as
before. Levin wanted to break this passivity by dividing the land among

his peasants in exchange for a share of the crops; but the peasants only let the land deteriorate further. Here follows a quote:

> [Levin] read political economy and socialistic works . . . but, as he had expected, found nothing in them related to his undertaking. In the political economy books – in [John Stuart] Mill, for instance, whom he studied first and with great ardour, hoping every minute to find an answer to the questions that were engrossing him – he found only certain laws deduced from the state of agriculture in Europe; but he could not for the life of him see why these laws, which did not apply to Russia, should be considered universal. . . . Political economy told him that the laws by which Europe had developed and was developing her wealth were universal and absolute. Socialist teaching told him that development along those lines leads to ruin. And neither of them offered the smallest enlightenment as to what he, Levin, and all the Russian peasants and landowners were to do with their millions of hands and millions of acres, to make them as productive as possible for the common good.

In the summer of 1991, the Russian lands yielded a record harvest, but a large share of it rotted in the fields because no people were to be found for harvesting. The passivity is still there, and not only among the peasants. And the heirs of John Stuart Mill (whom we met before as one of the early analysts of 'management') again present their universal recipes which simply do not apply.

Citing Tolstoy, I implicitly suggest that management theorists cannot neglect the great literature of the countries they want their ideas to apply to. The greatest novel in the Chinese literature is considered Cao Xueqin's *The Story of the Stone*, also known as *The Dream of the Red Chamber* which appeared around 1760. It describes the rise and fall of two branches of an aristocratic family in Beijing, who live in adjacent plots in the capital. Their plots are joined by a magnificent garden with several pavilions in it, and the young, mostly female members of both families are allowed to live in them. One day the management of the garden is taken over by a young woman, Tan-Chun, who states:

> I think we ought to pick out a few experienced trust-worthy old women from among the ones who work in the Garden – women who know something about gardening already – and put the upkeep of the Garden into their hands. We needn't ask them to pay us rent; all we need ask them for is an annual share of the produce. There would be four advantages in this arrangement. In the first place, if we have people whose sole occupation is to look after trees and flowers and so on, the condition of the Garden will improve gradually year after year and there will be no more of those long periods of neglect followed by bursts of feverish activity when things have been allowed to get out of hand. Secondly there won't be the spoiling and wastage we get at present. Thirdly the women themselves will gain a little extra to add to

their incomes which will compensate them for the hard work they put in throughout the year. And fourthly, there's no reason why we shouldn't use the money we should otherwise have spent on nursery-men, rockery specialists, horticultural cleaners and so on for other purposes.

As the story goes on, the capitalist privatization – because that is what it is – of the Garden is carried through, and it works. When in the 1980s Deng Xiaoping allowed privatization in the Chinese villages, it also worked. If we remember what Chinese entrepreneurs are able to do once they have become Overseas Chinese, we shouldn't be too surprised. But what works in China – and worked two centuries ago – does not have to work in Russia, not in Tolstoy's days and not today. I am not offering a solution: I only protest against a naive universalism that knows only one recipe for development, the one supposed to have worked in the United States.

A Theory of Culture in Management

There is something in all countries called 'management,' but its meaning differs to a larger or smaller extent from one country to the other, and it takes considerable historical and cultural insight into local conditions to understand its processes, philosophies, and problems. If already the word may mean so many different things, how can we expect one country's theories of management to apply abroad? One should be extremely careful in making this assumption, and test it before considering it proven. Management is not a phenomenon that can be isolated from other processes taking place in a society. It interacts with what happens in the family, at school, in politics, and government. It is obviously also related to religion and to beliefs about science. Theories of management always had to be interdisciplinary, but if we cross national borders they should become more interdisciplinary than ever.

As the word culture plays such an important role in my theory, let me give you my definition, which differs from some other very respectable definitions. Culture to me is *the collective programming of the mind which distinguishes one group or category of people from another*. In the part of my work I am referring to now, the category of people is the nation.

Cultural differences between nations can be, to some extent, described using five bipolar dimensions. The position of a country on these dimensions allows us to make some predictions on the way their society operates, including their management processes and the kind of theories applicable to their management.

The first dimension is labeled *power distance*, and it can be defined as the degree of inequality among people which the population of a country considers as normal: from relatively equal (that is, small power distance) to extremely unequal (large power distance). All societies are unequal, but some are more unequal than others.

The second dimension is labeled *individualism*, and it is the degree to which people in a country prefer to act as individuals rather than as members of groups. The opposite of individualism can be called *collectivism*, so collectivism is low individualism. The way I use the word it has no political connotations. In collectivist societies a child learns to respect the group to which it belongs, usually the family, and to differentiate between in-group members and out-group members (that is, all other people). When children grow up they remain members of their group, and they expect the group to protect them when they are in trouble. In return, they have to remain loyal to their group throughout life. In individualist societies, a child learns very early to think of itself as 'I' instead of a part of 'we'. It expects one day to have to stand on its own feet and not to get protection from its group any more; and therefore it also does not feel a need for strong loyalty.

The third dimension is called *masculinity* and its opposite pole *femininity*. It is the degree to which tough values like assertiveness, performance, success and competition, which in nearly all societies are associated with the role of men, prevail over tender values like the quality of life, maintaining warm personal relationships, service, care for the weak, and solidarity, which in nearly all societies are more associated with women's roles. Women's roles differ from men's roles in all countries; but in tough societies, the differences are larger than in tender ones.

The fourth dimension is labeled *uncertainty avoidance*, and it can be defined as the degree to which people in a country prefer structured over unstructured situations. Structured situations are those in which there are clear rules as to how one should behave. These rules can be written down, but they can also be unwritten and imposed by tradition. In countries that score high on uncertainty avoidance, people tend to show more nervous energy, while in countries that score low, people are more easy-going. A (national) society with strong uncertainty avoidance can be called rigid; one with weak uncertainty avoidance, flexible. In countries where uncertainty avoidance is strong a feeling prevails of 'what is different, is dangerous.' In weak uncertainty avoidance societies, the feeling would rather be 'what is different, is curious.'

The fifth dimension is labeled *long-term versus short-term orientation*. On the long-term side one finds values oriented towards the future, like thrift (saving) and persistence. On the short-term side one finds values rather oriented towards the past and present, like respect for tradition and fulfilling social obligations.

Table 1.2 lists the scores on all five dimensions for the United States and for the other countries we just discussed. The table shows that each country has its own configuration on the four dimensions. Some of the values in the table have been estimated based on imperfect replications or personal impressions. The different dimension scores do not 'explain' all the differences in management I described earlier. To understand management in a country, one should have both knowledge of and empathy with the entire local scene. However, the scores should make us aware that people in other countries may think, feel, and act very differently from us when confronted with basic problems of society.

Idiosyncrasies of American Management Theories

In comparison to other countries, the US culture profile presents itself as below average on power distance and uncertainty avoidance, highly individualistic, fairly masculine, and short-term oriented. The Germans show a stronger uncertainty avoidance and less extreme individualism; the Japanese are different on all dimensions, least on power distance; the French show larger power distance and uncertainty avoidance, but are less individualistic and somewhat feminine, the Dutch resemble the Americans on the first three dimensions, but score extremely feminine

TABLE 1.2
Culture dimension scores for 10 countries

	PD	ID	MA	UA	LT
USA	40 L	91 H	62 H	46 L	29 L
Germany	35 L	67 H	66 H	65 M	31 M
Japan	54 M	46 M	95 H	92 H	80 H
France	68 H	71 H	43 M	86 H	30*L
Netherlands	38 L	80 H	14 L	53 M	44 M
Hong Kong	68 H	25 L	57 H	29 L	96 H
Indonesia	78 H	14 L	46 M	48 L	25*L
West Africa	77 H	20 L	46 M	54 M	16 L
Russia	95*H	50*M	40*L	90*H	10*L
China	80*H	20*L	50*M	60*M	118 H

* estimated
Key: PD = Power Distance; ID = Individualism; MA = Masculinity; UA = Uncertainty Avoidance; LT = Long-Term Orientation
H = top third, M = medium third, L = bottom third (among 53 countries and regions for the first four dimensions; among 23 countries for the fifth)

and relatively long-term oriented; Hong Kong Chinese combine large power distance with weak uncertainty avoidance, collectivism, and are very long-term oriented; and so on.

The American culture profile is reflected in American management theories. I will just mention three elements not necessarily present in other countries: the stress on market processes, the stress on the individual, and the focus on managers rather than on workers.

The Stress on Market Processes

During the 1970s and 1980s it has become fashionable in the United States to look at organizations from a 'transaction costs' viewpoint. Economist Oliver Williamson has opposed 'hierarchies' to 'markets.' The reasoning is that human social life consists of economic transactions between individuals. We found the same in d'Iribarne's description of the US principle of the contract between employer and employee, the labor market in which the worker sells his or her labor for a price. These individuals will form hierarchical organizations when the cost of the economic transactions (such as getting information, finding out whom to trust etc.) is lower in a hierarchy than when all transactions would take place on a free market.

From a cultural perspective the important point is that the 'market' is the point of departure or base model, and the organization is explained from market failure. A culture that produces such a theory is likely to prefer organizations that internally resemble markets to organizations that internally resemble more structured models, like those in Germany or France. The ideal principle of control in organizations in the market philosophy is competition between individuals. This philosophy fits a society that combines a not-too-large power distance with a not-too-strong uncertainty avoidance and individualism; besides the USA, it will fit all other Anglo countries.

The Stress on the Individual

I find this constantly in the design of research projects and hypotheses; also in the fact that in the US psychology is clearly a more respectable discipline in management circles than sociology. Culture however is a collective phenomenon. Although we may get our information about culture from individuals, we have to interpret it at the level of collectivities. There are snags here known as the 'ecological fallacy' and the 'reverse ecological fallacy.' None of the US college textbooks on methodology I know deals sufficiently with the problem of multilevel analysis.

A striking example is found in the otherwise excellent book *Organizational Culture and Leadership* by Edgar H. Schein[9]. On the basis of his consulting experience he compares two large companies, nicknamed

'Action' and 'Multi.' He explains the difference in cultures between these companies by the group dynamics in their respective boardrooms. Nowhere in the book are any conclusions drawn from the fact that the first company is an American-based computer firm, and the second a Swiss-based pharmaceutical firm. This information is not even mentioned. A stress on interactions among individuals obviously fits a culture identified as the most individualistic in the world, but it will not be so well understood by the four-fifths of the world population for whom the group prevails over the individual.

One of the conclusions of my own multilevel research has been that culture at the national level and culture at the organizational level – corporate culture – are two very different phenomena and that the use of a common term for both is confusing. If we do use the common term, we should also pay attention to the occupational and the gender level of culture. National cultures differ primarily in the fundamental, invisible values held by a majority of their members, acquired in early childhood, whereas organization cultures are a much more superficial phenomenon residing mainly in the visible practices of the organization, acquired by socialization of the new members who join as young adults. National cultures change only very slowly if at all; organizational cultures may be consciously changed, although this isn't necessarily easy. This difference between the two types of culture is the secret of the existence of multinational corporations that employ employees with extremely different national cultural values. What keeps them together is a corporate culture based on common practices.

The Stress on Managers rather than Workers

The core element of a work organization around the world is the people who do the work. All the rest is superstructure, and I hope to have demonstrated to you that it may take many different shapes. In the US literature on work organization, however, the core element, if not explicitly then implicitly, is considered the manager. This may well be the result of the combination of extreme individualism with fairly strong masculinity, which has turned the manager into a cultural hero of almost mythical proportions. For example, he – not really she – is supposed to make decisions all the time. Those of you who are or have been managers must know that this is a fable. Very few management decisions are just 'made' as the myth suggests it. Managers are much more involved in maintaining networks; if anything, it is the rank-and-file worker who can really make decisions on his or her own, albeit on a relatively simple level.

Conclusion

This article started with Alice in Wonderland. In fact, the management theorist who ventures outside his or her own country into other parts of the world is like Alice in Wonderland. He or she will meet strange beings, customs, ways of organizing or disorganizing and theories that are clearly stupid, old-fashioned or even immoral – yet they may work, or at least they may not fail more frequently than corresponding theories do at home. Then, after the first culture shock, the traveler to Wonderland will feel enlightened, and may be able to take his or her experiences home and use them advantageously. All great ideas in science, politics and management have traveled from one country to another, and been enriched by foreign influences. The roots of American management theories are mainly in Europe: with Adam Smith, John Stuart Mill, Lev Tolstoy, Max Weber, Henri Fayol, Sigmund Freud, Kurt Lewin and many others. These theories were re-planted here and they developed and bore fruit. The same may happen again. The last thing we need is a Monroe doctrine for management.

Further Readings

As a follow up to this chapter, readers seeking a general survey of the fragmented field of strategic management might want to look at Henry Mintzberg's article 'Strategy Formation: Schools of Thought'. In this article, Mintzberg gives a broad overview of the strategy process literature and identifies ten schools of thought. Unfortunately, the same type of overview for the strategy content literature is lacking. However, Kathleen Conner's article 'A Historical Comparison of Resource Based Theory and Five Schools of Thought within Industrial Economics: Do We Have a New Theory of the Firm?' gives a useful summary of the predominant economics-based theoretical approaches in the strategy content area. For a good discussion on the pluriformity of strategy theories, Richard Whitley's article 'The Fragmented State of Management Studies: Reasons and Consequences' is recommended.

If readers are interested in tensions, paradoxes and the dialectical method, Richard Mason and Ian Mitroff's book *Challenging Strategic Planning Assumptions* is truly challenging. Charles Hampden-Turner's *Charting the Corporate Mind: From Dilemma to Strategy* is also a thought-provoking account of how dialectics can be employed as a problem-solving approach. For a more detailed account of wicked problems, readers should actually go back to Horst Rittel, who coined the term. His article, together with Melvin Webber, titled 'Dilemmas in a General Theory of Planning,' is a particularly readable essay.

On the topic of international cultural differences, Geert Hofstede's original book, *Culture's Consequences*, and its more popular follow up, *Cultures and Organizations: Software of the Mind*, are highly recommended. For a broader discussion of international differences in management and business systems, readers are advised to turn to *The Seven Cultures of Capitalism*, by Charles Hampden-Turner and Fons Trompenaars, *European Management Systems*, by Ronnie Lessem and Fred Neubauer, and *A European Management Model: Beyond Diversity*, by Roland Calori and Philippe de Woot.

Section II

Strategy Process

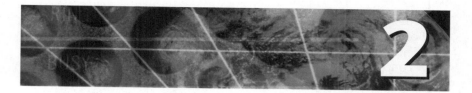

Strategic Thinking

When you have eliminated the impossible,
whatever remains, however improbable,
must be the truth.

(*Sherlock Holmes*, Arthur Conan Doyle 1859–1930; English novelist)

Imagination is more important
than knowledge.

(Albert Einstein 1879–1955; German-American physicist)

The Paradox of Logic and Creativity

At the beginning of Chapter 1 a concise definition of strategy was intentionally avoided. However, as the chapter progressed, it surfaced that strategy can be broadly conceived as a course of action for achieving an organization's purpose. It was argued that managers need strategies to solve the complicated, often wicked, problems with which they are confronted.

While the term *strategic problem* might have a negative connotation to some, it is not intended to denote only troublesome situations. It is a more general term, that refers to any challenging situation encountered by an organization that demands a reconsideration of the current course of action, either to profit from observed opportunities or to respond to perceived threats. The term *problem-solving* also has a connotation to many, namely, finding the optimal answer to a puzzle. However, what was said of strategy tensions in Chapter 1 can be extended to strategic problems in general – there might not be one best solution. Therefore, problem-solving should not be interpreted as the activity of finding *the* solution to a problem, but as the activity of finding *a* solution.

This chapter deals with the mode of thinking employed by people when confronted with strategic problems. Two issues will be central to this discussion on strategic thinking. First, how do people *define* strategic problems – how are problems identified and conceptualized? Second, how do people actually *solve* strategic problems – how are potential solutions generated, evaluated, and decided on? On both issues it is of interest to know what people really do (descriptive) and to know what people should do to be successful (prescriptive). Both an understanding of what is commonly done, and what leads to the best results, is of importance.

So, what is the fundamental nature of strategic thought processes? How does the mind of the strategist work and how should readers themselves think strategically? Opinions on this matter differ considerably, both among practitioners and theorists (who will jointly be referred to as *strategists* throughout this book). A whole spectrum of views exists, without any coherent clusters or schools of thought identifiable. However, two diametrically opposed positions can be observed at the extremes of the spectrum. On the one hand, there are strategists who argue that strategic thinking is one of the most advanced forms of analytical reasoning, requiring the consistent and rigorous use of logic. We shall refer to this point of view as the *rational thinking* perspective. On the other hand, there are strategists who argue that the essence of strategic thinking is the ability to break through orthodox beliefs, requiring the use of creativity. This point of view will be referred to as the *generative thinking* perspective.

Based on these two extremes, it seems that the disagreement between strategists revolves around the question whether strategic thinking is primarily logical or creative. These two factors are opposites and might be (partially) contradictory. To explore this paradox of logic and creativity, this chapter will proceed by means of *dialectical inquiry* – that is, a debate will be staged between the two opposite perspectives, with the intention of gaining a better understanding of the issues under discussion. In the next few pages, the rational and generative thinking perspectives will be further explained, and summarized in Table 2.1.

The Rational Thinking Perspective

Strategists employing the rational thinking perspective argue that strategic thinking is predominantly a 'logical activity'[1]. To deal with strategic problems the strategist must first consciously and thoroughly analyze the problem situation. Data must be gathered on all developments external to the organization, and this data must be processed to pinpoint the opportunities and threats in the organization's environment. Further-

TABLE 2.1
Rational thinking versus generative thinking perspective

	Rational Thinking Perspective	Generative Thinking Perspective
Emphasis on	Logic over creativity	Creativity over logic
Cognitive style	Analytical	Intuitive
Reasoning follows	Formal, fixed rules	Informal, variable rules
Nature of reasoning	Computational	Imaginative
Direction of reasoning	Vertical	Lateral
Value placed on	Consistency and rigor	Unorthodoxy and vision
Reasoning hindered by	Incomplete information	Adherence to current ideas
Assumption about reality	Objective, (partially) knowable	Subjective, (partially) createable
Decisions based on	Calculation	Judgement
Metaphor	Strategy as science	Strategy as art

more, the organization itself must be appraised, to uncover its strengths and weaknesses and to establish which resources are available. Once the problem has been defined, a number of alternative strategies can be identified by matching external opportunities to internal strengths. Then, the strategic options must be extensively screened, by evaluating them on a number of criteria, such as consistency, consonance, advantage, feasibility, potential return and risks. The best strategy can be selected by comparing the scores of all options and determining the level of risk the strategist is willing to take. The chosen strategy can subsequently be implemented.

This type of intellectual effort requires well-developed analytical skills. Strategists must be able to rigorously, consistently and objectively comb through huge amounts of data, interpreting and combining findings to arrive at a complete picture of the current problem situation. Possible solutions require critical appraisal and all possible contingencies must be logically thought through. Advocates of the rational perspective argue that such thinking strongly resembles the problem-solving approach of chess grand masters. They also thoroughly assess their competitive position, sift through a variety of options and calculate which course of action brings the best chances of success. Therefore, the thought processes of chess grand masters can be used as an analogy for what goes on in the mind of the strategist.

While depicted here as a purely linear process of analysis, evaluation and choice, proponents of the rational thinking perspective note that in reality strategists often have to backtrack and redo some of these steps, as new information becomes available or chosen strategies do not work out. Strategists attempt to be as comprehensive, consistent and rigorous as possible in their analyses and calculations, but of course they cannot know everything and their conclusions are not always perfect. Even with the most advanced forecasting techniques, not all developments can be foreseen. Even with state of the art market research, some trends can be missed. Even with cutting edge test marketing, scenario analyses, competitive simulations and net present value calculations, some selected strategies can turn out to be failures. Strategists are not all-knowing, and do make mistakes – their rationality is limited by incomplete information and imperfect cognitive facilities. Yet, strategists try to be as rational as possible. Simon[2] refers to this as *bounded rationality* – 'people act intentionally rational, but only limitedly so.' This coincides with Ambrose Bierce's famous sarcastic definition of logic as 'the art of thinking and reasoning in strict accordance with the limitations and incapacities of the human misunderstanding.'

The (boundedly) rational strategist must sometimes improvise to make up for a lack of information, but will try to do this as logically as possible. Inferences and speculation will always be based on the facts as known. By articulating assumptions and explicitly stating the facts and arguments on which conclusions have been based, problem definitions and solutions can be debated within the firm, to confirm that they have been arrived at using sound reasoning.

The alternative to a rational approach, it is often pointed out, is to be irrational and illogical, which surely cannot be a desirable alternative for the strategist. Non-rational thinking comes in a variety of forms. For instance, people's thinking can be guided by their *emotions*. Feelings such as love, hate, guilt, regret, pride, anxiety, frustration, and embarrassment, can all cloud the strategist's understanding of a problem situation and the possible solutions. Adherents of the rational thinking perspective do not dispute the importance of emotions – the purpose of an organization is often based on 'personal values, aspirations and ideals,' while the motivation to implement strategies is also rooted in human emotions. However, the actual determination of the optimal strategy is a 'rational undertaking' *par excellence*[3].

Another form of non-rationality is to let conscious thinking be largely superseded by *routine* and *habit*. Routines are programmed courses of action that originally were deliberately conceived, but are subsequently internalized and used automatically[4]. Habits are programmed courses of action that have developed unconsciously. Humans approach many everyday problems by reverting to routine and habit, which is a good thing, because conscious deliberation would cost too much time and effort. There is always a danger that routines can become outdated and that habits are totally nonsense, but there is a value to programmed behavior in some realms of human activity. However, strategic management is not one of these.

Intuition is sometimes also seen as a form of non-rational reasoning. Intuition has been defined in many ways[5], but in general it can be understood as the opposite of formal analysis[6]. Intuition is informal and synthetic. Informal means that the reasoning is largely unconscious and based on assumptions, variables and causal relationships not explicitly identifiable by those doing the thinking. Synthetic means that the thinker does not aim at unravelling phenomena into their constituent parts, but rather maintains a more holistic view of reality. Many management theorists have noted that the opposites of analysis and intuition pose a paradox in themselves – when should managers use analysis and when intuition, or can both be combined?[7] However, in this discussion on strategic thinking it is important to point out that intuition is not necessarily irrational. If intuition is viewed as a set of unconscious and uncodified decision rules largely derived from experience[8], intuitive judgements can be quite logical. Decision rules based on extensive experience are often correct, even if they have been arrived at unconsciously. For example, Simon argues that even chess grand masters make many decisions intuitively, based on tacit (that is, unarticulated) rules of thumb, formulated through years of experience. Unconscious does not mean illogical and therefore most proponents of the rational perspective do not dismiss intuition out of hand.

However, intuitive judgements are viewed with great suspicion, as they are difficult to verify and infamously unreliable[9]. Where possible, intuitive reasoning should be made explicit – the *cognitive map* in the strategist's head[10] should be captured on paper[11], so that the reasoning of the strategist can be checked for logical inconsistencies.

In short, advocates of the rational thinking perspective argue that strategic thinking should not be based on emotions, routines, habit or pure intuition, but on explicit logical reasoning, just like a science. Scientific methods of research, analysis, theorizing and falsification are all directly applicable to developing strategy. Consequently, the best preparation for strategic thinking is to be trained in the scientific tradition.

The Generative Thinking Perspective

Strategists taking a generative thinking perspective are strongly at odds with the unassailable position given to logic in the rational perspective. They agree that logic is important, but stress that logical reasoning is often more a hindrance than a help. The heavy emphasis placed on rationality can actually stifle creativity, while creativity is essential for generating novel insights, new ways of defining problems and innovative solutions[12]. Therefore, proponents of the generative perspective argue that strategists should not get too caught up in rational approaches to strategic thinking, but should nurture creativity as their primary cognitive asset.

The generative thinking perspective is based on the assumption that strategic problems are *wicked*[13]. It is believed that strategic problems cannot be easily and objectively defined, but that they are open to interpretation from a limitless variety of angles. The same is true for the possible solutions – there is no fixed set of problem solutions from which the strategist must select the best one. Defining and solving strategic problems, it is believed, is fundamentally a creative activity. As such, strategic thinking has very little in common with the thought processes of the aforementioned chess grand master, as was presumed by the rationalists. Playing chess is a *tame* problem. The problem definition is clear and all options are known. In the average game of chess, consisting of 40 moves, 10^{120} possibilities have to be considered[14]. This makes it a difficult game for humans to play, because of their limited computational capacities. Chess grand masters are better at making these calculations than other people and are particularly good at computational short-cuts – recognizing which things to figure out and which not. However, even the best chess grand masters have been beaten at the game by highly logical computers with a superior number crunching capability. For the poor chess grand master, the rules of the game are fixed and there is little room for redefining the problem or introducing innovative approaches.

Engaging in business strategy is an entirely different matter. Strategic problems are wicked. Problem definitions are highly subjective and there are no fixed solution sets. It is therefore impossible to 'identify' the problem and 'calculate' an optimal solution. Opportunities and threats do not exist, waiting for the analyst to discover them. A strategist believes that a situation can be viewed as an opportunity and sees that certain factors can be threatening if not approached properly. Neither can strengths and weaknesses be objectively determined – a strategist can employ a company characteristic as a strength, but can also turn a unique company quality into a weakness by a lack of vision. Hence, doing a SWOT analysis (Strengths, Weaknesses, Opportunities and Threats) actually has little to do with logical analysis, but in reality is nothing less than a creative interpretation of a problem situation. Which factors in the environment and the organization are seen to be important and how they should be evaluated depends on the idiosyncratic views held by strategists.

Likewise, it is a fallacy to believe that strategic options follow more or less logically from the characteristics of the firm and its environment.

Strategic options are not 'identified' or selected from a 2×2 matrix, but are dreamt up. Strategists must be able to use their imaginations to generate previously unknown solutions. If more than one strategic option emerges from the mind of the strategist, these can also not be simply scored and ranked to choose the optimal one. Some analyses can be done, but ultimately the strategist will have to intuitively judge which vision for the future has the best chance of being created in reality.

Hence, the major limitation of logic, according to adherents of the generative thinking perspective, is that it entraps strategists in the current orthodoxy. Logical reasoning can be an intellectual straight-jacket. 'Being logical' means engaging in consistent reasoning based on a number of accepted theories, ideas and assumptions about reality. When a group of people share such premises that shape how they view specific situations or problems, it is said that they have a common *paradigm*[15]. Prahalad and Bettis[16] speak of the *dominant logic* within a group, while others speak of a shared *cognitive map*[17] or *belief system*[18]. Rational thinking, then, is nothing other than interpreting problems and selecting solutions in accordance with the prevailing paradigm. Breaking out of the status quo requires that strategists question and contradict established wisdom. To find innovative ways of defining and solving problems, it is imperative that strategists think creatively – they must make leaps of imagination, that are not logical from the perspective of the current paradigm. Strategists must be willing to leave the intellectual safety of generally-accepted concepts to explore new ideas, guided by little else than their intuition. De Bono[19] refers to such generative, frame-breaking reasoning as *lateral thinking*, as opposed to vertical thinking, which remains neatly within the existing paradigm.

To proponents of the generative thinking perspective, it is essential for strategists to have a slightly contrarian[20], revolutionary predisposition[21]. Strategists must enjoy the challenge of thinking 'out of the box', even when this is disruptive of the status quo and not much appreciated by those with their two feet (stuck) on the ground. As Picasso once remarked, 'every act of creation is first of all an act of destruction' – strategists must enjoy the task of demolishing old paradigms and confronting the defenders of these beliefs.

In short, advocates of the generative perspective argue that the essence of strategic thinking is the ability to creatively challenge 'the tyranny of the given'[22] and to generate new and unique ways of understanding and doing things. As such, strategic thinking closely resembles the frame-breaking behavior common in the arts. In fields such as painting, music, motion pictures, dancing and architecture, artists are propelled by the drive to challenge convention and to seek out innovative approaches. Many of their methods, such as brainstorming, experimentation, openness to intuition, and the use of metaphors, contradictions and paradoxes, are directly applicable to developing strategy. Consequently, the best preparation for strategic thinking is to be trained in the artistic tradition of creativity and mental flexibility.

The question within the field of strategic management is, therefore, whether strategic thinking is primarily a rational activity or has more to do with ingenuity and imagination. Should strategists train themselves to follow *procedural rationality* – rigorously analyzing problems using scientific methods and calculating the optimal course of action? Or should strategists boldly think *out of the box* – inventing entirely new courses of action? Not all strategists give the same answers to these questions. This places readers in the position that they themselves must think about the nature of strategic thinking. Together, logic and creativity present a paradox that strategists, and prospective strategists, must come to terms with.

Defining the Issues: Cognition and Reasoning

Before proceeding with the 'debate' between proponents of the rational and generative thinking perspectives, it is useful to clarify the key topics under discussion. As will be seen, the disagreements between the two extreme points of view revolve around two major issues: the nature of *cognition* and the nature of *reasoning*. In the next paragraphs these two issues will be further explored, to set the stage for the debates that follow.

The Nature of Cognition

The mind of the strategist is a complex and fascinating apparatus, that never fails to astonish and dazzle on the one hand, and disappoint and frustrate on the other. We are often surprised by the power of the human mind, but equally often stunned by its limitations. For the discussion at hand it is not necessary to unravel all of the mysteries surrounding the functioning of the human brain, but a short overview of the capabilities and limitations of the human mind will greatly help to focus the debate.

The human ability to know is referred to as *cognition*. Knowledge that people have is stored in their minds in the form of *cognitive maps*, also referred to as *cognitive schemata*[23]. These cognitive maps are representations in the mind of an individual of how the world works. A cognitive map of a certain situation reflects a person's beliefs about the importance of the issues and about the cause and effect relationships between them. Cognitive maps are formed over time through education, experience and interaction with others.

It is clear that people are not omniscient – they do not have infinite knowledge. The cognitive abilities of humans are limited. These *cognitive limitations* are largely due to three factors:

■ *Limited information processing capacity.* As was clear in the chess example cited earlier, humans do not have unlimited data processing abilities. Thinking through problems with many variables and huge amounts of data is a task that people find extremely difficult to perform. Approaching every activity in this way would totally overload a person's brain. For this reason, humans hardly ever think through a problem with full use of all available data, but make extensive use of mental shortcuts, referred to as *cognitive heuristics*[24]. Cognitive heuristics are mental 'rules of thumb' that simplify a problem, so that it can be more quickly understood and solved. Cognitive heuristics focus a person's attention on a number of key variables that are believed to be most important, and present a number of simple decision rules to rapidly resolve an issue. The set of possible solutions to be considered is also limited in advance. The specific cognitive heuristics used by individuals are rooted in their cognitive maps.

■ *Limited information sensing ability.* Human cognition is also severely handicapped by the limitations of people's senses. While the senses – touch, smell, taste, hearing and seeing – are bombarded with stimuli, much of reality remains unobservable to humans. This is partially due to the physical inability to be everywhere, all the time, noticing everything. However, people's limited ability to register the structure of reality is also due to the inherent superficiality of the senses and the complexity of reality. The human senses cannot directly identify the way the world works and the underlying causal relationships. Only the physical consequences of the complex interactions between elements in reality can be picked up by a person's sensory system. Therefore, the mental representations of the world that individuals build up in their minds are based on circumstantial evidence. Cognitive maps are formed by inferring causal relationships, making guesses about unobservable factors and resolving inconsistencies between the bits of information received. Hence, the models of reality constructed in the minds of individuals are highly subjective. In turn, people's cognitive maps steer their senses – while cognitive maps are built on past sensory data, they will consequently direct which new information will be sought and perceived. A person's cognitive map will focus attention on particular phenomena, while blocking out other data as noise, and will quickly explain how a situation should be perceived. In this way, a cognitive map provides an *interpretive filter*, aiding the senses in selecting and understanding external stimuli[25].

■ *Limited information storage capacity.* Another human cognitive shortcoming is poor memory. People have only a limited capacity for storing information. Remembering all individuals, events, dates, places and circumstances is beyond the ability of the human brain. Therefore, people must store information very selectively and organize this information in a way that it can be easily retrieved when necessary. Here, again, cognitive heuristics are at play – 'rules of thumb' make the memorization process manageable in the face of severe capacity limitations. Such heuristics help to simplify complex clusters of data into manageable chunks and help to categorize, label and store this information so that it can be recalled at a later moment.

With these drawbacks, humans can never be as perfectly rational as computers. Even when people try to be as rational as possible – that is, they avoid emotional, routine and intuitive behavior – they will still be hindered by these cognitive limitations. Two types of problems, in particular, confront the boundedly rational thinker:

■ *Cognitive biases.* As was stated earlier, cognitive heuristics are mental shortcuts, needed to cope with limited information processing and storage capacity. Everyone uses them for a large part of their thinking. Yet, these shortcuts are 'quick and dirty' – efficient, but imprecise. They help people to intuitively jump to conclusions without thorough analysis, which increases speed, but also increases the risk of drawing faulty conclusions. The main danger of cognitive heuristics is that they are inherently biased, as they focus attention on only a few variables and interpret them in a particular way, even when this is not appropriate[26]. For this reason, many academicians urge practitioners to bolster their intuitive judgements with more explicit rational analysis. Especially in the case of strategic decisions, time and energy should be made available to avoid falling prey to common cognitive biases[27]. Others are quick to point out that without extensive use of cognitive heuristics, and all the dangers involved, strategists would grind to a halt, overloaded by the sheer complexity of the analyses that would need to be carried out – a situation of rationality gone rampant, usually referred to as *paralysis by analysis*[28]. This has led to an on-going debate on how to balance rational analysis and intuitive judgement.

■ *Cognitive rigidities.* A second problem is that people are generally not inclined to change their minds – cognitive maps exhibit a high level of rigidity. Once people's cognitive maps have formed, and they have a grip on reality, they become resistant to signals that challenge their conceptions. As McCaskey[29] remarks, the mind 'strives mightily to bring order, simplicity, consistency, and stability to the world it encounters,' and is therefore reluctant to welcome the ambiguity presented by contradicting data. People tend to significantly overestimate the value of information that confirms their cognitive map, underestimate disconfirming information, and they actively seek out evidence that supports their current beliefs[30]. Once an interpretive filter is in place, seeing is not believing, but believing is seeing. Cognitive rigidity is particularly strong when an individual's cognitive map is supported by similar beliefs shared within a social group or organization. How rigid cognitive maps actually are and how open people can be to evidence and new ideas is, however, an on-going debate within the fields of (strategic) management and (social) psychology.

The main question in this chapter is whether cognitive rigidities present a major problem to strategists. Do strategists need to 'change their minds' in significant ways or is it sufficient for strategists to build on their current understanding, with occasional minor adaptations? Must strategists consistently try to break through cognitive rigidities, by creatively generating other ways of understanding the world, or should they progress rationally, by logically extending their existing cognitive maps? Is it necessary for strategists to be intellectual revolutionaries, overthrowing the established order, or should they respect accepted knowledge and build on these foundations?

The issue, therefore, is how realistic or constraining strategists' cognitive maps actually are. If the cognitive maps employed by strategists are faithful representations of the world and strategists are relatively open to any dissonant signals indicating that their maps are incorrect, then they will have *objective knowledge* of reality. All thinking should then take this objective knowledge as a starting point and rationally build on these premises. New insights, new ideas, and new strategies should be arrived at by analytical reasoning, making them logically consistent with what is known to be objectively true.

However, if in fact the cognitive maps used by strategists are highly colored representations of the world and strategists are often immune to dissonant signals that do not fit in with their beliefs, then their knowledge of the world will be *subjective*. Their understanding of reality will be slanted. As people do not develop their cognitive maps in isolation, but in interaction with other individuals, their subjective understanding of the world will be largely *socially constructed*[31]. When people within a social group construct a common worldview, based on shared assumptions about reality, this is referred to as a *paradigm*. Thinking within the boundaries of a paradigm is usually very 'logical'. Once the subjective assumptions and the reasoning rules have been accepted, people proceed to think rationally – that is, they try to avoid logical inconsistencies. Challenging a paradigm's fundamental assumptions, however, cannot be done in a way that is logically consistent with the paradigm. Contradicting a paradigm is illogical from the point of view of those who accept the paradigm. Therefore, changing a rigid and subjective cognitive map, rooted in a shared paradigm, would require strategists to imagine new ways of understanding the world, that do not logically follow from past beliefs. Strategists would have to be willing and able to break with orthodoxy and make leaps of imagination, that are not logically justified, but needed to generate novel ways of looking at old problems. Strategic thinking would require a large dose of creativity – that is, the ability to understand problems and formulate solutions in a way that contradicts conventional wisdom. Strategists with a strong preference to remain rational would, in practice, become prisoners of their own rigid cognitive maps.

Which portrayal of cognition is right? As unanimity is lacking, readers will have to form an opinion of their own. Which position in this debate each reader takes will ultimately depend on their view of the nature of reality (which philosophers refer to as the issue of *ontology*) and the nature of knowledge (the issue of *epistemology*).

The Nature of Reasoning

Reasoning and cognition are intimately related – reasoning is the thought process leading to knowing. As a process, reasoning involves a number of mental activities taking place over time. In the context of strategy, reasoning is the thought process used to define and solve strategic problems.

Most strategists, whether of rational or generative inclination, agree that reasoning about strategic problems can be decomposed into four broad categories of mental activities (see Figure 2.1). These four elements of strategic reasoning are:

1   *Identifying*. Before strategists can move to benefit from opportunities or to counter threats, they must be aware of these challenges and acknowledge their importance. This part of the thought process is variably referred to as identifying, recognizing or sense-making.

2   *Diagnosing*. To come to grips with a problem, strategists must try to understand the structure of the problem and its underlying causes. This part of the thought process is variably referred to as diagnosing, analyzing or reflecting.

3   *Conceiving*. To deal with a strategic problem, strategists must come up with a potential solution. If more than one solution is available, the strategist must select the most promising one. This part of the thought process is variably referred to as conceiving, formulating or envisioning.

4   *Realizing*. A strategic problem is only really solved once concrete actions are undertaken that achieve results. Strategists must therefore carry out problem-solving activities and evaluate whether the consequences are positive. This part of the thought process is variably referred to as realizing, implementing or acting.

What strategists do not agree on, is how each activity is carried out and in what order. From the rational thinking perspective, it is logical to start by identifying problems and then to move from diagnosing to conceiving solutions and realizing them (clockwise movement in Figure 2.1). In general, adherents of the rational thinking perspective believe that identifying strategic problems requires extensive external and internal scanning, thorough sifting of incoming information, and leave selecting of priority issues. In the next mental phase, the major strategic problems that have been recognized are diagnosed by gathering more detailed data, and further analyzing and refining this information. Once the problem has been properly defined, a strategy can be formulated by evaluating the

FIGURE 2.1
Elements of strategic thought process

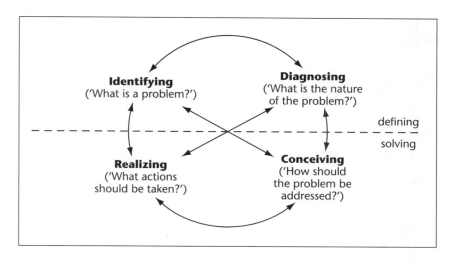

available options and deciding which solution is the best. In the final phase of realization, the strategist must ensure execution of the proposed solution by consciously planning and controlling implementation activities. Therefore, in the vocabulary of the rational thinking perspective the four elements of the strategic thought process are usually referred to as *recognizing, analyzing, formulating* and *implementing*.

Proponents of the generative thinking perspective do not believe that strategists reason in this linear (or actually circular) fashion. They do not accept that the four categories of mental activities are phases. In their view, reasoning is usually far more messy, with identifying, diagnosing, conceiving and realizing intermingled with one another and often going on at the same time. The more creative, the less linear are the thought processes (clockwise movement in Figure 2.1 is literally far too mechanical for the creative thinker). Nor do the advocates of the generative thinking perspective agree with the rationalist's characterization of the four groups of mental activities. In the generative view, identifying strategic problems is not about recognizing, but interpreting – by looking at the world from a particular angle, strategists see and value particular strengths, weaknesses, opportunities and threats. Such sense-making activities lead to attention being paid to some issues, while others do not make the *strategic agenda*[32]. Likewise, diagnosing strategic problems is not a straightforward analytical process. Reflecting on strategic problems may involve explicit analysis, but also intuition – understanding problems through unconscious and synthetic reasoning.

Conceiving strategic solutions is equally messy and creative, according to supporters of the generative perspective. Solutions are not lying around, waiting to be discovered, but are envisioned – strategists imagine how things could be done. Such idea generation may involve reasoning by analogy or metaphor, brainstorming, or pure fantasizing. New solutions may come to the strategist in a flash (eureka!) or emerge over time, but usually require a period of incubation beforehand, and a period of nurturing afterwards. Which new idea will be the best solution is, however, not something that can be objectively evaluated and decided. Therefore judgement, not calculation, will determine which idea will win the upper hand.

Finally, it is emphasized that realization-oriented thinking does not come last, as straightforward implementation. Acting does not wait for a problem to be precisely defined and for a solution to be fully conceived. Often, to really understand a problem, people must first act – they must have experience with a problem and know that the current strategy will not be able to overcome the problem. To generate a solution it is often also necessary to test certain assumptions in practice and to experiment. In short, in the generative thinking perspective the four elements of the strategic thought process are thoroughly intertwined, and best understood as *sense-making*, *reflecting*, *envisioning* and *acting*.

EXHIBIT 2.1
Mercedes-Benz and Swatch case

MERCEDES-BENZ AND SWATCH: A SMART MOVE?

Among the flurry of strategic alliances initiated during the last few years, the collaboration between the luxury car manufacturer Mercedes-Benz, and the Swiss watch producer SMH (known for its brands Swatch and Omega) has stood out as exceptionally eye-catching. At a press conference in May 1995, it was announced to surprised business journalists that the two companies had embarked on a major joint venture, with the intention of developing and manufacturing a revolutionary new automobile. The new firm, Micro Compact Car (MCC), would be 51 percent owned by Mercedes Benz, and would be endowed with DM 1.5bn ($1bn) of equity from the parent companies. The car would be called 'Smart,' which according to Hans Jürgen Schör, head of the MCC joint venture, combines the first letters of the two collaborating companies, Swatch (S) and Mercedes-Benz (M), with the way they are working together.

It is not very likely that anyone is going to spot Jürgen Hubbert, the chief executive of Mercedes-Benz, and Nicolas Hayek, chairman of SMH, taking long drives together in the Smart car. Not necessarily due to their relationship, but because of the dimensions of this micro car. With a length of 2.5 metres (8'4") and a width of 1.4 metres (4'8"), the Smart is going to be the world's smallest production vehicle, hardly sufficient to lure Mr. Hubbert out of his chauffeur-driven Mercedes. Yet, size may not even be the most unconventional characteristic of this tiny two seater urban vehicle. The original concept involves changeable car body panels, to match the color of the car with your favorite wardrobe items. On top of that, the little giant will have the right green credentials. The eco turbo diesel engines will offer unprecedented fuel economy and there will even be a battery-powered version, together with a diesel/electric hybrid, allowing the car to operate in zero-emission areas such as downtown LA.

The background of this venture is equally surprising. In 1990, Nicolas Hayek came up with the idea of diversifying SMH into the automobile industry, driven by an urgent desire to make driving fashionable, more in line with environmental constraints and, most of all, more fun. Yet, for a watchmaker it is not an easy job to build an automobile plant on its own, so SMH had to search for a reliable and sincere partner. Originally, Hayek tried to strike up a relationship with Volkswagen, the German manufacturer of medium-sized cars, for whom a micro compact might be a logical range extension. However, both parties had differing ideas and Volkswagen was financially restrained, so the brief flirt was quickly ended. Unexpectedly, Mercedes-Benz, which only produces high quality, top of the range cars, was particularly interested in Hayek's concept and willing to team up with this industry outsider.

To intrigued industry analysts, the motives of both companies are not entirely clear. Swatch seems to be propelled by the vision of its CEO, Nicolas Hayek. He feels that it is his personal responsibility to 'prevent the world from being out of oxygen in ten years,' and therefore he is determined to build a cleaner, more fuel-efficient car, which implies a significant decrease in size compared to regular vehicles. Of course, Hayek also believes that Swatch has many of the critical capabilities needed to make Smart a success, especially in the area of design, miniaturization, sensing the wishes of young people and marketing. Smart is an excellent opportunity for SMH to leverage these capabilities and to become less dependent on the watch-making business. Critics, however, point out that the Smart project might also have been intended to appease SMH shareholders, who have recently been confronted with declining profits and falling dividends.

Industry analysts are even more curious about the cooperative rationale of Mercedes-Benz. Why would a prestigious, conservative and highly rational firm like Mercedes-Benz collaborate with a fashion-driven, progressive and highly creative Swiss watchmaker? It seems clear that the company is currently locked into a narrow product range, resulting in a very limited target audience and few opportunities for growth. As Mr. Hubbert admits, demand is stagnant in the big luxury car segment, which includes Mercedes-Benz' flagship S Class saloon. In his view, significant growth will be limited to smaller, cheaper models. As a company that wants to expand, Mercedes-Benz needed to find a way to break into these segments. For such a move its image could be both an asset and a liability. The Smart project fits the needs of Mercedes-Benz exactly, because it can leverage its quality image, without suffering from its conservative connotations. At the same time, it is hoped, the company's traditional and loyal customer base will not be upset by a dilution of the Mercedes-Benz brand name.

However, it is not only a matter of piggy-backing on Swatch's fashionable image. The top management of Mercedes-Benz seems to recognize that its production skills and engineering excellence are not the only capabilities needed to successfully enter the small market segment. The company's rationalist culture is ill-suited to the development of other needed capabilities, such as the radical rethinking of the automobile concept, imaginative design, and creative marketing. These are exactly the qualities that Swatch can also bring in to the joint venture.

It is from this perspective that the decision must be understood to establish the Smart production location in France, instead of near Mercedes-Benz' main manufacturing hub in Stuttgart, Germany. Production will be located at Hambach, near Sarreguimes in north-eastern France, where a start has been made to build a plant with a capacity of 200,000 vehicles. This location, just across the French-German border, should be physically close enough to keep the Smart factory connected to the core company, to ensure quality, financial control and just-in-time delivery by Mercedes suppliers. However, it should also be far enough to allow a new culture to evolve combining the best of both worlds – Mercedes-Benz' analytical rigor on the one hand, and Swatch's creative capabilities on the other. Significant additional benefits are the lower French wages and energy prices, and the weaker French currency.

Yet, some market analysts have expressed their reservations about the success potential of the new-born joint venture. They question whether a car manufacturer and a watchmaker could ever make a compatible couple, even under the best of circumstances. Their doubts are even larger given the enormous cultural gap between the rationally-inclined managers at Mercedes-Benz and the creatively-inclined people at Swatch. Isn't it likely that their relationship will crack under the first real strains, as the Smart cars reach the market? Managers from both companies have had experience in cooperative ventures, Hayek as a coordinator within the network of Swiss companies producing watches, and Mercedes-Benz managers in joint new product development projects with suppliers (such as Bosch, with whom they developed an advanced Anti-Blocking System (ABS) for brakes). However, this collaborative venture is of a more structural nature and the partners are more strongly divergent. Many analysts wondered whether the companies' differences would be complementary or contradictory – whether the tensions created would be constructive or destructive.

Ultimately, the question which Mercedes-Benz and Swatch will have to ask themselves is whether logic and creativity can be, and need to be, combined in MCC's culture and strategy process. And, if so, which of the two should, or will dominate? The answers to these questions will determine whether we will see Mercedes-Benz and Swatch racing ahead together, or one partner towing the other, or even the joint venture crashing before completing its first lap.

Sources: *Financial Times*, various issues 1996.

The Debate and the Readings

As stated at the outset of this chapter, few authors make a point of explaining their rational thinking perspective. The position of logical reasoning is so strong in much of the literature, that many strategists adopt the rational perspective without making this choice explicit. It is, therefore, not possible to present a vocal defender of this perspective to get a nicely polarized debate going. Instead, as the first debate contribution to this chapter, a classic work has been selected that is a good example of the rational perspective on strategic thinking. This reading, 'The Concept of Corporate Strategy,' by Kenneth Andrews, has been drawn from one of the most influential textbooks in the field of strategy, *Business Policy: Text and Cases*[33]. Andrews is arguably one of the godfathers of strategic management and this chapter from his book has had considerable impact on theorists and practitioners alike. True to the rational thinking perspective, Andrews argues that strategy analysis and formulation should be conducted consciously, explicitly and rationally. In his view, strategic thinking is a 'logical activity,' while subsequent strategy implementation 'comprises a series of subactivities that are primarily administrative.' It should be noted that in this reading Andrews is positioning himself in opposition to incrementalists (see Chapter 3), not *vis-à-vis* proponents of the generative thinking perspective. Therefore, he does not counter any of the major arguments raised by advocates of this perspective.

The second reading in this chapter, highlighting the views of the generative thinking perspective, is 'The Mind of the Strategist,' by Kenichi Ohmae. Ohmae, formerly head of McKinsey's Tokyo office, is one of Japan's most well-known strategy authors. In this contribution, taken from the book of the same name[34], Ohmae argues that the mind of the strategist is not dominated by linear, logical thinking. On the contrary, a strategist's thought processes are 'basically creative and intuitive rather than rational.' In his view, 'great strategies . . . originate in insights that are beyond the reach of conscious analysis.' He does not dismiss logic as unnecessary, but notes that it is insufficient for arriving at innovative strategies. Yet, he observes that in most large companies creative strategists 'are being pushed to the sidelines in favor of rational, by-the-numbers strategic and financial planners,' leading to a withering of strategic thinking ability.

Which of the two positions gives the best explanation of the nature of strategic thinking? It is up to readers to weigh both sets of arguments and decide for themselves how to deal with the paradox of logic and creativity.

Reading 1 The Concept of Corporate Strategy

By Kenneth Andrews[†]

Corporate strategy is the pattern of decisions in a company that determines and reveals its objectives, purposes, or goals, produces the principal policies and plans for achieving those goals, and defines the range of business the company is to pursue, the kind of economic and human organization it is or intends to be, and the nature of the economic and noneconomic contribution it intends to make to its shareholders, employees, customers and communities. In an organization of any size or diversity, *corporate strategy* usually applies to the whole enterprise, while *business strategy*, less comprehensive, defines the choice of product or service and market of individual businesses within the firm. Business strategy is the determination of how a company will compete in a given business and position itself among its competitors. Corporate strategy defines the businesses in which a company will compete, preferably in a way that focuses resources to convert distinctive competence into competitive advantage. Both are outcomes of a continuous process of strategic management that we will later analyze in detail.

The strategic decision contributing to this pattern is one that is effective over long periods of time, affects the company in many different ways, and focuses and commits a significant portion of its resources to the expected outcomes. The pattern resulting from a series of such decisions will probably define the central character and image of a company, the individuality it has for its members and various publics, and the

[†]Source: This article was adapted with permission from chapter 2 of *The Concept of Corporate Strategy*, Irwin, Homewood, 1987.

position it will occupy in its industry and markets. It will permit the specification of particular objectives to be attained through a timed sequence of investment and implementation decisions and will govern directly the deployment or redeployment of resources to make these decisions effective.

Some aspects of such a pattern of decisions may be in an established corporation unchanging over long periods of time, like a commitment to quality, or high technology, or certain raw materials, or good labor relations. Other aspects of a strategy must change as or before the world changes, such as a product line, manufacturing process, or merchandising and styling practices. The basic determinants of company character, if purposefully institutionalized, are likely to persist through and shape the nature of substantial changes in product-market choices and allocation of resources.

It would be possible to extend the definition of strategy for a given company to separate a central character and the core of its special accomplishment from the manifestations of such characteristics in changing product lines, markets, and policies designed to make activities profitable from year to year. *The New York Times*, for example, after many years of being shaped by the values of its owners and staff, is now so self-conscious and respected an institution that its nature is likely to remain unchanged, even if the services it offers are altered drastically in the direction of other outlets for its news-processing capacity.

It is important, however, not to take the idea apart in another way, that is, to separate goals from the policies designed to achieve those goals. The essence of the definition of strategy I have just recorded is pattern. The interdependence of purposes, policies, and organized action is crucial to the particularity of an individual strategy and its opportunity to identify competitive advantage. It is the unity, coherence, and internal consistency of a company's strategic decisions that position the company in its environment and give the firm its identity, its power to mobilize its strengths, and its likelihood of success in the marketplace. It is the interrelationship of a set of goals and policies that crystallizes from the formless reality of a company's environment a set of problems an organization can seize upon and solve.

What you are doing, in short, is never meaningful unless you can say or imply what you are doing it for: the quality of administrative action and the motivation lending it power cannot be appraised without knowing its relationship to purpose. Breaking up the system of corporate goals and the character-determining major policies for attainment leads to narrow and mechanical conceptions of strategic management and endless logic chopping.

We should get on to understanding the need for strategic decisions and for determining the most satisfactory pattern of goals in concrete instances. Refinement of definition can wait, for you will wish to develop definition in practice in directions useful to you.

Summary Statements of Strategy

Before we proceed to clarification of this concept by application, we should specify the terms in which strategy is usually expressed. A summary statement of strategy will characterize the product line and services offered or planned by the company, the markets and market segments for which products and services are now or will be designed, and the channels through which these markets will be reached. The means by which the operation is to be financed will be specified, as will the profit objectives and the emphasis to be placed on the safety of capital versus level of return. Major policy in central functions such as marketing, manufacturing, procurement, research and development, labor relations, and personnel, will be stated where they distinguish the company from others, and usually the intended size, form, and climate of the organization will be included.

Each company, if it were to construct a summary strategy from what it understands itself to be aiming at, would have a different statement with different categories of decision emphasized to indicate what it wanted to be or do.

Reasons for Not Articulating Strategy

For a number of reasons companies seldom formulate and publish a complete strategy statement. Conscious planning of the long-term development of companies has been until recently less common than individual executive responses to environmental pressure, competitive threat, or entrepreneurial opportunity. In the latter mode of development, the unity or coherence of corporate effort is unplanned, natural, intuitive, or even nonexistent. Incrementalism in practice sometimes gives the appearance of consciously formulated strategy, but may be the natural result of compromise among coalitions backing contrary policy proposals or skillful improvisatory adaptation to external forces. Practicing managers who prefer muddling through to the strategic process would never commit themselves to an articulate strategy.

Other reasons for the scarcity of concrete statements of strategy include the desirability of keeping strategic plans confidential for security reasons and ambiguous to avoid internal conflict or even final decision. Skillful incrementalists may have plans in their heads that they do not reveal, to avoid resistance and other trouble in their own organization. A company with a large division in an obsolescent business that it intends to drain of cash until operations are discontinued could not expect high morale and cooperation to follow publication of this intent. In a dynamic company, moreover, where strategy is continually evolving, the official statement of strategy, unless couched in very general terms, would be as hard to keep up to date as an organization chart. Finally, a firm that has internalized its strategy does not feel the need to keep saying what it is, valuable as that information might be to new members.

Deducing Strategy from Behavior

In your own company you can do what most managements have not done. In the absence of explicit statements and on the basis of your experience, you may deduce from decisions observed what the pattern is and what the company's goals and policies are, on the assumption that some perhaps unspoken consensus lies behind them. Careful examination of the behavior of competitors will reveal what their strategy must be. At the same time none of us should mistake apparent strategy visible in a pattern of past incremental decisions for conscious planning for the future. What will pass as the current strategy of a company may almost always be deduced from its behavior, but a strategy for a future of changed circumstances may not always be distinguishable from performance in the present. Strategists who do not look beyond present behavior to the future are vulnerable to surprise.

Formulation of Strategy

Corporate strategy is an organization process, in many ways inseparable from the structure, behavior, and culture of the company in which it takes place. Nevertheless, we may abstract from the process two important aspects, interrelated in real life but separable for the purposes of analysis. The first of these we may call formulation, the second implementation. Deciding what strategy should be may be approached as a rational undertaking, even if, as in life, emotional attachments (to metal skis or investigative reporting) may complicate choice among future alternatives (for ski manufacturers or alternative newspapers). The principle subactivities of strategy formulation as a logical activity include indentifying opportunities and threats in the company's environment and attaching some estimate or risk to the discernible alternatives. Before a choice can be made, the company's strengths and weaknesses should be appraised together with the resources on hand and available. Its actual or potential capacity to take advantage of perceived market needs or to cope with attendant risks should be estimated as objectively as possible. The strategic alternative that results from matching opportunity and corporate capability at an acceptable level of risk is what we may call an *economic strategy*.

The process described thus far assumes that strategists are analytically objective in estimating the relative capacity of their company and the opportunity they see or anticipate in developing markets. The extent to which they wish to undertake low or high risk presumably depends on their profit objectives. The higher they set the latter, the more willing they must be to assume a correspondingly high risk that the market opportunity they see will not develop or that the corporate competence required to excel competition will not be forthcoming.

So far we have described the intellectual processes of ascertaining what a company *might do* in terms of environmental opportunity, of deciding what it *can do* in terms of ability and power, and of bringing these two considerations together in optimal equilibrium. The determination of strategy also requires consideration of what alternatives are preferred by the chief executive and perhaps by his or her immediate associates as well, quite apart from economic considerations. Personal values, aspirations and ideals do, and in our judgment quite properly should, influence the final choice of purposes. Thus what the executives of a company *want to do* must be brought into the strategic decision.

Finally strategic choice has an ethical aspect – a fact much more dramatically illustrated in some industries than in others. Just as alternatives may be ordered in terms of the degree of risk they entail, so may they be examined against the standards of responsiveness to the expectations of society the strategist elects. Some alternatives may seem to the executive considering them more attractive than others when the public good or service to society is considered. What a company *should do* thus appears as a fourth element of the strategic decision.

The ability to identify the four components of strategy – (a) market opportunity, (b) corporate competence and resources, (c) personal values and aspirations, and (d) acknowledged obligations to segments of society other than stockholders – is easier to exercise than the art of reconciling their implications in a final choice of purpose. Taken by itself each consideration might lead in a different direction.

If you put the various aspirations of individuals in your own organization against this statement you will see what I mean. Even in a single mind contradictory aspirations can survive a long time before the need to calculate trade-offs and integrate divergent inclinations becomes clear. Growth opportunity attracted many companies to the computer business after World War II. The decision to diversify out of typewriters and calculators was encouraged by growth opportunity and excitement that captivated the managements of RCA, General Electric, and Xerox, among others. But the financial, technical, and marketing requirements of this business exceeded the capacity of most of the competitors of IBM. The magnet of opportunity and the incentive of desire obscured the calculations of what resources and competence were required to succeed. Most crucially, where corporate capability leads, executives do not always want to go. Of all the components of strategic choice, the combination of resources and competence is most crucial to success.

The Implementation of Strategy

Since effective implementation can make a sound strategic decision ineffective or a debatable choice successful, it is as important to examine the processes of implementation as to weigh the advantages of available strategic alternatives. The implementation of strategy comprises a series of subactivities that are primarily administrative. If purpose is determined, then the resources of a company can be mobilized to accomplish it. An organizational structure appropriate for the efficient performance of the required tasks must be made effective by information systems and relationships permitting coordination of subdivided activities. The organizational processes of performance measurement, compensation, management development – all of them enmeshed in systems of incentives and controls – must be directed toward the kind of behavior required by organizational purpose. The role of personal leadership is important and sometimes decisive in the accomplishment of strategy. Although we know that organizational structure and processes of compensation, incentives, control, and management development influence and constrain the formulation of strategy, we should look first at the logical proposition that structure should follow strategy in order to cope later with the organizational reality that strategy also follows structure. When we have examined both tendencies, we will understand and to some extent be prepared to deal with the interdependence of the formulation and implementation of corporate purpose. Figure 2.1 (see page 67) may be useful in understanding the analysis of strategy as a pattern of interrelated decisions.

Criteria for Evaluation

How is the actual or proposed strategy to be judged? How are we to know that one strategy is better than another? A number of important questions can regularly be asked. As is already evident, no infallible

FIGURE 2.2
The strategy process

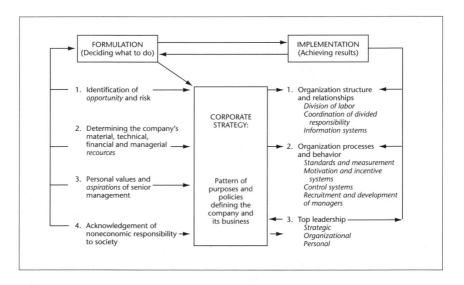

indicators are available. With practice they will lead to reliable intuitive discriminations.

■ *Is the strategy identifiable and has it been made clear either in words or in practice?* The degree to which attention has been given to the strategic alternatives available to a company is likely to be basic to the soundness of its strategic decision. To cover in empty phrases ('Our policy is planned profitable growth in any market we can serve well') an absence of analysis of opportunity or actual determination of corporate strength is worse than to remain silent, for it conveys the illusion of a commitment when none has been made. The unstated strategy cannot be tested or contested and is likely therefore to be weak. If it is implicit in the intuition of a strong leader, the organization is likely to be weak and the demands the strategy makes upon it are likely to remain unmet. A strategy must be explicit to be effective and specific enough to require some actions and exclude others.

■ *Does the strategy exploit fully domestic and international environmental opportunity?* The relation between market opportunity and organizational development is a critical one in the design of future plans. Unless growth is incompatible with the resources of an organization or the aspirations of its management, it is likely that a strategy that does not purport to make full use of market opportunity will be weak also in other aspects. Vulnerability to competition is increased by lack of interest in market share.

- *Is the strategy consistent with corporate competence and resources, both present and projected?* Although additional resources, both financial and managerial, are available to companies with genuine opportunity, the availability of each must be finally determined and programmed along a practicable time scale. This may be the most difficult question in this series.

- *Are the major provisions of the strategy and the program of major policies of which it is comprised internally consistent?* One advantage of making as specific a statement of strategy as is practicable is the resultant availability of a careful check on fit, unity, coherence, compatibility, and synergy – the state in which the whole of anything can be viewed as greater than the sum of its parts.

- *Is the chosen level of risk feasible in economic and personal terms?* The riskiness of any future plan should be compatible with the economic resources of the organization and the temperament of the managers concerned.

- *Is the strategy appropriate to the personal values and aspirations of the key managers?* Conflict between personal preferences, aspirations, and goals of the key members of an organization and the plan for its future is a sign of danger and a harbinger of mediocre performance or failure.

- *Is the strategy appropriate to the desired level of contribution to society?* To the extent that the chosen economic opportunity of the firm has social costs, such as air or water pollution, a statement of intention to deal with these is desirable and prudent.

- *Does the strategy constitute a clear stimulus to organizational effort and commitment?* Generally speaking, the bolder the choice of goals and the wider range of human needs they reflect, the more successfully they will appeal to the capable membership of a healthy and energetic organization.

- *Are there early indications of the responsiveness of markets and market segments to the strategy?* A strategy may pass with flying colors all the tests so far proposed, and may be in internal consistency and uniqueness an admirable work of art. But if within a time period made reasonable by the company's resources and the original plan the strategy does not work, then it must be weak in some way that has escaped attention.

A business enterprise guided by a clear sense of purpose rationally arrived at and emotionally ratified by commitment is more likely to have a successful outcome, in terms of profit and social good, than a company whose future is left to guesswork and chance. Conscious strategy does not preclude brilliance of improvisation or the welcome consequences of good fortune. Its cost is principally thought and work for which it is hard but not impossible to find time.

Reading 2   The Mind of the Strategist

By Kenichi Ohmae[†]

As a consultant I have had the opportunity to work with many large Japanese companies. Among them are many companies whose success you would say must be the result of superb strategies. But when you look more closely, you discover a paradox. They have no big planning staffs, no elaborate, gold-plated strategic planning processes. Some of them are painfully handicapped by lack of the resources – people, money, and technology – that seemingly would be needed to implement an ambitious strategy. Yet despite all these handicaps, they are outstanding performers in the marketplace. Year after year, they manage to build share and create wealth.

How do they do it? The answer is easy. They may not have a strategic planning staff, but they do have a strategist of great natural talent: usually the founder or chief executive. Often – especially in Japan, where there is no business school – these outstanding strategists have had little or no formal business education, at least at the college level. They may never have taken a course or read a book on strategy. But they have an intuitive grasp of the basic elements of strategy. They have an idiosyncratic mode of thinking in which company, customers, and competition merge in a dynamic interaction out of which a comprehensive set of objectives and plans for action eventually crystallizes.

Insight is the key to this process. Because it is creative, partly intuitive, and often disruptive of the status quo, the resulting plans might not even hold water from the analyst's point of view. It is the creative element in these plans and the drive and will of the mind that conceived them that give these strategies their extraordinary competitive impact.

Both in Japan and in the West, this breed of natural or instinctive strategist is dying out or at least being pushed to the sidelines in favor of rational, by-the-numbers strategic and financial planners. Today's giant institutions, both public and private, are by and large not organized for innovation. Their systems and processes are all oriented toward incremental improvement – doing better what they are doing already. In the United States, the pressure of innumerable social and governmental constraints on corporate activities – most notably, perhaps, the proliferation

[†] Source: This article was adapted with permission from chapter 1 and 17, and the introduction to *The Mind of the Strategist: The Art of Japanese Business*, McGraw-Hill, New York, 1982.

of government regulations during the 1960s and 1970s – has put a premium on the talent for adaptation and reduced still further the incentive to innovate. Advocates of bold and ambitious strategies too often find themselves on the sidelines, labeled as losers, while the rewards go to those more skilled at working within the system. This is especially true in mature industries, where actions and ideas often move in narrow grooves, forcing out innovators. Conversely, venture capital groups tend to attract the flexible, adaptive minds.

In all times and places, large institutions develop cultures of their own, and success is often closely tied to the ability to conform. In our day, the culture of most business corporations exalts logic and rationality; hence, it is analysts rather than innovators who tend to get ahead. It is not unreasonable to say that many large US corporations today are run like the Soviet economy. In order to survive, they must plan ahead comprehensively, controlling an array of critical functions in every detail. They specify policies and procedures in meticulous detail, spelling out for practically everyone what can and what cannot be done in particular circumstances. They establish hurdle rates, analyze risks, and anticipate contingencies. As strategic planning processes have burgeoned in these companies, strategic thinking has gradually withered away.

My message, as you will have guessed by now, is that successful business strategies result not from rigorous analysis but from a particular state of mind. In what I call the mind of the strategist, insight and a consequent drive for achievement, often amounting to a sense of mission, fuel a thought process which is basically creative and intuitive rather than rational. Strategists do not reject analysis. Indeed they can hardly do without it. But they use it only to stimulate the creative process, to test the ideas that emerge, to work out their strategic implications, or to ensure successful execution of high potential 'wild' ideas that might otherwise never be implemented properly. Great strategies, like great works of art or great scientific discoveries, call for technical mastery in the working out but originate in insights that are beyond the reach of conscious analysis.

If this is so – if the mind of the strategist is so deeply at odds with the culture of the corporation – how can an already institutionalized company recover the capacity to conceive and execute creative business strategies? In a book entitled *The Corporate Strategist* that was published in Japan in 1975, I attempted to answer that question in a specifically Japanese context.

In Japan, a different set of conditions from those in the West inhibits the creation of bold and innovative strategies. In the large Japanese company, promotion is based on tenure; there is no fast track for brilliant performers. No one reaches a senior management post before the mid-fifties, and chief executives are typically over 60 – well past the age when they are likely to be able to generate dynamic strategic ideas. At the same time, the inventive, often aggressive younger people have no means of contributing in a significant way to the strategy of the corporation. The result: strategic stagnation or the strong probability of it.

How, I asked myself, could the mind of the strategist, with its inventive élan, be reproduced in this kind of corporate culture? What were the ingredients of an excellent strategist, and how could they be reproduced in the Japanese context? These were the questions I addressed in my book. The answer I came up with involved the formation within the corporation of a group of young 'samurais' who would play a dual role. On the one hand they would function as real strategists, giving free rein to their imagination and entrepreneurial flair in order to come up with bold and innovative strategic ideas. On the other hand they would serve as staff analysts, testing out, digesting, and assigning priorities to the ideas, and providing staff assistance to line managers in implementing the approved strategies. This 'samurai' concept has since been adopted in several Japanese firms with great success.

Such a solution would not fit the circumstances of the typical American or European company. Yet it seems to me that the central notion of my book and of a sequel published in Japan 18 months later is relevant to the problem of strategic stagnation in any organization. There are ways in which the mind of the strategist can be reproduced, or simulated, by people who may lack a natural talent for strategy. Putting it another way, although there is no secret formula for inventing a successful strategy, there are some specific concepts and approaches that can help anyone develop the kind of mentality that comes up with superior strategic ideas. Thus the reader will find in this reading no formulas for successful business strategy. What I will try to supply in their place is a series of hints that may help him or her develop the capacity for and the habit of strategic thinking.

Analysis: The Starting Point

Analysis is the critical starting point of strategic thinking. Faced with problems, trends, events, or situations that appear to constitute a harmonious whole or come packaged as a whole by the common sense of the day, the strategic thinker dissects them into their constituent parts. Then, having discovered the significance of these constituents, he reassembles them in a way calculated to maximize his advantage.

In business as on the battlefield, the object of strategy is to bring about the conditions most favorable to one's own side, judging precisely the right moment to attack or withdraw and always assessing the limits of compromise correctly. Besides the habit of analysis, what marks the mind of the strategist is an intellectual elasticity or flexibility that enables him to come up with realistic responses to changing situations, not simply to discriminate with great precision among different shades of gray.

In strategic thinking, one first seeks a clear understanding of the particular character of each element of a situation and then makes the fullest possible use of human brainpower to restructure the elements in the most advantageous way. Phenomena and events in the real world do not always fit a linear model. Hence the most reliable means of dissecting a situation into its constituent parts and reassembling them in the desired pattern is not a step-by-step methodology such as systems analysis. Rather, it is that ultimate nonlinear thinking tool, the human brain. True strategic thinking thus contrasts sharply with the conventional mechanical systems approach based on linear thinking. But it also contrasts with the approach that stakes everything on intuition, reaching conclusions without any real breakdown or analysis (Figure 2.3).

No matter how difficult or unprecedented the problem, a breakthrough to the best possible solution can come only from a combination of rational analysis, based on the real nature of things, and imaginative reintegration of all the different items into a new pattern, using nonlinear brainpower. This is always the most effective approach to devising strategies for dealing successfully with challenges and opportunities, in the market arena as on the battlefield.

Determining the Critical Issue

The first stage in strategic thinking is to pinpoint the critical issue in the situation. Everyone facing a problem naturally tries in his or her own way to penetrate to the key issue. Some may think that one way is as good as another and that whether their efforts hit the mark is largely a matter of luck. I believe it is not a question of luck at all but of attitude and method. In problem solving, it is vital at the start to formulate the question in a way that will facilitate the discovery of a solution.

Suppose, for example, that overtime work has become chronic in a company, dragging down profitability. If we frame the question as: What should be done to reduce overtime? Many answers will suggest themselves:

- work harder during the regular working hours;

- shorten the lunch period and coffee breaks;

- forbid long private telephone conversations.

Such questioning is often employed by companies trying to lower costs and improve product quality by using zero defect campaigns and quality control (QC) circles that involve the participation of all employees. Ideas

FIGURE 2.3
Three kinds of thinking process

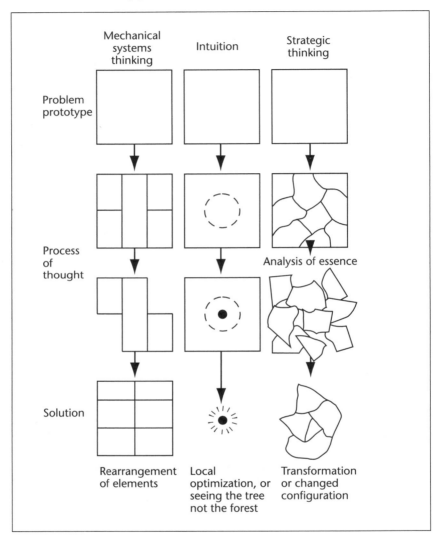

are gathered, screened, and later incorporated in the improvement program. But this approach has an intrinsic limitation. *The questions are not
framed to point toward a solution; rather, they are directed toward finding
remedies to symptoms.*

Returning to our overtime problem, suppose we frame the question
in a more solution-oriented way: Is this company's work force large

enough to do all the work required? To this question there can be only one of two answers – yes or no. To arrive at the answer yes, a great deal of analysis would be needed, probably including a comparison with other companies in the same industries, the historical trend of workload per employee, and the degree of automation and computerization and their economic effectiveness. On the other hand, if – after careful perusal of the sales record, profit per employee, ratio between direct and indirect labor, comparison with other companies, and so on – the answer should turn out to be no (i.e. the company is currently understaffed), this in itself would be tantamount to a solution of the original problem. This solution – an increase in personnel – will be validated by all the usual management indicators. And if the company adopts this solution, the probability increases that the desired outcome will actually follow. This way, objective analysis can supplant emotional discussions.

That is not the only way the question could have been formulated, however. We might have asked it this way: Do the capabilities of the employees match the nature of the work? This formulation, like the previous one, is oriented toward deriving a possible solution. Here too, a negative answer would imply a shortage of suitable personnel, which would in turn suggest that the solution should be sought either in staff training or in recruiting capable staff from elsewhere. On the other hand, if the answer is yes, this indicates that the problem of chronic overtime lies not in the nature of the work but in the amount of the workload. Thus, not training but adding to the work force would then be the crucial factor in the solution.

If the right questions are asked in a solution-oriented manner, and if the proper analyses are carried out, the final answer is likely to be the same, even though it may have started from a differently phrased question and may have been arrived at by a different route. In either case, a question concerning the nature and amount of work brings the real issue into focus and makes it easy to arrive at a clear-cut verdict.

It is hard to overstate the importance of formulating the question correctly. People who are trained and motivated to formulate the right questions will not offer vague proposals for 'improvements,' as are seen in many suggestion boxes. They will come up with concrete, practical ideas.

By failing to grasp the critical issues, too many senior managers today impose great anxiety on themselves and their subordinates, whose efforts end in failure and frustration. Solution-oriented questions can be formulated only if the critical issue is localized and grasped accurately in the first place. A clear common understanding of the nature of a problem that has already been localized provides a critical pressure to come up with creative solutions. When problems are poorly defined or vaguely comprehended, one's creative mind does not work sharply. The greater one's tolerance for lukewarm solutions, half measures and what the

British used to call muddling through, the more loosely the issue is likely to be defined. For this reason, isolating the crucial points of the problem – in other words, determining the critical issue – is most important to the discovery of a solution. The key at this initial stage is to *narrow down the issue by studying the observed phenomena closely.*

Figure 2.4 illustrates one method often used by strategists in the process of abstraction, showing how it might work in the case of a large, established company faced with the problem of declining competitive vigor.

The first step in the abstraction process is to use such means as brainstorming and opinion polls to assemble and itemize the respects in which the company is at a disadvantage *vis-à-vis* its competitors. These points can then be classified under a smaller number of headings (shown in Figure 2.4 as Concrete Phenomena) according to their common factors.

Next, phenomena sharing some common denominator are themselves combined into groups. Having done this, we look once again at each group as a unit and ask ourselves what crucial issue each unit poses. The source of the problem must be understood before any real solution can be found, and the process of abstraction enables us to bring the crucial issues to light without the risk of overlooking anything important.

Once the abstraction process has been completed, we must next decide on the right approach to finding a solution. Once we have determined the solution in principle, there remains the task of working out implementation programs and then compiling detailed action plans. No solution, however perfectly it may address the critical issue, can be of the slightest use until it is implemented. Too many companies try to short-circuit the necessary steps between identification of critical issues and line implementation of solutions by skipping the intermediate steps: planning for operational improvement and organizing for concrete actions. Even the most brilliant line manager cannot translate an abstract plan into action in a single step.

The Art of Strategic Thinking

Most of us are familiar with Thomas Alva Edison's recipe for inventive genius: '1 percent inspiration, 99 percent perspiration.' The same ratio holds true for creativity in any endeavor, including the development of business strategy. Don't be misled by the ratio. That spark of insight *is* essential. Without it, strategies disintegrate into stereotypes. But to bring insight to fruition as a successful strategy takes method, mental discipline, and plain hard work.

FIGURE 2.4
Narrowing down the issue

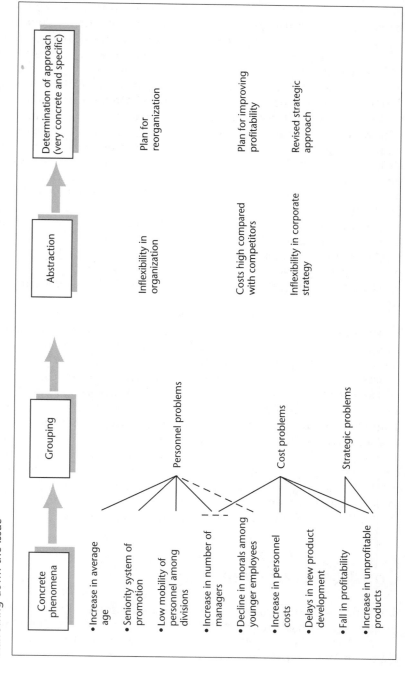

So far we have been exploring the mental processes or thought patterns for the 'grunt' part of the strategy. When we come to creative inspiration, however, our task becomes exceedingly difficult. Insight is far easier to recognize than define. Perhaps we might say that creative insight is the ability to combine, synthesize, or reshuffle previously unrelated phenomena in such a way that you get more out of the emergent whole than you have put in.

What does this all mean to the strategist? Can creativity be taught? Perhaps not. Can it be cultivated consciously? Obviously I believe so, or I wouldn't have written this article. Inventive geniuses such as Thomas Edison or Edwin Land are by definition rare exceptions. For most of us, creative insight is a smoldering ember that must be fanned constantly to glow. I strongly believe that when all the right ingredients are present – sensitivity, will, and receptiveness – they can be nurtured by example, direction, and conditioning. In short, creativity cannot be taught, but it can be learned.

Putting it more prosaically, we need to identify and stimulate those habits or conditions which nurture creativity and at the same time to crystallize the constraints or boundaries defining our probability of success. In my experience, there are at least three major constraints to which the business strategist needs to be sensitive. I think of them as the essential Rs: reality, ripeness, and resources.

Let's begin with *reality*. Unlike scientific conceptualizers or creative artists, business strategists must always be aware of the customer, the competition, and the company's field of competence. *Ripeness*, or timing, is the second key consideration that the business strategist must address. Unless the time is ripe for the proposed strategy, it is virtually certain to fail. *Resources*, my third R, constitute such an obvious constraint that it is amazing that they should be ignored or neglected by strategists. Yet examples abound of strategies that failed because their authors were not sensitive to their own resource limitations. Take diversification as a case in point. Few food companies trying to move into pharmaceuticals, chemical companies moving into foods, or electronic component manufacturers moving into final assembly have succeeded. The basic reason in most cases has been that the companies involved were not sensitive to the limitations of their own internal resources and skills.

Conditions of Creativity

Being attuned to the three Rs is a necessary precondition of creative insight, but in itself it will not fan the spark of creative power within us. For that, other elements are needed. Obviously, there is no single approach that will dependably turn anyone into a superstrategist, but there are certain things we can consciously do to stretch or stimulate our creative prowess. Most important, I believe, we need to cultivate three interrelated conditions: an initial charge, directional antennae, and a capacity to tolerate static.

Call it what you will – vision, focus, inner drive – the initial charge must be there. It is the mainspring of intuitive creativity. We have seen how Yamaha, originally a wood-based furniture company, was transformed into a major force in the leisure industry by just such a vision, born of one man's desire to bring positive enrichment into the lives of the work-oriented Japanese. From this vision he developed a totally new thrust for Yamaha.

An entire family of musical instruments and accessories – organs, trumpets, cornets, trombones, guitars, and so on – was developed to complement Yamaha's pianos. These were followed by stereo equipment, sporting goods, motorcycles and pleasure boats. Music schools were established. Then came the Yamaha Music Camp, complete with a resort lodge complex, a game reserve, an archery range, and other leisure-oriented pursuits. Today, Yamaha plans concerts and is involved with concert hall management as well, reaping profits while enriching the lives of millions of Japanese.

If the initial charge provides the creative impetus, directional antennae are required to recognize phenomena which, as the saying goes, are in the air. These antennae are the component in the creative process that uncovers and selects, among a welter of facts and existing conditions, potentially profitable ideas that were always there but were visible only to eyes not blinded by habit.

Consider how these directional antennae work for Dr Kazuma Tateishi, founder and chairman of Omron Tateishi Electronics. Tateishi has an uncanny flair for sensing phenomena to which the concept of flow can be applied. He perceived the banking business as a flow of cash, traffic jams and congested train stations as blocked flows of cars and people, and production lines as a physical flow of parts. From these perceptions evolved the development of Japan's first automated banking system, the introduction of sequence controllers that automatically regulate traffic according to road conditions and volume, and the evolution of the world's first unmanned railroad station based on a completely automatic system that can exchange bills for coins, issue tickets and season passes, and adjust fares and operate turnstiles. Today, Omron's automated systems are used in many industrial operations from production to distribution. Dr Tateishi is a remarkable example of a man whose directional antennae have enabled him to implement his youthful creed: 'Man should do only what only man can do.'

Creative concepts often have a disruptive as well as a constructive aspect. They can shatter set patterns of thinking, threaten the status quo, or at the very least stir up people's anxieties. Often when people set out to sell or implement a creative idea, they are taking a big risk of failing, losing money, or simply making fools of themselves. That is why the will to cope with criticism, hostility, and even derision, while not necessarily a condition of creative thinking, does seem to be an important characteristic of successful innovative strategists. To squeeze the last drop out of my original metaphor, I call this the static-tolerance component of creativity.

Witness the static that Soichiro Honda had to tolerate in order to bring his clean-engine car to market. Only corporate insiders can tell how much intracompany interference he had to cope with. That the government vainly brought severe pressure on him to stay out of the auto market is no secret, however. Neither is the public ridicule he bore when industry experts scoffed at his concept.

Dr Koji Kobayashi of NEC tolerated static of a rather different kind. Despite prevailing industry trends, he clung fast to his intuitive belief (some 20 years ahead of its time) that computers and telecommunications would one day be linked. To do so, he had to bear heavy financial burdens, internal dissension, and scorn. All this leads me to a final observation. Strategic success cannot be reduced to a formula, nor can anyone become a strategic thinker merely by reading a book. Nevertheless, there are habits of mind and modes of thinking that can be acquired through practice to help you free the creative power of your subconscious and improve your odds of coming up with winning strategic concepts.

The main purpose of this contribution is to encourage you to do so and to point out the directions you should pursue. The use of Japanese examples to illustrate points and reinforce assertions may at times have given it an exotic flavor, but that is ultimately of no importance. Creativity, mental productivity and the power of strategic insight know no national boundaries. Fortunately for all of us, they are universal.

Strategic Thinking in International Perspective

Rational, adj. Devoid of all delusions
save those of observation, experience and
reflection.
(*The Devil's Dictionary*, Ambrose Bierce 1842–1914; American columnist)

From the preceding contributions it has become clear that opinions differ sharply about what goes on, and should go on, in the mind of the strategist. There are strongly conflicting views on how managers deal with the paradox of logic and creativity. It is up to each reader to judge whether the rational or the generative perspective is more valuable for understanding strategic thinking. Yet, we hope that readers will feel challenged to consider the possibility that both perspectives may be useful at the same time. Although they are opposites, and partially contradictory, both perspectives might reveal crucial aspects of strategic thinking that need to be combined to achieve superior results. Blending logic and creativity in ingenious ways might allow strategists to get 'the best of both worlds.' What such syntheses of logic and creativity in the mind of the strategist could be like, will remain a matter for debate – with strategists using their own logical and/or creative thinking to come up with answers.

Hence, this last part of the chapter is not intended to present a grand synthesis. Readers will have to grapple with the paradox of logic and creativity themselves, by contrasting the thesis (the rational thinking perspective) and the antithesis (the generative thinking perspective). In this final part of the chapter it is the intention to view the topic of strategic thinking from an international perspective. The explicit question that must be added to the debate on the mind of the strategist is whether there are discernible national differences in approaches to strategic thinking. Are there specific national preferences for the rational or the generative perspective, or are the differing views spread randomly across the globe? Are each of the perspectives rooted in a particular national context, making it difficult to extend them to other countries, or are they universally applicable? In short, are views on strategic thinking the same all around the world?

Unfortunately, this question is easier asked than answered. Little cross-cultural research has been done in the field of strategic management and hardly any on this specific topic. This may be partially due to the difficulty of international comparative research, but it probably also reflects the implicit assumption by most that theories on strategic thinking are universally applicable. Few of the authors cited in this chapter suggest that there are international differences or note that their theories might be culturally biased and of limited validity in other national settings.

Yet, the assumption that strategic thinking is viewed in the same way around the world should be questioned. The human inclination to suppose that all others are the same as ourselves, is well known – it is a common cognitive bias. In international affairs, however, such an assumption must always be challenged. Internationally-operating strategists cannot afford the luxury of assuming that their views are universally accepted and applicable. Therefore, the thought must be entertained that strategists in some countries are more attracted to the rational perspective, while in other countries the generative perspective is more pervasive.

As a stimulus to the debate whether there are such national preferences in perspective on strategic thinking, we would like to bring forward a number of factors that might be of influence on how the paradox of logic and creativity is tackled in different countries. It goes almost without saying that more concrete international comparative research is needed to give this debate a firmer footing.

Position of Science

Science and the scientific method do not play the same role, and are not accorded the same value, in all societies. In some countries, science and scientists are held in high esteem, and scientific inquiry is believed to be the most fruitful way for obtaining new knowledge. Typical for these nations is that the scientific method has come to pervade almost all aspects of life. Objective knowledge and skill in analytical reasoning are widely believed to be the critical success factors in most professions – even to become a nurse, a journalist, a sports instructor, an actor or a musician requires a university education. Managers, too, are assumed to be scientifically trained, often specializing in management studies. Much of this education strongly promotes formal, explicit, analytical thinking, and pays little attention to creativity, imagination and intuition. In these nations a more pronounced preference for the rational thinking perspective might be expected.

In other countries, science holds a less predominant position[35]. Scientific methods might shed some light on issues, both other ways of obtaining new insights – such as through experience, intuition, philosophizing, fantasizing, and drawing analogies – are also valued[36]. Socially acceptable reasoning is less constrictive than in more rationalist nations. Leaps of imagination and logical inconsistencies are tolerated, as normal aspects in the messy process of sense-making[37]. In general, thinking is viewed as an art and therefore science has not made deep inroads into most of the professions. Managers, in particular, do not require a specific scientific training, but need to be broadly-developed generalists with flexible minds[38]. In these countries, a stronger preference for the generative thinking perspective can be expected.

Level of Uncertainty Avoidance

National cultures also differ with regard to their tolerance for ambiguity. As Hofstede points out in Chapter 1, reading 2, some societies feel uncomfortable with uncertain situations and strive for security. Countries that score high on Hofstede's *uncertainty avoidance dimension* typically try to suppress deviant ideas and behaviors, and institute rules that everyone must follow. People in these countries exhibit a strong intellectual need to believe in absolute truths and they place great trust in experts[39]. They have a low tolerance for the ambiguity brought on by creative insights, novel interpretations and 'wild ideas' that are not analytically sound. Therefore, it can be expected that strategists in high uncertainty avoidance cultures will be more inclined towards the rational thinking perspective than in nations with a low score.

Level of Individualism

As stated at the beginning of this chapter, strategists with a generative inclination are slightly rebellious. They show little reverence for the status quo, by continuously questioning existing cognitive maps and launching creative reinterpretations. As the dissenting voice, they often stand alone, and are heavily criticized by the more orthodox. This lonely position is difficult to maintain under the best of circumstances, but is especially taxing in highly collectivist cultures. If strategists wish to be accepted within their group, organization and community, they cannot afford to stick out too much. There will be a strong pressure on the strategist to conform. In more individualist cultures, however, there is usually a higher tolerance for individual variety. People find it easier to have their own ideas, independent of their group, organization and community (see Hofstede's individualism dimension). This gives strategists more intellectual and emotional freedom to be the 'odd man out.' Therefore, it can be expected that strategists in more individualist cultures will be more inclined towards the generative perspective than those in collectivist cultures.

Position of Strategists

Countries also differ sharply with regard to the hierarchical position of the managers engaged in strategy. In many countries strategic problems are largely defined and solved by the upper echelons of management. To reach this hierarchical position requires many years of hands on experience and climbing through the ranks. Therefore, by the time managers are in the position of being a strategist they are middle-aged and thoroughly familiar with their business – with the danger of being set in their ways. They will also have been promoted several times by senior managers who believe that they will function well within the organization. In general, the effect is that competent and conformist managers are promoted to strategy positions, while innovative dissidents are selected out along the way. In such countries, creative strategic thinking often does not take place within large organizations, but within small start ups, to which the creatively-inclined flee.

In cultures that score lower on Hofstede's power distance dimension, managers throughout the organization are often involved in strategy discussions. The responsibility for strategy is spread more widely among the ranks. Younger, less experienced managers are expected to participate in strategy formation processes, together with their senior colleagues. In general, this leads to a more open, messy and lively debate about the organization's strategy and provokes more creative strategic thinking. Therefore, it can be expected that in less hierarchical cultures the generative thinking perspective will be more popular than in cultures with stronger hierarchical relations.

Further Readings

Anyone interested in the topic of strategic thinking will sooner or later run into the work of Herbert Simon. His concept of bounded rationality was originally explored in the book *Models of Man*, which is still interesting reading, but *Organizations*, written together with James March, is a more comprehensive and up-to-date source with which to start. Also a good introduction to (bounded) rationality is given by Niels Noorderhaven, in his book *Strategic Decision Making*, which additionally covers the topics of emotions, intuition and cognition in relationship to the strategy process.

For a more in-depth discussion on the interplay between cognition and strategic decision-making, a stimulating book is R. Hogarth's *Judgement and Choice: The Psychology of Decision*. Also an excellent book is *The Essence of Strategic Decision Making*, by Charles Schwenk, in particular with regard to the discussion of cognitive biases. On the topic of the social construction of reality, Karl Weick's *The Social Psychology of Organizing* is still the classic that should be read.

Readers interested in the link between creativity and strategic thinking might want to start with *Creative Management*, an excellent reader edited by John Henry, which contains many classic articles on creativity from a variety of different disciplines. A second step would be to read Gareth Morgan's imaginative book *Imaginization: The Art of Creative Management*, or John Kao's *Jamming: The Art and Discipline of Business Creativity*, both of which make challenging proposals for improving an organization's creative thinking. Also stimulating is the book *Strategic Innovation*, by Charles Baden-Fuller and Martyn Pitt, which contains a large number of cases on companies exhibiting creative thinking. For a good follow-up article that strongly advocates the generative perspective, readers are advised to turn to the article 'Strategy as Revolution' by Gary Hamel.

Strategy Formation

Plans are nothing. Planning is everything.

(Dwight D. Eisenhower 1890–1969; American general and president)

It is a mistake to look too far ahead.
Only one link of the chain of destiny
can be handled at a time.

(Winston Churchill 1874–1965; British prime minister and writer)

The Paradox of Deliberateness and Emergentness

While the previous chapter dealt with the strategy processes going on in the minds of individuals, this chapter is concerned with the strategy processes going on in organizations. The central question here is how strategies are made in organizations – how the process of *strategy formation* takes place. It will be debated how organizations form their strategies in practice, as well as how the process of strategy formation can be made most effective.

Many conflicting opinions have been voiced about the best way of forming strategies. However, the debate between these rival points of view has not been very transparent. Much confusion has been caused by the fact that authors employ strongly differing definitions of what strategy actually is. Naturally, theorists starting with different implicit assumptions of what strategy is, will also disagree on how 'strategy' should be made. The most confusion has been between theorists who define strategy as a *pattern of decisions* and those who view strategy as a *pattern of actions*. Many authors speak of a strategy when an organization has decided on a consistent course of action, that it intends to pursue. Other authors speak of strategy when an organization has actually exhibited a consistent course of action in practice. To distinguish these two definitions[1] of strategy, Mintzberg and Waters[1] have proposed to refer to the former as *intended strategy* and the latter as *realized strategy*. Intended strategies are the patterns of decisions that organizations plan to execute, while realized strategies are the patterns of action that have been accomplished.

In this chapter, both intended and realized strategy are important, as are the links between them. As Figure 3.1 indicates, one would expect that intended strategy would lead to realized strategy. Where realized strategies were fully intended, Mintzberg and Waters speak of *deliberate strategy*. However, they argue that realized strategies can also come about 'despite, or in the absence of, intentions,' which they label *emergent strategy*. Strategies can emerge unintentionally as strategists take one step at a time trying to piece together a viable course of action. Patterns of action unfold over time as strategists gradually learn and come to agree on a particular direction.

This distinction between deliberate and emergent strategy goes to the heart of the debate on the topic of strategy formation. While theorists disagree on many points, the crucial issue is whether strategy formation should be more deliberate or more emergent. A wide variety of opinions exists, each dealing with the tension between deliberateness and emergentness in a different way. At the extremes in this debate, two radically

FIGURE 3.1
Forms of strategy (Source: Mintzberg and Waters, 1985)

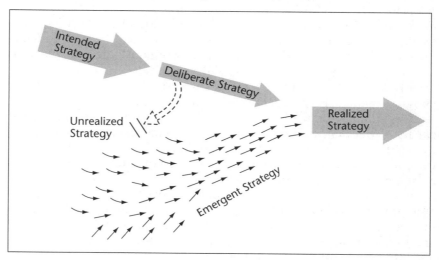

opposite positions can be identified. On the one hand, there are strategists who argue that organizations should strive to make strategy in a highly deliberate manner, by first explicitly formulating comprehensive plans, and only then implementing them. In accordance with common usage, we shall refer to this point of view as the *planning* perspective. On the other hand, there are strategists who argue that in reality most new strategies emerge over time and that organizations should facilitate this messy, fragmented, piecemeal formation process. This point of view shall be referred to as the *incrementalism* perspective.

Following the debate model introduced in Chapter 2, the inquiry into the nature of effective strategy formation in this chapter will also be structured by contrasting these two extremes. By comparing the two opposite ways of dealing with the paradox of deliberateness and emergentness, a better understanding of the issues under discussion should be gained. In the next few pages, the planning and incrementalism perspectives will be further explained, and finally summarized in Table 3.1.

The Planning Perspective

Advocates of the planning perspective argue that strategies should be deliberately planned and executed. In their view, anything that emerges unplanned is not really strategy. A successful pattern of action that was not intended cannot be called strategy, but should be seen for what it is – brilliant improvisation or just plain luck[2]. However, strategists cannot afford to count on their good fortune or skill at muddling through. They must put time and effort into consciously formulating an explicit plan, making use of all available information and weighing all of the strategic alternatives. Tough decisions need to be made and priorities need to be set, before action is taken. 'Think before you act' is the planning perspective's motto. But once a strategic plan has been adopted, action should be swift, efficient and controlled. Implementation must be secured by detailing the activities to be undertaken, assigning responsibilities to managers and holding them accountable for achieving results.

Hence, in the planning perspective, strategies are intentionally designed, much as an engineer designs a bridge. Building a bridge requires a long formulation phase, including extensive analysis of the situation, the drawing up of a number of rough designs, evaluation of these alternatives, choice of a preferred design, and further detailing in the form of a blueprint. Only after the design phase has been completed, do the construction companies take over and build according to plan. Characteristic of such a planning approach to producing bridges and strategies is that the entire process can be disassembled into a number of distinct steps, that need to be carried out in a sequential and orderly manner. Only by going through these steps in a conscious and structured manner will the best results be obtained.

A planning approach to strategy formation has many advantages over *ad hoc* management, it is argued. First, plans give an organization *direction*, instead of letting it drift. Organizations cannot act rationally without intentions – if you do not know where you are going, any behavior is fine. By first setting a goal and then choosing a strategy to get there, organizations can be given a clear sense of direction. Managers can then select actions that are efficient and effective within the context of the strategy. This leads to a second, related advantage, namely, that plans allow for organizational *programming*. The clearer the plan, the better a company can get itself organized for execution. A structure can be chosen, tasks can be assigned, responsibilities can be divided, budgets can be allotted, and targets can be set. Not unimportantly, a control system can be created to measure results in comparison to the plan, so that corrective action can be taken.

A further advantage of planning is that it helps to achieve *optimization*. By explicitly considering all available options before making a decision, organizations can allocate their scarce resources to the most promising course of action. Not only can options be compared within a business area, but planning facilitates the corporate-wide comparison between strategic options in different businesses. Another related advantage is that planning also expedites *coordination* between all of the involved parties. By having to agree on a joint plan before action is taken, differences of opinion can be ironed out, activities can be mutually adjusted, and a consistent organization-wide strategy can be pursued.

A planning approach to strategy formation also allows for the *formalization* and *differentiation* of strategy tasks. Because of its highly structured and sequential nature, planning lends itself well to formalization. The steps of the planning approach can be captured in planning systems[3], and procedures can be developed to further enhance and organize the strategy formation process. In such planning systems, not all elements of strategy formation need to be carried out by one and the same person, but can be divided among a number of people. The most important division of labor is often between those formulating the plans and those implementing them. In many large companies the managers proposing the plans are also the ones implementing them, but deciding on the plans is passed up to a higher level. Often other tasks are also spun off or shared with others, such as analysis (staff department or external consultants), evaluation (corporate planner) and implementation (staff departments). Such task differentiation and specialization, it is argued, can lead to a better use of management talent, much as the division of labor has improved the field of production.

Last, but not least, an advantage of planning is that it encourages *long-term thinking* and *commitment*. *Ad hoc* management is short-term oriented, dealing with issues of strategic importance as they come up or as a crisis develops. Planning, on the other hand, directs attention to the future. Managers making strategic plans have to take a more long-term view and are stimulated to prepare for, or even create, the future[4]. Instead of just muddling through, planning challenges strategists to define a desirable future and to work towards it. Instead of wavering and opportunism, planning commits the organization to a course of action and allows for investments to be made now that may only pay off in the long run.

One of the difficulties of planning, advocates of this perspective will readily admit, is that plans will always be based on assumptions about how future events will unfold. Plans require *forecasts*. And as the Danish physicist Niels Bohr once joked, 'prediction is very difficult, especially about the future.' Even enthusiastic planners acknowledge that forecasts will be inaccurate. As Makridakis, the most prolific writer on the topic of forecasting, writes[5], 'the future can be predicted only by extrapolating from the past, yet it is fairly certain that the future will be different from the past.' Consequently, it is clear that rigid long-range plans based on such unreliable forecasts would amount to nothing less than Russian roulette. Most proponents of the planning perspective therefore caution for overly deterministic plans. Some argue in favor of *contingency planning*, whereby a number of alternative plans are held in reserve in case key variables in the environment suddenly change. These contingency plans are commonly based on different future *scenarios*[6]. Others argue that organizations should stage regular reviews, and realign the strategic plans to match the altered circumstances. This is usually accomplished by going through the planning cycle every year, and adapting plans to fit with the new forecasts.

As the attentive reader may have already discerned, the planning perspective shares many of the assumptions underlying the rational perspective discussed in Chapter 2. Both perspectives value systematic, orderly, consistent, logical reasoning and assume that humans are capable of forming a fairly good understanding of reality. And both are based on a calculative and optimizing view of strategy making. It is, therefore, not surprising that many strategists who are rationally inclined also exhibit a distinct preference for the planning perspective in this debate.

The Incrementalism Perspective

To advocates of the incrementalism perspective, the planners' faith in deliberateness is misplaced and counterproductive. In reality, incrementalists argue, new strategies largely emerge over time, as managers proactively piece together a viable course of action or reactively adapt to unfolding circumstances. The formation process is not about comprehensively *figuring out* strategy in advance, but about actively *finding out* by doing and gradually blending together initiatives into a coherent pattern of actions. Making strategy involves sense-making, reflecting, learning, envisioning, experimenting and changing the organization, which cannot be neatly organized and programmed. Strategy formation is messy, fragmented, and piecemeal – much more like the unstructured and unpredictable processes of exploration and invention, than like the orderly processes of design and production.

Yet proponents of the planning perspective prefer to press strategy formation into an orderly, mechanistic straight-jacket. Strategies must be intentionally designed and executed. According to incrementalists, this excessive emphasis on deliberateness is due to planners' obsession with rationality and control[7]. Planners are often compulsive in their desire for order, predictability and efficiency. It is the intention of planning to predict, analyse, optimize and program – to deliberately fine-tune and control the organization's future behavior. For them, 'to manage' is 'to control' and therefore only deliberate patterns of action constitute good strategic management[8].

Incrementalists do not question the value of planning and control as a means for managing some organizational processes, but point out that strategy formation is not one of them. In general, planning and control are valuable for routine activities that need to be efficiently organized (e.g. production or finance). But planning is less suitable for non-routine activities – that is, for doing new things. Planning is not appropriate for *innovation*. Just as R&D departments cannot plan the invention of new products, strategists cannot plan the development of new strategies. Innovation, whether in products or strategies, is not a process that can be neatly structured and controlled. Novel insights and creative ideas cannot be generated on demand, but surface at unexpected moments, often in unexpected places. Neither are new ideas born full grown, ready to be evaluated and implemented. In reality, innovation requires brooding, tinkering, experimentation, testing and patience, as new ideas grow and take shape. Throughout the innovation process it remains unclear which ideas might evolve into blockbuster strategies and which will turn out to be miserable disappointments. No one can objectively determine ahead of time which strategic initiatives will 'fly' and which will 'crash'. Therefore, strategists engaged in the formation of new strategies must move incrementally, letting novel ideas crystallize over time, and increase commitment as ideas gradually prove their viability in practice. This demands that strategists behave not as planners, but as *inventors* – searching, experimenting, learning, doubting, and avoiding premature closure and lock-in to one course of action.

Recognizing that strategy formation is essentially an innovation process has more consequences. Innovation is inherently subversive, rebelling against the status quo and challenging those who are emotionally, intellectually or politically wedded to the current state of affairs. Creating new strategies involves confronting people's cognitive maps, questioning the organizational culture, threatening individuals' current interests and disrupting the distribution of power within the organization[9]. None of these processes can be conducted in an orderly fashion, let alone be incorporated into a planning system. Changing people's cognitive maps, as discussed in Chapter 2, requires complex processes of unlearning and learning. Cultural and political change, which will be discussed in Chapter 4, are also difficult processes to program. Even for the most powerful CEO, managing cognitive, cultural and political changes is not a matter of deliberate control, but of incremental shaping. Less powerful strategists will have even a weaker grip on the unfolding cognitive, cultural and political reality in their organization, and therefore will be even less able to plan. In short, strategists understanding that strategy formation is essentially a disruptive process of organizational change, will move incrementally, gradually molding the organization into a satisfactory form. This demands that strategists behave not as commanders, but as *organizational developers* – questioning assumptions, challenging ideas, getting points on the strategic agenda, encouraging learning, championing new initiatives, supporting change and building political support.

Incrementalists point out that planning is particularly inappropriate when dealing with *wicked problems*. While solving tame problems can often be planned and controlled, strategists rarely have the luxury of using generic solutions to fix clearly recognizable strategic problems. As Mason and Mitroff argued in reading 1.1, strategic problems are inherently wicked – they are essentially unique, highly complex, linked to other problems, can be defined and interpreted in many ways, have no correct answer, nor a delimited set of possible solutions. The planning approach of recognizing the problem, fully analyzing the situation, formulating a comprehensive plan and then implementing the solution, is sure to choke on a wicked problem. A number of weaknesses of planning show up when confronted with a wicked problem.

First, problems cannot be simply recognized and analyzed, but can be interpreted and defined in many ways, depending on how the strategist looks at it. Therefore, half the work of strategists is *making sense* out of complex problems. Or, as Rittel and Webber[10] put it, the definition of a wicked problem *is* the problem! Strategists must search for new ways for understanding old problems and must be aware of how others are reinterpreting what they see. This inhibits planning and encourages incrementalism.

Second, a full analysis of a wicked problem is impossible. Due to a wicked problem's complexity and links to other problems, a full analysis would take, literally, forever. And there would always be more ways of interpreting the problem, requiring more analysis. Planning based on the complete understanding of a problem in advance therefore necessarily leads to paralysis by analysis[11]. In reality, however, strategists move proactively despite their incomplete understanding of a wicked problem, *learning* as they go along. By acting and thinking at the same time strategists can focus their analyses on what seems to be important and realistic in practice, gradually shaping their understanding along the way.

Third, developing a comprehensive plan to tackle a wicked problem is asking for trouble. Wicked problems are very complex, consisting of many subproblems. Formulating a master plan to solve all subproblems in one blow would require a very high level of planning sophistication and an organization with the ability to implement plans in a highly coordinated manner – much like the circus performers who can keep ten plates twirling at the ends of poles at the same time. Such organizations are rare at best, and the risk of a grand strategy failing is huge – once one plate falls, the rest usually comes crashing down. This is also known as Knagg's law: the more complex a plan, the larger the chance of failure. Incrementalists therefore argue that it is wiser to tackle *subproblems* individually, and gradually blend these solutions into a cohesive pattern of action.

Finally, planners who believe that formulation and implementation can be separated underestimate the extent to which wicked problems are interactive. As soon as an organization starts to implement a plan, its actions will induce counteractions. Customers will react, competitors will change behavior, suppliers will take a different stance, regulatory agencies might come into action, unions will respond, the stockmarkets will take notice and company employees will draw conclusions. Hence, action by the organization will change the nature of the problem. And since the many counterparties are intelligent players, capable of acting strategically, their responses will not be entirely predictable. Planners will not be able to forecast and incorporate other parties' reactions into the plans. Therefore, plans will be outdated as soon as implementation starts. For this reason, incrementalists argue that action must always be swiftly followed by redefinition of the problem and reconsideration of the course of action being pursued. Over time, this iterative process of *action-reaction-reconsideration* will lead to the emergence of a pattern of action, which is the best possible result given the interactive nature of wicked problems.

This last point, on the unpredictability of external and internal reactions to a plan, leads up to a weakness of planning that is possibly its most obvious one – strategy has to do with the future and the future is inherently unknown. Developments cannot be clearly forecast, future opportunities and threats cannot be predicted, nor can future strengths and weaknesses be accurately foreseen. In such unknown terrain, it is foolhardy to commit oneself to a preset course of action unless absolutely necessary. It makes much more sense in new and unpredictable circumstances to remain flexible and adaptive, postponing fixed commitments for as long as possible. An unknown future requires not the mentality of a train conductor, but of an *explorer* – curious, probing, venturesome, and entrepreneurial, yet moving cautiously, step-by-step, ready to shift course when needed.

To proponents of the incrementalism perspective, it is a caricature to call such behavior *ad hoc* or muddling through. Rather, it is behavior that acknowledges the fact that strategy formation is a process of innovation and organizational development in the face of wicked problems in an unknown future. Under these circumstances, strategies must be allowed to emerge and 'strategic planning' must be seen for what it is – a contradiction in terms.

The question within the field of strategic management is, therefore, whether strategy formation is primarily a deliberate process or more of an emergent one. Should strategists strive to formulate and implement strategic plans, supported by a formalized planning and control system? Or should strategists move incrementally, behaving as inventors, organizational developers and explorers? Not all strategists agree on the answers to these questions, leaving readers in the position of having to draw their own conclusions on the nature of strategy formation. Readers themselves will have to wrestle with the paradox of deliberateness and emergentness (see Table 3.1).

Defining the Issues: Plans and Planning

Before moving on to the 'debate readings,' the dispute between the proponents of the planning and the incrementalism perspectives can be greatly clarified by distinguishing between two major issues on which the parties disagree. First, the two sides are at odds about the need for explicit *plans*. Obviously, advocates of the planning perspective are in favor of articulating intended courses of action. Supporters of the incrementalism perspective doubt the value of plans and focus on the emergence of strategy in the absence of explicit intentions. The second issue revolves around the need for formal *planning*. Here, proponents of the planning perspective champion the establishment of formal planning systems, while incrementalists dismiss such systems as counterproductive, favoring a less structured approach to strategy formation. In the next few paragraphs, these two issues will be further explored, to set the stage for the debate articles that follow.

The Need for Explicit Plans

A plan is an intended course of action. It stipulates which measures a person or organization deliberately proposes to take. In common usage, plans are assumed to be articulated (made explicit) and documented

TABLE 3.1
Planning versus incrementalism perspective

	Planning Perspective	Incrementalism Perspective
Emphasis on	Deliberateness over emergentness	Emergentness over deliberateness
Nature of strategy	Intentionally designed	Gradually shaped
Nature of strategy formation	Figuring out	Finding out
Formation process	Formally structured and comprehensive	Unstructured and fragmented
Formation process steps	First think, then act	Thinking and acting intertwined
Focus on strategy as a	Pattern of decisions (plan)	Pattern of actions (behavior)
Decision-making	Hierarchical	Political
Decision-making focus	Optimal resource allocation & coordination	Experimentation and parallel initiatives
View of future developments	Forecast and anticipate	Partially unknown and unpredictable
Posture towards the future	Make commitments, prepare for the future	Postpone commitments, remain flexible
Implementation focused on	Programming (organizational efficiency)	Learning (organizational development)
Strategic change	Implemented top-down	Requires broad cultural and cognitive shifts

(written down), although strictly speaking this is not necessary to qualify as a plan.

As intended courses of action, plans are means towards an end. Plans detail which actions will be undertaken to reach a particular objective. In practice, however, plans can exist without explicit objectives. In such cases, the objectives are implicitly wrapped up in the plan – the plan incorporates both ends and means.

The first issue dividing planners and incrementalists is whether organizations need plans at all. More accurately, the question is which organizational activities benefit from plans and which do not. To clarify this issue, the aforementioned advantages of plans will be revisited and contrasted with corresponding advantages of not having plans. This leads to five sets of opposites that strategists must consider – five tensions, or we would say paradoxes, embedded within the paradox of deliberateness and emergentness.

- *Direction vs. Latitude.* Planners argue that plans are needed to give organizations direction. Without plans, incorporating objectives, organizations would be adrift. If organizations do not decide where they want to go, any direction and any activity is fine. People in organizations would not know what they were working towards and therefore would not be able to judge what constitutes effective managerial behavior. Incrementalists counter that direction-setting plans can lead to single-minded behavior. Plans, they argue, work as blinkers, blocking out peripheral vision, keeping organizations sharply, yet myopically, focused on one course of action[12]. Thus, plans limit organizations' ability to be open to new opportunities and threats as these unfold and to deviate from a set course as the organization interacts with its environment and learns. The absence of plans does give strategists this latitude for responsive action.

- *Commitment vs. Flexibility.* Planners argue that early commitment to a course of action is highly beneficial. By setting objectives and drawing up a plan to accomplish these, organizations can invest resources, train people, build up production capacity and take a clear position within their environment. Plans allow organizations to mobilize themselves and to dare to take actions that are difficult to reverse and have a long payback period[13]. Incrementalists, however, point out that commitment has a flip-side, inflexibility. Plans, they argue, indeed encourage strategists to take irreversible actions, locking the organization in to a preset course of action[14]. Plans, therefore, inhibit organizations' ability to adapt to changing circumstances. The absence of plans does give strategists the flexibility to easily change course.

- *Coordination vs. Autonomy.* Plans also have the benefit of coordinating all strategic initiatives within an organization into a single cohesive pattern. An organization-wide master plan can ensure that differences of opinion are ironed out and one consistent course of action is followed throughout the entire organization, avoiding overlapping,

conflicting and contradictory behavior. Yet, according to incrementalists, master plans usually lead to the squashing of initiative, either
purposely or inadvertently. Coordination usually means centralization
and unification, leaving little room for autonomous action by entrepreneurs within the organization[15]. Bringing together all strategic action
into one grand scheme, does not encourage an internal market for
ideas, where managers pursue contrarian initiatives and try to sell these
to the rest of the organization. The absence of a comprehensive plan
does give strategists within an organization the autonomy to act as an
intrapreneur[16] and develop new courses of action. This issue will resurface in Chapter 6.

■ *Optimization vs. Learning.* Planners point out that plans also facilitate
optimal resource allocation. Drawing up a plan disciplines strategists to
explicitly consider all available information and consciously evaluate
all available options. This allows strategists to choose the optimal
course of action, before committing resources. Documented plans also
permit corporate-level strategists to compare the courses of action proposed by their various business units and to allocate scarce resources to
the most promising initiatives. Incrementalists counter that plans place
a disproportionate emphasis on thinking over action. Enormous
amounts of time and effort are put into analyses, paperwork, meetings
and presentations, trying to arrive at the optimal plan. Often the result
is that producing a plan develops into an end in itself. Action is seen
merely as operationalizing the plan, instead of as the primary input
into further strategy formation. The absence of explicit plans, therefore,
gives strategists the opportunity to merge thinking and acting, and to
form strategies through learning.

■ *Programming vs. Self-organization.* Last, but not least, plans are a means
for programming all organizational activities in advance. Having
detailed plans allows organizations to be run with the clockwork precision, reliability and efficiency of a machine. Activities that might
otherwise be plagued by poor organization, inconsistencies, redundant
routines, random behavior, helter-skelter fire-fighting and chaos, can be
programmed and controlled if plans are drawn up[17]. Incrementalists,
however, frown on planners' worship of top-down control. According
to incrementalists, using plans to pre-program all activities within an
organization grossly overestimates the extent to which an organization
can be run like a machine. For adaptation, experimentation and learning to take place and for new ideas to emerge from within the organization, a certain measure of chaos might actually be beneficial[18]. Top-
down control by means of plans denies that 'implementers' can be
anything more than cogs in the machine. The absence of detailed
top-down plans encourages employees to be responsible, entrepreneurial and combine thinking and action. In this way, new strategic initiatives are not organized and controlled top-down, but emerge
spontaneously through bottom-up processes of self-organization[19].
This issue will resurface in Chapter 9.

While for the sake of discussion these five paradoxes have been disentangled, in practice they are highly intertwined. A position taken in one debate will influence how the other pairs of opposites are dealt with.

The Need for Formal Planning

In the first pages of this chapter a sixth advantage of the planning approach was mentioned, namely that it facilitates process formalization and task differentiation. It was argued that strategy formation by means of planning lends itself well to formalization. By its very nature, planning is a very structured and sequential activity, and therefore can be readily organized by employing formal procedures. Extensive formalization can culminate in the establishment of a strategic planning system. In such a system, strategy formation steps can be scheduled, tasks can be specified, responsibilities can be assigned, decision-making authority can be clarified, budgets can be allocated and control mechanisms can be installed. It was also argued that formalization goes hand in hand with a division of labor within the strategy process. By pulling the strategy formation process apart into a number of formal, sequential activities, strategy-making tasks can be divided among a larger group of people and specializations can develop.

Obviously, not everyone agrees that formal planning systems are worth instituting. Some incrementalists regard them as a mixed blessing[20], while others are outright hostile[21]. Even some authors who value explicit plans, are not enthusiastic about formal planning[22]. The debate between supporters and detractors of formal planning systems revolves around two major tensions. These two paradoxes are

■   *Formal vs. Informal Process.* The advantage of formalization, according to advocates of the planning perspective, is that it structures and disciplines the strategy formation process[23]. Formalization facilitates tighter organization, unambiguous responsibilities, clearer accountability and stricter review of performance. A formal planning system forces managers to comply with a planned approach to strategy formation. It also gives top management more control over the organization, as all major activities must be in approved plans and the implementation of plans is checked. However, incrementalists challenge the value of such extensive procedures. In their view, formal planning systems are attempts to use bureaucratic means to make strategy. Formalization strongly overemphasizes those aspects which can be neatly organized such as meetings, writing reports, giving presentations, making decisions, allocating resources and reviewing progress, while marginalizing essential strategy-making activities that are difficult to capture in procedures. Important aspects such as creating new insights, learning, innovation, building political support and entrepreneurship are side-lined or crushed by the rote bureaucratic mechanisms used to produce strategy. Moreover, planning bureaucracies, once established, come to live a life of their own, creating rules, regulations, procedures, checks, paperwork, schedules, deadlines, and doublechecks, making the system inflexible, unresponsive, ineffective and demotivating.

■ *Differentiated vs. Integrated Tasks.* Many advocates of the planning perspective also believe that a division of labor within strategy formation processes is an important advantage of formal planning systems. The most important split facilitated by planning systems is between those who formulate the plans and those who implement them. Formulation can also be divided into the task of developing plans and the task of deciding which plans should be implemented. Of course, other specialized functions can also be created such as strategic planner, competitive intelligence analyst, new business developer and controller. A major benefit of task differentiation is that the best managers are liberated from time-consuming operational matters, so that they can focus on strategic issues. Furthermore, a certain measure of isolation from day-to-day operations gives the manager formulating strategy the necessary distance to judge a business more objectively. Supporters of the incrementalism perspective, however, point out that such isolation of the cerebral strategy formulator from the reality of the business is the main reason why so few strategies are successfully implemented. According to incrementalists, separating formulation and implementation tasks seriously inhibits the formation of novel strategies. If strategists need to be explorers, inventors and organizational developers, they cannot afford to view formulation and implementation as distinct activities, but must approach them as tasks that should be integrated.

As noted, not all proponents of explicit plans are convinced of the need for formal planning systems. Writers, such as Andrews in Chapter 2, who believe that plans should be drawn up by the CEO or a small group of top managers, feel uneasy about rigid corporate-wide planning systems. In general, they argue that such extensive formalization creates bureaucracy and reduces top management's freedom to manoever. Their preference is to retain a certain level of organizational flexibility, despite the existence of plans, by keeping enough power in the hands of top management to push through a change of course on command. This position has variably been referred to as the entrepreneurial, command, managerial autocracy, and design approach[24].

EXHIBIT 3.1
Ceteco case

CETECO: A DURABLE CONQUISTADOR?

La Curacao, Tropigas, Ventura . . . To some, these might sound like tasty cocktails, but in fact these are names of large retailers of consumer durables in Latin America. La Curacao has about 200 stores selling white goods (e.g. stoves, refrigerators, washing machines and airconditioners), consumer electronics, household appliances and furniture throughout Central America and the Caribbean. Tropigas has 60 stores selling these items in Guatemala, El Salvador and Honduras, while Ventura has 12 stores in Argentina. What all three have in common is that they are part of Ceteco, one of the leading retailers in Latin America. Ceteco also owns about 100 stores in Venezuela (Imgeve and Lehaca), Ecuador (Orve Hogar) and Peru (Total Artefactos). In 1997, their turnover was approximately US$ 400 million and they employed over 7000 people.

Oddly enough, Ceteco is a Dutch company, headquartered in Utrecht, the Netherlands. Their history is equally curious. Ceteco was established in 1890 as the Curacao Trading Company, initially to profit from the lucrative trading opportunities between the Netherlands and its Caribbean colonies (the main island of the six being Curacao). After a period of trading simple goods, the company also became a local dealer for the Dutch firm Philips and branched out into Central America. Following the Second World War, the company added dealerships for the Japanese companies National and Sharp, and Korea's Samsung and Goldstar to its activities. Ceteco became involved in what Spanish-speakers call *meubleria*, everything needed to run a household. When in the 1960s many Latin American countries began to protect their own 'infant industries' behind high tariff walls, Ceteco started assembling its own electrical appliances. To this day, about a quarter of Ceteco's revenues are from its white goods production, assembly and wholesaling operations.

By the 1980s, Ceteco was a highly diversified trading company, importing all types of commodities such as milk, steel and paper into Latin America and acting as the local representative for larger scale projects by Dutch companies in Africa, the Middle East and South America. It had also become active in retailing through its La Curacao stores. To avoid a hostile takeover, Ceteco's management decided in 1987 to proactively merge with a strong parent company that would support it with good management and solid finances. The willing parent they found was the Dutch shipping and storage company Van Ommeren, which was seeking a related diversification opportunity. However, it soon turned out that the two were not at all 'related'. Ceteco's flexible, free-wheeling, deal-making, relationship-based approach to business collided head-on with Van Ommeren's solid, disciplined, investment-oriented culture. In 1992 Van Ommeren sold

Ceteco to another Dutch trading company, Borsumij Wehry, for 50 million guilders (approximately US$ 25 million), taking a loss of 92 million guilders.

One advantage of the five-year Van Ommeren reign, according to Ceteco CEO Frits Eigenfeld, was that Van Ommeren demanded a more focused approach. Ceteco was forced to re-evaluate its highly scattered activities and pick out the most attractive ones. As a consequence, Ceteco withdrew from Africa and the Middle East, and sharply shifted its emphasis from trading to retailing. The company realized that it was a capable importer and wholesaler, but that its modest retailing activities were an unpolished gem. Through years of experience in the turbulent and idiosyn-cratic markets of Central America, Ceteco had gradually developed a durable goods retailing ability that no one could match. However, in its focused portfolio of activities, this unique capability had been buried under a moun-tain of other opportunities the company could pursue, and therefore received insufficient attention.

It became clear to Ceteco's management that it actually had a poten-tial retailing formula on its hands that was well-suited to the entire Latin American market, and differed significantly from the approaches taken by American and European retailers. For instance, Ceteco had learned that low purchasing power does not mean that consumers in Latin America are willing to settle for inferior appliances. Most people prefer quality brands, but need to buy these products on credit. While local banks often do not lend money for consumption purposes, Ceteco is a willing banker, selling over 70 per cent of its products on credit. Only 3 per cent of all loans are not paid back – a percentage that would satisfy most commercial bankers. Furthermore, Ceteco has a nose for choosing the right locations, building smaller stores closer to less mobile consumers and adapting store designs to suit local tastes.

Retailing in Latin America was especially appealing to Ceteco because local competitors were not yet very strong, while the continent had been more or less shunned by other internationalizing retailers. As a Dutch company, Ceteco also had the benefit of not being perceived by local partners and acquisition candidates as a conquistador, but as a neutral party. Cross-border acquisitions are still very rare and delicate in Latin America, and therefore being from a far away country, without a bad reputation, is a significant advantage.

After the divorce from Van Ommeren in 1992, Ceteco was asked by its new owner, Borsumij Wehry, to indicate in which direction it wanted to develop. Eager to capitalize on the retailing formula it had just defined as its core business, Mr Eigenfeld and his top management team formulated a general course of action, which they labelled the Ceteco Turbo 2000 plan. In this plan, Ceteco articulated its ambitions to be Latin America's leading retailer in the year 2000. More specifically, Ceteco defined its objective as capturing a 10 per cent share of the US$ 5 billion spent annually on durable household goods in the Spanish-speaking countries of Latin America. In terms of concrete actions, the Turbo 2000 plan indicated that Ceteco would expand from its Central American base to Mexico, Venezuala, Equador, Peru, and Argentina, largely through acquisitions. Portugese-speaking Brazil, good for US$ 3 billion sales annually, was believed to be too big to consider yet. All acquired chains would be reorganized to fit with the evolving La Curacao concept, while retaining their own name and a certain measure of local autonomy to adapt to specific national demands.

Of course, making acquisitions is not something that can be easily scheduled. Candidates have to be available, and the price has to be right. Sometimes a courtship is short and intensive, while sometimes the acquiree is unwilling or plays 'hard-to-get'. In Mexico, the intention to expand locally had to be shelved for a few years, following the economic crisis there. According to Mr Eigenfeld, it's all in the game. 'The core of the Turbo plan was to articulate our desire to become the leading retailer in South America,' he remarks. 'We understand that not everything can be realized at once and we accept differences per country.'

By 1997, most of the Turbo 2000 objectives had been realized. Large-scale acquisitions had been made in Venezuela, Equador, and Peru, while first steps had been set in Mexico and Argentina. Ceteco's retail turnover had more than tripled in five years. Part of the company had been brought to the Amsterdam stock exchange to raise capital for the acquisitions and the stock price indicated that Ceteco was valued at approximately a billion guilders (US$ 500 million), twenty times higher than Van Ommeren's selling price in 1992. For Mr Eigenfeld the question was, what now? A broad Turbo 2005 plan, or something more specific? Until now, he had acted as a entrepreneur, piecing together an empire, but would his style need to change now the company had grown so large? Strategy formation was largely incremental and informal, based on frequent visits to the subsidiaries, personal contact and an exchange of ideas. There were regular events, where country managers met each other and compared best practices. In this way, rather than through top-down standardization, a common retail formula was gradually evolving. But, Mr Eigenfeld wondered, would this approach to strategy formation remain the most appropriate in future?

Sources: Company documents and interview with Mr Eigenfeld.

The Debate and the Readings

As the opening reading in this debate, 'Managing the Strategy Process,' by Balaji Chakravarthy and Peter Lorange, has been selected to represent the planning perspective. Lorange is one of the most well-known writers on the topic of formal planning systems[25] and this article is taken from the textbook he co-authored with Chakravarthy, entitled *Managing the Strategy Process: A Framework for a Multibusiness Firm*[26]. As most proponents of the planning perspective, Chakravarthy and Lorange do not actively defend their assumption that explicit plans and formal planning are beneficial. Rather, basing themselves on this supposition, they concentrate on outlining a framework for effectively structuring strategic planning activities. Their ideal is an extensive strategic planning system, comprising a number of distinct steps, procedures, mechanisms and roles. However, they go further than only structuring strategic planning. In their view, a formal planning system will not lead to effective strategy formation if it is not linked to other organizational systems. In particular, the strategic planning system needs to interact with the monitoring, control, and learning system, the incentives system, and the staffing system. As such, Chakravarthy and Lorange champion a highly comprehensive and structured approach to strategic planning.

As spokesman for the incrementalism perspective, James Brian Quinn has been chosen. Together with Henry Mintzberg, Quinn has been one of the most influential pioneers on the topic of emergent strategy. Quinn's contribution, 'Logical Incrementalism,' that is reprinted here, and his subsequent book *Strategies for Change*[27], are widely accepted as having been instrumental in developing the incrementalism perspective. In his reading, Quinn explains some of the key shortcomings of formal strategic planning and goes on to make a case for incrementalism. Important in his argument is that incrementalism is distinguished from muddling through. Incrementalism is a proactive approach to strategy formation – strategists can intentionally choose to let unintended strategies emerge. Muddling through is also incremental in nature, but reactive and *ad hoc* – opportunistic decisions are made to deal with unplanned and poorly controllable circumstances. To make this distinction more explicit, Quinn refers to the proactive strain of incremental behavior as *logical incrementalism*. By 'logical' he means 'reasonable and well-considered'. However, logical incrementalism is not always logical by the definition used in Chapter 2 – incremental behavior is not necessarily 'dictated by formal logic'. To avoid confusion, therefore, in this book we shall refer to reasonable and well-considered incrementalism simply as incrementalism.

Again readers must hear the arguments from both sides and ask themselves what the true nature of strategy formation is. Readers must form their own judgment of how to deal with the paradox of deliberateness and emergentness.

Reading 1 Managing the Strategy Process

By Balaji Chakravarthy and Peter Lorange[†]

Steps in the Strategy Process

There are five distinct steps in the strategy process (see Figure 3.2). The first three steps involve the strategic planning system; the final two steps cover the role of the monitoring, control, and learning system and the incentives and staffing systems, respectively.

The Strategic Planning System

The purpose of the first step in the planning system, *objectives setting*, is to determine a strategic direction for the firm and each of its divisions and business units. Objectives setting calls for an open-ended reassessment of

FIGURE 3.2
The strategy process

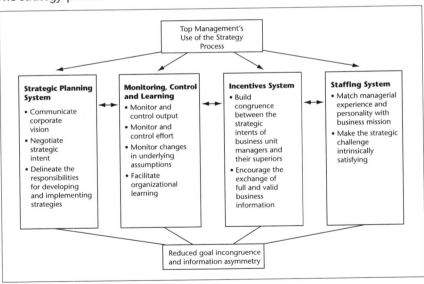

[†]Source: This article was adapted with permission from chapter 1 of *Managing the Strategy Process: A Framework for a Multibusiness Firm*, Prentice Hall, Englewood Cliffs, New Jersey, © 1991.

the firm's business environments and its strengths in dealing with these environments. At the conclusion of this step, there should be agreement at all levels of the organization on the goals that should be pursued and the strategies that will be needed to meet them. It is worth differentiating here between objectives and goals. Objectives refer to the strategic intent of the firm in the long run. Goals, on the other hand, are more specific statements of the achievements targeted for certain deadlines – goals can be accomplished, and when that happens the firm moves closer to meeting its objectives. Objectives represent a more enduring challenge.

The second step, *strategic programming*, develops the strategies identified in the first step and defines the cross-functional programs that will be needed to implement the chosen strategies. Cross-functional cooperation is essential to this step. At the end of the strategic programming step a long-term financial plan is drawn up for the firm as a whole and each of its divisions, business units, and functions. On top of the financial projections from existing operations, the long-term financial plan overlays both the expenditures and revenues associated with the approved strategic programs of an organizational unit. The time horizon for these financial plans is chosen to cover the typical lead times that are required to implement the firm's strategic programs. A five-year financial plan is, however, very common. The purpose of the five-year financial plan is to ensure that the approved strategic programs can be funded through either the firm's internally generated resources or externally financed resources.

The third step, *budgeting*, defines both the strategic and operating budgets of the firm. The strategic budget helps identify the contributions that the firm's functional departments, business units, and divisions will be expected to make in a given fiscal year in support of the firm's approved strategic programs. It incorporates new product/market initiatives. The operating budget, on the other hand, provides resources to functional departments, business units, and divisions so that they can sustain their existing momentum. It is based on projected short-term activity levels, given past trends. Failure to meet the operating budget will hurt the firm's short-term performance, whereas failure to meet the strategic budget will compromise the firm's future.

The Monitoring, Control, and Learning System

The fourth step in the strategy process is *monitoring, control, and learning*. Here the emphasis is not on output but on meeting key milestones in the strategic budget and on adhering to planned spending schedules. Strategic programs, like strategic budgets, are monitored for the milestones reached and for adherence to spending schedules. In addition, the key assumptions underlying these programs are validated periodically. As a natural extension to this validation process, even the agreed-on goals at various levels are reassessed in the light of changes to the resources of the firm and its business environment.

The Incentives and Staffing Systems

The fifth and final step in the strategy process is *incentives and staffing*. One part of this is the award of incentives as contracted to the firm's managers. If the incentives system is perceived to have failed in inducing the desired performance, redesigning the incentives system and reassessing the staffing of key managerial positions are considered at this step.

Linking Organizational Levels and Steps in Strategic Planning

An effective strategy process must allow for interactions between the organizational levels and iterations between the process steps. Figure 3.3 describes some of the interactions and iterations in the strategic planning steps. The formal interactions in the process are shown in the figure by the solid line that weaves up and down through the organizational levels and across the three steps. The informal interactions that complement the formal interactions are shown by dotted loops.

Objectives Setting

The first formal step of the strategy process commences soon after top management reaffirms or modifies the firm's objectives at the beginning of each fiscal year. Embedded in these objectives should be the vision of the chief executive officer (CEO) and his or her top management team. Top management's vision helps specify what will make the firm great. An elaboration of this vision can be done through a formal statement of objectives. However, it is not the formality of a firm's objectives but rather the excitement and challenge that top management's vision can bring to a firm's managers that is important to the strategy process.

Along with its communication of corporate objectives, top management must provide a forecast on key environmental factors. Assumptions on exchange rates, inflation, and other economic factors – as well as projections on the political risks associated with each country – are best compiled centrally so as to ensure objectivity and consistency. These objectives and forecasts are then discussed with a firm's divisional and business unit managers.

Once the corporate objectives are decided, top management negotiates, for each division and business unit in the firm, goals that

FIGURE 3.3

Steps in the strategy process

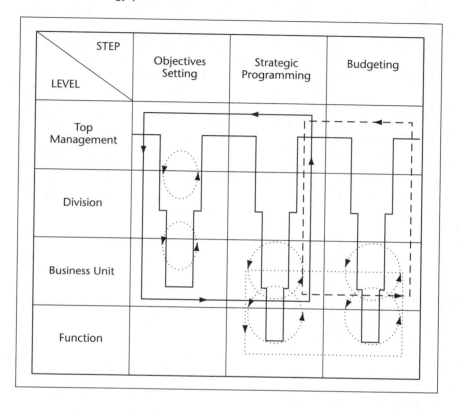

are consistent with these objectives. The nature of these negotiations can vary. In some firms, top management may wish to set goals in a top-down fashion; in others, it may invite subordinate managers to participate in the goal-setting process. Managers are encouraged to examine new strategies and modify existing ones in order to accomplish their goals. The proposed strategies are approved at each higher level in the organizational hierarchy, then eventually by top management. Top management tries to make certain that the strategies as proposed are consistent with the firm's objectives and can be supported with the resources available to the firm. Modifications, where necessary, are made to the objectives, goals, and strategies in order to bring them in alignment. Another important outcome of the objectives-setting step is to build a common understanding across the firm's managerial hierarchy of the goals and strategies that are intended for each organizational unit.

The objectives-setting step in Figure 3.3 does not include the functional departments. As we observed earlier, the primary role of these departments is a supporting one. They do not have a profit or growth responsibility, and their goals cannot be decided until the second step, when strategic programs in support of approved business unit goals begin to be formed. It is not uncommon, however, for key functional managers to be invited to participate in the objectives-setting step either as experts in a corporate task force or, more informally, as participants in the deliberations that are held at the business unit level.

It is important that divisional proposals be evaluated on an overall basis as elements of a corporate portfolio and not reviewed in a sequential mode. In the latter case, the resulting overall balance in the corporate portfolio would be more or less incidental, representing the accumulated sum of individual approvals. It makes little sense to attempt to judge in isolation whether a particular business family or business strategy is attractive to the corporate portfolio. That will depend on a strategy's fit with the rest of the portfolio and on the competing investment opportunities available to the firm in its business portfolio.

Strategic Programming

The second step in the process has two purposes:

1   To forge an agreement between divisional, business unit, and functional managers on the strategic programs that have to be implemented over the next few years.

2   To deepen the involvement of functional managers in developing the strategies that were tentatively selected in the first step.

The strategic programming step begins with a communication from top management about the goals and strategies that were finally approved for the firm's divisions and business units. The divisional manager then invites his or her business unit and functional managers to identify program alternatives in support of the approved goals and strategies. Examples of strategic programs include increasing market share for an existing product, introducing a new product, and launching a joint marketing campaign for a family of divisional products. As in these examples, a strategic program typically requires the cooperation of multiple functional departments.

However, the functional specialties within a firm often represent different professional cultures that do not necessarily blend easily. Further, day-to-day operating tasks can be so demanding that the functional managers may simply find it difficult to participate in the time-consuming cross-functional teamwork. A key challenge for both divisional and business managers is to bring about this interaction.

The proposed strategic programs travel up the hierarchy for approval at each level. At the division level, the programs are evaluated not only for how well they support the approved strategies but also for how they promote synergies within the firm. Synergies can come from two sources: through economies of scale and/or economies of scope. The creation of synergies based on economies of scale calls for a sharing of common functional activities – such as research and development (R&D), raw materials procurement, production, and distribution – so as to spread over a larger volume the overhead costs associated with these functions. The creation of economies of scope, on the other hand, requires a common approach to the market. Examples of such an approach include the development of a common trademark, the development of products/services that have a complementary appeal to a customer group, and the ability to offer a common regional service organization for the firm's diverse businesses.

At the corporate level, the proposed strategic programs provide an estimate of the resources that will be required to support the divisional and business unit goals. These goals, as well as their supporting strategies, are once again reassessed; and where needed, modifications are sought in the proposed strategic programs. As noted earlier, a long-term financial plan is drawn at this stage for the firm as a whole and each of its organizational units. The approved strategic programs are communicated to the divisions, business units, and functional departments at the beginning of the budgeting cycle.

Budgeting

When top management decides on the strategic programs that the firm should pursue, it has de facto allocated all of the firm's human, technological, and financial resources that are available for internal development. This allocation influences the strategic budgets that may be requested at each level in the organizational hierarchy.

The strategic budgets, together with the operating budgets of the various organizational units, are consolidated and sent up for top management approval. When top management finally approves the budgets of the various organizational units, before the start of a new budget year, it brings to a close what can be a year-long journey through the three steps of the strategy-making subprocess. The strategy implementation subprocess is then set into motion. Even though the two subprocesses are described sequentially here, it is important to mention that even as the budget for a given year is being formed, the one for the prior year will be under implementation. Midcourse corrections to the prior year's budget can have an impact on the formulation of the current budget.

If the actual accomplishments fall short of the strategic budget, in particular, the negative variance may suggest that the firm's managers failed to implement its chosen strategy efficiently. But it can also suggest that the strategic programs that drive this budget may have been ill conceived or even that the goals underlying these programs may have been specified incorrectly. The monitoring, control, and learning system provides continuous information on both the appropriateness of a strategic budget and the efficiency with which the budget is implemented. This information, based on the implementation of the prior year's strategic budget, can trigger another set of iterations between the three strategy-making steps, calling into question the goals and strategies on which the current year's budget are based. These iterations are shown by the dotted rectangles in Figure 3.1.2.

Reading 2   Logical Incrementalism

By James Quinn[†]

> When I was younger I always conceived of a room where all these [strategic] concepts were worked out for the whole company. Later I didn't find any such room . . . . The strategy [of the company] may not even exist in the mind of one man. I certainly don't know where it is written down. It is simply transmitted in the series of decisions made.
>
> (Interview quote)

When well-managed major organizations make significant changes in strategy, the approaches they use frequently bear little resemblance to the rational-analytical systems so often touted in the planning literature. The full strategy is rarely written down in any one place. The processes used to arrive at the total strategy are typically fragmented, evolutionary, and largely intuitive. Although one can usually find embedded in these fragments some very refined pieces of formal strategic analysis, the real strategy tends to evolve as internal decisions and external events flow together to create a new, widely shared consensus for action among key members of the top management team. Far from being an abrogation of good management practice, the rationale behind this kind of strategy formulation is so powerful that it perhaps provides the normative model for strategic decision making, rather than the step-by-step 'formal systems planning' approach so often espoused.

[†] Source: This article was originally published as 'Strategic Change: "Logical Incrementalism,"' in *Sloan Management Review* (Fall 1978). Reproduced by permission of John Wiley and Sons Limited.

The Formal Systems Planning Approach

A strong normative literature states what factors should be included in a systematically planned strategy and how to analyze and relate these factors step-by-step. The main elements of this 'formal' planning approach include:

- analyzing one's own internal situation: strengths, weaknesses, competencies, problems;

- projecting current product lines, profits, sales, investment needs into the future;

- analyzing selected external environments and opponents' actions for opportunities and threats;

- establishing broad goals as targets for subordinate groups' plans;

- identifying the gap between expected and desired results;

- communicating planning assumptions to the divisions;

- requesting proposed plans from subordinate groups with more specific target goals, resource needs, and supporting action plans;

- occasionally asking for special studies of alternatives, contingencies, or longer-term opportunities;

- reviewing and approving divisional plans and summing these for corporate needs;

- developing long-term budgets presumably related to plans;

- implementing plans;

- monitoring and evaluating performance (presumably against plans, but usually against budgets).

While this approach is excellent for some purposes, it tends to focus unduly on measurable quantitative factors and to underemphasize the vital qualitative, organizational, and power-behavioral factors that so often determine strategic success in one situation versus another. In practice, such planning is just one building block in a continuous stream of events that really determine corporate strategy.

The Power-Behavioral Approach

Other investigators have provided important insights on the crucial psychological, power, and behavioral relationships in strategy formulation. Among other things, these have enhanced understanding about: the multiple goal structures of organizations, the politics of strategic decisions, executive bargaining and negotiation processes, 'satisficing' (as opposed to maximizing) in decision making, the role of coalitions in strategic management, and the practice of 'muddling' in the public sphere. Unfortunately, however, many power-behavioral studies have been conducted in settings far removed from the realities of strategy formulation. Others have concentrated solely on human dynamics, power relationships, and organizational processes and ignored the ways in which systematic data analysis shapes and often dominates crucial aspects of strategic decisions. Finally, a few have offered much normative guidance for the strategist.

The Study

Recognizing the contributions and limitations of both approaches, I attempted to document the dynamics of actual strategic change processes in some 10 major companies as perceived by those most knowledgeably and intimately involved in them. Several important findings have begun to emerge from these investigations:

- Neither the power-behavioral nor the formal systems planning paradigm adequately characterizes the way successful strategic processes operate.

- Effective strategies tend to emerge from a series of 'strategic subsystems,' each of which attacks a specific class of strategic issue (e.g. acquisitions, divestitures, or major reorganizations) in a disciplined way, but which blends incrementally and opportunistically into a cohesive pattern that becomes the company's strategy.

- The logic behind each subsystem is so powerful that to some extent it may serve as a normative approach for formulating these key elements of strategy in large companies.

- Because of cognitive and process limits, almost all of these subsystems – and the formal planning activity itself – must be managed and linked together by an approach best described as logical incrementalism.

- Such incrementalism is not muddling. It is a purposeful, effective, proactive management technique for improving and integrating both the analytical and behavioral aspects of strategy formulation.

This article will document these findings, suggest the logic behind several important subsystems for strategy formulation, and outline some of the management and thought processes executives in large organizations use to synthesize them into effective corporate strategies. Such strategies embrace those patterns of high-leverage decisions (on major goals, policies, and action sequences) that affect the viability and direction of the entire enterprise or determine its competitive posture for an extended time period.

Critical Strategic Issues

Although certain 'hard data' decisions (e.g. on product-market position or resource allocations) tend to dominate the analytical literature, executives identified other 'soft' changes that have at least as much importance in shaping their concern's strategic posture. Most often cited were changes in the company's

- overall organizational structure or its basic management style;

- relationships with the government or other external interest groups;

- acquisition, divestiture, or divisional control practices;

- international posture and relationships;

- innovative capabilities or personnel motivations as affected by growth;

- worker and professional relationships reflecting changed social expectations and values;

- past or anticipated technological environments.

When executives were asked to 'describe the processes through which their company arrived at its new posture' *vis-à-vis* each of these critical domains, several important points emerged. First, a few of these issues lent themselves to quantitative modeling techniques or perhaps even formal financial analyses. Second, successful companies used a different subsystem to formulate strategy for each major class of strategic issues, yet these subsystems were quite similar among companies even in very different industries. Finally, no single formal analytical process could handle all strategic variables simultaneously on a planned basis. Why?

Precipitating Events

Often external or internal events over which managements had essentially no control would precipitate urgent, piecemeal, interim decisions that inexorably shaped the company's future strategic posture. One clearly observes this phenomenon in the decisions forced on General Motors by the 1973–74 oil crisis; the shift in posture pressed upon Exxon by sudden nationalizations; or the dramatic opportunities allowed for Haloid Corporation and Pilkington Brothers Ltd by the unexpected inventions of xerography and float glass.

In these cases, analyses from earlier formal planning cycles did contribute greatly, as long as the general nature of the contingency had been anticipated. They broadened the information base available (as in Exxon's case), extended the options considered (Haloid-Xerox), created shared values to guide decisions about precipitating events in consistent directions (Pilkington), or built up resource bases, management flexibilities, or active search routines for opportunities whose specific nature could not be defined in advance (General Mills, Pillsbury). But no organization – no matter how brilliant, rational, or imaginative – could possibly foresee the timing, severity, or even the nature of all such precipitating events. Further, when these events did occur there might be neither time, resources, nor information enough to undertake a full formal strategic analysis of all possible options and their consequences. Yet early decisions made under stress conditions often meant new thrusts, precedents, or lost opportunities that were difficult to reverse later.

An Incremental Logic

Recognizing this, top executives usually consciously tried to deal with precipitating events in an incremental fashion. Early commitments were kept broadly formative, tentative, and subject to later review. In some cases neither the company nor the external players could understand the full implications of alternative actions. All parties wanted to test assumptions and have an opportunity to learn from and adapt to the others' responses. For example: Neither the potential producer nor user of a completely new product or process (like xerography or float glass) could fully conceptualize its ramifications without interactive testing. All parties benefited from procedures that purposely delayed decisions and allowed mutual feedback. Some companies, like IBM or Xerox, have formalized this concept into 'phase program planning' systems. They make concrete decisions only on individual phases (or stages) of new product developments, establish interactive testing procedures with customers, and postpone final configuration commitments until the latest possible moment.

Similarly, even under pressure, most top executives were extremely sensitive to organizational and power relationships and consciously mananged decision processes to improve these dynamics. They often purposely delayed initial decisions, or kept such decisions vague, in order to encourage lower-level participation, to gain more information from specialists, or to build commitment to solutions. Even when a crisis atmosphere tended to shorten time horizons and make decisions more goal oriented than political, perceptive executives consciously tried to keep their options open until they understood how the crisis would affect the power bases and needs of their key constituents.

Incrementalism in Strategic Subsystems

One also finds that an incremental logic applies in attacking many of the critical subsystems of corporate strategy. Those subsystems for considering diversification moves, divestitures, major reorganizations, or government-external relations are typical and will be described here. In each case conscious incrementalism helps to

1   cope with both the cognitive and process limits on each major decision;

2   build the logical-analytical framework these decisions require;

3   create the personal and organizational awareness, understanding, acceptance, and commitment needed to implement the strategies effectively.

The Diversification Subsystem

Strategies for diversification, either through research and development (R&D) or acquisitions, provide excellent examples. The formal analytical steps needed for successful diversification are well documented. However, the precise directions that R&D may project the company can only be understood step-by-step as scientists uncover new phenomena, make and amplify discoveries, build prototypes, reduce concepts to practice, and interact with users during product introductions. Similarly, only as each acquisition is sequentially identified, investigated, negotiated for, and integrated into the organization can one predict its ultimate impact on the total enterprise.

A step-by-step approach is clearly necessary to guide and assess the strategic fit of each internal or external diversification candidate. Incremental processes are also required to manage the crucial psychological and power shifts that ultimately determine the program's overall direction and consequences. These processes help unify both the analytical and behavioral aspects of diversification decisions. They create the broad conceptual consensus, the risk-taking attitudes, the organizational and resource flexibilities, and the adaptive dynamism that determine both the timing and direction of diversification strategies. Most important among these processes are:

■   *Generating a genuine, top-level psychological commitment to diversification.* General Mills, Pillsbury, and Xerox all started their major diversification programs with broad analytical studies and goal-setting exercises designed both to build top-level consensus around the need to diversify and to establish the general directions for diversification. Without such action, top-level bargaining for resources would have continued to support only more familiar (and hence apparently less risky) old lines, and this could delay or undermine the entire diversification endeavor.

■   *Consciously preparing to move opportunistically.* Organizational and fiscal resources must be built up in advance to exploit candidates as they randomly appear. And a 'credible activist' for ventures must be developed and backed by someone with commitment power. All successful acquirers created the potential for profit centered divisions within their organizational structures, strengthened their financial-controllership capabilities, took action to create low-cost capital access, and maintained the shortest possible communication lines from the acquisitions activist to the resource-committing authority. All these actions integrally determined which diversifications actually could be made, the timing of their accession, and the pace at which they could be absorbed.

- *Building a 'comfort factor' for risk taking.* Perceived risk is largely a function of one's knowledge about a field. Hence well-conceived diversification programs should anticipate a trial-and-error period during which top managers reject early proposed fields or opportunities until they have analyzed enough trial candidates to 'become comfortable' with an initial selection. Early successes tend to be 'sure things' close to the companies' past (real or supposed) expertise. After a few successful diversifications, managements tend to become more confident and accept other candidates – farther from traditional lines – at a faster rate. Again, the way this process is handled affects both the direction and pace of the actual program.

- *Developing a new ethos.* If new divisions are more successful than the old – as they should be – they attract relatively more resources and their political power grows. Their most effective line managers move into corporate positions, and slowly the company's special competency and ethos change. Finally, the concepts and products that once dominated the company's culture may decline in importance or even disappear. Acknowledging these ultimate consequences to the organization at the beginning of a diversification program would clearly be impolitic, even if the manager both desired and could predict the probable new ethos. These factors must be handled adaptively, as opportunities present themselves and as individual leaders and power centers develop.

Each of the above processes interacts with all others (and with the random appearance of diversification candidates) to affect action sequences, elapsed time, and ultimate results in unexpected ways. Complexities are so great that few diversification programs end up as initially envisioned. Consequently, wise managers recognize the limits to systematic analysis in diversification, and use formal planning to build the 'comfort levels' executives need for risk taking and to guide the program's early directions and priorities. They then modify these flexibly, step-by-step, as new opportunities, power centers, and developed competencies merge to create new potentials.

The Divestiture Subsystem

Similar practices govern the handling of divestitures. Divisions often drag along in a less-than-desired condition for years before they can be strategically divested. In some cases, ailing divisions might have just enough yield or potential to offer hoped-for viability. In others, they might represent the company's vital core from earlier years, the creations of a powerful person nearing retirement, or the psychological touch-stones of the company's past traditions.

Again, in designing divestiture strategies, top executives had to reinforce vaguely felt concerns with detailed data, build up managers' comfort levels about issues, achieve participation in and commitment to decisions, and move opportunistically to make actual changes. In many cases, the precise nature of the decision was not clear at the outset. Executives often made seemingly unrelated personnel shifts or appointments that changed the value set of critical groups, or started a series of staff studies that generated awareness or acceptance of a potential problem. They might then instigate goal assessment, business review, or 'planning' programs to provide broader forums for discussion and a wider consensus for action. Even then they might wait for a crisis, a crucial retirement, or an attractive sale opportunity to determine the timing and conditions of divestiture. In some cases, decisions could be direct and analytical. But when divestitures involved the psychological centers of the organization, the process had to be much more oblique and carefully orchestrated.

The Major Reorganization Subsystem

It is well recognized that major organizational changes are an integral part of strategy. Sometimes they constitute a strategy themselves, sometimes they precede and/or precipitate a new strategy, and sometimes they help to implement a strategy. However, like many other important strategic decisions, macro-organizational moves are typically handled incrementally and outside of formal planning processes. Their effects on personal or power relationships preclude discussion in open forums and reports of such processes.

In addition, major organizational changes have timing imperatives (or 'process limits') all their own. In making any significant shifts, executives must think through the new roles, capabilities, and probable individual reactions of the many principals affected. They may have to wait for the promotion or retirement of a valued colleague before consummating any change. They then frequently have to bring in, train, or test new people for substantial periods before they can staff key posts with confidence. During this testing period they may substantially modify their original concept of the reorganization, as they evaluate individuals' potentials, their performance in specific roles, their personal drives, and their relationships with other team members.

Because this chain of decisions affects the career development, power, affluence, and self-image of so many, executives tend to keep close counsel in their discussions, negotiate individually with key people, and make final commitments as late as possible in order to obtain the best matches between people's capabilities, personalities, and aspirations and their new roles. Typically, all these events do not come together at one convenient time, particularly the moment annual plans are due. Instead executives move opportunistically, step-by-step, selectively moving people toward a broadly conceived organizational goal, which is constantly modified and rarely articulated in detail until the last pieces fit together.

The Government-External Relations Subsystem

Almost all companies cited government and other external activist groups as among the most important forces causing significant changes in their strategic postures during the periods examined. However, when asked 'How did your company arrive at its own strategy *vis-à-vis* these forces?' it became clear that few companies had cohesive strategies (integrated sets of goals, policies, and programs) for government-external relations, other than lobbying for or against specific legislative actions. To the extent that other strategies did exist, they were piecemeal, *ad hoc* and had been derived in a very evolutionary manner. Yet there seemed to be very good reasons for such incrementalism. The following are two of the best short explanations of the way these practices develop:

> We are a very large company, and we understand that any massive overt action on our part could easily create more public antagonism than support for our viewpoint. It is also hard to say in advance exactly what public response any particular action might create. So we tend to test a number of different approaches on a small scale with only limited or local company identification. If one approach works, we'll test it further and amplify its use. If another bombs, we try to keep it from being used again. Slowly we find a series of advertising, public relations, community relations actions that seem to help. Then along comes another issue and we start all over again. Gradually the successful approaches merge into a pattern of actions that becomes our strategy.

> I [the president] start conversations with a number of knowledgeable people . . . . I collect articles and talk to people about how things get done in Washington in this particular field. I collect data from any reasonable source. I begin wide-ranging discussions with people inside and outside the corporation. From these a pattern eventually emerges. It's like fitting together a jigsaw puzzle. At first the vague outline of an approach appears like the sail of a ship in a puzzle. Then suddenly the rest of the puzzle becomes quite clear. You wonder why you didn't see it all along. And once it's crystallized, it's not difficult to explain to others.

In this realm, uncontrollable forces dominate. Data are very soft, often can be only subjectively sensed, and may be costly to quantify. The possible responses of individuals and groups to different stimuli are difficult to determine in advance. The number of potential opponents with power is very high, and the diversity in their viewpoints and possible modes of attack is so substantial that it is physically impossible to lay out probabilistic decision diagrams that would have much meaning. Results are unpredictable and error costs extreme. Even the best intended and most rational-seeming strategies can be converted into disasters unless they are thoroughly and interactively tested.

Formal Planning in Corporate Strategy

What role do classical formal planning techniques play in strategy formulation? All companies in the sample do have formal planning procedures embedded in their management direction and control systems. These serve certain essential functions. In a process sense, they

- provide a discipline forcing managers to take a careful look ahead periodically;

- require rigorous communications about goals, strategic issues, and resource allocations;

- stimulate longer-term analyses than would otherwise be made;

- generate a basis for evaluating and integrating short-term plans;

- lengthen time horizons and protect long-term investments such as R&D;

- create a psychological backdrop and an information framework about the future against which managers can calibrate short-term or interim decisions.

In a decision-making sense, they

- fine-tune annual commitments;

- formalize cost-reduction programs;

- help implement strategic changes once decided on (for example, co-ordinating all elements of Exxon's decision to change its corporate name).

Formal Plans Also 'Increment'

Although individual staff planners were often effective in identifying potential problems and bringing them to top management's attention, the annual planning process itself was rarely (if ever) the initiating source of really new key issues or radical departures into new product/market realms. These almost always came from precipitating events, special studies, or conceptions implanted through the kinds of 'logical incremental' processes described above.

In fact, formal planning practices actually institutionalize incrementalism. There are two reasons for this. First, in order to utilize specialized expertise and to obtain executive involvement and commitment, most planning occurs from the bottom up in response to broadly defined assumptions or goals, many of which are longstanding or negotiated well in advance. Of necessity, lower-level groups have only a partial view of the corporation's total strategy, and command only a fragment of its resources. Their power bases, identity, expertise, and rewards also usually depend on their existing products or processes. Hence, these products or processes, rather than entirely new departures, should and do receive their primary attention. Second, most managements purposely design their plans to be 'living' or 'evergreen.' They are intended only as frameworks to guide and provide consistency for future decisions made incrementally. To act otherwise would be to deny that further information could have a value. Thus, properly formulated formal plans are also a part of an incremental logic.

Special Studies

Formal planning was most successful in stimulating significant change when it was set up as a special study on some important aspect of corporate strategy. For example, when it became apparent that Pilkington's new float glass process would work, the company formed a Directors' Float Glass Committee consisting of all internal directors associated with float glass 'to consider the broad issues of float glass [strategy] in both the present and the future.' The committee did not attempt detailed plans. Instead, it tried to deal in broad concepts, identify alternate routes, and think through the potential consequences of each route some 10 years ahead. Of some of the key strategic decisions it was later remarked, 'It would be difficult to identify an exact moment when the decision was made. . . . Nevertheless, over a period of time a consensus crystallized with great clarity.'

Such special strategic studies represent a subsystem of strategy formulation distinct from both annual planning activities and the other subsystems exemplified above. Each of these develops some important aspect of strategy, incrementally blending its conclusions with those of other subsystems, and it would be virtually impossible to force all these together to crystallize a completely articulated corporate strategy at any one instant.

Total Posture Planning

Occasionally, however, managements do attempt very broad assessments of their companies' total posture. Shortly after becoming CEO of General Mills, James McFarland decided that his job was 'to take a very good company and move it to greatness,' but that it was up to his management group, not himself alone, to decide what a great company was and how to get there. Consequently he took some 35 of the company's topmost managers away for a three-day management retreat. On the first day, after agreeing to broad financial goals, the group broke up into units of six to eight people. Each unit was to answer the question 'What is a great company?' from the viewpoints of stockholders, employees, suppliers, the public, and society. Each unit reported back at the end of the day, and the whole group tried to reach a consensus through discussion.

On the second day the groups, in the same format, assessed the company's strengths and weaknesses relative to the defined posture of 'greatness.' The third day focused on how to overcome the company's weaknesses and move it toward a great company. This broad consensus led, over the next several years, to the surveys of fields for acquisition, the building of management's initial comfort levels with certain fields, and the acquisition-divestiture strategy that characterized the McFarland era at General Mills.

Yet even such a major endeavor is only a portion of a total strategic process. Values that had been built up over decades stimulated or constrained alternatives. Precipitating events, acquisitions, divestitures, external relations, and organizational changes developed important segments of each strategy incrementally. Even the strategies articulated left key elements to be defined as new information became available, polities permitted, or particular opportunities appeared. Major product thrusts proved unsuccessful. Actual strategies therefore evolved as each company overextended, consolidated, made errors, and rebalanced various thrusts over time. And it was both logical and expected that this would be the case.

Logical Incrementalism

All of the above suggest that strategic decisions do not lend themselves to aggregation into a single massive decision matrix where all factors can be treated relatively simultaneously in order to arrive at a holistic optimum. Many have spoken of the cognitive limits that prevent this. Of equal importance are the process limits – that is, the timing and sequencing imperatives necessary to create awareness, build comfort levels, develop consensus, select and train people, and so forth – that constrain the system yet ultimately determine the decision itself. Unlike the preparation of a fine banquet, it is virtually impossible for the manager to orchestrate all internal decisions, external environmental events, behavioral and power relationships, technical and informational needs, and actions of intelligent opponents so that they come together at any precise moment.

Can the Process Be Managed?

Instead, executives usually deal with the logic of each subsystem of strategy formulation largely on its own merits and usually with a different subset of people. They try to develop or maintain in their own minds a consistent pattern among the decisions made in each subsystem. Knowing their own limitations and the unknowability of the events they face, they consciously try to tap the minds and psychic drives of others. They often purposely keep questions broad and decisions vague in early stages to avoid creating undue rigidities and to stimulate others' creativity. Logic, of course, dictates that they make final commitments *as late as possible* consistent with the information they have.

Consequently, many successful executives will initially set only broad goals and policies that can accommodate a variety of specific proposals from below, yet give a sense of guidance to the proposers. As they come forward the proposals automatically and beneficially attract the support and identity of their sponsors. Being only proposals, the executives can treat these at less politically charged levels, as specific projects rather than as larger goal or policy precedents. Therefore, they can encourage, discourage, or kill alternatives with considerably less political exposure. As events and opportunities emerge, they can incrementally guide the pattern of escalated or accepted proposals to suit their own purposes without getting prematurely committed to a rigid solution set that unpredictable events might prove wrong or that opponents find sufficiently threatening to coalesce against.

A Strategy Emerges

Successful executives link together and bring order to a series of strategic processes and decisions spanning years. At the beginning of the process it is literally impossible to predict all the events and forces that will shape the future of the company. The best executives can do is to forecast the forces most likely to impinge on the company's affairs and the ranges of their possible impact. They then attempt to build a resource base and a corporate posture so strong in selected areas that the enterprise can survive and prosper despite all but the most devastating events. They consciously select market/technological/product segments the concern can dominate given its resource limits, and place some side bets in order to decrease the risk of catastrophic failure or to increase the company's flexibility for future options.

They then proceed incrementally to handle urgent matters, start longer-term sequences whose specific future branches and consequences are perhaps murky, respond to unforeseen events as they occur, build on successes, and brace up or cut losses on failures. They constantly reassess the future, find new congruencies as events unfurl, and blend the organization's skills and resources into new balances of dominance and risk aversion as various forces intersect to suggest better – but never perfect – alignments. The process is dynamic, with neither a real beginning nor end.

Strategy deals with the unknowable, not the uncertain. It involves forces of such great number, strength, and combinatory powers that one cannot predict events in a probabilistic sense. Hence logic dictates that one proceed flexibly and experimentally from broad concepts toward specific commitments, making the latter concrete as late as possible in order to narrow the bands of uncertainty and to benefit from the best available information. This is the process of logical incrementalism.

Strategy Formation in International Perspective

To plan, v. To bother about the best
method of accomplishing an accidental result.
(*The Devil's Dictionary*, Ambrose Bierce 1842–1914; American columnist)

From the preceding contributions it has become evident that views differ sharply as to whether strategies should be formed by means of planning or incrementalism. It is clear that a wide variety of approaches exists to deal with the paradox of deliberateness and emergentness. None of the authors, however, suggest that their views may be more appropriate in some countries than in others. Nor do any of them mention the possibility that an organization's choice of approach may be influenced by national circumstances. In other words, so far the international angle has been conspicuously absent. It has generally been assumed that international differences are a non-issue.

Yet, the question whether there are specific national preferences for the planning or the incrementalism perspective seems quite legitimate. In the past, a few international comparative studies have been done that show significantly different levels of formal planning across various industrialized countries. For instance, Steiner and Schollhammer[28] reported that planning was found to be most common and most formalized in the United States, with other English-speaking countries (Britain, Canada and Australia) also exhibiting a high score. At the other extreme were Italy and Japan, where very little formal planning was witnessed. The low propensity to engage in formal planning in Japan has been noted by a number of other authors as well[29]. Hayashi[30] remarks that Japanese firms 'distrust corporate planning in general,' while Ohmae[31] characterizes Japanese companies as 'less planned, less rigid, but more vision- and mission-driven' than Western companies. Unfortunately, there are no cross-cultural studies of a more recent date to confirm that these international dissimilarities still exist. However, many observers have suggested that there remain discernible national differences in approaches to strategy formation[32].

Although it is difficult to generalize at the national level, since there can be quite a bit of variance within a country, it is challenging to pursue these observed international dissimilarities. Are there really national strategy formation styles and what factors might influence their existence? As a stimulus to the international dimension of this debate, we put forward the following country characteristics as possible influences on how the paradox of deliberateness and emergentness is dealt with in different national settings. As we noted at the end of Chapter 2, these propositions are intended to encourage discussion, but more concrete international comparative research is needed to give this debate a firmer footing.

Level of Professionalization

The high incidence of formal planning systems in Australia, Britain, Canada, New Zealand, and the United States seems odd, given their high level of individualism and their strong preference for a market economy. One might expect that the English-speaking countries' fondness of unplanned markets would be a reflection of a general dislike of planning. Yet, strangely, 'most large US corporations are run like the Soviet economy' of yesteryear, with strong central plans and top-down control, Ohmae concludes[33].

One explanation might be that formalized planning and control systems are a logical consequence of having professional management[34]. Nowhere in the industrialized world, with the exception of France, has there been a stronger development of a distinct managerial class than in the English-speaking countries[35]. These professional managers run companies on behalf of the owners, who are usually distant from the operations (i.e. often minority shareholders). In the division of labor, the managers perform the 'thinking' tasks – analyzing, planning, coordinating, leading, budgeting, motivating, controlling – while the workforce concentrates on performing the primary activities. This makes it possible for large, complex production processes to be controlled by a hierarchy of professional managers. It is commonly believed that these managers possess general skills that allow them to run a wide variety of different businesses.

In companies with professional management, the split between thinking and doing is made more explicit than in other organizations. The managers are the officers who formulate the strategies and the personnel on the workfloor are the troops that must implement them – 'management' has intentions that the 'employees' must realize. This requires formal planning to guide workers' actions and a tight control system to ensure compliance. This mechanism is usually employed all the way up the hierarchy, as higher level managers use a planning and control system to steer and coordinate the behavior of lower level managers. All the way at the top, senior management must also make plans to win the approval of the shareholders.

This stratified organizational model, that Mintzberg[36] dubs the machine bureaucracy, is also prevalent in France, where the distinction between *cadre* employees and *non-cadre* personnel is also very strong[37]. In many other countries, however, the split between managerial and non-managerial tasks is not as radical. For instance, in Germany and Japan, senior employees are expected to be involved in operational matters, while junior employees are expected to contribute to strategy formation, by coming up with ideas and passing on information to seniors. In such countries, there is less need to use formal planning and control mechanisms to manage employees, since the 'managers' have direct and informal links with those 'managed'. Usually these managers have risen through the ranks, giving them the richness of information and contacts needed to manage without highly formalized systems. In these nations, consensus-building and personal control are the important management skills, and these are not readily transferable to another industry or even another organization.

In yet other countries, the dominant form of organization is that of direct control by one person or a family. This usually means that organizations remain relatively small, although they can compensate by linking up into networks based on personal connections between the top bosses. This organizational model, common in Italy and among the overseas Chinese will be further discussed in Chapter 7. Here it is sufficient to conclude that in such organizations there is also little need for formalized planning and control systems to manage employees. The top boss, who is usually also the owner, steers the firm personally, with little regard for 'professional' methods.

The conclusion is that the national propensity to engage in formal planning is probably influenced by the level of professionalization of management within the country. In nations where the machine bureaucracy is the predominant organizational model, a stronger inclination towards formal planning systems can be expected.

Preference for Internal Control

While the previous section discussed different *types* of internal control, and the related organizational models, it should be noted that countries can also differ with regard to the *level* of internal control their citizens prefer. In some cultures, people have a strong desire for order and structure – clear tasks, responsibilities, powers, rules and procedures. Ambiguous situations and uncertain outcomes are disliked and therefore management strives to control organizational processes. Management can reduce uncertainty in a number of ways. Structure can be offered by strictly following traditions or by imposing top-down paternalistic rule. However, uncertainty can also be reduced by planning[38]. By setting direction, coordinating initiatives, committing resources, and programming activities, structure can be brought to the organization. In this way, planning can help to alleviate people's anxiety about 'disorganization'. In cultures that are more tolerant towards ambiguity and uncertainty, one can expect a weaker preference for planning.

The importance of planning as a means for structuring and controlling is particularly important in cultures where there is little confidence in self-organization. This is especially true in individualistic cultures, where organizational members cannot always be counted on to work towards the common good. In these countries, extensive planning and control systems are often used as a formal means for getting people to cooperate, coordinate and serve the organization's interests. Strategic plans function as internal contracts, to limit dysfunctional opportunistic behavior[39]. In cultures with a stronger group-orientation, there is usually more trust that individuals will be team players, making formal control mechanisms redundant[40]. Therefore, in general, one can expect a weaker preference for planning in collectivist cultures.

Preference for External Control

Cultures also differ with regard to the level of control that organizational members prefer to have over their environment. At the one extreme are cultures in which people strive to manage or even dominate their surroundings. In these countries, there is a strong desire to create the future and a fear of losing control of one's destiny. George Bernard Shaw's famous remark that 'to be in hell is to drift, to be in heaven is to steer,' neatly summarizes these feelings. The consequence is that organizations in these nations are strongly drawn to proactive and deliberate strategy making, under the motto 'plan or be planned for'[41]. Drawing up plans to actively engage the outside world meets people's need to determine their own fate. This cultural characteristic is particularly pronounced in Western countries[42].

At the other extreme are cultures in which most people passively accept their destiny. They believe that most external events are out of their hands and that they exert no control over the future. In such highly fatalistic cultures people tend to approach opportunities and threats reactively, on a day to day basis. Such muddling through behavior rarely leads to emergent strategy, but more often to disjointed, unpatterned action.

In the middle are cultures in which people believe neither in domination of, nor submission to, external circumstances. In these cultures people accept that events are unpredictable and that the environment cannot be tightly controlled, yet trust that individuals and organizations can proactively seek their own path among these uncertainties. The environment and the firm, it is thought, co-evolve through interaction and mutual adjustment, often in unforeseen ways. This requires firms to 'develop an attitude of receptivity and high adaptability to changing conditions'[43]. This way of thinking is particularly pronounced in South-East Asia, and leads to a stronger inclination towards the incrementalism perspective[44].

Time Orientation

A culture's time orientation can also be expected to influence national preferences for dealing with the paradox of deliberateness and emergentness. There are a number of dimensions along which cultures' perception of time can differ. Cultures can be more involved with the past, the present or the future, whereby some make a strong linear separation between these phases, while others emphasize the continuity of time or even its cyclical nature. With regard to the future, a distinction can also be made between cultures with a more short-term or long-term orientation[45].

In general, it can be expected that people in cultures that heavily accentuate the past, or the present, over the future, will be less inclined to think and act strategically. In cultures that emphasize the near future, however, it is likely that individuals and organizations will exhibit a preference for planning. A focus on the not-too-distant future, which is more predictable than the long-term future, fits well with a planning approach. In these countries, intentions are formulated, courses of action are determined and resources are committed, but with a relatively short planning horizon. Plans will only be adopted if results can be expected in the 'foreseeable' future. As Hofstede reports, the English-speaking countries belong to this category of short-term oriented cultures[46].

In cultures with a stronger long-term orientation, incrementalism can be expected to be a more predominant perspective. Since the long-term future is inherently unknown, planning for the future is seen as an inappropriate response. In these countries, it is generally believed that the unpredictability of the long-term future must be accepted and accommodated. This requires an attitude of caution and flexibility, linked to curiosity, learning and persistence. Actions are often taken that are not optimal in the short run, but point in the right long-term direction. As Hofstede reports, many South-East Asian countries fall into this category, as do some European countries.

Further Readings

Readers interested in an overview of the strategy formation literature have a number of good, although rather academically-oriented, articles they can choose from. 'How Strategies Develop in Organisations,' by Andy Bailey and Gerry Johnson, and 'An Integrative Framework for Strategy-Making Processes,' by Stuart Hart, both present short reviews of the main approaches to the topic of strategy process. However, if readers have more time, Henry Mintzberg's much longer article 'Strategy Formation: Schools of Thought' is also highly recommended.

There are many books that give a detailed rendition of how strategic planning should be conducted within organizations. Igor Ansoff's well-known textbook *Implanting Strategic Management* is an excellent, yet taxing, description of strategy making from a planning perspective, while George Steiner's *Strategic Planning: What Every Manager Must Know* is a more down to earth prescription. Between these two extremes is a whole range of widely-sold textbooks, such as Arthur Thompson and A.J. Strickland's *Strategic Management: Concepts and Cases*, and Thomas Wheelen and David Hunger's *Strategic Management and Business Policy*. For further reading on formal planning systems, Balaji Chakravarthy and Peter Lor-ange's book *Managing the Strategy Process: A Framework for a Multibusiness Firm* is a good place to start. On the link between planning and forecast-ing, the book *Forecasting, Planning, and Strategy for the 21st Century*, by Spiro Makridakis, provides a useful introduction.

The most articulate critic of planning is probably Henry Mintzberg, whose book *The Rise and Fall of Strategic Planning* makes for thought-provoking reading. David Hurst's article 'Why Strategic Management is Bankrupt' also provides many interesting arguments against strategic planning. For a more extensive description of the incrementalism per-spective, James Brian Quinn's book *Strategies for Change* is still a good starting point. Ralph Stacey's excellent *Strategic Management and Organi-zational Dynamics* is one of the only textbooks incorporating incremen-talist approaches. Also highly recommended are Ikujiro Nonaka's article 'Toward Middle-Up-Down Management: Accelerating Information Crea-tion' and Robert Burgelman's article 'Corporate Entrepreneurship and Strategic Management: Insights from a Process Study.'

For a better understanding of the political processes involved in strategy formation the reader might want to turn to Andrew Pettigrew's article 'Strategy Formulation as a Political Process,' or to Jeffrey Pfeffer's book *Power in Organizations*. Graham Allison's book *The Essence of Deci-sion: Explaining the Cuban Missile Crisis* is also highly recommended. The cultural processes are vividly described in Gerry Johnson's *Strategic Change and the Management Process*, and more popularly in Rosabeth Moss Kanter's *The Change Masters*. Further readings that explore the link between strategy formation and strategic change are presented at the end of Chapter 4.

Strategic Change

*Every act of creation is first of all an
act of destruction.*

(Pablo Picasso 1881–1973; Spanish artist)

Slow and steady wins the race.

(*The Hare and the Tortoise*, Aesop c. 620–c. 560 BC; Greek writer)

The Paradox of Revolution and Evolution

As became clear in the previous chapter, strategy formation is concerned
with the realization of change. In a world of changing technologies,
transforming economies, shifting demographics, reforming governments, fluctuating consumer preferences, and dynamic competition,
making strategy means making organizations change. In such a turbulent
environment, an organization's mission might remain unaltered for a
long period of time, but its objectives and behavior will repeatedly
need to change. For strategists, it is not an issue of whether organizations
must change, but of where, how and in what direction they must change.

In Chapter 3, the strategy formation debate focused on the question
whether realized strategic changes are arrived at deliberately or emer-
gently. Proponents of the planning perspective argued that strategic
change should be deliberately conceived, while supporters of the incrementalism perspective championed the case of emergent strategic
change. The disagreement between the two sides centered on the issue
of *intentions* – should strategic changes be planned in advance or unfold
in the absence of intentions?

In this chapter, the discussion will move to the issue of *continuity*

– should strategic changes gradually evolve out of the current state of affairs, or mark a radical departure from the organization's past? Should strategic change be *evolutionary*, that is, piecemeal and continuous, or *revolutionary*, which is dramatic and discontinuous? What is the nature of effective strategic change processes? Again, opinions differ considerably, and the subject is hotly contested by both practitioners and theorists. There is a wide range of differing views, each dealing with the tension between revolution and evolution in a different way. However, at the extreme poles of this debate, two diametrically opposed positions can be identified. On the one hand, there are strategists who argue that strategic change in organizations should be pushed through in a revolutionary manner, by taking radical, comprehensive and swift action. We shall refer to this point of view as the *discontinuous change* perspective. On the other hand, there are strategists who argue that strategic change should not be a one-shot, big bang affair, but should be approached in an evolutionary manner, with an emphasis on permanent learning and constant upgrading. This point of view will be referred to as the *continuous change* perspective.

Following the familiar debate model, the inquiry in this chapter into the nature of effective strategic change will be structured by contrasting these two extremes. By comparing the two opposite ways of dealing with the paradox of revolution and evolution, a better understanding of the issues under discussion should be gained. In the next few pages, the discontinuous change and continuous change perspectives will be further explained, and finally summarized in Table 4.1.

The Discontinuous Change Perspective

According to advocates of the discontinuous change perspective, it is a common misconception that organizations develop gradually. It is often assumed that organizations move fluidly from one state to the next, encountering minimal friction. In reality, however, organizational change is arduous and encounters significant resistance. Pressure must be exerted, and tension must mount, before a major shift can be accomplished. Movement, therefore, is not steady and constant, as a current in the sea, but abrupt and dramatic, as in an earthquake, where resistance gives way and tension is released in a short shock. In general, the more significant a change is, the more intense the shock will be.

Proponents of this perspective argue that people and organizations exhibit a natural reluctance to change. Humans have a strong preference for stability. Once general policy has been determined, most organizations are inclined to settle into a fixed way of working. The organizational structure will solidify, formal systems will be installed, standard operating procedures will be defined, key competence areas will be identified, a distribution of power will emerge, and a corporate culture will become established. The stability of an organization will be especially high if all of these elements form a consistent and cohesive configuration. Moreover, if an organization experiences a period of success, this usually strongly reinforces the existing way of working[1].

It must be emphasized that stability is not inherently harmful, as it allows people to 'get to work'. A level of stability is required to function efficiently[2]. Constant upheaval would only create an organizational mess. There would be prolonged confusion about tasks and authority, poorly structured internal communication and coordination, and a lack of clear standards and routines. The instability brought on by such continuously changing processes, procedures, and structures would lead to widespread insecurity, political manoevering, and interdepartmental conflicts.

Advocates of the discontinuous change perspective, therefore, argue that periods of relative stability are necessary for the proper functioning of organizations. However, the downside of stability is *inertia* – the unwillingness and/or inability to change, even when it is urgently required. An unwillingness to change can be due to the uncertainty and ambiguity that unavoidably accompany strategic shifts[3]. It is also common that individuals or departments resist change because they believe that their interests will be damaged[4]. An inability to change can be caused by *lock-in* factors, such as fixed investments, inflexible standards and long-term commitments[5]. However, change is often also impeded by the tenacity of organizational belief systems – cognitive maps shared by members of an organization are not easily adapted, as discussed in Chapter 2.

When change is needed and inertia must be overcome, a series of small nudges will not be sufficient to get the organization into motion. A big shove will be needed. For strategic change to really happen, measures must be radical and comprehensive. A coordinated assault is usually required to decisively break through organizational defenses and 'shock therapy' is needed to fundamentally change people's cognitive maps. Solving lock-in problems generally also demands a quick, organization-wide switch-over to a new system. For instance, *business process reengineering* must involve all aspects of the value chain at once. However, proponents of the discontinuous change perspective emphasize that the period of turmoil must not take too long. People cannot be indefinitely confronted with high levels of uncertainty and ambiguity, and a new equilibrium is vital for a new period of efficient operations.

Therefore, the long-term pattern of organizational change is not gradual, but episodic. Periods of relative stability are interrupted by short and dramatic periods of instability, during which revolutionary changes take place[6]. This pattern of development has also been recognized in a variety of other sciences[7]. Following the natural historians Eldredge and Gould, it is often referred to as the *punctuated equilibrium* view.

Some authors taking this view argue that strategists proactively seek the benefits of discontinuous change. In a competitive environment, they state, many firms will attempt to gain an advantage over their rivals by innovating. Staying one step ahead of other companies in the competitive game by means of technological or organizational innovation is regarded by many as a key success factor (see Chapter 5). Firms that can pull off major innovations in a short period of time will be the winners in the competitive sweepstakes. Such innovation, it must be noted, is inherently revolutionary. Creating novel products, processes, and business formulas requires a sharp break with the past. Old ways must be discarded, before new methods can be adopted. This is the essence of what Schumpeter[8] referred to as the process of *creative destruction*, inherent in the capitalist system. This process is not orderly and protracted, but disruptive and intense. Therefore, it is argued, to be a competitive success, firms must learn to master the skill of revolutionary change[9]. Rapid implementation of system-wide change is an essential organizational capability.

Other authors argue that discontinuous change is usually the reaction to an organizational crisis. In their view, inertia is usually too strong to be overcome by will-power alone. Organizations tend to stay close to stability, making minor changes where necessary, but not upsetting the basic beliefs, processes, systems and power structures. For significant changes to take place, a crisis is needed – either real or induced. A major environmental jolt can be the reason for a sudden crisis[10], but often a misalignment between the firm and its environment grows over a longer period of time[11]. As tension mounts, the organization becomes more receptive for painful changes. This increased willingness to change under crisis circumstances coincides with the physical law that 'under pressure things become fluid'. As long as the pressure persists, revolutionary change is possible, but as soon as the pressure lets up the organization will resolidify in a new form, inhibiting any further major changes[12].

It can be concluded that strategic change, whether proactive or reactive, requires an abrupt break with the status quo. Change management demands strong leadership to rapidly push through stressful, discomforting and risky shifts in an organization's structure, culture, processes and behavior. Battling the sources of inertia and turning crisis into opportunity are the key qualities needed by strategists implementing strategic change. Ultimately, strategists should know when to change and when it is more wise to seek stability – they should know when to trigger an 'earthquake' and when to avoid one.

The Continuous Change Perspective

According to proponents of the continuous change perspective, if organizations shift by 'earthquake', it is usually their own 'fault'. The problem with revolution is that it commonly leads to the need for further revolution at a later time – discontinuous change creates its own boom-and-bust cycle. Revolutionary change is generally followed by a strong organizational yearning for stability. The massive, organization-wide efforts to implement agonizing changes can often only be sustained for a short period of time, after which change momentum collapses. Any positive inclination towards change among employees will have totally disappeared by the time the reorganizations are over. Consequently, the organization lapses back into a stable state, in which only minor changes occur. This stable situation is maintained until the next round of shock therapy becomes necessary, to jolt the organization out of its ossified state.

To supporters of the continuous change perspective, the boom-and-bust approach to strategic change is like running a marathon by sprinting and then standing still to catch one's breath. Yet, marathons are not won by good sprinters, but by runners with endurance and persistence, who can keep a steady pace – runners who are more inspired by the tortoise than by the hare. The same is true for companies in the marathon of competition. Some companies behave like the hare in Aesop's fable, showing off their ability to take great leaps, but burdened by a short span of attention. Other companies behave more like the tortoise, moving gradually and undramatically, but unrelentingly and without interruption, focusing on the long-term goal. In the short run, the hares might dash ahead, suggesting that making big leaps forward is the best way to compete. But in the long run, the most formidable contenders will be the diligent tortoises, whose ability to maintain a constant speed will help them to win the race.

Therefore, the 'big ideas', 'frame-breaking innovations' and 'quantum leaps' that so mesmerize proponents of the discontinuous change perspective, are viewed with suspicion by supporters of continuous change. Revolution not only causes unnecessary disruption and dysfunctional crises, but is usually the substitute of diligence. If organizations do not have the stamina to continuously improve themselves, quick fix discontinuous change can be used as a short-term remedy. Where organizations do not exhibit the drive to permanently upgrade their capabilities, revolutionary innovations can be used as the short cut to renewed competitiveness. In other words, the lure of revolutionary change is that of short-term results. By abruptly and dramatically making major changes, managers hope to rapidly book tangible progress – and instantly win recognition and promotion.

To advocates of the continuous change perspective, a preference for revolution usually reflects an unhealthy obsession with the short term. Continuous change, on the other hand, is more long term in orientation. Development is gradual, piecemeal and undramatic, but as it is constantly maintained over a longer period of time, the aggregate level of change can still be significant. Three organizational characteristics are important for keeping up a steady pace of change. First, all employees within the firm should be committed to *continuously improve*. Everyone within the organization should be driven by constructive dissatisfaction with the status quo. This attitude, that things can always be done better, reflects a rejection of stability and the acceptance of bounded instability[13] – everything is open to change.

Second, everyone in the firm must be motivated to *continuously learn*[14]. People within the organization must constantly update their knowledge-base, which not only means acquiring new information, but also challenging accepted company wisdom. Learning goes hand in hand with unlearning – changing the cognitive maps shared within the organization. In this respect, it is argued that an atmosphere of crisis actually inhibits continuous change. In a situation of crisis, it is not a matter of 'under pressure things become fluid', but 'in the cold everything freezes'. Crisis circumstances might lower people's resistance to imposed change, but it also blunts their motivation for experimenting and learning, as they brace themselves for the imminent shock. Crisis encourages people to seek security and to focus on the short term, instead of opening up and working towards long-term development.

Third, everyone in the firm must be motivated to *continuously adapt*. Constant adjustment to external change and fluid internal realignment should be pursued. To this end, the organization must actively avoid inertia, by combating the forces of ossification. Strategists should strive to create flexible structures and systems, to encourage an open and tolerant corporate culture, and to provide sufficient job and career security for employees to accept other forms of ambiguity and uncertainty[15].

These three characteristics of an evolutionary organization – continuous improvement, learning and adaptation – have in common the fact that basically everyone in the organization is involved. Revolutionary change can be initiated by top management, possibly assisted and urged on by a few external consultants, and carried by a handful of change agents or champions[16]. Evolutionary change, on the other hand, requires an organization-wide effort. Leaders cannot learn on behalf of their organizations, nor can they orchestrate all of the small improvements and adaptations needed for continuous change. Strategists must realize that evolution can be led from the top, but not imposed from the top. For strategists to realize change, hands-on guidance of organizational developments is more important than commanding organizational actions.

The question within the field of strategic management is, therefore, whether strategic change is primarily a revolutionary or an evolutionary process. Should strategists strive to implement radical, comprehensive and dramatic changes, or should they emphasize continuous improvement, learning and adaptation? Not all strategists agree on the answers to

TABLE 4.1
Discontinuous change versus continuous change perspective

	Discontinuous Change Perspective	Continuous Change Perspective
Emphasis on	Revolution over evolution	Evolution over revolution
Strategic change as	Disruptive innovation/ turnaround	Uninterrupted improvement
Strategic change process	Creative destruction	Organic adaptation
Magnitude of change	Radical, comprehensive and dramatic	Moderate, piecemeal and undramatic
Pace of change	Abrupt, unsteady and intermittent	Gradual, steady and constant
Fundamental change requires	Sudden break with status quo	Permanent learning and flexibility
Reaction to environmental jolts	Shock therapy	Continuous adjustment
View of organizational crises	Under pressure things become fluid	In the cold everything freezes
Long-term change dynamics	Stable and unstable states alternate	Persistent transient state
Long-term change pattern	Punctuated equilibrium	Gradual development

these questions, leaving readers with the challenge of formulating their own conclusions with regard to the nature of strategic change. Readers will have to come to terms themselves with the paradox of revolution and evolution (see Table 4.1).

Defining the Issues: Magnitude and Pace

Before proceeding with the 'debate' between proponents of the discontinuous and continuous change perspectives, it is useful to clarify the key topics under discussion. As will be seen, the disagreements between the two extreme points of view revolve around two major issues: the *magnitude* of change and the *pace* of change. In the next paragraphs these two issues will be further explored, to set the stage for the debate articles that follow.

The Magnitude of Change

Change does not happen everywhere in the same way. Even to the casual observer, it is obvious that processes of change differ according to the thing being changed – the process of changing a satellite's orbit is inherently different than the process of changing one's socks. For anything useful to be said about change, it must be specified what the object is that is being changed. This is particularly true for the poorly defined topic of 'strategic change'. To have an insightful debate in this chapter, it is essential to clarify which elements of an organization are the objects of change, and what qualifies as 'strategic'. Only then can the discussion turn to the determination of the best type of strategic change process.

Organizations are complex systems, consisting of many different elements, each of which can be changed. Many frameworks exist that disassemble organizations into a number of components, to assist analysts in gaining an overview of an organization's complex composition. For instance, the 7S framework, put forward by Waterman, Peters and Phillips[17], divides the organization into seven interconnected elements, that can all be changed: structure, strategy, systems, style, staff, skills and superordinate goals. For the discussion in this chapter, however, the simple framework proposed by Mintzberg and Westley[18] is particularly insightful (see Figure 4.1).

Mintzberg and Westley first distinguish between change in the spheres of organization and strategy. Altering the *state* of the organization has traditionally been the focus of the field of organizational behavior, while changing the *direction* of the organization has been central to

FIGURE 4.1
Levels and spheres of organizational change (Mintzberg and Westley, 1992)

	Changes in Organization (State)	Changes in Strategy (Direction)
More Conceptual (Thought)	Culture	Vision
↕	Structure	Positions
	Systems	Programs
More Concrete (Action)	People	Facilities

the field of strategic management. Obviously the two spheres are linked and both must be discussed to understand organizational change. However, it is important to note that changes in one sphere are not always accompanied by full and simultaneous changes in the other.

Second, Mintzberg and Westley distinguish between different levels of change, from the broadest, most conceptual level, all the way down to the narrowest, most concrete. At the highest level, the collective mindset within the organization can be the object of change, both in the form of the organizational culture and the strategic vision. One level lower, it can be the organizational structure and corresponding strategic positions that need to be altered. Even more concrete is the next level of organizational systems and strategic programs, at which tangible change efforts can be directed. Finally, at the most concrete level, are the actual operations that can be the target of adjustment. At this level of action, it can be the actors (the people or their jobs) and the activities (the value-adding processes or the facilities) that are changed. Clearly, changes at the various levels are linked and understanding organizational change requires a holistic view of the entire range. However, not all organizational changes are strategic. Autonomous operational changes with no impact on the top two levels do not qualify as strategic. For instance, downsizing is usually not strategic, since vision and position (and culture and structure) are not altered. Only changes that affect the top two levels constitute strategic change.

If the elements in Figure 4.1 are the major aspects of the organization that can be changed, the first question to be asked in this debate is how major the changes to these elements should be? What should be the *magnitude of change*? This issue can be divided into two component parts.

1   *Scope of change*. The first bone of contention is whether all eight aspects of the organization need to be shifted in unison, or whether bits and pieces can be changed one after the other. The two perspectives take diametrically opposed positions on this point. In the discontinuous change perspective, revolution demands comprehensive action on all eight fronts – the scope of change must be broad. In the continuous change perspective, evolution demands a high number of piecemeal adjustments to be made over a prolonged period of time. Therefore, while the accumulated changes might be broad in scope, the scope of each individual change is rather narrow.

2   *Amplitude of change*. The second point of disagreement is whether the eight aspects of Figure 4.1 need to be changed in a radical or moderate manner. Again the two perspectives express diametrically opposed opinions. In the discontinuous change perspective, revolution demands a radical departure from the present situation – the amplitude of change should be high. In the continuous change perspective, evolution demands gradual development out of the present situation by means of moderate steps – the amplitude of changes should be low.

These two dimensions together determine the magnitude of change, as illustrated in Figure 4.2. What this diagram emphasizes, is that in terms of magnitude, revolution and evolution are the two extreme cases of change. In practice, a wide variety of possibilities exists between these two poles.

The Pace of Change

The second question dividing the two perspectives is how change should take place over time. The two parties disagree on what the *pace of change* should be. This issue can also be decomposed into two related parts.

1 *Tempo of change.* The first matter of dispute is whether change should take place in short bursts or should be realized over a longer period of time. Again the two perspectives adopt opposing vantage points. In the discontinuous change perspective, revolution demands fast action within a short timespan, after which the rate of change tapers off, until the next 'storming' effort is needed. This leads to an unsteady tempo of change. In the continuous change perspective, evolution demands a constant rate of change that is maintained indefinitely, without interruption. In other words, the tempo of change should be steady.

FIGURE 4.2
The magnitude of change

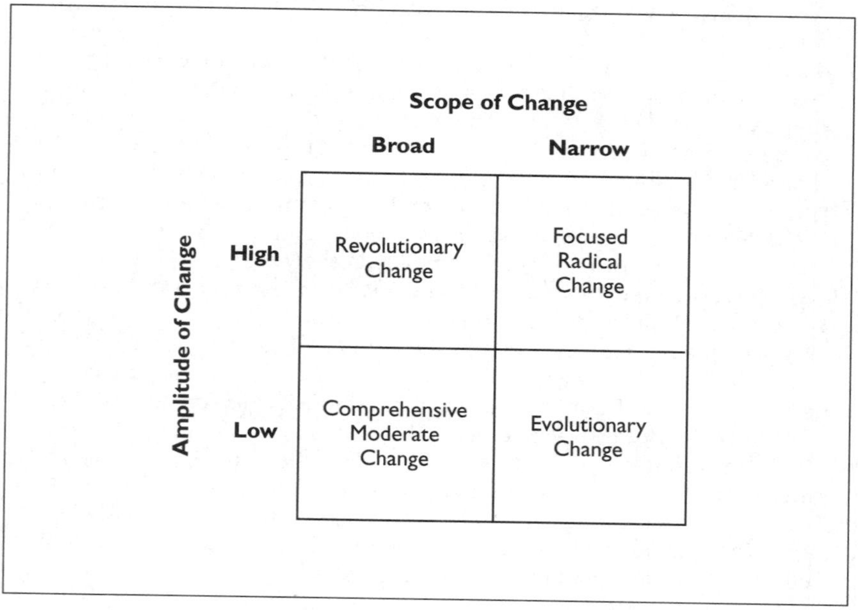

2   *Timing of change.* The second topic of debate has to do with the moment at which change should be realized. The question is whether change requires immediate action or can be gradually implemented over a longer period of time. Supporters of the discontinuous change perspective are inclined to view all strategic changes as highly urgent – the faster a change is pushed through, the sooner the competitive benefits of the change can be enjoyed. If a strategic change is a proactive innovation, then a rapid *transformation* can result in a major lead over rival firms. If the strategic change is a reaction to an organizational crisis, then a rapid *turnaround* is highly advantageous. Therefore, the timing of change should usually be 'as soon as possible'. Proponents of the continuous change perspective, on the other hand, tend to emphasize the need for persistent change over the need for immediate change. In their view, getting off to a flying start is not that difficult, but carrying a change all the way through is the challenge. Therefore, enough time should be taken to gradually improve, learn and adapt. Crises requiring immediate action should be avoided, where possible, by maintaining a flexible and proactive stance.

EXHIBIT 4.1
Morgan Motor Company case

MORGAN MOTOR COMPANY: (W)RECKLESS DRIVING?

Henry Fredrick Stanley Morgan was an apprentice engineer at the Great Western Railways works in Swindon, Great Britain, at the start of the 20th century, as were two other young men, whose names have become motor industry icons – Henry Royce and W.O. Bentley. All three went on to establish their own automobile manufacturing firm, but Morgan Motor Company, founded in 1909, is the only one that has survived as an independent company. In fact, all of the famous British car makers, such as Aston Martin, Jaguar, Austin Healey, Triumph, MG and Rover, have disappeared or have been acquired by larger foreign firms. Yet, Morgan remains as the last independent British car manufacturer and can also claim the title of oldest privately-owned motor company in the world.

Morgan currently produces about 480 cars per year and has three basic models, which are all small, open-topped, classic English sports cars. The smallest model is the 'Four-Four' (four wheels and four cylinders), introduced in 1936 to replace its long tradition of three-wheeled vehicles. The basic design of the Four-Four has survived with only minor modifications since the first cars were produced, giving them a vintage 1930s look. The slightly larger and faster model is called the 'Plus Four,' while the largest model is the 'Plus Eight,' which refers to the car's V-8 engine. The Plus Eight can accelerate as fast as a Ferrari, but is only about a third of the price. The Plus Eight sells for £26,000 (about US$ 50,000), while the Four-Four has a list price of approximately £18,000.

Morgan's production facilities in Malvern Link were established in 1919 and have remained largely unchanged since then. The construction of the cars is largely done by hand. Each Monday morning the chassis frames for 9 or 10 new cars are placed on saw horses, and in the subsequent nine weeks dedicated and highly skilled craftsmen complete the car. The frame of the coach is made of 100-year old ash wood, requiring precision carpentry. The exterior is finished with steel or aluminium sheet metal, demanding excellent metal working skills. All of this work is labor-intensive. Labor cost is estimated at 30–40 percent of the total cost. This mode of production also depends heavily on the abilities of the approximately 100 craftsmen employed by the company. Therefore, emphasis is placed on training and taking in a constant flow of apprentices. While a high proportion of the parts are made in-house, other components, such as the engine, rear axles, chassis, transmissions, windshields and electric parts, are all obtained from outside suppliers. By integrating these state-of-the-art components into its classic design, Morgan combines the best of both worlds – tradition and up-to-date technology.

In the market place, Morgan also seems to be cruising at a constant speed. While the company only has the capacity to produce 480 cars per year, there is a waiting list of about 3000 eager buyers, who on average have to wait six years before they can come to Malvern Link to see their car being produced. And these are the people who take the trouble to order and wait. Many more potential customers give up or change their minds once the long delivery time becomes apparent. The demand is so strong, that second-hand Morgans sell for almost the same price as new ones – sometimes even higher! Half of the cars are sold abroad, mostly in Western Europe, but also in Japan and North America. The other half are sold in Britain, and all quite profitably. Morgan earns a pre-tax profit of over £2000 (US$ 4000) per vehicle, while the large car manufacturers typically make a little over £300.

While Morgan sounds relatively successful, not everyone believes that the company is developing in the right way. Some analysts believe the company is squandering its enormous potential. One outspoken outsider has been Sir John Harvey-Jones, the well-known former CEO of ICI, the giant British chemical company. In the early 1990s, Harvey-Jones starred in a series of television programs produced by the BBC called 'The Trouble-shooter'. In these programs Harvey-Jones went into small firms and made suggestions for improvement. One of the companies he visited for an episode was the Morgan Motor Company. His conclusion was that gradual modifications to Morgan's production system and market strategy would not be enough to secure the company's future. Radical changes would be needed for Morgan to remain prosperous. In the opinion of Harvey-Jones, the profits at Morgan were too low to give it the stamina to survive the shock of changes in the environment. His suggestion was to increase production to at least 600 cars per year by moving to a more up-to-date production facility. New production technologies could be introduced and the firm would be less dependent on scarce craftsmen. The investment in a new plant could be financed by significantly raising the price of the cars. The fact that people were willing to wait for years or pay more than the list price to obtain a Morgan, indicated to Harvey-Jones that the cars were underpriced and that the market would easily accept price increases. Using a waiting list to cushion the firm against swings in demand seemed to Harvey-Jones to be overly cautious.

Yet, Peter and Charles Morgan, the son and grandson of the firm's founder, have remained unrepentant. They have fiercely resisted the pressure to raise production levels and prices. 'Our objective is to be in business for another 50 years,' has been Charles Morgan's stern response. In reaction to the suggestions by Harvey-Jones in 'The Troubleshooter,' Charles Morgan sent an open letter to a newspaper, writing: 'It is Sir John's view that we should double production in a short time scale, paying for this by increasing the price of the car and investing in an expensive new plant. His methods would result in making many changes in the way the Morgan is built. We strongly disagree with his solution, and believe the Morgan policy of gradual and carefully considered change will enable us to maintain the car's qualities, and unique appeal, and thereby ensure its survival for the foreseeable future. Sir John's criticisms have been noted, but they are unworthy of us.'

Morgan's approach has been to strive for gradual improvement. For instance, the car designs have been modified to facilitate airbags and a computerized just-in-time stock control system has been introduced. Alterations in the plant layout and minor changes in production practices are considered, but Morgan is not receptive to any large-scale reengineering efforts or bold strategic initiatives. The question is, however, whether these minor adaptations will be enough to keep Morgan healthy in the long run. Are the changes being made adequate to keep up with shifts in the environment? If a downturn hits the industry, will Morgan be sufficiently robust to survive or will it then pay for its unwillingness to make big changes in the fat years? In short, is the pace and magnitude of change within Morgan high enough, or should Charles Morgan reconsider the value of revolutionary change?

Sources: Morgan Website; *The Economist*, December 25th 1993; Goulet and Rappaport, 1992.

The Debate and the Readings

As opening contribution in the 'virtual debate', Michael Hammer's 'Re-engineering Work: Don't Automate, Obliterate'[20] has been selected to represent the discontinuous change perspective. This paper was published in *Harvard Business Review* in 1990 and was followed in 1993 by the highly influential book *Reengineering the Corporation: A Manifesto for Business Revolution*, that Hammer co-authored with James Champy[21]. In this article, Hammer explains the concept of reengineering in much the same way as in the best-selling book. 'At the heart of reengineering,' he writes, 'is the notion of discontinuous thinking – of recognizing and breaking away from the outdated rules and fundamental assumptions that underlie operations.' In his view, radically redesigning business processes 'cannot be planned meticulously and accomplished in small and cautious steps. It's an all-or-nothing proposition with an uncertain result.' He exhorts managers to 'think big,' by setting high goals, taking bold steps and daring to accept a high risk. In short, he preaches business revolution, and the tone of his article is truly that of a manifesto – impassioned, fervent, with here and there 'a touch of fanaticism.'

Equally impassioned is the argumentation in the second reading, 'Kaizen', by Masaaki Imai[22], which has been selected to represent the continuous change perspective. This article has been taken from Imai's famous book *Kaizen: The Key to Japan's Competitive Success*. Kaizen (pronounced Ky'zen) is a Japanese term, that is best translated as continuous improvement. Imai argues that it is this continuous improvement philosophy that best explains the competitive strength of so many Japanese companies. In his view, Western companies have an unhealthy obsession with one-shot innovations and revolutionary change. They are fixated on the great-leap forward, while disregarding the power of accumulated small changes. Imai believes that innovations are also important for competitive success, but that they should be embedded in an organization that is driven to continuously improve.

After reviewing the arguments put forward by these two discussants it will be up to readers to determine which perspective is most valuable. Both authors have convincing arguments and they just might change your mind – either moderately or dramatically. Whichever way, it is up to readers to form their own judgment on how to deal with the paradox of revolution and evolution.

Reading 1   Reengineering Work: Don't Automate, Obliterate

By Michael Hammer[†]

Despite a decade or more of restructuring and downsizing, many US companies are still unprepared to operate in the 1990s. In a time of rapidly changing technologies and ever-shorter product life cycles, product development often proceeds at a glacial pace. In an age of the customer, order fulfilment has high error rates and customer inquiries go unanswered for weeks. In a period when asset utilization is critical, inventory levels exceed many months of demand.

The usual methods for boosting performance – process rationalization and automation – haven't yielded the dramatic improvements companies need. In particular, heavy investments in information technology have delivered disappointing results – largely because companies tend to use technology to mechanize old ways of doing business. They leave the existing processes intact and use computers simply to speed them up.

But speeding up those processes cannot address their fundamental performance deficiencies. Many of our job designs, work flows, control mechanisms, and organizational structures came of age in a different competitive environment and before the advent of the computer. They are geared toward efficiency and control. Yet the watchwords of the new decade are innovation and speed, service and quality.

It is time to stop paving the cow paths. Instead of embedding outdated processes in silicon and software, we should obliterate them and start over. We should 'reengineer' our businesses: use the power of modern information technology to radically redesign our business processes in order to achieve dramatic improvements in their performance.

Every company operates according to a great many unarticulated rules. 'Credit decisions are made by the credit department.' 'Local inventory is needed for good customer service.' 'Forms must be filled in completely and in order.' Reengineering strives to break away from the old rules about how we organize and conduct business. It involves recognizing and rejecting some of them and then finding imaginative new ways to accomplish work. From our redesigned processes, new rules will emerge that fit the times. Only then can we hope to achieve quantum leaps in performance.

[†] Source: This article was adapted with permission from *Harvard Business Review*, July/August 1990.

Reengineering cannot be planned meticulously and accomplished in small and cautious steps. It's an all-or-nothing proposition with an uncertain result. Still, most companies have no choice but to muster the courage to do it. For many, reengineering is the only hope for breaking away from the antiquated processes that threaten to drag them down. Fortunately, managers are not without help. Enough businesses have successfully reengineered their processes to provide some rules of thumb for others.

What Ford and MBL Did

Japanese competitors and young entrepreneurial ventures prove every day that drastically better levels of process performance are possible. They develop products twice as fast, utilize assets eight times more productively, respond to customers ten times faster. Some large, established companies also show what can be done. Businesses like Ford Motor Company and Mutual Benefit Life Insurance have reengineered their processes and achieved competitive leadership as a result. Ford has reengineered its accounts payable processes, and Mutual Benefit Life, its processing of applications for insurance.

In the early 1980s, when the American automotive industry was in a depression, Ford's top management put accounts payable – along with many other departments – under the microscope in search of ways to cut costs. Accounts payable in North America alone employed more than 500 people. Management thought that by rationalizing processes and installing new computer systems, it could reduce the head count by some 20 percent.

Ford was enthusiastic about its plan to tighten accounts payable – until it looked at Mazda. While Ford was aspiring to a 400-person department, Mazda's accounts payable organization consisted of a total of five people. The difference in absolute numbers was astounding, and even after adjusting for Mazda's smaller size, Ford figured that its accounts payable organization was five times the size it should be. The Ford team knew better than to attribute the discrepancy to callisthenics, company songs, or low interest rates.

Ford managers ratcheted up their goal: accounts payable would perform with not just a hundred but many hundreds fewer clerks. It then set out to achieve it. First, managers analyzed the existing system. When Ford's purchasing department wrote a purchase order, it sent a copy to accounts payable. Later, when material control received the goods, it sent a copy of the receiving document to accounts payable. Meanwhile, the vendor sent an invoice to accounts payable. It was up to accounts payable, then, to match the purchase order against the receiving document and the invoice. If they matched, the department issued payment.

The department spent most of its time on mismatches, instances where the purchase order, receiving document, and invoice disagreed. In these cases, an accounts payable clerk would investigate the discrepancy, hold up payment, generate documents, and all-in-all gum up the works.

One way to improve things might have been to help the accounts payable clerk investigate more efficiently, but a better choice was to prevent the mismatches in the first place. To this end, Ford instituted 'invoiceless processing.' Now when the purchasing department initiates an order, it enters the information into an on-line database. It doesn't send a copy of the purchase order to anyone. When the goods arrive at the receiving dock, the receiving clerk checks the database to see if they correspond to an outstanding purchase order. If so, he or she accepts them and enters the transaction into the computer system. (If receiving can't find a database entry for the received goods, it simply returns the order.)

Under the old procedures, the accounting department had to match 14 data items between the receipt record, the purchase order, and the invoice before it could issue payment to the vendor. The new approach requires matching only three items – part number, unit of measure, and supplier code – between the purchase order and the receipt record. The matching is done automatically, and the computer prepares the check, which accounts payable sends to the vendor. There are no invoices to worry about since Ford has asked its vendors not to send them.

Ford didn't settle for the modest increases it first envisioned. It opted for radical change – and achieved dramatic improvement. Where it has instituted this new process, Ford has achieved a 75 percent reduction in head count, not the 20 percent it would have gotten with a conventional program. And since there are no discrepancies between the financial record and the physical record, material control is simpler and financial information is more accurate.

Mutual Benefit Life, the country's eighteenth largest life carrier, has reengineered its processing of insurance applications. Prior to this, MBL handled customers' applications much as its competitors did. The long, multistep process involved credit checking, quoting, rating, underwriting, and so on. An application would have to go through as many as 30 discrete steps, spanning five departments and involving 19 people. At the very best, MBL could process an application in 24 hours, but more typical turnarounds ranged from five to 25 days – most of the time spent passing information from one department to the next. (Another insurer estimated that while an application spent 22 days in process, it was actually worked on for just 17 minutes.)

MBL's rigid, sequential process led to many complications. For instance, when a customer wanted to cash in an existing policy and purchase a new one, the old business department first had to authorize the treasury department to issue a check made payable to MBL. The check would then accompany the paperwork to the new business department.

The president of MBL, intent on improving customer service, decided that this nonsense had to stop and demanded a 60 percent improvement in productivity. It was clear that such an ambitious goal would require more than tinkering with the existing process. Strong measures were in order, and the management team assigned to the task looked to technology as a means of achieving them. The team realized that shared databases and computer networks could make many different kinds of information available to a single person, while expert systems could help people with limited experience make sound decisions. Applying these insights led to a new approach to the application-handling process, one with wide organizational implications and little resemblance to the old way of doing business.

MBL swept away existing job definitions and departmental boundaries and created a new position called a case manager. Case managers have total responsibility for an application from the time it is received to the time a policy is issued. Unlike clerks, who performed a fixed task repeatedly under the watchful gaze of a supervisor, case managers work autonomously. No more handoffs of files and responsibility, no more shuffling of customer inquiries.

Case managers are able to perform all the tasks associated with an insurance application because they are supported by powerful PC-based workstations that run an expert system and connect to a range of automated systems on a mainframe. In particularly tough cases, the case manager calls for assistance from a senior underwriter or physician, but these specialists work only as consultants and advisers to the case manager, who never relinquishes control.

Empowering individuals to process entire applications has had a tremendous impact on operations. MBL can now complete an application in as little as four hours, and average turnaround takes only two to five days. The company has eliminated 100 field office positions, and case managers can handle more than twice the volume of new applications the company previously could process.

The Essence of Reengineering

At the heart of reengineering is the notion of discontinuous thinking – of recognizing and breaking away from the outdated rules and fundamental assumptions that underlie operations. Unless we change these rules, we are merely rearranging the deckchairs on the Titanic. We cannot achieve breakthroughs in performance by cutting fat or automating existing processes. Rather, we must challenge old assumptions and shed the old rules that made the business underperform in the first place.

Every business is replete with implicit rules left over from earlier decades. 'Customers don't repair their own equipment.' 'Local warehouses are necessary for good service.' 'Merchandising decisions are made at headquarters.' These rules of work design are based on assumptions about technology, people, and organizational goals that no longer hold. The contemporary repertoire of available information technologies is vast and quickly expanding. Quality, innovation, and service are now more important than cost, growth, and control. A large portion of the population is educated and capable of assuming responsibility, and workers cherish their autonomy and expect to have a say in how the business is run.

It should come as no surprise that our business processes and structures are outmoded and obsolete: our work structures and processes have not kept pace with the changes in technology, demographics, and business objectives. For the most part, we have organized work as a sequence of separate tasks and employed complex mechanisms to track its progress. This arrangement can be traced to the Industrial Revolution, when specialization of labor and economies of scale promised to overcome the inefficiencies of cottage industries. Businesses disaggregated work into narrowly defined tasks, reaggregated the people performing those tasks into departments, and installed managers to administer them.

Our elaborate systems for imposing control and discipline on those who actually do the work stem from the postwar period. In that halcyon period of expansion, the main concern was growing fast without going broke, so businesses focused on cost, growth, and control. And since literate, entry-level people were abundant but well-educated professionals hard to come by, the control systems funneled information up the hierarchy to the few who presumably knew what to do with it.

These patterns of organizing work have become so ingrained that, despite their serious drawbacks, it's hard to conceive of work being accomplished any other way. Conventional process structures are fragmented and piecemeal, and they lack the integration necessary to maintain quality and service. They are breeding grounds for tunnel vision, as people tend to substitute the narrow goals of their particular department for the larger goals of the process as a whole. When work is handed off from person to person and unit to unit, delays and errors are inevitable. Accountability blurs, and critical issues fall between the cracks. Moreover, no one sees enough of the big picture to be able to respond quickly to new situations. Managers desperately try, like all the king's horses and all the king's men, to piece together the fragmented pieces of business processes.

Managers have tried to adapt their processes to new circumstances, but usually in ways that just create more problems. If, say, customer service is poor, they create a mechanism to deliver service but overlay it on the existing organization. Bureaucracy thickens, costs rise, and enterprising competitors gain market share.

In reengineering, managers break loose from outmoded business processes and the design principles underlying them and create new ones. Ford had operated under the old rule that 'We pay when we receive the invoice.' While no one had ever articulated or recorded it, that rule determined how the accounts payable process was organized. Ford's re-engineering effort challenged and ultimately replaced the rule with a new one: 'We pay when we receive the goods.'

Reengineering requires looking at the fundamental processes of the business from a cross-functional perspective. Ford discovered that reengineering only the accounts payable department was futile. The appropriate focus of the effort was what might be called the goods acquisition process, which included purchasing and receiving as well as accounts payable.

One way to ensure that reengineering has a cross-functional per-spective is to assemble a team that represents the functional units involved in the process being reengineered and all the units that depend on it. The team must analyze and scrutinize the existing process until it really understands what the process is trying to accomplish. The point is not to learn what happens to form 73B in its peregrinations through the company but to understand the purpose of having form 73B in the first place. Rather than looking for opportunities to improve the current process, the team should determine which of its steps really add value and search for new ways to achieve the result.

The reengineering team must keep asking Why? and What if? Why do we need to get a manager's signature on a requisition? Is it a control mechanism or a decision point? What if the manager reviews only requi-sitions above $500? What if he or she doesn't see them at all? Raising and resolving heretical questions can separate what is fundamental to the process from what is superficial. The regional offices of an East Coast insurance company had long produced a series of reports that they regularly sent to the home office. No one in the field realized that these reports were simply filed and never used. The process outlasted the circumstances that had created the need for it. The reengineering study team should push to discover situations like this.

In short, a reengineering effort strives for dramatic levels of improvement. It must break away from conventional wisdom and the constraints of organizational boundaries and should be broad and cross-functional in scope. It should use information technology not to auto-mate an existing process but to enable a new one.

Principles of Reengineering

Creating new rules tailored to the modern environment ultimately requires a new conceptualization of the business process – which comes down to someone having a great idea. But reengineering need not be haphazard. In fact, some of the principles that companies have already discovered while reengineering their business processes can help jump start the effort for others.

Organize Around Outcomes, Not Tasks

This principle says to have one person perform all the steps in a process. Design that person's job around an objective or outcome instead of a single task. The redesign at Mutual Benefit Life, where individual case managers perform the entire application approval process, is the quintessential example of this.

The redesign of an electronics company is another example. It had separate organizations performing each of the five steps between selling and installing the equipment. One group determined customer requirements, another translated those requirements into internal product codes, a third conveyed that information to various plants and warehouses, a fourth received and assembled the components, and a fifth delivered and installed the equipment. The process was based on the centuries-old notion of specialized labor and on the limitations inherent in paper files. The departments each possessed a specific set of skills, and only one department at a time could do its work.

The customer order moved systematically from step to step. But this sequential processing caused problems. The people getting the information from the customer in step one had to get all the data anyone would need throughout the process, even if it wasn't needed until step five. In addition, the many handoffs were responsible for numerous errors and misunderstandings. Finally, any questions about customer requirements that arose late in the process had to be referred back to the people doing step one, resulting in delay and rework.

When the company reengineered, it eliminated the assembly-line approach. It compressed responsibility for the various steps and assigned it to one person, the 'customer service representative.' That person now oversees the whole process – taking the order, translating it into product codes, getting the components assembled, and seeing the product delivered and installed. The customer service rep expedites and coordinates the process, much like a general contractor. And the customer has just one contact, who always knows the status of the order.

Have Those Who Use the Output of the Process Perform the Process

In an effort to capitalize on the benefits of specialization and scale, many organizations established specialized departments to handle specialized processes. Each department does only one type of work and is a 'customer' of other groups' processes. Accounting does only accounting. If it needs new pencils, it goes to the purchasing department, the group specially equipped with the information and expertise to perform that role. Purchasing finds vendors, negotiates price, places the order, inspects the goods, and pays the invoice – and eventually the accountants get their pencils. The process works (after a fashion), but it's slow and bureaucratic.

Now that computer-based data and expertise are more readily available, departments, units, and individuals can do more for themselves. Opportunities exist to reengineer processes so that the individuals who need the result of a process can do it themselves. For example, by using expert systems and databases, departments can make their own purchases without sacrificing the benefits of specialized purchasers. One manufacturer has reengineered its purchasing process along just these lines. The company's old system, whereby the operating departments submitted requisitions and let purchasing do the rest, worked well for controlling expensive and important items like raw materials and capital equipment. But for inexpensive and nonstrategic purchases, which constituted some 35 percent of total orders, the system was slow and cumbersome; it was not uncommon for the cost of the purchasing process to exceed the cost of the goods being purchased.

The new process compresses the purchase of sundry items and pushes it on to the customers of the process. Using a database of approved vendors, an operating unit can directly place an order with a vendor and charge it on a bank credit card. At the end of the month, the bank gives the manufacturer a tape of all credit card transactions, which the company runs against its internal accounting system.

When an electronics equipment manufacturer reengineered its field service process, it pushed some of the steps of the process on to its customers. The manufacturer's field service had been plagued by the usual problems: technicians were often unable to do a particular repair because the right part wasn't on the van, response to customer calls was slow, and spare-parts inventory was excessive.

Now customers make simple repairs themselves. Spare parts are stored at each customer's site and managed through a computerized inventory-management system. When a problem arises, the customer calls the manufacturer's field-service hot line and describes the symptoms to a diagnostician, who accesses a diagnosis support system. If the problem appears to be something the customer can fix, the diagnostician tells the customer what part to replace and how to install it. The old part is picked up and a new part left in its place at a later time. Only for complex problems is a service technician dispatched to the site, this time without having to make a stop at the warehouse to pick up parts.

When the people closest to the process perform it, there is little need for the overhead associated with managing it. Interfaces and liaisons can be eliminated, as can the mechanisms used to coordinate those who perform the process with those who use it. Moreover, the problem of capacity planning for the process performers is greatly reduced.

Subsume Information-Processing Work into the Real Work that Produces the Information

The previous two principles compress linear processes. This principle suggests moving work from one person or department to another. Why doesn't an organization that produces information also process it? In the past, people didn't have the time or weren't trusted to do both. Most companies established units to do nothing but collect and process information that other departments created. This arrangement reflects the old rule about specialized labor and the belief that people at lower organizational levels are incapable of acting on information they generate. An accounts payable department collects information from purchasing and receiving and reconciles it with data that the vendor provides. Quality assurance gathers and analyzes information it gets from production.

Ford's redesigned accounts payable process embodies the new rule. With the new system, receiving, which produces the information about the goods received, processes this information instead of sending it to accounts payable. The new computer system can easily compare the delivery with the order and trigger the appropriate action.

Treat Geographically Dispersed Resources as Though They Were Centralized

The conflict between centralization and decentralization is a classic one. Decentralizing a resource (whether people, equipment, or inventory) gives better service to those who use it, but at the cost of redundancy, bureaucracy, and missed economies of scale. Companies no longer have to make such trade-offs. They can use databases, telecommunications networks, and standardized processing systems to get the benefits of scale and coordination while maintaining the benefits of flexibility and service.

At Hewlett-Packard, for instance, each of the more than 50 manufacturing units had its own separate purchasing department. While this arrangement provided excellent responsiveness and service to the plants, it prevented H-P from realizing the benefits of its scale, particularly with

STRATEGIC CHANGE **163**

regard to quantity discounts. H-P's solution is to maintain the divisional purchasing organizations and to introduce a corporate unit to coordinate them. Each purchasing unit has access to a shared database on vendors and their performance and issues its own purchase orders. Corporate purchasing maintains this database and uses it to negotiate contracts for the corporation and to monitor the units. The payoffs have come in a 150 percent improvement in on-time deliveries, 50 percent reduction in lead times, 75 percent reduction in failure rates, and a significantly lower cost of goods purchased.

Link Parallel Activities Instead of Integrating Their Results

H-P's decentralized purchasing operations represent one kind of parallel processing in which separate units perform the same function. Another common kind of parallel processing is when separate units perform different activities that must eventually come together. Product development typically operates this way. In the development of a photocopier, for example, independent units develop the various subsystems of the copier. One group works on the optics, another on the mechanical paperhandling device, another on the power supply, and so on. Having people do development work simultaneously saves time, but at the dreaded integration and testing phase, the pieces often fail to work together. Then the costly redesign begins.

Or consider a bank that sells different kinds of credit – loans, letters of credit, asset-based financing – through separate units. These groups may have no way of knowing whether another group has already extended credit to a particular customer. Each unit could extend the full $10 million credit limit.

The new principle says to forge links between parallel functions and to coordinate them while their activities are in process rather than after they are completed. Communications networks, shared databases, and teleconferencing can bring the independent groups together so that coordination is ongoing. One large electronics company has cut its product development cycle by more than 50 percent by implementing this principle.

Put the Decision Point Where the Work is Performed, and Build Control into the Process

In most organizations, those who do the work are distinguished from those who monitor the work and make decisions about it. The tacit assumption is that the people actually doing the work have neither the time nor the inclination to monitor and control it and that they lack the knowledge and scope to make decisions about it. The entire hierarchical management structure is built on this assumption. Accountants, auditors, and supervisors check, record, and monitor work. Managers handle any exceptions.

The new principle suggests that the people who do the work should make the decisions and that the process itself can have built-in controls. Pyramidal management layers can therefore be compressed and the organization flattened.

Information technology can capture and process data, and expert systems can to some extent supply knowledge, enabling people to make their own decisions. As the doers become self-managing and self-controlling, hierarchy – and the slowness and bureaucracy associated with it – disappears.

When Mutual Benefit Life reengineered the insurance application process, it not only compressed the linear sequence but also eliminated the need for layers of managers. These two kinds of compression – vertical and horizontal – often go together; the very fact that a worker sees only one piece of the process calls for a manager with a broader vision. The case managers at MBL provide end-to-end management of the process, reducing the need for traditional managers. The managerial role is changing from one of controller and supervisor to one of supporter and facilitator.

Capture Information Once and at the Source

This last rule is simple. When information was difficult to transmit, it made sense to collect information repeatedly. Each person, department, or unit had its own requirements and forms. Companies simply had to live with the associated delays, entry errors, and costly overhead. But why do we have to live with those problems now? Today when we collect a piece of information, we can store it in an on-line database for all who need it. Bar coding, relational databases, and electronic data interchange (EDI) make it easy to collect, store, and transmit information. One insurance company found that its application review process required that certain items be entered into 'stovepipe' computer systems supporting different functions as many as five times. By integrating and connecting these systems, the company was able to eliminate this redundant data entry along with the attendant checking functions and inevitable errors.

Think Big

Reengineering triggers changes of many kinds, not just of the business process itself. Job designs, organizational structures, management systems – anything associated with the process must be refashioned in an integrated way. In other words, reengineering is a tremendous effort that mandates change in many areas of the organization.

When Ford reengineered its payables, receiving clerks on the dock had to learn to use computer terminals to check shipments, and they had to make decisions about whether to accept the goods. Purchasing agents also had to assume new responsibilities – like making sure the purchase orders they entered into the database had the correct information about where to send the check. Attitudes toward vendors also had to change: vendors could no longer be seen as adversaries; they had to become partners in a shared business process. Vendors too had to adjust. In many cases, invoices formed the basis of their accounting systems. At least one Ford supplier adapted by continuing to print invoices, but instead of sending them to Ford threw them away, reconciling cash received against invoices never sent.

The changes at Mutual Benefit Life were also widespread. The company's job-rating scheme could not accommodate the case manager position, which had a lot of responsibility but no direct reports. MBL had to devise new job-rating schemes and compensation policies. It also had to develop a culture in which people doing work are perceived as more important than those supervising work. Career paths, recruitment and training programs, promotion policies – these and many other management systems are being revised to support the new process design.

The extent of these changes suggests one factor that is necessary for reengineering to succeed: executive leadership with real vision. No one in an organization wants reengineering. It is confusing and disruptive and affects everything people have grown accustomed to. Only if top-level managers back the effort and outlast the company cynics will people take reengineering seriously. As one wag at an electronics equipment manufacturer has commented, 'Every few months, our senior managers find a new religion. One time it was quality, another it was customer service, another it was flattening the organization. We just hold our breath until they get over it and things get back to normal.' Commitment, consistency – maybe even a touch of fanaticism – are needed to enlist those who would prefer the status quo.

Considering the inertia of old processes and structures, the strain of implementing a reengineering plan can hardly be overestimated. But by the same token, it is hard to overestimate the opportunities, especially for established companies. Big, traditional organizations aren't necessarily dinosaurs doomed to extinction, but they are burdened with layers of unproductive overhead and armies of unproductive workers. Shedding them a layer at a time will not be good enough to stand up against sleek startups or streamlined Japanese companies. US companies need fast change and dramatic improvements.

We have the tools to do what we need to do. Information technology offers many options for reorganizing work. But our imaginations must guide our decisions about technology – not the other way around. We must have the boldness to imagine taking 78 days out of an 80–day turnaround time, cutting 75 percent of overhead, and eliminating 80 percent of errors. These are not unrealistic goals. If managers have the vision, reengineering will provide a way.

Reading 2   Kaizen

By Masaaki Imai[†]

Back in the 1950s, I was working with the Japan Productivity Center in Washington, D.C. My job mainly consisted of escorting groups of Japanese businessmen who were visiting American companies to study 'the secret of American industrial productivity.' Toshiro Yamada, now Professor Emeritus of the Faculty of Engineering at Kyoto University, was a member of one such study team visiting the United States to study the industrial-vehicle industry. Recently, the members of his team gathered to celebrate the silver anniversary of their trip.

At the banquet table, Yamada said he had recently been back to the United States in a 'sentimental journey' to some of the plants he had visited, among them the River Rouge steelworks in Dearborn, Michigan. Shaking his head in disbelief, he said, 'You know, the plant was exactly the same as it had been 25 years ago.'

These conversations set me to thinking about the great differences in the ways Japanese and Western managers approach their work. It is inconceivable that a Japanese plant would remain virtually unchanged for over a quarter of a century.

I had long been looking for a key concept to explain these two very different management approaches, one that might also help explain why many Japanese companies have come to gain their increasingly conspicuous competitive edge. For instance, how do we explain the fact that while most new ideas come from the West and some of the most advanced plants, institutions, and technologies are found there, there are also many plants there that have changed little since the 1950s?

Change is something which everybody takes for granted. Recently, an American executive at a large multinational firm told me his company chairman had said at the start of an executive committee meeting: 'Gen-

[†] Source: This article was adapted with permission from chapter 1 and 2 of *Kaizen: The Key to Japan's Competitive Success*, McGraw-Hill, New York, 1986.

tlemen, our job is to manage change. If we fail, we must change management.' The executive smiled and said, 'We all got the message!'

In Japan, change is a way of life, too. But are we talking about the same change when we talk about managing change or else changing management? It dawned on me that there might be different kinds of change: gradual and abrupt. While we can easily observe both gradual and abrupt changes in Japan, gradual change is not so obvious a part of the Western way of life. How are we to explain this difference?

This question led me to consider the question of values. Could it be that differences between the value systems in Japan and the West account for their different attitudes toward gradual change and abrupt change? Abrupt changes are easily grasped by everyone concerned, and people are usually elated to see them. This is generally true in both Japan and the West. Yet what about the gradual changes? My earlier statement that it is inconceivable that a Japanese plant would remain unchanged for years refers to gradual change as well as abrupt change.

Thinking all this over, I came to the conclusion that the key difference between how change is understood in Japan and how it is viewed in the West lies in the Kaizen concept – a concept that is so natural and obvious to many Japanese managers that they often do not even realize that they possess it! The Kaizen concept explains why companies cannot remain the same for long in Japan. Moreover, after many years of studying Western business practices, I have reached the conclusion that this Kaizen concept is non-existent, or at least very weak, in most Western companies today. Worse yet, they reject it without knowing what it really entails. It's the old 'not invented here' syndrome. And this lack of Kaizen helps explain why an American or European factory can remain exactly the same for a quarter of a century.

The essence of Kaizen is simple and straightforward: Kaizen means improvement. Moreover, Kaizen means ongoing improvement involving everyone, including both managers and workers. The Kaizen philosophy assumes that our way of life – be it our working life, our social life, or our home life – deserves to be constantly improved.

In trying to understand Japan's postwar 'economic miracle,' scholars, journalists, and businesspeople alike have dutifully studied such factors as the productivity movement, total quality control (TQC), small-group activities, the suggestion system, automation, industrial robots, and labor relations. They have given much attention to some of Japan's unique management practices, among them the lifetime employment system, seniority-based wages, and enterprise unions. Yet I feel they have failed to grasp the very simple truth that lies behind the many myths concerning Japanese management.

The essence of most 'uniquely Japanese' management practices – be they productivity improvement, TQC (Total Quality Control) activities, QC (Quality Control) circles, or labor relations – can be reduced to one word: Kaizen. Using the term Kaizen in place of such words as productivity, TQC, ZD (Zero Defects), *kamban*, and the suggestion system paints a far clearer picture of what has been going on in Japanese industry. Kaizen is an umbrella concept covering most of those 'uniquely Japanese' practices that have recently achieved such world-wide fame.

The implications of TQC or CWQC (Company-Wide Quality Control) in Japan have been that these concepts have helped Japanese companies generate a process-oriented way of thinking and develop strategies that assure continuous improvement involving people at all levels of the organizational hierarchy. The message of the Kaizen strategy is that not a day should go by without some kind of improvement being made somewhere in the company.

The belief that there should be unending improvement is deeply ingrained in the Japanese mentality. As the old Japanese saying goes, 'If a man has not been seen for three days, his friends should take a good look at him to see what changes have befallen him.' The implication is that he must have changed in three days, so his friends should be attentive enough to notice the changes.

After World War II, most Japanese companies had to start literally from the ground up. Every day brought new challenges to managers and workers alike, and every day meant progress. Simply staying in business required unending progress, and Kaizen has become a way of life. It was also fortunate that the various tools that helped elevate this Kaizen concept to new heights were introduced to Japan in the late 1950s and early 1960s by such experts as W. E. Deming and J. M. Juran. However, most new concepts, systems, and tools that are widely used in Japan today have subsequently been developed in Japan and represent qualitative improvements upon the statistical quality control and total quality control of the 1960s.

Kaizen and Management

Figure 4.3 shows how job functions are perceived in Japan. As indicated, management has two major components: maintenance and improvement. Maintenance refers to activities directed toward maintaining current technological, managerial, and operating standards; improvement refers to those directed toward improving current standards.

Under its maintenance functions, management performs its assigned tasks so that everybody in the company can follow the established SOP (Standard Operating Procedure). This means that management must first establish policies, rules, directives, and procedures for all major operations and then see to it that everybody follows SOP. If people are able to follow the standard but do not, management must

FIGURE 4.3
Japanese perceptions of job functions

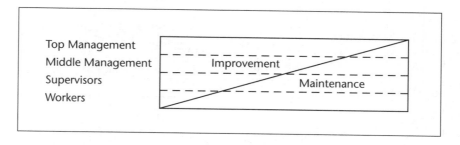

introduce discipline. If people are unable to follow the standard, management must either provide training or review and revise the standard so that people can follow it.

In any business, an employee's work is based on existing standards, either explicit or implicit, imposed by management. Maintenance refers to maintaining such standards through training and discipline. By contrast, improvement refers to improving the standards. The Japanese perception of management boils down to one precept: maintain and improve standards.

The higher up the manager is, the more he is concerned with improvement. At the bottom level, an unskilled worker working at a machine may spend all his time following instructions. However, as he becomes more proficient at his work, he begins to think about improvement. He begins to contribute to improvements in the way his work is done, either through individual suggestions or through group suggestions.

Ask any manager at a successful Japanese company what top management is pressing for, and the answer will be, 'Kaizen' (improvement). Improving standards means establishing higher standards. Once this is done, it becomes management's maintenance job to see that the new standards are observed. Lasting improvement is achieved only when people work to higher standards. Maintenance and improvement have thus become inseparable for most Japanese managers.

What is improvement? Improvement can be broken down between Kaizen and innovation. Kaizen signifies small improvements made in the status quo as a result of ongoing efforts. Innovation involves a drastic improvement in the status quo as a result of a large investment in new technology and/or equipment. Figure 4.4 shows the breakdown among maintenance, Kaizen, and innovation as perceived by Japanese management.

On the other hand, most Western managers' perceptions of job

FIGURE 4.4
Japanese vs Western perceptions of job functions

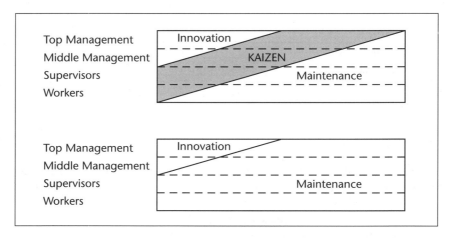

functions are as shown in Figure 4.4. There is little room in Western management for the Kaizen concept.

Sometimes, another type of management is found in the high-technology industries. These are the companies that are born running, grow rapidly, and then disappear just as rapidly when their initial success wanes or markets change.

The worst companies are those which do nothing but maintenance, meaning there is no internal drive for Kaizen or innovation, change is forced on management by market conditions and competition and management does not know where it wants to go.

Implications of QC for Kaizen

While management is usually concerned with such issues as productivity and quality, the thrust of this article is to look at the other side of the picture – at Kaizen.

The starting point for improvement is to recognize the need. This comes from recognition of a problem. If no problem is recognized, there is no recognition of the need for improvement. Complacency is the archenemy of Kaizen. Therefore, Kaizen emphasizes problem-awareness and provides clues for identifying problems.

Once identified, problems must be solved. Thus Kaizen is also a problem-solving process. In fact, Kaizen requires the use of various problem-solving tools. Improvement reaches new heights with every problem that is solved. In order to consolidate the new level, however, the improvement must be standardized. Thus Kaizen also requires standardization.

Such terms as QC (Quality Control), SQC (Statistical Quality Control), QC circles, and TQC (or CWQC) often appear in connection with Kaizen. To avoid unnecessary confusion, it may be helpful to clarify these terms here.

The word *quality* has been interpreted in many different ways, and there is no agreement on what actually constitutes quality. In its broadest sense, quality is anything that can be improved. In this context, quality is associated not only with products and services but also with the way people work, the way machines are operated, and the way systems and procedures are dealt with. It includes all aspects of human behavior. This is why it is more useful to talk about Kaizen than about quality or productivity.

The English term *improvement* as used in the Western context more often than not means improvement in equipment, thus excluding the human elements. By contrast, Kaizen is generic and can be applied to every aspect of everybody's activities. This said, however, it must be admitted that such terms as quality and quality control have played a vital role in the development of Kaizen in Japan.

In March 1950, the Union of Japanese Scientists and Engineers (JUSE) started publishing its magazine *Statistical Quality Control*. In July of the same year, W. E. Deming was invited to Japan to teach statistical quality control at an eight-day seminar organized by JUSE. Deming visited Japan several times in the 1950s, and it was during one of those visits that he made his famous prediction that Japan would soon be flooding the world market with quality products.

Deming also introduced the 'Deming cycle,' one of the crucial QC tools for assuring continuous improvement, to Japan. The Deming cycle is also called the Deming wheel or the PDCA (Plan-Do-Check-Action) cycle (see Figure 4.5). Deming stressed the importance of constant interaction among research, design, production, and sales in order for a company to arrive at better quality that satisfies customers. He taught that this wheel should be rotated on the ground of quality-first perceptions and quality-first responsibility. With this process, he argued, the company could win consumer confidence and acceptance and prosper.

In July 1954, J.M. Juran was invited to Japan to conduct a JUSE seminar on quality-control management. This was the first time QC was dealt with from the overall management perspective.

In 1956, Japan Shortwave Radio included a course on quality control as part of its educational programming. In November 1960, the first national quality month was inaugurated. It was also in 1960 that Q-marks and Q-flags were formally adopted. Then in April 1962 the magazine *Quality Control for the Foreman* was launched by JUSE, and the first QC circle was started that same year.

FIGURE 4.5
Deming wheel

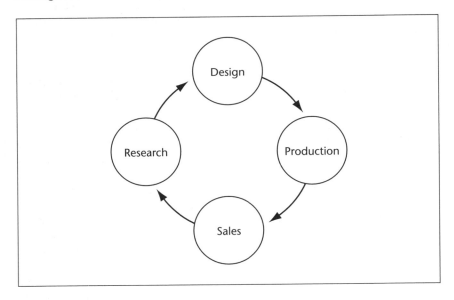

A QC circle is defined as a small group that *voluntarily* performs quality-control activities within the shop. The small group carries out its work continuously as part of a company-wide program of quality control, self-development, mutual education, and flow-control and improvement within the workshop. The QC circle is only *part* of a company-wide program; it is never the whole of TQC or CWQC.

Those who have followed QC circles in Japan know that they often focus on such areas as cost, safety, and productivity, and that their activities sometimes relate only indirectly to product-quality improvement. For the most part, these activities are aimed at making improvements in the workshop.

There is no doubt that QC circles have played an important part in improving product quality and productivity in Japan. However, their role has often been blown out of proportion by overseas observers who believe that QC circles are the mainstay of TQC activities in Japan. Nothing could be further from the truth, especially when it comes to Japanese management. Efforts related to QC circles generally account for only 10 percent to 30 percent of the overall TQC effort in Japanese companies.

What is less visible behind these developments is the transformation of the term quality control, or QC, in Japan. As is the case in many Western companies, quality control initially meant quality control applied to the manufacturing process, particularly the inspections for rejecting defective incoming material or defective outgoing products at the end of the production line. But very soon the realization set in that inspection alone does nothing to improve the quality of the product, and that product quality should be built at the production stage. 'Build quality into the process' was (and still is) a popular phrase in Japanese quality control. It is at this stage that control charts and the other tools for statistical quality control were introduced after Deming's lectures.

Juran's lectures in 1954 opened up another aspect of quality control: the managerial approach to quality control. This was the first time the term QC was positioned as a vital management tool in Japan. From then on, the term QC has been used to mean both quality control and the tools for overall improvement in managerial performance.

Initially, QC was applied in heavy industries such as the steel industry. Since these industries required instrumentation control, the application of SQC tools was vital for maintaining quality. As QC spread to the machinery and automobile industries, where controlling the process was essential in building quality into the product, the need for SQC became even greater.

At a later stage, other industries started to introduce QC for such products as consumer durables and home appliances. In these industries, the interest was in building quality in at the design stage to meet changing and increasingly stringent customer requirements. Today, management has gone beyond the design stage and has begun to stress the importance of quality product development, which means taking customer-related information and market research into account from the very start.

All this while, QC has grown into a full-fledged management tool for Kaizen involving everyone in the company. Such company-wide activities are often referred to as TQC (total quality control) or CWQC (company-wide quality control). No matter which name is used, TQC and CWQC mean company-wide Kaizen activities involving everyone in the company, managers and workers alike. Over the years, QC has been elevated to SQC and then to TQC or CWQC, improving managerial performance at every level. Thus it is that such words as QC and TQC have come to be almost synonymous with Kaizen. This is also why I constantly refer to QC, TQC, and CWQC in explaining Kaizen.

On the other hand, the function of quality control in its original sense remains valid. Quality assurance remains a vital part of management, and most companies have a QA (quality assurance) department for this. To confuse matters, TQC or CWQC activities are sometimes administered by the QA department and sometimes by a separate TQC office. Thus it is important that these QC-related words be understood in the context in which they appear.

Kaizen and TQC

Considering the TQC movement in Japan as part of the Kaizen movement gives us a clearer perspective on the Japanese approach. First of all, it should be pointed out that TQC activities in Japan are not concerned solely with quality control. People have been fooled by the term 'quality control' and have often construed it within the narrow discipline of product-quality control. In the West, the term QC is mostly associated with inspection of finished products, and when QC is brought up in discussion, top managers, who generally assume they have very little to do with quality control, lose interest immediately.

It is unfortunate that in the West TQC has been dealt with mainly in technical journals when it is more properly the focus of management journals. Japan has developed an elaborate system of Kaizen strategies as management tools within the TQC movement. These rank among this century's most outstanding management achievements. Yet because of the limited way in which QC is understood in the West, most Western students of Japanese QC activities have failed to grasp their real significance and challenge. At the same time, new TQC methods and tools are constantly being studied and tested.

TQC in Japan is a movement centered on the improvement of managerial performance at all levels. As such, it has typically dealt with:

1   quality assurance;

2   cost reduction;

3   meeting production quotas;

4   meeting delivery schedules;

5   safety;

6   new-product development;

7   productivity improvement;

8   supplier management.

More recently, TQC has come to include marketing, sales, and service as well. Furthermore, TQC has dealt with such crucial management concerns as organizational development, cross-functional management, policy deployment, and quality deployment. In other words, management has been using TQC as a tool for improving overall performance.

Those who have closely followed QC circles in Japan know that their activities are often focused on such areas as cost, safety and productivity, and that their activities may only indirectly relate to product-quality improvement. For the most part, these activities are aimed at making improvements in the workplace.

Management efforts for TQC have been directed mostly at such areas as education, systems development, policy deployment, cross-functional management and, more recently, quality deployment.

Kaizen and the Suggestion System

Japanese management makes a concerted effort to involve employees in Kaizen through suggestions. Thus, the suggestion system is an integral part of the established management system, and the number of workers' suggestions is regarded as an important criterion in reviewing the performance of these workers' supervisor. The manager of the supervisors is in turn expected to assist them so that they can help workers generate more suggestions.

Most Japanese companies active in Kaizen programs have a quality-control system and a suggestion system working in concert. The role of QC circles may be better understood if we regard them collectively as a group-oriented suggestion system for making improvements.

One of the outstanding features of Japanese management is that it generates a great number of suggestions from workers and that management works hard to consider these suggestions, often incorporating them into the overall Kaizen strategy. It is not uncommon for top management of a leading Japanese company to spend a whole day listening to presentations of activities by QC circles, and giving awards based on predetermined criteria. Management is willing to give recognition to employees' efforts for improvements and makes its concern visible wherever possible. Often, the number of suggestions is posted individually on the wall of the work-place in order to encourage competition among workers and among groups.

Another important aspect of the suggestion system is that each suggestion, once implemented, leads to a revised standard. For instance, when a special foolproof device has been installed on a machine at a worker's suggestion, this may require the worker to work differently and, at times, more attentively.

However, inasmuch as the new standard has been set up by the worker's own volition, he takes pride in the new standard and is willing to follow it. If, on the contrary, he is told to follow a standard imposed by management, he may not be as willing to follow it.

Thus, through suggestions, employees can participate in Kaizen in the workplace and play a vital role in upgrading standards. In a recent interview, Toyota Motor chairman Eiji Toyoda said, 'One of the features of the Japanese workers is that they use their brains as well as their hands.

Our workers provide 1.5 million suggestions a year, and 95 percent of them are put to practical use. There is an almost tangible concern for improvement in the air at Toyota.'

Kaizen vs. Innovation

There are two contrasting approaches to progress: the gradualist approach and the great-leap-forward approach. Japanese companies generally favor the gradualist approach and Western companies the great-leap approach – an approach epitomized by the term 'innovation'.

Western management worships at the altar of innovation. This innovation is seen as major changes in the wake of technological breakthroughs, or the introduction of the latest management concepts or production techniques. Innovation is dramatic, a real attention-getter. Kaizen, on the other hand, is often undramatic and subtle, and its results are seldom immediately visible. While Kaizen is a continuous process, innovation is generally a one-shot phenomenon.

In the West, for example, a middle manager can usually obtain top management support for such projects as CAD (computer-aided design), CAM (computer-aided manufacture), and MRP (materials requirements planning), since these are innovative projects that have a way of revolutionizing existing systems. As such, they offer ROI (return on investment) benefits that managers can hardly resist.

However, when a factory manager wishes, for example, to make small changes in the way his workers use the machinery, such as working out multiple job assignments or realigning production processes (both of which may require lengthy discussions with the union as well as re-education and retraining of workers), obtaining management support can be difficult indeed.

Table 4.2 compares the main features of Kaizen and of innovation. One of the beautiful things about Kaizen is that it does not necessarily require sophisticated technique or state-of-the-art technology. To implement Kaizen, you need only simple, conventional techniques. Often, common sense is all that is needed. On the other hand, innovation usually requires highly sophisticated technology, as well as a huge investment.

Kaizen is like a hotbed that nurtures small and ongoing changes, while innovation is like magma that appears in abrupt eruptions from time to time.

One big difference between Kaizen and innovation is that while Kaizen does not necessarily call for a large investment to implement it, it does call for a great deal of continuous effort and commitment. The difference between the two opposing concepts may thus be likened to

TABLE 4.2
Features of Kaizen and innovation

	Kaizen	Innovation
1. Effect	Long-term and long-lasting but undramatic	Short-term but dramatic
2. Pace	Small steps	Big steps
3. Timeframe	Continuous and incremental	Intermittent and non-incremental
4. Change	Gradual and constant	Abrupt and volatile
5. Involvement	Everybody	Select few 'champions'
6. Approach	Collectivism, group efforts, systems approach	Rugged individualism, individual ideas and efforts
7. Mode	Maintenance and improvement	Scrap and rebuild
8. Spark	Conventional know-how and state of the art	Technological break-throughs, new inventions, new theories
9. Practical requirements	Requires little investment but great effort to maintain it	Requires large investment but little effort to maintain it
10. Effort orientation	People	Technology
11. Evaluation criteria	Process and efforts for better results	Results and profits
12. Advantage	Works well in slow-growth economy	Better suited to fast-growth economy

that of a staircase and a slope. The innovation strategy is supposed to bring about progress in a staircase progression. On the other hand, the Kaizen strategy brings about gradual progress. I say the innovation strategy 'is supposed to' bring about progress in a staircase progression, because it usually does not. Instead of following the staircase pattern, the actual progress achieved through innovation will generally follow the pattern shown in Figure 4.5, if it lacks the Kaizen strategy to go along with it. This happens because a system, once it has been installed as a result of new innovation, is subject to steady deterioration unless continuing efforts are made first to maintain it and then to improve on it.

In reality, there can be no such thing as a static constant. All systems are destined to deteriorate once they have been established. One of the famous Parkinson's Laws is that an organization, once it

FIGURE 4.5
Innovation alone

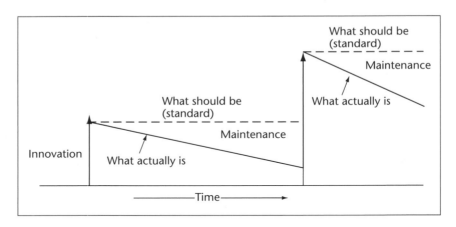

has built its edifice, begins its decline. In other words, there must be a continuing effort for improvement to even maintain the status quo.

When such effort is lacking, decline is inevitable (see Figure 4.5). Therefore, even when an innovation makes a revolutionary standard of performance attainable, the new performance level will decline unless the standard is constantly challenged and upgraded. Thus, whenever an innovation is achieved, it must be followed by a series of Kaizen efforts to maintain and improve it (see Figure 4.6).

Whereas innovation is a one-shot deal whose effects are gradually eroded by intense competition and deteriorating standards, Kaizen is an ongoing effort with cumulative effects marking a steady rise as the years go by. If standards exist only in order to maintain the status quo, they will not be challenged so long as the level of performance is acceptable. Kaizen, on the other hand, means a constant effort not only to maintain but also to upgrade standards. Kaizen strategists believe that standards are by nature tentative, akin to stepping stones, with one standard leading to another as continuing improvement efforts are made. This is the reason why QC circles no sooner solve one problem than they move on to tackle a new problem. This is also the reason why the so-called PDCA (plan-do-check-action) cycle receives so much emphasis in Japan's TQC movement.

Another feature of Kaizen is that it requires virtually everyone's personal efforts. In order for the Kaizen spirit to survive, management must make a conscious and continuous effort to support it. Such support is quite different from the fanfare recognition that management accords to people who have achieved a striking success or breakthrough. Kaizen is

FIGURE 4.6
Innovation plus Kaizen

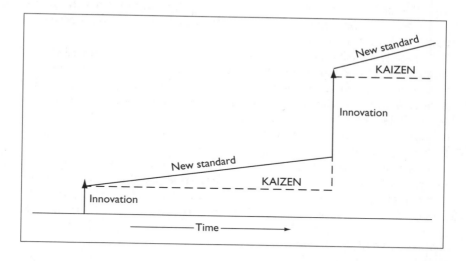

concerned more with the process than with the result. The strength of Japanese management lies in its successful development and implementation of a system that acknowledges the ends while emphasizing the means.

Thus Kaizen calls for a substantial management commitment of time and effort. Infusions of capital are no substitute for this investment in time and effort. Investing in Kaizen means investing in people. In short, Kaizen is people-oriented, whereas innovation is technology- and money-oriented.

Finally, the Kaizen philosophy is better suited to a slow-growth economy, while innovation is better suited to a fast-growth economy. While Kaizen advances inch-by-inch on the strength of many small efforts, innovation leaps upward in hopes of landing at a much higher plateau in spite of gravitational inertia and the weight of investment costs. In a slow-growth economy characterized by high costs of energy and materials, overcapacity, and stagnant markets, Kaizen often has a better payoff than innovation does.

As one Japanese executive recently remarked, 'It is extremely difficult to increase sales by 10 percent. But it is not so difficult to cut manufacturing costs by 10 percent to even better effect.'

I argued that the concept of Kaizen is nonexistent or at best weak in most Western companies today. However, there was a time, not so long ago, when Western management also placed a high priority on Kaizen-like improvement-consciousness. Older executives may recall that before the phenomenal economic growth of the late 1950s and early 1960s, management attended assiduously to improving all aspects of the business, particularly the factory. In those days, every small improvement was counted and was seen as effective in terms of building success.

People who worked with small, privately owned companies may recall with a touch of nostalgia that there was a genuine concern for improvement 'in the air' before the company was bought out or went public. As soon as that happened, the quarterly P/L (profit/loss) figures suddenly became the most important criterion, and management became obsessed with the bottom line, often at the expense of pressing for constant and unspectacular improvements.

For many other companies, the greatly increased market opportunities and technological innovations that appeared during the first two decades after World War II meant that developing new products based on the new technology was much more attractive or 'sexier' than slow, patient efforts for improvement. In trying to catch up with the ever-increasing market demand, managers boldly introduced one innovation after another, and they were content to ignore the seemingly minor benefits of improvement.

Most Western managers who joined the ranks during or after those heady days do not have the slightest concern for improvement. Instead, they take an offensive posture, armed with professional expertise geared toward making big changes in the name of innovation, bringing about immediate gains, and winning instant recognition and promotion. Before they knew it, Western managers had lost sight of improvement and put all their eggs in the innovation basket.

Another factor that has abetted the innovation approach has been the increasing emphasis on financial controls and accounting. By now, the more sophisticated companies have succeeded in establishing elaborate accounting and reporting systems that force managers to account for every action they take and to spell out the precise payout or ROI of every managerial decision. Such a system does not lend itself to building a favorable climate for improvement.

Improvement is by definition slow, gradual, and often invisible, with effects that are felt over the long run. In my opinion, the most glaring and significant shortcoming of Western management today is the lack of improvement philosophy. There is no internal system in Western management to reward efforts for improvement; instead, everyone's job performance is reviewed strictly on the basis of results. Thus it is not uncommon for Western managers to chide people with, 'I don't care what you do or how you do it. I want the results – and now!' This emphasis on results has led to the innovation-dominated approach of the West. This is not to say that Japanese management does not care about innovation. But Japanese managers have enthusiastically pursued Kaizen even when they were involved in innovation.

Strategic Change in International Perspective

Wisdom lies neither in fixity nor in change, but in the dialectic between the two.

(Octavio Paz 1914–1998; Mexican poet and essayist)

Again it has become clear that there is little consensus within the field of strategic management. Views on the best way to accomplish strategic change differ sharply. Even authors from one and the same country exhibit strikingly divergent perspectives on how to deal with the paradox of revolution and evolution.

Provocatively, the article by Imai explicitly introduced the international dimension, suggesting that there are specific national preferences in approach to strategic change. He argues that 'Japanese companies generally favor the gradualist approach and Western companies the great-leap approach – an approach epitomized by the term innovation. Western management worships at the altar of innovation.' This general, yet fundamental, distinction is supported by other researchers such as Ouchi, Pascale and Athos, and Kagono *et al.*[23], although all of these international comparative studies concentrate only on US–Japanese differences. The extensive study by Kagono and his colleagues among the top 1000 American and Japanese companies concludes that there are clearly different national change styles: 'The US-style elite-guided, logical, deductive approach achieves major innovation in strategies geared to surpass other companies. In contrast, the Japanese inductive, step-wise gradual adjustment approach seeks to steadily build upon the existing strengths to *evolve* strategy'[24]. Other authors suggest that the US and Japan seem to represent the two extremes, while most other industrialized countries seem to be somewhere in between[25].

Such pronounced international variance raises the question of cause. Why do firms in different countries prefer such significantly different approaches to strategic change? Which factors determine the existence of national strategic change styles? Answers to these questions might assist in defining the most appropriate context for discontinuous change, as opposed to circumstances in which continuous change would be more fitting. Understanding international dissimilarities and their roots should help to clarify whether firms in different countries can borrow practices from one another, or are limited by their national context.

As a stimulus to the international dimension of this debate, a short overview will be given of the country characteristics mentioned in the literature as the major influences on how the paradox of revolution and evolution is dealt with in different national settings. It should be noted, however, that cross-cultural research on this topic has not been extensive. Therefore, the propositions brought forward here should be viewed as tentative explanations, intended to encourage further discussion and research.

Prevalence of Mechanistic Organizations

At the end of Chapter 3, the international differences in organizing work were briefly discussed. It was argued that in some countries the machine bureaucracy is a particularly dominant form of organization, while in other countries organizations are more organic. The machine bureaucracy, that is more predominant in English-speaking countries and France, is characterized by clear hierarchical authority relationships, strict differentiation of tasks, and highly formalized communication, information, budgeting, planning and decision-making systems. In such organizations, there is a relatively clear line separating the officers (management) from the troops, and internal relationships are depersonalized and calculative. In more organic forms of organization, management and production activities are not strictly separated, leading to less emphasis on top-down decision-making, and more on bottom-up initiatives. Job descriptions are less strictly defined and control systems are less sophisticated. Integration within the organization is not achieved by these formal systems, but by extensive informal communication and consultation, both horizontally and vertically, and by a strong common set of beliefs and a shared corporate vision. Internal relationships are based on trust, cooperation and a sense of community, leading Ouchi[26] to call such organizations clans. This type of organization is more prevalent in Japan, and to a lesser extent in, for example, Germany, the Netherlands and the Nordic countries.

Various researchers have suggested that machine bureaucracies exhibit a high level of inertia[27]. Once formal systems have been created, they become difficult to change. As soon as particular tasks are specified and assigned to a person or group, it becomes their turf, while all else is 'not their business'. Once created, hierarchical positions, giving status and power, are not easily abolished. The consequence, it is argued, is that machine bureaucracies are inherently more resistant to change than clan-like organizations[28]. Therefore, revolution is usually the potent mode of change needed to make any significant alterations. It can be expected that in countries where organizations are more strongly mechanistic, the preference for the discontinuous change perspective will be more pronounced.

Clan-like organizations, on the other hand, are characterized by a strong capacity for self-organization – the ability to exhibit organized behavior without a boss being in control[29]. They are better at fluidly, and spontaneously, reorganizing around new issues because of a lack of rigid structure, the close links between management and production tasks, the high level of group-oriented information-sharing and consensual decision-making, and the strong commitment of individuals to the organization, and vice versa. In countries where organizations are more organic in this way, a stronger preference for the continuous change perspective can be expected. This issue will be discussed in more length in Chapter 9.

Position of Employees

This second factor is partially linked to the first. A mechanistic organization, it could be said, is a system, into which groups of people have been brought, while an organic organization is a group of people, into which some system has been brought. In a machine bureaucracy, people are human resources *for* the organization, while in a clan, people *are* the organization. These two conceptions of organization represent radically different views on the position and roles of employees within organizations.

In mechanistic organizations, employees are seen as valuable, yet expendable, resources utilized by the organization. Salaries are determined by the prices on the labor market and the value-added by the individual employee. In the contractual relationship between employer and employee, it is a shrewd bargaining tactic for employers to minimize their dependence on employees. Organizational learning should, therefore, be captured in formalized systems and procedures, to avoid the irreplaceability of their people. Employees, on the other hand, will strive to make themselves indispensable for the organization, for instance by not sharing their learning. Furthermore, calculating employees will not tie themselves too strongly to the organization, but will keep their options open to job-hop to a better paying employer. None of these factors contribute to the long-term commitment and receptiveness for ambiguity and uncertainty needed for continuous change.

In clan-like organizations the tolerance for ambiguity and

uncertainty is higher, because employees' position within the organization is more secure. Information is more readily shared, as it does not need to be used as a bargaining chip and acceptance within the group demands being a team player. Employers can invest in people instead of systems, since employees are committed and loyal to the organization. These better trained people can consequently be given more decision-making power and more responsibility to organize their own work to fit with changing circumstances. Therefore, clan-like organizations, with their emphasis on employees as permanent co-producers, instead of temporary contractors, are more conducive to continuous change. It is in this context that Imai concludes that 'Investing in Kaizen means investing in people . . . Kaizen is people-oriented, whereas innovation is technology- and money-oriented.'

A number of factors have been brought forward to explain these international differences in the structuring of work and the position of employees. Some authors emphasize cultural aspects, particularly the level of individualism. It is argued that the mechanistic-organic distinction largely coincides with the individualism-collectivism division[30]. In this view, machine bureaucracies are the logical response to calculative individuals, while clans are more predominant in group-oriented cultures. Other authors point to international differences in labor markets[31]. High mobility of personnel would coincide with the existence of mechanistic organizations, while low mobility (e.g. life time employment) fits with organic forms. Yet others suggest that the abundance of skilled workers is important. Machine bureaucracies are suited to dealing with narrowly trained individuals requiring extensive supervision. Clan-like organizations, however, need skilled, self-managing workers, who can handle a wide variety of tasks with relative autonomy. Kogut[32] reports that the level of workers within a country with these qualifications 'has been found to rest significantly upon the quality of education, the existence of programs of apprenticeship and worker qualifications, and the elimination of occupational distinctions.'

Based on these arguments it can be proposed that the discontinuous change perspective will be more prevalent in countries with a more individualistic culture, high labor mobility, and less skilled workers. Conversely, the continuous change perspective will be more strongly rooted in countries with a group-oriented culture, low labor mobility, and skilled, self-managing workers.

Role of Top Management

The third factor is also related to the previous points. Various researchers have observed important international differences in leadership styles and the role of top management. In some countries, top management is looked at as the 'central processing unit' of the company, making the key decisions and commanding the behavior of the rest of the organizational machine. Visible top-down leadership is the norm and, therefore, strategic innovation and change are viewed as top management responsibilities[33]. Strategic changes are formulated by top managers and then implemented by lower levels. Top managers are given significant power and discretion to develop bold new initiatives and to overcome organizational resistance to change. If organizational advances are judged to be insufficient or if an organization ends up in a crisis situation, a change of top management is often viewed as a necessary measure to transform or turnaround the company[34]. In nations where people exhibit a strong preference for this commander type of leadership, an inclination towards the discontinuous change perspective can be expected.

In other countries, top managers are viewed as the captains of the team and leadership is less direct and less visible[35]. The role of top managers is to facilitate change and innovation among the members of the group. It is not necessarily the intention that top managers initiate entrepreneurial activities themselves. Change comes from within the body of the organization, instead of being imposed upon it by top management. Therefore, change under this type of leadership will usually be more evolutionary than revolutionary. In nations where people exhibit a strong preference for this servant type of leadership, an inclination towards the continuous change perspective is more likely.

Time Orientation

At the end of Chapter 3, a distinction was made between cultures that are more oriented towards the past, the present, and the future. Obviously, it can be expected that cultures with a past or present orientation will be much less inclined towards change, than future-oriented cultures. Among these future-minded cultures, a further division was made between those with a long-term and a short-term orientation.

Various researchers have argued that short-term oriented cultures exhibit a much stronger preference for fast, radical change than cultures with a longer time horizon. In short-term oriented cultures, such as the English-speaking countries, there are significant pressures for rapid results, which predisposes managers towards revolutionary change. The sensitivity to stock prices especially is often cited as a major factor encouraging firms to focus on short spurts of massive change and pay much less attention to efforts and investments with undramatic long-term benefits. Other contributing factors mentioned include short-term oriented bonus systems, stock option plans and frequent job-hopping[36].

In long-term oriented cultures, such as Japan, China and South Korea, there is much less pressure to achieve short-term results. There is broad awareness that firms are running a competitive marathon and that a high, but steady, pace of motion is needed. Generally, more emphasis is placed on facilitating long-term change processes, instead of intermittently moving from short-term change to short-term change. Frequently mentioned factors contributing to this long-term orientation include long-term employment relationships, the lack of short-term bonus systems and most importantly the accent on growth, as opposed to profit, as firms' prime objective[37]. This topic will be discussed at more length in Chapter 11.

Further Readings

Many excellent writings on the topic of strategic change are available, although most carry other labels, such as innovation, entrepreneurship, reengineering, renewal, revitalization, rejuvenation and learning. For a good overview of the literature, readers can consult 'Environmental Jolts and Industry Revolutions: Organizational Responses to Discontinuous Change,' by Alan Meyer, Geoffry Brooks and James Goes. Paul Strebel's book *Breakpoints: How Managers Exploit Radical Business Change* also provides a broad introduction to much of the work on change.

In the discontinuous change literature, Larry Greiner's article 'Evolution and Revolution as Organizations Grow' is a classic well worth reading. Danny Miller and Peter Friesen's landmark book *Organizations: A Quantum View* is also stimulating, although not easily accessible. More readable books on radical change are *Rejuvenating the Mature Business* by Charles Baden-Fuller and John Stopford; *Sharpbenders: The Secrets of Unleashing Corporate Potential*, by Peter Grinyer, David Mayes and Peter McKiernan; *Crisis and Renewal*, by David Hurst. More 'hands-on' is Rosabeth Moss Kanter's *When Giants Learn to Dance*, and of course *Reengineering the Corporation: A Manifesto for Business Revolution*, by Michael Hammer and James Champy, which expands on the ideas discussed in Hammer's contribution in this chapter.

On the topic of innovation, Jim Utterback's book *Mastering the Dynamics of Innovation* provides a good overview, as does *Managing Innovation: Integrating Technological, Market and Organizational Change*, by Joe Tidd, John Bessant and Keith Pavitt. An excellent collection of cases is provided by Charles Baden-Fuller and Martyn Pitt, in their book *Strategic Innovation*.

Literature taking a continuous change perspective is less abundant, but no less interesting. Masaaki Imai's article in this chapter has been taken from his book *Kaizen: The Key to Japan's Competitive Success*, which is highly recommended. A more academic work that explains the continuous change view in detail is *Strategic vs. Evolutionary Management: A US-Japan Comparison of Strategy and Organization*, by Tadao Kagono, Ikujiro Nonaka, Kiyonori Sakakibara, and Akihiro Okumura. Ikujiro Nonaka's article 'Creating Organizational Order Out of Chaos: Self-Renewal in Japanese Firms' gives a good summary of this way of thinking. Peter Senge's book *The Fifth Discipline: The Art and Practice of the Learning Organization*, is also highly advised.

Finally, the award-winning article 'Ambidextrous Organizations: Managing Evolutionary and Revolutionary Change,' by Michael Tushman and Charles O'Reilly must be mentioned as a delightful reading, in particular with regard to the way in which the authors explicitly wrestle with the paradox of revolution and evolution. Their book *Winning Through Innovation: A Practical Guide to Leading Organizational Change and Renewal* is equally stimulating.

Strategy Content

Business Level Strategy

One does not gain much by mere cleverness.

(Marquis de Vauvenargues 1715–1747; French soldier and moralist)

Drive thy business; let it not drive thee.

(Benjamin Franklin 1706–1790; American writer and statesman)

The Paradox of Markets and Resources

The central question in this chapter is quite simple: 'What is the basis of a good strategy?' Are there characteristics that effective strategies have in common, that could be used as criteria for developing new strategies? Are there fundamental laws of strategy that could function as guiding principles for strategists? In short, what are the qualities of a successful strategy?

While the question may be straightforward, the answer seems less so, if the diversity of opinions among strategy theorists is taken as a measure. The variety of views on the topic is dauntingly large. Yet, at a fundamental level, two different perspectives on strategy can be identified, that underlie the broad spectrum of views observed within the field of strategic management. These two opposing outlooks are the *outside-in perspective* and the *inside-out perspective*. As in previous chapters, these two poles are based on diametrically opposed assumptions and arrive at distinct interpretations of actual behavior and recommended action. It is the intention of this chapter to structure the debate on the basic characteristics of a good strategy by presenting a limited number of readings illuminating the major differences between these two perspectives.

To understand the differences between the outside-in and inside-out perspectives, it is useful to start with their similarities. Both views accept four broad criteria that need to be met by a good strategy, as outlined by Rumelt[1]. Strategies must be *feasible* (implementable) and *consistent* (no mutually exclusive goals or policies), as well as capable of providing a competitive *advantage*. Furthermore, strategies must achieve *consonance* – a fit between the organization and its environment. It is the interpretation of these last two principles that forms the dividing line between the outside-in and inside-out perspectives.

While both views share the assumption that an alignment between the firm and the outside world must be established and maintained that assures competitive advantage, what divides them is their way of achieving such a fit. Should a company adapt itself to its surroundings or should it attempt to adapt the surroundings to itself? Should strategists take the environment as starting point, choose an advantageous market position and obtain the resources needed to implement this choice? Or should strategists take the organization's resource base (physical assets, competences and relationships) as starting point, selecting and/or adapting an environment to fit with these strengths? Creating alignment to achieve competitive advantage can go both ways, but which way is preferable?

This issue can also be expressed in terms of the classic SWOT framework, that suggests that a sound strategy should match the firm's strengths (S) and weaknesses (W) to the opportunities (O) and threats (T) encountered in the firm's environment. When striving for this match, should the firm be primarily strength driven or opportunity driven? What should be leading and what should be lagging?

The Outside-in Perspective

Strategists adopting an outside-in perspective believe that firms should not be self-centered, but should continuously take their environment as starting point when determining their strategy. Successful companies, it is argued, are *externally-oriented* and *market-driven*[2]. Such companies take their cues from customers and competitors, and use these signals to determine their own game plan. Strategists analyze the environment to identify attractive market opportunities. They search for potential customers whose needs could be better satisfied than currently done by other firms. The most attractive buyers are those willing and able to pay a premium price, and whose loyalty could be won, despite the efforts of the competition. Once these customers have been won over and a market position has been established, the firm must consistently defend or build on this position by adapting itself to changes in the environment. Shifts in customers' demands must be met, challenges from rival firms must be countered, impending market entries by outside firms must be rebuffed and excessive pricing by suppliers must be resisted. In short, to the outside-in strategist the game of strategy is about market positioning and understanding and responding to external developments. For this reason, the outside-in perspective is sometimes also referred to as the *positioning approach*[3].

Positioning is not short-term opportunistic behavior, but requires a strategic perspective, because superior market positions are difficult to attain, but once conquered can be the source of sustained profitability. Some proponents of the outside-in perspective argue that in each market a number of different positions can yield sustained profitability. For instance, Porter[4] suggests that companies that focus on a particular niche, and companies that strongly differentiate their product offering, can achieve strong and profitable market positions, even if another company has the lowest cost position. Other authors emphasize that the position of being market leader is particularly important[5]. Companies with a high market share profit more from economies of scale, benefit from risk aversion among customers, have more bargaining power towards buyers and suppliers, and can more easily flex their muscles to prevent new entrants and block competitive attacks.

Unsurprisingly, outside-in strategists argue that insight into markets and industries is essential. Not only the general structure of markets and industries needs to be analyzed, but also the specific demands, strengths, positions and intentions of all major forces need to be determined. For instance, buyers must be understood, with regard to their needs, wants, perceptions, decision-making processes and bargaining chips. The same holds true for suppliers, competitors, potential market and/or industry entrants, and providers of substitute products. Once a strategist knows 'what makes the market tick' – sometimes referred to as the *rules of the game* – a position can be identified within the market that could give the firm bargaining power *vis-à-vis* suppliers and buyers, while keeping competitors at bay. Of course, the wise strategist will not only emphasize winning under the current rules with the current players, but will attempt to anticipate market and industry developments, and position the firm to benefit from these. Many outside-in advocates even advise firms to initiate market and industry changes, so that they can be the first to benefit from the altered rules of the game (this issue will be discussed in further length in Chapter 8).

Proponents of the outside-in perspective readily acknowledge the importance of firm resources for cashing in on market opportunities the firm has identified. If the firm does not have, or is not able to develop or obtain, the necessary resources to implement a particular strategy, then specific opportunities will be unrealizable. Therefore, strategists should always keep the firm's strengths and weaknesses in mind when choosing an external position, to ensure that it remains feasible. Yet, to the outside-in strategist, the firm's current resource base should not be the starting point when determining strategy, but should merely be acknowledged as a potentially limiting condition on the firm's ability to implement the best market strategy. In general, therefore, the outside-in approach can be summarized as that of 'resource base follows market position' – the organization's resource base is adapted to fit the market position selected.

The Inside-out Perspective

Strategists adopting an inside-out perspective argue that strategies should not be built around external opportunities, but around a company's strengths. They believe that organizations should focus on the development of difficult-to-imitate competences and/or on the acquisition of exclusive assets. This unique resource base should be used as the starting point of strategy formation. Markets should subsequently be chosen, adapted or created to exploit these specific strengths. Identifying which company resources have to be further developed and applying them to various environmental opportunities is what strategy is all about.

Many strategists taking an inside-out perspective tend to emphasize the importance of the firm's competences over its tangible resources (physical assets). Their views are more specifically referred to as *competence-based*[6] or *capabilities-based*[7] perspectives on strategy. They argue that building up unique abilities is a strenuous and lengthy process, that can have both positive and negative consequences. On the positive side, once a company has developed a distinctive ability, it is usually difficult for competitors to imitate such a strength. And while rivals try to catch up, a company with an initial lead can try to upgrade its competences in the race to stay ahead[8]. On the negative side, the laborious task of building up competences makes it difficult to switch to other competences if that is what the market demands[9]. In the same way, few concert pianists are able (and willing) to switch to playing saxophone when they are out of a job. From an inside-out perspective, both companies and concert pianists should first try to build on their unique competences and attempt to find or create a more suitable market, instead of reactively adapting to the unpredictable whims of the current environment. In other words, the approach is that of 'market position follows resource base' – the market position selected is adapted to fit the organization's resource base.

The question for the field of strategic management is, therefore, whether business strategies are formed and should be formed outside-in or inside-out. Is it better to be market-driven or resource-driven? As in all previous paradoxes, it is compelling to want both at the same time, while their premises are contradictory and possibly even mutually exclusive. Therefore, strategists will have to somehow resolve the paradox of markets and resources (see Table 5.1).

TABLE 5.1
Outside-in versus inside-out perspective

	Outside-in Perspective	Inside-out Perspective
Emphasis on	Markets over resources	Resources over markets
Orientation	Market/Industry-driven	Resource-driven
Starting point	Market/Industry structure	Firm's resource infrastructure
Fit through	Adaptation to environment	Adaptation of environment
Strategic focus	Attaining advantageous position	Attaining distinctive resources
Strategic moves	Market/Industry positioning	Developing resource base
Tactical moves	Attaining necessary resources	Industry entry and positioning
Competitive weapons	Bargaining power and mobility barriers	Superior resources and imitation barriers

Defining the Issues: Adaptation and Advantage

Most strategists agree that the key question of business level strategy is 'how should a firm be related to its environment to achieve success?' In other words, how can the current, and potential, strengths and weaknesses of the organization be aligned with the current, and potential, opportunities and threats in the environment, in such a way that the firm will be able to reach its aims? The answer to this question must be sought in the issues of *adaptation* and *advantage*. 'Alignment of firm and environment' entails that they must be adapted to one another, while 'achieving success' necessitates the existence of an advantage over the firm's rivals.

Before proceeding to the readings, the nature of these two issues will first be more closely examined. In particular, what is the environment that must be adapted or adapted to, and what are firm resources?

Positioning in Industries, Markets and Businesses

While strategists generally agree that a firm must be aligned to its environment, the question is which external factors are the most relevant for the firm – which part of the environment should the firm be positioning in? Here there is a difference in emphasis among strategists, which requires that a distinction be made between various parts of the environment. Unfortunately, there is not yet a generally accepted set of concepts within the field of strategic management with which to describe the external environment of the firm. Terms such as industry, market and business are defined differently, or more often, not defined at all. Many of the contributions in this book actually use some of these terms interchangeably. However, to aid the debate, we suggest that the following distinction between the concepts of industry, market and business could be made:

■ *Industry*. An industry is defined as a group of firms making a similar type of product or employing a similar set of value-adding processes or resources. In other words, an industry consists of producers that are much alike – there is *supply side similarity* (Kay, 1993). The simplest way to draw an industry boundary is to use product similarity as delineation criterion. For instance, British Airways can be said to be in the air transportation industry, along with many other providers of the same product, such as Delta, Singapore Airlines and Air UK. Porsche can be placed in the automobile industry. However, an industry can also be defined on the basis of value-chain similarity (e.g. consulting industry and retailing industry) or resource similarity (e.g. information technology industry and oil industry). Economic statisticians tend to favor industry categories based on product similarity and therefore most figures available about industries are product-category based. However, a strategist may want to define an industry on the basis of underlying value-adding processes or resources. For instance, in which industry should Swatch be classified? If one focuses on the physical product and the production process, one would be inclined to situate Swatch in the watch industry. However, if a Swatch is seen as a fashion accessory and emphasis is placed on the key value-adding activities of fashion design and marketing, then Swatch would have to be categorized as a member of the fashion industry. For the strategist, the realization that Swatch can be viewed in both ways is an important insight[10].

■ *Market*. While economists see the market as a place where supply and demand meet, in the business world a market is usually defined as a group of customers with similar needs. In other words, a market consists of buyers whose demands are much alike – *demand side similarity*. For instance, there is a market for air transportation between London and Jamaica, which is a different market than for air transportation between London and Paris – the customer needs are different and therefore these products can not be substituted for one another. But customers can substitute a British Airways flight London–Paris for one by Air France, indicating that both companies are serving the same market. Yet, this market definition (London–Paris air transport) might not be the most appropriate, if in reality many customers are willing to substitute air travel by rail travel, taking Le Shuttle through the channel tunnel, or by ship or hovercraft. In this case, there is a broader London–Paris transportation market, and air transportation is a specific *market segment*. If many customers are willing to substitute physical travel by teleconferencing or other telecommunications methods, the market might need to be defined as the 'London-Paris meeting market'. For the strategist, the realization that all these market definitions might be useful is an important insight (see Figure 5.1).

■ *Business.* A business is defined as a set of related product-market combinations. The term 'business' refers neither to a set of producers nor a group of customers, but to the domain where the two meet. In other words, a business is a competitive arena where companies offering similar products serving similar needs rival against one another for the favor of the buyers. Hence, a business is delineated in both industry and market terms. Typically, a business is narrower than the entire industry and the set of markets served is also limited. For instance, within the airline industry the charter business is usually recognized as rather distinct. In the charter business, a subset of the airline services is offered to a number of tourist markets. Cheap flights from London to Jamaica and from London to Benidorm fall within this business, while service levels will be different than in other parts of the airline industry. It should be noted, though, that just as with industries and markets, there is no best way to define the boundaries of a business[11].

FIGURE 5.1
Industries, markets and businesses

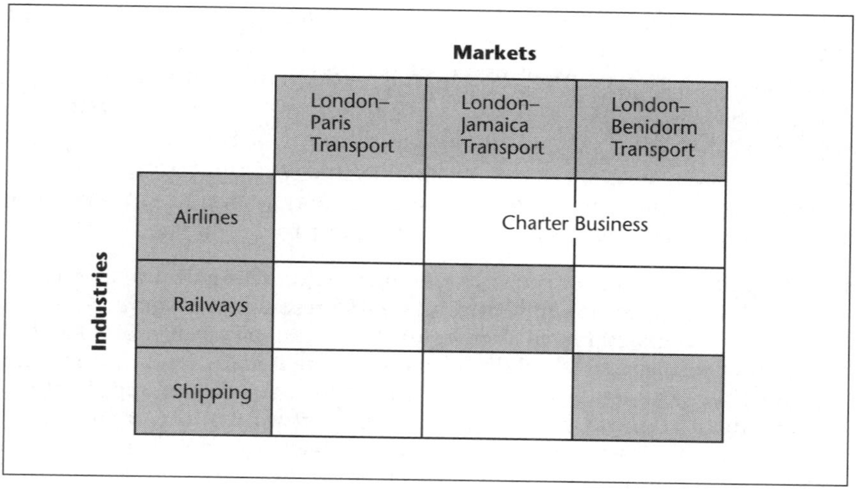

		Markets		
		London–Paris Transport	London–Jamaica Transport	London–Benidorm Transport
Industries	Airlines		Charter Business	
	Railways			
	Shipping			

A firm positioning itself in the external environment will need to define which industries, markets and businesses it is currently in and 'what makes them tick'. Based on this understanding, the strategist may want to strengthen the firm's existing position, or may prefer to reposition the firm within the current, or a newly-defined, industry, market or business.

An important distinction within the outside-in perspective can be made between strategists focusing on *positioning within a market* and those emphasizing *positioning within an industry*. When firms target a product or brand at a particular group of customers, they are positioning within a market. This is also referred to as *product positioning* and/or *brand positioning*. The key issue when positioning in a market is to meet customer demands in a manner that alternative products or services will not be selected. Emphasis is placed on the need to be market-driven, that is, responsive to the specific demands evolving within the market. This issue is central to the marketing discipline, and marketing strategists write extensively on such positioning challenges[12].

On the other hand, when a firm more generally distinguishes itself from other firms producing similar goods or services, they are positioning within an industry. A strategist dealing with *firm positioning* necessarily takes a broader view than that of individual products and markets. The firm's overall position within its industry, and more particularly a business unit's position within its business, are of concern. While marketing writers have also contributed to this topic, much of the underlying theory has its origins in the economic discipline of industrial organization[13]. In this chapter, both types of positioning will be considered.

Developing Tangible and Intangible Resources

Under the broad umbrella of *resource-based view of the firm*, there has been a wide range of research into the importance of resources for the success and even existence of firms[14]. Until now, no classification of firm resources has emerged that is generally accepted within the field of strategic management. Some authors don't even speak of *resources*, when referring to all the means at the disposal of the firm, but prefer the term *assets*[15]. Despite the lack of consensus on terminology, we would suggest that there are a number of major distinctions between types of resources that need to be pointed out to clarify the debate:

- *Tangible vs. intangible resources*. The first major distinction that could be made is between tangible and intangible resources. Tangible resources are all means available to the firm that can physically be observed ('touched'), such as buildings, machines, materials, land and money. Tangibles can be referred to as the 'hardware' of the organization. Intangibles, on the other hand, are the 'software' of the organization. Intangible resources cannot be touched, but are largely carried within the people in the organization. In general, tangible resources need to be purchased, while intangibles need to be developed. Therefore, tangible resources are often more readily transferable, easier to price and usually are placed on the balance sheet. For this reason, *assets* (with the connotation of ownership) is an appropriate term for tangible resources.

- *Relational resources vs. competences.* Within the category of intangible resources, relational resources and competences can be distinguished. Relational resources are all of the means available to the firm derived from the firm's interaction with its environment[16]. The firm can cultivate specific *relationships* with individuals and organizations in the environment, such as buyers, suppliers, competitors and government agencies, that can be instrumental in achieving the firm's goals. As attested by the old saying 'it's not what you know, but who you know,' relationships can often be an essential resource (see Chapter 7 for a further discussion). Besides direct relationships, a firm's *reputation* among other parties in the environment can also be an important resource. Competence, on the other hand, refers to the firm's fitness to perform in a particular field. A firm has a competence if it has the knowledge, capabilities and attitude needed to successfully operate in a specific area.

This description of competences is somewhat broad and therefore difficult to employ. However, the distinction between knowledge, capability and attitude[17] can be used to shed more light on the nature of competences:

- *Knowledge.* Knowledge can be defined as the whole of rules (know-how, know-what, know-where and know-when) and insights (know-why) that can be extracted from, and help make sense of, information. In other words, knowledge flows from, and influences, the interpretation of information. Examples of knowledge that a firm can possess are market insight, competitive intelligence, technological expertise, and understanding of political and economic developments.

- *Capability.* Capability refers to the organization's potential for carrying out a specific activity or set of activities. Sometimes the term *skill* is used to refer to the ability to carry out a narrow (functional) task or activity, while the term capability is reserved for the quality of combining a number of skills. For instance, a firm's capability-base can include narrower abilities such as market research, advertising and production skills, that if co-ordinated could result in a capability for new product development.

- *Attitude.* Attitude refers to the outlook prevalent within an organization. Sometimes the terms *disposition* and *will* are used in the same sense, to indicate how an organization views and relates to the world. Although ignored by some writers, every sports coach will acknowledge the importance of attitude as a resource. A healthy body (tangible resource), insight into the game (knowledge), speed and dexterity (capabilities) – all are important, but without the winning mentality a team will not get to the top. Some attitudes may change rapidly within firms, yet others may be entrenched within the cultural fabric of the organization – these in particular can be important resources for the firm. A company's attitude can, for instance, be characterized as quality-driven, internationally-oriented, innovation-minded and/or competitively-aggressive.

It must be noted that in practice the term 'competences' is used in many different ways, partially due to the ambiguous definition given by its early proponents. It is often used as a synonym for capabilities, while Prahalad and Hamel[18] seem to focus more on technologically-oriented capabilities ('how to coordinate diverse production skills and integrate multiple streams of technologies'). Others (e.g. Durand[19]) have suggested that a firm has a competence in a certain area, when the firm's underlying knowledge-base, capabilities and attitude are all aligned. So, Honda's engine competence is built on specific knowledge, development capabilities and the right predisposition. Walmart's inventory control competence depends on specific information technology knowledge, coordination capabilities and a conducive state of mind. Virgin Airway's service competence combines customer knowledge, adaptation capabilities and a customer-oriented attitude.

As in the case of industries, markets, and businesses, employing the concepts of tangible and intangible resources is quite difficult in practice. Two problems need to be overcome – resources are difficult to categorize, but worse yet, often difficult to recognize. The issue of categorization is a minor one. For some resources it is unclear how they should be classified. Are *human resources* tangible or intangible? Problematically, both. In humans, hardware and software are intertwined – if an engineer's expertise is required, the physical person usually needs to be hired. Knowledge, capabilities and attitudes need human carriers. Sometimes it is possible to separate hardware and software, by making the intangibles more tangible. This is done by 'writing the software down'. In such a manner, knowledge can be codified, for instance in a patent, a capability can be captured in a computer program and a relationship can be formalized in a contract (see Figure 5.2 for further examples).

More important is the problem of resource identification. Tangible resources, by their very nature, are relatively easy to observe. Accountants keep track of the financial resources, production managers usually know the quality of their machinery and stock levels, while the personnel department will have an overview of all people on the pay role. Intangible resources, on the other hand, are far more difficult to identify[20]. With whom does the firm have a relationship and what is the state of this relationship? What is the firm's reputation? These relational resources are hard to pin down. Competences are probably even more difficult to determine. How do you know what you know? Even for an individual it is a formidable task to outline areas of expertise, let alone for a more complex organization. Especially the *tacit* (non-articulated) nature of much organizational knowledge makes it difficult to identify the firm's knowledge-base[21]. The same is true for a firm's capabilities, which have developed in the form of organizational *routines*[22]. Likewise, the firm's attitudes are difficult to discern, because all people sharing the same disposition will tend to consider themselves normal and will tend to believe that their outlook is 'a matter of common sense' (see Chapter 2). Hence, firms intent on identifying their competences find that this is not an easy task.

While an overview of the firm's resource-base is important in itself, a strategist will want to know how the firm's resources compare to other companies. In other words, are the firm's resources unique, superior to, or inferior to the resources of (potential) competitors? In which resource areas does the firm have a relative strength and where does it have a relative weakness? This type of analysis is particularly difficult, as comparison requires insight into other firms' resource bases. Especially the identification of other firms' intangible resources can be quite arduous.

Creating a Sustainable Competitive Advantage

A firm has a competitive advantage when it has the means to edge out rivals when vying for the favor of customers. A competitive advantage is said to be sustainable if it cannot be copied or eroded by the actions of rivals, and is not made redundant by environment developments[23].

The question to be debated is how a sustainable competitive advantage can be created. Should generals create a sustainable competitive

FIGURE 5.2
Types of firm resources

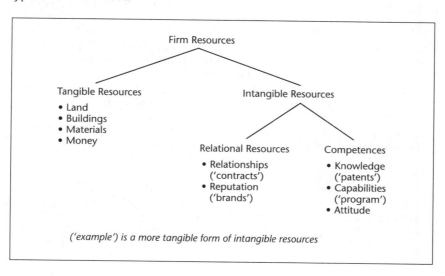

('*example*') *is a more tangible form of intangible resources*

advantage by first selecting a superior environmental position (e.g. a mountain pass) and then adapting their military resources to this position, or should generals develop armies with unique resources and then try to let the battle take place where these resources can best be employed? Should football coaches first determine how they want the game to be played on the field and then attract and train players to fit with this style, or should coaches develop uniquely talented players and then adapt the team's playing style to make the best use of these resources? Whether a military, sports or business strategist, an approach to creating competitive advantage must be chosen.

EXHIBIT 5.1
Avon case

AVON: KEEPING THOSE DOORBELLS RINGING?

When James Preston became chairman and CEO of Avon Products in 1989, the company was in dire straits. Many analysts doubted whether the well-known door-to-door vendor of cosmetics would make it into the 1990s as an independent company. Under Preston's predecessor, Avon had branched out of the mature cosmetics business, into the growing market for healthcare products, acquiring a number of companies along the way. However, this diversification move was not particularly successful, with the added disadvantage of tying up cash and siphoning off the profits made in cosmetics. As a consequence, Avon itself became an attractive candidate for acquisition and the company was forced to fight off some hostile take-over attempts. One of Preston's first tasks at the helm was to resist the aggressive bids by Mary Kay, one of Avon's most prominent cosmetics competitors, and Amway, a similar direct sales company, with a broad product portfolio. In an effort to retain Avon's independence, Preston also took drastic downsizing measures to restore profitability. The healthcare business was sold off and a number of production and distribution facilities in the cosmetics business were closed, putting over a thousand people out of a job. Preston realized, however, that recovery would not result from 'surgery' alone – Avon would need to strengthen its slipping position in the cosmetics markets of the US and Western Europe, as well as seek growth elsewhere. Naturally, the challenge facing Preston and his company was how this could be achieved. What competitive advantage would Avon have to concentrate on to return the firm to healthy profitability?

Avon did have a number of things going for it. Avon's direct sales system is probably its most valuable asset. Almost 100 percent of Avon's total turnover is generated through direct sales to consumers, using a network of over two million sales representatives around the world (445,000 in the US alone). These 'Avon ladies' are not employed by the company, but are 'independent entrepeneurs' paid on a commission basis. In 1995 this legion of sales reps took 650 million orders, in more than 120 countries, good for approximately $4.5 billion worth of beauty products. Selling through this system of 'virtual stores' has some important advantages over traditional retailing methods. Expanding and maintaining a network of virtual stores can be done at a fraction of the cost, and within a fraction of the time, of opening real stores. It is possible to reach almost anyone anywhere, because the 'virtual store' comes to the buyer, instead of vice versa. Selling Avon products can be done at home, but elsewhere as well. For instance, in the US 30 percent of sales are signed up at work. Furthermore, Avon's 'virtual stores' do not need a critical mass of potential buyers within a sales area. Avon ladies can sell as much as they want, wherever they want – and their straight commission income is a large incentive to ensure that they will be creative in seeking customers.

On the other hand, Avon's image in North America and Western Europe was stale and down market. While still popular among older women, more fashion-conscious younger women steered clear of Avon products. Preston himself recognized that this was a significant problem: 'I am well aware that there are many women who would not want to open their purses and pull out Avon lipstick.' Furthermore, customers increasingly demand instantaneous satisfaction. Ordering a product from Avon could take weeks, while products in the shop can be taken directly. This problem was aggravated by the growing trend toward 'recreational shopping'. Young women, especially, were exhibiting a growing preference for visiting stores as a leisure activity. By the early 1990s this had resulted in stagnant sales in the US and even declining sales in Western Europe.

Preston decided to counter these developments with a number of moves. First, slipping sales in mature markets could be more than off-set by expansion in fast-growing markets outside the developed economies. Demand for beauty products is booming in many 'emerging markets', as more women in these countries have enough cash at their disposal to make discretionary purchases. But even the lesser developed economies, where GNP growth is low, are in Preston's words 'Avon Heaven'. Where the retailing infrastructure is poor and conventional shops are difficult to set up, Avon's sales ladies have an even stronger advantage than usual. Avon needs only basic transportation and distribution facilities to get up and running. Moreover, there are usually plenty of eager sales people in less developed economies, willing to work hard to provide their family with some additional income. Between 1989 and 1995 Avon entered 14 new markets and plans to proceed at the same pace until it has global coverage. An interesting spin-off has been that the company now has one of the best sales forces in many countries, so that many firms, such as Reader's Digest, use Avon as their local sales organization.

Yet, Preston also refused to give up on the established markets. Avon's image needed to be upgraded and Preston set a two-day order processing time as new standard. Emphasis was also placed on getting to know its customers better. 'We do not want to build transactions, we want to build relationships,' according to Preston. Avon wanted to strengthen relations by being *the* resource for women, helping them in any way possible, for instance by providing seminars on household management and by offering education about abuse and breast cancer.

By 1995, the company seemed at a crossroads. Despite the afore-mentioned efforts, growth in the mature markets remained lacklustre. Preston seemed to be faced with two major options for achieving further growth. One would be to abandon direct sales as the company's primary sales method and to develop multiple channels. Avon could actually go into traditional retailing, catalogue sales, direct mail, telephone sales or even Internet sales, if this were what the market demanded. However, this partial repositioning would require the firm to develop many new skills. Alternatively, Avon could build on its direct sales ability and add related products to its sales portfolio. Glassware and bedware were suggested as potentially suitable product lines. The question facing Preston was which avenue of expansion to choose. What would be the advantages and dis-advantages of each alternative, both in the short and in the long run? In a nutshell, he had to choose whether Avon would primarily be a cosmetics company or a direct sales company – which wasn't an easy choice to make.

Sources: *The Economist*, July 13 1996; *Forbes*, December 2 1996.

The Debate and the Readings

The opening reading in the debate, 'Competitive Strategy', has been taken from Michael Porter's 1985 book *Competitive Advantage*, but its central concepts were originally introduced in his first book, *Competitive Strategy*[24]. Since Porter is considered by all to be the most important theorist in the positioning tradition, it seems only logical to start with him as representative of the outside-in perspective. In his contribution, Porter argues that 'two central questions underlie the choice of compe-titive strategy.' First, strategists must select a competitive domain with attractive characteristics and then they must position the firm *vis-à-vis* the five competitive forces encountered. These five forces impinging on the firm's profit potential are 'the entry of new competitors, the threat of substitutes, the bargaining power of buyers, the bargaining power of suppliers, and the rivalry among the existing competitors.' Long run above-average performance results from selecting one of the three defend-able positions available to the strategist: *cost leadership*, *differentiation* or *focus*. According to Porter, these three options, or *generic strategies*, are the only feasible ways of achieving a sustainable competitive advantage. A firm that does not make a clear choice between one of the three generic strategies, is 'stuck in the middle' and will suffer below-average performance. For the debate in this chapter it is important to note that Porter does not explicitly advocate an exclusively outside-in approach. However, he strongly emphasizes competitive positioning as leading strategy principle and treats the development of firm resources as a derivative activity. Indirectly, therefore, his message to strategists is that in the game of strategy it is essential to be focused on the external dynamics.

As representative of the inside-out perspective, the reading 'Competing on Capabilities,' by George Stalk, Philip Evans and Lawrence Shulman[25] has been selected. They argue that the key to competitive success lies in identifying and developing 'the hard-to-imitate organizational capabilities that distinguish a company from its competitors in the eyes of the customers.' In their view, the positioning way of looking at the world is too static. Competition, they believe, is increasingly unlike chess, a 'war of position,' and more like an interactive video game, a 'war of movement.' Therefore, a company should not build static market share, but should develop organizational capabilities that allow the firm to 'move quickly in and out of products, markets, and even entire businesses.' The flexibility gained by superior capabilities can be used to consistently change the rules of the competitive game in one's own industry, but can also be employed to rewrite the rules in entirely different industries. Stalk, Evans and Shulman refer to companies seeking to transfer their most important business processes to different industries as *capabilities predators*. The capabilities-based approach is, therefore, not only an important approach to business strategy, but also to corporate strategy (in Chapter 6, Prahalad and Hamel expand on this point).

Again it is up to readers to judge the arguments brought forward by both debaters and to conclude for themselves what the best way would be to create business level strategy. Each individual will have to determine whether one of the perspectives 'has a competitive advantage', or whether a synthesis of the two is preferable.

Reading 1   Competitive Strategy

By Michael Porter[†]

Competition is at the core of the success or failure of firms. Competition determines the appropriateness of a firm's activities that can contribute to its performance, such as innovations, a cohesive culture, or good

---

[†] Source: This article was adapted with permission from *Competitive Advantage: Creating and Sustaining Superior Performance*, Free Press, New York, 1985.

implementation. Competitive strategy is the search for a favorable competitive position in an industry, the fundamental arena in which competition occurs. Competitive strategy aims to establish a profitable and sustainable position against the forces that determine industry competition.

Two central questions underlie the choice of competitive strategy. The first is the attractiveness of industries for long-term profitability and the factors that determine it. Not all industries offer equal opportunities for sustained profitability, and the inherent profitability of its industry is one essential ingredient in determining the profitability of a firm. The second central question in competitive strategy is the determinants of relative competitive position within an industry. In most industries, some firms are much more profitable than others, regardless of what the average profitability of the industry may be.

Neither question is sufficient by itself to guide the choice of competitive strategy. A firm in a very attractive industry may still not earn attractive profits if it has chosen a poor competitive position. Conversely, a firm in an excellent competitive position may be in such a poor industry that it is not very profitable, and further efforts to enhance its position will be of little benefit. Both questions are dynamic; industry attractiveness and competitive position change. Industries become more or less attractive over time, and competitive position reflects an unending battle among competitors. Even long periods of stability can be abruptly ended by competitive moves.

Both industry attractiveness and competitive position can be shaped by a firm, and this is what makes the choice of competitive strategy both challenging and exciting. While industry attractiveness is partly a reflection of factors over which a firm has little influence, competitive strategy has considerable power to make an industry more or less attractive. At the same time, a firm can clearly improve or erode its position within an industry through its choice of strategy. Competitive strategy, then, not only responds to the environment but also attempts to shape that environment in a firm's favor.

The Structural Analysis of Industries

The first fundamental determinant of a firm's profitability is industry attractiveness. Competitive strategy must grow out of a sophisticated understanding of the rules of competition that determine an industry's attractiveness. The ultimate aim of competitive strategy is to cope with and, ideally, to change those rules in the firm's favor. In any industry, whether it is domestic or international or produces a product or a service, the rules of competition are embodied in five competitive forces: the entry

FIGURE 5.3
Elements of industry structure

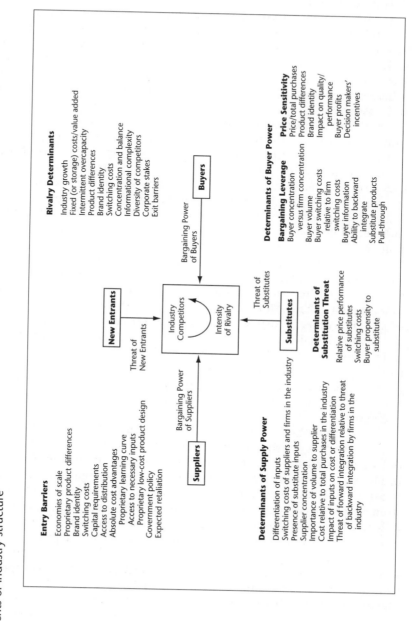

Entry Barriers

Economies of scale
Proprietary product differences
Brand identity
Switching costs
Capital requirements
Access to distribution
Absolute cost advantages
  Proprietary learning curve
  Access to necessary inputs
  Proprietary low-cost product design
Government policy
Expected retaliation

Rivalry Determinants

Industry growth
Fixed (or storage) costs/value added
Intermittent overcapacity
Product differences
Brand identity
Switching costs
Concentration and balance
Informational complexity
Diversity of competitors
Corporate stakes
Exit barriers

Determinants of Supply Power

Differentiation of inputs
Switching costs of suppliers and firms in the industry
Presence of substitute inputs
Supplier concentration
Importance of volume to supplier
Cost relative to total purchases in the industry
Impact of inputs on cost or differentiation
Threat of forward integration relative to threat
  of backward integration by firms in the
  industry

Determinants of Substitution Threat

Relative price performance
  of substitutes
Switching costs
Buyer propensity to
  substitute

Determinants of Buyer Power

Bargaining Leverage

Buyer concentration
  versus firm concentration
Buyer volume
Buyer switching costs
  relative to firm
  switching costs
Buyer information
Ability to backward
  integrate
Substitute products
Pull-through

Price Sensitivity

Price/total purchases
Product differences
Brand identity
Impact on quality/
  performance
Buyer profits
Decision makers'
  incentives

Suppliers

New Entrants

Buyers

Substitutes

Industry Competitors

Intensity of Rivalry

Threat of New Entrants

Bargaining Power of Suppliers

Bargaining Power of Buyers

Threat of Substitutes

of new competitors, the threat of substitutes, the bargaining power of buyers, the bargaining power of suppliers, and the rivalry among the existing competitors.

The collective strength of these five competitive forces determines the ability of firms in an industry to earn, on average, rates of return on investment in excess of the cost of capital. The strength of the five forces varies from industry to industry, and can change as an industry evolves. The result is that all industries are not alike from the standpoint of inherent profitability. In industries where the five forces are favorable, such as pharmaceuticals, soft drinks, and database publishing, many competitors earn attractive returns. But in industries where pressure from one or more of the forces is intense, such as rubber, steel, and video games, few firms command attractive returns despite the best efforts of management. Industry profitability is not a function of what the product looks like or whether it embodies high or low technology, but of industry structure. Some very mundane industries such as postage meters and grain trading are extremely profitable, while some more glamorous, high-technology industries such as personal computers and cable television are not profitable for many participants.

The five forces determine industry profitability because they influence the prices, costs, and required investment of firms in an industry – the elements of return on investment. Buyer power influences the prices that firms can charge, for example, as does the threat of substitution. The power of buyers can also influence cost and investment, because powerful buyers demand costly service. The bargaining power of suppliers determines the costs of raw materials and other inputs. The intensity of rivalry influences prices as well as the costs of competing in areas such as plant, product development, advertising, and sales force. The threat of entry places a limit on prices, and shapes the investment required to deter entrants.

The strength of each of the five competitive forces is a function of *industry structure*, or the underlying economic and technical characteristics of an industry. Its important elements are shown in Figure 5.3. Industry structure is relatively stable, but can change over time as an industry evolves. Structural change shifts the overall and relative strength of the competitive forces, and can thus positively or negatively influence industry profitability. The industry trends that are the most important for strategy are those that affect industry structure.

If the five competitive forces and their structural determinants were solely a function of intrinsic industry characteristics, then competitive strategy would rest heavily on picking the right industry and understanding the five forces better than competitors. But while these are surely important tasks for any firm, and are the essence of competitive strategy in some industries, a firm is usually not a prisoner of its industry's structure. Firms, through their strategies, can influence the five forces.

If a firm can shape structure, it can fundamentally change an industry's attractiveness for better or for worse. Many successful strategies have shifted the rules of competition in this way.

Figure 5.3 highlights all the elements of industry structure that may drive competition in an industry. In any particular industry, not all of the five forces will be equally important and the particular structural factors that are important will differ. Every industry is unique and has its own unique structure. The five-forces framework allows a firm to see through the complexity and pinpoint those factors that are critical to competition in its industry, as well as to identify those strategic innovations that would most improve the industry's – and its own – profitability. The five-forces framework does not eliminate the need for creativity in finding new ways of competing in an industry. Instead, it directs managers' creative energies toward those aspects of industry structure that are most important to long-run profitability. The framework aims, in the process, to raise the odds of discovering a desirable strategic innovation.

Strategies that change industry structure can be a double-edged sword, because a firm can destroy industry structure and profitability as readily as it can improve it. A new product design that undercuts entry barriers or increases the volatility of rivalry, for example, may undermine the long-run profitability of an industry, though the initiator may enjoy higher profits temporarily. Or a sustained period of price cutting can undermine differentiation. In the tobacco industry, for example, generic cigarettes are a potentially serious threat to industry structure. Generics may enhance the price sensitivity of buyers, trigger price competition, and erode the high advertising barriers that have kept out new entrants. Joint ventures entered into by major aluminum producers to spread risk and lower capital cost may have similarly undermined industry structure. The majors invited a number of potentially dangerous new competitors into the industry and helped them overcome the significant entry barriers to doing so. Joint ventures also can raise exit barriers because all the participants in a plant must agree before it can be closed down.

Often firms make strategic choices without considering the long-term consequences for industry structure. They see a gain in the competitive position if a move is successful, but they fail to anticipate the consequences of competitive reaction. If imitation of a move by major competitors has the effect of wrecking industry structure, then everyone is worse off. Such industry 'destroyers' are usually second-tier firms that are searching for ways to overcome major competitive disadvantages, firms that have encountered serious problems and are desperately seeking solutions, or 'dumb' competitors that do not know their costs or have unrealistic assumptions about the future. In the tobacco industry, for example, the Liggett Group (a distant follower) has encouraged the trend toward generics.

The ability of firms to shape industry structure places a particular burden on industry leaders. Leaders' actions can have a disproportionate impact on structure, because of their size and influence over buyers, suppliers, and other competitors. At the same time, leaders' large market shares guarantee that anything that changes overall industry structure will affect them as well. A leader, then, must constantly balance its own competitive position against the health of the industry as a whole. Often leaders are better off taking actions to improve or protect industry structure rather than seeking greater competitive advantage for themselves. Such industry leaders as Coca-Cola and Campbell's Soup appear to have followed this principle.

Industry Structure and Buyer Needs

It has often been said that satisfying buyer needs is at the core of success in business endeavor. How does this relate to the concept of industry structural analysis? Satisfying buyer needs is indeed a prerequisite to the viability of an industry and the firms within it. Buyers must be willing to pay a price for a product that exceeds its cost of production, or an industry will not survive in the long run.

Satisfying buyer needs may be a prerequisite for industry profitability, but in itself is not sufficient. The crucial question in determining profitability is whether firms can capture the value they create for buyers, or whether this value is competed away to others. Industry structure determines who captures the value. The threat of entry determines the likelihood that new firms will enter an industry and compete away the value, either passing it on to buyers in the form of lower prices or dissipating it by raising the costs of competing. The power of buyers determines the extent to which they retain most of the value created for themselves, leaving firms in an industry only modest returns. The threat of substitutes determines the extent to which some other product can meet the same buyer needs, and thus places a ceiling on the amount a buyer is willing to pay for an industry's product. The power of suppliers determines the extent to which value created for buyers will be appropriated by suppliers rather than by firms in an industry. Finally, the intensity of rivalry acts similarly to the threat of entry. It determines the extent to which firms already in an industry will compete away the value they create for buyers among themselves, passing it on to buyers in lower prices or dissipating it in higher costs of competing.

Industry structure, then, determines who keeps what proportion of the value a product creates for buyers. If an industry's product does not create much value for its buyers, there is little value to be captured by firms regardless of the other elements of structure. If the product creates a lot of value, structure becomes crucial. In some industries such as automobiles and heavy trucks, firms create enormous value for their buyers but, on average, capture very little of it for themselves through profits. In other industries such as bond rating services, medical equipment, and oil field services and equipment, firms also create high value for their buyers but have historically captured a good proportion of it. In oil field services and equipment, for example, many products can significantly reduce the cost of drilling. Because industry structure has been favorable, many firms in the oil field service and equipment sector have been able to retain a share of these savings in the form of high returns. Recently, however, the structural attractiveness of many industries in the oil field services and equipment sector has eroded as a result of falling demand, new entrants, eroding product differentiation, and greater buyer price sensitivity. Despite the fact that products offered still create enormous value for the buyer, both firm and industry profits have fallen significantly.

Industry Structure and the Supply/Demand Balance

Another commonly held view about industry profitability is that profits are a function of the balance between supply and demand. If demand is greater than supply, this leads to high profitability. Yet, the long-term supply/demand balance is strongly influenced by industry structure, as are the consequences of a supply/demand imbalance for profitability. Hence, even though short-term fluctuations in supply and demand can affect short-term profitability, industry structure underlies long-term profitability.

Supply and demand change constantly, adjusting to each other. Industry structure determines how rapidly competitors add new supply. The height of entry barriers underpins the likelihood that new entrants will enter an industry and bid down prices. The intensity of rivalry plays a major role in determining whether existing firms will expand capacity aggressively or choose to maintain profitability. Industry structure also determines how rapidly competitors will retire excess supply. Exit barriers keep firms from leaving an industry when there is too much capacity, and prolong periods of excess capacity. In oil tanker shipping, for example, the exit barriers are very high because of the specialization of assets. This has translated into short peaks and long troughs of prices. Thus industry structure shapes the supply/demand balance and the duration of imbalances.

The consequences of an imbalance between supply and demand for industry profitability also differs widely depending on industry structure. In some industries, a small amount of excess capacity triggers price wars and low profitability. These are industries where there are structural pressures for intense rivalry or powerful buyers. In other industries, periods of excess capacity have relatively little impact on profitability because of favorable structure. In oil tools, ball valves, and many other oil field equipment products, for example, there has been intense price cutting during the recent sharp downturn. In drill bits, however, there has been relatively little discounting. Hughes Tool, Smith International, and Baker International are good competitors operating in a favorable industry structure. Industry structure also determines the profitability of excess demand. In a boom, for example, favorable structure allows firms to reap extraordinary profits, while a poor structure restricts the ability to capitalize on it. The presence of powerful suppliers or the presence of substitutes, for example, can mean that the fruits of a boom pass to others. Thus industry structure is fundamental to both the speed of adjustment of supply to demand and the relationship between capacity utilization and profitability.

Generic Competitive Strategies

The second central question in competitive strategy is a firm's relative position within its industry. Positioning determines whether a firm's profitability is above or below the industry average. A firm that can position itself well may earn high rates of return even though industry structure is unfavorable and the average profitability of the industry is therefore modest.

The fundamental basis of above-average performance in the long run is *sustainable competitive advantage*. Though a firm can have a myriad strengths and weaknesses *vis-à-vis* its competitors, there are two basic types of competitive advantage a firm can possess: low cost or differentiation. The significance of any strength or weakness a firm possesses is ultimately a function of its impact on relative cost or differentiation. Cost advantage and differentiation in turn stem from industry structure. They result from a firm's ability to cope with the five forces better than its rivals.

The two basic types of competitive advantage combined with the scope of activities for which a firm seeks to achieve them lead to three *generic strategies* for achieving above-average performance in an industry: cost leadership, differentiation, and focus. The focus strategy has two variants, cost focus and differentiation focus. The generic strategies are shown in Figure 5.4.

Each of the generic strategies involves a fundamentally different route to competitive advantage, combining a choice about the type of competitive advantage sought with the scope of the strategic target in which competitive advantage is to be achieved. The cost leadership and differentiation strategies seek competitive advantage in a broad range of industry segments, while focus strategies aim at cost advantage (cost focus) or differentiation (differentiation focus) in a narrow segment.

FIGURE 5.4
Three generic strategies

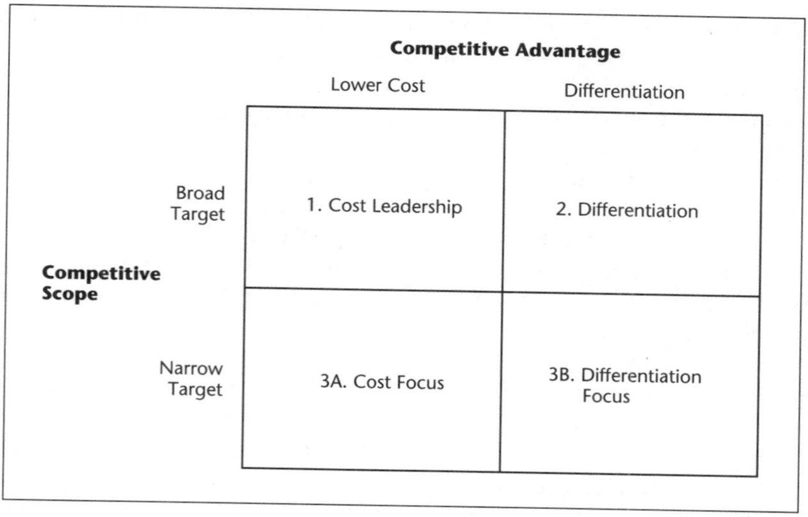

The specific actions required to implement each generic strategy vary widely from industry to industry, as do the feasible generic strategies in a particular industry. While selecting and implementing a generic strategy is far from simple, they are the logical routes to competitive advantage that must be probed in any industry.

The notion underlying the concept of generic strategies is that competitive advantage is at the heart of any strategy, and achieving competitive advantage requires a firm to make a choice – if a firm is to attain a competitive advantage, it must make a choice about the type of competitive advantage it seeks to attain and the scope within which it will attain it. Being all things to all people is a recipe for strategic mediocrity and below-average performance, because it often means that a firm has no competitive advantage at all.

Cost Leadership

Cost leadership is perhaps the clearest of the three generic strategies. In it, a firm sets out to become *the* low-cost producer in its industry. The firm has a broad scope and serves many industry segments, and may even operate in related industries – the firm's breadth is often important to its cost advantage. The sources of cost advantage are varied and depend on the structure of the industry. They may include the pursuit of economies of scale, proprietary technology, preferential access to raw materials, and other factors. In TV sets, for example, cost leadership requires efficient-size picture tube facilities, a low-cost design, automated assembly, and global scale over which to amortize research and development (R&D). In security guard services, cost advantage requires extremely low overhead, a plentiful source of low-cost labor, and efficient training procedures because of high turnover. Low-cost producer status involves more than just going down the learning curve. A low-cost producer must find and exploit all sources of cost advantage. Low-cost producers typically sell a standard, or no-frills, product and place considerable emphasis on reaping scale or absolute cost advantages from all sources.

If a firm can achieve and sustain overall cost leadership, then it will be an above-average performer in its industry provided it can command prices at or near the industry average. At equivalent or lower prices than its rivals, a cost leader's low-cost position translates into higher returns. A cost leader, however, cannot ignore the bases of differentiation. If its product is not perceived as comparable or acceptable by buyers, a cost leader will be forced to discount prices well below competitors' to gain sales. This may nullify the benefits of its favorable cost position. Texas Instruments (in watches) and Northwest Airlines (in air transportation) are two low-cost firms that fell into this trap. Texas Instruments could not overcome its disadvantage in differentiation and exited the watch industry. Northwest Airlines recognized its problem in time, and has instituted efforts to improve marketing, passenger service, and service to travel agents to make its product more comparable to those of its competitors.

A cost leader must achieve *parity or proximity* in the bases of differentiation relative to its competitiors to be an above-average performer, even though it relies on cost leadership for its competitive advantage. Parity in the bases of differentiation allows a cost leader to translate its cost advantage directly into higher profits than competitors'. Proximity in differentiation means that the price discount necessary to achieve an acceptable market share does not offset a cost leader's cost advantage and hence the cost leader earns above-average returns.

The strategic logic of cost leadership usually requires that a firm be *the* cost leader, not one of several firms vying for this position. Many firms have made serious strategic errors by failing to recognize this. When there is more than one aspiring cost leader, rivalry among them is usually fierce because every point of market share is viewed as crucial. Unless one firm can gain a cost lead and 'persuade' others to abandon their strategies, the consequences for profitability (and long-run industry structure) can be disastrous, as has been the case in a number of petrochemical industries. Thus cost leadership is a strategy particularly dependent on preemption, unless major technological change allows a firm to radically change its cost position.

Differentiation

The second generic strategy is differentiation. In a differentiation strategy, a firm seeks to be unique in its industry along some dimensions that are widely valued by buyers. It selects one or more attributes that many buyers in an industry perceive as important, and uniquely positions itself to meet those needs. It is rewarded for its uniqueness with a premium price.

The means for differentiation are peculiar to each industry. Differentiation can be based on the product itself, the delivery system by which it is sold, the marketing approach, and a broad range of other factors. In construction equipment, for example, Caterpillar Tractor's differentiation is based on product durability, service, spare parts availability, and an excellent dealer network. In cosmetics, differentiation tends to be based more on product image and the positioning of counters in the stores.

A firm that can achieve and sustain differentiation will be an above-average performer in its industry if its price premium exceeds the extra costs incurred in being unique. A differentiator, therefore, must always seek ways of differentiating that lead to a price premium greater than the cost of differentiating. A differentiator cannot ignore its cost position, because its premium prices will be nullified by a markedly inferior cost position. A differentiator thus aims at cost parity or proximity relative to its competitors by reducing cost in all areas that do not affect differentiation.

The logic of the differentiation strategy requires that a firm choose attributes in which to differentiate itself that are *different* from its rivals'. A firm must truly be unique at something or be perceived as unique if it is to expect a premium price. In contrast to cost leadership, however, there can be more than one successful differentiation strategy in an industry if there are a number of attributes that are widely valued by buyers.

Focus

The third generic strategy is focus. This strategy is quite different from the others because it rests on the choice of a narrow competitive scope within an industry. The focuser selects a segment or group of segments in the industry and tailors its strategy to serving them to the exclusion of others. By optimizing its strategy for the target segments, the focuser seeks to achieve a competitive advantage in its target segments even though it does not possess a competitive advantage overall.

The focus strategy has two variants. In *cost focus* a firm seeks a cost advantage in its target segment, while in *differentiation focus* a firm seeks differentiation in its target segment. Both variants of the focus strategy rest on *differences* between a focuser's target segments and other segments in the industry. The target segments must either have buyers with unusual needs or else the production and delivery system that best serves the target segment must differ from that of other industry segments. Cost focus exploits differences in cost behavior in some segments, while differentiation focus exploits the special needs of buyers in certain segments. Such differences imply that the segments are poorly served by broadly targeted competitors who serve them at the same time as they serve others. The focuser can thus achieve competitive advantage by dedicating itself to the segments exclusively. Breadth of target is clearly a matter of degree, but the essence of focus is the exploitation of a narrow target's differences from the balance of the industry. Narrow focus in and of itself is not sufficient for above-average performance.

A good example of a focuser who has exploited differences in the production process that best serves different segments is Hammermill Paper. Hammermill has increasingly been moving toward relatively low-volume, high-quality speciality papers, where the larger paper companies with higher volume machines face a stiff cost penalty for short production runs. Hammermill's equipment is more suited to shorter runs with frequent setups.

A focuser takes advantage of suboptimization in either direction by broadly targeted competitors. Competitors may be *underperforming* in meeting the needs of a particular segment, which opens the possibility for differentiation focus. Broadly targeted competitors may also be *overperforming* in meeting the needs of a segment, which means that they are bearing higher than necessary cost in serving it. An opportunity for cost focus may be present in just meeting the needs of such a segment and no more.

If a focuser's target segment is not different from other segments, then the focus strategy will not succeed. In soft drinks, for example, Royal Crown has focused on cola drinks, while Coca-Cola and Pepsi have broad product lines with many flavored drinks. Royal Crown's segment, however, can be well served by Coke and Pepsi at the same time they are serving other segments. Hence Coke and Pepsi enjoy competitive advantages over Royal Crown in the cola segment due to the economies of having a broader line.

If a firm can achieve sustainable cost leadership (cost focus) or differentiation (differentiation focus) in its segment and the segment is structurally attractive, then the focuser will be an above-average performer in its industry. Segment structural attractiveness is a necessary condition because some segments in an industry are much less profitable than others. There is often room for several sustainable focus strategies in an industry, provided that focusers choose different target segments. Most industries have a variety of segments, and each one that involves a different buyer need or a different optimal production or delivery system is a candidate for a focus strategy.

Stuck in the Middle

A firm that engages in each generic strategy but fails to achieve any of them is 'stuck in the middle.' It possesses no competitive advantage. This strategic position is usually a recipe for below-average performance. A firm that is stuck in the middle will compete at a disadvantage because the cost leader, differentiators, or focusers will be better positioned to compete in any segment. If a firm that is stuck in the middle is lucky enough to discover a profitable product or buyer, competitors with a sustainable competitive advantage will quickly eliminate the spoils. In most industries, quite a few competitors are stuck in the middle.

A firm that is stuck in the middle will earn attractive profits only if the structure of its industry is highly favorable, or if the firm is fortunate enough to have competitors that are also stuck in the middle. Usually, however, such a firm will be much less profitable than rivals achieving one of the generic strategies. Industry maturity tends to widen the performance differences between firms with a generic strategy and those that are stuck in the middle, because it exposes ill-conceived strategies that have been carried along by rapid growth.

Becoming stuck in the middle is often a manifestation of a firm's unwillingness to make *choices* about how to compete. It tries for competitive advantage through every means and achieves none, because achieving different types of competitive advantage usually requires inconsistent actions. Becoming stuck in the middle also afflicts successful firms, who compromise their generic strategy for the sake of growth or prestige. A classic example is Laker Airways, which began with a clear cost-focus strategy based on no-frills operation in the North Atlantic market, aimed at a particular segment of the traveling public that was extremely price sensitive. Over time, however, Laker began adding frills, new services, and new routes. It blurred its image, and suboptimized its service and delivery system. The consequences were disastrous, and Laker eventually went bankrupt.

The temptation to blur a generic strategy, and therefore become stuck in the middle, is particularly great for a focuser once it has dominated its target segments. Focus involves deliberately limiting potential sales volume. Success can lead a focuser to lose sight of the reasons for its success and compromise its focus strategy for growth's sake. Rather than compromise its generic strategy, a firm is usually better off finding new industries in which to grow where it can use its generic strategy again or exploit interrelationships.

Pursuit of More Than One Generic Strategy

Each generic strategy is a fundamentally different approach to creating and sustaining a competitive advantage, combining the type of competitive advantage a firm seeks and the scope of its strategic target. Usually a firm must make a choice among them, or it will become stuck in the middle. The benefits of optimizing the firm's strategy for a particular target segment (focus) cannot be gained if a firm is simultaneously serving a broad range of segments (cost leadership or differentiation). Sometimes a firm may be able to create two largely separate business units within the same corporate entity, each with a different generic strategy. A good example is the British hotel firm Trusthouse Forte, which operates five separate hotel chains each targeted at a different segment. However, unless a firm strictly separates the units pursuing different generic strategies, it may compromise the ability of any of them to achieve its competitive advantage. A suboptimized approach to competing, made likely by the spillover among units of corporate policies and culture, will lead to becoming stuck in the middle.

Achieving cost leadership and differentiation is also usually inconsistent, because differentiation is usually costly. To be unique and command a price premium, a differentiator deliberately elevates costs, as Caterpillar has done in construction equipment. Conversely, cost leadership often requires a firm to forgo some differentiation by standardizing its product, reducing marketing overhead, and the like.

Reducing cost does not always involve a sacrifice in differentiation. Many firms have discovered ways to reduce cost not only without hurting their differentiation but while actually raising it, by using practices that are both more efficient and effective or employing a different technology. Sometimes dramatic cost savings can be achieved with no impact on differentiation at all if a firm has not concentrated on cost reduction previously. However, cost reduction is not the same as achieving a cost advantage. When faced with capable competitors also striving for cost leadership, a firm will ultimately reach the point where further cost reduction requires a sacrifice in differentiation. It is at this point that the generic strategies become inconsistent and a firm must make a choice.

If a firm can achieve cost leadership and differentiation simultaneously, the rewards are great because the benefits are additive – differentiation leads to premium prices at the same time that cost leadership implies lower costs. An example of a firm that has achieved both a cost advantage and differentiation in its segments is Crown Cork and Seal in the metal container industry. Crown has targeted the so-called hard-to-hold uses of cans in the beer, soft drink, and aerosol industries. It manufactures only steel cans rather than both steel and aluminium. In its target segments, Crown has differentiated itself based on service, technological assistance, and offering a full line of steel cans, crowns, and canning machinery. Differentiation of this type would be much more difficult to achieve in other industry segments that have different needs. At the same time, Crown has dedicated its facilities to producing only the types of cans demanded by buyers in its chosen segments and has aggressively invested in modern two-piece steel-canning technology. As a result, Crown has probably also achieved low-cost producer status in its segments.

Sustainability

A generic strategy does not lead to above-average performance unless it is sustainable *vis-à-vis* competitors, though actions that improve industry structure may improve industrywide profitability even if they are imitated. The sustainability of the three generic strategies demands that a firm's competitive advantage resist erosion by competitor behavior or industry evolution. Each generic strategy involves different risks, which are shown in Table 5.2.

The sustainability of a generic strategy requires that a firm possess some barriers that make imitation of the strategy difficult. Since barriers to imitation are never insurmountable, however, it is usually necessary for a firm to offer a moving target to its competitors by investing in order to continually improve its position. Each generic strategy is also a potential threat to the others – as Table 5.2 shows, for example, focusers must worry about broadly targeted competitors and vice versa.

Table 5.2 can be used to analyze how to attack a competitor that employs any of the generic strategies. A firm pursuing overall differentiation, for example, can be attacked by firms that open up a large cost gap, narrow the extent of differentiation, shift the differentiation desired by buyers to other dimensions, or focus. Each generic strategy is vulnerable to different types of attacks.

In some industries, industry structure or the strategies of competitors eliminate the possibility of achieving one or more of the generic strategies. Occasionally no feasible way for one firm to gain a significant cost advantage exists, for example, because several firms are equally placed with respect to scale economies, access to raw materials, or other cost drivers. Similarly, an industry with few segments or only minor differences among segments, such as low-density polyethylene, may offer few opportunities for focus. Thus the mix of generic strategies will vary from industry to industry.

In many industries, however, the three generic strategies can profitably coexist as long as firms pursue different ones or select different bases

TABLE 5.2
Risks of the generic strategies

Risks of Cost Leadership	Risks of Differentiation	Risks of Focus
Cost leadership is not sustained • competitors imitate • technology changes • other bases for cost leadership erode	Differentiation is not sustained • competitors imitate • bases for differentiation become less important to buyers	The focus strategy is imitated The target sement becomes structually unattractive • structure erodes • demand disappears
Proximity in differentiation is lost	Cost proximity is lost	Broadly targeted competitors overwhelm the segment • the segment's differences from other segments narrow • the advantages of a broad line increase
Cost focusers achieve even lower cost in segments	Differentiation focusers achieve even greater differentiation in segments	New focusers subsegment the industry

for differentiation or focus. Industries in which several strong firms are pursuing differentiation strategies based on different sources of buyer value are often particularly profitable. This tends to improve industry structure and lead to stable industry competition. If two or more firms choose to pursue the same generic strategy on the same basis, however, the result can be a protracted and unprofitable battle. The worst situation is where several firms are vying for overall cost leadership. The past and present choice of generic strategies by competitors, then, has an impact on the choices available to a firm and the cost of changing its position.

The concept of generic strategies is based on the premise that there are a number of ways in which competitive advantage can be achieved, depending on industry structure. If all firms in an industry followed the principles of competitive strategy, each would pick different bases for competitive advantage. While not all would succeed, the generic strategies provide alternate routes to superior performance. Some strategic planning concepts have been narrowly based on only one route to competitive advantage, most notably cost. Such concepts not only fail to explain the success of many firms, but they can also lead all firms in an industry to pursue the same type of competitive advantage in the same way – with predictably disastrous results.

Reading 2   Competing on Capabilities

By George Stalk, Philip Evans and Lawrence Shulman[†]

In the 1980s, companies discovered time as a new source of competitive advantage. In the 1990s, they will learn that time is just one piece of a more far-reaching transformation in the logic of competition.

Companies that compete effectively on time – speeding new products to market, manufacturing just in time, or responding promptly to customer complaints – tend to be good at other things as well: for instance, the consistency of their product quality, the acuity of their insight into evolving customer needs, the ability to exploit emerging markets, enter new businesses, or generate new ideas and incorporate them in innovations. But all these qualities are mere reflections of a more fundamental characteristic: a new conception of corporate strategy that we call capabilities-based competition.

Four Principles of Capabilities-Based Competition

In industry after industry, established competitors are being outmaneuvered and overtaken by more dynamic rivals. In the years after World War II, Honda was a modest manufacturer of a 50cc engine designed to be attached to a bicycle. Today it is challenging General Motors and Ford for dominance of the global automobile industry. Xerox invented xerography

[†] Source: Reprinted by permission of *Harvard Business Review*. 'Competing on Capabilities' by George Stalk, Philip Evans and Lawrence Shulman, March/April 1992. Copyright © 1992 by the President and Fellows of Harvard College. All rights reserved.

and the office copier market. But between 1976 and 1982, Canon introduced more than 90 new models, cutting Xerox's share of the midrange copier market in half. Today Canon is a key competitor not only in midrange copiers but also in high-end color copiers.

The greatest challenge to department store giants like Macy's comes neither from other large department stores nor from small boutiques but from The Limited, a $5.25 billion design, procurement, delivery, and retailing machine that exploits dozens of consumer segments with the agility of many small boutiques. Citicorp may still be the largest US bank in terms of assets, but Banc One has consistently enjoyed the highest return on assets in the US banking industry and now enjoys a market capitalization greater than Citicorp's.

These examples represent more than just the triumph of individual companies. They signal a fundamental shift in the logic of competition, a shift that is revolutionizing corporate strategy.

When the economy was relatively static, strategy could afford to be static. In a world characterized by durable products, stable customer needs, well-defined national and regional markets, and clearly identified competitors, competition was a 'war of position' in which companies occupied competitive space like squares on a chessboard, building and defending market share in clearly defined product or market segments. The key to competitive advantage was *where* a company chose to compete. *How* it chose to compete was also important but secondary, a matter of execution.

Few managers need reminding of the changes that have made this traditional approach obsolete. As markets fragment and proliferate, 'owning' any particular market segment becomes simultaneously more difficult and less valuable. As product life cycles accelerate, dominating existing product segments becomes less important than being able to create new products and exploit them quickly. Meanwhile, as globalization breaks down barriers between national and regional markets, competitors are multiplying and reducing the value of national market share.

In this more dynamic business environment, strategy has to become correspondingly more dynamic. Competition is now a 'war of movement' in which success depends on anticipation of market trends and quick response to changing customer needs. Successful competitors move quickly in and out of products, markets, and sometimes even entire businesses – a process more akin to an interactive video game than to chess. In such an environment, the essence of strategy is not the structure of a company's products and markets but the dynamics of its behavior. And the goal is to identify and develop the hard-to-imitate organizational capabilities that distinguish a company from its competitors in the eyes of customers.

Companies like Wal-Mart, Honda, Canon, The Limited, or Banc One have learned this lesson. Their experience and that of other successful companies suggest four basic principles of capabilities-based competition:

- The building blocks of corporate strategy are not products and markets but business processes.

- Competitive success depends on transforming a company's key processes into strategic capabilities that consistently provide superior value to the customer.

- Companies create these capabilities by making strategic investments in a support infrastructure that links together and transcends traditional strategic business units (SBUs) and functions.

- Because capabilities necessarily cross functions, the champion of a capabilities-based strategy is the chief executive officer (CEO).

A capability is a set of business processes strategically understood. Every company has business processes that deliver value to the customer. But few think of them as the primary object of strategy. Capabilities-based competitors identify their key business processes, manage them centrally, and invest in them heavily, looking for a long-term payback.

What transforms a set of individual business processes into a strategic capability? The key is to connect them to real customer needs. A capability is strategic only when it begins and ends with the customer. Of course, just about every company these days claims to be 'close to the customer.' But there is a qualitative difference in the customer focus of capabilities-driven competitors. These companies conceive of the organization as a giant feedback loop that begins with identifying the needs of the customer and ends with satisfying them.

As managers have grasped the importance of time-based competition, for example, they have increasingly focused on the speed of new product *development*. But as a unit of analysis, new product development is too narrow. It is only part of what is necessary to satisfy a customer and, therefore, to build an organizational capability. Better to think in terms of new product *realization*, a capability that includes the way a product is not only developed but also marketed and serviced. The longer and more complex the string of business processes, the harder it is to transform them into a capability – but the greater the value of that capability once built because competitors have more difficulty imitating it.

Weaving business processes together into organizational capabilities in this way also mandates a new logic of vertical integration. At a time when cost pressures are pushing many companies to outsource more and more activities, capabilities-based competitors are integrating vertically to ensure that they, not a supplier or distributor, control the performance of key business processes. Even when a company doesn't actually own every link of the capability chain, the capabilities-based competitor works to tie these parts into its own business systems.

Another attribute of capabilities is that they are collective and cross-functional – a small part of many people's jobs, not a large part of a few.

This helps explain why most companies underexploit capabilities-based competition. Because a capability is 'everywhere and nowhere,' no one executive controls it entirely. Moreover, leveraging capabilities requires a panoply of strategic investments across SBUs and functions far beyond what traditional cost–benefit metrics can justify. Traditional internal accounting and control systems often miss the strategic nature of such investments. For these reasons, building strategic capabilities cannot be treated as an operating matter and left to operating managers, to corporate staff, or still less to SBU heads. It is the primary agenda of the CEO. The prize will be companies that combine scale and flexibility to outperform the competition along five dimensions:

1 *Speed.* The ability to respond quickly to customer or market demands and to incorporate new ideas and technologies quickly into products.

2 *Consistency.* The ability to produce a product that unfailingly satisfies customers' expectations.

3 *Acuity.* The ability to see the competitive environment clearly and thus to anticipate and respond to customers' evolving needs and wants.

4 *Agility.* The ability to adapt simultaneously to many different business environments.

5 *Innovativeness.* The ability to generate new ideas and to combine existing elements to create new sources of value.

Becoming a Capabilities-Based Competitor

Few companies are fortunate enough to begin as capabilities-based competitors. For most, the challenge is to become one.

The starting point is for senior managers to undergo the fundamental shift in perception that allows them to see their business in terms of strategic capabilities. Then they can begin to identify and link together essential business processes to serve customer needs. Finally, they can reshape the organization – including managerial roles and responsibilities – to encourage the new kind of behavior necessary to make capabilities-based competition work.

The experience of a medical-equipment company we'll call Medequip illustrates this change process. An established competitor, Medequip recently found itself struggling to regain market share it had lost to a new competitor. The rival had introduced a lower-priced, lower-performance version of the company's most popular product. Medequip had developed a similar product in response, but senior managers were hesitant to launch it. Their reasoning made perfect sense according to the traditional competitive logic. As managers saw it, the company faced a classic no-win situation. The new product was lower priced but also lower profit. If the company promoted it aggressively to regain market share, overall profitability would suffer.

But when Medequip managers began to investigate their competitive situation more carefully, they stopped defining the problem in terms of static products and markets. Increasingly, they saw it in terms of the organization's business processes. Traditionally, the company's functions had operated autonomously. Manufacturing was separate from sales, which was separate from field service. What's more, the company managed field service the way most companies do – as a classic profit center whose resources were deployed to reduce costs and maximize profitability. For instance, Medequip assigned full-time service personnel only to those customers who bought enough equipment to justify the additional cost.

However, a closer look at the company's experience with these steady customers led to a fresh insight: at accounts where Medequip had placed one or more full-time service representatives on-site, the company renewed its highly profitable service contracts at three times the rate of its other accounts. When these accounts needed new equipment, they chose Medequip twice as often as other accounts did and tended to buy the broadest mix of Medequip products as well. The reason was simple. Medequip's on-site service representatives had become expert in the operations of their customers. They knew what equipment mix best suited the customer and what additional equipment the customer needed. So they had teamed up informally with Medequip's salespeople to become part of the selling process. Because the service reps were on-site full-time, they were also able to respond quickly to equipment problems. And of course, whenever a competitor's equipment broke down, the Medequip reps were on hand to point out the product's shortcomings.

This new knowledge about the dynamics of service delivery inspired top managers to rethink how their company should compete. Specifically, they redefined field service from a stand-alone function to one part of an integrated sales and service capability. They crystallized this new approach in three key business decisions.

First, Medequip decided to use its service personnel not to keep costs low but to maximize the life-cycle profitability of a set of targeted accounts. This decision took the form of a dramatic commitment to place at least one service rep on-site with selected customers – no matter how little business each account currently represented.

The decision to guarantee on-site service was expensive, so choosing which customers to target was crucial; there had to be potential for considerable additional business. The company divided its accounts into three categories: those it dominated, those where a single competitor dominated, and those where several competitors were present. Medequip protected the accounts it dominated by maintaining the already high level of service and by offering attractive terms for renewing service contracts. The company ignored those customers dominated by a single competitor – unless the competitor was having serious problems. All the remaining resources were focused on those accounts where no single competitor had the upper hand.

Next Medequip combined its sales, service, and order entry organizations into cross-functional teams that concentrated almost exclusively on the needs of the targeted accounts. The company trained service reps in sales techniques so they could take full responsibility for generating new sales leads. This freed up the sales staff to focus on the more strategic role of understanding the long-term needs of the customer's business. Finally, to emphasize Medequip's new commitment to total service, the company even taught its service reps how to fix competitor's equipment.

Once this new organizational structure was in place, Medequip finally introduced its new low-price product. The result: the company has not only stopped its decline in market share but also *increased* share by almost 50 percent. The addition of the lower-priced product has reduced profit margins, but the overall mix still includes many higher-priced products. And absolute profits are much higher than before.

This story suggests four steps by which any company can transform itself into a capabilities-based competitor.

Shift the Strategic Framework to Achieve Aggressive Goals

At Medequip, managers transformed what looked like a no-win situation – either lose share or lose profits – into an opportunity for a major competitive victory. They did so by abandoning the company's traditional function, cost, and profit-center orientation and by identifying and managing the capabilities that link customer need to customer satisfaction. The chief expression of this new capabilities-based strategy was the decision to provide on-site service reps to targeted accounts and to create cross-functional sales and service teams.

Organize around the Chosen Capability and Make Sure Employees Have the Necessary Skills and Resources to Achieve It

Having set this ambitious competitive goal, Medequip managers next set about reshaping the company in terms of it. Rather than retaining the existing functional structure and trying to encourage coordination through some kind of matrix, they created a brand new organization – Customer Sales and Service – and divided it into 'cells' with overall responsibility for specific customers. The company also provided the necessary training so that employees could understand how their new roles would help achieve new business goals. Finally, Medequip created systems to support employees in their new roles. For example, one information system uses CD-ROMs to give field-service personnel quick access to information about Medequip's product line as well as those of competitors.

Make Progress Visible and Bring Measurements and Reward into Alignment

Medequip also made sure that the company's measurement and reward systems reflected the new competitive strategy. Like most companies, the company had never known the profitability of individual customers. Traditionally, field-service employees were measured on overall service profitability. With the shift to the new approach, however, the company had to develop a whole new set of measures – for example, Medequip's 'share-by-customer-by-product,' the amount of money the company invested in servicing a particular customer, and the customer's current and estimated lifetime profitability. Team members' compensation was calculated according to these new measures.

Do Not Delegate the Leadership of the Transformation

Becoming a capabilities-based competitor requires an enormous amount of change. For that reason, it is a process extremely difficult to delegate. Because capabilities are cross-functional, the change process can't be left to middle managers. It requires the hands-on guidance of the CEO and the active involvement of top line managers. At Medequip, the heads of sales, service, and order entry led the subteams that made the actual recommendations, but it was the CEO who oversaw the change process, evaluated their proposals, and made the final decision. His leading role ensured senior management's commitment to the recommended changes.

This top-down change process has the paradoxical result of driving business decision making down to those directly participating in key processes – for example, Medequip's sales and service staff. This leads to a high measure of operational flexibility and an almost reflex-like responsiveness to external change.

EXHIBIT 5.2

HOW CAPABILITIES DIFFER FROM CORE COMPETENCIES: THE CASE OF HONDA

In their influential 1990 HBR article, 'The Core Competencies of the Corporation,' (see chapter 6) Gary Hamel and C.K. Prahalad mount an attack on traditional notions of strategy that is not so dissimilar from what we are arguing here. For Hamel and Prahalad, however, the central building block of corporate strategy is 'core competence.' How is a competence different from a capability, and how do the two concepts relate to each other?

Hamel and Prahalad define core competence as the combination of individual technologies and production skills that underly a company's myriad product lines. Sony's core competence in miniaturization, for example, allows the company to make everything from the Sony Walkman to videocameras to notebook computers. Canon's core competencies in optics, imaging, and microprocessor controls have enabled it to enter markets as seemingly diverse as copiers, laser printers, cameras, and image scanners.

As the above examples suggest, Hamel and Prahalad use core competence to explain the ease with which successful competitors are able to enter new and seemingly unrelated businesses. But a closer look reveals that competencies are not the whole story.

Consider Honda's move from motorcycles into other businesses, including lawn mowers, outboard motors, and automobiles. Hamel and Prahalad attribute Honda's success to its underlying competence in engines and power trains. While Honda's engine competence is certainly important, it alone cannot explain the speed with which the company has successfully moved into a wide range of businesses over the past 20 years. After all, General Motors (to take just one example) is also an accomplished designer and manufacturer of engines. What distinguishes Honda from its competitors is its focus on capabilities.

One important but largely invisible capability is Honda's expertise in 'dealer management' – its ability to train and support its dealer network with operating procedures and policies for merchandising, selling floor planning, and service management. First developed for its motorcycle business, this set of business processes has since been replicated in each new business the company has entered.

Another capability central to Honda's success has been its skill at 'product realization.' Traditional product development separates planning, proving, and executing into three sequential activities: assessing the market's needs and whether existing products are meeting those needs; testing the proposed product; then building a prototype. The end result of this process is a new factory or organization to introduce the new product. This traditional approach takes a long time – and with time goes money.

Honda has arranged these activities differently. First, planning and proving go on continuously and in parallel. Second, these activities are clearly separated from execution. At Honda, the highly disciplined execution cycle schedules major product revisions every four years and minor revisions every two years. The 1990 Honda Accord, for example, which is the first major redesign of that model since 1986, incorporates a power train developed two years earlier and first used in the 1988 Accord. Finally, when a new product is ready, it is released to existing factories and organizations, which dramatically shortens the amount of time needed to launch it. As time is reduced, so are cost and risk.

Consider the following comparison between Honda and GM. In 1984, Honda launched its Acura division; one year later, GM created Saturn. Honda chose to integrate Acura into its existing organization and facilities. In Europe, for example, the Acura Legend is sold through the same sales force as the Honda Legend. The Acura division now makes three models – the Legend, Integra, and Vigor – and is turning out 300,000 cars a year. At the end of 1991, seven years after it was launched, the division had produced a total of 800,000 vehicles. More important, it had already introduced eight variations of its product line.

By contrast, GM created a separate organization and a separate facility for Saturn. Production began in late 1990, and 1991 will be its first full model year. If GM is lucky, it will be producing 240,000 vehicles in the next year or two and will have two models out.

As the Honda example suggests, competencies and capabilities represent two different but complementary dimensions of an emerging paradigm for corporate strategy. Both concepts emphasize 'behavioral' aspects of strategy in contrast to the traditonal structural model. But whereas core competence emphasizes technological and production expertise at specific points along the value chain, capabilities are more broadly based, encompassing the entire value chain. In this respect, capabilities are visible to the customer in a way that core competencies rarely are.

Like the 'grand unified theory' that modern-day physicists are searching for to explain physical behavior at both the subatomic level and that of the entire cosmos, the combination of core competence and capabilities may define the universal model for corporate strategy in the 1990s and beyond.

A New Logic of Growth: The Capabilities Predator

Once managers reshape the company in terms of its underlying capabilities, they can use these capabilities to define a growth path for the corporation. At the center of capabilities-based competition is a new logic of growth.

In the 1960s, most managers assumed that when growth in a company's basic business slowed, the company should turn to diversification. This was the age of the multibusiness conglomerate. In the 1970s and 1980s, however, it became clear that growth through diversification was difficult. And so, the pendulum of management thinking swung once again. Companies were urged to 'stick to their knitting' – that is, to focus on their core business, identify where the profit was, and get rid of everything else. The idea of the corporation became increasingly narrow.

Competing on capabilities provides a way for companies to gain the benefits of both focus and diversification. Put another way, a company that focuses on its strategic capabilities can compete in a remarkable diversity of regions, products, and businesses and do it far more coherently than the typical conglomerate can. Such a company is a 'capabilities predator' – able to come out of nowhere and move rapidly from nonparticipant to major player and even to industry leader.

Capabilities-based companies grow by transferring their essential business processes – first to new geographic areas and then to new businesses. Wal-Mart CEO David Glass alludes to this method of growth when he characterizes Wal-Mart as 'always pushing from the inside out; we never jump and backfill.'

Strategic advantages built on capabilities are easier to transfer geographically than more traditional competitive advantages. Honda, for example, has become a manufacturer in Europe and the United States with relatively few problems. The quality of its cars made in the United States is so good that the company is exporting some of them back to Japan.

But the big payoff for capabilities-led growth comes not through geographical expansion but through rapid entry into whole new businesses. Capabilities-based companies do this in at least two ways. The first is by 'cloning' their key business processes. Again, Honda is a typical example.

Most people attribute Honda's success to the innovative design of its products or the way the company manufactures them. These factors are certainly important. But the company's growth has been spearheaded by less visible capabilities. For example, a big part of Honda's original success in motorcycles was due to the company's distinctive capability in 'dealer management,' which departed from the traditional relationship between motorcycle manufacturers and dealers. Typically, local dealers were motorcycle enthusiasts who were more concerned with finding a way to support their hobby than with building a strong business. They were not particularly interested in marketing, parts-inventory management, or other business systems.

Honda, by contrast, managed its dealers to ensure that they would become successful businesspeople. The company provided operating procedures and policies for merchandising, selling, floor planning, and service management. It trained all its dealers and their entire staffs in these new management systems and supported them with a computerized dealer-management information system. The part-time dealers of competitors were no match for the better prepared and better financed Honda dealers.

Honda's move into new businesses, including lawn mowers, outboard motors, and automobiles, has depended on recreating this same dealer-management capability in each new sector. Even in segments like luxury cars, where local dealers are generally more service oriented than those in the motorcycle business, Honda's skill at managing its dealers is transforming service standards. Honda dealers consistently receive the highest ratings for customer satisfaction among auto companies selling in the United States. One reason is that Honda gives its dealers far more autonomy to decide on the spot whether a needed repair is covered by the warranty (see Exhibit 5.2).

But the ultimate form of growth in the capabilities-based company may not be cloning business processes so much as creating processes so flexible and robust that the same set can serve many different businesses.

The Future of Capabilities-Based Competition

For the moment, capabilities-based companies have the advantage of competing against rivals still locked into the old way of seeing the competitive environment. But such a situation won't last forever. As more and more companies make the transition to capabilities-based competition, the simple fact of competing on capabilities will become less important than the specific capabilities a company has chosen to build. Given the necessary long-term investments, the strategic choices managers make will end up determining a company's fate.

Business Level Strategy in International Perspective

Whoever is winning at the moment will always seem to be invincible.
(George Orwell 1903–1950; English novelist)

Just as in the previous debates, it has become clear that there are various ways of dealing with the paradox of markets and resources. Each of the authors has argued a particular point of view, and it is the reader's task to judge which approach will yield the highest strategic dividends, under which set of circumstances. And as before, the chapter is concluded by explicitly looking at the issue from an international angle.

The difference between this and other chapters is that comparative management researchers have not reported specific national preferences for an inside-out or an outside-in perspective. This may be due to the fact that there actually are no distinct national inclinations when dealing with this paradox. However, it might also be the case that the late emergence of resource-based theories (starting in the early 1990s) has not yet allowed for cross-national comparisons.

As a stimulus to the debate whether there are national differences in the approach to business level strategies, we would like to bring forward a number of factors that might be of influence on how the paradox of markets and resources is tackled in different countries. It goes almost without saying that more international research is needed to give this discussion a firmer footing.

Mobility Barriers

In general, industry and market positions will be of more value if there are high mobility barriers within the environment[26]. Some of these mobility barriers can be specifically national in origin. Government regulation, in particular, can be an important source of mobility barriers. For instance, import quotas and duties, restrictive licensing systems, and fiscal regulations and subsidies, can all – knowingly or unknowingly – result in protection of incumbent firms. Such government intervention enhances the importance of obtained positions.

Other national sources of mobility barriers can be unions' resistance to change and high customer loyalty. In some economies high mobility barriers might also be imposed by powerful groups or families.

In such economies, which are more rigid due to high mobility barriers, strategists might have a strong preference to think in terms of market positions first, since these are more difficult to obtain than the necessary resources. The opposite would be true in more dynamic economies, where market positions might easily be challenged by competitors, unless they are based on distinctive and difficult to imitate resources.

Resource Mobility

A second international difference might be found in the types of resources employed across countries. In nations where the dominant industries are populated by firms using relatively simple and abundant resources, market positions are far more important, since acquisition of the necessary resources is hardly a worry. However, if a national economy is composed of industries using complex bundles of resources, requiring many years of painstaking development, there might be a tendency to emphasize the importance of resources over market positions.

Further Readings

Although many textbooks give an overview of the variety of approaches to the topic of business level strategy, none of these introductions are as crisp as John Kay's book *Foundations of Corporate Success: How Corporate Strategies Add Value*, which can be highly recommended as further reading. In the category of textbooks, Robert Grant's *Contemporary Strategy Analysis* is suggested as a good overview of business strategy approaches.

Most of what has been published on the topic of business level strategy has implicitly or explicitly made reference to the work of Michael Porter. Therefore, any follow up readings should include his benchmark works *Competitive Strategy* and *Competitive Advantage*. It is also interesting to see how his thinking has developed and has embraced some of the resource-based concepts. In particular his articles 'Towards a Dynamic Theory of Strategy,' and 'What is Strategy?' are stimulating works. Also highly recommended is the book by Robert Buzzell and Bradley Gale, *The PIMS Principles: Linking Strategy to Performance*, which is well known for linking market share to performance.

For a better insight into the resource-based approach, readers might want to go back to Edith Penrose's classic book *The Theory of the Growth of the Firm*, which has recently been republished. For a more recent introduction, Robert Grant's article 'The Resource-Based Theory of Competitive Advantage: Implications for Strategy Formulation' can be advised. David Collis and Cynthia Montgomery have also written an accessible article explaining the resource-based view, titled 'Competing on Resources: Strategy in the 1990s.' Other important works that are more academically-oriented are 'A Historical Comparison of Resource-Based Theory and Five Schools of Thought Within Industrial Organization Economics: Do We Have a New Theory of the Firm?' by Kathleen Conner; 'Strategic Assets and Organizational Rent' by Raphael Amit and Paul Schoemaker; 'The Cornerstones of Competitive Advantage: A Resource-Based View' by Margaret Peteraf.

Last, but not least, the works of Gary Hamel and C.K. Prahalad should be mentioned. Many of their articles in *Harvard Business Review*, such as 'Strategic Intent,' 'Strategy as Stretch and Leverage,' and 'The Core Competence of the Corporation' (reading 6.2 in this book) have had a major impact, both on practitioners and academics, and are well worth reading. Many of the ideas expressed in these articles have been brought together in their book *Competing for the Future*, which is therefore highly recommended.

Corporate Level Strategy

Consider the little mouse, how sagacious
an animal it is which never entrusts its
life to one hole only.

(Plautus 254–184 BC; Roman playwright)

None ever got ahead of me
except the man of one task.

(Azariah Rossi 1513–1578; Italian physician)

The Paradox of Responsiveness and Synergy

Just as mice see the benefit of more than one hole, so many companies believe in the virtue of being active in more than one business. These firms have chosen to diversify based on the assumption that multibusiness involvement will lead to synergies that outweigh the extra costs of managing a more complex organization. *Multibusiness level*, or *corporate*, strategy deals with the identification and realization of these synergies. Or as Porter[1] puts it, 'corporate strategy is what makes the corporate whole add up to more than the sum of its business unit parts.'

Synergies occur when firms are able to productively share resources among two or more businesses (also referred to as *economies of scope*). If resource productivity gains are achieved by such sharing, this is called *resource leveraging*[2]. All types of company resources can potentially be leveraged. For example, if two business units use the same production facilities, savings might be achieved. Other tangible resources may also be jointly employed, such as buildings, equipment, materials, land and money. Besides these tangibles, business units may share intangible resources as well. Joint use can be made of relational resources (e.g. bargaining power *vis-à-vis* suppliers, reputation among customers, contacts with regulatory agencies), while competences can also be leveraged (sharing knowledge, capabilities and business outlook).

Synergies can also be achieved by linking the market strategies of two or more business units. Such coordination of business units' externally oriented behavior, with the intention of creating added-value, can be referred to as *strategy alignment*. Both vertically- and horizontally-related business units might benefit from aligning their market strategies with one another. Two vertically-related business units might develop a symbiotic supplier-buyer relationship between them, with a high level of specialized investment and dependence, without the threat of one misusing this power over the other. Two horizontally-related business units (i.e. selling similar types of products) might, for example, coordinate their attack on a common competitor, join forces to create market entry barriers and build acceptance for a common standard in the market.

To realize such synergies, a firm must to some extent coordinate the activities carried out in its various business units. The autonomy of the business units must be partially limited, in the interest of concerted action. However, coordination comes with a price tag. An extra level of management is required, more meetings, extra complexity, potential conflicts of interest, turf wars, additional bureaucracy – alignment costs money and diminishes a business unit's ability to precisely tailor its strategy to its specific business environment. In other words, *coordination* with other business units and meddling by the corporate center can blunt a business unit's *responsiveness* to its own business[3].

Multibusiness level strategy is concerned with realizing more value creation by means of synergy than value destruction through loss of responsiveness. To achieve this, corporate strategists must wrestle with the paradox of responsiveness and synergy. Although there are many different views on how these two objectives might be balanced or pursued simultaneously, two opposite perspectives stand out in the debate. These two views, the *portfolio* and the *core competence* perspectives, are almost at opposite ends of the spectrum, with many other strategists taking up intermediate positions. While these two perspectives do not monopolize the real-life debate, they do represent the two extremes to which strategists are willing to go (see Table 6.1). Therefore, the debate in this chapter will start with these two poles.

The Portfolio Perspective

In the portfolio perspective, responsiveness is strongly emphasized over synergy. Strategists taking this perspective usually argue that each business has its own unique characteristics and demands. Firms operating in different businesses must therefore develop a specific strategy for each business and assign the responsibility for each business strategy to a specific part of the organization – a *strategic business unit* (SBU). In this manner, the (strategic) business units can be highly responsive to the competitive dynamics in the business, while being a clear unit of accountability towards the corporate center. High responsiveness, however, requires freedom from corporate center interference and freedom from cross-business coordination. Hence, a high level of business unit autonomy is required, with the corporate center's influence limited to arm's length financial control.

In the portfolio perspective, the main reason for a number of highly autonomous business units to be in one firm is to *leverage financial resources*. The only synergies emphasized are financial synergies. Actually, the term 'portfolio' entered the business vocabulary via the financial sector, where it refers to an investor's *collection of shareholdings* in different companies, purchased to spread investment risks. Transferred to corporate strategy, the portfolio perspective views the corporate center as an active investor with financial stakes in a number of stand-alone business units. The role of the center is one of selecting a promising portfolio of businesses, keeping tight financial control, and allocating available capital – redirecting flows of cash from business units where prospects are dim ('cash cows' or 'dogs'), to other business units where higher returns can be expected ('stars' or 'question marks'). The strategic mission of each business unit is, therefore, also financial in orientation – grow, hold, milk or divest, depending on the business unit's position on the portfolio grid. A good corporate strategy strives for a balanced portfolio of mature cash producers and high potential ROI cash users, at an acceptable level of overall risk. The business units do not necessarily need to be 'related' in any other way than financial. In practice, the business units can be related, that is, there can be resource leveraging and strategy alignment opportunities that are seized. The portfolio perspective does not reject the pursuit of other forms of synergy, but neither does it accommodate such efforts[4].

New businesses can be entered by means of internal growth, but the portfolio approach to corporate strategy is particularly well suited to diversification through acquisition. In a multibusiness firm run on portfolio principles, acquired companies are simple to integrate into the corporation, because they can be largely left as stand-alone units and only need to be linked to corporate reporting and control systems. Proponents of the portfolio perspective argue that such nonsynergistic acquisitions can be highly profitable[5]. Excess cash can be routed to more attractive investment opportunities than the corporation has internally. Moreover, the acquiring corporation can shake up the management of the acquired company and can function as a strategic sounding board for the new people[6].

The portfolio perspective is particularly well known for the analytical techniques that have been developed to support it. A large number of portfolio grids are in widespread use as graphical tools for visualizing the composition of the corporation and for determining the position of each of the business units. All of these portfolio grids are based on the same fundamental concept, that the profit and growth potential of individual business units can be measured along two dimensions – attractiveness of the business, and competitive strength of the business unit. For instance, the Boston Consulting Group matrix (see reading 6.1) uses business growth as a measure of attractiveness and relative market share as a measure of competitive strength. The General Electric business screen uses a larger number of factors to determine a score on both dimensions. The Arthur D. Little matrix, on the other hand, uses industry maturity instead of industry attractiveness as one of its two dimensions. These portfolio tools have proven to be popular and much used[7], even among strategists who are not proponents of the portfolio perspective.

The Core Competence Perspective

The core competence perspective is fundamentally at odds with the portfolio perspective's minimalist interpretation of corporate strategy. In the core competence perspective, multibusiness firms should be more than a loose federation of businesses held together by a common investor. Actually, corporations should be quite the opposite – a common resource-base that is applied to various businesses. As the name of the perspective indicates, it is a set of shared competences that is believed to be the best central core for a multibusiness company. It is argued that these core competences should be leveraged as much as possible, by using them in all of the firm's business units. Such use in a specific business setting will, in turn, improve the core competence, leading to a virtuous circle of competence upgrading, profiting the entire corporation.

As all business units should both tap into, and contribute to, the corporation's core competences, the business units' autonomy is necessarily limited. The creation and leveraging of core competences requires that the business units remain close team players. Prahalad and Hamel's[8] metaphor for the corporation is not an investor's portfolio, but a large tree – 'the trunk and major limbs are core products, the smaller branches are business units, the leaves, flowers and fruit are end products; the root system that provides nourishment, sustenance and stability is the core competence.' Business unit branches can be cut off and new ones can grow on, but all spring from the same tree. And it is the corporate center's role to nurture this tree, building up the core competences and ensuring that the firm's critical resources and competence carriers can easily be redeployed across business units. Unavoidably, the responsiveness to the specific characteristics of each business does suffer from this emphasis on coordination.

Yet the loss of responsiveness to business demands is more than compensated by the benefits of resource leveraging. In line with the inside-out perspective discussed in Chapter 5, proponents of the core competence perspective argue that long-term competitiveness depends more on the continual upgrading of unique bundles of resources within a corporation, than on occupying specific market positions. Competitive wars are fought out between corporations, each trying to build better competence bases – skirmishes in particular markets are only battles in this broader war. From this angle, building the corporation's core competences is strategic, while engaging other corporations in specific markets is tactical. The corporate center is therefore the nexus of

TABLE 6.1
Portfolio versus core competence perspective

	Portfolio Perspective	Core Competence Perspective
Emphasis on	Responsiveness over synergy	Synergy over responsiveness
View of competition	Firms compete within a business	Corporations compete across businesses
Competitive strategy at	Business level	Corporate level
Key success factor	Responsiveness to business demands	Competence leveraging
Corporate composition	Potentially unrelated (diverse)	Shared competence-base (focused)
Multibusiness synergy	Cash flow optimization	Rapid competence building
Primary task corporate center	Capital allocation to SBUs	Competence development and application
Position of business units	Highly autonomous (independent)	Highly integrated (interdependent)
Coordination between SBUs	Low, incidental	High, structural
Corporate control style	Setting financial objectives	Joint strategy development
Diversification acquisitions	Simple to accommodate	Difficult to integrate

competitive strategy, instead of the business units, that are literally divisions in the overall campaign. It follows that some loss of responsiveness to specific business pressures is an acceptable price to pay.

The question for the field of strategic management is, therefore, whether multibusiness level strategies should be formed based on the portfolio or the core competence perspective. Should corporate strategists limit themselves to achieving financial synergies, leaving SBU managers to 'mind their own business'? Or should corporate strategists strive to build a multibusiness firm around a shared set of competences, intricately weaving all business units into a highly coordinated whole? In short, strategists have to deal with yet another fundamental challenge, the paradox of responsiveness and synergy.

Defining the Issues: Composition and Coordination

Most strategists agree that the two key questions of corporate strategy are: What businesses should the corporation be in and how should this array of businesses be managed? These two central questions can be referred to as the issues of *composition* and *coordination*. Before proceeding to the readings, the nature of these two issues will first be more closely examined.

The Issue of Corporate Composition

A multibusiness firm is composed of two or more businesses. When a corporation enters yet another line of business, either by starting up new activities (*internal growth*) or by buying another firm (*acquisition*), this is referred to as *diversification*. There are two general categories of diversification moves, *vertical* and *horizontal*. Vertical diversification, usually called *vertical integration*, is when a firm enters other businesses within its own business system – it can strive for backward integration by getting involved in supplier businesses or it can initiate forward integration by entering the businesses of its buyers. When a firm expands outside of its current business system(s), this is referred to as horizontal diversification (see Figure 6.1).

The issue of corporate composition deals with the question whether a firm should diversify, and if so, into which businesses. This issue can be examined by looking at the conditions under which diversification results in value creation. According to Porter[9] entering into another business (by acquisition or internal growth) can only lead to increased shareholder value if three essential tests are passed:

FIGURE 6.1
Directions of diversification

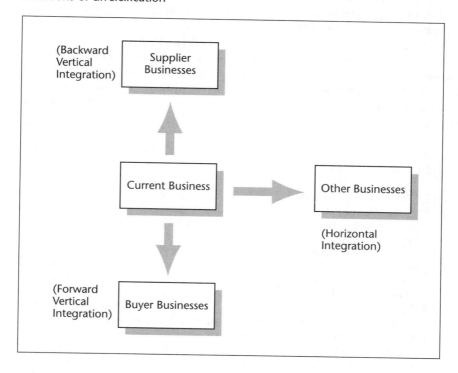

- *The attractiveness test.* The business 'must be structurally attractive, or capable of being made attractive.' In other words, the business must be potentially profitable (see Chapter 5).

- *The cost-of-entry test.* 'The cost of entry must not capitalize all the future profits.' In other words, it must be possible to recoup the investment made.

- *The better-off test.* 'Either the new unit must gain competitive advantage from its link with the corporation or vice versa.' In other words, it must be possible to create synergy.

It is around this last test that the debate in the area of corporate strategy revolves. What types of synergies can realistically be achieved, without paying a heavier penalty in terms of coordination costs? To answer this question, it must first be clear what synergy is.

For quite some time, strategists have known that potential for synergy has something to do with *relatedness*[10]. Diversification moves that were unrelated, for example a food company's entrance into the bicycle rental business, were deemed to be less profitable, in general, than moves that were related, such as car makers' diversification into the car rental business. However, the problem has been to determine the nature of 'relatedness'. Superficial signs of relatedness do not indicate that there is potential for synergy. Drilling for oil and mining might seem highly related (both are 'extraction businesses'), but Shell found out the hard way that they are not, selling the acquired mining company Billiton to Gencor after they were unable to add value. Chemicals and pharmaceuticals seem like similar businesses (especially if pharmaceuticals are labelled 'specialty chemicals'), but ICI decided to split itself in two (into ICI and Zeneca), because it couldn't achieve sufficient synergy between these two business areas.

Strategists have therefore attempted to pin down the exact nature of relatedness[11]. Two areas of 'potential relatedness'[12] are generally identified:

■ *Opportunities for resource leveraging.* Two businesses are related if resources can be productively shared between them. All types of resources can be shared, both tangible and intangible. Resource leveraging can be achieved in three ways. First, resources can be physically transferred from one business unit to the other, where better use can be made of them (*resource reallocation*). For instance, money and personnel are often shifted between business units, depending on where they are needed. Second, resources can be copied from one business unit to the other, so that the same resource can be used many times over (*resource replication*). This happens, for example, when competences are copied between business units. Third, resources can be employed simultaneously by two or more business units, where joint use is more efficient and/or more effective (*resource pooling*). For instance, business units can initiate shared activities, such as production or marketing, or can make use of the same brand name.

■ *Opportunities for strategy alignment.* Two businesses are related if the alignment of their market strategies creates added-value. Coordinated behavior between business units can be preferable to independent, uncoordinated behavior under a number of circumstances. Horizontally related business units working together as a team can often multiply their effective market power by 'ganging up' on competitors, buyers or suppliers. Coordination within one firm can also prevent a number of business units from fighting fiercely amongst one another, which might have happened if all units were independent companies. Vertically related business units linked to each other in one firm may also be preferable to independent buyers and suppliers. Especially where close vertical cooperation is needed and relation-specific investments need to be made, *vertical integration* has a high potential for synergy, by avoiding the threats of mistrust and power misuse.

In this chapter the focus is on the potential for resource leveraging across business units. The advantages and disadvantages of strategy alignment across businesses are studied in more depth in Chapter 7.

FIGURE 6.2
Corporate coordination mechanisms

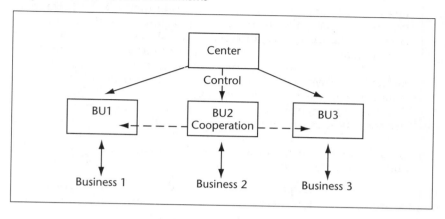

The Issue of Corporate Coordination

Coordination is about attaining the potential synergies. In other words, the question is how the business units must be managed to achieve the envisioned added value. Recognizing the possible benefits of working together under a corporate umbrella is one thing, but developing coordination mechanisms that do not cost more than they yield is another. Therefore, corporate strategists need to carefully design organizational systems that facilitate resource leveraging and/or strategy alignment, without excessive costs in terms of overhead, bureaucracy, slow decision-making, political infighting and bland compromises.

Many forms of coordination exist and many classifications have been put forward[13]. For the debate in this chapter, however, the most important distinction is between cooperation and control mechanisms (see Figure 6.2).

- *Control mechanisms.* An obvious way to facilitate resource leveraging and strategy alignment across businesses is to appoint someone as coordinator and to place that person hierarchically above the units that need to be coordinated. Such a central figure (a division-level or corporate-level manager), with formal power over the individual business units, can then enforce coordination by hierarchical control. Such control can be exerted in many ways. It can be *direct* (telling business units what to do), but often it is more indirect, by giving business units objectives that must be met. Campbell and Goold[14] distinguish between financial and strategic objectives. The negotiation, setting and monitoring of financial objectives is referred to as *financial control*, while they speak of *strategic control* when the guiding objectives are of a strategic nature.

■   *Cooperation mechanisms.* Coordination between business units can also
    be achieved without the use of hierarchical authority. Business units
    might be willing to cooperate because it is in their interest to do so, or
    because they recognize the overall corporate interests. If business units
    believe in the importance of certain synergies, sometimes identifying
    these potential synergies themselves, this can be a powerful impetus to
    coordinate. Corporate strategists interested in such coordination by
    mutual adjustment will focus on creating the organizational circum-
    stances under which such *self-organization* can take place (see Chapters
    3 and 4). For instance, they might strengthen formal and informal ties
    between the business units, to enhance mutual understanding and
    encourage the exchange of ideas and joint initiatives. They may also
    support cross-business career paths and try to instil a corporation-wide
    culture, to facilitate the communication between business units.

It is the task of the corporate strategist to determine the right mix of
control and cooperation mechanisms, needed to bring about the synergies envisioned. Of course, which mechanisms are emphasized depends
on the perspective taken by the corporate center. Advocates of the portfolio perspective, arguing that very little coordination is needed at all,
strongly prefer arm's length financial control over more direct interference and 'fuzzy' cooperation. Proponents of the core competence perspective, believing in the importance of tight coordination, stress the
need for directer control by the corporate center, supported by strong
cooperation mechanisms.

EXHIBIT 6.1
Philips case

PHILIPS: REWIRE OR SHORTCIRCUIT?

On October 1st 1996, Cor Boonstra took over as president and CEO of
Philips Electronics NV, headquartered in Eindhoven, the Netherlands.
Boonstra had only joined the top management team at Philips in 1994,
after leaving the American fast-moving consumer goods company, Sara
Lee. His appointment was a surprise to many, both in and outside the
company, as he edged out internal Philips candidates and other recently
hired industry outsiders, such as Pierre Everaert (from food-retailing
multinational Ahold) and Henk Bodt (from copier-maker Océ van der
Grinten). In the business press it was suggested that Boonstra had been
selected because of his strong marketing background, ability to make
tough decisions and lack of emotional and political attachment to the
current Philips businesses and way of doing things.

Boonstra succeeded Jan Timmer, under whose leadership Philips had
been pulled back from the brink of collapse. When taking the helm in 1990,
Timmer had been confronted with a severe crisis, brought on by intense

competition in most of the industries in which Philips was active, and compounded by a high level of bureaucracy and political infighting. Timmer, a long-time company man, had built up a reputation for restructuring ailing divisions and was appointed to apply the same medicine to the entire company. He initiated a major restructuring plan, code-named 'Operation Centurion,' involving major cost and job cutting programs. Throughout its world-wide operations, Philips chopped 59,000 jobs, most of them in high-cost regions, such as North America and Europe, reducing the work force to a level of 238,000 at the beginning of 1995. Timmer also gave the company some financial breathing space by divesting non-core activities. The white goods division (mainly refrigerators and washing machines) was sold to Whirlpool and a minority stake in the Japanese electronics giant Matsushita was sold back to this company.

Due to these efforts, the $2.3 billion loss (including restructuring costs) suffered in 1990 had been transformed into a modest profit by 1994, allowing Philips to pay a small dividend to its shareholders for the first time in four years. Three of the five product sectors (Light, Other Consumer Products, and Components and Semiconductors) were profitable, while the other two product sectors (Consumer Electronics and Professional Products) still showed negative results (for a large part due to problems within their German Grundig subsidiary).

While the emphasis of the Centurion program had been on operational efficiency, Timmer had also endorsed a number of high profile new product initiatives, to ensure future areas of growth. Especially in Philips' key consumer electronics division new products were needed to compensate for the low growth and cut-throat competition in the 'traditional' product groups, such as televisions, radios, and audio and video equipment. In this area, three new initiatives were launched. To reinvigorate sales in the area of television, Philips took a leading role in the development of high definition television (HDTV); to bring cassette players into the digital age, Philips introduced the digital compact cassette (DCC) player; and as a venture into the world of multimedia, Philips created the interactive CD player (CD-I). However, as Boonstra took over from Timmer, he was forced to conclude that none of these innovations had evolved into the blockbuster products needed to revive Philips', and the industry's, fortunes. Neither did Timmer's decision to pour hundreds of millions of guilders into the fast-growing mobile telephones market result in a strong profit-generator for the future. As a late entrant into this industry, Philips was finding it just too difficult to catch up with the top three, Ericsson, Nokia and Motorola.

Unfortunately, Philips' move into 'software' creation and distribution hadn't proven to be particularly successful either. The purchase in 1991 of Superclub, the video rental chain with 430 stores in the US and 86 stores in Europe (mostly in Belgium) was very costly, especially due to unforeseen reorganization costs. In 1993 the American stores were sold. Philips also invested in the acquisition of television cable companies, particularly in the Netherlands, spending approximately a billion guilders ($600 million).

However, these holdings were fragmented geographically, and didn't help to turn Timmer's pet project, a cable sports channel called Sport7, into a success. The channel, in which Philips had a minority stake, and of which Timmer was chairman, went bankrupt in 1996, after only a few months. Only Philips' music company PolyGram, already in the business of 'content,' was moderately successful in its diversification into the motion picture industry. When compared to the track records of Philips' arch rivals Sony and Matsushita, who both lost billions of dollars by acquiring major Hollywood film studios, PolyGram's results looked even better.

Given these developments, it was clear to Boonstra that besides continued cost cutting, significant strategic changes would have to be made. Obviously, at the business level Philips would need to improve its competitive position and find growth oppportunities, despite the intense rivalry and sluggish demand in many of its markets. Particularly worrying were the consumer electronics business units and the medical products (due to reduced health care budgets). At the corporate level, the tough choices confronting Boonstra were even more challenging. Overseeing this strongly diversified company, with 60 different units, Boonstra had to ask himself why the company existed in its current composition. What was the 'wiring' keeping the corporation together and was it actually creating added-value? Wouldn't Philips be worth more to its shareholders if split up and sold to the highest bidder, instead of kept together as one firm? Maybe less drastically than a split up, should Philips divest certain business units or even entire divisions?

In other words, Boonstra had to grapple with the task of determining what Philips' core businesses should be and what types of synergies he wished to pursue between these businesses. The company's array of businesses was quite wide. Within the product sector consumer electronics (34 percent of sales), Philips was divided into Sound & Vision (television, audio, video and personal communication), Car Systems (car stereo, car navigation, automotive electronics), Business Electronics (monitors, broadcast TV systems, video distribution networks, digital video communication, dictation systems), and Grundig (TV, audio, video, car stereo and professional electronics). The Other Consumer Products sector (19 percent of sales) consisted of Domestic Appliances and Personal Care (vacuum cleaners, irons, air cleaners, shavers, hair dryers, electric toothbrushes, etc.), Philips Media (software, services, interactive media systems and cable television systems) and PolyGram. Professional Products and Systems (13 percent of sales) was another diverse product sector, spanning Medical Systems (x-ray, tomography, magnetic resonance, ultrasound, and radiotherapy), Communication Systems (business communication, personal communication, wide-area paging, smart cards and private mobile radio), and Industrial Electronics (x-ray, communication and security systems, electronic manufacturing technology, electron optics, automation systems, weighing systems and integrated projects). The sector Components and Semiconductors (17 percent of sales), true to its name, contained Components (display, passive components, magnetic products, active-matrix LCDs, LCD cells, and key modules) and Semiconductors. Lighting (13 percent of sales) was a distinct sector (lamps, luminaries, lighting electronics, automotive lamps and batteries), while the company also had a category Miscellaneous (e.g. ASM Lithography, Philips Plastics and Metalware Factories).

Could resources be leveraged more effectively across such a variety of businesses without succumbing to even more bureaucracy than already burdening Philips? One of the first things Boonstra had noticed when entering Philips was that there were too many layers of middle management 'clay' in which initiatives tended to get stuck. Should the solution be to de-emphasize cross-business coordination and to liberate the business units from the shackles of corporate interference, so that they can get on with their own business? In short, should Boonstra attempt to 'rewire' Philips into a more integrated company, or would a 'shortcircuiting' of the company be fine, leaving each business to operate autonomously as a stand alone unit? Which ever way it went, it promised to be an electrifying time.

Sources: *Fortune*, March 31, 1997; *Advertising Age*, November, 1996; *Electronic Business Today*, February, 1997.

The Debate and the Readings

To open the debate on behalf of the portfolio perspective, Barry Hedley's reading 'Strategy and the Business Portfolio' has been selected. Hedley was an early proponent of the portfolio perspective, together with other consultants from the Boston Consulting Group (BCG), such as Bruce Henderson[15]. In this contribution, he explains the strategic principles underlying the famed growth-share grid, that is commonly known as the BCG matrix. His argument is based on the premise that a complex corporation can be viewed as a portfolio of businesses, with each business having its own competitive arena to which it must be responsive. By disaggregating a corporation into its business unit components, separate strategies can be devised for each. The overarching role of the corporate level can then be defined as that of portfolio manager. The major task of the corporate headquarters is to manage the allocation of scarce financial resources over the business units, to achieve the highest returns at an acceptable level of risk. Each business unit can be given a strategic mission to grow, hold or milk, depending on their prospects compared to the businesses in the corporate portfolio. This is where portfolio analysis comes in. Hedley argues that the profit and growth potential of each business unit depends on two key variables: the growth rate of the total business and the relative market share of the business unit within its business. When these two variables are put together in a grid, this forms the BCG matrix. This graphical tool can be used to visualize the composition of the corporation and to determine the position of each of the business units. For the discussion in this chapter, the precise details of the BCG portfolio technique are less relevant than the basic corporate strategy perspective that Hedley advocates – running the multibusiness firm as a hands-on investor.

Selecting a representative for the core competence perspective was a simple choice. In 1990, C.K. Prahalad and Gary Hamel published an article in *Harvard Business Review* with the title 'The Core Competence of the Corporation.'[16] This has had a profound impact on the debate surrounding the topic of corporate strategy, and has inspired a considerable amount of research and writing taking a core competence perspective. Obviously, this article has been selected as reading 6.2. In this contribution, and in their subsequent book, *Competing for the Future*[17], Prahalad and Hamel explicitly dismiss the portfolio perspective as a viable approach to corporate strategy. Prahalad and Hamel acknowledge that diversified corporations have a portfolio of businesses, but they do not believe that this implies the need for a portfolio management approach, in which the business units are highly autonomous. In their view, 'the primacy of the SBU – an organizational dogma for a generation – is now clearly an anachronism.' Drawing mainly on Japanese examples, they carry on to argue that corporations should be built around a core of shared competences (note that one of the few Western companies they mention is Philips, featured in Exhibit 6.1 above). Business units should use and help to further develop these core competences. The consequence is that the role of corporate level management is much more far reaching than in the portfolio perspective. The corporate center must 'establish objectives for competence building' and must ensure that this 'strategic architecture' is carried through.

Again, it is up to each strategist to weigh the arguments put forward by the two discussants and judge what would be the best approach to corporate level strategy. As before, readers may choose either point of view or arrive at a synthesis of the two.

Reading 1   Strategy and the Business Portfolio

By Barry Hedley[†]

All except the smallest and simplest companies comprise more than one business. Even when a company operates within a single broad business area, analysis normally reveals that it is, in practice, involved in a number of product-market segments which are distinct economically. These must be considered separately for purposes of strategy development.

The fundamental determinant of strategy success for each individual business segment is relative competitive position. As a result of the experience curve effect the competitor with high market share in the segment relative to competition should be able to develop the lowest cost position and hence the highest and most stable profits. This will be true regardless of changes in the economic environment. Hence relative competitive position in the appropriately defined business segment forms a simple but sound strategic goal. Almost invariably, any company which reviews its various businesses carefully in this light will discover that they occupy widely differing relative competitive positions. Some businesses will be competitively strong already, and may appear to present no strategic problem; others will be weak, and the company must face the question of whether it would be worthwhile to attempt to improve their position, making whatever investments might be required to achieve this; if this is not done, the company can only expect poor performance from the business and the best option economically will be divestment.

Even in quite small companies, the total number of possible combinations of individual business strategies can be extremely large. The difficulty of making a firm final choice on strategy for each business is normally compounded by the fact that most companies must operate within constraints established by limited resources, particularly cash resources.

The Business Portfolio Concept

At its most basic, the importance of growth in shaping strategy choice is twofold. First, the growth of a business is a major factor influencing the

[†] Source: This article was adapted with permission from 'Strategy and the "Business Portfolio"', *Long Range Planning*, Vol. 10, February 1977, pp. 9–15.

likely ease – and hence cost of gaining market share. In low-growth businesses, any market share gained will tend to require an actual volume reduction in competitors' sales. This will be very obvious to the competitors and they are likely to fight to prevent the throughput in their plants dropping. In high-growth businesses, on the other hand, market share can be gained steadily merely by securing the largest share of the growth in the business: expanding capacity earlier than the competitors, ensuring product availability and effective selling support despite the strains imposed by the *growth*, and so forth. Meanwhile competitors may even be unaware of their share loss because their actual volume of throughput has been well maintained. Even if aware of their loss of share, the competitors may be unconcerned by it given that their plants are still well loaded. This is particularly true of competitors who do not understand the strategic importance of market share for long term profitability resulting from the experience curve effect.

An unfortunate example of this is given by the history of the British motorcycle industry. British market share was allowed to erode in motorcycles world-wide for more than a decade, throughout which the British factories were still fairly full: British motorcycle production volumes held up at around 80,000 units per year throughout the sixties; in sharp contrast, Japanese export volumes leapt from only about 60,000 in 1960 to 2.5 million in 1973; their total production volumes roughly tripled in the same period. The long term effect was that while Japanese real costs were falling rapidly British costs were not: somewhat oversimplified, this is why the British motorcycle industry faced bankruptcy in the early seventies.

The second important factor concerning growth is the opportunity it provides for investment. Growth businesses provide the ideal vehicles for investment, for ploughing cash into a business in order to see it compound and return even larger amounts of cash at a later point in time. Of course this opportunity is also a need: the faster a business grows, the more investment it will require just to maintain market share. Yet the experience curve effect means that this is essential if its profitability is not to decline over time.

Whilst these growth considerations affect the rate at which a business will use cash, the relative competitive position of the business will determine the rate at which the business will generate cash: the stronger the company's position relative to its competitors the higher its margins should be, as a result of the experience curve effect. The simplest measure of relative competitive position is, of course, relative market share. A company's relative market share in a business can be defined as its market share in the business divided by that of the largest other competitor. Thus only the biggest competitor has a relative market share greater than one. All the other competitors should enjoy lower profitability and cash generation than the leader.

The Growth-Share Matrix

Individual businesses can have very different financial characteristics and face different strategic options depending on how they are placed in terms of growth and relative competitive position. Businesses can basically fall into any one of four broad strategic categories, as depicted schematically in the growth-share matrix in Figure 6.3.

■   *Stars*. High growth, high share – are in the upper left quadrant. Growing rapidly, they use large amounts of cash to maintain position. They are also leaders in the business, however, and should generate large amounts of cash. As a result, star businesses are frequently roughly in balance on net cash flow, and can be self-sustaining in growth terms. They represent probably the best profit growth and investment opportunities available to the company, and every effort should therefore be made to maintain and consolidate their competitive position. This will sometimes require heavy investment beyond their own generation capabilities and low margins may be essential at times to deter competition, but this is almost invariably worthwhile for the longer term: when the growth slows, as it ultimately does in all businesses, very large cash returns will be obtained if share has been maintained so that the business drops into the lower left quadrant of the matrix, becoming a cash cow. If star businesses fail to hold share, which

FIGURE 6.3
The business portfolio or growth–share matrix

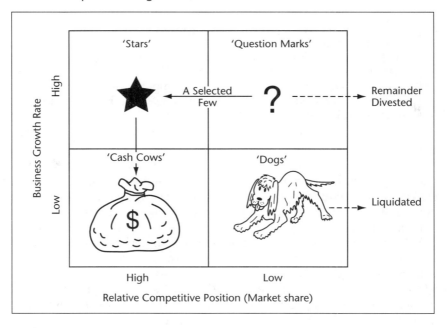

frequently happens if the attempt is made to net large amounts of cash from them in the short and medium term (e.g. by cutting back on investment and raising prices, creating an 'umbrella' for competitors), they will ultimately become dogs (lower right quadrant). These are certain losers.

■   *Cash cows.* Low growth, high share – should have an entrenched superior market position and low costs. Hence profits and cash generation should be high, and because of the low growth reinvestment needs should be light. Thus large cash surpluses should be generated by these businesses. Cash cows pay the dividends and interest, provide the debt capacity, pay for the company overhead and provide the cash for investment elsewhere in the company's portfolio of businesses. They are the foundation on which the company rests.

■   *Dogs.* Low growth, low share – represent a tremendous contrast. Their poor competitive position condemns them to poor profits. Because the growth is low, there is little potential for gaining sufficient share to achieve a viable cost position at anything approaching a reasonable cost. Unfortunately, the cash required for investment in the business just to maintain competitive position, though low, frequently exceeds that generated, especially under conditions of high inflation. The business therefore becomes a 'cash trap' likely to absorb cash perpetually unless further investment in the business is rigorously avoided. The colloquial term 'dog' describing these businesses, though undoubtedly pejorative, is thus rather apt. A company should take every precaution to minimize the proportion of its assets that remain in this category.

■   *Question marks.* High growth, low share – have the worst cash characteristics of all. In the upper right quadrant, their cash needs are high because of their growth, but their cash generation is small because of their low share. If nothing is done to change its market share, the question mark will simply absorb large amounts of cash in the short term and later, as the growth slows, become a dog. Following this sort of strategy, the question mark is a cash loser throughout its existence. Managed this way, a question mark becomes the ultimate cash trap.

In fact there is a clear choice between only two strategy alternatives for a question mark, hence the name. Because growth is high, it should be easier and less costly to gain share here than it would be in a lower growth business. One strategy is therefore to make whatever investments are necessary to gain share, to try to fund the business to dominance so that it can become a star and ultimately a cash cow when the business matures. This strategy will be very costly in the short term – growth rates will be even higher than if share were merely being maintained, and additional marketing and other investments will be required to make the share actually change hands – but it offers the only way of developing a sound business from the question mark over the long term. The only logical alternative is divestment. Outright sale is preferable; but if this is not possible, then a firm decision must be taken not to invest further in the business and it must be allowed simply to generate whatever cash it can while none is reinvested. The business will then decline, possibly quite rapidly if market growth is high, and will have to be shut down at some point. But it will produce cash in the short term and this is greatly preferable to the error of sinking cash into it perpetually without improving its competitive position.

These then, are the four basic categories to which businesses can belong. Some companies tend to fit almost entirely into a single quadrant. General Motors and English China Clays are examples of predominantly cash cow companies. Chrysler, by comparison, is a dog which compounded its fundamental problem of low share in its domestic US market by acquiring further mature low share competitors in other countries (e.g. Rootes which became Chrysler UK). IBM in computers, Xerox in photocopiers, BSR in low cost record autochangers, are all examples of predominantly star businesses. Xerox's computer operation, XDS, was clearly a question mark, however, and it is not surprising that Xerox recently effectively gave it away free to Honeywell, and considered itself lucky to escape at that price! When RCA closed down its computer operation, it had to sustain a write-off of about $490m. Question marks are costly.

Portfolio Strategy

Most companies have their portfolio of businesses scattered through all four quadrants of the matrix. It is possible to outline quite briefly and simply what the appropriate overall portfolio strategy for such a company should be. The first goal should be to maintain position in the cash cows, but to guard against the frequent temptation to reinvest in them excessively. The cash generated by the cash cows should be used as a first priority to maintain or consolidate position in those stars which are not self sustaining. Any surplus remaining can be used to fund a selected number of question marks to dominance. Most companies will find they have inadequate cash generation to finance market share-gaining strategies in all their question marks. Those which are not funded should be divested either by sale or liquidation over time.

Finally, virtually all companies have at least some dog businesses. There is nothing reprehensible about this, indeed on the contrary, an absence of dogs probably indicates that the company has not been sufficiently adventurous in the past. It is essential, however, that the fundamentally weak strategic position of the dog be recognized for what it is. Occasionally it is possible to restore a dog to viability by a creative business segmentation strategy, rationalizing and specializing the business into a small niche which it can dominate. If this is impossible, however, the only thing which could rescue the dog would be an increase in share taking it to a position comparable to the leading competitors in the segment. This is likely to be unreasonably costly in a mature business, and therefore the only prospect for obtaining a return from a dog is to manage it for cash, cutting off all investment in the business. Management should be particularly wary of expensive 'turn around' plans developed for a dog if these do not involve a significant change in fundamental competitive position. Without this, the dog is a sure loser. An indictment of many corporate managements is not the fact that their companies have dogs in the portfolio, but rather that these dogs are not managed according to logical strategies. The decision to liquidate a business is usually even harder to take than that of entering a new business. It is essential, however, for the long-term vitality and performance of the company overall that it be prepared to do both as the need arises.

Thus the appropriate strategy for a multibusiness company involves striking a balance in the portfolio such that the cash generated by the cash cows, and by those question marks and dogs which are being liquidated, is sufficient to support the company's stars and to fund the selected question marks through to dominance. This pattern of strategies is indicated by the arrows in Figure 6.3. Understanding this pattern conceptually is, however, a far cry from being able to implement it in practice. What any Company should do with its own specific businesses is of course a function of the precise shape of the company's portfolio, and the particular opportunities and problems it presents. But how can a clear picture of the company's portfolio be developed?

The Matrix Quantified

Based on careful analysis and research it is normally possible to divide a company into its various business segments appropriately defined for purposes of strategy development. Following this critical first step, it is usually relatively straightforward to determine the overall growth rate of each individual business (i.e. the growth of the market, not the growth of the company within the market), and the company's size (in terms of turnover or assets) and relative competitive position (market share) within the business.

Armed with these data it is possible to develop a precise overall picture of the company's portfolio of businesses graphically. This can greatly facilitate the identification and resolution of the key strategic issues facing the company. It is a particularly useful approach where companies are large, comprising many separate businesses. Such complex portfolios often defy description in more conventional ways.

The nature of the graphical portfolio display is illustrated by the example in Figure 6.4. In this chart, growth rate and relative competitive

FIGURE 6.4

Growth rate and relative competitive position

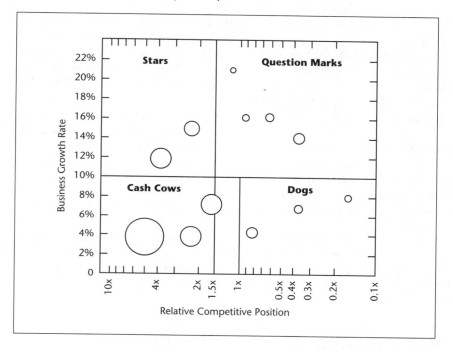

position are plotted on continuous scales. Each circle in the display represents a single business or business segment, appropriately defined. To convey an impression of the relative significance of each business, size is indicated by the area of the circle, which can be made proportional to either turnover or assets employed. Relative competitive position is plotted on a logarithmic scale, in order to be consistent with the experience curve effect, which implies that profit margin or rate of cash generation differences between competitors will tend to be related to the ratio of their relative competitive positions (market shares). A linear axis is used for growth, for which the most generally useful measure is volume growth of the business concerned, as in general rates of cash use should be directly proportional to growth.

The lines dividing the portfolio into four quadrants are inevitably somewhat arbitrary. 'High growth', for example, is taken to include all businesses growing in excess of 10 percent per annum in volume terms. Certainly, above this growth rate market share tends to become fairly fluid and can be made to change hands quite readily. In addition many companies have traditionally employed a figure of 10 percent for their discount rate in times of low inflation, and so this also tends to be the growth rate above which investment in market share becomes particularly attractive financially.

The line separating areas of high and low relative competitive position is set at 1.5 times. Experience in using this display has been that in high-growth businesses relative strengths of this magnitude or greater are necessary in order to ensure a sufficiently dominant position that the business will have the characteristic of a star in practice. On the other hand, in low-growth businesses acceptable cash generation characteristics are occasionally, but not always, observed at relative strengths as low as 1 times; hence the addition of a second separating line at 1 times in the low growth area, to reflect this. These lines should, of course, be taken only as approximate guides in characterizing businesses in the portfolio as dogs and question marks, cash cows and stars. In actuality, businesses cover a smooth spectrum across both axes of the matrix. There is obviously no 'magic' which transforms a star into a cash cow as its growth declines from 10.5 to 9.5 percent. It is undeniably useful, however, to have some device for broadly indicating where the transition points occur within the matrix, and the lines suggested here have worked well in practical applications of the matrix in a large number of companies.

Portfolio Approaches in Practice

The company shown in Figure 6.4 would be a good example of a potentially well-balanced portfolio. With a firm foundation in the form of two or three substantial cash cows, this company has some well-placed stars to provide growth and to yield high cash returns in the future when they mature. The company also has some question marks, at least two of which are probably sufficiently well placed that they offer a good chance of being funded into star positions at a reasonable cost, not out of proportion to the company's resources. The company is not without dogs, but properly managed there is no reason why these should be a drain on cash.

The Sound Portfolio, Unsoundly Managed

Companies with an attractive portfolio of this kind are not rare in practice. In fact Figure 6.4 is a disguised version of a representation of an actual UK company analyzed in the course of a Boston Consulting Group assignment. What is much rarer, however, is to find that the company has made a clear assessment of the matrix positioning and appropriate strategy for each business in the portfolio.

Ideally, one would hope that the company in Figure 6.4 would develop strategy along the following lines. For the stars, the key objectives should be the maintenance of market share; current profitability should be accorded a lower priority. For the cash cows, however, current profitability may well be the primary goal. Dogs would not be expected to be as profitable as the cash cows, but would be expected to yield cash. Some question marks would be set objectives in terms of increased market share; others, where gaining dominance appeared too costly, would be managed instead for cash.

The essence of the portfolio approach is therefore that strategy objectives must vary between businesses. The strategy developed for each business must fit its own matrix position and the needs and capabilities of the company's overall portfolio of businesses. In practice, however, it is much more common to find all businesses within a company being operated with a common overall goal in mind. 'Our target in this company is to grow at 10 percent per annum and achieve a return of 10 percent on capital'. This type of overall target is then taken to apply to every business in the company. Cash cows beat the profit target easily, though they frequently miss on growth. Nevertheless, their managements are praised and they are normally rewarded by being allowed to plough back what only too frequently amounts to an excess of cash into their 'obviously attractive' businesses. Attractive businesses, yes: but not for growth investment. Dogs on the other hand rarely meet the profit target. But how often is it accepted that it is in fact unreasonable for them ever to hit the target? On the contrary, the most common strategic mistake is that major investments are made in dogs from time to time in hopeless attempts to turn the business around without actually shifting market share. Unfortunately, only too often question marks are regarded very much as dogs, and get insufficient investment funds ever to bring them to dominance. The question marks usually do receive some investment, however, possibly even enough to maintain share. This is throwing money away into a cash trap. These businesses should either receive enough support to enable them to achieve segment dominance, or none at all.

These are some of the strategic errors which are regularly committed even by companies which have basically sound portfolios. The result is a serious sub-optimization of potential performance in which some businesses (e.g. cash cows) are not being called on to produce the full results of which they are actually capable, and resources are being mistakenly squandered on other businesses (dogs, question marks) in an attempt to make them achieve performance of which they are intrinsically incapable without a fundamental improvement in market share. Where mismanagement of this kind becomes positively dangerous, is when it is applied within the context of a basically unbalanced portfolio.

The Unbalanced Portfolio

The disguised example in Figure 6.5 is another actual company. This portfolio is seriously out of balance. As shown in Figure 6.5(a), the company has a very high proportion of question marks in its portfolio, and an inadequate base of cash cows. Yet at the time of investigation this company was in fact taking such cash as was being generated by its mature businesses and spreading it out amongst all the high-growth businesses, only one of which was actually receiving sufficient investment to enable it even to maintain share! Thus the overall relative competitive position of the portfolio was on average declining. At the same time, the balance in the portfolio was shifting: as shown in the projected portfolio in Figure 6.5(b), because of the higher relative growth of the question marks their overall weight in the portfolio was increasing, making them even harder to fund from the limited resources of the mature businesses.

If the company continued to follow the same strategy of spreading available funds between all the businesses, then the rate of decline could only increase over time leading ultimately to disaster.

This company was caught in a vicious circle of decline. To break out of the circle would require firm discipline and the strength of will to select only one or two of the question marks and finance those, whilst cutting off investment in the remainder. Obviously the choice of which should receive investment involves rather more than selection at random from the portfolio chart. It requires careful analysis of the actual nature of the businesses concerned and particularly the characteristics and behavior of the competitors faced in those businesses. However, the nature of the strategic choice facing the company is quite clear, when viewed in portfolio terms. Without the clarity of view provided by the matrix display, which focuses on the real fundamentals of the businesses and their relationships to each other within the portfolio, it is impossible to develop strategy effectively in any multibusiness company.

FIGURE 6.5
An unbalanced portfolio

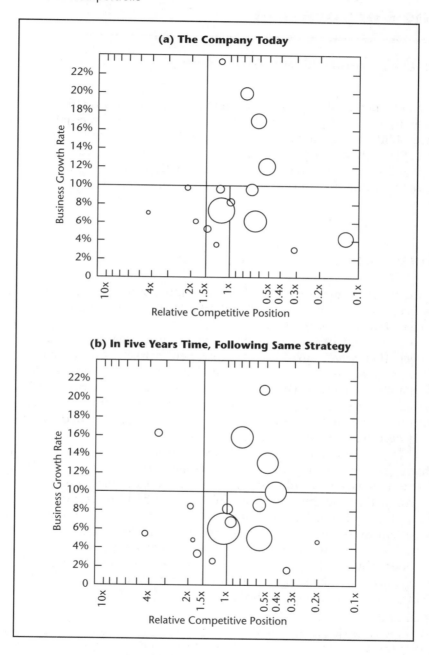

Reading 2   The Core Competence of the Corporation

By C.K. Prahalad and Gary Hamel[†]

The most powerful way to prevail in global competition is still invisible to many companies. During the 1980s, top executives were judged on their ability to restructure, declutter, and delayer their corporations. In the 1990s, they'll be judged on their ability to identify, cultivate, and exploit the core competencies that make growth possible – indeed, they'll have to rethink the concept of the corporation itself.

Rethinking the Corporation

Once, the diversified corporation could simply point its business units at particular end-product markets and admonish them to become world leaders. But with market boundaries changing ever more quickly, targets are elusive and capture is at best temporary. A few companies have proven themselves adept at inventing new markets, quickly entering emerging markets, and dramatically shifting patterns of customer choice in established markets. These are the ones to emulate. The critical task for management is to create an organization capable of infusing products with irresistible functionality or, better yet, creating products that customers need but have not yet even imagined.

This is a deceptively difficult task. Ultimately, it requires radical change in the management of major companies. It means, first of all, that top managements of western companies must assume responsibility for competitive decline. Everyone knows about high interest rates, Japanese protectionism, outdated antitrust laws, obstreperous unions, and impatient investors. What is harder to see, or harder to acknowledge, is how little added momentum companies actually get from political or macroeconomic 'relief.' Both the theory and practice of Western management have created a drag on our forward motion. It is the principles of management that are in need of reform.

The Roots of Competitive Advantage

In the short run, a company's competitiveness derives from the price/performance attributes of current products. But the survivors of the first wave of global competition, Western and Japanese alike, are all converging on similar and formidable standards for product cost and quality – minimum hurdles for continued competition, but less and less important as sources of differential advantage. In the long run, competitiveness derives from an ability to build, at lower cost and more speedily than competitors, the core competencies that spawn unanticipated products. The real sources of advantage are to be found in management's ability to consolidate corporate-wide technologies and production skills into competencies that empower individual businesses to adapt quickly to changing opportunities.

Senior executives who claim that they cannot build core competencies either because they feel the autonomy of business units is sacrosanct or because their feet are held to the quarterly budget fire should think again. The problem in many Western companies is not that their senior executives are any less capable than those in Japan or that Japanese companies possess greater technical capabilities. Instead, it is their adherence to a concept of the corporation that unnecessarily limits the ability of individual businesses to fully exploit the deep reservoir of technological capability that many American and European companies possess.

The diversified corporation is a large tree. The trunk and major limbs are core products, the smaller branches are business units; the leaves, flowers, and fruit are end products. The root system that provides nourishment, sustenance, and stability is the core competence. You can miss the strength of competitors by looking only at their end products, in the same way you miss the strength of a tree if you look only at its leaves (see Figure 6.6).

Core competencies are the collective learning in the organization, especially how to coordinate diverse production skills and integrate multiple streams of technologies. Consider Sony's capacity to miniaturize or Philips's optical-media expertise. The theoretical knowledge to put a radio on a chip does not in itself assure a company the skill to produce a miniature radio no bigger than a business card. To bring off this feat, Casio must harmonize know-how in miniaturization, microprocessor design, materials science, and ultrathin precision casing – the same skills it applies in its miniature card calculators, pocket TVs, and digital watches.

If core competence is about harmonizing streams of technology, it is also about the organization of work and the delivery of value. Among Sony's competencies is miniaturization. To bring miniaturization to its products, Sony must ensure that technologists, engineers, and marketers

FIGURE 6.6
Competencies as the roots of competitiveness

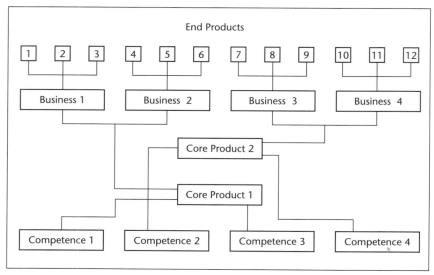

have a shared understanding of customer needs and of technological possibilities. The force of core competence is felt as decisively in services as in manufacturing. Citicorp was ahead of others investing in an operating system that allowed it to participate in world markets 24 hours a day. Its competence in systems has provided the company the means to differentiate itself from many financial service institutions.

Core competence is communication, involvement, and a deep commitment to working across organizational boundaries. It involves many levels of people and all functions. World-class research in, for example, lasers or ceramics can take place in corporate laboratories without having an impact on any of the businesses of the company. The skills that together constitute core competence must coalesce around individuals whose efforts are not so narrowly focused that they cannot recognize the opportunities for blending their functional expertise with those of others in new and interesting ways.

Core competence does not diminish with use. Unlike physical assets, which do deteriorate over time, competencies are enhanced as they are applied and shared. But competencies still need to be nurtured and protected; knowledge fades if it is not used. Competencies are the glue that binds existing businesses. They are also the engine for new business development. Patterns of diversification and market entry may be guided by them, not just by the attractiveness of markets.

Consider 3M's competence with sticky tape. In dreaming up

businesses as diverse as 'Post-it' note pads, magnetic tape, photographic film, pressure-sensitive tapes, and coated abrasives, the company has brought to bear widely shared competencies in substrates, coatings, and adhesives and devised various ways to combine them. Indeed, 3M has invested consistently in them. What seems to be an extremely diversified portfolio of businesses belies a few shared core competencies.

In contrast, there are major companies that have had the potential to build core competencies but failed to do so because top management was unable to conceive of the company as anything other than a collection of discrete businesses. General Electric sold much of its consumer electronics business to Thomson of France, arguing that it was becoming increasingly difficult to maintain its competitiveness in this sector. That was undoubtedly so, but it is ironic that it sold several key businesses to competitors who were already competence leaders – Black & Decker in small electrical motors, and Thomson, which was eager to build its competence in microelectronics and had learned from the Japanese that a position in consumer electronics was vital to this challenge.

Management trapped in the strategic business unit (SBU) mind-set almost inevitably finds its individual businesses dependent on external sources for critical components, such as motors or compressors. But these are not just components. They are core products that contribute to the competitiveness of a wide range of end products. They are the physical embodiments of core competencies.

How Not to Think of Competence

Since companies are in a race to build the competencies that determine global leadership, successful companies have stopped imagining themselves as bundles of businesses making products. Canon, Honda, Casio, or NEC may seem to preside over portfolios of businesses unrelated in terms of customers, distribution channels, and merchandising strategy. Indeed, they have portfolios that may seem idiosyncratic at times: NEC is the only global company to be among leaders in computing, telecommunications, and semiconductors *and* to have a thriving consumer electronics business.

But looks are deceiving. In NEC, digital technology, especially VLSI and systems integration skills, is fundamental. In the core competencies underlying them, disparate businesses become coherent. It is Honda's core competence in engines and power trains that gives it a distinctive advantage in car, motorcycle, lawn mower, and generator businesses. Canon's core competencies in optics, imaging, and microprocessor controls have enabled it to enter, even dominate, markets as seemingly diverse as copiers, laser printers, cameras, and image scanners. Philips worked for more than 15 years to perfect its optical-media (laser disc) competence, as did JVC in building a leading position in video recording. Other examples of core competencies might include mechantronics (the ability to marry mechanical and electronic engineering), video displays, bioengineering, and microelectronics. In the early stages of its competence building, Philips could not have imagined all the products that would be spawned by its optical-media competence, nor could JVC have anticipated miniature camcorders when it first began exploring videotape technologies.

Unlike the battle for global brand dominance, which is visible in the world's broadcast and print media and is aimed at building global 'share of mind,' the battle to build world-class competencies is invisible to people who aren't deliberately looking for it. Top management often tracks the cost and quality of competitors' products, yet how many managers untangle the web of alliances their Japanese competitors have constructed to acquire competencies at low cost? In how many Western boardrooms is there an explicit, shared understanding of the competencies the company must build for world leadership? Indeed, how many senior executives discuss the crucial distinction between competitive strategy at the level of a business and competitive strategy at the level of an entire company?

Let us be clear. Cultivating core competence does not mean outspending rivals on research and development. In 1983, when Canon surpassed Xerox in world-wide unit market share in the copier business, its R&D budget in reprographics was but a small fraction of Xerox's. Over the past 20 years, NEC has spent less on R&D as a percentage of sales than almost all of its American and European competitors.

Nor does core competence mean shared costs, as when two or more SBUs use a common facility – a plant, service facility, or sales force – or share a common component. The gains of sharing may be substantial, but the search for shared costs is typically a post hoc effort to rationalize production across existing businesses, not a premeditated effort to build the competencies out of which the businesses themselves grow.

Building core competencies is more ambitious and different than integrating vertically, moreover. Managers deciding whether to make or buy will start with end products and look upstream to the efficiencies of the supply chain and downstream toward distribution and customers. They do not take inventory of skills and look forward to applying them in nontraditional ways. (Of course, decisions about competencies *do* provide a logic for vertical integration. Canon is not particularly integrated in its copier business, except in those aspects of the vertical chain that support the competencies it regards as critical.)

Identifying Core Competencies – And Losing Them

At least three tests can be applied to identify core competencies in a company. First, a core competence provides potential access to a wide variety of markets. Competence in display systems, for example, enables a company to participate in such diverse businesses as calculators, miniature TV sets, monitors for laptop computers, and automotive dashboards – which is why Casio's entry into the handheld TV market was predictable. Second, a core competence should make a significant contribution to the perceived customer benefits of the end product. Clearly, Honda's engine expertise fills this bill.

Finally, a core competence should be difficult for competitors to imitate. And it will be difficult if it is a complex harmonization of individual technologies and production skills. A rival might acquire some of the technologies that comprise the core competence, but it will find it more difficult to duplicate the more-or-less comprehensive pattern of internal coordination and learning. JVC's decision in the early 1960s to pursue the development of a videotape competence passed the three tests outlined here. RCA's decision in the late 1970s to develop a stylus-based video turntable system did not.

Few companies are likely to build world leadership in more than five or six fundamental competencies. A company that compiles a list of 20 to 30 capabilities has probably not produced a list of core competencies. Still, it is probably a good discipline to generate a list of this sort and to see aggregate capabilities as building blocks. This tends to prompt the search for licensing deals and alliances through which the company may acquire, at low cost, the missing pieces.

Most Western companies hardly think about competitiveness in these terms at all. It is time to take a tough-minded look at the risks they are running. Companies that judge competitiveness, their own and their competitors', primarily in terms of the price/performance of end products are courting the erosion of core competencies – or making too little effort to enhance them. The embedded skills that give rise to the next generation of competitive products cannot be 'rented in' by outsourcing and original equipment manufacturer (OEM) supply relationships. In our view, too many companies have unwittingly surrendered core competencies when they cut internal investment in what they mistakenly thought were just 'cost centers' in favor of outside suppliers.

Of course, it is perfectly possible for a company to have a competitive product line up but be a laggard in developing core competencies – at least for a while. If a company wanted to enter the copier business today, it would find a dozen Japanese companies more than willing to supply copiers on the basis of an OEM private label. But when fundamental technologies changed or if its supplier decided to enter the market directly and become a competitor, that company's product line, along with all of its investments in marketing and distribution, could be vulnerable. Outsourcing can provide a shortcut to a more competitive product, but it typically contributes little to building the people-embodied skills that are needed to sustain product leadership.

Nor is it possible for a company to have an intelligent alliance or sourcing strategy if it has not made a choice about where it will build competence leadership. Clearly, Japanese companies have benefited from alliances. They've used them to learn from Western partners who were not fully committed to preserving core competencies of their own. Learning within an alliance takes a positive commitment of resources – travel, a pool of dedicated people, test-bed facilities, time to internalize and test what has been learned. A company may not make this effort if it doesn't have clear goals for competence building.

Another way of losing is forgoing opportunities to establish competencies that are evolving in existing businesses. In the 1970s and 1980s, many American and European companies – like General Electric, Motorola, GTE, Thorn, and General Electric Company (GEC) – chose to exit the color television business, which they regard as mature. If by 'mature' they meant that they had run out of new product ideas at precisely the moment global rivals had targeted the TV business for entry, then yes, the industry was mature. But it certainly wasn't mature in the sense that all opportunities to enhance and apply video-based competencies had been exhausted.

In ridding themselves of their television businesses, these companies failed to distinguish between divesting the business and destroying their video media-based competencies. They not only got out of the TV business but they also closed the door on a whole stream of future opportunities reliant on video-based competencies.

There are two clear lessons here. First, the costs of losing a core competence can be only partly calculated in advance. The baby may be thrown out with the bath water in divestment decisions. Second, since core competencies are built through a process of continuous improvement and enhancement that may span a decade or longer, a company that has failed to invest in core competence building will find it very difficult to enter an emerging market, unless, of course, it will be content simply to serve as a distribution channel.

American semiconductor companies like Motorola learned this painful lesson when they elected to forgo direct participation in the 256k generation of DRAM chips. Having skipped this round, Motorola, like most of its American competitors, needed a large infusion of technical help from Japanese partners to rejoin the battle in the 1-megabyte generation. When it comes to core competencies, it is difficult to get off the train, walk to the next station, and then reboard.

From Core Competencies to Core Products

The tangible link between identified core competencies and end products is what we call the core products – the physical embodiments of one or more core competencies. Honda's engines, for example, are core products, linchpins between design and development skills that ultimately lead to a proliferation of end products. Core products are the components or subassemblies that actually contribute to the value of the end products. Thinking in terms of core products forces a company to distinguish between the brand share it achieves in end product markets (for example, 40 percent of the US refrigerator market) and the manufacturing share it achieves in any particular core product (for example, five percent of the world share of compressor output).

It is essential to make this distinction between core competencies, core products, and end products because global competition is played out by different rules and for different stakes at each level. To build or defend leadership over the long term, a corporation will probably be a winner at each level. At the level of core competence, the goal is to build world leadership in the design and development of a particular class of product functionality – be it compact data storage and retrieval, as with Philips's optical-media competence, or compactness and ease of use, as with Sony's micromotors and microprocessor controls.

To sustain leadership in their chosen core competence areas, these companies *seek to maximize their world manufacturing share in core products*. The manufacture of core products for a wide variety of external (and internal) customers yields the revenue and market feedback that, at least partly, determines the pace at which core competencies can be enhanced and extended. This thinking was behind JVC's decision in the mid-1970s to establish VCR supply relationships with leading national consumer electronics companies in Europe and the United States. In supplying Thomson, Thorn, and Telefunken (all independent companies at that time) as well as US partners, JVC was able to gain the cash and the diversity of market experience that ultimately enabled it to outpace Philips and Sony. (Philips developed videotape competencies in parallel with JVC, but it failed to build a world-wide network of OEM relationships that would have allowed it to accelerate the refinement of its videotape competence through the sale of core products.)

JVC's success has not been lost on Korean companies like Goldstar, Samsung, Kia, and Daewoo, who are building core product leadership in areas as diverse as displays, semiconductors, and automotive engines through their OEM-supply contracts with western companies. Their avowed goal is to capture investment initiative away from potential competitors, often US companies. In doing so, they accelerate their competence-building efforts while 'hollowing out' their competitors. By focusing on competence and embedding it in core products, Asian competitors have built up advantages in component markets first and have then leveraged off their superior products to move downstream to build brand share. And they are not likely to remain the low-cost suppliers forever. As their reputation for brand leadership is consolidated, they may well gain price leadership. Honda has proven this with its Acura line, and other Japanese carmakers are following suit.

Control over core products is critical for other reasons. A dominant position in core products allows a company to shape the evolution of applications and end markets. Such compact audio disc-related core products as data drives and lasers have enabled Sony and Philips to influence the evolution of the computer-peripheral business in optical-media storage. As a company multiplies the number of application arenas for its core products, it can consistently reduce the cost, time, and risk in new product development. In short, well-targeted core products can lead to economies of scale and scope.

The Tyranny of the SBU

The new terms of competitive engagement cannot be understood using analytical tools devised to manage the diversified corporation of 20 years ago, when competition was primarily domestic (GE versus Westinghouse, General Motors versus Ford) and all the key players were speaking the language of the same business schools and consultancies. Old prescriptions have potentially toxic side effects. The need for new principles is most obvious in companies organized exclusively according to the logic of SBUs. The implications of the two alternate concepts of the corporation are summarized in Table 6.2.

Obviously, diversified corporations have a portfolio of products and a portfolio of businesses. But we believe in a view of the company as a portfolio of competencies as well. United States companies do not lack the technical resources to build competencies, but their top management often lacks the vision to build them and the administrative means for assembling resources spread across multiple businesses. A shift in commitment will inevitably influence patterns of diversification, skill deployment, resource allocation priorities, and approaches to alliances and outsourcing.

We have described the three different planes on which battles for global leadership are waged: core competence, core products, and end

TABLE 6.2
Two concepts of the corporation

	SBU	Core Competence
Basis for competition	Competitiveness of today's products	Interfirm competition to build competencies
Corporate structure	Portfolio of businesses related in product-market terms	Portfolio of competencies, core products, and businesses
Status of the business unit	Autonomy is sacrosanct; the SBU 'owns' all resources other than cash	SBU is a potential reservoir of core competencies
Resource allocation	Discrete businesses are the unit of analysis; capitial is allocated business by business	Businesses and competencies are the unit of analysis: top management allocates capital and talent
Value added of top management	Optimizing corporate returns through capital allocation trade-offs among businesses	Enunciating strategic architecture and building competencies to secure the future

products. A corporation has to know whether it is winning or losing on each plane. By sheer weight of investment, a company might be able to beat its rivals to blue-sky technologies yet still lose the race to build core competence leadership. If a company is winning the race to build core competencies (as opposed to building leadership in a few technologies), it will almost certainly outpace rivals in new business development. If a company is winning the race to capture world manufacturing share in core products, it will probably outpace rivals in improving product features and the price/performance ratio.

Determining whether one is winning or losing end-product battles is more difficult because measures of product market share do not necessarily reflect various companies' underlying competitiveness. Indeed, companies that attempt to build market share by relying on the competitiveness of others, rather than investing in core competencies and world core-product leadership, may be treading on quicksand. In the race for global brand dominance, companies like 3M, Black & Decker, Canon, Honda, NEC, and Citicorp have built global brand umbrellas by proliferating products out of their core competencies. This has allowed their individual businesses to build image, customer loyalty, and access to distribution channels.

When you think about this reconceptualization of the corporation, the primacy of the SBU – an organizational dogma for a generation – is now clearly an anachronism. Where the SBU is an article of faith, resistance to the seductions of decentralization can seem heretical. In many companies, the SBU prism means that only one plane of the global competitive battle, the battle to put competitive products on the shelf *today*, is visible to top management. What are the costs of this distortion?

Underinvestment in Developing Core Competencies and Core Products

When the organization is conceived of as a multiplicity of SBUs, no single business may feel responsible for maintaining a viable position in core products or be able to justify the investment required to build world leadership in some core competence. In the absence of a more comprehensive view imposed by corporate management, SBU managers will tend to underinvest. Recently, companies such as Kodak and Philips have recognized this as a potential problem and have begun searching for new organizational forms that will allow them to develop and manufacture core products for both internal and external customers.

SBU managers have traditionally conceived of competitors in the same way they've seen themselves. On the whole, they've failed to note the emphasis Asian competitors were placing on building leadership in core products or to understand the critical linkage between world manufacturing leadership and the ability to sustain development pace in core competence. They've failed to pursue OEM-supply opportunities or to look across their various product divisions in an attempt to identify opportunities for coordinated initiatives.

Imprisoned Resources

As an SBU evolves, it often develops unique competencies. Typically, the people who embody this competence are seen as the sole property of the business in which they grew up. The manager of another SBU who asks to borrow talented people is likely to get a cold rebuff. SBU managers are not only unwilling to lend their competence carriers but they may actually hide talent to prevent its redeployment in the pursuit of new opportunities. This may be compared to residents of an underdeveloped country hiding most of their cash under their mattresses. The benefits of competencies, like the benefits of the money supply, depend on the velocity of their circulation as well as on the size of the stock the company holds.

Western companies have traditionally had an advantage in the stock of skills they possess. But have they been able to reconfigure them quickly to respond to new opportunities? Canon, NEC, and Honda have had a lesser stock of the people and technologies that compose core competencies but could move them much quicker from one business unit to another. Corporate R&D spending at Canon is not fully indicative of the size of Canon's core competence stock and tells the casual observer nothing about the velocity with which Canon is able to move core competencies to exploit opportunities.

When competencies become imprisoned, the people who carry the competencies do not get assigned to the most exciting opportunities, and their skills begin to atrophy. Only by fully leveraging core competencies can small companies like Canon afford to compete with industry giants like Xerox. How strange that SBU managers, who are perfectly willing to compete for cash in the capital budgeting process, are unwilling to compete for people – the company's most precious asset. We find it ironic that top management devotes so much attention to the capital budgeting process yet typically has no comparable mechanism for allocating the human skills that embody core competencies. Top managers are seldom able to look four or five levels down into the organization, identify the people who embody critical competencies, and move them across organizational boundaries.

Bounded Innovation

If core competencies are not recognized, individual SBUs will pursue only those innovation opportunities that are close at hand – marginal product-line extensions or geographic expansions. Hybrid opportunities like fax machines, laptop computers, handheld televisions, or portable music keyboards will emerge only when managers take off their SBU blinkers. Remember, Canon appeared to be in the camera business at the time it was preparing to become a world leader in copiers. Conceiving of the corporation in terms of core competencies widens the domain of innovation.

Developing Strategic Architecture

The fragmentation of core competencies becomes inevitable when a diversified company's information systems, patterns of communication, career paths, managerial rewards, and processes of strategy development do not transcend SBU lines. We believe that senior management should spend a significant amount of its time developing a corporate-wide strategic architecture that establishes objectives for competence building. A strategic architecture is a road map of the future that identifies which core competencies to build and their constituent technologies.

By providing an impetus for learning from alliances and a focus for internal development efforts, a strategic architecture like NEC's C&C (computers and communication) can dramatically reduce the investment needed to secure future market leadership. How can a company make partnerships intelligently without a clear understanding of the core competencies it is trying to build and those it is attempting to prevent from being unintentionally transferred?

Of course, all of this begs the question of what a strategic architecture should look like. The answer will be different for every company. But it is helpful to think again of that tree, of the corporation organized around core products and, ultimately, core competencies. To sink sufficiently strong roots, a company must answer some fundamental questions: How long could we preserve our competitiveness in this business if we did not control this particular core competence? How central is this core competence to perceived customer benefits? What future opportunities would be foreclosed if we were to lose this particular competence?

The architecture provides a logic for product and market diversification, moreover. An SBU manager would be asked: Does the new market opportunity add to the overall goal of becoming the best player in the world? Does it exploit or add to the core competence? At Vickers, for example, diversification options have been judged in the context of becoming the best power and motion control company in the world.

The strategic architecture should make resource allocation priorities transparent to the entire organization. It provides a template for allocation decisions by top management. It helps lower-level managers understand the logic of allocation priorities and disciplines senior management to maintain consistency. In short, it yields a definition of the company and the markets it serves. 3M, Vickers, NEC, Canon, and Honda all qualify on this score. Honda knew it was exploiting what it had learned from motorcycles – how to make high-revving, smooth-running, lightweight engines – when it entered the car business. The task of creating a strategic architecture forces the organization to identify and commit to the technical and production linkages across SBUs that will provide a distinct competitive advantage.

It is consistency of resource allocation and the development of an administrative infrastructure appropriate to it that breathes life into a strategic architecture and creates a managerial culture, teamwork, a capacity to change, and a willingness to share resources, to protect proprietary skills, and to think long term. That is also the reason the specific architecture cannot be copied easily or overnight by competitors. Strategic architecture is a tool for communicating with customers and other external constituents. It reveals the broad direction without giving away every step.

Redeploying to Exploit Competencies

If the company's core competencies are its critical resource and if top management must ensure that competence carriers are not held hostage by some particular business, then it follows that SBUs should bid for core competencies in the same way they bid for capital. We've made this point glancingly. It is important enough to consider more deeply.

Once top management (with the help of divisional and SBU managers) has identified overarching competencies, it must ask businesses to identify the projects and people closely connected with them. Corporate officers should direct an audit of the location, number, and quality of the people who embody competence.

This sends an important signal to middle managers: core competencies are corporate resources and may be reallocated by *corporate* management. An individual business doesn't own anybody. SBUs are entitled to the services of individual employees so long as SBU management can demonstrate that the opportunity it is pursuing yields the highest possible payoff on the investment in their skills. This message is further underlined if each year in the strategic planning or budgeting process, unit managers must justify their hold on the people who carry the company's core competencies.

Also, reward systems that focus only on product-line results and career paths that seldom cross SBU boundaries engender patterns of behavior among unit managers that are destructively competitive. At NEC, divisional managers come together to identify next-generation competencies. Together they decide how much investment needs to be made to build up each future competence and the contribution in capital and staff support that each division will need to make. There is also a sense of equitable exchange. One division may make a disproportionate contribution or may benefit less from the progress made, but such short-term inequalities will balance out over the long term.

Incidentally, the positive contribution of the SBU manager should be made visible across the company. An SBU manager is unlikely to surrender key people if only the other business (or the general manager of that business who may be a competitor for promotion) is going to benefit from the redeployment. Cooperative SBU managers should be celebrated as team players. Where priorities are clear, transfers are less likely to be seen as idiosyncratic and politically motivated.

Transfers for the sake of building core competence must be recorded and appreciated in the corporate memory. It is reasonable to expect a business that has surrendered core skills on behalf of corporate opportunities in other areas to lose, for a time, some of its competitiveness. If these losses in performance bring immediate censure, SBUs will be unlikely to assent to skills transfers next time.

Finally, there are ways to wean key employees off the idea that they belong in perpetuity to any particular business. Early in their careers, people may be exposed to a variety of businesses through a carefully planned rotation program.

Competence carriers should be regularly brought together from across the corporation to trade notes and ideas. The goal is to build a strong feeling of community among these people. To a great extent, their loyalty should be to the integrity of the core competence area they represent and not just to particular businesses. In traveling regularly, talking frequently to customers, and meeting with peers, competence carriers may be encouraged to discover new market opportunities.

Core competencies are the wellspring of new business development. They should constitute the focus for strategy at the corporate level. Managers have to win manufacturing leadership in core products and capture global share through brand-building programs aimed at exploiting economies of scope. Only if the company is conceived of as a hierarchy of core competencies, core products, and market-focused business units will it be fit to fight.

Nor can top management be just another layer of accounting consolidation, which it often is in a regime of radical decentralization. Top management must add value by enunciating the strategic architecture that guides the competence acquisition process. We believe an obsession with competence building will characterize the global winners of the 1990s. With the decade underway, the time for rethinking the concept of the corporation is already overdue.

Corporate Level Strategy in International Perspective

Growth for the sake of growth is the ideology of the cancer cell.

(Edward Abbey 1927–1989; American author)

As with the topic in the previous chapter, scarce attention has been paid to international differences in multibusiness level strategies. Despite the high media profile of major corporations from different countries and despite researchers' fascination with large companies, little comparative research has been done. Yet, it seems not unlikely that corporate strategy practices and preferences vary across national boundaries, although these differences are not blatant. Casual observation of the major corporations around the globe quickly makes clear that one cannot easily divide the world into portfolio-oriented and core competence-oriented countries. However, Campbell, Goold and Alexander do observe that there are relatively few companies in the United Kingdom, the United States, and other Western countries that pursue a highly-integrated corporate strategy while it is 'the most popular style among leading Japanese companies'[18].

As an input to the debate whether there are international differences in corporate strategy perspectives, we would like to put forward a number of factors that might be of influence on how the paradox of responsiveness and synergy is managed in different countries. It should be noted, however, that these propositions must be viewed as tentative explanations, intended to encourage further discussion and research.

Functioning of Capital and Labor Markets

One of the arguments levelled against the portfolio perspective is that there is no need for corporations that merely act as investors. With efficiently-operating capital markets, investing should be left to 'real' investors. Stock markets are an excellent place for investors to spread their risks and for growing firms to raise capital. Start-up companies with viable plans can easily find venture capitalists to assist them. And all these capital providers can perform the task of financial control – portfolio-oriented corporations have nothing else to add but overhead costs. Add to this the argument that large corporations no longer have an advantage in terms of professional management skills. While in the past large firms could add value to smaller units by injecting more sophisticated managers, flexible labor markets now allow small firms to attract the same talent themselves.

Even if this general line of argumentation is true, the extent to which capital and labor markets are 'efficient' varies widely across countries. Porter[19], an outspoken detractor of the portfolio perspective, acknowledges that 'in developing countries, where large companies are few, capital markets are undeveloped, and professional management is scarce, portfolio management still works.' However, he quickly adds that portfolio thinking 'is no longer a valid model for corporate strategy in advanced economies.' But are capital and labor markets equally efficient across all so-called advanced economies? Few observers would argue that venture capital markets in Asia and Europe work as well as in the US, and the terms under which large corporations can raise capital on these continents are usually far better than for smaller companies. Neither does holding shares of a company through the stock markets of Asia and Europe give investors as much influence over the company as in the US. In short, even in the group of developed economies, various gradations of capital market efficiency seem to exist, suggesting varying degrees to which corporations can create value by adopting the role of investors.

The same argument can be put forward for the efficiency of 'managerial labor' markets. Even if Porter is right when stating that smaller companies can attract excellent professional managers through flexible labor markets, this conclusion is not equally true across advanced economies. Lifetime employment might be a declining phenomenon in most of these countries, but not to the same extent. Job-hopping between larger and smaller companies is far more common in the US, than in many European and Asian countries[20]. In many advanced economies large corporations still command a more sophisticated core of professional managers, through superior recruiting and training practices, higher compensation and status, and greater perceived career opportunities and job security. Hence, even within this group of countries, different degrees of labor market flexibility exist, suggesting that corporations in some countries might be able to create more value as developers and allocators of management talent than in other countries.

Leveraging of Relational Resources and Strategy Alignment

With the portfolio perspective focusing on the leveraging of financial resources and the core competence perspective favoring the leveraging of competences, the leveraging of relational resources is a topic receiving far less attention within the field of strategic management. It is widely acknowledged that 'umbrella' brands can often be stretched to include more product categories and that the corporation's reputation can commonly be employed to the business units' benefit. However, in the areas of political science and industrial organization much more attention is paid to the corporation as leverager of contacts and aligner of power. In many circumstances knowing the right people, being able to bring parties together, being able to force compliance and having the power to influence government regulations, are essential aspects of doing business. Often, corporations, either by their sheer size, or by their involvement in many businesses, will have more clout and essential contacts than can be mustered by individual businesses.

Here the international differences come in. As put forward at the end of Chapter 5, in some countries relational resources are more important than in others. Influence over government policy making, contacts with the bureaucrats applying the rules, power over local authorities and institutions, connections with the ruling elite, access to informal networks of companies – the importance of these factors can differ from country to country. Therefore, it stands to reason that the clustering of businesses around key external relationships and power bases will vary strongly across nations.

Costs of Coordination

Coordination comes at a cost, it is argued. Individual business units usually have to participate in all types of corporate systems, file reports, ask permission, attend meetings and adapt their strategy to fit with the corporate profile. This can result in time delays, lack of fit with the market, less entrepreneurial action, a lack of accountability and a low morale. On top of this, business units have to pay a part of corporate overhead as well. The benefits of coordination should be higher than these costs.

This argument might be suffering from a cultural bias, as it assumes that individuals and businesses are not naturally inclined to coordinate. However, control by the corporate center and cooperation with other business units is not universally viewed as a negative curtailment of individual autonomy. In many countries coordination is not an unfortunate fact of life, but a natural state of affairs. Coordination within the corporate whole is often welcomed as motivating, not demotivating, especially in cultures that are more group-oriented[21]. As observed in Chapter 4, if the common form of organization in a country resembles a clan, coordination might not be as difficult and costly as in other nations. Therefore, on the basis of this argument, it is reasonable to expect a stronger preference for the portfolio perspective in countries that favor mechanistic organizations.

Preference for Control

The last point of international difference ties into the discussion of the next chapter. If the essence of corporate strategy is about realizing synergies between businesses, is it not possible for these businesses to coordinate with one another and achieve synergies without being a part of the same corporation? In other words, is it necessary to be owned and controlled by the same parent in order to leverage resources and align strategies? Or could individual businesses band together and work as if they were one company – acting as a *virtual corporation*?

In Chapter 7 it will be argued that there are significant international differences on this account. In some countries there is a strong preference to have hierarchical control over two businesses that need to be coordinated. In other countries there is a preference for businesses to use various forms of cooperation to achieve synergies with other businesses, while retaining the flexibility of independent ownership. Preference for control, it will be argued, depends on how managers deal with the paradox of competition and cooperation.

Further Readings

Readers who would like to gain a better overview of the literature on the topic of corporate level strategy have a number of good sources from which to choose. Two scholarly reviews are 'Strategy and Structure in the Multiproduct Firm' by Charles Hill and Robert Hoskisson, and 'Research on Corporate Diversification: A Synthesis,' by Vasudevan Ramanujam and P. Varadarajan, although both have become somewhat dated. A more recent review is 'Why Diversify? Four Decades of Management Thinking,' by Michael Goold and Kathleen Luchs. Mark Sirower's book *The Synergy Trap: How Companies Lose the Acquisition Game* also has an excellent overview of the literature as appendix.

Much of the strategy literature taking a portfolio perspective is from the end of the 1970s and the beginning of the 1980s. Bruce Henderson's popular book *On Corporate Strategy*, that explains the basic principles of the portfolio perspective, is from this period. However, a better review of the portfolio approach, and especially portfolio techniques, is given by Charles Hofer and Dan Schendel in *Strategy Formulation: Analytical Concepts*. Recently, there has been renewed interest in viewing the corporation as investor and restructurer. In this crop, the article 'Growth Through Acquisitions: A Fresh Look,' by Patricia Anslinger and Thomas Copeland is particularly provocative.

For further reading on the core competence perspective, Gary Hamel and C.K. Prahalad's book *Competing for the Future* is an obvious choice. The literature on the resource-based view of the firm mentioned at the end of Chapter 5 is also interesting in the context of this chapter. Also highly stimulating is Hiroyuki Itami's book *Mobilizing Invisible Assets*, in which he argues for sharing intangible resources throughout a multibusiness firm.

On the topic of acquisitions, a good overview of the arguments and quantitative research is provided by Anju Seth, in his article 'Value Creation in Acquisitions: A Re-Examination of Performance Issues.' Mark Sirower's earlier mentioned book is also an excellent choice. When it comes to issues in the area of post-acquisition integration, Philippe

Haspeslagh and David Jemison's *Managing Acquisitions: Creating Value Through Corporate Renewal* is the authoritative work in the field.

On the role of the corporate center, *Corporate-Level Strategy: Creating Value in the Multibusiness Company,* by Andrew Campbell, Michael Goold, and Marcus Alexander, is highly recommended. Also stimulating is Charles Hill's article 'The Functions of the Headquarters Unit in Multibusiness Firms.' For a more academic analysis, readers are advised to turn to Vijay Govindarajan's article 'A Contingency Approach to Strategy Implementation at the Business-Unit Level: Integrating Administrative Mechanisms with Strategy.'

7

Network Level Strategy

The strong one is most powerful alone.

(Friedrich von Schiller 1759–1805; German writer)

All for one, one for all.

(*The Three Musketeers* by Alexandre Dumas Jr. 1824–1895; French novelist)

The Paradox of Competition and Cooperation

Strategists generally agree that for an effective *business level* strategy it is necessary to integrate *functional level* strategies into a consistent whole. Marketing, operations, finance, logistics, human resource, procurement and research and development strategies need to be systematically aligned for a business to be successful. It is also generally accepted that when a number of businesses reside together in one corporation an overarching *multibusiness level* strategy is required. However, while the business strategy and corporate strategy concepts are largely uncontroversial, widespread consensus is lacking when the next level of aggregation is discussed. The issue arises whether or not an overarching strategy is required for a group of interacting companies. In other words, the question is posed whether a *network* or *multicompany level* strategy is necessary to align the strategies of a network of firms. The alternative to such a network strategy would be for all firms to 'go it alone,' without explicit coordination of their strategies and to interact with one another at arm's length.

This issue of developing strategy together with other firms has an impact on all aspects of a company's functioning. For example, should a company work closely with its suppliers on a common production strategy or is it better to keep one's distance and shop around for the best deals? Should a company build up long-term partnerships with its customers, or is it more sensible not to become a captive supplier? Should a company get involved in joint ventures with other firms to develop new technologies and products, or is it wiser to do all research and development independently? Is it beneficial for a company to determine its strategy together with its bankers or is it preferable to keep the money lenders at a distance? In each case the question is what type of *relationship* a company wants or needs to have with other organizations in its environment.

On the one hand, interorganizational relationships can be primarily *competitive*. Such antagonism between organizations can vary from open 'warfare' to more subtle forms of friction, tension and strain. Under conditions of competition, behavior between rivals is characterized by calculation, bargaining, maneuvering and the use of power to achieve results. Usually conflicting interests and/or objectives are the root of competitive relationships.

On the other hand, interorganizational relationships can be primarily *cooperative*. Such symbiosis between organizations can vary from occasional collaboration to virtual integration. Under conditions of cooperation, behavior between partners is characterized by trust, commitment, reciprocity and the use of coordination to achieve results. Usually the opportunity for mutual gain lies at the heart of cooperative relationships.

So, should strategists prefer more competitive or more cooperative relationships with the organizations in their environment? As before, two diametrically opposed positions can be identified on this issue. On the one side of the spectrum, there are strategists who believe that it is best for companies to be primarily competitive in their relationships to all outside forces. They argue that firms should remain independent and interact with other companies under market conditions. We shall refer to this point of view as the *discrete organization* perspective. At the other end of the spectrum, there are strategists who believe that companies should build up more cooperative relationships with key organizations in their environment. They argue that firms can reap significant benefits by surrendering a part of their independence and developing close relationships with a group of other organizations. This will be referred to as the *embedded organization* perspective.

Following the familiar debate model, this chapter will explore the nature of successful interfirm relationships by contrasting these two extreme views. By comparing the two opposite ways of dealing with the paradox of competition and cooperation, a better understanding of the issues under discussion should be gained. In the next few pages the discrete organization and embedded organization perspectives will be further explained, and finally summarized in Table 7.1.

The Discrete Organization Perspective

Strategists employing the discrete organization perspective view companies as independent entities competing with other organizations in a hostile market environment. Inspired by neo-classical economics, this perspective commonly emphasizes that individuals, and the organizations they form, are fundamentally motivated by aggressive self-interest and therefore that competition is the natural state of affairs. Suppliers will try to enhance their bargaining power *vis-à-vis* buyers with the aim of getting a better price, while conversely buyers will attempt to improve their negotiation position to attain better quality at lower cost. Competing firms will endeavour to gain the upperhand against their rivals if the opportunity arises, while new market entrants and manufacturers of substitute products will consistently strive to displace existing firms[1].

In such a hostile environment it is a strategic necessity for companies to strengthen their competitive position in relation to the external forces. The best strategy for each organization is to obtain the market power required to get good price/quality deals, ward off competitive threats and even determine the development of the industry. Effective power requires independence and heavy reliance on specific suppliers, buyers, financiers or public organizations should therefore be avoided. Coalitions are occasionally formed to create power blocks, if individual companies are not strong enough on their own, but such alliances of convenience are usually second best to doing things independently. In most cases, collaboration is the strategy of the weak, to be engaged in at one's own peril. Collaborative efforts, it is argued, are fraught with the hazard of opportunism. Due to the ultimately competitive nature of relationships, allies will be tempted to serve their own interests to the detriment of the others, by maneuvering, manipulating or cheating. The collaboration might even be a useful ploy, to cloak the company's aggressive intentions and moves. Collaboration, it is therefore concluded, is merely 'competition in a different form'[2].

Where collaboration is not the tool of the weak, it is often a conspiracy of the strong to inhibit competition. If two or more formidable companies collaborate, chances are that the alliance is actually ganging up on a third party, for instance on buyers. In such cases, it is argued, the term 'collaboration' is just a euphemism for collusion and not in the interest of the economy at large.

Worse yet, collaboration is usually also bad for a company's long-term health. A highly competitive environment is beneficial for a firm, because it provides the necessary stimulus for companies to continually improve and innovate. Strong adversaries push companies towards competitive fitness. As expressed by Porter[3], 'alliances are rarely a solution . . . no firm can depend on another independent firm for skills and assets that are central to its competitive advantage . . . Alliances tend to ensure mediocrity, not create world leadership.'

The label 'discrete organization' given to this perspective refers to the fact that each organization is seen as being entirely on its own in a game with a large number of other players. The competitive situation is believed to be *atomistic*, that is, each 'selfish' individual firm strives to satisfy its own interests, leading to rivalry and occasionally to shifting coalitions between antagonists. Furthermore, the competitive game is assumed to be largely of a *zero-sum* nature, that is, a fight for who gets how much of the pie. Under these circumstances, collaboration is tactical; strategically each individual firm tries to retain its independence.

The Embedded Organization Perspective

Strategists taking an embedded organization perspective are fundamentally at odds with the assumption that competition is the predominant factor determining the interaction between organizations. Business isn't war, so to approach all interactions from a conflictual angle is seen as overly pessimistic, even cynical. On the contrary, it is argued that relations between organizations are characterized by a dynamic mix of competitive and cooperative behavior. Rarely are the interests of firms completely opposed or entirely aligned. The natural state of affairs is that firms must balance competitive and cooperative postures in their relationships towards other organizations, depending on the circumstances. In some interactions a predominantly competitive posture might prevail, while in other situations a genuinely cooperative posture may be deemed more suitable. For example, a company may have a long-standing partnership with the supplier of one input, while the suppliers of another input are forced to compete fiercely for every new contract. Each relationship with a buyer, supplier, competitor, institution or government agency can be placed on the continuum from competitive to cooperative. Collaboration is not competition in disguise, but a real alternative means of dealing with other organizations[4].

In the embedded organization perspective it is argued that firms can, and many do, intentionally embed themselves in a web of durable collaborative relationships. In the most simple case, a firm can have a number of bilateral collaborative relationships, in the form of joint ventures, strategic alliances and value-adding partnerships. However, loose multilateral webs or tight federations of cooperating companies can also develop. These collaborative clusters of organizations, which can also include not-for-profit institutions such as government agencies and universities, are referred to as networks. The companies in such networks align their strategies, or even develop their strategies

TABLE 7.1

Discrete organization versus embedded organization perspective

	Discrete Organization Perspective	Embedded Organization Perspective
Emphasis on	Competition over cooperation	Cooperation over competition
Structure of the environment	Discrete organizations (atomistic)	Embedded organizations (networked)
Firm boundaries	Distinct	Fuzzy
Preferred position	Independence	Interdependence
Interaction outcomes	Mainly zero-sum (win/lose)	Often positive-sum (win/win)
Source of advantage	Bargaining power	Specialization and coordination
Multicompany level strategy	No	Yes
Use of collaboration	Temporary arrangement (tactical)	Durable partnership (strategic)
Basis of collaboration	Power and calculation	Trust and reciprocity
Structure of collaboration	Limited, well-defined, contract-based	Broad, open, relationship-based

jointly, in an effort to accrue system-wide benefits to the advantage of all network participants[5].

The fact that strategic coordination takes place within networks makes them an organizational form at a higher level of aggregation than the individual company. Networks are neither *markets* or *hierarchies*, to use Williamson's[6] classic distinction. The term 'hierarchies' is used to refer to regular companies, where internal relationships are governed by a central authority that has the formal power to coordinate strategy and solve interdepartmental disputes. 'Markets,' on the other hand, refers to the situation where transactional relationships are not governed by the 'visible,' but by the 'invisible hand.' Independent firms interact with one another under competitive conditions, without any explicit coordination or dispute settlement mechanism. A network is in between markets and hierarchies[7]. Strategies are coordinated and disputes resolved, not through formal top-down power, but by mutual adaptation. To extend the above metaphor, networks rely neither on the visible nor invisible hand to guide relationships, but rather employ the continuous hand-shake[8].

To proponents of the embedded organization perspective, there-fore, atomistic competition is a neo-classical theoretical abstraction, that seriously mischaracterizes the nature of relationships between orga-nizations. In reality, companies have some competitive relationships, but they are also characterized by their *embeddedness* in webs of durable partnerships, whereby the game is potentially *positive-sum*, that is, a win-win situation. In turn, networks can compete against other net-works[9], or build up cooperative relationships where appropriate. Colla-boration can be tactical, but also strategic; companies can accept a measure of interdependence if the cooperating network achieves more than the companies independently.

The question for the field of strategic management is, therefore, whether network level strategies are formed and should be formed. Is market power and independence the best approach to the environment? Or is a web of durable cooperative relationships the best way forward for companies? In short, strategists must grapple with the paradox of com-petition and cooperation.

Defining the Issues: Boundaries and Relationships

The two major issues under discussion in this chapter are to which activities the firm wishes to limit itself and how it wishes to interact with organizations or individuals in its environment. These are referred to as the issues of *boundaries* and *relationships*. The issue of organizational boundaries revolves around the questions of *scope* and *scale*[10] – how many different activities should a firm be involved in and how much of each activity should a firm want to perform? The issue of interorgani-zational relationships deals with the nature of the interactions that a firm would like to have with external parties. Before launching into the debate, both issues will be examined more closely.

Relationships between the Firm and its Environment

In Figure 7.1 an overview is given of the eight major groups of external parties with which the firm can, or must, interact. A distinction has been made between *market* and *contextual* actors. The market actors are those individuals and organizations that perform value-adding activities and/or consume the outputs of these activities. The contextual actors are those parties whose behavior, intentionally or unintentionally, sets the conditions under which the market actors must operate. The four main categories of relationships between the firm and other market parties are the following[11]:

- *Upstream vertical (supplier) relations.* Every company has suppliers of some sort. In a narrow definition these include the providers of raw materials, parts, machinery, and business services. In a broader definition the providers of all production factors (land, capital, labor, technology, information and entrepreneurship) can be seen as suppliers, if they are not part of the firm itself. All these suppliers can either be the actual producers of the input, or an intermediary (distributor or agent) trading in the product or service. Besides the suppliers with which the firm transacts directly (first-tier suppliers), the firm may also have relationships with suppliers further upstream in the business (value) system[12]. All these relationships are traditionally referred to as upstream vertical relations, because economists commonly draw the business system as a column.

- *Downstream vertical (buyer) relations.* On the output side, the firm has relationships with its customers. These clients can either be the actual users of the product or service, or intermediaries trading the output. Besides the buyers with which the firm transacts directly, it may also have relationships with parties further downstream in the business system.

- *Direct horizontal (competitor) relations.* This category includes the relations between the firm and other industry incumbents. Because these competitors produce similar goods or services, they are said to be at the same horizontal level in the industry column.

- *Indirect horizontal (industry outsider) relations.* Where a firm has a relationship with a company outside its industry, this is referred to as an indirect horizontal relation (or a diversification relation). For instance, the joint venture between Mercedes-Benz and Swatch discussed in Chapter 2 is a straightforward example of a relationship between two firms with roots in different industries. An indirect horizontal relation can develop between a firm and a potential industry entrant, whereby the incumbent firm can assist or attempt to block the entry of the industry outsider. A relation can also exist with the producer of a substitute good or service, either as an adversary or an ally. Furthermore, a firm can establish a relationship with a firm in another industry, with the intention of diversifying into that, or a third, industry. In reality, where industry boundaries are not clear, the distinction between direct and indirect horizontal relations is equally blurry.

Besides relationships with these market actors, there can be many contacts with condition-setting parties in the broader environment. Employ-

FIGURE 7.1
The firm and its relationships

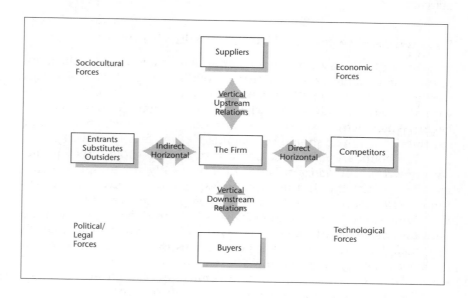

ing the classic SEPTember distinction, the following rough categories of contextual actors can be identified:

- *Sociocultural forces*. Individuals or organizations that have a significant impact on societal values, norms, beliefs and behaviors may interact with the firm. These could include the media, community groups, religious organizations, and opinion leaders.

- *Economic forces*. There can also be organizations influencing the general economic state of affairs, with which the firm interacts. Among others tax authorities, central banks, employers' federations, stock exchanges and unions may be of importance.

- *Political/legal forces*. The firm may also interact with organizations setting or influencing the regulations under which companies must operate. These could include governments, political parties, special interest groups, regulatory bodies and international institutions.

- *Technological forces*. There are also many organizations that influence the pace and direction of technological development and the creation of new knowledge. Among others, universities, research institutes, government agencies and standardization bodies may be important to deal with.

As Figure 7.1 visualizes, companies can choose, or are often forced, to interact with a large number of organizations and individuals in the environment. In the further discussion in this chapter, however, the focus will be primarily on the vertical and horizontal relationships between market parties.

Boundaries Between the Firm and its Environment

Closely tied to the issue of interorganizational relationships is the question of interorganizational boundaries. While the first topic deals with the 'how' of the interface between organizations, the second topic deals with the 'where.' Where should the firm end and the environment begin? Which activities should the firm carry out and which should be left to others? Where should the boundary of the firm be drawn?

The boundary issue, it could be said, revolves around the optimal level of *vertical* and *horizontal integration*. Vertically, the firm must determine which activities in the business system it deems necessary to perform itself, leaving all other activities to suppliers and buyers. Horizontally, the firm must assess what size it needs to have within the business (scale) and in which businesses it wishes to participate (scope).

Scale has already been a topic of discussion in Chapter 5. It was made clear by Porter in reading 5.1 that in many industries potential scale advantages exist that pressure companies to increase their size. These advantages include cost savings per unit produced, leveraging of resources, and increased bargaining power. Furthermore, large companies can set industry standards and influence regulatory agencies. However, it has also been acknowledged that severe scale disadvantages may exist, such as bureaucratic inertia, excessive coordination costs and lagging innovativeness. Moreover, antitrust authorities may intervene to cut companies down to size. Bigger is, therefore, not always better, but neither is small always beautiful. Each company must decide what its size within the industry should be and strive to achieve this optimal scale. The company's intended scale, in turn, will have a significant impact on the type of relationships the company will have with the other industry players. In general, the more intrusive a firm's size ambitions, the more conflictual will be its direct horizontal relations.

Scope has been discussed at length in Chapter 6. The central question was in what array of businesses a company should be involved. It was argued that there are potential scope advantages, that is, synergies between units operating in different businesses. Depending on the perspective taken, the leveraging of competences, the sharing of activities and financial synergies were mentioned as possible gains. On the other side of the balance, however, were the scope disadvantages, including coordination costs, slower decision-making and the corporate center's lack of specific business know-how. It was concluded that each company must continuously assess its optimal scope, and may need to enter and exit businesses accordingly. The company's intended scope, in turn, will have an impact on its relationships with other firms. Particularly in those businesses that a company is considering to enter, it must determine whether to cooperate with others, or to challenge all the incumbents.

An essential aspect of organizational scope, that was only touched on in Chapter 6, is that of vertical integration. In each business system there are a number of major production and distribution stages that take place between raw materials and final consumer. Each of these major stages consists of an enormous number of value-adding activities. Few companies are fully integrated 'from the mine to the customer's front door,' producing all goods and services *in-house*. Alternatively, it is also rare that a firm performs only one specific business system activity, *outsourcing* all other activities to outsiders. Companies seek the optimal level of activity *internalization* somewhere between these two extremes. Advantages of vertical integration, pressuring the firm to expand its boundaries upstream or downstream, may include[13]:

- *Avoidance of contracting costs.* Reaching a deal with a supplier or buyer and transferring the goods or services to the required location may be accompanied by significant direct costs. These can include the costs of negotiations, drawing up a contract, financial transfers, packaging, distribution and insurance. If a firm vertically integrates, many of these costs can be avoided, leading to potential savings.

- *Economies of scale.* Costs per unit can often be reduced by combining similar administrative, production, transport and information-processing activities. For instance, vertical integration can allow for the investment in more efficient large scale systems and can help to achieve learning curve savings.

- *Operational coordination.* Often it is necessary for various parts of the business system to be tightly coordinated, to ensure that the right components, meeting the right specification, are available in the right quantities, at the right moment, so that high quality and timely delivery can be achieved. To realize this level of coordination it might be necessary to gain control over a number of key activities in the business system.

- *Implementing system-wide changes.* Besides continual operational coordination, there may be a need to coordinate strategic changes throughout the business system. Switching over to new technologies, new production methods and new standards can sometimes only be implemented if there is commitment and a concerted effort in various parts of the business system. Vertical integration can give a firm the formal control needed to push through such changes.

- *Exploitation of dissipation-sensitive knowledge.* Know-how that is readily codifiable and transferable, but difficult to protect by means of patents, might best be exploited by applying it to a number of activities within the confines of one firm. Vertical integration minimizes the risk that such knowledge will quickly leak out to rival firms.

- *Exploitation of non-marketable capabilities.* Other knowledge may be tacit, that is, difficult to codify and transfer. This knowledge and the capabilities resulting from it, may be valuable to other activities, but difficult to sell, because they are wrapped up in the management systems, routines and culture of the firm. Vertical integration can be the best way to exploit these non-marketable capabilities. By internalizing various activities, a firm may be able to leverage these 'wrapped up' capabilities.

- *Increased bargaining power.* If a firm is facing a supplier or buyer with a disproportionately high level of bargaining power (for instance, a monopolist), vertical integration can be used to weaken or neutralize such a party. By fully or partially performing the activities in-house, the firm can lessen its dependence on a strong buyer or supplier. Alternatively, the firm may strive to acquire the other party, to avoid the bargaining situation altogether.

Counterbalancing these advantages of vertical integration are a number of important disadvantages. These drawbacks to internalization can include:

- *High governance costs.* Coordinating activities within a firm requires managers. Layers of management, and the bureaucratic processes that might entail, can lead to higher costs than if activities were outsourced.

- *Dulled incentives.* Operating units carrying out activities within the firm may not be as motivated to perform optimally, as when they would have to sell their wares on the open market. Internalizing activities can thus dull the incentive to excel, compared to the competitive stimulus offered by the market.

- *High capital investment.* Vertical integration requires extra capital to be invested. These funds may not be available, or may need to be withdrawn from investments in the core business. The additional risk of investing within one value system may also be judged to be too high.

- *Reduced flexibility.* Once integrated into one firm, operating units can become fully dependent on each other. However, each unit may be exposed to different environmental and technological changes, requiring different strategic responses. Their interdependence will limit the extent to which adaptation to these changes will be possible.

- *Reduced exposure to external know-how.* If the firm is more or less a closed system, it will be infrequently exposed to new insights and technologies adopted elsewhere. There may be a real threat of missing important external developments.

It is often argued that all of these reasons for not internalizing activities can be regarded as the strengths of the market system. In many situations, markets are the most efficient mechanism of conducting transactions. Where activities are performed by autonomous parties and sold in the market place, costs will often be lowest. As summarized by Ouchi[14], 'in a market relationship, the transaction takes place between the two parties and is mediated by a price mechanism in which the existence of a competitive market reassures both parties that the terms of exchange are equitable.'

Integration of activities into the firm is only necessary where markets do not function properly. All of the advantages of integration mentioned above refer to such cases of *market failure*. The firm must internalize activities, despite the disadvantages, because the invisible hand of the market cannot be trusted to be equitable and effective. Control over transactions by means of formal authority – the visible hand – is needed under these conditions.

Between Markets and Hierarchies

In the previous paragraphs, the firm and its environment have been presented as a clear dichotomy for argumentation's sake. Within a firm (a hierarchy, in transaction cost jargon) cooperative relationships were assumed to be prevalent, while in the market environment competitive relationships were assumed to be the norm. In reality, however, there are many organizational forms between markets and hierarchies. These are referred to as *hybrids*, *alliances* or *collaborative arrangements*. In Table 7.2, an overview of the most common types of collaborative arrangements is presented.

The intent of these collaborative arrangements is to profit from some of the advantages of vertical and horizontal integration, without incurring its costs. These organizational forms are truly hybrids, as they attempt to combine the benefits of integration with the benefits of the market. However, they might also combine the weaknesses of both, making their use an issue for heated debate.

Strategists taking a discrete organization perspective are not particularly fond of these collaborative arrangements. After all, they believe that the relationships between firms are fundamentally competitive and that other firms can never be fully trusted. Companies run the risk of opportunism, that is, '. . . self-interest seeking with guile. This includes but is scarcely limited to more blatant forms, such as lying, stealing and cheating . . . More generally, opportunism refers to the incomplete or distorted disclosure of information, especially to calculated efforts to mislead, distort, disguise, obfuscate, or otherwise confuse'[15]. Therefore, collaborative arrangements must be approached with caution and only used tactically under a limited set of circumstances. In particular, it is argued that collaborative efforts should be restricted to a well-defined area, with clear objectives, responsibilities, authority and results spelled out ahead of time, preferably in an explicit contract.

TABLE 7.2
Types of cooperative arrangements

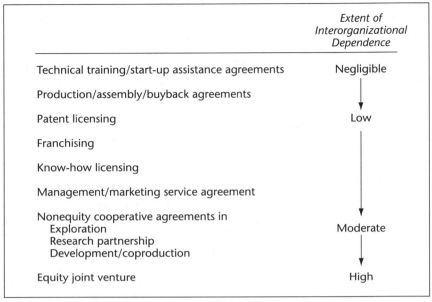

	Extent of Interorganizational Dependence
Technical training/start-up assistance agreements	Negligible
Production/assembly/buyback agreements	
Patent licensing	Low
Franchising	
Know-how licensing	
Management/marketing service agreement	
Nonequity cooperative agreements in Exploration Research partnership Development/coproduction	Moderate
Equity joint venture	High

Source: Contractor, F.J. and Lorange, P. (1988) *Cooperative Strategies in International Business*, Lexington Books, Lexington, MA.

In the embedded organization perspective, collaborative arrangements can evolve to such an extent that a group of cooperating companies actually functions as a *virtual corporation*[16]. A firm can become so embedded in a web of collaborative relationships, that the boundary between the firm and the environment is entirely fuzzy. This enthusiasm for collaborative forms is based on the belief that organizations can develop relationships based on trust, and that durable partnerships can grow. The more trust that exists between the partners, the more open-ended the collaboration can become. Objectives, responsibilities, authority and results needn't be fully determined in advance in a written contract, but can evolve and be adjusted over time, given all parties' sincere willingness to 'work on their relationship'[17]. This is what economists call an implicit contract and legal theorists refer to as a relational contract[18].

EXHIBIT 7.1
Merck case

MERCK: A MEDICINE AGAINST ANOREXIA?

Name an industry in which the average product takes 15 years to develop, at a cost of more than US$350 million a shot. Aerospace? Robotics? Logical choices, but the right answer is pharmaceuticals. Developing new drugs does not come easily or cheaply. The R&D budgets of the pharmaceutical giants are typically about 10–12 percent of sales, placing seven of them among the 25 biggest R&D spenders in the US. These high investments and long lead times make the pharmaceutical industry a competitive arena that should be avoided by the short-winded and faint-hearted. Raymond Gilmartin, however, does not need to reach for Prilosec, an ulcer drug – he only needs to sell the product and is doing so quite well. Gilmartin is CEO of Merck, the third largest pharmaceutical company in the world, after Glaxo Wellcome and Novartis, and arguably the most successful one. In 1996, Merck produced net profits of $3.9 billion on sales of $19.8 billion, which translates into profits of $79,000 for each of its 49,000 staff members, compared with $64,500 for the Swiss giant Roche and $57,500 for Britain's Glaxo Wellcome. In the same year, Merck was also ranked as best pharmaceutical company by US physicians and voted one of the 'most admired' companies in the US by managers.

Merck has competed in this high-stakes industry for more than a hundred years, initially as the US subsidiary of the German Merck company. During World War I the Merck subsidiary became separated from the parent company in Darmstadt, and to this day both companies use the Merck name (the German E. Merck has sales of approximately $4 billion, half of which in pharmaceuticals). Gilmartin was placed at the helm of Merck in 1994, as the first outsider in the company's history, coming from Becton Dickinson & Co., a modest-sized manufacturer of medical equipment. While the retirement of ex-CEO Roy Vagelos had been planned far in advance, the appointment of Gilmartin, and the bypassing of all senior managers within Merck by the board of directors had come as quite a shock. The resulting exodus of top management was accepted by the board as the necessary price for shaking up the company. It was the board's belief that Merck had become accustomed to easy expansion in the late 1980s, growing annually by 20 to 30 percent. Costs had risen sharply, while by the early 1990s growth was declining and competitive pressures were increasing. In the board's view, a sharp break with the past was needed and a more cost-conscious CEO was required to push through changes.

Since Gilmartin's arrival pressures for change at Merck have only increased, as the pharmaceutical industry has entered a tumultuous period. After years of unchallenged price hikes, governments now look at the drug firms as partially responsible for the soaring cost of health care. In the US, the rise of 'managed care' organizations has further enhanced the bargaining power of buyers, placing more pressure on prices. In the mean time, the pharmaceutical industry has had to double its spending on R&D in the five years between 1991 and 1996 to make up for the slowing stream of new products. Development costs per new drug are rapidly increasing, while the profitable 'monopoly' period after introduction is becoming ever shorter. Companies are not waiting to see whether their competitors' new drugs are successful before following in their footsteps, but are quickly investing in emerging areas as soon as others do. Therefore, innovative drugs are soon joined by similar products.

The high cost of getting the scientists' chemical compounds out of the test tube and on to the pharmacists' shelves is only partially attributable to the process of actually discovering a potential new drug. In general it takes about one to three years for a new preparation to be synthesized and tested. But once a preparation is in the pipeline, many further steps need to be taken before it becomes a sellable product. First, the preparation enters the preclinical development phase, which might involve animal testing. If, after a few years of tests, the results are promising, permission can be gained to proceed with clinical trials on human volunteers. At first, these are conducted on small groups, but if successful, they are enlarged to full-scale tests. The clinical trials can take 5 to 10 years before a drug is approved for broader use and sales can begin. On average, of the 20 preparations entering preclinical development, only one has come out of the pipeline as a marketable drug. Obviously, pharmaceutical companies would like to increase this yield and shorten the process, but this is not proving to be easy.

Merck has followed the industry trend by investing more heavily in R&D. In 1997, its R&D budget was more than $1.7 billion, compared to $1.1 billion in 1992. What Merck has consciously not done, is to follow the industry trend towards more alliances with small biotech firms. Merck's philosphy towards R&D is decidedly do-it-yourself. Not more than 5 percent of Merck's total research spending ends up outside of its own laboratories. This emphasis on doing everything in-house contrasts sharply with the direction being taken by the rest of the industry. All of Merck's rivals reserve between 10 and 20 percent of their R&D budgets for external work. In some cases only the laborious task of conducting clinical trials is outsourced, but increasingly the pharmaceutical giants are contracting out the development of new drugs to specialist firms. Some analysts are predicting that the proportion of R&D performed outside of the big companies could reach 80 percent. Sir Richard Sykes, head of Glaxo Wellcome, has suggested that the major drug firms will increasingly become 'virtual' companies, as they concentrate on the marketing of drugs developed by the legions of small independent biotech firms.

The enthusiasm of Merck's competitors for alliances with the creative independents is based on the view 'if you can't beat them, join them'. The number of small biotech firms has grown rapidly – in the United States alone there are more than 1200 firms active. All of these firms are so specialized, that at any one moment at least one of them will be ahead of any given big firm in any given technology. Most pharmaceutical giants believe that it is wise to tap in to this source of new products, especially if this speeds up the process of getting new drugs into their product portfolio. Moreover, licensing in new drugs from the small biotech firms can usually be achieved at a fraction of the cost of doing it in-house. Most biotech firms do not have the financial stamina to shepherd their products through the years of development and trials, nor do they have the marketing and distribution infrastructure needed to reap the benefits of their labors. This gives the big firms the negotiation position to snap up promising products for considerably less than they are worth. In 1996, over 170 deals were struck between small biotech firms and big drug companies, more than double the amount of just three years before.

Merck, however, is strongly opposed to this policy of hollowing out. According to Ed Scolnick, Merck's combative head of research and only remaining member of Vagelos' original top management team, the type of corporate anorexia its rivals are suffering from might end up to be fatal. He argues that without first class in-house scientific talent, a drug firm cannot tell which biotech ideas are worth buying. In his view, competitors are taking the easy route of shopping for new products simply because they are not clever enough to come up with their own.

Of course, the question is whether Scolnick and Gilmartin are right, while the rest of the industry is wrong. Is it necessary to keep all key activities in-house and to remain largely self-contained and independent from the outside world? Or are Merck's competitors right, when they argue that the pharmaceutical industry will come to resemble Hollywood, where the big studios are focusing more on marketing and distribution, while the films are increasingly being made by small production companies. Time will tell who is right, but maybe Gilmartin should keep a bottle of Prilosec handy, just in case.

Sources: *The Economist*, May 24 1997; *Medical Marketing and Media*, May 1996; *Drug Topics*, July 24 1995.

The Debate and the Readings

In Table 7.1 the two perspectives were summarized, to sharply contrast their divergent assumptions. As before, the readings in this chapter have been chosen as well-known representatives of these two perspectives. As representative of the discrete organization perspective, Michael Porter's reading in Chapter 5 could easily have been selected. In this reading, Porter states that 'the essence of strategy formulation is coping with competition,' and that there are five sources of competitive pressure, all impinging on a firm's profit potential. These competitive forces are the threat of new entrants, powerful buyers and suppliers, rivalry among existing competitors and the threat of substitute products. Porter asserts that a company's profitability depends on how well it is able to defend itself against these 'opponents'. It is this view of the firm, as a lone organization surrounded by hostile forces, that places this contribution clearly within the discrete organization perspective. While Porter does not denounce or warn against cooperative arrangements in this reading (as he does in his 1990 work), neither does he recognize cooperation as a possibility. His message is that of *realpolitik* – in inter-organizational relationships, conflict and power is the name of the game.

Because Porter's reading is already a part of Chapter 5, another classic, 'Collaborate with Your Competitors – and Win,'[19] has been selected as the opening contribution for this chapter. In this piece, the authors, Gary Hamel, Yves Doz and C.K. Prahalad, basically take the same stance as Porter, in assuming that interfirm relations are largely competitive and governed by power and calculation. However, while Porter makes little mention of, or is apprehensive about, collaboration with other organizations, Hamel, Doz and Prahalad see collaboration as a useful tool for improving the firm's competitive profile. They argue that alliances with competitors 'can strengthen both companies against outsiders even if it weakens one partner *vis-à-vis* the other,' and therefore that the net result can be positive. Yet they emphasize that companies should not be naive about the real nature of alliances – 'collaboration is competition in a different form.' An alliance is 'a constantly evolving bargain,' in which each firm will be fending for itself, trying to learn as much as possible from the other, while attempting to limit the partner's access to its knowledge and skills. The authors advise firms to proceed cautiously with alliances, only when they have clear objectives of what they wish to learn from their allies, a well-developed capacity to learn, and defenses against their allies' probing of their skills and technologies. While Hamel, Doz and Prahalad only focus on horizontal relationships in this article, their message is similar to that of Porter – competition in the environment is paramount and cooperation is merely an opportunistic move in the overall competitive game.

As representative of the embedded organization perspective, *Creating a Strategic Center for a Network of Firms* by Gianni Lorenzoni and Charles Baden-Fuller[20], has been selected. Lorenzoni and Baden-Fuller argue that the traditional conception of the fully-integrated, stand-alone corporation is heavily dated. In their view, a network of firms can closely work together as a virtual company, without the disadvantages of integration. In this reading they not only explain the reasoning behind spinning webs of relationships with other firms but they also outline how a network of firms can be created and maintained. Interestingly, they believe that networks can be deliberately assembled and require a strategic center to effectively coordinate activities. Of course, the question is whether this is always the case. Are networks designed by a central coordinating body, or might they gradually emerge, without any party being in control?

In any case, their message is that of *symbiosis* – in inter-organizational relations, cooperation and interdependence can often be mutually beneficial. Again, each reader must weigh the arguments brought forward by the discussants and may decide what the best approach is to inter-firm relationships. Readers must form their own judgment on how to deal with the paradox of competition and cooperation.

Reading 1   Collaborate with Your Competitors – and Win

By Gary Hamel, Yves Doz, and C.K. Prahalad[†]

Collaboration between competitors is in fashion. General Motors and Toyota assemble automobiles, Siemens and Philips develop semiconductors, Canon supplies photocopiers to Kodak, France's Thomson and Japan's JVC manufacture videocassette recorders. But the spread of what we call 'competitive collaboration' – joint ventures, outsourcing agreements, product licensings, cooperative research – has triggered unease about the long-term consequences. A strategic alliance can strengthen both companies against outsiders even as it weakens one partner *vis-à-vis* the other. In particular, alliances between Asian companies and Western rivals seem to work against the Western partner. Cooperation becomes a low-cost route for new competitors to gain technology and market access.

Yet the case for collaboration is stronger than ever. It takes so much money to develop new products and to penetrate new markets that few companies can go it alone in every situation. ICL, the British computer company, could not have developed its current generation of mainframes without Fujitsu. Motorola needs Toshiba's distribution capacity to break into the Japanese semiconductor market. Time is another critical factor.

Alliances can provide shortcuts for Western companies racing to improve their production efficiency and quality control.

We have spent more than five years studying the inner workings of 15 strategic alliances and monitoring scores of others. Our research involves cooperative ventures between competitors from the United States and Japan, Europe and Japan, and the United States and Europe. We did not judge the success or failure of each partnership by its longevity – a common mistake when evaluating strategic alliances – but by the shifts in competitive strength on each side. We focused on how companies use competitive collaboration to enhance their internal skills and technologies while they guard against transferring competitive advantages to ambitious partners.

There is no immutable law that strategic alliances *must* be a windfall for Japanese or Korean partners. Many Western companies do give away more than they gain – but that's because they enter partnerships without knowing what it takes to win. Companies that benefit most from competitive collaboration adhere to a set of simple but powerful principles.

- *Collaboration is competition in a different form.* Successful companies never forget that their new partners may be out to disarm them. They enter alliances with clear strategic objectives, and they also understand how their partners' objectives will affect their success.

- *Harmony is not the most important measure of success.* Indeed, occasional conflict may be the best evidence of mutually beneficial collaboration. Few alliances remain win-win undertakings forever. A partner may be content even as it unknowingly surrenders core skills.

- *Cooperation has limits.* Companies must defend against competitive compromise. A strategic alliance is a constantly evolving bargain whose real terms go beyond the legal agreement or the aims of top management. What information gets traded is determined day to day, often by engineers and operating managers. Successful companies inform employees at all levels about what skills and technologies are off-limits to the partner and monitor what the partner requests and receives.

- *Learning from partners is paramount.* Successful companies view each alliance as a window on their partners' broad capabilities. They use the alliance to build skills in areas outside the formal agreement and systematically diffuse new knowledge throughout their organizations.

Why Collaborate?

Using an alliance with a competitor to acquire new technologies or skills is not devious. It reflects the commitment and capacity of each partner to absorb the skills of the other. We found that in every case in which a

Japanese company emerged from an alliance stronger than its Western partner, the Japanese company had made a greater effort to learn.

Strategic intent is an essential ingredient in the commitment to learning. The willingness of Asian companies to enter alliances represents a change in competitive tactics, not competitive goals. NEC, for example, has used a series of collaborative ventures to enhance its technology and product competences. NEC is the only company in the world with a leading position in telecommunications, computers, and semiconductors – despite its investing less in research and development (R&D) (as a percentage of revenues) than competitors like Texas Instruments, Northern Telecom, and L.M. Ericsson. Its string of partnerships, most notably with Honeywell, allowed NEC to leverage its in-house R&D over the last two decades.

Western companies, on the other hand, often enter alliances to avoid investments. They are more interested in reducing the costs and risks of entering new businesses or markets than in acquiring new skills. A senior US manager offered this analysis of his company's venture with a Japanese rival: 'We complement each other well – our distribution capability and their manufacturing skill. I see no reason to invest upstream if we can find a secure source of product. This is a comfortable relationship for us.'

An executive from this company's Japanese partner offered a different perspective: 'When it is necessary to collaborate, I go to my employees and say, "This is bad, I wish we had these skills ourselves. Collaboration is second best. But I will feel worse if after four years we do not know how to do what our partner knows how to do." We must digest their skills.'

The problem here is not that the US company wants to share investment risk (its Japanese partner does too) but that the US company has no ambition beyond avoidance. When the commitment to learning is so one-sided, collaboration invariably leads to competitive compromise.

Many so-called alliances between Western companies and their Asian rivals are little more than sophisticated outsourcing arrangements. General Motors buys cars and components from Korea's Daewoo. Siemens buys computers from Fujitsu. Apple buys laser printer engines from Canon. The traffic is almost entirely one way. These original equipment manufacturer (OEM) deals offer Asian partners a way to capture investment initiative from Western competitors and displace customer-competitors from value-creating activities. In many cases this goal meshes with that of the Western partner: to regain competitiveness quickly and with minimum effort.

Consider the joint venture between Rover, the British automaker, and Honda. Some 25 years ago, Rover's forerunners were world leaders in small car design. Honda had not even entered the automobile business. But in the mid-1970s, after failing to penetrate foreign markets, Rover turned to Honda for technology and product development support.

Rover has used the alliance to avoid investments to design and build new cars. Honda has cultivated skills in European styling and marketing as well as multinational manufacturing. There is little doubt which company will emerge stronger over the long term.

Troubled laggards like Rover often strike alliances with surging late-comers like Honda. Having fallen behind in a key skills area (in this case, manufacturing small cars), the laggard attempts to compensate for past failures. The latecomer uses the alliance to close a specific skills gap (in this case, learning to build cars for a regional market). But a laggard that forges a partnership for short-term gain may find itself in a dependency spiral: as it contributes fewer and fewer distinctive skills, it must reveal more and more of its internal operations to keep the partner interested. For the weaker company, the issue shifts from, 'Should we collaborate?' to 'With whom should we collaborate?' to 'How do we keep our partner interested as we lose the advantages that made us attractive to them in the first place?'

There's a certain paradox here. When both partners are equally intent on internalizing the other's skills, distrust and conflict may spoil the alliance and threaten its very survival. That's one reason joint ventures between Korean and Japanese companies have been few and tempestuous. Neither side wants to 'open the kimono.' Alliances seem to run most smoothly when one partner is intent on learning and the other is intent on avoidance – in essence, when one partner is willing to grow dependent on the other. But running smoothly is not the point; the point is for a company to emerge from an alliance more competitive than when it entered it.

One partner does not always have to give up more than it gains to ensure the survival of an alliance. There are certain conditions under which mutual gain is possible, at least for a time:

■   *The partners' strategic goals converge while their competitive goals diverge.* That is, each partner allows for the other's continued prosperity in the shared business. Philips and Du Pont collaborate to develop and manufacture compact discs, but neither side invades the other's market. There is a clear upstream/downstream division of effort.

■   *The size and market power of both partners is modest compared with industry leaders.* This forces each side to accept that mutual dependence may have to continue for many years. Long-term collaboration may be so critical to both partners that neither will risk antagonizing the other by an overtly competitive bid to appropriate skills or competences. Fujitsu's 1 to 5 size disadvantage with IBM means it will be a long time, if ever, before Fujitsu can break away from its foreign partners and go it alone.

■   *Each partner believes it can learn from the other and at the same time limit access to proprietary skills.* JVC and Thomson, both of whom make VCRs, know that they are trading skills. But the two companies are looking for

very different things. Thomson needs product technology and manufacturing prowess; JVC needs to learn how to succeed in the fragmented
European market. Both sides believe there is an equitable chance for
gain.

How to Build Secure Defenses

For collaboration to succeed, each partner must contribute something
distinctive: basic research, product development skills, manufacturing
capacity, access to distribution. The challenge is to share enough skills
to create advantage *vis-à-vis* companies outside the alliance while preventing a wholesale transfer of core skills to the partner. This is a very
thin line to walk. Companies must carefully select what skills and technologies they pass to their partners. They must develop safeguards
against unintended, informal transfers of information. The goal is to
limit the transparency of their operations.

The type of skill a company contributes is an important factor in
how easily its partner can internalize the skills. The potential for transfer
is greatest when a partner's contribution is easily transported (in engineering drawings, on computer tapes, or in the heads of a few technical
experts); easily interpreted (it can be reduced to commonly understood
equations or symbols); and easily absorbed (the skill or competence is
independent of any particular cultural context).

Western companies face an inherent disadvantage because their
skills are generally more vulnerable to transfer. The magnet that attracts
so many companies to alliances with Asian competitors is their manufacturing excellence – a competence that is less transferable than most.
Just-in-time inventory systems and quality circles can be imitated, but
this is like pulling a few threads out of an oriental carpet. Manufacturing
excellence is a complex web of employee training, integration with
suppliers, statistical process controls, employee involvement, value engineering, and design for manufacture. It is difficult to extract such a subtle
competence in any way but a piecemeal fashion.

So companies must take steps to limit transparency. One approach
is to limit the scope of the formal agreement. It might cover a single
technology rather than an entire range of technologies; part of a product
line rather than the entire line; distribution in a limited number of
markets or for a limited period of time. The objective is to circumscribe
a partner's opportunities to learn.

Moreover, agreements should establish specific performance
requirements. Motorola, for example, takes an incremental, incentive-
based approach to technology transfer in its venture with Toshiba. The
agreement calls for Motorola to release its microprocessor technology

incrementally as Toshiba delivers on its promise to increase Motorola's penetration in the Japanese semiconductor market. The greater Motorola's market share, the greater Toshiba's access to Motorola's technology.

Many of the skills that migrate between companies are not covered in the formal terms of collaboration. Top management puts together strategic alliances and sets the legal parameters for exchange. But what actually gets traded is determined by day-to-day interactions of engineers, marketers, and product developers: who says what to whom, who gets access to what facilities, who sits on what joint committees. The most important deals ('I'll share this with you if you share that with me') may be struck four or five organizational levels below where the deal was signed. Here lurks the greatest risk of unintended transfers of important skills.

Consider one technology-sharing alliance between European and Japanese competitors. The European company valued the partnership as a way to acquire a specific technology. The Japanese company considered it a window on its partner's entire range of competences and interacted with a broad spectrum of its partner's marketing and product development staff. The company mined each contact for as much information as possible.

For example, every time the European company requested a new feature on a product being sourced from its partner, the Japanese company asked for detailed customer and competitor analyses to justify the request. Over time, it developed a sophisticated picture of the European market that would assist its own entry strategy. The technology acquired by the European partner through the formal agreement had a useful life of three to five years. The competitive insights acquired informally by the Japanese company will probably endure longer.

Limiting unintended transfers at the operating level requires careful attention to the role of gatekeepers, the people who control what information flows to a partner. A gatekeeper can be effective only if there are a limited number of gateways through which a partner can access people and facilities. Fujitsu's many partners all go through a single office, the 'collaboration section,' to request information and assistance from different divisions. This way the company can monitor and control access to critical skills and technologies.

We studied one partnership between European and US competitors that involved several divisions of each company. While the US company could only access its partner through a single gateway, its partner had unfettered access to all participating divisions. The European company took advantage of its free rein. If one division refused to provide certain information, the European partner made the same request of another division. No single manager in the US company could tell how much information had been transferred or was in a position to piece together patterns in the requests.

Collegiality is a prerequisite for collaborative success. But *too much* collegiality should set off warning bells to senior managers. CEOs or division presidents should expect occasional complaints from their counterparts about the reluctance of lower level employees to share information. That's a sign that the gatekeepers are doing their jobs. And senior management should regularly debrief operating personnel to find out what information the partner is requesting and what requests are being granted.

Limiting unintended transfers ultimately depends on employee loyalty and self-discipline. This was a real issue for many of the Western companies we studied. In their excitement and pride over technical achievements, engineering staffs sometimes shared information that top management considered sensitive. Japanese engineers were less likely to share proprietary information.

There are a host of cultural and professional reasons for the relative openness of Western technicians. Japanese engineers and scientists are more loyal to their company than to their profession. They are less steeped in the open give-and-take of university research since they receive much of their training from employers. They consider themselves team members more than individual scientific contributors. As one Japanese manager noted, 'We don't feel any need to reveal what we know. It is not an issue of pride for us. We're glad to sit and listen. If we're patient we usually learn what we want to know.'

Controlling unintended transfers may require restricting access to facilities as well as to people. Companies should declare sensitive laboratories and factories off-limits to their partners. Better yet, they might house the collaborative venture in an entirely new facility. IBM is building a special site in Japan where Fujitsu can review its forthcoming mainframe software before deciding whether to license it. IBM will be able to control exactly what Fujitsu sees and what information leaves the facility.

Finally, which country serves as 'home' to the alliance affects transparency. If the collaborative team is located near one partner's major facilities, the other partner will have more opportunities to learn – but less control over what information gets traded. When the partner houses, feeds, and looks after engineers and operating managers, there is a danger they will 'go native.' Expatriate personnel need frequent visits from headquarters as well as regular furloughs home.

Enhance the Capacity to Learn

Whether collaboration leads to competitive surrender or revitalization depends foremost on what employees believe the purpose of the alliance to be. It is self-evident: to learn, one must want to learn. Western companies won't realize the full benefits of competitive collaboration until they overcome an arrogance borne of decades of leadership. In short, Western companies must be more receptive.

We asked a senior executive in a Japanese electronics company about the perception that Japanese companies learn more from their foreign partners than vice versa. 'Our Western partners approach us with the attitude of teachers,' he told us. 'We are quite happy with this, because we have the attitude of students.'

Learning begins at the top. Senior management must be committed to enhancing their companies' skills as well as to avoiding financial risk. But most learning takes place at the lower levels of an alliance. Operating employees not only represent the front lines in an effective defense but also play a vital role in acquiring knowledge. They must be well briefed on the partner's strengths and weaknesses and understand how acquiring particular skills will bolster their company's competitive position.

This is already standard practice among Asian companies. We accompanied a Japanese development engineer on a tour through a partner's factory. This engineer dutifully took notes on plant layout, the number of production stages, the rate at which the line was running, and the number of employees. He recorded all this despite the fact that he had no manufacturing responsibility in his own company, and that the alliance didn't encompass joint manufacturing. Such dedication greatly enhances learning.

Collaboration doesn't always provide an opportunity to fully internalize a partner's skills. Yet just acquiring new and more precise benchmarks of a partner's performance can be of great value. A new benchmark can provoke a thorough review of internal performance levels and may spur a round of competitive innovation. Asking questions like, 'Why do their semiconductor logic designs have fewer errors than ours?' and 'Why are they investing in this technology and we're not?' may provide the incentive for a vigorous catch-up program.

Competitive benchmarking is a tradition in most of the Japanese companies we studied. It requires many of the same skills associated with competitor analysis: systematically calibrating performance against external targets; learning to use rough estimates to determine where a competitor (or partner) is better, faster, or cheaper; translating those estimates into new internal targets; and recalibrating to establish the rate of improvement in a competitor's performance. The great advantage of competitive collaboration is that proximity makes benchmarking easier.

Indeed, some analysts argue that one of Toyota's motivations in collaborating with GM in the much-publicized NUMMI venture is to gauge the quality of GM's manufacturing technology. GM's top manufacturing people get a close look at Toyota, but the reverse is true as well.

Toyota may be learning whether its giant US competitor is capable of closing the productivity gap with Japan.

Competitive collaboration also provides a way of getting close enough to rivals to predict how they will behave when the alliance unravels or runs its course. How does the partner respond to price changes? How does it measure and reward executives? How does it prepare to launch a new product? By revealing a competitor's management orthodoxies, collaboration can increase the chances of success in future head-to-head battles.

Knowledge acquired from a competitor-partner is only valuable after it is diffused through the organization. Several companies we studied had established internal clearinghouses to collect and disseminate information. The collaborations manager at one Japanese company regularly made the rounds of all employees involved in alliances. He identified what information had been collected by whom and then passed it on to appropriate departments. Another company held regular meetings where employees shared new knowledge and determined who was best positioned to acquire additional information.

Proceed with Care – But Proceed

After World War II, Japanese and Korean companies entered alliances with Western rivals from weak positions. But they worked steadfastly toward independence. In the early 1960s, NEC's computer business was one-quarter the size of Honeywell's, its primary foreign partner. It took only two decades for NEC to grow larger than Honeywell, which eventually sold its computer operations to an alliance between NEC and Group Bull of France. The NEC experience demonstrates that dependence on a foreign partner doesn't automatically condemn a company to also-ran status. Collaboration may sometimes be unavoidable; surrender is not.

Managers are too often obsessed with the ownership structure of an alliance. Whether a company controls 51 percent or 49 percent of a joint venture may be much less important than the rate at which each partner learns from the other. Companies that are confident of their ability to learn may even prefer some ambiguity in the alliance's legal structure. Ambiguity creates more potential to acquire skills and technologies. The challenge for Western companies is not to write tighter legal agreements but to become better learners.

Running away from collaboration is no answer. Even the largest Western companies can no longer outspend their global rivals. With leadership in many industries shifting toward the East, companies in the United States and Europe must become good borrowers – much like

Asian companies did in the 1960s and 1970s. Competitive renewal depends on building new process capabilities and winning new product and technology battles. Collaboration can be a low-cost strategy for doing both.

Reading 2   Creating a Strategic Center to Manage a Web of Partners

By Gianni Lorenzoni and Charles Baden-Fuller[†]

Strategic alliances and inter-firm networks have been gaining popularity with many firms for their lower overhead costs, increased responsiveness and flexibility, and greater efficiency of operations. Networks that are *strategically guided* are often fast-growing and on the leading edge. In 10 years, Sun Microsystems (founded in 1982) grew to $3.2 billion in sales and $284 million in profits. This remarkable growth has been achieved by Sun's strategic direction of a web of alliances.

Few would expect such rapid growth and technological success in an older and mature industry such as textiles. Yet Benetton, the famous global textile empire, is in many ways like Sun. Founded in 1964, it had by 1991 achieved more than $2 billion in sales and $235 million in profits. Benetton is widely admired in Europe and the Far East for its rapid growth and ability to change the industry's rules of the game through its strategy of 'mass fashion to young people.'

What creates and guides the successful, innovative, leading-edge interfirm network? Most research into inter-firm networks has emphasized how they can reconcile the flexibility of market relationships with the long-term commitment of hierarchically centralized management. Although all networks reflect the conscious decisions of some managers, it is becoming increasingly apparent that those networks that are not guided strategically by a 'center' are unable to meet the demanding challenges of today's markets. In this article, we are concerned with those strategic centers that have had a very significant impact on their sectors, especially as regards innovation. They are not confined to just a few isolated sectors, but have been observed in a wide variety of circumstances, some of which are listed in Table 7.3.

[†] Source: This article was adapted with permission from 'Creating A Strategic Center to Manage a Web of Partners,' *California Management Review*, Vol. 37, No. 3, Spring 1995.

In this reading, we examine three dimensions of the strategic center:

- as a creator of value for its partners;
- as leader, rule setter, and capability builder;
- as simultaneously structuring and strategizing.

The Role of the Strategic Center

The strategic center (or central firm) plays a critical role as a creator of value. The main features of this role are:

- *Strategic outsourcing.* Outsource and share with more partners than the normal broker and traditional firm. Require partners to be more than doers, expect them to be problemsolvers and initiators.

- *Capability.* Develop the core skills and competencies of partners to make them more effective and competitive. Force members of the network to share their expertise with others in the network, and with the central firm.

- *Technology.* Borrow ideas from others which are developed and exploited as a means of creating and mastering new technologies.

- *Competition.* Explain to partners that the principle dimension of competition is between value chains and networks. The network is only as strong as its weakest link. Encourage rivalry between firms inside the network, in a positive manner.

From Subcontracting to Strategic Outsourcing

All firms that act as brokers or operate networks play only a limited role in undertaking the production and delivery of the good or service to the markets in which the system is involved. What distinguishes central firms is both the extent to which they subcontract, and the way that they collect together partners who contribute to the whole system and whose roles are clearly defined in a positive and creative way.

Many organizations see their sub-contractors and partners as passive doers or actors in their quest for competitive advantage. They typically specify exactly what they want the partners to do, and leave little to the creative skills of others. They reserve a special creative role for only a few 'critical' partners. In strategic networks, it is the norm rather than an exception for partners to be innovators.

Typically each of these partnerships extends beyond a simple subcontracting relationship. Strategic centers expect their partners to do more than follow the rules, they expect them to be creative. For

TABLE 7.3

Some central firms and their activities

Name of Company and its Industry	Activities of Strategic Center	Activities of the Network
Apple (Computers)	Hardware Design Software Design Distribution	Principal subcontractors manufacture 3,000 software developers
Benetton (Apparel)	Designing Collections Selected Production Developing New Technology Systems	6,000 shops 400 subcontractors in production Principal joint ventures in Japan, Egypt, India, and others
Corning (Glass, Medical Products and Optical Fibers)	Technology Innovation Production	More than 30 joint ventures world-wide
Genentech (Biotechnology/ DNA)	Technology Innovation	J.V.s with drug companies for production and distribution, licensing in from universities
McDonald's (Fast Food)	Marketing Prototyping Technology and Systems	9,000 outlets, joint ventures in many foreign countries
McKesson (Drug Distribution)	Systems Marketing Logistics Consulting Advice	Thousands of retail drug outlets, and ties with drug companies, and government institutions
Nike (Shoes and Sportswear)	Design Marketing	Principal subcontractors world-wide
Nintendo (Video Games)	Design Prototyping Marketing	30 principal hardware subcontractors 150 software developers
Sun (Computers and Computer Systems)	Innovation of Technology Software Assembly	Licensor/licensees for software and hardware
Toyota (Automobiles)	Design Assembly Marketing	Principal subcontractors for complex components Second tier for other components Network of agents for distribution

example, Apple worked with Canon and Adobe to design and create a laser jet printer which then gave Apple an important position in its industry. In all the cases we studied, the strategic center looked to the partners to be creative in solving problems and being proactive in the relationships. They demanded more – and obtained more – from their partners than did their less effective counterparts that used traditional subcontracting.

Developing the Competencies of the Partners

How should the central firm see its own competencies *vis-à-vis* its partners? Most writers argue that current competencies should guide future decisions. Many have warned of the dangers in allowing the other partners in a joint venture or alliance to exploit the skills of the host organization. For example, Reich and Mankin[21] noted that joint ventures between Japanese and US firms often result in one side (typically the Japanese) gaining at the expense of the other. Bleeke and Ernst[22] found similar disappointment in that in only 51 percent of the cases they studied did both firms gain from alliances. In a study of cross border alliances, Hamel[23] found that the unwary partner typically found that its competencies were 'hollowed out' and that its collaborator became a more powerful competitor. Badaracco[24] examined the experiences of GM and IBM, who have signed multiple agreements, and explored the difficulties they face.

Traditional brokers and large integrated firms do not 'hand out' core skills, but the central firms we studied have ignored this advice and won. While keeping a very few skills and assets to themselves, the central firms were remarkable in their desire to transfer skill and knowledge adding value to their partners. Typically, they set out to build up the partners' ability and competencies. At Benetton, site selection and sample selection were skills which Benetton would offer to the new retail partners, either directly or through the agents. Skill transfers were also evident in the machinery networks and at Apple.

Nike brings its partners to its research site at Beaverton to show them the latest developments in materials, product designs, technologies, and markets. Sometimes the partners share some of the costs, but the prime benefit is to shorten cycle times and create a more vibrant system. Toyota's subcontractors may receive training from Toyota and are helped in their development of expertise in solving problems pertaining to their particular component. Not only does this encourage them to deliver better quality parts to the Toyota factories, but it also allows the Toyota system to generate an advantage over other car manufacturers.

In contrast to these companies, the less successful organizations we studied did not have groups of specialists to transfer knowledge to partners – nor, it seems, did they appreciate its importance. They did not enlist all their suppliers and customers to fight a common enemy. Moreover, their experiences did not encourage exploration of this approach. They spoke of past difficulties in alliances. Skill transfers between parties did not always result in mutual benefit. One defense contractor explained that their experience of skill transfers nearly always meant that the partner was strengthened and became a stronger rival.

Borrowing–Developing–Lending New Ideas

While all firms bring in new ideas from outside, the central firms we studied have adopted an unusual and aggressive perspective in this sphere. They scan their horizons for all sorts of opportunities and utilize a formula we call *borrow–develop–lend*. 'Borrow' means that the strategic center deliberately buys or licenses some existing technological ideas from a third party; 'develop' means that it takes these outside ideas and adds value by developing them further in its own organization. This commercialization can then be exploited or 'lent' with great rapidity through its stellar system, creating new adjuncts to leverage to the greatest advantage. Borrowing ideas, which are subsequently developed and exploited, stretches the organization and forces it to grow its capabilities and competencies. It demands a new way of thinking.

In the Italian packaging machinery sector, lead producers follow this strategy. They borrow designs of a new machine from specialist designers or customers. These designs are then prototyped. From these prototypes, small and medium-sized partners or specialists often improve the design in a unique way, such as improving the flows and linkages. The focal firm then re-purchases and exploits the modified design, licensing to producers for the final development and marketing phase. Thus we see a 'to-and-fro' pattern of development between the central firm and its many partners.

Sun also used the borrow–develop–lend approach in their project to build a new workstation delivering 'more power with less cost.' They borrowed existing technology from other parties, recombined and developed them further inside Sun, and then licensed them to third parties for development and sale under the Sun brand.

The borrow–develop–lend principle helps the central firm reduce the cost of development, make progress more quickly, and, most importantly, undertake projects which would normally lie outside its scope. This approach contrasts with the procedures used by other large firms. Although these firms may buy ideas from other sources, large firms usually have a slower pace of development and rarely match the speed of exploitation achieved through networking and re-lending the idea to third parties. The strategic center seems to avoid the *not-invented-here* syndrome, where innovations and ideas are rejected because they are not internally created and developed.

From the view of independent inventors, the strategic center is an attractive organization with which to do business. The central firms have a track record of rapid commercialization (usually offering large incentives to those with ideas). They emphasize moving quickly from ideas to market by a simultaneous learning process with partners, thereby offering a competitive advantage over other developers. Finally, the willingness to involve others means rapid diffusion with fast payback, thus lessening the risks.

Perceptions of the Competitive Process

Firms in the same industry experience varying degrees of competitive rivalry. The joint venture, formal agreements, or the use of cross shareholdings are mechanisms used to create common ties, encourage a common view, and unite firms against others in the industry. Strategic centers also create this sense of cooperation across competing enterprises.

Competitive success requires the integration of multiple capabilities (e.g. innovation, productivity, quality, responsiveness to customers) across internal and external organizational boundaries. Such integration is a big challenge to most organizations. Strategic centers rise to this challenge and create a sense of common purpose across multiple levels in the value chain and across different sectors. They achieve a combination of specialized capability and large-scale integration at the same time, despite the often destructive rivalry between buyers and customers. Strategic purchasing partnerships are commonly used to moderate this rivalry, but few firms are able to combine both horizontal and vertical linkages.

In building up their partner's capabilities and competencies, strategic

TABLE 7.4
Different kinds of competition across sectors and stages of the value chain

	Single Units Within the Sector	Multiple Units Within the Sector or Across Related Sectors
Multiple stages of the value chain	Vertical integration or value-added partnerships	Strategic centers and their webs of partners or large integrated multi-market organizations
Single stages of the value chain	Traditional adversarial firm	chain stores or simple networks

centers convey an unusual perspective to their partners on the nature of the competitive process. This perspective permits the partners to take a holistic view of the network, seeing the collective as a unit that can achieve competitive advantage. In this respect, the whole network acts like a complex integrated firm spanning many markets.

Table 7.4 illustrates how the actions of the strategic center differ from other organizations. Chain stores are a good example of organizations that coordinate activities across many actors, yet at a single stage of the value chain. In contrast, the narrowly defined, vertically integrated firm coordinates across many stages but not across many markets or actors. Only the strategic center and the large multi-market, vertically integrated organization are able to coordinate across many markets and many stages of the value chain.

Beyond the Hollow Organization

Although the strategic center outsources more activities than most organizations, it is not hollow. Unlike the traditional broker that is merely a glorified arranger, the central firms we studied understand that they have to develop some critical core competencies. These competencies are, in general, quite different from those stressed by most managers in traditional firms. The agenda for the central firm consists of:

■ *The idea.* Creating a vision in which partners play a critical role.

■ *The investment.* A strong brand image and effective systems and support.

■ *The climate.* Creating an atmosphere of trust and reciprocity.

■ *The partners.* Developing mechanisms for attracting and selecting partners.

Sharing a Business Idea

Most of the central firms we studied are small, lean, and focused operations. They employ comparatively few people and are very selective in what they do. Yet, they have an unusual ability to conceptualize a business idea that can be shared not only internally, but with other partners. In the case of Benetton, this idea has a few key elements such as: mass fashion for young people, and the notion of a strategic network to orchestrate and fulfill this vision. In food-machinery, the key idea of the central firms is to solve the client's problems, rather than selling existing competencies, while new partners are developed in response to customer needs – a novel notion in this sector. These simple ideas are not easy to create or sustain.

These ideas have been able to capture the imagination of the employees and their partners. They also encapsulate strategy and so contain, in the language of Prahalad and Hamel[25], the features of a clear strategic intent. Common to all the business ideas we studied, there is a notion of partnership which includes the creation of a learning culture and the promotion of systems experiments so as to outpace rival competing organizations. The strategic centers view their role as one of leading and orchestrating their systems. Their distinctive characteristics lie in their ability to perceive the full business idea and understand the role of all the different parties in many different locations across the whole value chain. The managers in the strategic center have a dream and they orchestrate others to fulfill that dream.

This vision of the organization is not just an idea in the minds of a few managers, it is a feature that is shared throughout the organization. Many of the strategic centers we studied admit that their visions have emerged over time, they are not the work of a moment. Their vision is dynamic, for as their network grows and as the environment changes, the organizational vision also changes. This is not the case in the less successful alliances. They showed the typical characteristics of most organizations, multifaceted views of the world and a less-than-clear expression of their vision.

Clearly, vision is reinforced by success. The ability of central firms to deliver profits and growth for the partners helps cement a vision in their minds and makes their claims credible. It creates a cycle where success breeds clarity, which in turn helps breed more success.

Brand Power and Other Support

To maintain the balance of power in the network, all central firms retain certain activities. The control of the brand names and the development of the systems that integrate the network are two activities that give the organization a pivotal role and allow it to exercise power over the system.

Some of the firms we observed were involved in consumer markets where branding is important. The brand name, owned by the central firm, was promoted by the activities of the partners, who saw the brand as a shared resource. They were encouraged to ensure its success, and quite often these efforts helped the brand become famous in a short period of time. While the brand and marketing are not so vital in producer goods markets, they are still important – and the strategic center neglects these at its peril. Its importance is highlighted by the experiences of one of the less successful organizations we studied. This aerospace firm had problems as a result of the inability of its members to relinquish many of the aspects of marketing to a single central firm.

To retain its power, the central firm must ensure that the information between partners flows freely and is not filtered. Communication is a costly activity, and developing effective communication systems is always the responsibility of the strategic center. These systems are not only electronically based, but include all other methods of communication. Often there is a style for meeting among the partners, which is set and monitored by the central firm. The quality of information is a key requirement if the central firm is to mandate effectively the stream of activities scattered among different firms.

Trust and Reciprocity

Leveraging the skills of partners is easy to conceive but hard to implement. The difficulties occur because it takes many partners operating effectively to make the system work, but the negative behavior of only a few can bring the whole system to a halt. The strategic vision requires all its members to contribute all the time without fail. This is a considerable demand. The typical organizational response to such a need is to circumscribe the contracts with outsiders in a tight legalistic manner. But this is not always wise; contract making and policing can be difficult and expensive. Formal contracts are relatively inflexible and are suitable only where the behavior is easy to describe and is relatively inflexible. But the relationships are creative and flexible and so very difficult to capture and enforce contractually.

The approach of the central firms we studied is to develop a sense of trust and reciprocity in the system. This trust and reciprocity is a dynamic concept and it can be very tight. The tightness is apparent in each party agreeing to perform its known obligations. This aspect has similarities to contracts in the sense that obligations are precisely understood. But Anglo-Saxon contracts are typically limited in the sense that partners are not expected to go beyond the contract. In contrast, in a network perspective, the behavior is prescribed for the unknown, each promising to work in a particular manner to resolve future challenges and difficulties as they arise. This means that each partner will promise to deliver what is expected, and that future challenges will also be addressed positively. If there are uncertainties and difficulties in the relationships, these will be resolved after the work is done. If one party goes beyond (in the positive sense) the traditional contract, others will remember and reciprocate at a later date.

Trust and reciprocity are complements, not substitutes, to other obligations. If partners do not subscribe to the trust system, they can hold the whole system hostage whenever they are asked to do something out of the ordinary, or even in the normal course of events. Such behavior will cause damage to all, and the system will break up. Only with trust can the system work in unison.

The Benetton franchising system is perhaps an extreme version of this trust system. In the continent of Europe, Benetton does not use legal contracts, rather it relies on the unwritten agreement. This, it claims, focuses everyone's attention on making the expectations clear. It also saves a great deal of time and expense. Many other strategic centers also rely on trust, but utilize contracts and formal controls as a complement. Central firms develop rules for settling disputes (for there will be disputes even in a trust system). The central firm also ensures that rewards are distributed in a manner which encourages partners to reinforce the positive circle. Benetton has encountered limits to its approach in the US, where the cultural emphasis on law and contracts has come into conflict with Benetton's strategy.

In sharp contrast are the other less successful systems we studied. There, trust was used on a very limited scale, since most organizations had difficulty in getting partners to deliver even that which was promised. Broken promises and failed expectations were common in the defense systems. Very low anticipated expectations of partner reciprocity were a common feature of the Scottish network and appliance sectors. Most organizations believed that anything crucial had to be undertaken in-house.

Trust is delicate, and it needs fostering and underpinning. One of the ways in which positive behavior is encouraged is to ensure that the profit-sharing relationship gives substantial rewards to the partners. None of the central firms we studied seeks to be the most profitable firm in the system; they are happy for others to take the bulk of the profit. In Benetton, a retailer may find his or her capital investment paid back in three years. In Corning, some partners have seen exceptional returns. This seemingly altruistic behavior, however, does not mean that the rewards to the central firm are small.

Partner Selection

The central firms we studied recognize that creating success and a long-term perspective must begin with the partner selection process. In building a network, partners must be selected with great care. Initially, the central firms followed a pattern of trial and error, but following successful identification of the key points the selection process, they became more deliberate. The many new styles of operation and new ways of doing things are not easy to grasp, and they are quite difficult to codify – especially at the early stages of the selection process. As time passes, a partner profile emerges together with a selection procedure aimed at creating the correct conditions for the relationships. These relationships require coordination among all the partners, a common long-term perspective, an acceptance of mutual adaptation, and incremental innovation.

When we looked at the details of the selection procedure, there was a difference between those central firms that had a few large partners and those that had many small-scale partners. In the case of the network composed of a few, large firm alliances, the selection criterion is typically based on careful strategic considerations. There is the question of matching capabilities and resources, as well as considerations of competition. However, most important are the organizational features based on a compatibility of management systems, decision processes, and perspectives – in short, a cultural fit.

The selection process must also be tempered by availability. Typically, there are few potential partners to fit the ideal picture. Perhaps it is for this reason that some Japanese and European firms start the process early on by deliberately spinning off some of their internal units to create potential partners. Typically these units will contain some of their best talents. However, these units will have a cultural affinity and a mutual understanding, which makes the partnership easier.

In the case of the large network composed of many small partners, the center acts as a developer of the community. Its managers must assume a different role. Apple called some of its managers 'evangelists' because they managed the relationships with 3,000 third-party developers. So that they could keep constant contact with them, they used images of the 'Figurehead' and the 'Guiding Light.'

Simultaneous Structuring and Strategizing

Of all the battles firms face, the most difficult is not the battle for position, nor is it even the battle between strong firms and weak firms following the same strategic approaches. Rather, it is the battle between firms adopting different strategies and different approaches to the market. In these battles, the winners are usually those who use fewer and different resources in novel combinations. The central firms we studied fit this category, for they have typically dominated their sectors by stretching and leveraging modest resources to great effect. In trying to understand these battles of stretch and leverage, others have stressed the technical achievements of central firms such as lean production, technical innovation, or flexible manufacturing and service delivery. To be sure, these advances are important and provide partial explanations for the success of Sun, Nintendo, Benetton, Apple, and others. Equally important, if not more important, are new ideas on the nature of strategizing and structuring. Strategizing is a shared process between the strategic center and its partners; structuring of the relationships between the partners goes hand in hand and is seen as a key part of the strategy.

Strategy conception and implementation of ideas is shared between central firms and their webs of partners. Here they differ from most conventional organizations, which neither share their conceptions of strategy with other organizations nor insist that their partners share their ideas with them in a constructive dialogue. While all firms form partnerships with some of their suppliers and customers, these linkages rarely involve sharing ideas systematically. Subcontracting relationships are usually deeper and more complex, and many firms share their notions of strategy with their subcontractors, but the sharing is nearly always limited. Alliances demand even greater levels of commitment and interchange, and it is common for firms involved in alliances to exchange ideas about strategy and to look for strategic fit and even reshaping of strategic directions. Networks can be thought of as a higher stage of alliances, for in the strategic center there is a conscious desire to influence and shape the strategies of the partners, and to obtain from partners ideas and influences in return.

This conscious desire to share strategy is reflected in the way in which central firms conceive of the boundaries of their operations. Most organizations view their joint ventures and subcontractors as beyond the boundaries of their firm, and even those involved in alliances do not think of partners as an integral part of the organization. Even firms that are part of a franchise system (and thus have a more holistic perspective) do not view their relationships as a pattern of multilateral contracts. Going beyond the franchise view, central firms and their participants communicate multilaterally across the whole of the value chain. In the words of Johanson and Mattsson[26], they have a 'network theory,' a perception of governing a whole system.

Strategizing and structuring in the central firms we studied reverses Chandler's famous dictum about structure following strategy. When partner's competencies are so crucial to the developments of the business idea of the strategic center, the winners are building strategy and structure simultaneously whereas the losers are signing agreements without changing their organizational forms to match them. When each partner's resources and competencies are so essential to the success of the enterprise, new forms must be designed. To achieve this, structuring must come earlier, alongside strategizing, and both require an interaction among partners to create a platform of flexibility and capability. This behavior challenges much of what is received managerial practice and avoids some of the traps that webs of alliances face.

Like the large integrated cohesive organization, networked firms are able to behave as a single competitive entity which can draw on considerable resources. However, the network form avoids many of the problems of large integrated firms, who typically find themselves paralyzed in the struggle between freedom and control. By focusing attention on the matters where commonality is important (e.g. product design) and by allowing each unit to have freedom elsewhere, cooperation is fostered, time and energy spent in monitoring is reduced, and resources are optimized. In this way, the networked organization succeeds in bridging the gap between centralization and decentralization. But cooperation can dull the edge of progress, and the organizations in our study have avoided this trap by fostering a highly competitive spirit.

Marketing and Information Sharing

The way in which information is collected and shared in the system reveals how structure and strategy go hand in hand. The gathering of information is a central activity in any organization. A strategic feature of a network of alliances is that the firms in the system are closely linked for the sharing of information. Members of the network exchange not only hard data about best practice, but also ideas, feelings, and thoughts about customers, other suppliers, and general market trends.

The central firm structures the information system so that knowledge is funneled to the areas that need it the most. Members specializing in a particular function have access to others in the system performing similar tasks, and share their knowledge. This creates a level playing field within the network system. It also provides the opportunity for the members to focus and encourage the development of competitive advantage over rivals.

One of the basic premises in our network view is that new information leading to new ways of doing things emerges in a process of interaction with people and real-life situations. It follows that the 'information ability' of the firm depends critically on a scheme of interactions. The difficulty is that the generation of new information cannot be planned, but has to emerge. Thus, the task of the manager is one of designing a structure which provides an environment favorable for interactions to form, and for new information to be generated. Such a structure is a network.

Our study found, as have others, that the availability of large amounts of high quality information on many aspects of the business facilitated more rapid responses to market opportunities. Information condensed through the network is 'thicker' than that condensed through the brokerage market, but is 'freer' than in the hierarchy.

The need for a sophisticated system was clear when we contrasted the central firms we studied with other firms. In these other firms, we often found that critical information was guarded, not shared. As is so common among organizations, individual players are either afraid of being exploited or they have a desire to exploit the power they have through knowledge. Even in traditional franchise systems, information is typically passed to the center for filtering before being shared. In the large integrated firm, centralization also causes unnecessary filtering. With centralization, the process of collecting and distributing information can be cumbersome and slow. Moreover, power to manipulate the information can be accidentally or intentionally misused by a small central group.

Some of the 'control group' of firms we studied did share their information, with adverse consequences. For example, defense contractors, unable to create an effective strategic network, found the partners sometimes used the shared information to their own advantage, and then did not reciprocate. The knowledge was exploited by partners to create superior bargaining positions. Opportunities to foster collective interest were missed, and in extreme cases, partners used the information to bolster a rival alliance to the detriment of the original information provider.

Learning Races

Whereas identifying opportunities for growth is facilitated by information sharing, responding to the opportunity is more difficult. Here we see some of the clearest evidence that structure and strategy go hand in hand. First and foremost, the central firms we studied reject the idea of doing everything themselves. Instead, they seek help from others to respond to the opportunities they face. When the knowledge and capabilities exist within the network, the role of the center is to orchestrate the response so that the whole system capitalizes on the opportunity.

It frequently happens that opportunities require an innovative response, and it is common for strategic centers to set up 'learning races.' Here, partners are given a common goal (say a new product or process development) with a prize for the first to achieve the target. The prize may be monetary, but more commonly it is the opportunity to lead off the exploitation of the new development. There is a catch, the development must be shared with others in the network. Learning races create a sense of competition and rivalry, but within an overall common purpose.

Nintendo uses carefully nurtured learning races with its partners to create high quality rapid innovation. Partners are typically restricted in the number of contributions they can make. In the case of software design, the limit may be three ideas a year. These restrictions force a striving for excellence, and the consequence is a formidable pace of progress.

Learning races can be destructive rather than constructive if the partners do not have the skills and resources. The strategic centers we studied get around these difficulties by sharing knowledge and in effect allowing the whole network to 'borrow' skills and competencies from each other.

It is important to understand the role of new members in the process of creating innovations. Many central firms follow the twin strategies of internal and external development. Internal development involves offering existing partners a possibility of sharing in the growth markets. External development involves the finding of new partners to fill the gaps and accelerate the possibilities. New partners typically fit the pattern set by existing partners. These newly found 'look alike' firms allow the strategic center to truncate development of the necessary capabilities, leveraging off earlier experiences developed by the existing partners. By making growth a race between old and new partners, speed is assured and scale effects exploited. Our strategic centers fostered positive rivalry rather than hostility by ensuring that both old and new partners share in the final gains. When pursuing rapid growth, the twin tracks of internal and external development can lessen tensions. Because they are independent, existing members can respond to the new demands as they wish. But, if they do not respond positively, the central firm can sign up new partners to fill the gaps. The stresses and strains of growth can thus be reduced for each of the members of the network.

Conclusions

The strategically minded central firms in our study view the boundaries of the organization differently because their conception and implementation of strategy are shared with a web of partners. This attitude contrasts sharply with most organizations, which view their joint ventures and subcontractors as existing beyond the boundaries of their firm. Even those involved in alliances typically do not think of partners as an integral part of their organization; they rarely share their conceptions of strategy and even fewer insist that their partners share their strategy with them in a constructive dialogue. In contrast, strategic centers communicate strategic ideas and intent multilaterally across the whole of the value chain. They have a network view of governing a whole system.

Strategic centers reach out to resolve classic organizational paradoxes. Many subcontracting and alliance relationships seem to be mired in the inability to reconcile the advantages of the market with those of the hierarchy. Strategic centers are able to create a system that has the flexibility and freedom of the market coupled with long-term holistic relationships, ensuring the requisite strategic capabilities across the whole system. Another paradox exists between creativity and discipline. Most organizations oscillate between having ample creativity and little discipline, or too much discipline and not enough creativity. Through their unusual attitude to structuring and strategizing, strategic centers attain leading-edge technological and market developments while retaining rapid decision-making processes.

All organizations have much to learn from studying strategic centers and their unusual conception of the managerial task. Strategic centers have taken modest resources and won leadership positions in a wide variety of sectors. They have brought a new way of thinking about business and organizing. Much of what they do is at the cutting edge, and they are shining examples of how firms can change the rules of the game by creative and imaginative thinking.

Network Level Strategy in International Perspective

Do as adversaries in law, strive mightily, but eat and drink as friends.
(William Shakespeare 1564–1616; English dramatist and poet)

Of all of the debates in the field of strategic management, this one has received the most attention from comparative management researchers. Almost all of these researchers have concluded that firms from different countries display widely divergent propensities to compete and co-operate. Many authors suggest that there are recognizable national inclinations, even national styles, when it comes to establishing interfirm relationships. For instance, Kanter[27] notes that

> North American companies, more than others in the world, take a narrow, opportunistic view of relationships, evaluating them strictly in financial terms or seeing them as barely tolerable alternatives to outright acquisition. Preoccupied with the economics of the deal, North American companies frequently neglect the political, cultural, organizational, and human aspects of the partnership. Asian companies are the most comfortable with relationships, and therefore they are the most adept at using and exploiting them. European companies fall somewhere in the middle.

Although Kanter's 'classification' is somewhat rough, most strategic management researchers who have done international comparative studies agree with the broad lines of her remark[28].

While it is difficult to generalize at the national level, since there can be quite a bit of variance within a country, it is challenging to debate these observed international dissimilarities. Are there really national interfirm relationship styles and what factors might influence their existence? As a stimulus to the international dimension of this debate, a number of country characteristics are put forward as possible influences on how the paradox of competition and cooperation is dealt with in different national settings. As noted before, it is the intention of these propositions to encourage further discussion and cross cultural research on the topic of interorganizational relationships.

Level of Individualism

At the most fundamental level, cultural values can place more emphasis on competition or on cooperation. Some researchers point out that this has much to do with a culture's orientation toward individuals or groups. More individualist cultures accentuate the position of each single person as a distinct entity, while more collectivist cultures stress people's group affiliations. In Hofstede's research (see reading 1.2), the United States surfaced as highest scoring nation in the world on the individualism scale, closely followed by the other English-speaking countries, Australia, Great Britain, Canada and New Zealand respectively. Hofstede argues that 'in the US individualist conception, the relationship between the individual and the organization is essentially calculative, being based on enlightened self-interest,' while in more collectivist cultures the relationship 'is not calculative, but moral: it is based not on self interest, but on the individual's loyalty toward the clan, organization, or society – which is supposedly the best guarantee of that individual's ultimate interest.' The willingness of individuals to forgo self-interested behavior for the good of the group, is believed to be the same cultural value spurring individual firms to cooperate for the good of an entire network[29]. Pascale and Athos[30] agree that in the highly group-oriented culture of Japan, interdependence is valued, while the 'self' is regarded as an obstacle to joint development. Group members feel indebted and obligated toward one another, and trust results from a shared understanding and acceptance of interdependence.

The strong orientation of the English-speaking ('Anglo-Saxon') cultures toward individualism and the Japanese cultural emphasis on group-affiliation, is also recognized by Lessem and Neubauer[31], who place these two cultures at the extreme ends of a continuum. In the socially atomistic Anglo-Saxon nations, individuals are seen as the building blocks of society and each person is inclined to optimize her/his own interests. In the socially symbiotic Japanese culture, the whole is more important than the individual parts, so that individuals are more likely to strive towards a group's common good. Interestingly, Lessem and Neubauer (following Albert[32]) argue that, on this point, German and Japanese cultures are strikingly similar. Both cultures exhibit a 'wholist' world view, in which 'management and banker, employer and employee, government and industry combine forces rather than engage in adversarial relations,' to the benefit of the entire system. This collectivist bent can be observed at the multi-company level (industrial networks/*keiretsu*), but also at the industry and national levels of aggregation, leading many analysts to speak of Japan Incorporated and Germany Incorporated.

Other cultures fall somewhere between these two extremes. Italy, for instance, is often cited for its high number of networked companies[33]. Besides the well-known example of Benetton, there are many networks in the textile industry of Prato, the ceramics industry of Sassuolo, the farm machine industry of Reggio-Emilia and motorcycle industry of Bologna. Similar to the Germans and Japanese, Italian culture is also characterized by a strong group-orientation, but the affiliations valued by Italians tend to be mostly family-like, based on blood-ties, friendships or ideological bonds between individuals. There is often a strong loyalty and trust within these family-like communities, but distrust toward the outside world. Therefore, cooperation tends to be high within these communities, but competition prevails beyond.

In France the situation is again different. In French culture, according to Lessem and Neubauer[34], there is 'an ingrained mistrust of the natural play of forces of a free economy.' People have a strong sense that cooperation in economic affairs is important, similar to the Japanese, Germans and Italians. However, the French are unwilling to depend on the evolution of cooperation between (semi-)independent firms. Generally, there is a preference to impose cooperation top-down, by integrating companies into efficiently working bureaucracies. Such structuring of the economy usually takes place under influence, or by direct intervention, of the French government. Such *dirigisme* is based on the opposite assumption as Williamson's work[35]: hierarchical coordination is usually preferable to market transactions. Former prime minister, Edouard Balladur, summarized this assumption far more graciously, when he remarked: 'What is the market? It is the law of the jungle, the law of nature. And what is civilisation? It is the struggle against nature' (*The Economist*, March 15th 1997). Based on this view, even relationships with firms not absorbed into the hierarchy are of a bureaucratic nature, that is, formal, rational and depersonalized.

Type of Institutional Environment

Of course, the cultural values described above are intertwined with the institutional structures that have developed in each country. Some comparative management researchers focus on these institutional forces, such as governments, banks, universities and unions, to explain the divergent national views on competition and cooperation. It is generally argued that most countries have developed an idiosyncratic economic system, that is, their own distinct brand of capitalism, with a different emphasis on competition and cooperation.

One prominent analysis is that of business historian Chandler[36], who has described the historical development of 'personal capitalism' in the United Kingdom, 'managerial capitalism' in the United States, 'co-operative capitalism' in Germany and 'group capitalism' in Japan from 1850 to 1950. The legacy of these separately evolving forms of capitalism is that, to this day, there are significantly different institutional philo-sophies, roles and behaviors in each of these countries. In the English-speaking nations, governments have generally limited their role to the establishment and maintenance of competitive markets. A shared belief in the basic tenets of classical economics has lead these governments to be suspect of competition-undermining collusion masquerading under the term 'cooperation.' For instance, in the United States the Sherman Antitrust Act was passed in 1890 and has been applied with vigor since then to guard the functioning of the market. Many companies that would like to cooperate have been discouraged from doing so[37].

In the German 'cooperative capitalism' system, the situation has been quite different. The government has major shareholdings in hundreds of companies outside the public services. According to Lessem and Neubauer[38] 'the attitude to government participation in industry is based not on ideology but on a sense of partnership with the business community. It extends to the local level where local authorities, schools, banks and businesses combine to establish policies of mutual benefit.' Especially the large German banks play an important role in guiding industrial development, promoting cooperation and defusing potentially damaging conflicts between companies. They have an intimate know-ledge of the business and have a long-term stake in each relationship, which is often expressed by a minority shareholding of the bank in the client company and/or a seat on its supervisory board. The officers of the largest bank, Deutsche Bank, hold roughly 400 seats on other companies' supervisory boards. It should be noted, however, that trade associations and unions also employ a long-term, cooperative perspective.

The Japanese 'group capitalism' system is somewhat akin to the German model. In Japan, too, business and social institutions have formed a partnership to promote mutually beneficial developments. However, in Japan, the government plays a more prominent role than in Germany, through its national industrial strategies. As Thurow[39] points out, the Japanese government is actively involved in the indirect protection of some domestic industries, the selection of other sectors as development priorities and the funding of related research and develop-ment. Furthermore, the keiretsu industry groups, such as Mitsui, Mitsubishi, Sanwa, Hitachi and Sumitomo, also form long-term networks of cooperating companies. While some consortia are formed to deal with a particular task at hand, firms within a keiretsu are familiar with one another through long historical association and have durable, opened-ended relationships, partially cemented by multilateral minority share-holdings.

In France, the dirigiste state planners play an even more prominent role than in Japan. The French model, which could be dubbed 'bureau-cratic capitalism,' focuses sharply on the State as industrial strategist, coordinating all major developments in the economy. It is the planners' job 'to maintain a constant pressure on industry – as part industrial consultant, part banker, part plain bully – to keep it moving in some desired direction'[40]. The unions, on the other hand, tend to be more antagonistic, particularly in their relationship to the government. On the work floor, however, a more cooperative attitude prevails.

Finally, in the 'familial capitalism' system of Italy, local networks of economic, political and social actors cooperate to create a mutually beneficial environment. Trade associations, purchasing cooperatives, educational institutions and cooperative marketing are often created to support a large number of small specialized firms working together as a loose federation. Trust within the network is often large, but institutions outside of these closed communities are mistrusted, especially the central government, tax authorities, bankers and the trade unions.

Market for Corporate Control

Linked to the general institutional environment, is how the issue of mergers, acquisitions and take-overs is viewed in each nation. In countries such as the United States and Britain, companies whose shares are traded on the stock exchange are exposed to the threat of a take-over. This relatively open market for corporate control facilitates vertical and horizontal integration. Companies can contemplate acquiring another firm, if they believe that internal coordination is preferable to a market-based relationship. In other countries, however, the market for corporate control is less open, if not entirely absent. Where horizontal or vertical integration is difficult to achieve, but working together is still beneficial, potential acquirers often only have collaborative arrangements as an alternative.

Type of Career Paths

Finally, a more down to earth reason why competition or cooperation might be more prevalent in a particular country may be found at the level of personnel policy. In general, the longer people know each other and the more they interact, the more trust and cooperativeness that evolves[41]. In countries such as Japan and Germany, where stable, long-term employment is common, individuals are in a better position to build up durable personal relationships with people in other firms. In nations where employees frequently shift between positions and companies, establishing personal ties and gradually building mutual trust is more difficult to achieve.

Another relationship-building mechanism can be the exchange of personnel, on a temporary or permanent basis. In Japan, for instance, it is not unusual to send an employee 'on assignment' to a partner firm for a long period of time, often simultaneously accepting 'external' employees in return. In some countries, the transfer of employees between partner organizations is more permanent. France and Japan are known for their public servants' mid-career shifts to the private sector (*pantouflage* and *amakudari*, respectively), which makes building public–private partnerships much easier.

Further Readings

No one who wishes to delve more deeply into the topic of organizational boundaries and inter-organizational relationships can avoid running into references to the classic in this area, Oliver Williamson's *Markets and Hierarchies: Analysis and Antitrust Implications*. Williamson's writings have inspired many researchers, especially economists. Others have remarked that Williamson's transaction cost economics largely ignores the political, social and psychological aspects of business relationships. As an antidote to Williamson's strongly rationalist view of the world, another classic can be advised. Jeffrey Pfeffer and Gerald Salancik's *The External Control of Organizations: A Resource Dependency Perspective* is an excellent book that emphasizes the political aspects of interorganizational relationships. However, both books are quite academic and not for the faint-hearted.

A more accessible overview of the topic of interorganizational cooperation is provided by Farok Contractor and Peter Lorange in their book *Cooperative Strategies in International Business*. For further reading on the subject of vertical relationships, Michael Best's *The New Competition*, and Carlos Jarillo's *Strategic Networks: Creating the Borderless Organization*, are both excellent choices. For horizontal relationships a good starting point would be *Strategic Alliances: Formation, Implementation and Evolution*, by Peter Lorange and Johan Roos, or *The Knowledge Link: How Firms Compete through Strategic Alliances*, by J. Badaracco. If the reader is interested in moving beyond dyadic relationships,

B. Axelsson and G. Easton's *Industrial Networks: A New View of Reality* is recommended.

All of the above works are positively inclined towards collaboration, largely adopting the embedded organization perspective. For a more critical appraisal of networks, alliances and close relationships, by authors taking the discrete organization perspective, readers are advised to start with the article 'Outsourcing and Industrial Decline,' by Richard Bettis, Stephen Bradley and Gary Hamel. Other critical accounts are John Hendry's article 'Culture, Community and Networks: The Hidden Cost of Outsourcing,' and S. MacDonald's 'Too Close for Comfort?: The Strategic Implications of Getting Close to the Customer.'

For a more thorough understanding of networks within the Japanese context, Michael Gerlach's *Alliance Capitalism: The Social Organization of Japanese Business* is a good book to begin with. T. Nishiguchi's book *Strategic Industrial Sourcing: The Japanese Advantage* is particularly interesting on the topic of Japanese supplier relationships. For the Chinese view on networks, Murray Weidenbaum and Samuel Hughes' book *The Bamboo Network: How Expatriate Chinese Entrepreneurs Are Creating a New Economic Superpower in Asia* is recommended, as is S. Redding's *The Spirit of Chinese Capitalism*. For an overview of European views, Ronnie Lessem and Fred Neubauer's *European Management Systems* is an excellent book, but also Roland Calori and Philippe de Woot's collection *A European Management Model: Beyond Diversity* provides challenging insights.

Strategy Context

8

The Industry Context

The pilot cannot mitigate the billows
or calm the winds.

(Plutarch c.46–c.120; Greek biographer and philosopher)

The reasonable man adapts himself to
the world; the unreasonable one
persists in trying to adapt the world
to himself. Therefore, all progress
depends on the unreasonable man.

(George Bernard Shaw 1856–1950; Irish playwright and critic)

The Paradox of Compliance and Choice

Is it unreasonable to want to change the world? Your answer to this question will largely depend on how adaptable you think the world is. Those who believe that the world develops following its own dynamics will argue that individuals must adapt to the world – it is better to buy an umbrella than to attempt to change the weather. If individuals do not 'follow the laws of nature' or 'play by the rules of the game', they do so at their own peril. On the other hand, those who believe that there are no unchangeable rules or laws, will argue that the world is actually quite adaptable – it is better to invent a new cure than to get used to the illness. Individuals who expose the 'rules' as mere conventions and show that the 'laws' are merely habits, can do so to their own (and others') advantage.

This chapter looks at the issue of environment adaptability at the industry level. The issue is the *malleability* of the industry context – the extent to which the industry context can be modified by a firm (or group of collaborating firms). If firms cannot influence the structure of the industry they are in, *compliance* to the rules of the game is the strategic imperative. Under these circumstances, wise strategists will adapt the firm to the industry environment. However, if firms do have the ability to manipulate the industry structure, they can try to change the 'terms of competition' in their own favor. In this type of situation, wise strategists will not comply to the existing industry rules, but exercise their freedom of *choice* to break the rules or create new rules.

How malleable are industries in practice? Should strategists take a predominantly compliance- or choice-oriented view? Opinions on this matter differ considerably. As in the previous debates, two diametrically opposed points of view can be identified, while many others take in intermediate positions. On the one hand, some argue that industry development is an autonomous process, to which firms must adjust or risk being selected out. We shall refer to this point of view as the *industry evolution* perspective. On the other hand, many strategists believe that the industry context can be moulded in an infinite variety of ways by innovative firms. This point of view will be referred to as the *industry creation* perspective.

As before, this chapter has been structured as a debate between the two opposite points of view. By comparing these two contradictory views on how the paradox of compliance and choice should be dealt with, a better understanding of the issues under discussion should be gained. In the next few pages, the industry evolution and industry creation perspectives will be further explained, and finally summarized in Table 8.1.

The Industry Evolution Perspective

To those taking an industry evolution perspective, the popular notion that individual firms have the power to shape their industry is an understandable, but quite misplaced, belief. Of course, the illusion of control is tempting – most people, especially managers, would like to control their own destiny. Most individuals assume they have a free will and can decide their own future. Many governments suppose that they can shape society and many cultures assume that they control nature. In the same way, it is seductive to believe that the individual firm can matter, by influencing the development of its industry.

Unfortunately, this belief is largely a fallacy, brought on by a poor understanding of the underlying industry dynamics. In reality, according to advocates of the industry evolution perspective, industries are complex systems, with a large number of forces interacting simultaneously, none of which can significantly direct the long-term development of the whole. Firms are relatively small players in a very large game – their behaviors may have some impact on industry development, but none can fundamentally shape the direction of changes. On the contrary, as industries evolve, all firms that do not meet the changing demands of the environment are weeded out. Firms not suited to the new circumstances die, while firms complying to the changing rules prosper. Hence, through *selection* the industry context determines the group of industry survivors and through the pressures for *adaptation* the behavior of the remaining firms is determined. In short, the industry shapes the firm, not the other way around.

The label 'industry evolution perspective' is derived from the parallel often drawn with biological evolution. Both evolutionary processes, it is argued, share a number of basic characteristics. In nature, as in business, the survival and growth of entities depends on their fit with the environment. Within each environment variations to a successful theme might come about. These new individuals will thrive, as long as they suit the existing circumstances, but as the environment changes, only those that meet the new demands will not be selected out. Hence, Darwin's well-known principle of 'survival of the fittest' is based on a cycle of *variation* and *environmental selection*. Some proponents of the industry evolution perspective think that this biological view of evolution is a good model for what happens in industries – new organizations arise as mutations and only the fittest mutations survive[1]. Others adopting the industry evolution perspective argue that there is a significant difference with biological evolution. Organizations do not vary 'at random,' but purposefully, and they possess the ability to adapt to selection pressures during the evolution process[2].

The upshot of the industry evolution perspective is that there is actually not very much that a strategist can do to improve the performance of a company. Industries follow an evolutionary trajectory, that no one controls. The current and future industry structure cannot be influenced, however cunning strategists believe they can be. With immutable rules of the game, strategy is reduced to playing well within the rules. This leaves only small margins within which to maneuver and predetermines the general level of profitability that a firm can achieve. Once in a poor industry, a firm's growth and profit potential are significantly limited. The best a firm can do is to score slightly above the industry average, by adapting better, and anticipating changes better, than competitors.

The Industry Creation Perspective

Strategists taking an industry creation perspective fundamentally disagree with the determinism inherent in the industry evolution perspective. Even in biology, breeders and genetic engineers consistently attempt to shape the natural world. Of course, in industries, as in biology, some rules are immutable. Certain economic, technological, social and political factors have to be accepted as hardly influenceable. But the remaining environmental factors that can be manipulated leave strategists with an enormous scope for moulding the industry of the future. This belief is reflected in the remark by the Dutch poet Jules Deelder that 'even within the limits of the possible, the possibilities are limitless.' It is up to the strategist to identify which rules of the game must be respected and which can be ignored in the search for new strategic options. The strategist must recognize both the limits on the possible and the limitless possibilities.

In the industry creation perspective, both the *strictness* and *rigidity* of the industry rules can be challenged. The 'strictness of rules' refers to the degrees of freedom available to the strategist. Strict rules imply that only very specific behavior is allowed – firms must closely follow the rules or face severe consequences. However, those taking an industry creation perspective argue that rules are usually not as strict as they seem. There is plenty of room for firms to 'do their own thing' within the existing industry structure. The 'rigidity of rules' refers to the extent to which strategists can actually alter the industry rules. Rigid rules cannot easily be changed, but must be accepted as a given. In the industry creation perspective, however, it is argued that rules can usually be broken by those who know where to apply pressure. In this way rule breakers can become the new rule makers, unless these new rules are again challenged by others.

It must be emphasized that, while rules are rooted in the underlying economics, technologies, politics and social structures of an industry, it is perception of the rules that guides firms' behavior. Companies make strategies based on their understanding of the rules. Over time, firms within an industry often tend to develop a common definition of the rules, also referred to as an *industry recipe*[3]. Proponents of the industry creation perspective argue that such shared beliefs are often a more significant barrier to changing the industry rules, than the underlying economic, technological, political and social factors themselves. In this manner, industry incumbents can become the victims of their own experience[4]. They lose the ability to question their own beliefs about the industry rules and therefore lose their ability to be innovative (see Chapter 2). Industry rule breaking therefore starts with mental frame breaking. Strategists striving to shape the rules must violate industry conventions by challenging their own cognitive preconceptions. Industry creation requires a significant amount of creativity.

Advocates of the industry creation perspective do not deny that in many industries developments are largely evolutionary. For an understanding of the dynamics in these industries, the industry evolution perspective offers a powerful explanatory 'lens.' However, these industries only followed an evolutionary path because no firms were creative and powerful enough to actively shape the direction of change. An evolutionary trajectory isn't a strategic given, but the result of a lack of strategy by the industry incumbents. Industry developments can be shaped, but it does require innovative companies.

The question for the field of strategic management is, therefore, whether the future of industries evolves or can be created. Must firms conform to the environmental demands placed upon them or can they shape their own environment? Should the industry context be understood from a deterministic or a voluntaristic point of view[5]? In short, strategists must come to terms with the paradox of compliance and choice (see Table 8.1).

Defining the Issues: Rules and Recipes

Debates between people with a voluntaristic inclination and those with a more deterministic perspective, are not limited to the field of strategy. In many areas, thinkers are in disagreement about the malleability of the environment. Macroeconomists, for example, debate to what extent governments can influence economic growth, inflation and unemployment, sociologists wrangle about the ability of political and social action

TABLE 8.1
Industry evolution versus industry creation perspective

	Industry Evolution Perspective	Industry Creation Perspective
Emphasis on	Compliance over choice	Choice over compliance
Industry changes	Uncontrollable evolutionary processes	Controllable creation processes
Change dynamics	Environment selects fit firms	Firm creates fitting environment
Firm success due to	Fitness to industry demands	Manipulation of industry demands
Industry malleability	Low, slow	High, fast
Normative implication	Play by the rules (adapt)	Change the rules (innovate)
Firm profitability	Industry-dependent	Firm-dependent
Point of view	Deterministic	Voluntaristic

groups to change society and historians argue about the power of great individuals to shape the course of history. In all cases, it cannot be simply and unambiguously established how much impact individuals or organizations can have on their environments and vice versa. Therefore, assumptions must be made – a perspective must be taken on the question of malleability.

Two issues are central to this discussion on 'who shapes whom'. The first issue, as already indicated above, is that of *industry rules*. Industry rules are the demands dictated to the organization by the industry context, that limit the scope of economically rational behavior. In other words, industry rules stipulate what must be done to survive and thrive in the chosen line of business – they determine under what conditions the competitive game will be played. Failure to adhere to the rules leads to being selected out.

The industry rules arise from the structure of the industry. All five forces can impose constraints on a firm's freedom of action. The main question for strategists is how strict and rigid these rules actually are. Are a firm's possibilities for maneuvering within the rules and changing the rules severely restricted, or should strategists be inspired by Napoleon's famous remark: 'Circumstances? I make circumstances!'?

The second issue in the debate is that of *industry recipes*[6]. An industry recipe is a widely held perception with regard to the industry rules. In other words, an industry recipe is the cognitive map that people have about the structure and demands of an industry (see Chapter 2). Industry recipes usually develop over time through shared experiences and interaction. A common understanding of the rules of the game grows among those involved. The issue in this chapter is whether most of the perceived industry rules are 'real' – that is, rooted in the underlying economics of the industry – or merely conventions. Does the industry recipe reflect actual constraints or largely the constraints of habit?

EXHIBIT 8.1
CarMax case

CARMAX: TO THE MAX!?

Picture this. After 150,000 miles (240,000 kilometers) of faithful service, your old car is ready to roll over and die. So you drive down the road to the local car dealer to look at the used cars on offer. As you kick the tires on the 50 vehicles on the lot – all of the same make – you suddenly hear a voice behind you: 'That one belonged to a little old lady. She hardly drove over 30mph with it.' Great, a used-car salesman. You're thrilled by the prospect of spending the rest of the day visiting other dealers, listening to unlikely stories and haggling over prices.

Richard Sharp and Austin Ligon are counting on this story sending a shiver down your spine. In 1993 they founded CarMax, a used car retailing company with a twist. Realizing that most people hate the hassle and uncertainty that seem so inherent to buying a second hand car, Sharp and Ligon introduced a different retailing concept: the auto superstore. Similar to food and electronics superstores, the giant CarMax outlets offer an enormous choice of 500 to 1500 cars of all makes, each no more than five model years old, with a past of no more than 70,000 miles (112,000 km). To be salesworthy, a car must pass the extensive CarMax 110-point inspection program. CarMax does not sell bottom line used cars because the small margins on these items are not sufficient to cover all service-related expenses. And service there is: the showroom floor is scattered with touch-screen computer terminals in which customers can enter their preferences, and there are supervised playrooms for the kids. While the potential buyers make a test drive in the vehicle of their choice, the salesperson checks out whether CarMax's own financing subsidiary can give them an accreditation for a loan, according to the customers' wishes. When the customers return, they can sign up for an extended service plan with warranty that covers all mechanical and electrical parts. When the customers climb into their clean, shiny used car, ready to drive off, the salesperson snaps their picture with a Polaroid.

But probably the most important difference is that CarMax outlets offer no room for haggling, by using fixed prices for their vehicles. The salespersons receive a fixed commission per car, independent of the price of the vehicle. That is why CarMax calls them 'consultants', using their time to smooth the process for the customer, instead of using it for bargaining over prices. Potential customers do not have to fear getting stuck with a lemon: each car comes with a 30-day warranty and is always sold below NADA's (National Automotive Dealers Association) prices. Sharp himself says: 'Once you remove the price negotiation process, the salesperson becomes someone who can assist you in making the right purchase.'

Results so far seem to indicate that CarMax is on to something big. Customers are giving CarMax a 90 percent favorable rating, a level that most dealers can only dream of. In its first operational year, 1993, the 'pilot' outlet in Richmond, Virginia, alone turned over more than 4000 cars to the tune of $55m. By 1995 there were seven CarMax locations, with sales of $288m. Driven by this success, Sharp is aiming for a nationwide retail chain by the end of the decade, consisting of 55 outlets, generating approximately $3.3bn in revenues. Eventually, CarMax hopes to go abroad and introduce its auto superstores to other parts of the world, starting in Europe.

Richard Sharp and Austin Ligon are not the young penniless entrepreneurs who are stereotypically associated with 'frame-breaking' innovations. Sharp is the CEO of Circuit City stores, the largest chain of brand name consumer electronics in the US, and Ligon is Circuit City's senior vice president of corporate planning and automotive. The first CarMax outlet in Richmond is less than a mile from Circuit City's 'big box' stores.

Sharp and Ligon had some convincing arguments for diversifying from electronics retailing (consumer electronics and computers) to used car retailing. The used-car market is the third largest market in the USA, after food and housing, but ahead of new cars. Total demand in the market for used cars is about $150bn a year. This demand is being boosted by all time high new car prices, on average $20,270 in 1995. The prices for used vehicles are significantly lower, with an average of $10,980 in 1995. Yet the profit margin per vehicle sold is almost the same, regardless of whether it is new or used. Furthermore, by selling used vehicles, CarMax can sell any brand it wants, without restrictions or commitments towards the producers or importers. The supply of used cars is tremendous due to the boom in leasing practices, each leasing company releasing its vehicles after just two or three years of use. Adding to this constant supply, CarMax buys its inventory from auctions, fleet holders (e.g. rental companies) and even from customers trading in their vehicles when they are looking for something else.

A $150 billion market, buoyant demand and a good bargaining position towards suppliers are all quite attractive, but could easily be overshadowed by cut-throat competition. However, Sharp and Ligon concluded that the competition was heavily fragmented, and that there was no 'category killer' chain, such as Toys 'R' Us or Walmart, that could spoil the fun. The main competitors were relatively small car dealerships, usually with an exclusive contract to sell one auto maker's new products in a certain geographic area. To aid the selling of new cars, dealers accept trade-ins of various makes, which they in turn will try to sell. The average dealer in the US has about 150 used vehicles on offer, compared to CarMax's 500 to 1500. So far, the response by the big three auto makers in Detroit has not been to come to the rescue of their dealers. Officially, CarMax's entry into the business has been welcomed by the car manufacturers as a needed stimulus to improve the service quality in the dealerships.

Unfortunately for CarMax, it is hard to keep a good idea to yourself nowadays, and they have to deal with other entrants. Blockbuster Entertainment's Wayne Huizenga, a man who can only get excited when the stakes are high, intends to go nationwide with his AutoNation USA secondhand car retailing chain, after the successful start of two Florida sites in 1996. And there is more to come. Waad J. Nadhir, an established shopping-mall developer, intends to copy the CarMax concept with his CarChoice.

Of course, the question is whether the launching of CarMax and other secondhand vehicle megastores heralds the structural transformation of the used car retailing industry, or whether this is all a storm in a glass of water. Has CarMax fundamentally changed the rules of the game, to which all other retailers must now comply? Or can the traditional car dealerships continue on the same footing, surrendering a small segment to these newcomers? Alternatively, could the dealerships innovate themselves and try to find new methods for competing against the megastores? In other words, how much room do the dealerships have to maneuver? And what can CarMax do to make its concept the predominant formula? It was not at all certain how the industry would evolve in the coming years, but the score so far was clear: CarMax 7 – traditional dealers NADA.

Sources: *The Economist*, July 12, 1997; *Forbes*, February 10, 1997; *Stores*, June 1996

The Debate and the Readings

Few strategists like to hear that they have little influence over their industry and that they should play by the rules. This message is hardly inspiring, if not outright frustrating. And it definitely does not sell books. This might partially explain why few proponents of the industry evolution perspective have written for an audience of practicing managers. Most contributions to the strategic management literature by researchers taking an industry evolution view have been written in academic journals and are hardly comprehensible to outsiders. There are many excellent works, but none that are accessible enough to act as opening reading in this debate.

As a compromise, therefore, the debate in this chapter will be started off by an author who is strongly affiliated with the industry evolution perspective, but who is not fully in their camp. This author is Michael Porter, and the contribution selected is appropriately titled 'Industry Evolution.'[7] In this reading taken from his classic book *Competitive Strategy*, Porter expands on his basic premises that were discussed in Chapter 5. In his view, a company's profitability is heavily influenced by the structure of the industry in which it competes. Some industries have a poor structure, making it difficult for even the best firms to make a profit. Other industries, however, have a more advantageous structure, making it much easier to show a good performance. In Porter's opinion, how the game of competition is played in each industry is largely determined by the underlying economics. The industry structure presents the strict rules to which companies must comply. As an industry's structure evolves, Porter sees two processes at work that determine which companies will survive and profit over the longer term. On the one hand, Porter recognizes 'natural selection' processes, whereby only the fittest survive and firms that are not suited to the new environment become extinct. For instance, Porter argues that the selection of fit companies is particularly strong as industries move into a mature phase of development: 'when growth levels off in an industry (. . .) there is a period of turmoil as intensified rivalry weeds out the weaker firms.' On the other hand, Porter also believes that companies can adapt themselves to changes in the industry's structure, although he emphasizes that they first must understand the drivers of change. So far, Porter's arguments fully coincide with the industry evolution perspective. However, besides compliance to the industry context, Porter mentions the possibility of 'co-makership' as well. Or, in his own terms, he believes that firms can have some influence on the evolution of the industry's structure. Thus, each company does have a certain degree of strategic freedom to determine its own fate, but ultimately the autonomous development of the industry structure is crucially important to the survival and profitability of the company.

To open the debate on behalf of the industry creation perspective, a reading by Charles Baden-Fuller and John Stopford has been selected, with the telling title 'The Firm Matters, Not the Industry.'[8] In a direct reference to Porter, they state that their view 'contrasts sharply with the popular, but misguided, school of thought that believes that the fortune of a business is closely tied to its industry.' They point out that only a fraction of the differences in profitability between companies can be attributed to industry characteristics, while more than half of the profit variations are due to the choice of strategy. Their conclusion is that the given industry circumstances are largely unimportant – it's how a firm plays the game that matters. In their opinion, high profitability is not the consequence of complying with some preset rules, but the result of acting creatively and imaginatively. For instance, they challenge the widely held belief that high market share is important for profitability. Nor do they agree that the competitive game dictates generic strategies, as Porter suggested in Chapter 5. They do not even believe that there is such a thing as a mature industry. In their view, the industry environment does not present any fixed rules, that can not be avoided or changed by innovative companies. Their advice, therefore, is to remain imaginative and to adopt approaches that counter traditional solutions.

With such strongly competing opinions on the nature of the industry context, readers may now want to 'select the fittest one'. Or maybe readers will have to conclude that one view has rewritten the rules of competition in the strategy industry. Whichever way, it is up to individual readers to form their own judgment on how to deal with the paradox of compliance and choice.

Reading 1   Industry Evolution

By Michael Porter[†]

Structural analysis gives us a framework for understanding the competitive forces operating in an industry that are crucial to developing competitive strategy. It is clear, however, that industries' structures change, often in fundamental ways. Entry barriers and concentration have gone up significantly in the US brewing industry, for example, and the threat of substitutes has risen to put a severe squeeze on acetylene producers.

Industry evolution takes on critical importance for formulation of strategy. It can increase or decrease the basic attractiveness of an industry as an investment opportunity, and it often requires the firm to make strategic adjustments. Understanding the process of industry evolution and being able to predict change are important because the cost of reacting strategically usually increases as the need for change becomes more obvious and the benefit from the best strategy is the highest for the first firm to select it. For example, in the early post-war farm equipment business, structural change elevated the importance of a strong exclusive dealer network backed by company support and credit. The firms that recognized this change first had their pick of dealers to choose from.

This article will present analytical tools for predicting the evolutionary process in an industry and understanding its significance for the formulation of competitive strategy.

Basic Concepts in Industry Evolution

The starting point for analyzing industry evolution is the framework of structural analysis (see Chapter 5). Industry changes will carry strategic significance if they promise to affect the underlying sources of the five competitive forces; otherwise changes are important only in a tactical sense. The simplest approach to analyzing evolution is to ask the following question: Are there any changes occurring in the industry that will affect each element of structure? For example, do any of the industry trends imply an increase or decrease in mobility barriers? An increase or decrease in the relative power of buyers or suppliers? If this question is

[†] Source: Reprinted with the permission of The Free Press, a Division of Macmillan, Inc., from *Competitive Strategy: Techniques for Analyzing Industries and Competitiors*, pp. 156–164, 184–188, by Michael E. Porter. Copyright © 1980 by The Free Press.

asked in a disciplined way for each competitive force and the economic causes underlying it, a profile of the significant issues in the evolution of an industry will result.

Although this industry-specific approach is the place to start, it may not be sufficient, because it is not always clear what industry changes are occurring currently, much less which changes might occur in the future. Given the importance of being able to predict evolution, it is desirable to have some analytical techniques that will aid in anticipating the pattern of industry changes we might expect to occur.

The Product Life Cycle

The grandfather of concepts for predicting the probable course of industry evolution is the familiar product life cycle. The hypothesis is that an industry passes through a number of phases or stages – introduction, growth, maturity, and decline – illustrated in Figure 8.1. These stages are defined by inflection points in the rate of growth of industry sales. Industry growth follows an S-shaped curve because of the process of innovation and diffusion of a new product. The flat introductory phase of industry growth reflects the difficulty of overcoming buyer inertia and stimulating trials of the new product. Rapid growth occurs as many buyers rush into the market once the product has proven itself successful. Penetration of the product's potential buyers is eventually reached, causing the rapid growth to stop and to level off to the underlying rate of growth of the relevant buyer group. Finally, growth will eventually taper off as new substitute products appear.

As the industry goes through its life cycle, the nature of competition will shift. I have summarized in Table 8.2 the most common predictions about how an industry will change over the life cycle and how this should affect strategy.

The product life cycle has attracted some legitimate criticism:

- The duration of the stages varies widely from industry to industry, and it is often not clear what stage of the life cycle an industry is in. This problem diminishes the usefulness of the concept as a planning tool.

- Industry growth does not always go through the S-shaped pattern at all. Sometimes industries skip maturity, passing straight from growth to decline. Sometimes industry growth revitalizes after a period of decline, as has occurred in the motorcycle and bicycle industries and recently in the radio broadcasting industry. Some industries seem to skip the slow takeoff of the introductory phase altogether.

- Companies can *affect* the shape of the growth curve through product innovation and repositioning, extending it in a variety of ways. If a

FIGURE 8.1
Stages of the life cycle

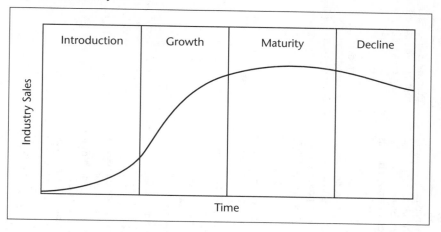

company takes the life cycle as given, it becomes an undesirable self-fulfilling prophesy.

■ The nature of competition associated with each stage of the life cycle is *different* for different industries. For example, some industries start out highly concentrated and stay that way. Others, like bank cash dispensers, are concentrated for a significant period and then become less so. Still others begin highly fragmented; of these some consolidate (automobiles) and some do not (electronic component distribution). The same divergent patterns apply to advertising, research and development (R&D) expenditures, degree of price competition, and most other industry characteristics. Divergent patterns such as these call into serious question the strategic implications ascribed to the life cycle.

The real problem with the product life cycle as a predictor of industry evolution is that it attempts to describe *one* pattern of evolution that will invariably occur. And except for the industry growth rate, there is little or no underlying rationale for why the competitive changes associated with the life cycle will happen. Since actual industry evolution takes so many different paths, the life cycle pattern does not always hold, even if it is a common or even the most common pattern of evolution. Nothing in the concept allows us to predict when it will hold and when it will not.

A Framework for Forecasting Evolution

Instead of attempting to describe industry evolution, it will prove more fruitful to look underneath the process to see what really drives it. Like

TABLE 8.2
Predictions of product life cycle theories about strategy, competition, and performance

	Introduction	Growth	Maturity	Decline
Buyers and Buyer Behavior	High-income purchaser Buyer inertia Buyers must be convinced to try the product	Widening buyer group Consumer will accept uneven quality	Mass market Saturation Repeat buying Choosing among brands is the rule	Customers are sophisticated buyers of the product
Products and Product Change	Poor quality Product design and development key Many different product variations; no standards Frequent design changes Basic product designs	Products have technical and performance differentiation Reliability key for complex products Competitive product improvements Good quality	Superior quality Less product differentiation Standardization Less rapid product changes – more minor annual model changes Trade-ins become significant	Little product differentiation Spotty product quality
Marketing	Very high advertising/sales (a/s) Creaming price strategy High marketing costs	High advertising, but lower percent of sales than introductory Most promotion of ethical drugs Advertising and distribution key for nontechnical products	Market segmentation Efforts to extend life cycle Broaden line Service and deals more prevalent Packaging important Advertising competition Lower a/s	Low a/s and other marketing
Manufacturing and Distribution	Overcapacity Short production runs High skilled-labor content High production costs Specialized channels	Undercapacity Shift toward mass production Scramble for distribution Mass channels	Some overcapacity Optimum capacity Increasing stability of manufacturing process Lower labor skills Long production runs with stable techniques Distribution channels pare down their lines to improve their margins High physical distribution costs due to broad lines Mass channels	Substantial over-capacity Mass production Specialty channels

R&D	Changing production techniques			
Foreign Trade	Some exports	Significant exports Few imports	Falling exports Significant imports	No exports Significant imports
Overall Strategy	Best period to increase market share R&D, engineering are key functions	Practical to change price or quality image Marketing the key function	Bad time to increase market share, particularly if low-share company Having competitive costs becomes key Bad time to change price image or quality image 'Marketing effectiveness' key	Cost control key
Competition	Few companies	Entry Many competitors Lots of mergers and casualties	Price competition Shakeout Increase in private brands	Exits Fewer competitors
Risk	High risk	Risks can be taken here because growth covers them up	Cyclicality sets in	
Margins and Profits	High prices and margins Low profits Price elasticity to individual seller not as great as in maturity	High profits Highest profits Fairly high prices Lower prices than introductory phase Recession resistant High P/Es Good acquisition climate	Falling prices Lower profits Lower margins Lower dealer margins Increased stability of market shares and price structure Poor acquisition climate – tough to sell companies Lowest prices and margins	Low prices and margins Falling prices Prices might rise in late decline

any evolution, industries evolve because some forces are in motion that create incentives or pressures for change. These can be called *evolutionary processes*.

Every industry begins with an *initial structure* – the entry barriers, buyer and supplier power, and so on that exist when the industry comes into existence. This structure is usually (though not always) a far cry from the configuration the industry will take later in its development. The initial structure results from a combination of underlying economic and technical characteristics of the industry, the initial constraints of small industry size, and the skills and resources of the companies that are early entrants. For example, even an industry like automobiles with enormous possibilities for economies of scale started out with labor-intensive, job-shop production operations because of the small volumes of cars produced during the early years.

The evolutionary processes work to push the industry toward its *potential structure*, which is rarely known completely as an industry evolves. Embedded in the underlying technology, product characteristics, and nature of present and potential buyers, however, there is a range of structures the industry might possibly achieve, depending on the direction and success of research and development, marketing innovations, and the like.

It is important to realize that instrumental in much industry evolution are the investment decisions by both existing firms in the industry and new entrants. In response to pressures or incentives created by the evolutionary process, firms invest to take advantage of possibilities for new marketing approaches, new manufacturing facilities, and the like, which shift entry barriers, alter relative power against suppliers and buyers, and so on. The luck, skills, resources, and orientation of firms in the industry can shape the evolutionary path the industry will actually take. Despite potential for structural change, an industry may not actually change because no firm happens to discover a feasible new marketing approach; or potential scale economies may go unrealized because no firm possesses the financial resources to construct a fully integrated facility or simply because no firm is inclined to think about costs. Because innovation, technological developments, and the identities (and resources) of the particular firms either in the industry or considering entry into it are so important to evolution, industry evolution will not only be hard to forecast with certainty but also an industry can potentially evolve in a variety of ways at a variety of different speeds, depending on the luck of the draw.

Evolutionary Processes

Although initial structure, structural potential, and particular firms' investment decisions will be industry-specific, we can generalize about what the important evolutionary processes are. There are some predictable (and interacting) dynamic processes that occur in every industry in one form or another, though their speed and direction will differ from industry to industry:

- long-run changes in growth;

- changes in buyer segments served;

- buyer's learning;

- reduction of uncertainty;

- diffusion of proprietary knowledge;

- accumulation of experience;

- expansion (or contraction) in scale;

- changes in input and currency costs;

- product innovation;

- marketing innovation;

- process innovation;

- structural change in adjacent industries;

- government policy change;

- entries and exits.

Key Relationships in Industry Evolution

In the context of this analysis, *how* do industries change? They do not change in a piecemeal fashion, because an industry is an *interrelated system*. Change in one element of an industry's structure tends to trigger changes in other areas. For example, an innovation in marketing might develop a new buyer segment, but serving this new segment may trigger changes in manufacturing methods, thereby increasing economies of scale. The firm reaping these economies first will also be in a position to start backward integration, which will affect power with suppliers – and so on. One industry change, therefore, often sets off a chain reaction leading to many other changes.

It should be clear from the discussion here that whereas industry evolution is always occurring in nearly every business and requires a strategic response, there is no one way in which industries evolve. Any single model for evolution such as the product life cycle should therefore be rejected. However, there are some particularly important relationships in the evolutionary process that I will examine here.

Will the Industry Consolidate?

It seems to be an accepted fact that industries tend to consolidate over time, but as a general statement, it simply is not true. In a broad sample of 151 four-digit US manufacturing industries in the 1963–72 time period, for example, 69 increased in four-firm concentration more than two percentage points, whereas 52 decreased more than two percentage points in the same period. The question of whether consolidation will occur in an industry exposes perhaps the most important interrelationships among elements of industry structure – those involving competitive rivalry, mobility barriers, and exit barriers.

Industry Concentration and Mobility Barriers Move Together

If mobility barriers are high or especially if they increase, concentration almost always increases. For example, concentration has increased in the US wine industry. In the standard-quality segment of the market, which represents much of the volume, the strategic changes (high advertising, national distribution, rapid brand innovation, and so on) have greatly increased barriers to mobility. As a result, the larger firms have gotten further ahead of smaller ones, and few new firms have entered to challenge them.

No Concentration Takes Place if Mobility Barriers are Low or Falling

Where barriers are low, unsuccessful firms that exit will be replaced by new firms. If a wave of exit has occurred because of an economic downturn or some other general adversity, there may be a temporary increase in industry concentration. But at the first signs that profits and sales in the industry are picking up, new entrants will appear. Thus a shakeout when an industry reaches maturity does not necessarily imply long-run consolidation.

Exit Barriers Deter Consolidation

Exit barriers keep companies operating in an industry even though they are earning subnormal returns on investment. Even in an industry with relatively high mobility barriers, the leading firms cannot count on reaping the benefits of consolidation if high exit barriers hold unsuccessful firms in the market.

Long-Run Profit Potential Depends on Future Structure

In the period of very rapid growth early in the life of an industry (especially after initial product acceptance has been achieved), profit levels are usually high. For example, growth in sales of skiing equipment was in excess of 20 percent per year in the late 1960s, and nearly all firms in the industry enjoyed strong financial results. When growth levels off in an industry, however, there is a period of turmoil as intensified rivalry weeds out the weaker firms. All firms in the industry may suffer financially during this adjustment period. Whether or not the remaining firms will enjoy above-average profitability will depend on the level of mobility barriers, as well as the other structural features of the industry. If mobility barriers are high or have increased as the industry has matured, the remaining firms in the industry may enjoy healthy financial results even in the new era of slower growth. If mobility barriers are low, however, slower growth probably means the end of above-average profits for the industry. Thus mature industries may or may not be as profitable as they were in their developmental period.

Changes in Industry Boundaries

Structural change in an industry is often accompanied by changes in industry boundaries. Industry evolution has a strong tendency to shift these boundaries. Innovations in the industry or those involving substitutes may effectively enlarge the industry by placing more firms into direct competition. Reduction in transportation cost relative to timber cost, for example, has made timber supply a world market rather than one restricted to continents. Innovations increasing the reliability and lowering the cost of electronic surveillance devices have put them into effective competition with security guard services. Structural changes making it easier for suppliers to integrate forward into the industry may well mean that suppliers effectively become competitors. Or buyers purchasing private label goods in large quantities and dictating product design criteria may become effective competitors in the manufacturing industry. Part of the analysis of the strategic significance of industry evolution is clearly an analysis of how industry boundaries may be affected.

Firms Can Influence Industry Structure

Industry structural change can be influenced by firms' strategic behavior. If it understands the significance of structural change for its position, the firm can seek to influence industry change in ways favorable to it, either through the way it reacts to strategic changes of competitors or in the strategic changes it initiates.

Another way a company can influence structural change is to be very sensitive to external forces that can cause the industry to evolve. With a head start, it is often possible to direct such forces in ways appropriate to the firm's position. For example, the specific form of regulatory changes can be influenced; the diffusion of innovations coming from outside the industry can be altered by the form that licensing or other agreements with innovating firms take; positive action can be initiated to improve the cost or supply of complementary products through providing direct assistance and help in forming trade associations or in stating their case to the government; and so on for the other important forces causing structural change. Industry evolution should not be greeted as a fait accompli to be reacted to, but as an opportunity.

Reading 2   The Firm Matters, Not the Industry

By Charles Baden-Fuller and John Stopford[†]

It is the firm that matters, not the industry. Successful businesses ride the waves of industry misfortunes; less successful businesses are sunk by them. This view contrasts sharply with the popular, but misguided, school of thought that believes that the fortune of a business is closely tied to its industry. Those who adhere to this view believe that some industries are intrinsically more attractive for investment than others. They (wrongly) believe that if a business is in a profitable industry, then its profits will be greater than if the business is in an unprofitable industry.

The Role of the Industry in Determining Profitability

Old views

■   Some industries are intrinsically more profitable than others.

■   In mature environments it is difficult to sustain high profits.

[†] Source: This article has been adapted from chapter 2 of *Rejuvenating the Mature Business*, Routledge, 1992, pp. 13–34. Used with permission.

- It is environmental factors that determine whether an industry is successful, not the firms in the industry.

New views

- There is little difference in the profitability of one industry versus another.

- There is no such thing as a mature industry, only mature firms; industries inhabited by mature firms often present great opportunities for the innovative.

- Profitable industries are those populated by imaginative and profitable firms; unprofitable industries have unusually large numbers of uncreative firms.

This notion that there are 'good' and 'bad' industries is a theme that has permeated many strategy books. As one famous strategy writer put it:

> The state of competition in an industry depends on five basic competitive forces. . . . The collective strength of these forces determines the ultimate profit potential in the industry, where profit potential is measured in terms of long-run return on invested capital. . . . The forces range from intense in industries like tires, paper and steel – where no firm earns spectacular returns – to relatively mild like oil-field equipment and services, cosmetics and toiletries – where high returns are quite common.[9]

Unfortunately, the writer overstates his case, for the evidence does not easily support his claim. Choosing good industries may be a foolish strategy; choosing good firms is far more sensible. As noted in Table 8.3, recent statistical evidence does not support the view that the choice of industry is important. At best only 10 percent of the differences in profitability between one business unit and another can be related to their choice of industry. By implication, nearly 90 percent of profitability variations are not explained by the choice of industry, and *at least half appear to be attributable to the choice of strategy*. Put simply, the correct choice of strategy appears to be at least five times more important than the correct choice of industry.

Mature Industries Offer Good Prospects for Success

It is often stated that market opportunities are created rather than found. Thus market research would never have predicted the large potential of xerography, laptop computers, or the pocket cassette recorder. Leaps of faith may be required. By analogy, low-growth mature markets or

TABLE 8.3
The role of industry factors determining firm performance

Percentage of Business Units' Profitability Explained by	
Choice of industry	8.3 percent
Choice of strategy	46.4 percent
Parent company	0.8 percent
Not explained – random	44.5 percent

Abstracted from Rumelt[10].

troubled industries are arguably ones that may offer greater chances of rewards than ones that appear to be glamorous and profitable. Our reasoning is simple. In general, profitable industries are more profitable because they are populated by more imaginative and more creative businesses. These businesses create an environment that attracts customers, grows the industry revenues, and makes the industry attractive. But creative and innovative businesses are also more fiercely competitive. To win in such environments may be difficult, as the pace of change may be rapid and the minimum standards high. In contrast, many less profitable industries are populated by sleepy, uncreative businesses that fail to innovate. In such environments, the potential for success by a creative newcomer is greater. The demands of competition may be less exacting and the potential for attracting customers is better.

We do not wish to overstate our case, but rather to force the reader to focus attention away from the mentality of labelling and prejudging opportunities based only on industry profitability. For example, outsiders often point to low-growth industries and suggest that the opportunities are less than those in high-growth industries. Yet the difference in growth rates may be dependent on the ability of businesses in these industries to be creative and innovative. Until Honda came, the motorcycle market was in steady decline. By their innovations – of new bicycles with attractive features sold at reasonable prices – the market was once again revived. Thus we suggest that the growth rate of the industry is a reflection of the kinds of businesses in the industry, not the intrinsic nature of the environment.

Large Market Share is the Reward, not the Cause of Success

We believe that many managers are mistaken in the value they ascribe to market share. A large share of the market is often the symptom of success, but it is not always its cause. Banc One and Cook achieved significant positions in their industries because they were successful. For these organizations the sequence of events was success followed by growth, which was then cemented into greater success. Banc One has been doing things differently from many of its competitors for many years. It emphasized operational efficiency and it quickly captured a significant position as a low cost, high quality data processor for other banks and financial service companies. It also emphasized service, in particular service to retail and commercial customers, which contrasted with the approach of many other banks that sought to compete solely on price or failed to appreciate what the customer really wanted. Mergers and growth have been an important part of Banc One's strategy, but in every case, the merged organizations have been changed to fit the philosophy of Banc One.

Market Share and Profitability

Old views

- Large market share brings lower costs and higher prices and so yields greater profits.

- Small-share firms cannot challenge leaders.

New views

- Large market share is the reward for efficiency and effectiveness.

- If they do things better, small-share firms can challenge the leaders.

For creative organizations we see an upward spiral (Figure 8.2), and for organizations that are not creative, we see the cycles shown in Figure 8.3.

FIGURE 8.2
Upward spiral of creative business

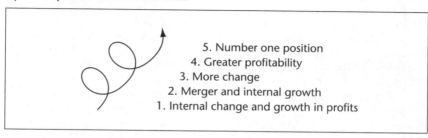

5. Number one position
4. Greater profitability
3. More change
2. Merger and internal growth
1. Internal change and growth in profits

FIGURE 8.3
Downward spiral of unchanging business

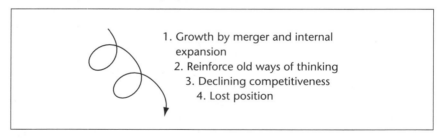

1. Growth by merger and internal
   expansion
2. Reinforce old ways of thinking
3. Declining competitiveness
4. Lost position

EXHIBIT 8.2
Market share and profitability

MARKET SHARE AND PROFITABILITY

There is a lively debate on the importance of market share in *explaining* business unit profitability. By *explaining* we do not mean *causing*. High market share could be the consequence of profitability, or the cause of both.

Those who advocate that large market share *leads* to greater profits point to the importance of several causal factors. First, large market share gives rise to the need to deliver large volumes of the service or good. These increased volumes in turn give rise to opportunities for costs savings by exploiting scale economies in production, service delivery, logistics, and marketing. Second, large market share permits the firm to benefit from experience or learning effects that also lower costs. Third, larger market share may allow the firm to charge higher prices. A product or service with a large share may seem intrinsically less risky to consumers. Finally, with a large market share, new entrants may be discouraged because they perceive the incumbent to have a substantial commitment to the industry through perceived or actual sunk costs.

In contrast, there are several who argue that these supposed benefits of large share are overrated. It is innovation that matters, innovators that realize new ways of competing can achieve their advantages by new approaches that do not necessarily need large market shares. However, those with new approaches may win market share, in which case large share is a reward for success. This Darwinian view of the market suggests that the competitive process is one where success goes to the firm that successfully innovates.

The strongest proponents of the importance of market share as a cause of success are Buzzell and Gale. Using the PIMS database drawn from a very large sample of business units across a range of industries, they asserted the existence of a strong relationship between relative market share and profitability. The figures below[11] suggest that a firm that has first rank in an industry will be more than twice as profitable as one of fourth rank.

Industry rank (by market share)	1	2	3	4	≤5
Pretax profits/sales (per cent)	12.7	9.1	7.1	5.5	4.5

However, these figures are misleading, for in a very large proportion of the industries studied, the firm with largest rank was *not* the most profitable. Often the picture is quite different; indeed according to the statistics published in Buzzell and Gale[12] only 4 percent of the differences in profitability of one business unit versus another could be explained by differences in market share. Schmalensee[13] in his extensive study of more than 400 firms in US manufacturing, found that less than 2 percent of the variations in profitability between one business and another could be explained by differences in market share. Market share effects appear to be relatively unimportant across a wide sample of industries. Of course, market share may be important in specific instances, but this only goes to reinforce our basic point that the critical success is dependent on getting the right strategy.

Our assertions run counter to much of what has been written in conventional books on strategy, and what is believed in many corporate boardrooms (see Exhibit 8.2). There is a common but incorrect belief among managers that being number one or number two in an industry gives the business unique advantages and that these are greatest in industries characterized by slow growth. With a large market share, it is often argued, the business can achieve lower costs and charge higher prices than its rivals. In slow-growth markets, it is argued, this may prove to be a decisive factor. This thinking ignores the importance of innovation, and believes that it is the size of the business that confers the advantage, not the new ways of doing things.

These false beliefs are widespread. They appear in many guises. At one extreme there are chief executives who say, 'We are only interested in industries where we hold a number one or number two position.' Such statements, if unaccompanied by an emphasis on innovation, will give out the wrong signal that high share will lead to success. At a more mundane level, managers are encouraged to write in their plans, 'We should dominate the industry and seek success by capturing a number one position.' Again, such statements are dangerous where the writer and reader believe that share by itself will bring success.

Growing market share is not the panacea for an organization's ills, not even in mature slow-growing markets. The belief that gaining market share will lead to greater profitability comes from confusing cause and effect. Many successful businesses do have a large market share, but the causality is usually from success to share, not the other way. Successful businesses often (but not always) grow because they have discovered an overwhelming source of competitive advantage, such as quality at low cost. Such advantages can be used to displace the market share of even the most entrenched incumbents.

Competing Recipes

The crucial battles amongst firms in an industry are often centered around differing approaches to the market. Even in the so-called mature industries, where incumbent strategies have evolved and been honed over long time periods, it is new ideas that displace the existing leaders. Traditional wisdom has overstated the power of the generic approach (see Exhibit 8.3) and underplayed the role of innovation. Banc One established its premier position by rejecting conventional orthodoxy and emphasizing aspects hitherto neglected by industry leaders. Cook won in the steel castings industry by emphasizing quality and service to the customer. Hotpoint emphasized variety and quality in its approach to both the retailers and the final consumers. No single approach works well in all industries, but rather a multiple set of approaches. Here we emphasize the more fundamental point: the real competitive battles are fought out between firms with a diversity of approaches to the market.

EXHIBIT 8.3
The fallacy of the generic strategy

THE FALLACY OF THE GENERIC STRATEGY

It has been fashionable to suggest that there are a few *stable generic strategies* that offer fundamental choices to the organization. Typically these are described as a choice between a *low cost strategy* or a *differentiated strategy*. The low cost strategy involves the sacrifice of something – speed, variety, fashion, or even quality – in order to keep costs low, the lowest in the industry. In contrast, the high cost, differentiated strategy involves the focus on the very factors ignored by the others. The advocates of generic strategy make an (implicit or explicit) assertion: that the opposites cannot be reconciled. According to the generic strategists, it is not possible to be both low cost and high quality, or low cost and fashionable, or low cost and speedy. Trying to reconcile the opposites means being *stuck in the middle*. This, it is suggested, is the worst of both worlds.

Generic strategies are a fallacy. The best firms are striving all the time to reconcile the opposites. Cook did find a way to be both high quality and low cost, so, too, many of the other creative firms we studied. At any point in time, there are some combinations that have not yet been resolved, but firms strive to resolve them. Until McDonald's, the idea of consistency and low price for fast food had not been achieved on a large scale. McDonald's solved that problem. Benetton was but one of many firms that resolved the dilemma of fashion at low cost. Given the enormous rewards that accrue to those who can resolve the dilemmas of the opposites, it is not surprising that there are no *lasting or enduring generic strategies*.

The Dynamics of Competition in Traditional Industries

Old view

- Competition is based on firms following well-defined traditional (or generic) approaches to the market.

New view

- The real battles are fought among firms taking different approaches, especially those that counter yesterday's ideas.

Conclusions

Organizations that have become mature and suffer from poor performance typically view themselves as prisoners of their environment. Often their managers blame everyone but themselves for their poor performance. Labelling their environment as mature or hostile, they identify excess capacity, unfair competition, adverse exchange rates, absence of demand, and a host of other factors to explain why they are doing badly. Alas, too often these external factors are not really the causes of their demise but rather the symptoms of their failure. This conclusion is not so new; others have made the point before, yet their words appear to have been forgotten. Hall[14] in an article in the *Harvard Business Review* noted:

> Even a cursory analysis of the leading companies in the eight basic industries leads to an important observation: survival and prosperity are possible even when the business environment turns hostile and industry trends change from favourable to unfavourable. In this regard, the casual advice frequently offered to competitors in basic industries – that is diversify, dissolve or be prepared for below average returns – seems oversimplified and even erroneous.

Of course all industries experience the roller coaster of economic upswings and downswings, but there are organizations that appear to ride the waves and others that appear to be submerged by them.

Those who are submerged all too often clutch at the wrong things in trying to escape their drowning. Seeking simple solutions such as industry recipes, the value of market share, or the need to amass large resources, they fail to appreciate the extent to which the rules of the game in an industry are always changing.

The Industry Context in International Perspective

How many things are looked upon as quite impossible until they have been actually effected.

(Pliny the Elder 23–79; Roman writer)

As stated in the introduction, debates between people with a deterministic predisposition and those favoring a more voluntaristic view can be witnessed in quite a few scientific fields. In the field of strategy, perspectives on the malleability of the industry context also differ sharply, although often implicitly – few authors or practicing strategists make a point of expounding their assumptions about the nature of the environment. For this reason, it is difficult to identify whether there are national preferences when it comes to industry context perspective. Yet, it seems not unlikely that strategists in different countries have different inclinations on this issue. Although it is always difficult to generalize, it seems that strategists in some nations gravitate more towards an industry creation perspective than in other nations.

As an input to the debate whether there are international differences in industry context perspective, we would like to put forward a number of factors that might be of influence on how the paradox of compliance and choice is viewed in different countries. It should be noted, however, that these propositions are intended to encourage discussion and constitute only tentative explanations for cross-cultural differences in perspective. More specific international research is needed to give this debate a firm footing.

Locus of Control

Culture researchers have long recognized international differences in how people perceive the power of individuals to shape their environments. In some cultures the view that an individual is at the mercy of external events is more predominant, while in other cultures there is a stronger belief in the freedom of individuals to act independent of the environment and even to create their own circumstances. Psychologists refer to this as the perceived *locus of control*[15]. People with an internal locus of control believe that they largely control their own fate. Their efforts will shape their circumstances – success is earned and failure is one's own fault. People with an external locus of control, on the other hand, believe that their fate is largely the result of circumstances beyond their control. Any effort to improve one's position, if at all possible, should be directed toward complying to external demands – fortune favors those who go with the flow. In the most extreme case, however, people with an external locus of control are fatalistic, that is, they assume no efforts will change that which is inevitable.

Obviously, in countries where the culture is more inclined towards an internal locus of control, it is reasonable to expect that the industry creation perspective will be more widespread. It is in such nations that one might expect remarks, such as that by the nineteenth century English essayist Sydney Smith: 'When I hear any man talk of an unalterable law, the only effect it produces on me is to convince me that he is an unalterable fool.' In cultures with a strong emphasis on external locus of control, the industry evolution perspective is likely to be more predominant.

Time Orientation

As was identified in Chapter 4, cultures can also differ with respect to their time orientation. Some cultures are directed towards the past, while others are more focused on the present or on the future. In countries with a future-orientation, the belief is widespread that change is progress. People generally welcome change as an opportunity for advancement. Therefore, in future-oriented cultures, people are even willing to initiate painful change processes, in the expectation that this will lead to future benefits. In these countries a strong inclination towards the industry creation perspective is most likely.

In past-oriented cultures, the belief is widespread that change is decay. People generally actively resist change and protect the status quo. In these cultures, external changes will only be adapted to if strictly necessary. In present-oriented cultures, the belief is widespread that change is relatively unimportant. People live for the day and adapt to changes as they come. In both types of culture, the industry evolution perspective is more likely to be more predominant.

Role of Government

Internationally, opinions also differ on the role that governments can play in encouraging the shaping of industries. In some countries the predominant view is that governments should facilitate industry change by creating good business circumstances and then staying out of the way of company initiatives. Governments are needed to set basic rules of business conduct, but firms should not be impeded by other governmental intervention in the functioning of industries and markets. Individual companies are seen as the primary drivers of industry innovation and if companies are given enough leeway, excellent ones can significantly shape their industry context. Such *economic liberalism* is particularly strong in the English-speaking nations, and it is here that governments attempt to actually facilitate firm's industry creation efforts. Unsurprisingly, the industry creation perspective is rather pronounced in these countries.

In other nations the predominant view is that Adam Smith's free market ideal often proves to be dysfunctional. A fully liberal market, it is believed, can lead to short-termism, negative social consequences, mutually-destructive competition, and an inability to implement industry-wide changes. Governments must therefore assume a more proactive role. They must protect weaker parties, such as workers and the environment, against the negative side-effects of the capitalist system, and actively create a shared infrastructure for all companies. Furthermore, the government can develop an industrial policy to encourage the development of new industries, force companies to work together where this is more effective, and push through industry-wide changes, if otherwise a stalemate would occur. Such a *managed competition* view is prevalent in Japan and France, and to a lesser extent in Germany[16]. In these countries the industry creation perspective is not as strongly held as in the English-speaking nations – industries can be shaped, but few companies have the power to do so without a good national industrial policy and government backing.

Network of Relationships

This factor is linked to the discussion in the previous chapter. In countries where the discrete organization perspective is predominant, companies often strive to retain their independence and power position *vis-à-vis* other companies. As these firms are not embedded in complex networks, but operate free from these constraining relationships, they are more at liberty to challenge the existing rules of the game. In other words, where firms are not entangled in a web of long-term relationships, they are better positioned for industry revolution – every firm can make a difference. In these countries an industry creation perspective is more prevalent.

However, in nations where firms are more inclined to operate in networks, each individual firm surrenders a part of its freedom in exchange for long-term relationships. The ability of the individual firm to shape its industry thus declines, as all changes must be discussed and negotiated with its partners. Hence, in these countries, the industry creation perspective is generally less strongly held than in the countries favoring discrete organizations. It should be noted that a group of firms, once in agreement, is often more powerful than each individual firm and therefore more capable of shaping the industry. However, it is acknowledged that getting the network partners to agree is a formidable task and a significant limit on the firm's ability to shape its environment.

Further Readings

For a good academic overview of the debate on 'who shapes whom' readers are advised to consult the special edition of *Academy of Management Review* (July 1990), that focused on this issue. Especially the article 'Market discipline and the discipline of management,' by Richard Bettis and Lex Donaldson, is very insightful. For a broader discussion on the issue of determinism and voluntarism, good readings are 'Central perspectives and debates in organization theory,' by W. Graham Astley and Andrew van der Ven, and 'Organizational adaptation: Strategic choice and environmental determinism,' by Lawrence Hrebiniak and William Joyce. Also useful is the recent work on managerial discretion, that attempts to measure how much leeway top managers have in shaping the future of their firm in different industries. Of these, the article 'Managerial Discretion: A Bridge Between Polar Views of Organizational Outcomes,' by Donald Hambrick and Sydney Finkelstein, is interesting for its theoretical base, while 'Assessing the Amount of Managerial Discretion in Different Industries: A Multimethod Approach,' by Donald Hambrick and Eric Abrahamson is interesting for its analysis of various industry environments. All of these readings, it should be mentioned, do not have an audience of practitioners in mind.

The same is true for all further readings taking an industry evolution perspective. A good follow up to Michael Hannan and John

Freeman's article is their book, *Organizational Ecology*. The collection of articles edited by Joel Baum and Jitendra Sigh, *Evolutionary Dynamics of Organizations*, is also a stimulating, yet arduous, work. Other constraints on the freedom of firms to shape their own fate are brought forward by institutional theory and resource dependence theory, both of which have not been represented in this debate. A good overview of these two approaches is given by Christine Oliver, in her article 'Strategic responses to institutional processes.' The classic in the field of institutional theory is Paul DiMaggio and Walter Powell's article 'The Iron Cage Revisited: Institutional Isomorphism and Collective Rationality in Organizational Fields.' The classic work in the field of resource dependence is Jeffrey Pfeffer and Gerald Salancik's book *The External Control of Organizations*.

Readers interested in the industry creation perspective might want to start by looking at J.C. Spender's book *Industry Recipes – An Enquiry into the Nature and Sources of Managerial Judgement*. The book from which Charles Baden-Fuller and John Stopford's article was taken, *Rejuvenating the Mature Business*, is also an excellent follow up reading. The same is true of Gary Hamel and C.K. Prahalad's book *Competing for the Future*. In this context, Richard D'Aveni's book *Hypercompetition* is also worth reviewing.

9

The Organizational Context

An institution is the lengthened
shadow of one man.

(Ralph Waldo Emerson 1803–1882; American essayist and poet)

We shape our environments, then
our environments shape us.

(Winston Churchill 1874–1965; British statesman and writer)

The Paradox of Control and Chaos

This chapter is the mirror image of Chapter 8. While the previous chapter dealt with the malleability of the company's *external* environment, this chapter focuses on the malleability of the company's *internal* environment. In other words, to what extent can strategists adapt the organization to fit with their wishes? Can the strategist shape the organization at will or does the organization have dynamics all its own, that can actually even shape the strategist?

If the firm's leader, responsible for deciding on strategy, is in absolute *control*, the organization can be fully geared to implement the strategy chosen. In such a case, the organization resembles a mechanical system, with the leader at the control panel. The leader has full command over the machine, within the limits of what is technically feasible. Under these circumstances, the wise strategist will first develop a strategy and then push through the necessary organizational changes. If, on the other hand, the strategist has hardly any influence on developments within the organization, there is a state of *chaos*. In such a case, the organization resembles a complex system, like the weather, in which events gradually evolve out of the current situation, depending on the intricate inter-actions between large numbers of influencing factors. The strategy is not selected by the strategist, but emerges from the complex dynamics within the organization. Strategy is not the result of free choice, but determined by the organizational context. Under these circumstances, even the wise strategist can do little more than marginally influence the unfolding system.

How malleable are organizations in practice? Should strategists take a predominantly control- or chaos-oriented view? Predictably, opinions on the matter are heavily divided. As in the previous debates, two opposite points of view can be identified, while many other authors take up intermediate positions. On the one hand, many strategists assume that leaders can have considerable control over organizations and therefore that leaders need not be restricted by the organizational context. We shall refer to this point of view as the *organizational leadership* perspective. On the other hand, some believe that leaders are actually the product of the organizational context and that they can have only a marginal impact on the strategy of the organization. This point of view will be referred to as the *organizational dynamics* perspective.

As in previous chapters, these two opposite points of view will be contrasted with one another to explore the real nature of the organiza-tional context. By staging a debate between these two contradictory views on the paradox of control and chaos, a better understanding of the issues under discussion should be gained. In the next few pages, the organizational leadership and organizational dynamics perspectives will be further explained, and finally summarized in Table 9.1.

The Organizational Leadership Perspective

To proponents of the organizational leadership perspective, individual managers, especially those at the top, can make a big difference. *Organi-zational inertia*[1] and *strategic drift*[2] are not normal and inevitable condi-tions, but result from a failure of leadership. Bureaucracy, organizational fiefdoms, hostile relationships, resilient corporate cultures, rigid competences, resistance to change – all of these organizational diseases exist, but they are not inherent to organizational life. Healthy organiza-tions try to avoid falling prey to such degenerative illnesses, and when symptoms do arise, it is a task of the leader to address them. If organiza-tions do go 'out of control', it is because weak leadership has failed to deal with a creeping ailment. The fact that there are many sick, poorly controlled, companies does not mean that sickness should be accepted as the natural state of affairs.

At the basis of the organizational leadership perspective lies the belief in the power of individuals to steer organizational processes, in particular strategy formation. It is usually argued that this power does not only stem from the formal position occupied by managers, but also from the forcefulness of their personality and the persuasiveness of their vision. Having a formal position of power, therefore, does not necessarily make someone a leader. Effective leaders must be able to get other people to follow them[3], by setting an appealing organizational direction, and aligning and motivating people to move together in that direction[4]. To gain control over the organization, and to 'lead the troops into battle', it is essential to convince the troops to let themselves be led.

This does not mean that the leader of an organization needs to engage in simple top-down management. Of course, there are circumstances where the CEO or the top management team designs strategies in isolation and then imposes them on the rest of the organization. This type of direct control is sometimes necessary to push through reorganizations or to make major acquisitions. In other circumstances, however, the top managers can control organizational behavior more indirectly. Initiatives can be allowed to emerge bottom-up, as long as top management retains its power to approve or 'kill' projects as soon as they become serious proposals. Some authors suggest that top management might even delegate decision-making powers to lower level managers, but still control outcomes by setting clear goals, developing a conducive incentive system and fostering a particular culture[5].

What leaders should not do, however, is to relinquish control over the direction of the organization. The strategies do not have to be their own ideas, nor do they have to carry everything out themselves. But they should take upon themselves the responsibility for leading the organization in a certain direction and achieving results. If leaders let go of the helm, organizations will be set adrift, and will be carried by the prevailing winds and currents in directions unknown. Someone has to be in control of the organization, otherwise its behavior will be erratic. Leadership is needed to ensure that the best strategy is followed.

In conclusion, the organizational leadership perspective holds that the upper echelons of management can, and should, control the strategy process, and by extension, the strategy content. The CEO, or the top management team[6], should have a grip on the organization's process of strategy formation and should be able to impose their will on the organization. Leaders should strive to overcome organizational inertia and adapt the organization to the strategic direction they intend. This type of controlled strategic behavior is what Chandler[7] had in mind when he coined the aphorism *structure follows strategy* – the organizational structure should be adapted to the strategy intended by the decision-maker. In the organizational leadership perspective it would be more fitting to expand Chandler's maxim to *organization follow strategy* – all aspects of the company should be matched to the strategist's intentions.

The Organizational Dynamics Perspective

To proponents of the organizational dynamics perspective, such an heroic depiction of leadership is understandable, but usually more myth than reality. There might be a few great, wise, charismatic managers that rise to the apex of organizations, but unfortunately, all other organizations have to settle for regular mortals. Strong leaders are an exception, not the norm, and even their ability to mould the organization at will is highly exaggerated – good stories for a best-selling (auto)-biography, but legend nevertheless[8]. Yet, the belief in the power of leadership is quite popular, among managers and the managed alike[9]. Managers like the idea that as leaders of an organization or organizational unit, they can make a difference. To most, 'being in control' is what management is about. They have a penchant for attributing organizational results to their own efforts[10]. Most other people in the organization, the managed, assume that they will be led and therefore have expectations about the characteristics of good leaders and the actions such leaders should take. In fact, both parties are subscribing to a seductively simple model of how organizations work. They see organizations as straightforward mechanical systems, whose behavior can be governed by a simple 'cause-and-effect' control system – to get an effect, one has to push the right button.

However seductive, this view of organizational functioning is rarely a satisfactory model. A top manager does not resemble a jockey riding a thoroughbred horse, but is more like a cowboy herding mules. Organizations are complex social systems, made up of many 'stubborn individuals' with their own ideas, interests, and agendas. Strategy formation is therefore an inherently political process[11], that leaders can only influence depending on their power base. The more dispersed the political power, the more difficult it is for a leader to control the organization's behavior. Even if leaders are granted, or acquire, significant political power to push through their favored measures, there may still be considerable resistance and guerrilla activities. Political processes within organizations do not signify the derailment of strategic decision-making – politics is the normal state of affairs.

Besides such political dynamics, a top manager's ability to control the direction of a company is also severely constrained by the organization's culture. Social norms will have evolved, relationships will have been formed, aspirations will have taken root and cognitive maps will have been shaped. A leader cannot ignore the cultural legacy of the organization's history, as this will be deeply etched into the minds of the organization's members. Any top manager attempting to radically alter the direction of a company will find out that changing the under-lying values, perceptions, beliefs and expectations is extremely difficult, if not next to impossible. As Weick[12] puts it, an organization does not have a culture, it is a culture – shared values and norms are what make an organization. And just as it is difficult to change someone's character, it is difficult to change an organization's culture[13]. Moreover, as most top managers rise through the ranks to the upper echelons, they themselves are a product of the existing organizational culture. Changing your own culture is like pulling yourself up by your own bootstraps – a great trick, too bad that nobody can do it.

In Chapters 5 and 6, a related argument was put forward, as part of the resource-based view of the firm. One of the basic assumptions of the resource-based view is that building up competences is an arduous task, requiring a relatively long period of time. Learning is a slow process under the best of circumstances, but even more difficult if learning one thing means unlearning something else. The stronger the existing cognitive maps (knowledge), routines (capabilities) and disposition (attitude), the more challenging it is to 'teach an old dog new tricks.' The leader's power to direct and speed up such processes, it was argued, is quite limited[14].

Taken together, the political, cultural and learning dynamics leave top managers with relatively little power over the system they want to steer, according to advocates of the organizational dynamics perspective. A leader might be able to nudge, but on the whole the strategy will be the result of the chaotic internal dynamics of the organizational system. Some leaders might think that they are in control and that they are consciously choosing the future direction of the organization, but this is often only an illusion. In reality, they are limited by a cognitive map of which they are not aware, trapped in a culture they think is normal, reigned in by the political interests of diverse groups, and stuck with competences and investments that are difficult to change. Under these circumstances, one could say *strategy follows organization*, instead of the other way around.

The question for the field of strategic management is, therefore, whether organization follows strategy or strategy follows organization[15]. Can top management of a firm shape the organization to fit with their intended strategy or does the organizational context determine the strategy actually followed? In short, strategists must come to terms with the paradox of control and chaos (see Table 9.1).

Defining the Issues: Inheritance and Initiative

As in Chapter 8, the debate between proponents of the organizational leadership perspective and supporters of the organizational dynamics

TABLE 9.1
Organizational leadership versus organizational dynamics perspective

	Organizational Leadership Perspective	Organizational Dynamics Perspective
Emphasis on	Control over chaos	Chaos over control
Organizational changes	Controllable creation processes	Uncontrollable evolutionary processes
Change process	Leader commands behavior	Behavior emerges from history
Change determinants	Leader's vision and skill	Political, cultural and learning dynamics
Form of change	Top-down, mechanistic	Interactive fermentation
Organizational malleability	High, fast	Low, slow
Direction of adaptation	Organization follows strategy	Strategy follows organization
Normative implication	Strategize, then organize	Strategizing and organizing intertwined
Point of view	Voluntaristic	Deterministic

perspective rests on the age-old question of voluntarism versus determinism. Are humans free to make their own choices and shape their own future, or is free will an illusion and is the future shaped by forces beyond an individual's grasp? Where people have the power to mold their direct environment as they see fit, they have control. Where their direct environment is shaped by dynamics that no one controls, there is a state of chaos. Whether control or chaos prevails – or whether both are simultaneously in evidence – is essential to the approach one takes to strategy process and strategy content. However, it is clear that the paradox of control and chaos is not easily resolved and therefore hotly disputed.

Two issues are central to this discussion on 'who shapes whom'. The first issue is that of *organizational inheritance*[16]. In organizations, just as in families, each new generation does not start from scratch, but inherits properties that belong to the group. In families, a part of this inheritance is in the form of genetic properties, but other elements are also passed on such as family traditions, myths, connections, feuds, titles, and possessions. Each person might think of themselves as a unique individual, but to some degree they are an extension of the family line, and their behavior is influenced by their inheritance. In organizations the same phenomenon is observable. New top managers may arrive on the scene, but they inherit a great deal from their predecessors. They inherit traditions and myths in the form of a culture. Internal and external connections and feuds shape the political constellation in which new leaders must function. And brands, skills and other resources are passed down to them.

The question is how heavily organizational inheritance predetermines an organization's future path. Can top managers, if necessary, compel the organization to break with its past, and transform it into something new? This would assume weak pressures of inheritance and high malleability. Or must top managers accept the fact that the influence of inherited characteristics is pervasive, and hence malleability limited?

The second issue in the debate is that of *managerial initiative*. While organizational inheritance refers to the 'momentum' present in the organizational system[17], managerial initiative refers to the power of managers to intervene in organizational processes. Only where managers lose all ability to take initiatives do they truly become mere spectators of organizational development. The more power that managers have to move proactively, the greater the chance of gaining control over organizational behavior. If top managers are able to accumulate enough political power, it might be possible to neutralize opposing coalitions in the organization and impose a new agenda. If leaders are capable of critical thought and dialogue, they might have the intellectual power to challenge the organizational belief system, and forge a new paradigm. If they are skilled in capturing the hearts and minds of the employees, they might be able to change the corporate culture and push the organization in a new direction. Even if organizational inheritance is a major factor, the power of top managers to take initiatives might be a sufficiently strong counterpressure to give leaders a real impact on shaping the organizational context.

EXHIBIT 9.1
Kodak case

KODAK: MANUAL OR AUTOFOCUS?

George Fisher was somewhat of a corporate celebrity in the US when he took over as Chairman, President, and Chief Executive Officer of Kodak in October 1993. His fame had been acquired while leading the restructuring of Motorola from a troubled firm into one of America's leading high-tech companies. Particularly eye-catching was how Fisher moved Motorola into the embryonic markets for cellular telephones and pagers just in time to ride the wave of exponential growth. Fisher had also gained widespread public attention in his efforts to combat what he believed to be unfair trade practices by Motorola's Japanese competitors. By intensively lobbying Washington, Fisher was able to extract concessions from the Japanese government to open up the Japanese market for Motorola's products, while Washington instituted measures to curb the 'dumping' of Japanese products on the American market. This success made Fisher one of the obvious choices to lead the necessary restructuring of Kodak.

The task facing Fisher was formidable. Kodak was a lumbering giant, with more than $12 billion in sales and over 100,000 employees world-wide. While the company, founded in 1881, had one of the world's most valuable brand names, it was slowly losing terrain in its core photographic film business and had not been particularly successful in its diversification efforts. Its main competitor in the photo film industry, the Japanese company Fuji, had been steadily nibbling away market share for years and Kodak had not demonstrated that it had the innovative capabilities to counter this trend. Moreover, the photographic film technology, on which Kodak's predominance in consumer markets rests, was being threatened by substitute technologies. Especially the emergence of digital imaging, using high resolution scanners and printers, posed a significant danger to Kodak's 'analog imaging' business. The company had been slow in its response to these developments, and the efforts that were been made resulted in lacklustre performance at best.

Between 1983 and 1993 Kodak had restructured several times, under changing leadership, but with little effect. In August 1993 a group of outside directors removed CEO, Kay Whitmore, because it was believed that not enough had been done to improve the company's performance and future outlook. It was felt that it was time to attract an outsider without Kodak photo chemicals in his veins. An outsider without an emotional attachment to the Kodak culture, without a stake in the current strategy and without political debts to repay, would have the freedom to reshape the firm as he saw fit. This person would be given *carte blanche* to wield the ax where necessary to bring about a rapid transformation of Kodak. Preferably this outsider would have a track record in transforming bogged down high-tech companies. According to the board of directors George Fisher fit the bill exactly. Or as Roberto C. Goizueta, Kodak board member and Chairman of Coca Cola, put it at the time: 'When we began this search, our No.1 candidate was God, and we stepped down from that'.

Fisher's mandate was to carry out all necessary changes at Kodak and turn around the company within three years. By 1996, Fisher had booked some impressive results. He had sold off $8.9 billion in non-core businesses, including Eastman Chemical Co. and a copier company. This had helped to reduce Kodak's debt from $7.5 billion to $1.5 billion. Sales grew to $16 billion and earnings reached $1.29 billion, more than double that of 1994. Investor confidence in Kodak's potential had also increased, as its stock reached a record high of $94 in January 1997, up 80 per cent since Fisher's arrival. In the 1996 annual report Fisher could reflect with satisfaction that 1996 had been a 'watershed' in his efforts to turn around the company. 'The picture at Kodak is clearly changing,' a proud Fisher reported to his shareholders.

However, as 1997 progressed, it became clear that all was not well at Kodak. On October 14 the firm announced results that shocked investors, and sent share prices in a nose dive to $63. Operating profits over 1997 were expected to be down by 25 per cent, with no immediate improvement foreseen. As a consequence, Fisher reduced the number of senior managers in the company by 20 per cent and unveiled plans to chop 16,000 of the company's 100,000 jobs. Analysts were quick to point out that massive bloodletting was long overdue. Kodak had been known for its bloated cost structure for years, yet during Fisher's reign the number of employees in continuing operations had actually grown by 3000. It is a tell-tale sign that Kodak's major rival, Fuji, accomplished twice the level of sales per employee. Furthermore, Kodak's overhead and administrative costs were at 27.5 per cent of sales, which was higher than most of its competitors.

While Kodak's efforts to significantly revamp its cost structure grabbed the headlines, other problems were dogging Fisher. Most importantly, Fisher's core strategy of expanding from analog to digital imaging, making Kodak an allround imaging company, was not running smoothly. Just as he had guided Motorola into the promising market for cellular phones, it was Fisher's intention to move Kodak into the emerging market for digital imaging. Yet, despite investments of some $500 million a year into research and product development, results were mixed at best. In terms of sales volume Fisher could point to a promising trend. In 1996 sales of digital products, such as digital cameras and scanners, went up 25 per cent to $1.5 billion, putting them ahead of the competition. The downside was that this lead was costing Kodak mountains of cash – in 1997 alone the losses were estimated at $200 million. Furthermore, Kodak was up against such ferocious competitors as Sony, Hewlett-Packard, Epson and Canon, as well as a pack of smaller companies, all accustomed to the break-neck pace of technological development in the information technology industry. Analysts point out that in this emerging business, where dominant formats for things like image compression and low-cost photo-quality printers still need to surface, competitors need to be fast and nimble. According to high-tech consultant Robert Krinsky 'to win at this game will require speed and flexibility – and that's not what I think of when I think of Kodak.'

Critics argue that this is the major difference between Kodak and Motorola. At Kodak Fisher has faced a far more ingrained and bureaucratic culture, more oriented to old-line manufacturing than to high-tech innovation. 'Fisher has been able to change the culture at the very top,' remarks one industry analyst in *Business Week*, 'but he hasn't been able to change the huge mass of middle managers, and they just don't understand this [digital] world.' Moreover, there is a fear among many Kodak managers that digital products will cannibalize the company's core business. This had led to caution, suspicion and sometimes even hostility towards the new direction.

To make things worse, Fisher could find no effective response to Fuji's continued onslaught in Kodak's core photo film business. Fuji's market share in the US market jumped from 11 per cent in 1996 to 16 per cent in 1997, due to extensive marketing efforts, steep price cuts, and an exclusive deal for Wal-Mart's photofinishing business. In 1997, Fuji also boldly opened a plant in South Carolina with a capacity to produce 100 million rolls of color film a year, which equals about 14 per cent of the US annual demand. While Kodak's US market share has dropped to about 70 per cent, it cannot afford to get caught up in a price war with Fuji to recover lost ground, as this would cut into the profits it needs to fuel its digital activities. Fisher's only ace in his poker game with Fuji was to lobby Washington again to seek action against unfair trade barriers in the Japanese market for photo film and paper. Fisher argued that hidden barriers in this second largest photo market in the world had limited Kodak's market share to 10 per cent, while Fuji enjoyed a profitable market share of 70 per cent, allowing Fuji to cross-subsidize aggressive pricing in other markets. However, while in his Motorola days Fisher pulled off a success, the World Trade Organization rejected Kodak's claims due to lack of proof, leaving Fisher furious, but empty handed.

All these developments have left many analysts wondering whether Fisher is the leader who can get Kodak back on track again. Or as *Business Week* titled an article on the company's problems: 'Can George Fisher Fix Kodak?' Is Fisher in control and can he push through the necessary changes, or is it time to unleash the headhunters again? Or is it an illusion to believe that anyone can 'fix Kodak' and must more attention be paid to influencing the organizational dynamics that are propelling the company? Whichever is the case, for the next little while few people at Kodak will be saying 'smile'.

Sources: *Business Week*, October 20, 1997; *New York Times*, May 5, 1994

The Debate and the Readings

The economic sociologist Duesenberry once remarked that 'economics is all about how people make choices; sociology is all about how they don't have any choices to make.' Although half in jest, his comment does ring true. Much of the literature within the field of economics assumes that people in organizations can freely make choices and have the power to shape their strategy – possible restraints on their freedom usually come from the environment. Sociological literature, but also psychological and political science work, often feature the limitations on individual's freedom. These different disciplinary inclinations are not absolute, but can be clearly recognized in the debate.

To open the debate on behalf of the organizational leadership perspective, a classic reading has been selected, 'The CEO: Leadership in Organizations,' by Roland Christensen, Kenneth Andrews, Joseph Bower, Richard Hamermesh and Michael Porter[18]. This contribution is a part of the same well-known Harvard textbook, *Business Policy*, as is Kenneth Andrew's reading in Chapter 2. In line with the organizational leadership literature, this reading emphasizes the role of the organization's leader as main strategic planner and chief strategy implementor. But while many other authors taking this perspective accord a large measure of importance to the broader top management team, Christensen and his colleagues focus on the pivotal position of the CEO. In their view, the president of the company is essential to the organization's success. They are skeptical of research, such as Henry Mintzberg's, that portray managers as 'harried, improvisatory, overworked performers of ten roles [who] do not really know what they are doing.' In their opinion, this says little about how effective leaders should work. CEOs are crucial in their roles as organizational leaders, personal leaders and chief architects of organizational purpose. Where organizations are led by individuals of 'great human skill, sensitivity, administrative capability . . . [and] analytic intelligence of a higher order,' above average organizational performance is much more likely. The organization is a vehicle in need of a driver, who knows where to go, how to get there and is capable of roadside repairs if anything breaks down on the way. Christensen and colleagues recognize that the organizational context is sometimes not entirely malleable and can limit the freedom of the CEO to make and implement strategy. However, this is not viewed as a disqualification of the organizational leadership perspective, but as a failure of the CEO to lead. In short, the leader matters, not the organizational context.

For a reading to represent the organizational dynamics perspective, the same problem exists as in Chapter 8 – most authors arguing that managers have little freedom to shape their future usually do not write for a managerial audience. Almost all of the literature with a strong determinist bent is quite academic, and therefore less suitable as a reading in this chapter. Therefore, an accessible contribution has been selected that is very close to the extreme pole of organizational dynamics, but is not fully deterministic. This reading by Ralph Stacey is mysteriously entitled 'Strategy as Order Emerging from Chaos.'[19] Stacey argues that top managers cannot, and should not even try, to control the organization and its strategy. In his view, the organizational dynamics involved in strategy formation, learning and change are too complex to simply be controlled by managers. He states that 'sometimes the best thing a manager can do is to let go and allow things to happen.' The resulting *chaos*, he argues, does not mean that the organization will be a mess – a lack of control does not mean that the organization will be adrift. His reasoning is that non-linear feedback systems, such as organizations, have a self-organizing ability, which 'can produce controlled behavior, even though no one is in control.' In his view, real strategic change requires the chaos of contention and conflict to destroy old recipes and to seek for new solutions. The 'self-organizing processes of political interaction and complex learning' ensure that chaos does not result in disintegration. Hence, in Stacey's opinion, it is management's task to help create a situation of bounded instability in which strategy can emerge. The role of leaders is to influence the organizational context in a way that new and unexpected strategies can develop spontaneously.

With such strongly differing views on the nature of the organizational context, it is up to readers to create order out of this chaos. Each individual will have to form their own opinion about the best way to deal with the paradox of control and chaos.

Reading 1 The CEO: Leadership in Organizations

By Roland Christensen, Kenneth Andrews, Joseph Bower, Richard Hamermesh, and Michael Porter[†]

Management we regard as leadership in the informed, planned, purposeful conduct of complex organized activity. *General management* is, in its simplest form, the management of a total enterprise or of an autonomous subunit. The senior general manager in any organization is its chief executive officer, who for the purposes of simplicity we will often call the *president*.

We will begin by considering the *roles* that presidents must play. We will examine the *functions* or characteristic and natural actions that they perform in the roles they assume. We will try to identify *skills* or abilities that put one's perceptions, judgment, and knowledge to effective use in executive performance. As we look at executive roles, functions and skills, we may be able to define more clearly aspects of the *point of view* that provide the most suitable perspective for high-level executive judgment.

[†] Source: This article has been adapted from 'The CEO: Leadership in Organization,' in *Business Policy: Text and Cases*, Sixth Edition, Irwin, Homewood, IL, 1987. Used with permission.

Many attempts to characterize executive roles and functions come to very little. Henri Fayol, originator of the classical school of management theory, identified the roles of planner, organizer, coordinator, and controller, initiating the construction by others of a later vocabulary of remarkable variety. Present-day students reject these categories as vague or abstract and indicative only of the objectives of some executive activity. Henry Mintzberg, who among other researchers has observed managers at work, identifies three sets of behavior – interpersonal, informational, and decisional. The interpersonal roles he designates as *figurehead* (for ceremonial duties), *leader* (of the work of his organization or unit), and *liaison agent* (for contacts outside his unit). Information roles can be designated as *monitor* (of information), *disseminator* (internally), and *spokesman* (externally). Decisional roles are called *entrepreneur, disturbance handler, resource allocator,* and *negotiator.*

Empirical studies of what managers do are corrective of theory but not necessarily instructive in educating good managers. That most unprepared managers act intuitively rather than systematically in response to unanticipated pressures does not mean that the most effective do so to the same extent. If in fact the harried, improvisatory, overworked performers of 10 roles do not really know *what* they are doing or have any priorities besides degree of urgency, then we are not likely to find out what more effective management is from categorizing their activities. On the other hand it is futile to offer unrealistic exhortations about long-range planning and organizing to real-life victims of forced expediency.

The simplification that will serve best our approach to policy will leave aside important but easily understood activities. The executive may make speeches, pick the silver pattern for the executive lunchroom, negotiate personally with important customers, and do many things human beings have to do for many reasons. Roles we may study in order to do a better job of general management can be viewed as those of *organization leader, personal leader,* and *chief architect of organization purpose.* As leader of persons grouped in a hierarchy of suborganizations, the president must be taskmaster, mediator, motivator, and organization designer. Since these roles do not have useful job descriptions saying what to do, one might better estimate the nature of the overlapping responsibility of the head of an organization than to draw theoretical distinctions between categories. The personal influence of leaders becomes evident as they play the role of communicator or exemplar and attract respect or affection. When we examine finally the president's role as architect of organization purpose, we may see entrepreneurial or improvisatory behavior if the organization is just being born. If the company is long since established, the part played may be more accurately designated as manager of the purpose-determining process or chief strategist.

The CEO as Organization Leader

Chief executives are first and probably least pleasantly persons who are responsible for results attained in the present as designated by plans made previously. Nothing that we will say shortly about their concern for the people in their organizations or later about their responsibility to society can gainsay this immediate truth. Achieving acceptable results against expectations of increased earnings per share and return on the stockholder's investment requires the CEO or president to be continually informed and ready to intervene when results fall below what had been expected. Changing circumstances and competition produce emergencies upsetting well-laid plans. Resourcefulness in responding to crisis is a skill that most successful executives develop early.

But the organizational consequences of the critical taskmaster role require presidents to go beyond insistence upon achievement of planned results. They must see as their second principal function the creative maintenance and development of the organized capability that makes achievement possible. This activity leads to a third principle – the integration of the specialist functions that enable their organizations to perform the technical tasks in marketing, research and development, manufacturing, finance, control, and personnel that proliferate as technology develops and tend to lead the company in all directions. If this coordination is successful in harmonizing special staff activities, presidents will probably have performed the task of getting organizations to accept and order priorities in accordance with the companies' objectives. Securing commitment to purpose is a central function of the president as organization leader.

The skills required by these functions reveal presidents not solely as taskmasters but as mediators and motivators as well. They need ability in the education and motivation of people and the evaluation of their performance, two functions that tend to work against one another. The former requires understanding of individual needs, which persist no matter what the economic purpose of the organization may be. The latter requires objective assessment of the technical requirements of the task assigned. The capability required here is also that required in the integration of functions and the mediation of the conflict bound to arise out of technical specialism. The integrating capacity of the chief executive extends to meshing the economic, technical, human, and moral dimensions of corporate activity and to relating the company to its immediate and more distant communities. It will show itself in the formal organizational designs that are put into effect as the blueprint of the required structured cooperation.

The perspective demanded of successful organization leaders embraces both the primacy of organizational goals and the validity of individual goals. Besides this dual appreciation, they exhibit an impartiality toward the specialized functions and have criteria enabling them to allocate organizational resources against documented needs. The point of view of the leader of an organization almost by definition requires an overview of its relations not only to its internal constituencies but to the relevant institutions and forces of its external environment. We will come soon to a conceptual solution of the problems encountered in the role of organization leader.

The CEO as Personal Leader

The functions, skills, and appropriate point of view of chief executives hold true no matter who they are or who makes up their organizations. The functions that accompany presidential performance of their role as communicator of purpose and policy, as exemplar, and as the focal point for the respect or affection of subordinates vary much more according to personal energy, style, character, and integrity. Presidents contribute as persons to the quality of life and performance in their organizations. This is true whether they are dynamic or colorless. By example they educate junior executives to seek to emulate them or simply to learn from their behavior what they really expect. They have the opportunity to infuse organized effort with flair or distinction if they have the skill to dramatize the relationship between their own activities and the goals of corporate effort.

All persons in leadership positions have or attain power that in sophisticated organizations they invoke as humanely and reasonably as possible in order to avoid the stultifying effects of dictatorship, dominance, or even markedly superior capacity. Formally announced policy, backed by the authority of the chief executive, can be made effective to some degree by clarity of direction, intensity of supervision, and the exercise of sanctions in enforcement. But in areas of judgment where policy cannot be specified without becoming absurdly overdetailed, chief executives establish in their own demeanor even more than in policy statements the moral and ethical level of performance expected.

The skills of the effective personal leader are those of persuasion and articulation made possible by saying something worth saying and by understanding the sentiments and points of view being addressed. Leaders cultivate and embody relationships between themselves and their subordinates appropriate to the style of leadership they have chosen or fallen into. Some of the qualities lending distinction to this leadership cannot be deliberately contrived, even by an artful schemer. The maintenance of personal poise in adversity or emergency and the capacity for development as an emotionally mature person are essentially innate and developed capabilities. It is probably true that some personal pre-eminence in technical or social functions is either helpful or essential in demonstrating leadership related to the president's personal contribution. Credibility and cooperation depend upon demonstrated capacity of a kind more tangible and attractive than, for example, the noiseless coordination of staff activity.

The CEO as Architect of Organization Purpose

To go beyond the organizational and personal roles of leadership, we enter the sphere of organization purpose, where we may find the atmosphere somewhat rare and the going less easy. We think students will note, as they see president after president cope or fail to cope with problems of various economic, political, social, or technical elements, that the contribution presidents make to their companies goes far beyond the apparently superficial activities that clutter their days.

The attention of presidents to organizations' needs must extend beyond answering letters of complaint from spouses of aggrieved employees to appraisal (for example) of the impact of their companies' information, incentive, and control systems upon individual behavior. Their personal contribution to their company goes far beyond easily understood attention to key customers and speeches to the Economic Club to the more subtle influence their own probity and character have on subordinates. We must turn now to activities even further out – away from immediate everyday decisions and emergencies. Some part of what a president does is oriented toward maintaining the development of a company over time and preparing for a future more distant than the time horizon appropriate to the roles and functions identified thus far.

The most difficult role – and the one we will concentrate on henceforth – of the chief executive of any organization is the one in which he serves as custodian of corporate objectives. The entrepreneurs who create a company know at the outset what they are up to. Their objectives are intensely personal, if not exclusively economic, and their passions may be patent protection and finance. If they succeed in passing successfully through the phase of personal entrepreneurship, where they or their bankers or families are likely to be the only members of the organization concerned with purpose, they find themselves in the role of planner, managing the process by which ideas for the future course of the company are conceived, evaluated, fought over, and accepted or rejected.

The presidential functions involved include establishing or presiding over the goal-setting and resource-allocation processes of the company, making or ratifying choice among strategic alternatives, and clarifying and defending the goals of the company against external attack or internal erosion. The installation of purpose in place of improvisation and the substitution of planned progress in place of drifting are probably the most demanding functions of the chief executive. Successful organization leadership requires great human skill, sensitivity, and administrative ability. Personal leadership is built upon personality and character. The capacity for determining and monitoring the adequacy of the organization's continuing purposes implies as well analytic intelligence of a high order. The president we are talking about is not a two-dimensional poster or television portrait.

The crucial skill of the president concerned with corporate purpose includes the creative generation or recognition of strategic alternatives made valid by developments in the marketplace and the capability and resources of the company. Along with this, in a combination not easily come by, runs the critical capacity to analyze the strengths and weaknesses of documented proposals. The ability to perceive with some objectivity corporate strengths and weaknesses is essential to sensible choice of goals, for the most attractive goal is not attainable without the strength to open the way to it through inertia and intense opposition, with all else that lies between.

Probably the skill most nearly unique to general management, as opposed to the management of functional or technical specialties, is the intellectual capacity to conceptualize corporate purpose and the dramatic skill to invest it with some degree of magnetism. As we will see, the skill can be exercised in industries less romantic than space, electronics, or environmental reclamation. No sooner is a distinctive set of corporate objectives vividly delineated than the temptation to go beyond it sets in. Under some circumstances it is the president's function to defend properly focused purpose against superficially attractive diversification or corporate growth that glitters like fool's gold. Because defense of proper strategy can be interpreted as mindless conservatism, wholly appropriate defense of a still valid strategy requires courage, supported by detailed documentation.

Continuous monitoring, in any event, of the quality and continued suitability of corporate purpose is over time the most sophisticated and essential of all the functions of general management alluded to here. The perspective that sustains this function is the kind of creative discontent that prevents complacency even in good times and seeks continuous advancement of corporate and individual capacity and performance. It requires also constant attention to the future, as if the present did not offer problems and opportunities enough.

Reading 2   Strategy as Order Emerging from Chaos

By Ralph Stacey[†]

There are four important points to make on the recent discoveries about the complex behavior of dynamic systems, all of which have direct application to human organizations.

Chaos is a Form of Instability Where the Specific Long-Term Future is Unknowable

Chaos in its scientific sense is an irregular pattern of behavior generated by well-defined nonlinear feedback rules commonly found in nature and human society. When systems driven by such rules operate away from equilibrium, they are highly sensitive to selected tiny changes in their environments, amplifying them into self-reinforcing virtuous and vicious circles that completely alter the behavior of the system. In other words, the system's future unfolds in a manner dependent upon the precise detail of what it does, what the systems constituting its environments do, and upon chance. As a result of this fundamental property of the system itself, specific links between cause and effect are lost in the history of its development, and the specific path of its long-term future development is completely unpredictable. Over the short term, however, it is possible to predict behavior because it takes time for the consequences of small changes to build up.

Is there evidence of chaos in business systems? We would conclude that there was if we could point to small changes escalating into large consequences; if we could point to self-reinforcing vicious and virtuous circles; if we could point to feedback that alternates between the amplifying and the damping. It is not difficult to find such evidence.

Creative managers seize on small differences in customer requirements and perceptions to build significant differentiators for their products. Customers may respond to this by switching from other product offerings, leading to a virtuous circle; or they may switch away, causing the kind of vicious circle that Coca-Cola found itself caught up in when it made that famous soft drink slightly sweeter.

Managers create, or at the very least shape, the requirements of

[†] Source: Reprinted with permission from *Long Range Planning*, Vol. 26, No. 1, 'Strategy as Order Emerging from Chaos,' pp. 10–17. © 1993, Pergamon Press Ltd. Oxford, England.

their customers through the product offerings they make. Sony created a requirement for personal hi-fi systems through its Walkman offering, and manufacturers and operators have created requirements for portable telephones. Sony and Matsushita created the requirement for video recorders, and when companies supply information systems to their clients, they rarely do so according to a complete specification – instead, the supplier shapes the requirement. When managers intentionally shape customer demands through the offerings they make, this feeds back into customer responses, and managers may increase the impact by intentionally using the copying and spreading effects through which responses to product offerings feed back into other customers' responses. When managers do this, they are deliberately using positive feedback – along with negative feedback controls to meet cost and quality targets, for example – to create business success.

A successful business is also affected by many amplifying feedback processes that are outside the control of its managers and produce effects that they did not intend. Successful businesses are quite clearly characterized by feedback processes that flip between the negative and the positive, the damping and the amplifying; that is, they are characterized by feedback patterns that produce chaos. The long-term future of a creative organization is absolutely unknowable, and no one can intend its future direction over the long term or be in control of it. In such a system long-term plans and visions of future states can be only illusions.

But in Chaos there are Boundaries Around the Instability

While chaos means disorder and randomness in the behavior of a system at the specific level, it also means that there is a qualitative pattern at a general, overall level. The future unfolds unpredictably, but it always does so according to recognizable family-like resemblances. This is what we mean when we say that history repeats itself, but never in the same way. We see this combination of unpredictable specific behavior within an overall pattern in snowflakes. As two nearby snowflakes fall to the earth, they experience tiny differences in temperature and air impurities. Each snowflake amplifies those differences as they form, and by the time they reach the earth they have different shapes – but they are still clearly snowflakes. We cannot predict the shape of each snowflake, but we can predict that they will be snowflakes. In business, we recognize patterns of boom and recession, but each time they are different in specific terms, defying all attempts to predict them.

Chaos is unpredictable variety within recognizable categories defined by irregular features, that is, an inseparable intertwining of order and disorder. It is this property of being bounded by recognizable qualitative patterns that makes it possible for humans to cope with chaos. Numerous tests have shown that our memories do not normally store information in units representing the precise characteristics of the individual shapes or events we perceive. Instead, we store information about the strength of connection between individual units perceived. We combine information together into categories or concepts using family resemblance-type features. Memory emphasizes general structure, irregular category features, rather than specific content. We remember the irregular patterns rather than the specific features and we design our next actions on the basis of these memorized patterns. And since we design our actions in this manner, chaotic behavior presents us with no real problem. Furthermore, we are adept at using analogical reasoning and intuition to reflect upon experience and adapt it to new situations, all of which is ideally suited to handling chaos.

Unpredictable New Order can Emerge from Chaos through a Process of Spontaneous Self-Organization

When nonlinear feedback systems in nature are pushed far from equilibrium into chaos, they are capable of creating a complex new order. For example, at some low temperature the atoms of a particular gas are arranged in a particular pattern and the gas emits no light. Then, as heat is applied, it agitates the atoms causing them to move, and as this movement is amplified through the gas it emits a dull glow. Small changes in heat are thus amplified, causing instability, or chaos, that breaks the symmetry of the atoms' original behavior. Then at a critical point, the atoms in the gas suddenly all point in the same direction to produce a laser beam. Thus, the system uses chaos to shatter old patterns of behavior, creating the opportunity for the new. And as the system proceeds through chaos, it is confronted with critical points where it, so to speak, makes a choice between different options for further development. Some options represent yet further chaos and others lead to more complex forms of orderly behavior, but which will occur is inherently unpredictable. The choice itself is made by spontaneous self-organization amongst the components of the system in which they, in effect, communicate with each other, reach a consensus, and commit to a new form of behavior. If a more complex form of orderly behavior is reached, it has what scientists call a dissipative structure, because continual attention and energy must be applied if it is to be sustained – for example, heat has to be continually pumped into the gas if the laser beam is to continue. If the system is to develop further, then the dissipative structure must be short-lived; to reach an even more complex state, the system will have to pass through chaos once more.

It is striking how similar the process of dealing with strategic issues in an organization is to the self-organizing phenomenon just outlined. The key to the effectiveness with which organizations change and develop new strategic directions lies in the manner in which managers handle what might be called their strategic issue agenda. That agenda is a dynamic, unwritten list of issues, aspirations, and challenges that key groups of managers are attending to. Consider the steps managers can be observed to follow as they handle their strategic issue agenda:

■ *Detecting and selecting small disturbances.* In open-ended strategic situations, change is typically the result of many small events and actions that are unclear, ambiguous, and confusing, with consequences that are unknowable. The key difficulty is to identify what the real issues, problems, or opportunities are, and the challenge is to find an appropriate and creative aspiration or objective. In these circumstances the organization has no alternative but to rely on the initiative of individuals to notice and pursue some issue, aspiration, or challenge. In order to do this, those individuals have to rely on their experience-based intuition and ability to detect analogies between one set of ambiguous circumstances and another.

■ *Amplifying the issues and building political support.* Once some individual detects some potential issue, that individual begins to push for organizational attention to it. A complex political process of building special interest groups to support an issue is required before it gains organizational attention and can thus be said to be on the strategic issue agenda.

■ *Breaking symmetries.* As they build and progress strategic issue agendas, managers are in effect altering old mental models, existing company and industry recipes, to come up with new ways of doing things. They are destroying existing perceptions and structures.

■ *Critical points and unpredictable outcomes.* Some issues on the agenda may be dealt with quickly, while others may attract attention, continuous or periodic, for a very long time. How quickly an issue is dealt with depends upon the time required to reach enough consensus and commitment to proceed to action. At some critical point, an external or internal pressure in effect forces a choice. The outcome on whether and how to proceed to action over the issue is unpredictable because it depends upon the context of power, personality, and group dynamic within which it is being handled. The result may or may not be action, and action will usually be experimental at first.

■ *Changing the frame of reference.* Managers in a business come to share memories of what worked and what did not work in the past – the organizational memory. In this way they build up a business philosophy, or culture, establishing a company recipe and in common with their rivals an industry recipe too. These recipes have a powerful effect on what issues will subsequently be detected and attended to; that is, they constitute a frame of reference within which managers interpret what to do next. The frame of reference has to be continually challenged and changed because it can easily become inappropriate to new circumstances. The dissipative structure of consensus and commitment is therefore necessarily short-lived if an organization is to be innovative.

These phases constitute a political and learning process through which managers deal with strategic issues, and the key point about these processes is that they are spontaneous and self-organizing: no central authority can direct anyone to detect and select an open-ended issue for attention, simply because no one knows what it is until someone has detected it; no one can centrally organize the factions that form around specific issues; nor can anyone intend the destruction of old recipes and the substitution of new ones since it is impossible to know what the appropriate new ones are until they are discovered. The development of new strategic direction requires the chaos of contention and conflict, and the self-organizing processes of political interaction and complex learning.

Chaos is a Fundamental Property of Nonlinear Feedback Systems, a Category that Includes Human Organizations

Feedback simply means that one action or event feeds into another; that is, one action or event determines the next according to some relationship. For example, one firm repackages its product and its rival responds in some way, leading to a further action on the part of the first, provoking in turn yet another response from the second, and so on. The feedback relationship may be linear, or proportional, and when this is the case, the first firm will repackage its product and the second will respond by doing much the same. The feedback relationship could be nonlinear, or nonproportional, however, so that when the first firm repackages its product, the second introduces a new product at a lower price; this could lead the first to cut prices even further, so touching off a price war. In other words, nonlinear systems are those that use amplifying (positive) feedback in some way. To see the significance of positive feedback, compare it with negative feedback.

All effective businesses use negative or damping feedback systems to control and regulate their day-to-day activities. Managers fix short-term targets for profits and then prepare annual plans or budgets, setting out the time path to reach the target. As the business moves through time, outcomes are measured and compared with annual plan projections to yield variances. Frequent monitoring of those variances prompts corrective action to bring performance indicators back onto their planned paths; that is, variances feed back into corrective action and the feedback takes a negative form, so that when profit is below target, for example, offsetting action is taken to restore it. Scheduling, budgetary, and planning systems utilize negative feedback to keep an organization close to a predictable, stable equilibrium path in which it is adapted to its environment. While negative feedback controls a system according to prior intention, positive feedback produces explosively unstable equilibrium where changes are amplified, eventually putting intolerable pressure on the system until it runs out of control.

The key discovery about the operation of nonlinear feedback systems, however, is that there is a third choice. When a nonlinear feedback system is driven away from stable equilibrium toward explosive unstable equilibrium, it passes through a phase of bounded instability – there is a border between stability and instability where feedback flips autonomously between the amplifying and the damping to produce chaotic behavior; a paradoxical state that combines both stability and instability.

All human interactions take the form of feedback loops simply because the consequences of one action always feed back to affect a subsequent one. Furthermore, all human interactions constitute nonlinear feedback loops because people under- and overreact. Since organizations are simply a vast web of feedback loops between people, they must be capable of chaotic, as well as stable and explosively unstable, behavior. The key question is which of these kinds of behaviors leads an organization to success. We can see the answer to this question if we reflect upon the fundamental forces operating on an organization.

All organizations are powerfully pulled in two fundamentally different directions:

- *Disintegration.* Organizations can become more efficient and effective if they divide tasks, segment markets, appeal to individual motivators, empower people, promote informal communication, and separate production processes in geographic and other terms. These steps lead to fragmenting cultures and dispersed power that pull an organization toward disintegration, a phenomenon that can be seen in practice as companies split into more and more business units and find it harder and harder to maintain control.

- *Ossification.* To avoid this pull to disintegration, and to reap the advantages of synergy and coordination, all organizations are also pulled to a state in which tasks are integrated, overlaps in market segments and production processes managed, group goals stressed above individual ones, power concentrated, communication and procedures formalized, and strongly shared cultures established. As an organization moves in this direction it develops more and more rigid structures, rules, procedures, and systems until it eventually ossifies, consequences that are easy to observe as organizations centralize.

Thus, one powerful set of forces pulls every organization toward a stable equilibrium (ossification) and another powerful set of forces pulls it toward an explosively unstable equilibrium (disintegration). Success lies at the border between these states, where managers continually alter systems and structures to avoid attraction either to disintegration or to ossification. For example, organizations typically swing to centralization in one period, to decentralization in another, and back again later on. Success clearly lies in a nonequilibrium state between stable and unstable equilibria; and for a nonlinear feedback system, that is chaos.

Eight Steps to Create Order Out of Chaos

When managers believe that they must pull together harmoniously in pursuit of a shared organizational intention established before they act, they are inevitably confined to the predictable – existing strategic directions will simply be continued or innovations made by others will simply be imitated. When, instead of this, managers create the chaos that flows from challenging existing perceptions and promote the conditions in which spontaneous self-organization can occur, they make it possible for innovation and new strategic direction to emerge. Managers create such conditions when they undertake actions of the following kind.

Develop New Perspectives on the Meaning of Control

The activity of learning in a group is a form of control that managers do not normally recognize as such. It is a self-organizing, self-policing form of control in which the group itself discovers intention and exercises control. Furthermore, we are all perfectly accustomed to the idea that the strategic direction of local communities, nation-states, and international communities is developed and controlled through the operation of political systems, but we rarely apply this notion to organizations. When we do, we see that a sequence of choices and actions will continue in a particular direction only while those espousing that direction continue to enjoy sufficient support. This constitutes a form of control that is as applicable to an organization when it faces the conflicts around open-ended change, as it is to a nation. The lesson is that self-organizing processes can produce controlled behavior even though no one is in control – sometimes the best thing a manager can do is to let go and allow things to happen.

Design the Use of Power

The distribution of power and the way in which it is used provide very important boundaries around the group learning process from which new strategic directions emerge. The application of power in particular forms has fairly predictable consequences for group dynamics. Where power is applied as force and consented to out of fear, the group dynamic will be one of submission, or where such power is not consented to, the group dynamic will be one of rebellion, either covert or overt. Power may be applied as authority, and the predictable group dynamic here is one in which members of the group suspend their critical faculties and accept instructions from those above them. Groups in states of submission, rebellion, or conformity are incapable of complex learning, that is, the development of new perspectives and new mental models.

The kind of group dynamics that are conducive to complex learning occur when highly competitive win/lose polarization is removed, and open questioning and public testing of assertions encouraged. When this happens, people use argument and conflict to move toward periodic consensus and commitment to a particular issue. That consensus and commitment cannot, however, be the norm when people are searching for new perspectives – rather, they must alternate between conflict and consensus, between confusion and clarity. This kind of dynamic is likely to occur when they most powerfully alternate the form in which they use their power: sometimes withdrawing and allowing conflict; sometimes intervening with suggestions; sometimes exerting authority.

Encourage Self-Organizing Groups

A group will be self-organizing only if it discovers its own challenges, goals, and objectives. Mostly, such groups need to form spontaneously – the role of top managers is simply to create the atmosphere in which this can happen. When top managers do set up a group to deal with strategic issues, however, they must avoid the temptation to write terms of reference, set objectives, or prod the group to reach some predetermined view. Instead top managers must present ambiguous challenges and take the chance that the group may produce proposals they do not approve of. For a group of managers to be self-organizing, it has to be free to operate as its members jointly choose, within the boundaries provided by their work together. This means that when they work together in this way, the normal hierarchy must be suspended for most of the time. Members are there because of the contributions they are able to make and the influence they can exert through those contributions and their own personalities. This suspension of the normal hierarchy can take place only if those on higher levels behave in a manner that indicates that they attach little importance to their position for the duration of the work of the group.

Provoke Multiple Cultures

One way of developing the conflicting countercultures required to provoke new perspectives is to rotate people between functions and business units. The motive here is to create cultural diversity as opposed to the current practice of using rotation to build a cadre of managers with the same management philosophy. Another effective way of promoting countercultures is that practiced by Canon and Honda, where significant numbers of managers are hired at the same time, midway through their careers in other organizations, to create sizeable pockets of different cultures that conflict with the predominant one.

Present Ambiguous Challenges Instead of Clear Long-Term Objectives or Visions

Agendas of strategic issues evolve out of the clash between different cultures in self-organizing groups. Top managers can provoke this activity by setting ambiguous challenges and presenting half-formed issues for others to develop, instead of trying to set clear long-term objectives. Problems without objectives should be intentionally posed to provoke the emotion and conflict that lead to active search for new ways of doing things. This activity of presenting challenges should also be a two-way one, where top executives hold themselves open to challenge from subordinates.

Expose the Business to Challenging Situations

Managers who avoid taking chances face the certainty of stagnation and therefore the high probability of collapse in the long term, simply because innovation depends significantly on chance. Running for cover because the future is unknowable is in the long run the riskiest response of all. Instead, managers must intentionally expose themselves to the most challenging of situations. In his study of international companies, Michael Porter concludes that those who position themselves to serve the world's most sophisticated and demanding customers, who seek the challenge of competing with the most imaginative and competent competitors, are the ones who build sustainable competitive advantage on a global scale.

Devote Explicit Attention to Improving Group Learning Skills

New strategic directions emerge when groups of managers learn together in the sense of questioning deeply held beliefs and altering existing mental models rather than simply absorbing existing bodies of knowledge and sets of techniques. Such a learning process may well be personally threatening and so arouse anxiety that leads to bizarre group dynamics – this is perhaps the major obstacle to effective organizational learning. To overcome it, managers must spend time explicitly exploring how they interact and learn together – the route to superior learning is self-reflection in groups.

Create Resource Slack

New strategic directions emerge when the attitudes and behavior of managers create an atmosphere favourable to individual initiative and intuition, to political interaction, and to learning in groups. Learning and political interaction are hard work, and they cannot occur without investment in spare management resources. A vital precondition for emergent strategy is thus investment in management resources to allow it to happen.

Conclusion

Practicing managers and academics have been debating the merits of organizational learning as opposed to the planning conceptualization of strategic management. That debate has not, however, focused clearly on the critical unquestioned assumptions upon which the planning approach is based, namely, the nature of causality. Recent discoveries about the nature of dynamic feedback systems make it clear that cause and effect links disappear in innovative human organizations, making it impossible to envision or plan their long-term futures. Because of this lack of causal connection between specific actions and specific outcomes, new strategic directions can only emerge through a spontaneous, self-organizing political and learning process. The planning approach can be seen as a specific approach applicable to the short-term management of an organization's existing activities, a task as vital as the development of a new strategic direction.

The Organizational Context in International Perspective

Chaos often breeds life, when order breeds habit.
(Henry Brooks Adams 1838–1919; American writer and historian)

Again it has become clear that there is little consensus within the field of strategic management. Views on the nature of the organizational context vary sharply. Even authors from one and the same country have contrasting opinions on the paradox of control and chaos. However, looking back on the articles in the sections on strategy process and strategy content, it is striking how few of the authors make a point of expounding their outlook on organizational malleability. The assumptions on which their theories are built are largely left implicit.

For this reason, it is difficult to identify whether there are national preferences when it comes to organizational context perspective. Yet, it seems not unlikely that strategists in different countries have different inclinations on this issue. In recent large-scale field work done by researchers at Cranfield Business School in the UK[20], significantly different 'leadership styles' were recognized among European executives. The predominant approach in Sweden and Finland was typified as the 'consensus' style (low power distance, low masculinity), while executives in Germany and Austria had a style that was labelled 'working towards a common goal' (specialists working together within a rule-bound structure). In France, the most popular style was 'managing from a distance' (focus on planning, high power distance), while executives from the UK, Ireland, and Spain preferred 'leading from the front.' This last leadership style, according to the researchers, relies 'on the belief that the charisma and skills of some particular individuals will lead to either the success or the failure of their organizations.' This finding suggests that the organizational leadership perspective will be more popular in these three countries (as well as in other 'Anglo-Saxon' and 'Latin' cultures), than in the rest of Europe. Other cross-cultural theorists also support this supposition.[21]

As an input to the debate whether there are international differences in perspective, we would like to put forward a number of factors that might be of influence on how the paradox of control and chaos is viewed in different countries. It should be noted, however, that these propositions are intended to encourage discussion and constitute only tentative explanations for cross-cultural differences in perspective. More specific international research is needed to give this debate a firm footing.

Locus of Control

This point can be kept short, as it was also raised in Chapter 8. People with an internal locus of control believe that they can shape events and have an impact on their environment. People with an external locus of control believe that they are caught up in events that they can hardly influence. Cross-cultural researchers have argued that cultures can differ significantly with regard to the perceived locus of control that is predominant among the population.

Obviously, in countries where the culture is more inclined towards an internal locus of control, it is reasonable to expect that the organizational leadership perspective will be more widespread. Managers in such 'just do it' cultures will be more strongly predisposed to believe that they can shape organizational circumstances. In cultures that are character-ized by a predominantly external locus of control, more support for the organizational dynamics perspective can be expected.

Level of Uncertainty Avoidance

A cultural characteristic related to the previous point, is the preference for order and structure that prevails in some countries. Hofstede[22] refers to this issue as uncertainty avoidance. In some cultures, there is a low tolerance for unstructured situations, poorly defined tasks and respon-sibilities, ambiguous relationships and unclear rules. People in these nations exhibit a distinct preference for order, predictability and security – they need to feel that things are 'in control'. In other cultures, however, people are less nervous about uncertain settings. The tolerance for situations that are 'unorganized', or 'self-organizing', is much higher – even in relatively chaotic circumstances, the call for 'law and order' will not be particularly strong. It can be expected that there will be a more pronounced preference for the organizational leadership perspective in countries that score high on uncertainty avoidance, than in nations with a low score.

Prevalence of Mechanistic Organizations

In Chapters 3 and 4, different international views on the nature of organizations were discussed. A simple distinction was made between mechanistic and organic conceptions of organizations. In the mechan-istic view, organizations exist as systems that are staffed with people, while in the organic view organizations exist as groups of people, into which some system has been brought.

When it comes to malleability, people taking a mechanistic view will see organizational leaders as mechanics – the organizational system can be redesigned, reengineered and restructured to pursue another course of action where necessary. Success will depend on leaders' design, engineering and structuring skills, and their ability to overcome resistance to change by the system's inhabitants. If a leader does not function well, a new one can be installed, and if employees are too resistant, they can be replaced. In countries where the mechanistic view of organizations is more predominant, a leaning towards the organizational leadership perspective can be expected.

People taking an organic view will see a leader as the head of the clan, bound by tradition and loyalty, but able to count on the emotional commitment of the members. Success in reshaping the organization will depend on reshaping the people – changing beliefs, ideas, visions, skills and interests. Important in reorienting and rejuvenating the organization is the leader's ability to challenge orthodox ideas, motivate people and manage the political processes. In countries where the organic view of organizations is more predominant, a leaning towards the organizational dynamics perspective can be expected.

Further Readings

Readers interested in pursuing the topics of leadership and organizational dynamics have a rich body of literature from which to choose. An excellent overview of the subject is provided by Sydney Finkelstein and Donald Hambrick, in their book *Strategic Leadership: Top Executives and Their Effects on Organizations*. Also highly recommended as overview of the leadership literature is *Bass and Stogdill's Handbook of Leadership*, by Bill Bass. In the category of more academically oriented works, the special issue of *Organization Studies* entitled 'Interpreting Organizational Leadership,' and edited by Susan Schneider gives a rich spectrum of ideas. The same is true for the special edition of the *Strategic Management Journal* entitled 'Strategic Leadership,' and edited by Donald Hambrick.

For more specific readings taking an organizational leadership perspective, the classics with which to start are John Kotter's *The General Managers* and Gordon Donaldson and Jay Lorsch's *Decision Making at the Top: The Shaping of Strategic Direction*. Good follow up readings are the book by Warren Bennis, *On Becoming a Leader*, and the book by Burt Nanus, *Visionary Leadership: Creating a Compelling Sense of Direction for Your Organization*. For leadership literature further away from the voluntarist extreme, readers are advised to turn to Peter Senge's book *The Fifth Discipline: The Art and Practice of the Learning Organization* and Edward Schein's *Organizational Culture and Leadership*. The book by Henry Sims and Peter Lorenzi, *The New Leadership Paradigm: Social Learning and Cognition in Organizations*, is also a challenging book, but not easy to read.

For a critical reaction to the leadership literature, Manfred Kets de Vries has many excellent contributions. His article 'The Leadership Mystique' is very good, as are his books with Danny Miller, entitled *The Neurotic Organization* and *Unstable at the Top*. Miller also has many thought-provoking works to his name, of which *The Icarus Paradox: How Excellent Companies Can Bring About Their Own Downfall* is highly recommended. In the more academic literature, stimulating commentaries are given in the articles 'The Romance of Leadership' by James Meindl, S. Ehrlich and J. Dukerich, and in 'The Ambiguity of Leadership,' by Jeffrey Pfeffer.

For a good reading highlighting the importance of organizational dynamics for both strategy process and strategy content, Ralph Stacey's book *Strategic Management and Organizational Dynamics* is a good place to start. Gerry Johnson's *Strategic Change and the Management Process* also provides provocative ideas about the relationship between strategy and the organizational context. Richard Pascale's *Managing on the Edge: How Successful Companies Use Conflict to Stay Ahead* is also stimulating reading. Finally, for the academically more adventurous, Joel Baum and Jitendra Singh's volume, *Evolutionary Dynamics of Organizations*, gives plenty of food for thought.

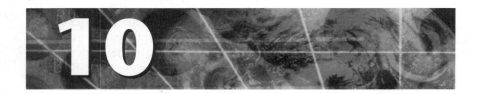

The International Context

You may say I'm a dreamer, but I'm not
the only one; I hope some day you'll join us,
and the world will live as one.

(John Lennon 1940–1980; British musician and songwriter)

When I am at Milan, I do as they do at
Milan; but when I go to Rome, I do as
Rome does.

(St. Augustine 354–430; Roman theologian and philosopher)

The Paradox of Globalization and Localization

Countries can differ from one another in may respects. They can vary with regard to consumer behavior, language, legal system, technological infrastructure, business culture, educational system, labor relations, political ideology, distribution structures and fiscal regime, to name just a few. The pluriformity of the international context is multi-faceted. Yet the question is how significant are these international differences? Do strategists need to adapt the organization's behavior to the international diversity encountered, or can strategists find ways of overcoming the constraints imposed by cross-border variety? This is one of the issues that will be discussed in this chapter.

A second issue with regard to the international context is that of *international linkages* – to what extent do events in one country have an impact on what happens in other countries? Countries might be quite different, yet developments in one nation might significantly influence developments elsewhere. For instance, if interest rates rise in the United States, this cannot be ignored by central bankers in most other countries. If the price of oil goes down on the spot market in Rotterdam, this will have a 'spill over effect' towards most other nations. And if a break-through chip technology is developed in Japan, this will send a shock-wave through the computer industry around the world. When a number of nations are tightly linked to one another in a particular area, this is referred to as *international integration*. If, on the other hand, there are very weak links between developments in one country and developments elsewhere, this is referred to as a situation of *international fragmentation*. The question for the strategist is how tightly linked are nations around the world? In the case of international fragmentation, a strategist can approach each country independently – as an isolated strategic issue. If nations are highly integrated, the strategist must view all countries as part of the same system – as squares on a chess board, not to be judged in isolation.

When looking at the variety and linkages within the international context, the question arises how these have been developing, and will develop further, over time. As might be expected by now, opinions on this matter, too, differ quite sharply. As in the previous debates, two opposite points of view can be identified, while many other strategists take up intermediate positions. On the one hand, there are strategists who believe that countries are becoming increasingly similar and more closely interrelated. This development towards lower international variety and tighter international linkages on a world-wide scale is referred to as the process of *globalization*. These strategists argue that globalization is already far advanced and will continue into the future, wiping out the importance of nations as it progresses. Therefore, it is wise to anticipate, and even encourage, a 'nationless' world. We shall refer to this point of view as the *global convergence* perspective. On the other hand, some strategists point out that important international differences will not change easily and that on many issues nations will not integrate with one another. In some circumstances, international variety might actually increase and international linkages might loosen, which is referred to as *localization*. Therefore, wise strategists should be willing to adapt them-selves to the complex variety and fragmentation that characterizes our world. We shall refer to this point of view as the *international diversity* perspective.

Hence, the debate in this chapter revolves around the current and future nature of the international context. Where are processes of globalization taking place, at what speed and with which consequences? And are there countercurrents of localization that need to be taken into account? While there are quite a few different answers to these questions, the discussion in this chapter will start by considering the two opposite poles in the debate, the global convergence and international diversity perspectives.

The Global Convergence Perspective

According to proponents of the global convergence perspective, the growing similarity and integration of the world can be argued by pointing to extensive economic statistics, showing significant rises in foreign direct investment and international trade. Yet, it is simpler to observe things directly around you. For instance, are you wearing clothing unique to your country, or could you mingle in an international crowd without standing out? Are the television you watch, the vehicle you drive, the telephone you use and the timepiece you wear specific to your nation, or based on the same technology and even produced by the same companies as those in other countries? Is the music you listen to made by local bands, unknown outside your country, or is this music also popular abroad? Is the food you eat unique to your region, or is even this served in other countries? Now compare your answers to what your parents would have answered 30 years ago – the difference is due to global convergence.

Global convergence, it is argued, is largely driven by the ease, low cost and frequency of international communication, transport and travel. This has diminished the importance of distance. In the past world of large distances, interactions between countries were few and international differences could develop in relative isolation. But the victory of technology over distance has created a 'global village', in which goods, services and ideas are easily exchanged, new developments spread quickly and the 'best practices' of one nation are rapidly copied in others. Once individuals and organizations interact with one another as if no geographic distances exist, an unstopable process towards cultural, political, technological and economic convergence is set in motion – countries will become more closely linked to one another and local differences will be superseded by new global norms.

Of course, in the short run there will still be international differences and nations will not be fully integrated into a 'world without borders'. Strategists taking a global convergence perspective acknowledge that such fundamental and wide ranging changes take time. There are numerous sources of inertia – e.g. vested interests, commitment to existing systems, emotional attachment to current habits, fear of change. The same type of change inhibitors could be witnessed during the industrial revolution, as well. Yet, these change inhibitors can only slow the pace of global convergence, not reverse its direction – the momentum caused by the shrinking of distance can only be braked, but not stopped. Therefore, firms thinking further than the short term should not let themselves be guided too much by current international diversity, but rather by the emerging global reality[1].

For individual firms, global convergence is changing the rules of the competitive game. In the past, most countries had their own distinct characteristics and there were few international economies of scale, while pressures to be locally responsive were high. But growing similarity between nations offers the enormous opportunity of leveraging resources across borders – e.g. production can be standardized to save costs, new product development can be done on an international scale to reduce the total investments required, and marketing knowledge can easily be exchanged to avoid reinventing the wheel in each country. In other words, growing international similarity allows firms to reap global scale economies through *standardization*.

Simultaneously, international integration facilitates the pursuit of global scale economies through *centralization*. Firms can centralize production in large-scale facilities at the most attractive locations, and supply world markets from there, unrestrained by international borders. In the same manner, all types of activities, such as R&D, marketing, sales and procurement, can be centralized to profit from world-wide economies of scale.

An equally important aspect of international integration is that suppliers, buyers and competitors can also increasingly operate as if there are no borders. The ability of buyers to shop around internationally makes the world one *global market*, in which global bargaining power is very important. The ability of suppliers and competitors to reap global economies of scale and sell everywhere around the world creates *global industries*, in which competition takes place on a world-wide stage, instead of in each nation separately. To deal with such global industries and global markets, the firm must be able to co-ordinate its strategy and activities across nations. In other words, firms must be capable of global *strategy alignment*.

These demands of standardization, centralization and alignment require a global firm, with a strong center responsible for the global strategy, instead of a federation of autonomous national subsidiaries focused on being responsive to their local circumstances. According to proponents of the global convergence perspective, such *global organizations*, or 'centralized hubs'[2], will become increasingly predominant over time. And as more companies switch to a global strategy and a global organizational form, this will in turn speed up the general process of globalization. By operating in a global fashion, these firms will actually contribute to a further decrease of international variety and fragmentation. In other words, globalizing companies are both the consequence and a major driver of further global convergence.

The International Diversity Perspective

To strategists taking an international diversity perspective, the 'brave new world' outlined above is largely science fiction. People around the world might be sporting a Swatch or a Rolex, munching Big Macs and drinking Coke, while sitting in their Toyota or Nissan, but to conclude that these are symptoms of global convergence is a leap of faith. Of course, there are some brand names and products more or less standardized around the world, and their numbers might actually be increasing. The question is whether these manufacturers are globalizing to meet increasing world-wide similarity, or whether they are actually finally utilizing the similarities between countries that have always existed. The actual level of international variety may really be quite consistent.

It is particularly important to recognize in which respects countries remain different. For instance, the world might be drinking the same soft drinks, but they are probably doing it in different places, at different times, under different circumstances and for different reasons in each country. The product might be standardized world-wide, but the cultural norms and values that influence its purchase and use remain diverse across countries. According to proponents of the international diversity perspective, it is precisely these fundamental aspects of culture that turn out to be extremely stable over time – habits change slowly, but cultural norms and values are outright rigid. Producers might be lucky to find one product that fits in with such cultural diversity, but it would be foolish to interpret this as world-wide cultural convergence.

Other national differences are equally resilient against the tides of globalization. No countries have recently given up their national language in favor of Esperanto or English. On the contrary, there has been renewed emphasis on the local language in many countries (e.g. Ireland and the Baltic countries) and regions (e.g. Catalonia and Quebec). In the same way, political systems have remained internationally diverse, with plenty of examples of localization, even within nations. For instance, in Russia and the US the shift of power to regional governments has increased policy diversity within the country. Similar arguments can be put forward for legal systems, fiscal regimes, educational systems and technological infrastructure – each is extremely difficult to change due to lock-in effects, vested interests, psychological commitment and complex decision-making processes. For each example of increasing similarity, a counterexample of local initiatives and growing diversity could be given. Some proponents of the international diversity perspective argue that it is exactly this interplay of divergence and convergence forces that creates a dynamic balance preserving diversity. While technologies, organizing principles, political trends and social habits disperse across borders, resulting in global convergence, new developments and novel systems in each nation arise causing international divergence[3]. Convergence trends are usually easier to spot than divergence – international dispersion can be more simply witnessed than new localized developments. To the casual observer, this might suggest that convergence trends have the upper hand, but after more thorough analysis, this conclusion must be cast aside.

Now add to this enduring international diversity the reality of international economic relations. Since World War II attempts have been made to facilitate the integration of national economies. There have been some regional successes (e.g. the North American Free Trade Association and the European Union) and some advances have been made on a world-wide scale (e.g. the World Trade Organization). However, progress has been slow and important political barriers remain.

The continued existence of international diversity and political obstacles, it is argued, will limit the extent to which nations can become fully integrated into one borderless world. International differences and barriers to trade and investment will frustrate firms' attempts to standardize and centralize, and will place a premium on firms' abilities to adapt and decentralize. Of course, there will be some activities for which global economies of scale can be achieved and for which strategy alignment is needed, but this will not become true for all activities. Empowering national managers to be responsive to specific local conditions will remain an important ingredient for international success. Balancing globalization and localization of the firm's activities will continue to be a requirement in the future international context.

Ideally, the internationally operating company should neither deny nor regret the existence of international diversity, but regard it as an opportunity that can be exploited. Each country's unique circumstances will pose different challenges, requiring the development of different competences. Different national 'climates' will create opportunities for different innovations. If a company can tap into each country's opportunities and leverage the acquired competences and innovations to other countries, this could offer the company an important source of competitive advantage. Naturally, these locally-leveraged competences and innovations would subsequently need to be adapted to the specific circumstances in other countries. This balancing act would require an organization that combined strong local responsiveness with the ability to exchange and coordinate internationally, even on a world-wide scale (globally-networked). International organizations blending these two elements are referred to as *transnational*[4], or *heterarchical*[5].

The question for the field of strategic management is, therefore, whether the international context is moving towards similarity and integration, or will it remain as diverse and fragmented as at the moment? Should strategists anticipate and encourage global convergence by emphasizing global standardization, centralization and strategy alignment, or should strategists acknowledge and exploit international diversity by emphasizing local adaptation, decentralization and international networking? In short, strategists must wrestle with the paradox of globalization and localization (see Table 10.1).

Defining the Issues: Dimensions and Subjects

Globalization is a term used by many, but specified by few. This lack of definition often leads to an unfocused debate, as different people employ the same term, but actually refer to different phenomena. To have a more structured debate, the term globalization (and its opposite, localization) needs to be explored and a broad common definition needs to be established. This stage-setting work will concentrate on two key questions, namely, globalization *dimensions* (what does globalization encompass?) and globalization *subjects* (what actually globalizes?).

TABLE 10.1
Global convergence versus international diversity perspective

	Global Convergence Perspective	International Diversity Perspective
Emphasis on	Globalization over localization	Localization over globalization
International variety	Growing similarity	Remaining diversity
International linkages	Growing integration	Remaining fragmentation
Major drivers	Technology and communication	Cultural and institutional inertia
Diversity and fragmentation	Costly, convergence can be encouraged	Reality, can be exploited
Strategic focus	Global-scale efficiency	Local responsiveness
Organizational preference	Standardize/centralize unless	Adapt/decentralize unless
Innovation process	Center-for-global	Locally-leveraged
Organizational structure	Global (centralized hub)	Transnational (globally-networked)

Globalization as Increasing International Scope, Similarity and Integration

Clearly, globalization refers to the process of becoming more global. But what is global? Although there is not full agreement on a single definition, most writers use the term to refer to one or more of the following elements:

- *International scope.* 'Global' can simply mean world-wide. For instance, a firm with operations around the world can be labeled a global company, to distinguish it from firms that are national (local) or regional in scope. In such a case, the term 'global' is primarily intended to describe the *spatial* dimension – the broadest possible international scope is to be global. When this definition of global is employed, globalization is the process of international expansion on a world-wide scale.

- *International similarity.* 'Global' can also refer to homogeneity around the world. For instance, if a company decides to sell the same product in all of its international markets, it is often referred to as a global product, as opposed to a locally-tailored product. In such a case, the term 'global' is primarily intended to describe the *variance* dimension – the ultimate level of international similarity is to be global. When this definition of global is employed, globalization is the process of declining international variety.

- *International integration.* 'Global' can also refer to the world as one tightly-linked system. For instance, a global market can be said to exist if events in one country are significantly impacted by events in other geographic markets. This is as opposed to local markets, where price levels, competition, demand and fashions are hardly influenced by developments in other nations. In such a case, the term 'global' is primarily intended to describe the *linkages* dimension – the ultimate level of international integration is to be global. When this definition of global is employed, globalization is the process of increasing international interconnectedness.

So, is for example McDonald's a global company? That depends along which of the above three dimensions the company is measured. When judging the international scope of McDonald's, it can be seen that the company is globalizing, but far from global. The company operates in approximately half the countries in the world, but in many of these only in one or a few large cities. Of McDonald's world-wide revenues, more than half is still earned in the United States. This predominance of the home country is even stronger if the composition of the company's top management is looked at. However, when judging McDonald's along the dimension of international similarity, it is simple to observe that the company is relatively global, as it takes a highly standardized approach to most markets around the world. Still, it should be noted that on some aspects as menu and interior design there is leeway for local adaptation.

Finally, when judging McDonald's along the dimension of international integration, the company is only slightly global, as it is not very tightly linked around the world. Some activities are centralized or coordinated, but in general there is relatively little need for concerted action.

In this chapter, all three possible dimensions of globalization will be examined. The opposites – localization as decreasing international scope, similarity and integration – will also be discussed. The reader is advised, however, to consider which dimension of globalization or localization each of the contributing authors place centrally in their analyses.

Globalization of Companies, Businesses and Economies

The second factor complicating the debate on the nature of the international context is that the concept of globalization is applied to a variety of subjects, while the differences are often not made explicit. Some people discuss globalization as a development in the economy at large, while others debate globalization as something potentially happening to industries, markets, products, technologies, fashions, production, competition and organizations. For the reader it is essential to identify the actual subject(s) under discussion. In general, debates on globalization tend to concentrate on one of three levels of analysis:

■ *Globalization of companies*. Some authors focus on the *micro* level, debating whether individual companies are becoming more global. Issues are the extent to which firms have a global strategy, structure, culture, workforce, management team and resource base. In more detail, the globalization of specific products and value-adding activities is often discussed. Here it is of particular importance to acknowledge that the globalization of one product or activity (e.g. marketing) does not necessarily entail the globalization of all others[6].

■ *Globalization of businesses*. Other authors are more concerned with the *meso* level, debating whether particular businesses are becoming more global. Here it is important to distinguish those who emphasize the globalization of markets, as opposed to those accentuating the globalization of industries (see Chapter 5 for this distinction). The issue of globalizing markets has to do with the growing similarity of world-wide *customer demand* and the growing ease of world-wide product flows. For example, the crude oil and foreign currency markets are truly global – the same commodities are traded at the same rates around the world. The markets for accountancy and hairdressing services, on the other hand, are very local – demand differs significantly, there is little cross-border trade and consequently prices vary sharply. The globalization of industries is quite a different issue, as it has to do with the emergence of a set of *producers* that compete with one another on a world-wide scale[7]. So, for instance, the automobile and consumer electronics industries are quite global – the major players in most countries belong to the same set of companies that compete against each other all around the world. Even the accountancy industry is relatively global, even though the markets for accountancy services are very local. On the other hand, the construction and retail banking industries are very local – the competitive scene in each country is relatively uninfluenced by competitive developments elsewhere.

- *Globalization of economies.* Yet other authors take a *macro* level of analysis, arguing whether or not the world's economies in general are experiencing a convergence trend. Many authors are interested in the macro economic dynamics of international integration and its consequences in terms of growth, employment, inflation, productivity, trade and foreign direct investment[8]. Others focus more on the political realities constraining and encouraging globalization[9]. Yet others are interested in the underlying dynamics of technological, institutional and organizational convergence[10]. None of these authors has been included in this chapter, but it should be noted that the discussions at this level of analysis are also important to the debate on the future of the international context.

Ultimately, the question in this chapter is not only whether economies, businesses and companies are actually globalizing, but whether these developments are a matter of choice. In other words, is global convergence or continued international diversity an uncontrollable evolutionary development to which firms (and governments) must comply, or can firms actively influence the globalization or localization of their environment?

EXHIBIT 10.1
IKEA case

IKEA: GLOBALIZATION BY DESIGN?

IKEA's bright yellow and blue home furnishing stores have become a common sight in most Western countries. With more than 125 stores in 25 countries, frequented by over 120 million people spending approximately $4.5 billion each year, IKEA is the world's largest home furnishing retailer. Their strong international presence is even more remarkable when compared to competitors and retailers in general. Retailing is a very local industry, with only a handful of companies that have successfully branched out to foreign markets, and in the home furnishings segment IKEA is virtually the only international player.

IKEA's success formula has remained surprisingly constant over the years, ever since founder Ingvar Kamprad set up a warehouse showroom in a disused factory in Almhult, Sweden, in 1953. Then, as now, furniture retailing was highly fragmented, split between department stores and small family-owned shops. Market power was in the hands of the furniture manufacturers and prices were high. Kamprad aimed to counter this situation and decided 'to offer a wide range of home furnishing items of good design and function at prices so low, that the majority of people can afford to buy them'. IKEA's way of achieving this was highly innovative. Instead of pushing a manufacturer's traditional wares, IKEA discussed with new and open-minded suppliers what types of products it could sell and at what prices. Manufacturers were encouraged to switch from hand-crafted items made of expensive woods, to mass-produced basic furniture of good quality, using local inexpensive softwoods such as pine and spruce, and new wood-based materials such as plywood and particle boards. Such pieces of furniture IKEA could sell in large quantities at low prices.

Long-term production agreements are still a hallmark of the IKEA concept. IKEA does not 'shop around for deals', but has established close relationships with more than 2000 suppliers around the world. These long-term partners are supported by IKEA when needed, but are also required to adapt to IKEA specifications and be very responsive to IKEA's needs. This is particularly important because the design and engineering of most products is carried out by IKEA itself in Sweden. Almost all of the 20,000 product items carried by IKEA have been specifically designed by or for the company. And all share a typical Scandinavian design – simple elegance achieved by clear lines and natural materials.

This is probably one of the most interesting aspects of IKEA's expansion outside of Scandinavia, which started in 1973, when the company entered the Swiss market. Although internationalizing, IKEA has remained quintessentially Swedish. Most products are of Swedish design, all have Swedish names, the store restaurants serve Swedish food and the company culture strongly reflects such Swedish values as equality, honesty, openness, modesty, reliability and simplicity. The company's home market provides IKEA with both image and identity – towards the marketplace IKEA's Swedishness is employed as a distinctive quality, while internally it provides much of the cultural glue keeping the company together. Approximately 90 percent of senior managers around the world are Swedes. The current CEO Anders Moberg is very clear about the importance of the Swedish culture within the organization: 'I would advise any foreign employee who really wants to advance in this company to learn Swedish. They will then get a completely different feeling for our culture, our mood, our values. We encourage them to have as much contact with Sweden as possible, for instance by going there for their holidays.'

One important reflection of the Swedish egalitarian culture is that there are only four levels of management separating Moberg from Willy the stockboy, even though IKEA employs more than 27,000 people. The company is flat, open and informal. Employees are encouraged to take initiatives and creatively challenge the status quo. IKEA managers operate with a large measure of autonomy from headquarters. The Swedish emphasis on ethical behavior is also highly valued and is expressed in such conduct as rigorous product safety measures, environmental responsibility and employment conditions.

IKEA's store formula reflects many of these qualities. While the aircraft-hangar-sized stores benefit from scale efficiencies, IKEA has been able to create a quality atmosphere through human-scale dimensions in the store lay-out. Visiting an IKEA store is intended to be more like a day out than a shopping trip. Fun and excitement for the entire family are paramount – there are play areas for the kids, changing rooms for babies, and a family restaurant. Customers are lead by a one-way lay-out through the entire store, past articles that are either self-service (can be taken off the self) or full-service (can be picked up on the way out from the warehouse). If necessary, customers can find assistance at information desks, but pay when exiting the store through supermarket-style check-outs. IKEA stores are normally situated outside cities on cheap land, but close to major roads and with plenty of space for parking, so that customers can easily transport most items home in their own vehicle (delivery is available for a fee). Transportation is made easy by presenting most furniture as flat-packs, that is, in its unassembled state. This also saves IKEA labor-intensive assembly and the cost of shipping and storing air.

Within the international organization the functions of purchasing, and product range and development are strongly controlled by headquarters. The functions of physical distribution and retailing are regionally divided (Northern Europe, Southern Europe, East Central Europe, North America, Australasia). Within this structure the Market Unit North America has a special status, due to the need to do things differently on the other side of the Atlantic. When IKEA first entered the American market in 1985, the American stores were set up and run in the same way as the European stores. Most of the products were also sourced from European suppliers. But after five years and five new stores, operations were still not breaking even. Then in 1991 the US dollar strongly depreciated and IKEA's low cost position became threatened. After a thorough diagnosis, Moberg concluded that IKEA had been 'behaving like all Europeans, as exporters, which meant that we are not really in the country.' Supply lines from Europe to the US were too long and too currency dependent, and many products clashed with American standards and tastes. For instance, all products were made in metric sizes and often did not fit with other American products (e.g. kitchens did not fit with appliances, beds did not fit customer's sheets). Many products were also too small (e.g. beds and kitchen cupboards were perceived as too narrow and glasses as too small). To remedy this situation, the new US chief executive Goran Carstedt was given more autonomy and he quickly moved to more closely adapt to US practices and by 1994 about half of IKEA's furniture sales were locally produced.

Now IKEA wants to grow further by moving to markets outside the western industrialized group of nations. In particular, Moberg believes that South-East Asia and Eastern Europe represent an enormous potential for IKEA. Moberg's vision is to gradually transform the company into a more global player. One of the first moves he has announced is the opening of ten stores in mainland China. This might seem like a radical step in the dark, but IKEA has gained some indirect experience in Asia, through a number of franchise stores in Hong Kong (6), Taiwan (1) and Singapore (1). In these markets IKEA is perceived as very Western and very trendy, and they have been able to lure young urban professionals into the stores. These experiences, together with the existing contacts with Chinese suppliers, have now emboldened IKEA to set up fully owned stores in mainland China. Yet the question is whether this move is foresight or fallacy. If global convergence is truly happening, IKEA might be at its forefront, actually even speeding up the process. Of course, IKEA would still need to make adjustments to the local circumstances, but it could transplant most of the IKEA formula to non-Western countries and benefit from being the first global home furnishing retailer. However, if international diversity remains high, IKEA will have to make enormous adaptations to its formula to be successful in China – possibly to the extent that one might wonder whether they will bring any competitive advantage with them at all. IKEA's entry into China might be an open invitation for local competitors to copy those aspects of IKEA's concept that are transferable, while retaining their stronger local responsiveness. Therefore the question facing IKEA is whether to enter China at all, and if they do choose to do so, whether they should take a more globally-integrated or locally-responsive approach.

Sources: *Financial Times*, various issues; *The Economist*, November 19 1994[11].

The Debate and the Readings

The international context has long been a topic receiving significant academic attention. It was not until the early 1980s, however, that the subject of globalization developed into a full-fledged debate at the center of strategic management. The article that has probably been the most influential at focusing this debate, by boldly advocating a global convergence perspective, has been 'The Globalization of Markets' by Theodore Levitt[12]. For this reason, Levitt's forceful article has been selected as the opening essay in this chapter, representing the global convergence perspective. In this contribution, Levitt provocatively predicts that the world is quickly moving towards a converging commonality. He believes that 'the world's needs and desires have been irrevocably homogenized.' The force driving this process is technology, which has facilitated communication, transport and travel, while allowing for the development of superior products at low prices. His conclusion is that 'the commonality of preference leads inescapably to the standardization of products, manufacturing, and the institutions of trade and commerce.' The old-fashioned multinational corporation, that adapted itself to local circumstances, is 'obsolete and the global corporation absolute.'

While a clear proponent of the global convergence perspective, it should be noted that Levitt's inspired prediction of global convergence is focused on the globalization of *markets*. In particular, he is intent on pointing out that converging consumer demand in international markets facilitates – even necessitates – the reaping of economies of scale through the standardization of products, marketing and production. With this emphasis on the demand side, Levitt pays far less attention to the supply side – the globalization of industries and the competition within industries – which other global convergence proponents tend to accentuate. And although he strongly advises companies to become 'global corporations,' he does not further detail what a global company should look like. Overall, Levitt views globalization more as growing international similarity, while paying less attention to the possibility of growing international integration, as some other authors do.

As a direct response to 'the sweeping and somewhat polemic character' of Levitt's argumentation, Susan Douglas and Yoram Wind have written 'The Myth of Globalization,'[13] that has been selected as representative of the international diversity perspective. Douglas and Wind believe that many of the assumptions underlying Levitt's global standardization philosophy are contradicted by the facts. They argue that the convergence of customer needs is not a one way street; *divergence* trends are also noticeable. Furthermore, they believe that Levitt is mistaken in arguing that economies of scale in production and marketing is an irreversible force driving globalization. According to Douglas and Wind, many new technologies have actually lowered the minimum efficient scale of operation, while there are also plenty of industries where economies of scale are not an important issue. The authors conclude by outlining the specific circumstances under which a strategy of global standardization might be effective. Under all other circumstances, Douglas and Wind reiterate, the international strategist will have to deal with the existence of international diversity and search for the right balance between global standardization and local adaptation.

Although these two debate articles only deal with the globalization of markets, they are quite representative of the broader debate going on among strategists. Therefore, they confront readers with the need to come to terms with the paradox of globalization and localization.

Reading 1   The Globalization of Markets

By Theodore Levitt[†]

A powerful force drives the world toward a converging commonality, and that force is technology. It has proletarianized communication, transport, and travel. It has made isolated places and impoverished peoples eager for modernity's allurements. Almost everyone everywhere wants all the things they have heard about, seen, or experienced via the new technologies.

The result is a new commercial reality – the emergence of global markets for standardized consumer products on a previously unimagined scale of magnitude. Corporations geared to this new reality benefit from enormous economies of scale in production, distribution, marketing, and management. By translating these benefits into reduced world prices, they can decimate competitors that still live in the disabling grip of old assumptions about how the world works.

Gone are accustomed differences in national or regional preference. Gone are the days when a company could sell last year's models – or lesser versions of advanced products – in the less developed world. And gone are the days when prices, margins, and profits abroad were generally higher than at home.

The globalization of markets is at hand. With that, the multinational commercial world nears its end, and so does the multinational corporation.

The multinational and the global corporation are not the same thing. The multinational corporation operates in a number of countries, and adjusts its products and practices in each – at high relative costs. The global corporation operates with resolute constancy – at low relative cost – as if the entire world (or major regions of it) were a single entity; it sells the same things in the same way everywhere.

Which strategy is better is not a matter of opinion but of necessity. World-wide communications carry everywhere the constant drumbeat of modern possibilities to lighten and enhance work, raise living standards, divert, and entertain. The same countries that ask the world to recognize and respect the individuality of their cultures insist on the wholesale transfer to them of modern goods, services, and technologies. Modernity is not just a wish but also a widespread practice among those who cling, with unyielding passion or religious fervor, to ancient attitudes and heritages.

Who can forget the televized scenes during the 1979 Iranian uprisings of young men in fashionable French-cut trousers and silky body shirts thirsting with raised modern weapons for blood in the name of Islamic fundamentalism?

In Brazil, thousands swarm daily from preindustrial Bahian darkness into exploding coastal cities, there quickly to install television sets in crowded corrugated huts and, next to battered Volkswagens, make sacrificial offerings of fruit and fresh-killed chickens to Macumban spirits by candlelight.

A thousand suggestive ways attest to the ubiquity of the desire for the most advanced things that the world makes and sells – goods of the best quality and reliability at the lowest price. The world's needs and desires have been irrevocably homogenized. This makes the multinational corporation obsolete and the global corporation absolute.

Living in the Republic of Technology

Daniel J. Boorstin, author of the monumental trilogy *The Americans*, characterized our age as driven by 'the Republic of Technology (whose) supreme law . . . is convergence, the tendency for everything to become more like everything else.'

In business, this trend has pushed markets toward global commonality. Corporations sell standardized products in the same way everywhere – autos, steel, chemicals, petroleum, cement, agricultural commodities and equipment, industrial and commercial construction, banking and insurance services, computers, semiconductors, transport, electronic instruments, pharmaceuticals, and telecommunications, to mention some of the obvious.

Nor is the sweeping gale of globalization confined to these raw material or high-tech products, where the universal language of customers and users facilitates standardization. The transforming winds whipped up by the proletarianization of communication and travel enter every crevice of life.

Commercially, nothing confirms this as much as the success of McDonald's from the Champs Elysées to the Ginza, of Coca-Cola in Bahrain and Pepsi-Cola in Moscow, and of rock music, Greek salad, Hollywood movies, Revlon cosmetics, Sony televisions, and Levi jeans everywhere. 'High-touch' products are as ubiquitous as high-tech.

Starting from opposing sides, the high-tech and the high-touch ends of the commercial spectrum gradually consume the undistributed middle in their cosmopolitan orbit. No one is exempt and nothing can stop the process. Everywhere everything gets more and more like everything else as the world's preference structure is relentlessly homogenized.

Consider the cases of Coca-Cola and Pepsi-Cola, which are globally standardized products sold everywhere and welcomed by everyone. Both successfully cross multitudes of national, regional, and ethnic taste buds trained to a variety of deeply ingrained local preferences of taste, flavor, consistency, effervescence, and aftertaste. Everywhere both sell well. Cigarettes, too, especially American-made, make year-to-year global inroads in territories previously held in the firm grip of other, mostly local, blends.

These are not exceptional examples. (Indeed their global reach would be even greater were it not for artificial trade barriers.) They exemplify a general drift toward the homogenization of the world and how companies distribute, finance, and price products. Nothing is exempt. The products and methods of the industrialized world play a single tune for all the world, and all the world eagerly dances to it.

Ancient differences in national tastes or modes of doing business disappear. The commonality of preference leads inescapably to the standardization of products, manufacturing, and the institutions of trade and commerce. Small nation-based markets transmogrify and expand. Success in world competition turns on efficiency in production, distribution, marketing, and management, and inevitably becomes focused on price.

The most effective world competitors incorporate superior quality and reliability into their cost structures. They sell in all national markets the same kind of products sold at home or in their largest export market. They compete on the basis of appropriate value – the best combinations of price, quality, reliability, and delivery for products that are globally identical with respect to design, function, and even fashion.

That, and little else, explains the surging success of Japanese companies dealing world-wide in a vast variety of products – both tangible products like steel, cars, motorcycles, hi-fi equipment, farm machinery, robots, microprocessors, carbon fibers, and now even textiles, and intangibles like banking, shipping, general contracting, and soon computer software. Nor are high-quality and low-cost operations incompatible, as a host of consulting organizations and data engineers argue with vigorous vacuity. The reported data are incomplete, wrongly analyzed, and contradictory. The truth is that low-cost operations are the hallmark of corporate cultures that require and produce quality in all that they do. High quality and low costs are not opposing postures. They are compatible, twin identities of superior practice.

To say that Japan's companies are not global because they export cars with left-side drives to the United States and the European continent, while those in Japan have right-side drives, or because they sell office machines through distributors in the United States but directly at home, or speak Portuguese in Brazil is to mistake a difference for a distinction. The same is true of Safeway and Southland retail chains operating effectively in the Middle East, and to not only native but also imported populations from Korea, the Philippines, Pakistan, India, Thailand, Britain, and the United States. National rules of the road differ, and so do distribution channels and languages. Japan's distinction is its unrelenting push for economy and value enhancement. That translates into a drive for standardization at high quality levels.

Vindication of the Model T

If a company forces costs and prices down and pushes quality and reliability up – while maintaining reasonable concern for suitability – customers will prefer its world-standardized products. The theory holds at this stage in the evolution of globalization, no matter what conventional market research and even common sense may suggest about different national and regional tastes, preferences, needs, and institutions. The Japanese have repeatedly vindicated this theory, as did Henry Ford with the Model T. Most important, so have their imitators, including companies from South Korea (television sets and heavy construction), Malaysia (personal calculators and microcomputers), Brazil (auto parts and tools), Colombia (apparel), Singapore (optical equipment), and yes, even from the United States (office copiers, computers, bicycles, castings), Western Europe (automatic washing machines), Rumania (housewares), Hungary (apparel), Yugoslavia (furniture), and Israel (pagination equipment).

Of course, large companies operating in a single nation or even a single city don't standardize everything they make, sell, or do. They have product lines instead of a single product version, and multiple distribution channels. There are neighborhood, local, regional, ethnic, and institutional differences, even within metropolitan areas. But although companies customize products for particular market segments, they know that success in a world with homogenized demand requires a search for sales opportunities in similar segments across the globe in order to achieve the economies of scale necessary to compete.

Such a search works because a market segment in one country is seldom unique; it has close cousins everywhere precisely because technology has homogenized the globe. Even small local segments have their global equivalents everywhere and become subject to global competition, especially on price.

The global competitor will seek constantly to standardize his offering everywhere. He will digress from this standardization only after exhausting all possibilities to retain it, and he will push for reinstatement of standardization whenever digression and divergence have occurred. He will never assume that the customer is a king who knows his own wishes.

Trouble increasingly stalks companies that lack clarified global focus and remain inattentive to the economics of simplicity and standardization. The most endangered companies in the rapidly evolving world tend to be those that dominate rather small domestic markets with high value-added products for which there are smaller markets elsewhere. With transportation costs proportionately low, distant competitors will enter the now-sheltered markets of those companies with goods produced more cheaply under scale-efficient conditions. Global competition spells the end of domestic territoriality, no matter how diminutive the territory may be.

When the global producer offers his lower costs internationally, his patronage expands exponentially. He not only reaches into distant markets, but also attracts customers who previously held to local preferences and now capitulate to the attractions of lesser prices. The strategy of standardization not only responds to world-wide homogenized markets but also expands those markets with aggressive low pricing. The new technological juggernaut taps an ancient motivation – to make one's money go as far as possible. This is universal – not simply a motivation but actually a need.

The Hedgehog Knows

The difference between the hedgehog and the fox, wrote Sir Isaiah Berlin in distinguishing between Dostoevski and Tolstoy, is that the fox knows a lot about a great many things, but the hedgehog knows everything about one great thing. The multinational corporation knows a lot about a great many countries and congenially adapts to supposed differences. It willingly accepts vestigial national differences, not questioning the possibility of their transformation, not recognizing how the world is ready and eager for the benefit of modernity, especially when the price is right. The multinational corporation's accommodating mode to visible national differences is medieval.

By contrast, the global corporation knows everything about one great thing. It knows about the absolute need to be competitive on a world-wide basis as well as nationally and seeks constantly to drive down prices by standardizing what it sells and how it operates. It treats the world as composed of few standardized markets rather than many customized markets. It actively seeks and vigorously works toward global convergence. Its mission is modernity and its mode, price competition, even when it sells top-of-the-line, high-end products. It knows about the one great thing all nations and people have in common: scarcity.

Nobody takes scarcity lying down; everyone wants more. This in part explains division of labor and specialization of production. They enable people and nations to optimize their conditions through trade. The median is usually money.

Experience teaches that money has three special qualities: scarcity, difficulty of acquisition, and transience. People understandably treat it with respect. Everyone in the increasingly homogenized world market wants products and features that everybody else wants. If the price is low enough, they will take highly standardized world products, even if these aren't exactly what mother said was suitable, what immemorial custom decreed was right, or what market-research fabulists asserted was preferred.

The implacable truth of all modern production – whether of tangible or intangible goods – is that large-scale production of standardized items is generally cheaper within a wide range of volume than small-scale production. Some argue that CAD/CAM (computer aided design/computer aided manufacturing) will allow companies to manufacture customized products on a small scale – but cheaply. But the argument misses the point. If a company treats the world as one or two distinctive product markets, it can serve the world more economically than if it treats it as three, four, or five product markets.

Different cultural preferences, national tastes and standards, and business institutions are vestiges of the past. Some inheritances die gradually; others prosper and expand into mainstream global preferences. So-called ethnic markets are a good example. Chinese food, pitta bread, country and western music, pizza, and jazz are everywhere. They are market segments that exist in world-wide proportions. They don't deny or contradict global homogenization but confirm it.

Many of today's differences among nations as to products and their features actually reflect the respectful accommodation of multinational corporations to what they believe are fixed local preferences. They believe preferences are fixed, not because they are but because of rigid habits of thinking about what actually is. Most executives in multinational corporations are thoughtlessly accommodating. They falsely presume that marketing means giving the customer what he says he wants rather than trying to understand exactly what he'd like. So they persist with high-cost, customized multinational products and practices instead of pressing hard and pressing properly for global standardization.

I do not advocate the systematic disregard of local or national differences. But a company's sensitivity to such differences does not require that it ignore the possibilities of doing things differently or better.

With persistence and appropriate means, barriers against superior technologies and economics have always fallen. There is no recorded exception where reasonable effort has been made to overcome them. It is very much a matter of time and effort.

A Failure in Global Imagination

Many companies have tried to standardize world practice by exporting domestic products and processes without accommodation or change – and have failed miserably. Their deficiencies have been seized on as evidence of bovine stupidity in the face of abject impossibility. Advocates of global standardization see them as examples of failures in execution.

In fact, poor execution is often an important cause. More important, however, is failure of nerve – failure of imagination.

Consider the case for the introduction of fully automatic home laundry equipment in Western Europe at a time when few homes had even semiautomatic machines.

The growing success of small, low-powered, low-speed, low-capacity, low-priced Italian machines, even against the preferred but highly priced and highly promoted brand in West Germany, was significant. It contained a powerful message that was lost on managers confidently wedded to a distorted version of the marketing concept according to which you give the customer what he says he wants. In fact the customers said they wanted certain features, but their behavior demonstrated they'd take other features provided the price and the promotion were right.

In this case it was obvious that under prevailing conditions, people preferred a low-priced automatic over any kind of manual or semi-automatic machine and certainly over higher priced automatics, even though the low-priced automatics failed to fulfil all their expressed preferences. The supposedly meticulous and demanding German consumers violated all expectations by buying the simple, low-priced Italian machines.

This case illustrates how the perverse practice of the marketing concept and the absence of any kind of marketing imagination let multi-national attitudes survive when customers actually want the benefits of global standardization. People were asked what features they wanted in a washing machine rather than what they wanted out of life. Selling a line of products individually tailored to each nation is thoughtless. Managers who took pride in practicing the marketing concept to the fullest did not, in fact, practice it at all. Data do not yield information except with the intervention of the mind. Information does not yield meaning except with the intervention of imagination.

Cracking the Code of Western Markets

Since the theory of the marketing concept emerged a quarter of a century ago, the more managerially advanced corporations have been eager to offer what customers clearly want rather than what is merely convenient. They have created marketing departments supported by professional market researchers of awesome and often costly proportions. And they have proliferated extraordinary numbers of operations and product lines – highly tailored products and delivery systems for many different markets, market segments, and nations.

Significantly, Japanese companies operate almost entirely without marketing departments or market research of the kind so prevalent in the West. Yet, in the colorful words of General Electric's chairman John F. Welch Jr., the Japanese, coming from a small cluster of resource-poor islands, with an entirely alien culture and an almost impenetrably complex language, have cracked the code of Western markets. They have done it not by looking with mechanistic thoroughness at the way markets are different but rather by searching for meaning with a deeper wisdom. They have discovered the one great thing all markets have in common – an overwhelming desire for dependable, world-standard modernity in all things, at aggressively low prices. In response, they deliver irresistible value everywhere, attracting people with products that market-research technocrats described with superficial certainty as being unsuitable and uncompetitive.

The wider a company's global reach, the greater the number of regional and national preferences it will encounter for certain product features, distribution systems, or promotional media. There will always need to be some accommodation to differences.

In its highly successful introduction of Contac 600 (the timed-release decongestant) into Japan, SmithKline Corporation used 35 wholesalers instead of the 1000-plus that established practice required. Daily contacts with the wholesalers and key retailers, also in violation of established practice, supplemented the plan, and it worked.

Denied access to established distribution institutions in the United States, Komatsu, the Japanese manufacturer of lightweight farm machinery, entered the market through over-the-road construction equipment dealers in rural areas of the Sunbelt, where farms are smaller, the soil sandier and easier to work. Here inexperienced distributors were able to attract customers on the basis of Komatsu's product and price appropriateness.

In cases of successful challenge to prevailing institutions and practices, a combination of product reliability and quality, strong and sustained support systems, aggressively low prices, and sales-compensation packages, as well as audacity and implacability, circumvented, shattered, and transformed very different distribution systems. Instead of resentment, there was admiration.

The differences that persist throughout the world despite its globalization affirm an ancient dictum of economics – that things are driven by what happens at the margin, not at the core. Thus, in ordinary competitive analysis, what's important is not the average price but the marginal price, what happens not in the usual case but at the interface of newly erupting conditions. What counts in commercial affairs is what happens at the cutting edge. What is most striking today is the underlying similarities of what is happening now to national preferences at the margin. These similarities at the cutting edge cumulatively form an overwhelming, predominant commonality everywhere.

To refer to the persistence of economic nationalism (protective and subsidized trade practices, special tax aids, or restrictions for home market producers) as a barrier to the globalization of markets is to make a valid point. Economic nationalism does have a powerful persistence. But, as with the present almost totally smooth internationalization of investment capital, the past alone does not shape or predict the future.

Reality is not a fixed paradigm, dominated by immemorial customs and derived attitudes, heedless of powerful and abundant new forces. The world is becoming increasingly informed about the liberating and enhancing possibilities of modernity. The persistence of the inherited varieties of national preferences rests uneasily on increasing evidence of, and restlessness regarding, their inefficiency, costliness, and confinement. The historic past, and the national differences respecting commerce and industry it spawned and fostered everywhere, is now subject to relatively easy transformation.

Cosmopolitanism is no longer the monopoly of the intellectual and leisure classes; it is becoming the established property and defining characteristic of all sectors everywhere in the world. Gradually and irresistibly it breaks down the walls of economic insularity, nationalism, and chauvinism. What we see today as escalating commercial nationalism is simply the last violent death rattle of an obsolete institution.

The successful global corporation does not abjure customization or differentiation for the requirements of markets that differ in product preferences, spending patterns, shopping preferences, and institutional or legal arrangements. But the global corporation accepts and adjusts to these differences only reluctantly, only after relentlessly testing their immutability, after trying in various ways to circumvent and reshape them.

Reading 2   The Myth of Globalization

By Susan Douglas and Yoram Wind[†]

In recent years, globalization has become a key theme in every discussion of international strategy. Proponents of the philosophy of 'global' products and brands, such as Professor Theodore Levitt of Harvard, and the highly successful advertising agency, Saatchi and Saatchi, argue that in a world of growing internationalization, the key to success is the development of global products and brands, in other words, a focus on standardized products and brands world-wide. Others, however, point to the numerous barriers to standardization, and suggest that greater returns are to be obtained from adapting products and marketing strategies to the specific characteristics of individual markets.

The growing integration of international markets as well as the growth of competition on a world-wide scale implies that adoption of a global perspective has become increasingly imperative in planning strategy. However, to conclude that this mandates the adoption of a strategy of universal standardization appears naive and oversimplistic. In particular, it ignores the inherent complexity of operations in inter-national markets, and the formulation of an effective strategy to penetrate these markets. While global products and brands may be appropriate for certain markets and in targeting certain segments, adopting such an approach as a universal strategy in relation to all markets may not be desirable, and may lead to major strategic blunders. Furthermore, it implies a product orientation, and a product-driven strategy, rather than a strategy grounded in a systematic analysis of customer behavior and response patterns and market characteristics.

The purpose of this article is thus to examine critically the notion that success in international markets necessitates adoption of a strategy of global products and brands. Given the restrictive characteristic of this philosophy, a somewhat broader perspective in developing global strategy is proposed which views standardization as merely one option in the range of possible strategies which may be effective in global markets.

[†] Source: *Columbia Journal of World Business*, Winter 1987. Copyright © 1987. Reprinted with permission.

The Traditional Perspective on International Strategy

Traditionally, discussion of international business strategy has been polarized around the debate concerning the pursuit of a uniform strategy world-wide versus adaptation to specific local market conditions. On the one hand, it has been argued that adoption of a uniform strategy world-wide enables a company to take advantage of the potential synergies arising from multicountry operations, and constitutes the multinational company's key competitive advantage in international markets. Others, however, have argued that adaptation of strategy to idiosyncratic national market characteristics is crucial to success in these markets.

Fayerweather in his seminal work in international business strategy described the central issue as one of conflict between forces toward unification and those resulting in fragmentation. He pointed out that within a multinational firm, internal forces created pressures toward the integration of strategy across national boundaries. On the other hand, differences in the sociocultural, political, and economic characteristics of countries as well as the need for effective relations with the host society, constitute fragmenting influences that favor adaptation to the local environment.

Recent discussion of global competitive strategy echoes the same theme of the dichotomy between the forces that have triggered the globalization of markets and those that constitute barriers to global competition. Factors such as economies of scale in production, purchasing, faster accumulation of learning from operating world-wide, decrease in transportation and distribution costs, reduced costs of product adaptation, and the emergence of global market segments have encouraged competition on a global scale. However, barriers such as governmental and institutional constraints, tariff barriers and duties, preferential treatment of local firms, transportation costs, differences in customer demand, and so on, call for nationalistic or 'protected niche' strategies.

Compromise solutions such as 'pattern standardization' have also been proposed. In this case, a global promotional theme or positioning is developed, but execution is adapted to the local market. Similarly, it has been pointed out that even where a standardized product is marketed in a number of countries, its positioning may be adapted in each market. Conversely, the positioning may be uniform across countries, but the product itself adapted or modified.

Although this debate first emerged in the 1960s, it has recently taken on a new vigor with the widely publicized pronouncements of proponents of 'global standardization' such as Professor Levitt and Saatchi & Saatchi.

The sweeping and somewhat polemic character of their argument has sparked a number of counterarguments as well as discussion of conditions under which such a strategy may be most appropriate. It has, for example, been pointed out that the potential for standardization may be greater for certain types of products such as industrial goods or luxury personal items targeted to upscale consumers, or products with similar penetration rates. Opportunities for standardization are also likely to occur more frequently among industrialized nations, and especially the Triad countries where customer interests as well as market conditions are likely to be more similar than among developing countries.

The role of corporate philosophy and organizational structure in influencing the practicality of implementing a strategy of global standardization has also been recognized. Here, it has been noted that few companies pursue the extreme position of complete standardization with regard to all elements of the marketing mix, and business functions such as R&D, manufacturing, and procurement in all countries throughout the world. Rather, some degree of adaptation is likely to occur relative to certain aspects of the firm's operations or in certain geographic areas. In addition, the feasibility of implementing a standardized strategy will depend on the autonomy accorded to local management. If local management has been accustomed to substantial autonomy, considerable opposition may be encountered in attempting to introduce globally standardized strategies.

An examination of such counterarguments suggests that there are a number of dangers in espousing a philosophy of global standardization for all products and services, and in relation to all markets world-wide. Furthermore, there are numerous difficulties and constraints to implementing such a strategy in many markets, stemming from external market conditions (such as government and trade regulation, competition, the marketing infrastructure, and so on), as well as from the current structure and organization of the firm's operations.

The Global Standardization Philosophy: The Underlying Assumptions

An examination of the arguments in favor of a strategy of global products and brands reveals three key underlying assumptions:

- Customer needs and interests are becoming increasingly homogeneous world-wide.

- People around the world are willing to sacrifice preferences in product features, functions, design, and the like for lower prices at high quality.

■   Substantial economies of scale in production and marketing can be achieved through supplying global markets.

There are, however, a number of pitfalls associated with each of these assumptions. These are discussed here in more detail.

Homogenization of the World's Wants

A key premise of the philosophy of global products is that customers' needs and interests are becoming increasingly homogeneous world-wide. But while global segments with similar interests and response patterns may be identified in some product markets, it is by no means clear that this is a universal trend. Furthermore, there is substantial evidence to suggest an increasing diversity of behavior within countries, and the emergence of idiosyncratic country-specific segments.

Lack of evidence of homogenization   In a number of product markets ranging from watches, perfume, and handbags to soft drinks and fast foods, companies have successfully identified global customer segments, and developed global products and brands targeted to these segments. These include such stars as Rolex, Omega and Le Baume & Mercier watches, Dior, Patou or Yves St. Laurent perfume. But while these brands are highly visible and widely publicized, they are often, with a few notable exceptions such as Classic Coke or McDonald's, targeted to a relatively restricted upscale international customer segment.

Numerous other companies, however, adapt lines to idiosyncratic country preferences, and develop local brands or product variants targeted to local market segments. The Findus frozen food division of Nestlé, for example, markets fish cakes and fish fingers in the United Kingdom, but beef bourguignon and coq au vin in France, and vitello con funghi and braviola in Italy. Similarly, Coca-Cola in Japan markets Georgia, cold coffee in a can, and Aquarius, a tonic drink, as well as Classic Coke and Hi-C.

Growth of intracountry segmentation price sensitivity   Furthermore, there is a growing body of evidence that suggests substantial heterogeneity within countries. In the United States, for example, the VALS (Value of American Lifestyles) study has identified nine value segments, while other studies have identified major differences in behavior between regions and subcultural segments. Many other countries are also characterized by substantial regional differences as well as different lifestyle and value segments.

Similarly, in industrial markets, while some global segments, often consisting of firms with international operations, can be identified, there also is considerable diversity within and between countries. Often local

THE INTERNATIONAL CONTEXT **421**

businesses constitute an important market segment and, especially in developing countries, may differ significantly in technological sophistication, business philosophy and strategy, emphasis on product quality, and service and price, from large multinationals.

The evidence thus suggests that the similarities in customer behavior are restricted to a relatively limited number of target segments, or product markets, while for the most part, there are substantial differences between countries. Proponents of standardization counter that the international strategist should focus on similarities among countries rather than differences. This may, however, imply ignoring a major part of a local market, and the potential profits that may be obtained from tapping other market segments.

Universal Preference for Low Price at Acceptable Quality

Another critical component of the argument for global standardization is that people around the world are willing to sacrifice preferences in product features, functions, design, and the like for lower prices, assuming equivalent quality. Aggressive low pricing for quality products that meet the common needs of customers in markets around the world is believed to further expand the global markets facing the firm. Although an appealing argument, this has three major problems.

Lack of evidence of increased price sensitivity   Evidence to suggest that customers are universally willing to trade off specific product features for a lower price is largely lacking. While in many product markets there is invariably a price-sensitive segment, there is no indication that this is on the increase. On the contrary, in many product and service markets, ranging from watches, personal computers, and household appliances to banking and insurance, an interest in multiple product features, product quality, and service appears to be growing.

Low price positioning is a highly vulnerable strategy   Also, from a strategic point of view, emphasis on price positioning may be undesirable, especially in international markets, since it offers no long-term competitive advantage. A price-positioning strategy is always vulnerable to new technological developments that may lower costs, as well as to attack from competitors with lower overhead, and lower operating or labor costs. Government subsidies to local competitors may also undermine the effectiveness of a price-positioning strategy. In addition, price-sensitive customers typically are not brand or source loyal.

Standardized low price can be overpriced in some countries and underpriced in others   Finally, a strategy based on a combination of a standardized product at a low price, when implemented in countries that vary in their competitive structure as well as the level of economic development, is likely to result in products that are overdesigned and overpriced for some markets and underdesigned and underpriced for others. Cost advantages may also be negated by transportation and distribution costs as well as tariff barriers and/or price regulation.

Economies of Scale of Production and Marketing

The third assumption underlying the philosophy of global standardization is that a key force driving strategy is product technology, and that substantial economies of scale can be achieved by supplying global markets. This does, however, neglect three critical and interrelated points:

1   Technological developments in flexible factory automation enable economies of scale to be achieved at lower levels of output and do not require production of a single standardized product.

2   Cost of production is only one and often not the critical component in determining the total cost of the product.

3   Strategy should not be solely product driven but should take into account the other components of a marketing strategy, such as positioning, packaging, brand name, advertising, PR, consumer and trade promotion and distribution.

Developments in flexible factory automation   Recent developments in flexible factory automation methods have lowered the minimum efficient scale of operation and have thus enabled companies to supply smaller local markets efficiently, without requiring operations on a global scale. However, diseconomies may result from such operations due to increased transportation and distribution costs, as well as higher administrative overhead, and additional communication and co-ordination costs.

Furthermore, decentralization of production and establishment of local manufacturing operations enables diversification of risk arising from political events, fluctuations in foreign exchange rates, or economic instability. Recent swings in foreign exchange rates, coupled with the growth of offshore sourcing have underscored the vulnerability of centralizing production in a single location. Government regulations relating to local component and/or offset requirements create additional pressures for local manufacturing. Flexible automation not only implies that decentralization of manufacturing and production may be cost efficient but also makes minor modifications in products of models in the latter stages of production feasible, so that a variety of model versions can be produced without major retooling. Adaptations to product design can thus be made to meet differences in preferences from one country to another without loss of economies of scale.

Production costs are often a minor component of total cost   In many consumer and service industries, such as cosmetics, detergents, pharmaceuticals, or financial institutions, production costs are a small fraction of total cost. The key to success in these markets is an understanding of the tastes and purchase behavior of target customers' distribution channels, and tailoring products and strategies to these rather than production efficiency. In the detergent industry, for example, mastery of mass-merchandising techniques and an effective brand management system are typically considered the key elements in the success of the giants in this field, such as Procter & Gamble (P&G) or Colgate-Palmolive.

The standardization philosophy is primarily product driven   The focus on product- and brand-related aspects of strategy in discussions of global standardization is misleading since it ignores the other key strategy variables. Strategy in international markets should also take into consideration other aspects of the marketing mix, and the extent to which these are standardized across country markets rather than adapted to local idiosyncratic characteristics.

Requisite Conditions for Global Standardization

The numerous pitfalls in the rationale underlying the global standardization philosophy suggests that such a strategy is far from universally appropriate for all products, brands, or companies. Only under certain conditions is it likely to prove a 'winning' strategy in international markets. These include:

- the existence of a global market segment;

- potential synergies from standardization;

- the availability of a communication and distribution infrastructure to deliver the firm's offering to target customers world-wide.

Existence of Global Market Segments

As noted previously, global segments may be identified in a number of industrial and consumer markets. In consumer markets these segments are typically luxury- or premium-type products. Global segments are, however, not limited to such product markets, but also exist in other types of markets, such as motorcycle, record, stereo equipment, and computer, where a segment with similar needs and wants can be identified in many countries.

In industrial markets, companies with multinational operations are particularly likely to have similar needs and requirements world-wide. Where the operations are integrated or coordinated across national boundaries, as in the case of banks or other financial institutions, compatibility of operational systems and equipment may be essential. Consequently, they may seek vendors who can supply and service their operations world-wide, in some cases developing global contrasts for such purchases. Similarly, manufacturing companies with world-wide operations may source globally in order to ensure uniformity in quality, service and price of components, and other raw materials throughout their operations.

Marketing of global products and brands to such target segments and global customers enables development of a uniform global image throughout the world. In some markets such as perfume or fashions, association with a specific country of origin or a foreign image in general may carry a prestige connotation. In other cases, for example, Sony electronic equipment, McDonald's hamburgers, Hertz or Avis car rental, IBM computers, or Xerox office equipment, it may help to develop a world-wide reputation for quality and service. Just as multinational corporations may seek uniformity in supply world-wide, some consumers who travel extensively may be interested in finding the same brand of cigarettes and soft drinks, or hotels, in foreign countries. This may be particularly relevant in product markets used extensively by international travelers.

While the existence of a potential global segment is a key motivating factor for developing a global product and brand strategy, it is important to note that the desirability of such a strategy depends on the size and economic viability of the segment in question, the strength of the segment's preference for the global brand, as well as the ability to reach the segment effectively and profitably.

Synergies Associated with Global Standardization

Global standardization may also have a number of synergistic effects. In addition to those associated with a global image noted above, opportunities may exist for the transfer of good ideas for products or promotional strategies from one country to another.

The standardization of strategy and operations across a number of countries may also enable the acquisition or exploitation of specific types of expertise that would not be feasible otherwise. Expertise in assessing country risk or foreign exchange risk, or in identifying and interpreting information relating to multiple country markets, for example, may be developed.

Such synergies are not, however, unique to a strategy of global standardization, but may also occur wherever operations and strategy are coordinated or integrated across country markets. In fact, only certain scale economies associated with product and advertising copy standardization, and the development of a global image as discussed earlier, are unique to global standardization.

Availability of an International Communication and Distribution Infrastructure

The effectiveness of global standardization also depends to a large extent on the availability of an international infrastructure of communications and distribution. As many corporations have expanded overseas, service organizations have followed their customers abroad to supply their needs world-wide.

Advertising agencies such as Saatchi & Saatchi, McCann Erickson, and Young & Rubicam now have an international network of operations throughout the world, while many research agencies can also supply services in major markets world-wide. With the growing integration of financial markets, banks, investment firms, insurance and other financial institutions are also becoming increasingly international in orientation and are expanding the scope of their operations in world markets. The physical distribution network of shippers, freight forwarding, export and import agents, customs clearing, invoicing and insurance agents is also becoming increasingly integrated to meet demand for international shipment of goods and services.

Improvements in telecommunications and in logistical systems have considerably increased capacity to manage operations on a global scale and hence facilitate adoption of global standardization strategies. The spread of telex and fax systems, as well as satellite linkages and international computer linkages, all contribute to the shrinking of distances and facilitate globalization of operations. Similarly, improvements in transportation systems and physical logistics such as containerization and computerized inventory and handling systems have enabled significant cost savings as well as reducing time required to move goods across major distances.

Operational Constraints to Effective Implementation of a Standardization Strategy

While adoption of a standardized strategy may be desirable under certain conditions, there are a number of constraints that severely restrict the firm's ability to develop and implement a standardized strategy.

External Constraints to Effective Standardization

The numerous external constraints that impede global standardization are well recognized. Here, three major categories are highlighted, namely

1   government and trade restrictions;

2   differences in the marketing infrastructure, such as the availability and effectiveness of promotional media;

3   the character of resource markets, and differences in the availability and costs of resources;

4   differences in competition from one country to another.

Government and trade restrictions Government and trade restrictions, such as tariff and other trade barriers, product, pricing or promotional regulation, frequently hamper standardization of the product line, pricing, or promotional strategy. Tariffs or quotas on the import of key materials, components, or other resources may, for example, affect production costs and thus hamper uniform pricing or alternatively result in the substitution of other components and modifications in product design. Local content requirements or compensatory export requirements, which specify that products contain a certain proportion of components manufactured locally or that a certain volume of production is exported to offset imports of components or other services, may have a similar impact.

The existence of cartels such as the European steel cartel, or the Swiss chocolate cartel, may also impede or exclude standardized strategies in countries covered by these agreements. In particular, they may affect adoption of a uniform pricing strategy as the cartel sets prices for the industry. Cartel members may also control established distribution channels, thus preventing use of a standardized distribution strategy. Extensive grey markets in countries such as India, Hong Kong, and South America may also affect administered pricing systems, and require adjustment of pricing strategies.

The nature of the marketing infrastructure Differences in the marketing infrastructure from one country to another may hamper use of a standardized strategy. These may, for example, include differences in the availability and reach of various promotional media, in the availability of certain distribution channels or retail institutions, or in the existence and efficiency of the communication and transportation network. Such factors may, therefore, require considerable adaptation of strategy of local market conditions.

Interdependencies with resource markets   Yet another constraint to the development of standardized strategies is the nature of resource markets, and their operation in different countries throughout the world as well as the interdependency of these markets with marketing decisions. Availability and cost of raw materials, as well as labor and other resources in different locations, will affect not only decisions regarding sourcing of and hence the location of manufacturing activities but also marketing strategy decisions such as product design. For example, in the paper industry, availability of cheap local materials such as jute and sugar cane may result in their substitution for wood fiber.

Cost differentials relative to raw materials, labor, management, and other inputs may also influence the trade-off relative to alternative strategies. For example, high packaging cost relative to physical distribution may result in use of cheaper packaging with a shorter shelf life and more frequent shipments. Similarly, low labor costs relative to media may encourage a shift from mass media advertising to labor-intensive promotion such as personal selling and product demonstration.

Availability of capital, technology, and manufacturing capabilities in different locations will also affect decisions about licensing, contract manufacturing, joint ventures, and other 'make–buy' types of decisions for different markets, as well as decisions about countertrade, reciprocity, and other long-term relations.

The nature of the competitive structure   Differences in the nature of the competitive situation from one country to another may also suggest the desirability of adaptation strategy. Even in markets characterized by global competition, such as agricultural equipment and motorcycles, the existence of low-cost competition in certain countries may suggest the desirability of marketing stripped-down models or lowering prices to meet such competition. Even where competitors are predominantly other multinationals, preemption of established distribution networks may encourage adoption of innovative distribution methods or direct distribution to short-circuit an entrenched position. Thus, the existence of global competition does not necessarily imply a need for global standardization.

All such aspects thus impose major constraints on the feasibility and effectiveness of a standardized strategy, and suggest the desirability or need to adapt to specific market conditions.

Internal Constraints to Effective Standardization

In addition to such external constraints on the feasibility of a global standardization strategy, there are also a number of internal constraints that may need to be considered. These include compatibility with the existing network of operations overseas, as well as opposition or lack of enthusiasm among local management toward a standardized strategy.

Existing international operations   Proponents of global standardization typically take the position of a novice company with no operations in international markets, and hence fail to take into consideration the fit of the proposed strategy with current international activities. In practice, however, many companies have a number of existing operations in various countries. In some cases, these are joint ventures, or licensing operations or involve some collaboration in purchasing, manufacturing or distribution with other companies. Even where foreign manufacturing and distribution operations are wholly owned, the establishment of a distribution network will typically entail relationships with other organizations, for example, exclusive distributor agreements.

Such commitments may be difficult if not impossible to change in the short run, and may constitute a major impediment to adoption of a standardized strategy. If, for example, a joint venture with a local company has been established to manufacture and market a product line in a specific country or region, resistance from the local partner (or government authorities) may be encountered if the parent company wishes to shift production or import components from another location. Similarly, a licensing contract will impede a firm from supplying the products covered by the agreement from an alternative location for the duration of the contract, even if it becomes more cost efficient to do so.

Conversely, the establishment of an effective dealer or distribution network in a country or region may constitute an important resource to a company. The addition of new products to the product line currently sold or distributed by this network may therefore provide a more efficient utilization of company resources than expanding to new countries or geographic regions with the existing line, as this would require substantial investment in the establishment of a new distribution network.

In addition, overseas subsidiaries may currently be marketing not only core products and brands from the company's domestic business, but may also have added or acquired local or regional products and brands in response to local market demand. In some cases, therefore, introduction of a global product or brand may be likely to cannibalize sales of local or regional brands.

Advocates of standardization thus need to take into consideration the evolutionary character of international involvement, which may render a universal strategy of global products and brands suboptimal.

Somewhat ironically, the longer the history of a multinational corporation's involvement in foreign or international markets, and the more diversified and far-flung its operations, the more likely it is that standardization will not lead to optimal results.

Local management motivation and attitudes Another internal constraint concerns the motivation and attitudes of local management with regard to standardization. Standardized strategies tend to facilitate or result in centralization in the planning and organization of international activities. Especially if input from local management is limited, this may result in a feeling that strategy is 'imposed' by corporate headquarters, and/or not adequately adapted or appropriate in view of specific local market characteristics and conditions. Local management is likely to take the view 'it won't work here – things are different,' which will reduce their motivation to implement a standardized strategy effectively.

A Framework for Classifying Global Strategy Options

The adoption of a global perspective should not be viewed as synonymous with a strategy of global products and brands. Rather, for most companies such a perspective implies consideration of a broad range of strategic options of which standardization is merely one.

In essence, a global perspective implies planning strategy relative to markets world-wide rather than on a country-by-country basis. This may result in the identification of opportunities for global products and brands and/or integrating and coordinating strategy across national boundaries to exploit potential synergies of operating on an international scale. Such opportunities should, however, be weighed against the benefits of adaptation to idiosyncratic customer characteristics.

The development of an effective global strategy thus requires a careful examination of all international options in terms of standardization versus adaptation open to the firm.

A firm's international operations are likely to be characterized by a mix of strategies, including not only global products and brands, but also some regional products and brands and some national products and brands. Similarly, some target segments may be global, others regional, and others national. Hybrid strategies of this nature thus enable a company to take advantage of the benefits of standardization and potential synergies from operating on an international scale, while at the same time not losing those afforded by adaptation to specific country characteristics and customer preferences.

The International Context in International Perspective

> *There never were, since the creation of the world, two cases exactly*
> *parallel.*
> (Philip Dormer Stanhope 1694–1773; English Secretary of State)

What a curious title, one might be inclined to think. 'The international context in international perspective' – isn't this a case of the snake biting itself in its own tail? Of course, the answer is no. Just as in all previous chapters, the debate between proponents of the global convergence perspective and those of the international diversity perspective can be viewed from an international angle. The question of interest is whether strategists in certain countries are more inclined towards a specific perspective on the international context than in others. In other words, are there nations where the global convergence perspective is more prevalent, while in other nations the international diversity perspective is more widespread?

This is a tantalizing question, but as before, it must be concluded that little comparative research has been done on the issue. As a stimulus to the debate whether there are national differences in international context perspective, we would like to put forward a number of factors that might be of influence on how the paradox of globalization and localization is dealt with in different countries. It goes without saying that more international comparative research is required before a clear picture can be formed about the actual international differences.

Of course, if the proponents of the global convergence perspective are entirely right, the factors mentioned below will become less and less important as countries grow more similar. All of the international differences in strategic management preferences discussed in the concluding pages of each of the preceeding chapters will also wither away. However, if international diversity remains a characteristic of our world, the way strategic management paradoxes are dealt with differently in each country will continue to be an important issue to discuss.

Level of Nationalism

The prospect of global convergence is a dream to some, but a nightmare to others. It is inspiring for those who would like to see a borderless world, in which like-minded people would see eye-to-eye. It is frightening for those who prefer to keep a diverse world, in which local autonomy and the retainment of national culture are highly valued. Although global convergence enthusiasts and detractors can be found in each country, some nations seem more troubled by the prospect of further globalization than others. In some countries the belief is widespread that foreign values, norms, habits and behaviors are being imposed, that are undermining the national culture, and that the country's ability to decide its own fate is being compromised. This leads many to argue that global convergence should be, and will be, curtailed. In other countries such nationalism is far less pronounced, and the advantages of globalization are more widely accepted. In general, it can be expected that strategists from countries with a strong streak of nationalism will gravitate more toward the international diversity perspective, while strategists from less nationalist countries will be more inclined toward the global convergence perspective.

Size of Country

In general, smaller countries are more exposed to the international context than larger countries. Smaller countries commonly export more of their gross domestic product than larger countries, and import more as well. Hence, their companies are more used to dealing with, and adapting to, a high number of foreign suppliers, customers and competitors. Moreover, companies from smaller countries, confronted with a limited home market, are forced to seek growth in foreign markets earlier than their counterparts in larger countries. During this early internationalization, these companies do not have the benefit of scale economies in the home market and therefore are usually more inclined to adapt themselves to the demands of foreign markets. Companies in larger markets normally grow to a significant size at home, thereby achieving certain economies of scale through national standardization, while also establishing a domestically-oriented management style. When they do move abroad, as a more mature company, their international activities will tend to be modest compared to domestic operations and therefore they will be less inclined to be locally adaptive.

It stands to reason that this difference in exposure to the international context has an influence on how strategists from different countries perceive developments in the international context. Generally, strategists from smaller countries, to whom adaptation to international variety has become second nature, will favor the view that international diversity will remain. Strategists from larger countries will be more inclined to emphasize the growing similarities and to seek opportunities for international standardization.

Preference for Central Decision-Making

This point is linked to the debate in the previous chapter, where the paradox of control and chaos was discussed. It was argued that in some countries there is a stronger emphasis on the role of top management in running the firm. In these countries there is usually a strong chain of command, with clear authority and responsibilities, and a well-developed control system. To remain manageable from the top, the organization must not become too complex to comprehend and steer. Usually this means that business units are structured along simple lines and that strategy is not too varied by product or geographic area. As soon as each product or geographic area requires its own specific strategy, the ability to run things centrally will diminish. Strategists with a strong preference for central decision-making will therefore be less inclined to acknowledge pressures for local responsiveness. Quite the opposite, they will be searching for opportunities to standardize their approach to different countries, which will allow for a more centralized decision-making structure. Strategists from countries with a tradition of more decentralized decision-making, are more likely to accept international diversity as a workable situation[14].

Further Readings

There have been few writers as radical as Levitt, but quite a large number of stimulating works from the global convergence perspective. A good place for the interested reader to start would be Kenichi Ohmae's *The Borderless World: Power and Strategy in the Interlinked Economy* and George Yip's *Total Global Strategy*. For a stronger balancing of perspectives, the reader should turn to *The Multinational Mission*, by C.K. Prahalad and Yves Doz, and *Competition in Global Industries* by Michael Porter. For a critical review of the globalization literature, *The Logic of International Restructuring*, by Winfried Ruigrok and Rob van Tulder makes for stimulating reading.

Most of this literature emphasizes strategy content issues, while largely neglecting strategy process aspects. A well-known exception is the article 'Strategic Planning for a Global Business,' by Balaji

Chakravarthy and Howard Perlmutter. With regard to the management of large international companies, *Managing Across Borders: The Transnational Solution*, by Christopher Bartlett and Sumantra Ghoshal, is highly recommended.

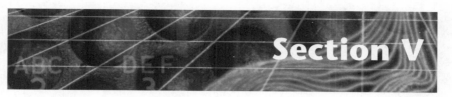

Section V

Purpose

Organizational Purpose

Corporation, *n. An ingenious device for*
obtaining individual profit without
individual responsibility.

(*The Devil's Dictionary*, Ambrose Bierce 1842 – 1914; American columnist)

A business that makes nothing but money
is a poor kind of business.

(Henry Ford 1863–1947; American industrialist)

The Paradox of Profitability and Responsibility

In Chapter 2 it was argued that strategy can be broadly conceived as a course of action for achieving an organization's purpose. Subsequently, nine chapters were spent looking at strategy from many different angles, but relatively little explicit attention was paid to the fundamental issue of organizational purpose – the focus was on means, not on ends. The various authors debated how to set a course for the organizational vessel through turbulent waters, but few raised the issue of why the journey was being undertaken in the first place. This lack of attention for the topic of organizational purpose may in part be due to the assumption by many that it is obvious why organizations exist. Others may avoid the topic because it is highly value-laden and somehow outside the realm of strategic management.

Yet, in practice, strategists must constantly seek solutions and make choices based on an understanding of what the organization is intended to achieve. Strategists are confronted by many different claimants, who believe that the organization exists to serve their interests. The demands placed on the organization by shareholders, employees, suppliers, customers, governments and communities must be weighed and priorities must be set, to guide organizational decision making. It is hardly possible for strategists to avoid taking a stance on what they judge to be the purpose of the organization. The topic of organizational purpose is not an irrelevant ivory tower subject, but an essential issue facing strategists. Therefore, a debate on organizational purpose in this chapter is justified and should prove valuable to both practitioners and academics.

Clearly, the debate on organizational purpose is not limited to the field of strategic management. Given the influential position of business organizations in modern society, the purpose they should serve is also discussed by theorists in the fields of economics, political science, sociology, ethics and philosophy. The enormous impact of corporations on the functioning of society also attracts political parties, labor unions, community representatives, environmentalists, the media and the general public to the debate. All take a position on the role that business organizations should play within society and the responsibilities that they ought to shoulder. In countries with a market economy, it is generally accepted that companies should pursue *profitability*, but also have certain *responsibilities* that must be fulfilled. But this is where the consensus ends. Opinions differ sharply with regard to the question to whom business organizations should be responsible and what the relative importance of profitability and responsibility should be.

Both within the field of strategic management, as in broader society, a wide variety of views exists on what the purpose of organizations should be. Although there are many aspects to this debate, the central tension appears to be between profitability and responsibility. These two elements seem to present a paradox, as they place partially conflicting and maybe even mutually exclusive pressures on firms. When focusing on this key aspect of the debate, a spectrum of opinions can be identified spanning the middle ground between two radically opposite points of view. At the one pole of the debate are those people who argue that corporations are established to serve the purposes of their owners. Generally, it is in the best interest of a corporation's shareholders to see the value of their stocks increase through the organization's pursuit of profitable business strategies. This point of view is commonly referred to as the *shareholder value* perspective. At the other end of the spectrum are those people who argue that corporations should be seen as joint ventures between shareholders, employees, banks, customers, suppliers, governments and the community. All of these parties hold a stake in the organization and therefore can expect that the corporation will take as its responsibility to develop business strategies that are in accordance with their interests and values. This point of view will be referred to as the *stakeholder values* perspective.

As before, this chapter will explore the topic under discussion by following a debate model. First, the two opposite ways of dealing with the paradox of profitability and responsibility will be compared, and then summarized in Table 11.1. Subsequently, three readings will be presented to kick off a 'virtual debate'.

The Shareholder Value Perspective

To proponents of the shareholder value perspective it is obvious that companies belong to their owners and therefore should act in accordance with the interests of the owners. Corporations are instruments, whose purpose it is to create economic value on behalf of those who invest risk-taking capital in the enterprise. This clear purpose should drive companies, irregardless of whether they are privately or publicly held. According to Rappaport[1], 'the idea that business strategies should be judged by the economic value they create for shareholders is well accepted in the business community. After all, to suggest that companies be operated in the best interests of its owners is hardly controversial.'

There is some disagreement between advocates of this perspective with regard to the best way of advancing the interests of the shareholders, particularly in publicly held companies. Many people taking this point of view argue that the well-being of the shareholders is served if the strategy of a company leads to higher share prices and/or higher dividends[2]. Others are less certain of the stock markets' ability to correctly value long-term investments, such as R&D spending and capital expenditures. In their view, the stock markets are excessively concerned with the short term and therefore share prices myopically overemphasize current results and heavily discount investments for the future. To avoid being pressured into short-termism, these people advocate that strategists must keep only one eye on the share prices, while the other is focused on the long-term horizon[3].

According to supporters of the shareholder value perspective, one of the major challenges in large corporations is to actually get top management to pursue the shareholders' interests. Where ownership and managerial control over a company have become separated, it is often difficult to get the managers to work on behalf of the shareholders, instead of letting their self-interest prevail. This is known as the *principal–agent* problem[4] – the managers are agents, working to further the interests of their principals, the shareholders, but are tempted to serve their own interests, even when this is to the detriment of the principal. This has led to a widespread debate in the academic and business communities, especially in Britain and the United States, about the best form of *corporate governance*. The subject of corporate governance, as opposed to corporate management, deals with the issue of governing the behavior of top management. The most important players in corporate governance are the outside, or non-executive, members on the board of directors. It is one of the tasks of these outsiders to check whether the executives are truly running the company in a way that maximizes the shareholders' wealth. For this reason, many proponents of the shareholder value perspective call for a majority of independent-minded outside directors in the board, preferably owning significant amounts of the company's stock themselves.

The emphasis placed on profitability as the fundamental purpose of firms does not mean that supporters of the shareholder value perspective are blind to the demands placed on firms by other stakeholders. On the contrary, most exponents of this view argue that it is in the interest of the shareholders to do a stakeholder analysis and even to actively manage stakeholder relations. Knowing the force field of stakeholders constraining the freedom of the company is important information for the strategy process. It is never advisable to ignore important external claimants such as labor unions, environmental activists, bankers, governmental agencies and community groups. Few strategists would doubt that proactive engagement is preferable to 'corporate isolationism'. However, recognizing that it is expedient to pay attention to stakeholders does not mean that it is the corporation's purpose to serve them. If parties have a strong bargaining position, a firm might be forced into all types of concessions, sacrificing profitability, but this has little to do with any moral responsibility of the firm towards these other powers. The only duty of a company is to maximize shareholder value, within the boundaries of what is legally permissible.

The important conclusion is that in this perspective it might be in the interest of shareholders to treat stakeholders well, but that there is no moral obligation to do so. For instance, it might be a good move for a troubled company not to lay off workers if the resulting loyalty and morale improve the chances of recovery and profitability later on. In this case the decision not to fire workers is based on profit-motivated calculation, not on a sense of moral responsibility towards the employees. Generally, proponents of the shareholder value perspective argue that society is best served by this type of economic rationale. By pursuing enlightened self-interest and maintaining market-based relationships between the firm and all stakeholders, societal wealth will be maximized. Responsibility for employment, local communities, the environment, consumer welfare and social developments are not an organizational matter, but issues for individuals and governments[5].

The Stakeholder Values Perspective

Advocates of the stakeholder values perspective do not see why the supplier of one ingredient in an economic value creation process has a stronger moral claim on the organization than the providers of other inputs. They challenge the assumption that individuals with an equity stake in a corporation have the right to demand that the entire organization work on their behalf. In the stakeholder values perspective, a company should not be seen as the instrument of shareholders, but as a coalition between various resource suppliers, with the intention of increasing their common wealth. An organization should be regarded as a joint-venture in which the suppliers of equity, loans, labor, management, expertise, parts and service all participate to achieve economic success. As all groups hold a stake in the joint-venture and are mutually dependent, it is argued that the purpose of the organization is to serve the interests of all parties involved[6].

According to endorsers of the stakeholder values perspective, shareholders have a legitimate interest in the firm's profitability. However, the emphasis shareholders place on stock price appreciation and dividends must be balanced against the legitimate demands of the other partners. These demands are not only financial, as in the case of the shareholders, but also qualitative, reflecting different values held by different groups. For instance, employees might place a high value on job security, occupational safety, holidays and working conditions, while a supplier of parts might prefer secure demand, joint innovation, shared risk-taking and prompt payment. Of course, balancing these interests is a challenging task, requiring an ongoing process of negotiation and compromise. The outcome will in part depend on the bargaining power of each stakeholder – how essential is their input to the economic success of the organization? However, the extent to which a stakeholder's interests are pursued will also depend on the perceived legitimacy of their claim. For instance, employees usually have a strong moral claim because they are heavily dependent on the organization and have a relatively low mobility, while most shareholders have a spread portfolio and can exit the corporation with a phone call[7].

In this view of organizational purpose, strategists must recognize their responsibility towards all constituents[8]. Maximizing shareholder value to the detriment of the other stakeholders would be unjust. Strategists in the firm have a moral obligation to consider the interests and values of all joint-venture partners. Managing stakeholder demands is not merely a pragmatic means to running a profitable business – serving stakeholders is an end in itself. These two interpretations of stakeholder management are often confused. Where it is primarily viewed as an approach or technique for dealing with the essential participants in the value-adding process, stakeholder management is *instrumental*. But if it is based on the fundamental notion that the organization's purpose is to serve the stakeholders, then stakeholder management is *normative*[9].

Most proponents of the stakeholder values perspective argue that, ultimately, pursuing the joint interests of all stakeholders it is not only more just, but also more effective for organizations[10]. Few stakeholders are filled with a sense of mission to go out and maximize shareholder value, especially if shareholders bear no responsibility for the other stakeholders' interests[11]. It is difficult to work as a motivated team, if it is the purpose of the organization to serve only one group's interests. Furthermore, without a stakeholder values perspective, there will be a deep-rooted lack of trust between all of the parties involved in the enterprise. Each stakeholder will assume that the others are solely motivated by self-interest and are tentatively cooperating in a calculative manner. All parties will perceive a constant risk that the others will use their power to gain a bigger slice of the pie, or even rid themselves of their 'partners'. The consequence is that all stakeholders will vigorously guard their own interests and will interact with one another as adversaries. To advocates of the stakeholder values perspective, this 'every person for themselves' model of organizations is clearly inferior to the partnership model, in which sharing, trust and symbiosis are emphasized. Cooperation between stakeholders is much more effective than competition (note the link with the embedded organization perspective in Chapter 7).

Some exponents of the stakeholder values perspective argue that the narrow economic definition of stakeholders given above is too constrictive. In their view, the circle of stakeholders with a legitimate claim on the organization should be drawn more widely. Not only should the organization be responsible to the direct participants in the economic value creation process (the *primary stakeholders*), but also to all parties affected by the organization's activities. For example, an organization's behavior might have an impact on local communities, governments, the environment and society in general, and therefore these groups have a stake in what the organization does. Most supporters of the stakeholder values perspective acknowledge that organizations have a moral responsibility towards these *secondary stakeholders*[12]. However, opinions differ whether it should actually be a part of business organizations' purpose to serve this broader body of constituents.

The implication of this view for corporate governance is that the board of directors should be able to judge whether the interests of all stakeholders are being justly balanced. This has led some advocates of the stakeholder values perspective to call for representatives of the most important stakeholder groups in the board[13]. Others argue more narrowly for a stronger influence of employees on the choices made by organizations[14]. Such *co-determination* of the corporation's strategy by management and workers can, for instance, be encouraged by establishing work councils (a type of organizational parliament or senate), as the European Union proposes. Yet others emphasize measures to strengthen corporate social responsibility in general. To improve *corporate social performance*, it is argued, companies should be encouraged to adopt internal policy processes that promote ethical behavior and responsiveness to societal issues[15]. Corporate responsibility should not be, to quote Ambrose Bierce's sarcastic definition, 'a detachable burden easily shifted to the shoulders of God, Fate, Fortune, Luck, or one's neighbor.'

Given these arguments for the two perspectives – shareholder value versus stakeholder values – the question for strategists is which one to choose. Should it be the purpose of business organizations to pursue profitability on behalf of their owners? Or should firms serve the interests and promote the values of all of their stakeholders in a balanced way? It is clear that both theorists and practitioners sharply disagree, again placing readers in the position of needing to make up their own minds. Readers themselves will have to come to terms with the paradox of profitability and responsibility (see Table 11.1).

TABLE 11.1
Shareholder value versus stakeholder values perspective

	Shareholder Value Perspective	Stakeholder Values Perspective
Emphasis on	Profitability over responsibility	Responsibility over profitability
Organizations seen as	Instruments	Joint-ventures
Organizational purpose	To serve owner	To serve all parties involved
Measure of success	Share price & dividends (shareholder value)	Satisfaction among stakeholders
Major difficulty	Getting agent to pursue principal's interests	Balancing interests of various stakeholders
Corporate governance through	Independent outside directors with shares	Stakeholder representation
Stakeholder management	Means	End and means
Social responsibility	Individual, not organizational matter	Both individual and organizational
Society best served by	Pursuing self-interest (economic efficiency)	Pursuing joint-interests (economic symbiosis)

Defining the Issues: Mission and Governance

Before proceeding with the 'debate' between proponents of the share-holder value and stakeholder values perspectives, it is useful to clarify the key topics under dispute. As will be seen, the disagreements in this discussion revolve around two key issues. First, the two sides take a different view on the reasons why companies exist and the business philosophy that should guide strategic choices. This is referred to as the issue of *corporate mission*. Second, there is no agreement on who should determine the corporate mission and who should ensure that strategies pursued are in accordance with the mission. This is referred to as the issue of *corporate governance*. In the next few paragraphs, these two issues will be further explored, to set the stage for the 'debate readings' that follow.

Purpose, Mission and Vision

Organizational purpose can be defined as the reason for which an organization exists. It can be expected that the perception that strategists have of their organization's purpose will give direction to the strategy process and influence the strategy content. Sometimes strategists might consciously reflect on, or question, the organizational purpose as they make strategic choices. However, more often their view of the organization's purpose will be a part of the broader business philosophy that steers their decision making. This enduring set of fundamental principles guiding strategic decision making in a firm is referred to as the *corporate mission*.

The corporate mission encompasses the basic points of departure that send the organization in a particular direction (from the Latin *mittere* – to send[16]). The purpose of an organization is arguably the most important point of departure for strategy making, but also influential are the values embodied in an organization's culture[17]. The values shared by an organization's members will shape what is seen as ethical behavior and moral responsibilities, and therefore have an impact on strategic choices[18]. Other authors emphasize 'hard' strategy principles as points of departure for the strategy process. Often mentioned is the need to define the businesses on which the corporation wishes to focus its efforts[19]. Others mention competitive ambitions or intentions as an important part of the mission[20].

The corporate mission can be articulated by means of a *mission statement*, but in practice not everything that is called a mission statement meets the above criteria[21]. However, firms can have a mission, even if it has not been explicitly encoded on paper, although this increases the chance of divergent interpretations within the organization.

In general, the corporate mission plays three important roles for a business organization. These roles are:

1   *Direction.* The corporate mission can point the organization in a certain direction, by defining the boundaries within which strategic choices and actions must take place. By specifying the fundamental principles on which strategies must be based, the corporate mission limits the scope of strategic options and sets the organization on a particular heading.

2   *Legitimization.* The corporate mission can convey to all stakeholders inside and outside the company that the organization is pursuing valuable activities in a proper way. By specifying the business philosophy that will guide the company, it is hoped that stakeholders will accept, support and trust the organization.

3   *Motivation.* The corporate mission can go a step further than legitimization, by actually inspiring individuals to work together in a particular way. By specifying the fundamental principles driving organizational actions, an *esprit de corps* can evolve, with the powerful capacity to motivate people over a prolonged period of time.

A concept that is often confused with mission is *vision*. Individuals or organizations have a vision if they picture a future state of affairs they wish to achieve (from the Latin *vide* – to see[23]). While the corporate mission outlines the basic points of departure, a corporate vision outlines the desired future at which the company hopes to arrive. In other words, vision provides a business aim, while mission provides a business philosophy.

Generally, a company vision is a type of goal that is less specific than an objective. Vision is usually defined as a broad conception of a desirable future state, of which the details must still be determined[24]. As such, corporate vision can play the same type of roles as corporate mission. A corporate vision can point the firm in a particular direction, can legitimize the organization's existence and actions, and can motivate individuals to work together towards a shared end.

Corporate Governance

While the first question in this debate is '*What* should be the corporate mission?', the second question is '*Who* should determine the corporate mission and regulate the activities of the corporation?'. This second issue is that of corporate governance. The subject of corporate governance, as opposed to corporate management, deals with the issue of governing the strategic choices and actions of top management. Popularly stated, corporate governance is about managing top management – building in checks and balances to ensure that the senior executives pursue strategies that are in accordance with the corporate mission. Corporate governance encompasses all tasks and activities that are intended to supervise and steer the behavior of top management.

In the common definition, corporate governance 'addresses the issues facing boards of directors'[25]. In this view, corporate governance is the task of the directors and therefore attention must be paid to their roles and responsibilities[26]. Others have argued that this definition is too narrow, and that in practice there are more forces that govern the activities of top management. In this broader view, boards of directors are only a part of the *governance system*. For instance, regulation by local and national authorities, as well as pressure from societal groups, can function as the checks and balances limiting top management's discretion[27].

Whether employing a narrow or broad definition, three important corporate governance functions can be distinguished[28]:

- *Forming function.* The first function of corporate governance is to influence the forming of the corporate mission. The task of corporate governance is to shape, articulate and communicate the fundamental principles that will drive the organization's activities. Determining the purpose of the organization and setting priorities among claimants are part of the forming function. The board of directors can conduct this task by, for example, questioning the basis of strategic choices, influencing the business philosophy, and explicitly weighing the advantages and disadvantages of the firm's strategies for various constituents[29].

- *Performance function.* The second function of corporate governance is to contribute to the strategy process with the intention of improving the future performance of the corporation. The task of corporate governance is to judge strategy initiatives brought forward by top management and/or to actively participate in strategy development. The board of directors can conduct this task by, for example, engaging in strategy discussions, acting as a sounding board for top management, and networking to secure the support of vital stakeholders[30].

- *Conformance function.* The third function of corporate governance is to ensure corporate conformance to the stated mission and strategy. The task of corporate governance is to monitor whether the organization is undertaking activities as promised and whether performance is satisfactory. Where management is found lacking, it is a function of corporate governance to press for changes. The board of directors can conduct this task by, for example, auditing the activities of the corporation, questioning and supervising top management, determining remuneration and incentive packages, and even appointing new managers[31].

How these corporate governance functions should be operationalized in practice is the second issue central to the debate in this chapter. There is considerable disagreement on how boards of directors should be run.

Three characteristics of boards of directors are of particular importance:[32]

- *Board structure.* Internationally, there are major differences between countries requiring a two-tier board structure (e.g. Germany, the Netherlands and Finland), countries with a one-tier board (e.g. United States, Britain and Japan), and countries in which companies are free to choose (e.g. France and Switzerland). In a two-tier system there is a formal division of power, with a management board made up of the top executives and a distinct supervisory board made up of non-executives, with the task of monitoring and steering the management board. In a one-tier (or unitary) board system, executive and non-executive (outside) directors sit together on one board.

- *Board membership.* The composition of boards of directors can vary sharply, from company to company, and country to country. Some differences are due to legal requirements that are not the same internationally. For instance, in Germany by law half of the membership of a supervisory board must represent labor, while the other half represents the shareholders. In French companies labor representatives are given observer status on the board. In other countries there are no legal imperatives, yet differences have emerged. In some cases outside (non-executive) directors from other companies are common, while in other nations fewer outsiders are involved. Even within countries differences can be significant, especially with regard to the number, stature and independence of outside (non-executive) directors.

- *Board tasks.* The tasks and authority of boards of directors also differ quite significantly between companies. In some cases boards meet infrequently and are merely asked to vote on proposals put in front of them. Such boards have little formal or informal power to contradict the will of the CEO. In other companies, boards meet regularly and play a more active role in corporate governance, by formulating proposals, proactively selecting new top managers, and determining objectives and incentives. Normally, the power of outside (non-executive) directors to monitor and steer a company only partly depends on their formally defined tasks and authority. To a large degree their impact is determined by how proactive they define their own role.

The question in the context of this chapter is how a board of directors should be run to ensure that the organization's purpose is best achieved. What should be the structure, membership and tasks of the board of directors, to realize the ends for which the organization exits?

More than all other debates in this book, the disagreements between the proponents of the two perspectives are strongly influenced by national culture. Each country has its own system of corporate governance and the international differences are significant. Therefore, instead of an international perspective section at the end of the chapter, an extra key reading on the international differences has been selected.

EXHIBIT 11.1
Daimler-Benz case

DAIMLER-BENZ: BURNT AT THE STAKE?

On January 6, 1997, Jürgen Schrempp, Chairman of Daimler-Benz AG, stepped forward to address the members of the Economic Club of Detroit. He spoke at length of the major changes being implemented within Daimler-Benz, the largest industrial company in Germany. His message was clear:

> We have learned in Europe the same lessons you all have, there's no hiding from the global economy. We must go out to meet it, by unshackling the creativity of our employees and managers and encouraging them to be the best they can be.

He continued by explaining how his Stuttgart-based corporation was adopting measures to restructure after taking a $4.5 billion loss over 1995. This heavily disappointing financial result, the worst in the company's long history, had for a large part been due to major write-offs in the company's aerospace unit, DASA. The collapse of defense spending had hit DASA hard and had necessitated major reorganizations, the outsourcing of production to low wage US locations, wage concessions and a reduction in the DASA workforce from 40,000 to 25,000 employees. DASA had also been forced to halt financial support to its ailing regional aircraft manufacturing affiliate, Fokker, in which it held a 51 percent controlling stake. This withdrawal, which led to Fokker's bankruptcy, cost Daimler-Benz about $1.55 billion. Furthermore, Schrempp had divested Dornier aircraft and had pushed through a restructuring of the corporation's AEG electrical engineering subsidiary, which had cost another $1.1 billion. Luckily, the company's core business of Mercedes-Benz cars and trucks, good for 80 percent of the $75 billion in revenues, had been reasonably profitable. He carried on:

> All the changes I have mentioned were aggravating and painful for a German company and for our people. And, may I add, far from popular. The initial reaction demonstrated the obvious contrast in perceptions between the German public, trade unions, politicians and media on the one hand, and the international financial community on the other. Germany has been historically an economic success because we achieved a system of pragmatic consensus between labor and business. This emphasis on social stability paid off for the Germans. The model used to provide fast and continuously growing prosperity . . . I want to repeat that the German system of consensus should under no circumstances be abandoned . . . We need to modify the 'German model' so that we not only reap the benefits of consensus but also adapt ourselves successfully to a world that has significantly changed . . .

While in Germany we initially faced criticism and there was a lack of understanding for our actions, the international financial markets responded positively. This year we achieved a 40 percent increase in the value of our shares. And I like to think that the consistent rise in our share price in recent months is a result of the growing trust of the financial markets.

A part of this trust was due to the promising strategies being pursued by Daimler-Benz and the wave of new products hitting the market. Schrempp could point to the sophisticated and stylish Mercedes-Benz CLK coupe being premiered in Detroit, but also to the new SLK roadster, which had just been awarded the title of 1997 North America car of the year. Schrempp was also proud of the new M-Class sport utility vehicle, set to be produced at Mercedes' brand new production facility in Tuscaloosa, Alabama. In the pipeline were also the A-Class compact Mercedes (more affectionately known as the 'Baby Benz') and the even smaller Smart car. The Mercedes-Benz truck division, together with its American Freightliner subsidiary, were also doing well and had the position of world market leader in sales. Daimler's railroad systems joint-venture with ABB, Adtranz, also occupied the global top spot. Furthermore, it was starting to look more likely that the Airbus consortium in which DASA participated, would be reformed into a stronger, unified company.

Daimler-Benz had also significantly improved its standing in the international financial community by boldly going where no German company had gone before – to Wall Street. In 1993 the company had negotiated a deal with the Securities and Exchange Commission to get a listing on the New York Stock Exchange. This deal pushed Daimler-Benz to adopt US generally accepted accounting principles (GAAP), in return for exemption from the rules requiring the publication of quarterly results. The importance of this switch in bean counting method became directly obvious in the first year of reporting. In 1994 Daimler's German accounts showed a DM500 million profit, while in the US a DM2 billion loss was reported. Since then, the company had introduced a new system of performance measurement and management accounting that aligns internal and external reporting based on US GAAP.

Even more importantly, Schrempp had openly professed his dedication to creating shareholder value. Each business unit within Daimler-Benz had been given the task of achieving a minimum return on capital employed of 12 percent by 1998 and were instructed to aim for profitability levels close to those of their most profitable competitors. According to analysts, this conversion to the importance of shareholder value was not only instigated by pressures from Wall Street, but also from Deutsche Bank, the company's largest shareholder. Deutsche Bank has a 24 percent share of Daimler-Benz, worth roughly $6 billion, and its chief executive, Hilmar Kopper, is the chairman of Daimler's *aufsichtsrat* (board of supervisors). Since Deutsche Bank has a poor return on capital of approximately 8 percent, compared to 20 percent at many large American banks such as Citicorp, Kopper is

rumoured to be pressing Daimler-Benz to place more emphasis on profitability. To his Detroit audience Schrempp remarked:

> Profitability can no longer be a ghost word in Europe. Only profitable
> companies can ensure jobs and benefits. However, we do not think of
> profitability over the short-term . . . Value is not created just by
> paying out dividends to shareholders. Value creation is organic to a
> growing and profitable business.

However, Schrempp had to admit that the German labor unions, media,
politicians and general public were slow at accepting Daimler's new
message. In some circles, reactions had been vehement – just short of
burning top management at the stake. At the other end, however, there
were some shareholder activists, mainly in the US, arguing that Schrempp
hadn't gone far enough. Criticisms were also levelled at the corporate
governance structure at Daimler, where the twenty-person board of
supervisors included only two people with experience in running a major
manufacturer (half the board, by law, consists of labor representatives).
Schrempp's position, he stated in his address, was to balance the two
extremes:

> The imperatives that drive Anglo-American business are also making
> shareholder value an issue for European industry. However, we can-
> not simply graft Anglo-American business practices on to European
> industry. Rather, we must harness the best elements of both worlds.

As Schrempp concluded his speech, and the audience applauded, many in
the room were impressed by Schrempp's words. But some wondered
whether striving to get the 'best of both worlds' isn't a recipe for getting
'stuck in the middle'.

Sources: *The Economist*, February 15 1997; *Forbes*, April 22 1996; *Business Week*,
February 5 1996

The Debate and the Readings

Selecting the first reading to represent the shareholder value perspective
was a simple task. Alfred Rappaport's highly influential book *Creating
Shareholder Value*[32] is the classic reading in the field. Although the largest
part of his book details how the shareholder value approach can be
applied to planning and performance evaluation processes, the first
chapter is a compelling exposition of his underlying views on the purpose
of a business organization. This first chapter, entitled 'Shareholder Value
and Corporate Purpose', has been reprinted here. Rappaport's argument is
straightforward – the primary purpose of corporations should be to
maximize shareholder value. Therefore, 'business strategies should be
judged by the economic returns they generate for shareholders, as

measured by dividends plus the increase in the company's share price.' Unlike some other proponents of the shareholder value perspective, Rappaport does not explicitly claim that shareholders have the moral right to demand the primacy of profitability. His argument is more pragmatic – failing to meet the objective of maximizing shareholder value will be punished by more expensive financing. A company's financial power is ultimately determined by the stock markets. Hence, management's ability to meet the demands of the various corporate constituencies depends on the continuing support of its shareholders. Creating shareholder value, therefore, precedes the satisfaction of all other claims on the corporation. It should be noted, however, that Rappaport's arrows are not directed at the demands of employees, customers, suppliers or debtholders, but at top management. He carefully states that senior executives may in some situations pursue objectives that are not to the benefit of shareholders. His preferred solution is not to change corporate governance structures, but to more tightly align the interests of both groups, for example by giving top managers a relatively large ownership position and by tying their compensation to shareholder return performance (in later writings he does favor more structural reforms[33]).

The opening reading on behalf of the stakeholder values perspective is also a classic, 'Stockholders and Stakeholders: A New Perspective on Corporate Governance,' by Edward Freeman and David Reed[34]. This article in *California Management Review* and Freeman's subsequent book *Strategic Management: A Stakeholder Approach*[35] were instrumental in popularizing the stakeholder concept. In their article, Freeman and Reed challenge 'the view that stockholders have a privileged place in the business enterprise.' They deplore the fact that 'it has long been gospel that corporations have obligations to stockholders . . . that are sacrosanct and inviolable.' They argue that there has also been a long tradition of management thinkers who believe that corporations have a broader responsibility towards other stakeholders than only the suppliers of equity financing. It is their conviction that such a definition of the corporation, as a system serving the interests of multiple stakeholders, is superior to the shareholder perspective. Their strong preference for the stakeholder concept is largely based on the pragmatic argument that in reality stakeholders have the power to seriously affect the continuity of the corporation. Stakeholder analysis is needed to understand the actual claims placed by constituents on the firm and to evaluate each stakeholder's power position. Stakeholder management is a practical response to the fact that corporations cannot afford to ignore or down-play the interests of the claimants. Only here and there do Freeman and Reed hint that corporations have the moral responsibility to work on behalf of all stakeholders (which Freeman does more explicitly in some of his later works[36]). In their opinion, the consequence of the stakeholder concept for corporate governance is that 'there are times when stakeholders must participate in the decision-making process.' However, they believe that if boards of directors adopt a stakeholder outlook and become more responsive to the demands placed on corporations, structural reforms to give stakeholders a stronger role in corporate governance will not be necessary.

The third reading is intended to bring the international perspective directly into the debate, instead of introducing possible cross-cultural differences at the end of the chapter. The title of the article by Masaru Yoshimori, 'Whose Company Is It? The Concept of the Corporation in Japan and the West,'[37] reflects the essence of the debate on corporate purpose. The ultimate issue dividing the shareholder value and stakeholder values perspectives is their conception of organization ownership. Yoshimori has looked at this issue by asking middle managers in Britain, France, Germany, the US, and Japan the simple question 'In whose interest should the firm be managed?'. He reports that the countries studied fall into three categories. In Britain and the US the shareholder value perspective, which he refers to as the monistic concept of the corporation, is most prevalent. In Japan, on the other hand, the stakeholder values perspective is by far the predominant outlook. In the Japanese pluralistic concept of the corporation, the employees' interests take precedence, closely followed by those of the main banks, major suppliers, subcontractors, and distributors. According to Yoshimori, most managers in Germany and France exhibit a dualistic concept of the corporation, in which shareholder and employee interests are both taken into consideration. Yoshimori carries on to explain the most important differences between these five countries, and he weighs the costs and benefits of each. He concludes that in all countries corporate governance is poorly developed, and that nations have a lot to learn from one another. In his opinion, international cross-fertilization will lead to a partial convergence of corporate governance systems in the various countries. However, 'the concept of the corporation is firmly rooted in the historic, economic, political and even socio-cultural traditions of the nation,' and therefore it is improbable 'that any one concept should drive out another at least in the foreseeable future.'

Once again, readers are faced with diametrically opposed arguments convincingly put forward by discussants. This places readers once more in the position of needing to look for their own judgment on how to deal with a paradox, that of profitability and responsibility.

Reading 1   Shareholder Value and Corporate Purpose

By Alfred Rappaport[†]

Corporate mission statements proclaiming that the primary responsibility of management is to maximize shareholders' total return via dividends and increases in the market price of the company's shares abound. While the principle that the fundamental objective of the business corporation is to increase the value of its shareholders' investment is widely accepted, there is substantially less agreement about how this is accomplished.

On the cover of its 1984 annual report Coca-Cola states that 'to increase shareholder value over time is the objective driving this enterprise'. On the very next page the company goes on to say that to accomplish its objective 'growth in annual earnings per share and increased return on equity are still the names of the game.' In contrast, Hillenbrand Industries, a producer of caskets and hospital equipment, also declares its intention to provide a superior return to its shareholders, but to accomplish that objective management is focusing not on earnings but rather on creating 'shareholder value,' which, it explains in the 1984 annual report, 'is created when a company generates free cash flow in excess of the shareholders' investment in the business.'

Both Coca-Cola and Hillenbrand Industries acknowledge their responsibility to maximize return to their respective shareholders. However, Coca-Cola emphasizes accounting indicators, earnings-per-share growth, and return on equity, while Hillenbrand Industries emphasizes the cash-flow based shareholder value approach to achieve shareholder returns. There are material differences between these two approaches to assessing a company's investment opportunities. Maximizing earnings-per-share growth or other accounting numbers may not necessarily lead to maximizing return for shareholders.

The Growing Interest

Numerous surveys indicate that a majority of the largest industrial companies have employed the shareholder value approach in capital

[†] Source: This article was adapted with permission from Chapter 1 of *Creating Shareholder Value: The New Standard for Business Performance*, The Free Press, New York, 1986, pp. 1–13.

budgeting for some time. Capital budgeting applications deal with investment projects such as capacity additions rather than total investment at the business level. Thus, we sometimes see a situation where capital projects regularly exceed the minimum acceptable rate of return, while the business unit itself is a 'problem' and creates little or no value for shareholders. This situation can arise because capital expenditures typically represent only a small percentage of total company outlays. For example, capital expenditures amount to about 10 percent of total outlays at General Motors, a particularly capital intensive company.

During the past 10 years, the shareholder value approach has been frequently applied not only to internal investments such as capacity additions, but also to opportunities for external growth such as mergers and acquisitions. Recently a number of major companies such as American Hospital Supply, Combustion Engineering, Hillenbrand Industries, Libbey-Owens-Ford, Marriott, and Westinghouse have found that the shareholder value approach can be productively extended from individual projects to the entire strategic plan. A strategic business unit (SBU) is commonly defined as the smallest organizational unit for which integrated strategic planning, related to a distinct product that serves a well-defined market, is feasible. A strategy for an SBU may then be seen as a collection of product-market related investments and the company itself may be characterized as a portfolio of these investment-requiring strategies. By estimating the future cash flows associated with each strategy, a company can assess the economic value to shareholders of alternative strategies at the business unit and corporate levels.

The interest in shareholder value is gaining momentum as a result of several recent developments.

■   The threat of corporate take-overs by those seeking undervalued, under-managed assets.

■   Impressive endorsements by corporate leaders who have adopted the approach.

■   The growing recognition that traditional accounting measures such as EPS and ROI are not reliably linked to increasing the value of the company's shares.

■   Reporting of returns to shareholders along with other measures of performance in the business press such as *Fortune's* annual ranking of the 500 leading industrial firms.

■   A growing recognition that executives' long-term compensation needs to be more closely tied to returns to shareholders.

Endorsements of the shareholder value approach can be found in an increasing number of annual reports and other corporate publications. One of the more thoughtful statements appears in Libbey-Owens-Ford's 1983 annual report and is reproduced as Exhibit 11.2. Combustion

EXHIBIT 11.2
Libbey-Owens-Ford

A Greater Emphasis on Shareholder Value

Libbey-Owens-Ford's mission statement specifies that its primary responsibility is to its shareholders, and that the company has a continuing requirement to increase the value of our shareholders' investment in LOF. This is not just a contemporary business phrase, but the basis for a long-term company strategy. It evaluates business strategies and plans in terms of value to our shareholders, not just on the incremental income that the results will contribute to the bottom line. It requires a greater emphasis on developing strategies and plans that will increase shareholder value as measured by the market appreciation of our stock and dividends.

Traditional Accounting Measures May Not Tell the Entire Story

Traditionally, the most popular way to determine whether a company is performing well is through such accounting measurements as earnings per share (EPS) and return on investment. These measures do, of course, give an indication of a company's performance, but they can be misleading in that often they do not measure the increase or decrease in shareholder value. Sustained growth as measured by EPS does not necessarily reflect an increase in stock value.

This occurs because earnings do not reflect changes in risk and inflation, nor do they take into account the cost of added capital that may have been invested in the business to finance its growth. Yet these are critical considerations when you are striving to increase the value of the shareholders' investment.

Cash Flow Analysis is Emphasized

LOF stresses the importance of cash flow measurement and performance. Individual operating companies must analyze the cash flow effects of running their businesses. Where cash comes from and what cash is used for must be simply and clearly set forth. LOF's cash and short-term investments increased $46.3 million during 1983.

The Shareholder Value Approach

The shareholder value approach taken by LOF emphasized economic cash flow analysis in evaluating individual projects and in determining the economic value of the overall strategy of each business unit and the corporation as a whole. Management looks at the business units and the corporation and determines the minimum operating return necessary to create value. It then reviews the possible contribution of alternative strategies and evaluates the financial feasibility of the strategic plan, based on the company's cost of capital, return on assets, the cash flow stream and other important measurements.

This disciplined process allows LOF to objectively evaluate all its corporate investments, including internal projects and acquisitions, in light of our primary goal to increase shareholder value.

Engineering's vice president for finance states that 'a primary financial objective for Combustion Engineering is to create shareholder value by earning superior returns on capital invested in the business. This serves as a clear guide for management action and is the conceptual framework on which CE's financial objectives and goals are based.'

Whether or not executives agree with the well-publicized tactics of raiders such as Carl Icahn and T. Boone Pickens, they recognize that the raiders characterize themselves as champions of the shareholders. The raiders attack on two fronts. First, they are constantly searching for poorly managed companies, where aggressive changes in strategic directions could dramatically improve the value of the stock. Second, they identify undervalued assets that can be redeployed to boost the stock price. As a result, many executives recognize a new and compelling reason to be concerned with the performance of their company's stock.

Executives have also become increasingly aware that many accrual-based accounting measures do not provide a dependable picture of the current and future performance of an organization. Numerous companies have sustained double-digit EPS growth while providing minimal or even *negative* returns to shareholders. Hillenbrand Industries, for example, points out in its 1984 annual report (p. 4) that 'public companies that focus on achieving short-term earnings to meet external expectations sometimes jeopardize their ability to create long-term value.'

Considerable attention has focused recently on the problems associated with rewarding executives on the basis of short-term accounting-based indicators. As a reflection of the increasing scrutiny under which executive compensation has come, business publications such as *Fortune* and *Business Week* have begun to publish compensation surveys that examine the correlation between the executives' pay and how well their companies have performed based on several measures-including returns to shareholders. For example, *Business Week*'s executive compensation scoreboard now includes a 'pay-performance index' for 255 companies in 36 industries. The index shows how well the top two executives in each company were paid relative to how shareholders fared. The index is the ratio of the executive's three-year total pay as a percent of the industry average to the shareholders' total three-year return as a percent of the industry average. If an executive's pay and shareholders' return are both at the industry average, the index is 100. The lower the index, the better shareholders fared. The broad range in the pay-performance index, even within industries, has further fueled the interest in achieving shareholder value. For the 1982–1984 period, for example, *Business Week* reported a pay-performance index of 59 for Roger Smith, CEO of General Motors, and an index of 160 for Phillip Caldwell, CEO of Ford Motor.

When the shareholder value approach first gained attention toward the end of the 1970s, even the executives who found the concept an intriguing notion tended to think that the approach would be very difficult to implement. The task of educating managers seemed substantial, and they were also not eager to develop a new planning system if it might involve upheaval in the corporate information system. Recent advances in technology have put impressive analytical potential at management's disposal. Managers' decisions are now greatly facilitated by microcomputer software. New approaches thus can more readily be incorporated without displacing existing information systems.

Management versus Shareholder Objectives

It is important to recognize that the objectives of management may in some situations differ from those of the company's shareholders. Managers, like other people, act in their self-interest. The theory of a market economy is, after all, based on individuals promoting their self-interests via market transactions to bring about an efficient allocation of resources. In a world in which principals (e.g. stockholders) have imperfect control over their agents (e.g. managers), these agents may not always engage in transactions solely in the best interests of the principals. Agents have their own objectives and it may sometimes pay them to sacrifice the principals' interests. The problem is exacerbated in large corporations where it is difficult to identify the interests of a diverse set of stockholders ranging from institutional investors to individuals with small holdings.

Critics of large corporations often allege that corporate managers have too much power and that they act in ways to benefit themselves at the expense of shareholders and other corporate constituencies. The argument is generally developed along the following lines. Responsibility for administering companies or 'control' is vested in the hands of professional managers and thereby has been separated from 'ownership.' Since the ownership of shares in large corporations tends to be diffused, individual shareholders are said to have neither influence on nor interest in corporate governance issues such as the election of board members. Therefore, boards are largely responsive to management which, in turn, can ignore shareholders and run companies as they see fit.

The foregoing 'separation of ownership and control' argument advanced by Berle and Means in 1932[38] has been a persistent theme of corporate critics during the intervening years. There are, however, a number of factors that induce management to act in the best interests of shareholders. These factors derive from the fundamental premise that the greater the expected unfavorable consequences to the manager who decreases the wealth of shareholders, the less likely it is that the manager will, in fact, act against the interests of shareholders.

Consistent with the above premise, at least four major factors will induce management to adopt a shareholder orientation: (1) a relatively large ownership position, (2) compensation tied to shareholder return performance, (3) threat of take-over by another organization, and (4) competitive labor markets for corporate executives.

Economic rationality dictates that stock ownership by management motivates executives to identify more closely with the shareholders' economic interests. Indeed, we would expect that the greater the proportion of personal wealth invested in company stock or tied to stock options, the greater would be management's shareholder orientation. While the top executives in many companies often have relatively large percentages of their wealth invested in company stock, this is much less often the case for divisional and business unit managers. And it is at the divisional and business unit levels that most resource allocation decisions are made in decentralized organizations.

Even when corporate executives own shares in their company, their viewpoint on the acceptance of risk may differ from that of shareholders. It is reasonable to expect that many corporate executives have a lower tolerance for risk. If the company invests in a risky project, stockholders can always balance this risk against other risks in their presumably diversified portfolios. The manager, however, can balance a project failure only against the other activities of the division or the company. Thus, managers are hurt by the failure more than shareholders.

The second factor likely to influence management to adopt a shareholder orientation is compensation tied to shareholder return performance. The most direct means of linking top management's interests with those of shareholders is to base compensation, and particularly the incentive portion, on market returns realized by shareholders. Exclusive reliance on shareholder returns, however, has its own limitations. First, movements in a company's stock price may well be greatly influenced by factors beyond management control such as the overall state of the economy and stock market. Second, shareholder returns may be materially influenced by what management believes to be unduly optimistic or pessimistic market expectations at the beginning or end of the performance measurement period. And third, divisional and business unit performance cannot be directly linked to stock price.

Rather than linking incentive compensation directly to the market returns earned by shareholders, most Fortune 500 companies tie annual bonuses and long-term performance plans to internal financial goals such as earnings or accounting return on investment. These accounting criteria can often conflict with the way corporate shares are valued by the market. If incentives were largely based on earnings, for example, management might well be motivated to pursue economically unsound strategies when viewed from the perspective of shareholders. In such a situation what is economically irrational from the shareholder viewpoint may be a perfectly rational course of action for the decision-making executives.

The third factor affecting management behavior is the threat of take-over by another company. Tender offers have become a commonly employed means of transferring corporate control. Moreover the size of the targets continues to become larger. During the 1979–1985 period, 77 acquisitions each in excess of $1 billion were completed. The threat of take-over is an essential means of constraining corporate managers who might choose to pursue personal goals at the expense of shareholders. Any significant exploitation of shareholders should be reflected in a lower stock price. This lower price, relative to what it might be with more efficient management, offers an attractive take-over opportunity for another company which in many cases will replace incumbent management. An active market for corporate control places limits on the divergence of interests between management and shareholders and thereby serves as an important counterargument to the 'separation of ownership and control' criticisms.

The fourth and final factor influencing management's shareholder orientation is the labor market for corporate executives. Managerial labor markets are an essential mechanism for motivating management to function in the best interests of shareholders. Managers compete for positions both within and outside of the firm. The increasing number of executive recruiting firms and the length of the 'Who's News' column in the *Wall Street Journal* are evidence that the managerial labor market is very active. What is less obvious is how managers are evaluated in this market. Within the firm, performance evaluation and incentive schemes are the basic mechanisms for monitoring managerial performance. As seen earlier, the question here is whether these measures are reliably linked to the market price of the company's shares.

How managers communicate their value to the labor market outside of their individual firms is less apparent. While the performance of top-level corporate officers can be gleaned from annual reports and other publicly available corporate communications, this is not generally the case for divisional managers. For corporate level executives, the question is whether performance for shareholders is the dominant criterion in assessing their value in the executive labor market. The question in the case of division managers is, first, how does the labor market monitor and gain insights about their performance and second, what is the basis for valuing their services.

'Excellence' and Restructuring

Two of the most visible business phenomena of the first half of the 1980s have been the publication of Peters and Waterman's *In Search of*

Excellence[39] and the unprecedented surge in the restructuring of companies. The 'excellence phenomenon' certainly provided no obvious encouragement for management to link its decisions more closely with the objective of maximizing returns to shareholders. In contrast, the more recent restructuring movement is clearly a manifestation of top management's growing concern with its company's share price and shareholder returns.

As US corporations began the 1980s, saddled with a decade of inflation and lagging productivity, nothing could have come as better news than the idea that not all excellent companies are Japanese. It was in this climate that *In Search of Excellence*, published in 1982, became an absolute sensation. Its longevity on the top of the best-seller list along with its wide coverage in the business press provided an extraordinary platform for the authors' ideas.

The basic purpose of *In Search of Excellence* was to identify key attributes of corporate excellence that are common among successful American corporations. To choose the 'excellent' companies, Peters and Waterman began by assembling a list of 62 US companies that were considered 'successful' by business leaders, consultants, members of the business press, and business school professors. From that list they selected 36 'excellent' companies based on superior performance for such financial measures as return on total capital, return on equity, return on sales, and asset growth. Eight attributes of corporate excellence were identified – a bias for action; staying close to the customer; autonomy and entrepreneurship; productivity through people; hands-on, value-driven management; sticking to the knitting; simple organization form and lean staff; and simultaneous loose–tight properties.

Even though the 'excellent' firms exhibited superior financial (accounting) performance over the 1960–1980 period, they did not provide consistently superior returns to shareholders via dividends plus share price appreciation. The excellent companies did not perform significantly better than the market. Indeed, they did not consistently outperform their respective industry groups or closest competitors. These results once again raise questions about the use of accounting measures to gauge the economic performance of corporations. Since the eight attributes of corporate excellence are not associated with systematically superior returns to shareholders, efforts to emulate these attributes may be ill-advised.

While *In Search of Excellence* became 'must reading' in many organizations during 1982 and 1983, a certain degree of disenchantment set in during the following two years as a number of 'excellent' companies experienced strategic setbacks. Atari, Avon Products, Caterpillar Tractor, Digital Equipment, Hewlett-Packard, Levi Strauss, and Texas Instruments serve as examples.

But if emulating excellent companies has lost some of its luster, a new focal point of interest has captured the imagination of management during the past couple of years – restructuring. Hardly a day passes without some company announcing a major restructuring of its businesses or capital structure. Restructuring involves diverse activities such as divestiture of underperforming businesses or businesses that do not 'fit,' spin-offs directly to shareholders, acquisitions paid with 'excess cash,' stock repurchases, debt swaps, and liquidation of overfunded pension funds. In many cases, these restructurings are motivated by a desire to foil a take-over bid by so-called 'raiders' who look for undermanaged companies where changes in strategic direction could dramatically increase the value of the stock, and for companies with high liquidation values relative to their current share price. There is, of course, no better means of avoiding a take-over than increasing the price of the stock. Thus, increasing share price has become the fundamental purpose of corporate restructuring.

In contrast to the earlier euphoria over emulating excellent companies, the current restructuring movement is solidly based on shareholder value creation principles. In 1985, the Standard & Poor's 500 appreciated 26 percent in price. Goldman Sachs estimates that corporate restructuring accounted for about 30 percent of that price change. However, the early stage of the restructuring movement, which I call 'Phase I restructuring,' is largely based on one-time transactions such as those listed above rather than changes in day-to-day management of the business.

The necessary agenda for the second half of the 1980s seems clear. Companies need to move from Phase I restructuring to Phase II restructuring. In Phase II, the shareholder value approach is employed not only when buying and selling businesses or changing the company's capital structure, but also in the planning and performance monitoring of all business strategies on an ongoing basis. Frequently, the most difficult issue in this area is how to go about estimating the impact of strategies on shareholder value. Fortunately, relatively straightforward approaches do exist for estimating the shareholder value created by a business strategy, and an increasing number of major companies have begun to use them.

Most companies already use the same discounted cash-flow techniques used in the shareholder value approach to assess the attractiveness of capital investment projects and to value prospective acquisition targets. This approach can be extended to estimate the value creation potential of individual business units and the strategic plan for the entire company.

In Phase II restructuring it will also become increasingly important that executive compensation be tied closely to the shareholder value driven plans so that management will be strongly motivated to make decisions consistent with creating maximum returns to shareholders. A successful implementation of Phase II restructuring not only ensures that management has met its fiduciary responsibility to develop corporate performance evaluation systems consistent with the parameters investors use to value the company, but also minimizes the Phase I concern that a take-over of an undermanaged company is imminent.

Rationale for Shareholder Value Approach

Business strategies should be judged by the economic returns they generate for shareholders, as measured by dividends plus the increase in the company's share price. As management considers alternative strategies, those expected to develop the greatest sustainable competitive advantage will be those that will also create the greatest value for shareholders. The 'shareholder value approach' estimates the economic value of an investment (e.g. the shares of a company, strategies, mergers and acquisitions, capital expenditures) by discounting forecasted cash flows by the cost of capital. These cash flows, in turn, serve as the foundation for shareholder returns from dividends and share-price appreciation.

The case for why management should pursue this objective is comparatively straightforward. Management is often characterized as balancing the interests of various corporate constituencies such as employees, customers, suppliers, debtholders, and stockholders. As Treynor[40] points out, the company's continued existence depends upon a financial relationship with each of these parties. Employees want competitive wages. Customers want high quality at a competitive price. Suppliers and debtholders each have financial claims that must be satisfied with cash when they fall due. Stockholders as residual claimants of the firm look for cash dividends and the prospect of future dividends which is reflected in the market price of the stock.

If the company does not satisfy the financial claims of its constituents, it will cease to be a viable organization. Employees, customers, and suppliers will simply withdraw their support. Thus, a going concern must strive to enhance its cash-generating ability. The ability of a company to distribute cash to its various constituencies depends on its ability to generate cash from operating its businesses and on its ability to obtain any additional funds needed from external sources.

Debt and equity financing are the two basic external sources. The company's ability to borrow today is based on projections of how much cash will be generated in the future. Borrowing power and the market value of the shares both depend on a company's cash-generating ability. The market value of the shares directly impacts the second source of financing, that is, equity financing. For a given level of funds required, the higher the share price, the less dilution will be borne by current shareholders. Therefore, management's financial power to deal effectively with corporate claimants also comes from increasing the value of the shares. Treynor, a former editor of the *Financial Analysts Journal*, summarizes this line of thinking best.

> Those who criticize the goal of share value maximization are forgetting that stockholders are not merely the beneficiaries of the corporation's financial success, but also the referees who determine management's financial power.
>
> Any management – no matter how powerful and independent – that flouts the financial objective of maximizing share value does so at its own peril.

Reading 2 Stockholders and Stakeholders: A New Perspective on Corporate Governance

By Edward Freeman and David Reed[†]

Management thought has changed dramatically in recent years. There have been, and are now underway, both conceptual and practical revolutions in the ways that management theorists and managers think about organizational life. The purpose of this article is to understand the implications of one of these shifts in world view; namely, the shift from 'stockholder' to 'stakeholder.'

The Stakeholder Concept

It has long been gospel that corporations have obligations to stockholders, holders of the firm's equity, that are sacrosanct and inviolable.

[†] Source: This article was adapted with permission from 'Stockholders and Stakeholders: A new perspective on Corporate Governance' *California Management Review*, Vol. 25, No. 3, Spring 1993, pp. 88–106.

Corporate action or inaction is to be driven by attention to the needs of its stockholders, usually thought to be measured by stock price, earnings per share, or some other financial measure. It has been argued that the proper relationship of management to its stockholders is similar to that of the fiduciary to the *cestui gue trustent*, whereby the interests of the stockholders should be dutifully cared for by management. Thus, any action taken by management must ultimately be justified by whether or not it furthers the interests of the corporation and its stockholders.

There is also a long tradition of departure from the view that stockholders have a privileged place in the business enterprise. Berle and Means[41] were worried about the 'degree of prominence entitling (the corporation) to be dealt with as a major social institution.' Chester Barnard argued that the purpose of the corporation was to serve society, and that the function of the executive was to instill this sense of moral purpose in the corporation's employees[42]. Public relations and corporate social action have a history too long to be catalogued here. However, a recent development calls for a more far-reaching change in the way that we look at corporate life, and that is the good currency of the idea of 'stakeholders.'

The stakeholder notion is indeed a deceptively simple one. It says that there are other groups to whom the corporation is responsible in addition to stockholders: those groups who have a stake in the actions of the corporation. The word *stakeholder*, coined in an internal memorandum at the Stanford Research Institute (SRI) in 1963, refers to 'those groups without whose support the organization would cease to exist.' The list of stakeholders originally included shareowners, employees, customers, suppliers, lenders, and society. Stemming from the work of Igor Ansoff and Robert Stewart (in the planning department at Lockheed) and, later, Marion Doscher and Stewart (at SRI), stakeholder analysis served and continues to serve an important function in the SRI corporate planning process.

From the original work at SRI, the historical trail diverges in a number of directions. In his now classic *Corporate Strategy: An Analytic Approach to Business Policy for Growth and Expansion*, Igor Ansoff[43] makes limited use of the theory:

> While as we shall see later, 'responsibilities' and 'objectives' are not synonymous, they have been made one in a 'stakeholder theory' of objectives. This theory maintains that the objectives of the firm should be derived by balancing the conflicting claims of the various 'stakeholders' in the firm: managers, workers, stockholders, suppliers, vendors.

Ansoff goes on to reject the stakeholder theory in favor of a view which separates objectives into 'economic' and 'social' with the latter being a 'secondary modifying and constraining influence' on the former.

In the mid-1970s, researchers in systems theory, led by Russell Ackoff[44] 'rediscovered' stakeholder analysis, or at least took Ansoff's admonition more seriously. Propounding essentially an open systems view of organizations, Ackoff argues that many social problems can be solved by the redesign of fundamental institutions with the support and interaction of stakeholders in the system.

A second trail from Ansoff's original reference is the work of William Dill[45] who, in concert with Ackoff, sought to move the stakeholder concept from the periphery of corporate planning to a central place. In 1975 Dill argued:

> For a long time, we have assumed that the views and the initiative of stakeholders could be dealt with as externalities to the strategic planning and management process: as data to help management shape decisions, or as legal and social constraints to limit them. We have been reluctant, though, to admit the idea that some of these outside stakeholders might seek and earn active roles with management to make decisions. The move today is from *stakeholder influence towards stakeholder participation*.

Dill went on to set out a role for strategic managers as communicators with stakeholders and considered the role of adversary groups such as Nader's Raiders in the strategic process. For the most part, until Dill's paper, stakeholders had been assumed to be nonadversarial, or adversarial only in the sense of labor-management relations. By broadening the notion of stakeholder to 'people outside ... who have ideas about what the economic and social performance of the enterprise should include,' Dill set the stage for the use of the stakeholder concept as an umbrella for strategic management.

A related development is primarily responsible for giving the stakeholder concept a boost; namely, the increase in concern with the social involvement of business. The corporate social responsibility movement is too diverse and has spawned too many ideas, concepts, and techniques to explain here. Suffice it to say that the social movements of the sixties and seventies – civil rights, the antiwar movement, consumerism, environmentalism, and women's rights – served as a catalyst for rethinking the role of the business enterprise in society. From Milton Friedman to John Kenneth Galbraith, there is a diversity of arguments. However, one aspect of the corporate social responsibility debate is particularly relevant to understanding the good currency of the stakeholder concept.

In the early 1970s the Harvard Business School undertook a project on corporate social responsibility. The output of the project was voluminous, and of particular importance was the development of a pragmatic model of social responsibility called 'the corporate social responsiveness model.'[46] It essentially addressed Dill's question with respect to social issues: 'How can the corporation respond proactively to the increased pressure for positive social change?' By concentrating on responsiveness instead of responsibility, the Harvard researchers were able to link the analysis of social issues with the traditional areas of strategy and organization.

By the late 1970s the need for strategic management processes to take account of nontraditional business problems in terms of government, special interest groups, trade associations, foreign competitors, dissident shareholders, and complex issues such as employee rights, equal opportunity, environmental pollution, consumer rights, tariffs, government regulation, and reindustrialization had become obvious. To begin to develop these processes, The Wharton School began, in 1977 in its Applied Research Center, a 'stakeholder project.' The objectives of the project were to put together a number of strands of thought and to develop a theory of management which enabled executives to formulate and implement corporate strategy in turbulent environments. Thus, an action research model was used whereby stakeholder theory was generated by actual cases.

To date the project has explored the implications of the stakeholder concept on three levels: as a management theory; as a process for practitioners to use in strategic management; and as an analytical framework.

At the theoretical level the implications of substituting *stakeholder* for *stockholder* needs to be explicated. The first problem at this level is the actual definition of *stakeholder*. SRI's original definition is too general and too exclusive to serve as a means of identifying those external groups who are strategically important. The concentration on generic stakeholders, such as society and customers, rather than specific social interest groups and specific customer segments produces an analysis which can only be used as a background for the planning process. Strategically useful information about the actions, objectives, and motivations of specific groups, which is needed if management is to be responsive to stakeholder concerns, requires a more specific and inclusive definition.

We propose two definitions of *stakeholder*: a wide sense, which includes groups who are friendly or hostile, and a narrow sense, which captures the essence of the SRI definition but is more specific.

- *The wide sense of stakeholder.* Any identifiable group or individual who can affect the achievement of an organization's objectives or who is affected by the achievement of an organization's objectives. (Public interest groups, protest groups, government agencies, trade associations, competitors, unions, as well as employees, customer segments, shareowners, and others are stakeholders, in this sense.)

- *The narrow sense of stakeholder.* Any identifiable group or individual on which the organization is dependent for its continued survival. (Employees, customer segments, certain suppliers, key government agencies, shareowners, certain financial institutions, as well as others are all stakeholders in the narrow sense of the term.)

While executives are willing to recognize that employees, suppliers, and customers have a stake in the corporation, many resist the inclusion of adversary groups. But from the standpoint of corporate strategy, *stakeholder* must be understood in the wide sense: strategies need to account for those groups who can affect the achievement of the firm's objectives. Some may feel happier with other words, such as *influencers, claimants, publics, or constituencies.* Semantics aside, if corporations are to formulate and implement strategies in turbulent environments, theories of strategy must have concepts, such as the wide sense of *stakeholder*, which allow the analysis of all external forces and pressures whether they are friendly or hostile. In what follows we will use *stakeholder* in the wide sense, as our primary objective is to elucidate the questions of corporate governance from the perspective of strategic management.

A second issue at the theoretical level is the generation of prescriptive propositions which explain actual cases and articulate regulative principles for future use. Thus, a *post hoc* analysis of the brewing industry and the problem of beverage container legislation, combined with a similar analysis of the regulatory environments of public utilities have led to some simple propositions which serve as a philosophical guideline for strategy formulation. For example:

- Generalize the marketing approach: understand the needs of each stakeholder, in a similar fashion to understanding customer needs, and design products, services, and programs to fulfill those needs.

- Establish negotiation processes: understand the political nature of a number of stakeholders, and the applicability of concepts and techniques of political science, such as coalition analysis, conflict management, and the use and abuse of unilateral action.

- Establish a decision philosophy that is oriented towards seizing the initiative rather than reacting to events as they occur.

- Allocate organizational resources based on the degree of importance of the environmental turbulence (the stakeholders' claims).

Other prescriptive propositions can be put forth, especially with respect to issues of corporate governance. One proposition that has been discussed is to 'involve stakeholder groups in strategic decisions,' or 'invite stakeholders to participate in governance decisions.' While propositions like this may have substantial merit, we have not examined enough cases nor marshalled enough evidence to support them in an unqualified manner. There are cases where participation is appropriate.

Some public utilities have been quite successful in the use of stakeholder advisory groups in matters of rate setting. However, given the breadth of our concept of stakeholder we believe that co-optation through participation is not always the correct strategic decision.

The second level of analysis is the use of stakeholder concepts in strategy formulation processes. Two processes have been used so far: the *Stakeholder Strategy Process* and the *Stakeholder Audit Process*. The Stakeholder Strategy Process is a systematic method for analyzing the relative importance of stakeholders and their cooperative potential (how they can help the corporation achieve its objectives) and their competitive threat (how they can prevent the corporation from achieving its objectives). The process is one which relies on a behavioral analysis (both actual and potential) for input, and an explanatory model of stakeholder objectives and resultant strategic shifts for output. The Stakeholder Audit Process is a systematic method for identifying stakeholders and assessing the effectiveness of current organizational strategies. By itself, each process has a use in the strategic management of an organization. Each analyzes the stakeholder environment from the standpoint of organizational mission and objectives and seeks to formulate strategies for meeting stakeholder needs and concerns.

The use of the stakeholder concept at the analytical level means thinking in terms which are broader than current strategic and operational problems. It implies looking at public policy questions in stakeholder terms and trying to understand how the relationships between an organization and its stakeholders would change given the implementation of certain policies.

One analytical device depicts an organization's stakeholders on a two-dimensional grid map. The first dimension is one of 'interest' or 'stake' and ranges from an equity interest to an economic interest or marketplace stake to an interest or stake as a 'kibitzer' or influencer. Shareowners have an equity stake; customers and suppliers have an economic stake; and single-issue groups have an influencer stake. The second dimension of a stakeholder is its power, which ranges from the formalistic or voting power of stockholders to the economic power of customers to the political power of special interest groups. By *economic power* we mean 'the ability to influence due to marketplace decisions' and by *political power* we mean 'the ability to influence due to use of the political process.'

Figure 11.2 represents this stakeholder grid graphically. It is of course possible that a stakeholder has more than one kind of both stake and power, especially in light of the fact that there are stakeholders who have multiple roles. An employee may be at once shareholder, customer, employee, and even kibitzer. Figure 11.1 represents the prevailing world view. That is, shareholders and directors have formal or voting power; customers, suppliers, and employees have economic power; and govern-

FIGURE 11.1
Classical grid

Stake/Power	Formal or Voting	Economic	Political
Equity	• Stockholders • Directors • Minority interests		
Economic		• Customers • Competitors • Suppliers • Debt holders • Unions	• Foreign governments
Influencers			• Consumer advocates • Government • Nader's Raiders • Sierra Club • Trade associations

ment and special interest groups have political power. Moreover, management concepts and principles have evolved to treat this 'diagonal case.' Managers learn how to handle stockholders and boards via their ability to vote on certain key decisions, and conflicts are resolved by the procedures and processes written into the corporate charter or by methods which involve formal legal parameters. Strategic planners, marketers, financial analysts, and operations executives base their decisions on marketplace variables, and an entire tradition of management principles is based on the economic analysis of the marketplace. Finally, public relations and public affairs managers and lobbyists learn to deal in the political arena. As long as the real world approximately fits into the diagonal, management processes may be able to deal effectively with them. A more thoughtful examination, however, reveals that Figure 11.2 is either a straw man or that shifts of position have occurred. In the auto industry, for instance, one part of government has acquired economic power in terms of the imposition of import quotas or the trigger price mechanism. The Securities and Exchange Commission might be looked at as a kibitzer with formal power in terms of disclosure and accounting rules. Outside directors do not necessarily have an equity stake, especially those women, minorities, and academics who are becoming more and more normal for the boards of large corporations. Some kibitzer groups are buying stock and acquiring an equity stake, and while they also acquire formal power, their

FIGURE 11.2
'Real world' stakeholder grid

Stake/Power	Formal or Voting	Economic	Political
Equity	• Stockholders • Directors • Minority interests		• Dissident stockholders
Economic		• Suppliers • Debt holders • Customers • Unions	• Local governments • Foreign governments • Consumer groups • Unions
Influencers	• Government • SEC • Outside directors	• EPA/OSHA	• Nader's Raiders • Government • Trade associations

main source of power is still political. Witness the marshalling of the political process by church groups in bringing up, at annual meetings, issues such as selling infant formula in the Third World or investing in South Africa. Unions are using their political power as well as their formal clout as managers of large portions of pension funds to influence the company. Customers are being organized by consumer advocates to exercise the voice option and to politicize the marketplace. In short, the real world looks more like Figure 11.2. (Of course, each organization will have its own individual grid.) Thus, the search for alternative applications of traditional management processes must begin, and new concepts and techniques are needed to understand the shifts that have occurred and to manage in the new environment.

There is a need to develop new and innovative management processes to deal with the current and future complexities of management issues. At the theoretical level, stakeholder analysis has been developed to enrich the economic approach to corporate strategy by arguing that kibitzers with political power must be included in the strategy process. At the strategic level, stakeholder analysis takes a number of groups into account and analyzes their strategic impact on the corporation.

Stakeholder Analysis and Corporate Democracy

The debate on corporate governance and, in particular, corporate democracy has recently intensified. Proposals have been put forth to make the corporation more democratic, to encourage shareholder participation and management responsiveness to shareholder needs, and to make corporations more responsive to other stakeholder needs and, hence, to encourage the participation of stakeholders in the governance process. Reforms from cumulative voting to audit committees have been suggested.

Corporate democracy has come to have at least three meanings over the years, which prescribe that corporations should be made more democratic: by increasing the role of government, either as a watchdog or by having public officials on boards of directors; by allowing citizen or public participation in the managing of its affairs via public interest directors and the like; or by encouraging or mandating the active participation of all or many of its shareholders. The analysis of the preceding section has implications for each of these levels of democratization.

The propositions of stakeholder analysis advocate a thorough understanding of a firm's stakeholders (in the wide sense) and recognize that there are times when stakeholders must participate in the decision-making process. The strategic tools and techniques of stakeholder analysis yield a method for determining the timing and degree of such participation. At the absolute minimum this implies that boards of directors must be aware of the impact of their decisions on key stakeholder groups. As stakeholders have begun to exercise more political power and as marketplace decisions become politicized, the need for awareness to grow into responsiveness has become apparent. Thus, the analytical model can be used by boards to map carefully the power and stake of each group. While it is not the proper role of the board to be involved in the implementation of tactical programs at the operational level of the corporation, it must set the tone for how the company deals with stakeholders, both traditional marketplace ones and those who have political power. The board must decide not only whether management is managing the affairs of the corporation, but indeed, what are to count as the affairs of the corporation. This involves assessing the stake and power of each stakeholder group.

Much has been written about the failure of senior management to think strategically, competitively, and globally. Some have argued that American businesspersons are 'managing [their] way to economic decline'[47]. Executives have countered the critics with complaints about the increase in the adversarial role of government and in the number of hostile external interest groups. Yet if the criteria for success for senior executives remains fixated on economic stakeholders with economic power and on short-term performance on Wall Street, the rise of such a turbulent political environment in a free and open society should come as no surprise. If the board sees itself as responsive only to the shareholder in the short term, senior management will continue to manage towards economic decline.[‡] We have argued that the problem of governing the corporation in today's world must be viewed in terms of the entire grid of stakeholders and their power base. It is only by setting the direction for positive response and negotiation at the board level that the adversarial nature of the business–government relationship can be overcome.

If this task of stakeholder management is done properly, much of the air is let out of critics who argue that the corporation must be democratized in terms of increased direct citizen participation. Issues which involve both economic and political stakes and power bases must be addressed in an integrated fashion. No longer can public affairs, public relations, and corporate philanthropy serve as adequate management tools. The sophistication of interest groups who are beginning to use formal power mechanisms, such as proxy fights, annual meetings, the corporate charter, to focus the attention of management on the affairs of the corporation has increased. Responsive boards will seize these opportunities to learn more about those stakeholders who have chosen the option of voice over the Wall Street Rule. As boards direct management to respond to these concerns, to negotiate with critics, to trade off certain policies in return for positive support, the pressure for mandated citizen participation will subside.

Reading 3   Whose Company is it? The Concept of the Corporation in Japan and the West

By Masaru Yoshimori[†]

Available evidence seems to suggest that in terms of corporate governance countries may be divided into three groups: with monistic, dualistic

---

[‡] It is arguable whether responsiveness to nonmarket stakeholders is in the long-term interest of the corporation. We believe that there is no need to appeal to utilitarian notions of greatest social good or altruism or social responsibility. Rather the corporation fulfills its obligations to shareholders in the long term only through proper stakeholder management. In short we believe that enlightened self-interest gives both reasons why (personal motivation) and reasons for (social justification) taking stakeholder concerns into account. The development of this argument is, however, beyond our present scope.

[†] Source: This article was adapted with permission from *Long Range Planning*, Vol. 28, No. 4, 1995, pp. 33–44.

and pluralistic concepts of the corporation. The monistic outlook is shareholder-oriented and looks at the firm as the private property of its owners. This concept is prevalent in the United States and the UK. The dualistic concept also puts a premium on the shareholder interest, but the interests of employees are taken into account as well. This is an adapted form of the monistic concept and is widely shared in Germany and to a lesser degree in France. The view that the firm is a social institution where people develop themselves freely ranked first among six alternative definitions, according to Albach's survey of leading German companies in 1975, though it slipped to the third rank in 1991[48].

The pluralistic approach assumes that the firm belongs to all the stakeholders, with the employees' interests taking precedence. This is the concept specific to Japan which manifests itself in the form of long-term employment for employees and long-term trading relations among various other stakeholders (the main bank, major suppliers, sub-contractors, distributors), loosely called *Keiretsu*.

This three-part categorization is supported by the results of a mail survey undertaken by the author with managers and executives in the five countries under review. The shareholder-centred Anglo-American outlook starkly contrasts with the employee-centred Japanese perspective, with Germany and France in between but significantly more oriented towards 'shareholder value' than Japan. The findings on Japan

FIGURE 11.3
Whose company is it?

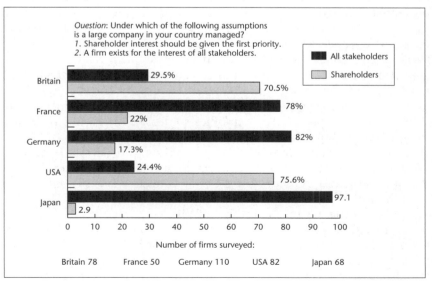

are consistent with the results of other studies. For instance, a survey carried out in 1990 by *Nippon Keizai Shimbun* on 104 employees of large corporations showed a majority of 80 percent replying that the company belongs to its employees; 70 percent believed that the company exists for the benefit of society as a whole. The concept that the firm is the property of shareholders ranked third with 67 percent.

Clearly Japan puts the interest of employees before that of shareholders. Her current unemployment rate of around 3 percent even in a prolonged recession is a testimony to this. Though increasingly challenged, job security is still defended as the mainstream ideology, as two major spokesmen of the Japanese business community recently proclaimed: Fumio Sato, Chairman of Toshiba Corporation, said that to discharge employees is 'the most serious sin' a president can commit and Takeshi Moroi, Chairman of Chichibu Cement, said that job security is the 'responsibility of the corporation'.

Key Implications of the Different Approaches

The central characteristic of the Japanese pluralistic concept is the alignment of the company's goals and interests with those of the stakeholders. This leads to a higher degree of cohesion between the firm's stakeholders, i.e. shareholders, management, employees, the main bank, major suppliers and distributors. They pull together toward a common purpose: the company's survival and prosperity. They share the implicit consensus that their respective interests are realized and promoted through their long-term commitment and cooperation with the firm. Maximization of general benefit, or the firm's 'wealth maximizing capacity', as Drucker[49] puts it, and not self-interest, is the name of the game. Michael Porter characterizes such relationship as 'a greater community of interest' and categorizes it as 'quasi integration', that is an intermediate form between long-term contracts and full ownership. According to Porter[50], this type of interdependent relationship among the stakeholders combines some of the benefits of vertical integration without incurring the corresponding costs. Suzuki and Wright[51] argue that a Japanese company, though legally independent, should be regarded rather as a division of a big conglomerate. This 'network structure' provides a system of collective security in time of crisis, as will be illustrated later.

Within the Japanese concept of the corporation, the company president is the representative of both the employees and the other stakeholders. The source of legitimacy of the president is derived primarily from his role as the defender of job security for the employees. This is understandable given the fact that the employees constitute the most

FIGURE 11.4
Job security or dividends?

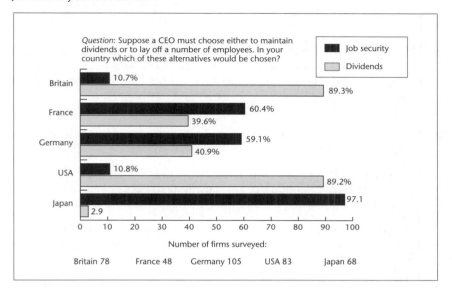

Question: Suppose a CEO must choose either to maintain dividends or to lay off a number of employees. In your country which of these alternatives would be chosen?

■ Job security
▢ Dividends

Britain — 10.7% / 89.3%
France — 60.4% / 39.6%
Germany — 59.1% / 40.9%
USA — 10.8% / 89.2%
Japan — 97.1 / 2.9

Number of firms surveyed:

Britain 78   France 48   Germany 105   USA 83   Japan 68

important power base for the president, as Figure 11.4 indicates. His secondary role is as the arbitrator for the divergent interests of the stakeholders so that a long-term balance of interests is achieved.

In contrast, under the Anglo-American 'monistic' concept where shareholders' interests are given primacy, the CEO represents the interests of the shareholders as their 'ally', according to Abegglen and Stalk[52], though their respective objectives may diverge at times. Understandably other stakeholders also seek to maximize their respective interests. In this 'zero-sum game', the firm ends up as a mere vehicle by which to satisfy the self-centred needs of the different stakeholders. The company then becomes an organization 'external' to the interests of its stakeholders, as Abegglen and Stalk point out, with no one caring about the long-term destiny of the firm itself. This makes a turnaround process more difficult, once a firm is confronted with financial difficulties.

The Relationship Between the Firm and Its Main Bank

In the Japanese *Keiretsu* the main bank assumes a pivotal role owing to its monitoring and disciplinary function based on its financial and equity claims. The main bank is not to be confused with the *Zaibatsu*[†] *institution, as any bank, whether Zaibatsu or non-Zaibatsu* in origin, can assume this role. The firm's main bank relations are characterized as follows:

- The main bank is typically the largest or one of the largest providers of loans and makes available on a preferential basis long-term and comprehensive financial services covering deposits, discounting of notes, foreign exchange transactions, advice in financial planning, agents on other loans, etc.

- Cross-shareholdings and interlocking directorships result in information sharing through official and personal contacts.

- The rescue of a client firm is attempted when it is targeted in a hostile take-over bid. Thus none of the hostile take-over attempts by a well-known raider, Minebea, were successful. An attempt to acquire Janome, a sewing machine maker, was thwarted by its main bank, Saitama Bank, another raid on Sankyo Seiki was frustrated by its main bank, Mitsubishi Bank who later arranged for an equity participation by Nippon Steel.

- Direct intervention in the turnaround process occurs in case the borrower company faces serious financial distress.

This main bank support is the most important motivation for Japanese firms to have a main bank. Typically the bailout measures range from the provision of emergency finance at an early stage in the crisis to, if the situation becomes more serious, the reduction of or exemption from interest payments, the engineering of a financial reorganization, the bank sending its own executives to supervise the reorganization, and finally the replacement of ineffectual management, the reorganization of the assets and an arrangement for an alliance or merger with another firm. The intervention by the main bank may have effects similar to an external take-over.

A recent mail survey of 305 listed companies excluding financial corporations suggests that 70 percent of them believe that their main bank would provide them with support in case of a crisis. The results of another poll of 354 corporations of Nikkeiren (The Japanese Federation of Employers' Associations) published in August 1994, indicated that 81.6 percent are in favour of maintaining the main bank system.

[†] *Zaibatsu* is a prewar conglomerate under family ownership and control. Mitsubishi, Mitsui, Sumitomo, and other *Zaibatsu* controlled a majority of Japan's large industrial, financial and service firms before World War II. They were broken up by the Occupation forces after the war. Today the firms of a former *Zaibatsu* form a loose federation based on their common tradition and business relationship.

FIGURE 11.5
The Japanese CEO's most important power base

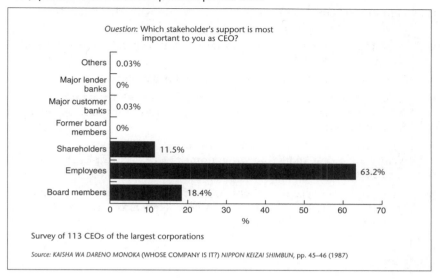

Survey of 113 CEOs of the largest corporations

Source: *KAISHA WA DARENO MONOKA* (WHOSE COMPANY IS IT?) *NIPPON KEIZAI SHIMBUN*, pp. 45–46 (1987)

A Japan–US Comparison of Stakeholder Relations

The relations among stakeholders in Japan, in particular the firm–main bank relations, may be better understood when a firm faces a crisis. The turnaround processes of Toyo Kogyo, manufacturer of Mazda passenger cars, and of Chrysler are contrasted.

Toyo Kogyo

In 1974, Toyo Kogyo was confronted with a financial crisis due to its large stockpile of unsold cars. Mazda cars powered by Wankel rotary engines were less fuel-efficient, a serious disadvantage after the first oil crisis of 1973. Sumitomo Bank, the main bank, played a vital role in the bailout operations.

■ Sumitomo Bank made a public assurance to stand by the distressed company, and a commitment to carry any new loans.

■ Sumitomo Bank sent a team of seven directors to control and implement the reorganization process.

- Sumitomo Bank replaced the president with a new, more competent successor.

- Sumitomo Bank co-ordinated negotiations with the other lenders to establish a financial package.

- Sumitomo group companies switched their car purchases to Mazda and bought 8000 vehicles over six years.

- No lay-off of employees but factory operators joined the sales force.

- The suppliers and subcontractors agreed to extend payment terms from 189 to 210 days, resulting in estimated savings in interest payments of several billion Yen.

- They also agreed to price reductions of 14 percent over two and a half years. Joint cost reduction programmes were also implemented, with cost reductions of ¥123 billion over 4 years.

- The employees accepted rescheduling of bonus payments, contributing ¥4 billion in increased annual cash flow. They also agreed to restraints in wage and bonus increases.

Chrysler

In the turnaround process at Chrysler, the stakeholders – the banks, the union, and the dealers – distrusted each other, were afraid of being stuck with an unfair burden and shunned responsibility for saving the firm. Its lead bank, Manufacturers Hanover Trust, did not or could not make an assurance to bail Chrysler out, although the bank's chairman had been on the Chrysler board for years. The chairman declared that he would approve no more unguaranteed loans to Chrysler because of its fiduciary responsibility to its shareholders and depositors. Lack of solidarity of the lenders and other stakeholders made the turnaround process dependent on government guarantees. As Iacocca sarcastically wrote, 'it took longer to get $655 million in concessions from the four hundred lending institutions than it did to get the loan guarantees of $1.5 billion passed by the entire US Congress'. For him, 'the congressional hearings were as easy as changing a flat tire on a spring day, compared to dealing with the banks'. Such financial concerns occupied top management for most of one year.

- Manufacturers Hanover Trust arranged for an agreement on a $455 million revolving credit with 80 American banks.

- Manufacturers Hanover Trust's chairman pleaded in Congress for a Federal loan guarantee for Chrysler.

- Manufacturers Hanover Trust urged its colleagues to accept Chrysler's packages of concessions.

- The Labour union agreed to a wage restraint and curtailment of paid days off.

- Suppliers agreed to price reductions.

Legal Restrictions on Banks in the United States

Contrary to Japan and Germany, the United States traditionally put a premium on investor protection by insisting on complete and accurate disclosure of company information, portfolio diversification and on a sharp line of demarcation between investor and manager roles. Thus the Glass-Steagall Act, the Bank Holding Company Act of 1956, the Investment Company Act of 1940, the ERISA Act of 1974 and finally the rules against insider trading all combine to prohibit or inhibit investing funds of banks and pension plans in the stock of any single corporation, and participation in the management of the portfolio and borrower companies. This legal framework coupled with banks' preference for liquidity over investment has made the US financial market the most transparent, fair, efficient, liquid and low-cost in the world. The downside is fragmented equity holding, and arm's length or even antagonistic relations between shareholders and management.

The Roles of the German 'Hausbank'

In Germany where the Hausbank has a similar role to the Japanese main bank, many firms regard it as a kind of 'insurance, bearing appropriate premiums in good times and offering corresponding protection when things go less well', according to Schneider-Linné, a member of the Management Board of Deutsche Bank. German main banks do take initiatives to reorganize their client firms in financial distress. Their part in rescuing companies, however, seems to be more limited in scope and commitment than that of Japanese main banks. The most significant difference is that the German main bank does not get directly involved in the management of the distressed firm and that the rescue concept itself is usually left to management consultancy firms. The German bank usually confines itself to rescheduling interest and principal payments or reducing interest charges and debts, giving advice to management and bringing in suitable new management.

The Flaws in the Japanese Concept of the Corporation

Needless to say, Japan's close-knit, inward-looking concept of the corporation has its downsides. The most serious one is inefficient monitoring of top management. Indeed, there has been practically no control exercised over top management except through the product market. Through cross-shareholdings, cross-directorships and long-term business relations, Japanese managers have isolated themselves from take-over threats and shareholder pressures and thus have been able to pursue expansionist strategies throughout the post-war period, particularly during the high-growth period up until the mid-1970s. Certainly their growth-oriented strategies have been beneficial to companies, as many Japanese firms rose to dominant positions in the international market. In the process managers have not generally sought to maximize their personal income as in some other countries. The remuneration level of Japanese top executives is much lower than international levels.

But the potential risk of ineffective monitoring of top management was inherent in the Japanese governance system, as it is also in Germany. This flaw became apparent in the second half of the 1980s in horrendous wastes of capital through reckless and unrelated diversifications and investments, and illegal or unethical behavior of many large firms. We now examine major dysfunctions of the Japanese monitoring system.

Ritualized General Meeting of Shareholders

The Japanese general meeting of shareholders is without doubt the least effective among the countries under review as a monitor over management. It has degenerated into a mere formality, as nearly everything is decided between the management and the major shareholders before the meeting takes place.

A mail survey carried out in June 1993 by the Japan Association of Statutory Auditors on 1106 public corporations revealed that nearly 80 percent of their general meetings of shareholders ended in less than half an hour including recess time. Less than 3 percent last for more than an hour. At the meeting not a single question was posed by shareholders in 87 percent of the companies studied, not to speak of shareholder proposals which were not made at all in 98 percent of the companies.

Limited Monitoring Power of the Chairman of the Board

Unlike in Anglo-American and French companies, board chairmanship and presidency of Japanese corporations are seldom assumed concurrently by the same person. At first sight, therefore, the supervisory function of the chairman and the executive function of the president seem to be clearly separated. Theoretically the chairman is expected to exercise control over the president. But this is not the case, because the Japanese board chairmanship is usually an honorary, symbolic or advisory position, the last step on the ladder before retirement from the company after having been president for several years. The chairman rarely interferes with the day-to-day managerial activities of the president, though his advice may be occasionally sought on major strategic decisions or on the appointment of key managerial positions. He spends most of his time representing the firm at external functions and activities, such as meetings of trade and economic associations, government commissions, etc. This 'half-retired' position of the chairman of the board is well illustrated by the fact that in 96 percent of the firms the president, not the chairman, presides over the general meeting of shareholders.

Board Members Are Appointed by the President

The fundamental cause of the board's dysfunction is that in most large firms nearly all of the board members are appointed by the president and naturally pledge their allegiance to him. In addition there are no or very few outside directors. If any, they are typically representatives from affiliated companies such as suppliers, subcontractors, etc. with little influence on the president. There is no distinction, therefore, between directors and officers. The board members are supposed to monitor the president who is their immediate superior, with obvious adverse consequences.

Boards Are Too Large

The average board in Japanese companies is larger than in any of the other industrialized nations examined here. Sakura Bank, second largest bank in revenue in 1993, is the champion with 62 board members. The average board size for the top three construction firms is about 52, for the top three trading companies close to 50, and for the three largest automobile and banking companies around 43.

This inflation of board sizes is due to the fact that board membership is often a reward for long and faithful service or major contributions to the company. The title of board member is useful to obtain business from major customers. In short, the Japanese board of directors has been transformed into a motivating and marketing tool. With such a large board with most directors engaged in day-to-day line activities, it is practically impossible to discuss any matter of importance in detail, let alone advise and sanction the president.

Ineffective Statutory Auditors

Large listed corporations are legally subject to two monitoring mechanisms: statutory auditors and independent certified public accountants. Neither is functioning properly. The primary auditing function of statutory auditors is to prevent any decisions by the directors to be taken or implemented which are judged to be in violation of laws or articles of incorporation, or otherwise detrimental to the company. Statutory auditors thus perform both accounting and operating audits to protect the interests of the company and the stakeholders by forestalling any adverse decisions and actions before it is too late. On paper they are given powerful authority, including the right to suspend illegal actions by a board member. But actual use of this power is unheard of. The root cause of the lack of monitoring by the statutory auditors is that they are selected by the president whom they are supposed to monitor.

A study conducted by Kobe University reveals that 57 percent of statutory auditors are selected by the president and 33 percent by directors or the executive committee and endorsed by the president. This shows that 90 percent of the statutory auditors are indeed chosen by the president for perfunctory approval at the shareholders' meeting.

Flawed Corporate Governance in the West

Nor do the monitoring capabilities of Western boards function perfectly due firstly to the CEO assuming the board chairmanship (except in Germany where this is legally prohibited), secondly due to the psychological and even economic dependence of outside (non-executive) directors on the CEO/chairman, and lastly due to multiple directorships.

CEO/Chairman Duality – USA, UK, and France

These three countries share the same problem as expressed by the chairman of Delta Metal; 'The problem with British companies is that the chairman marks his own papers'. In the United States, 75 percent of large manufacturing companies are run by the CEO-chairman, according to a survey by Rechner and Dalton[53]. CEO duality is also prevalent in the UK where in 60 percent of large firms including financial corporations the chairman is also the CEO, according to a Korn Ferry International survey. In France firms can opt either for the conventional single board or the two-tier board system inspired by the German model. An overwhelming majority of large firms have the traditional single board where in most cases the chairman is also the CEO, as the title Président Directeur-Général indicates.

In Germany the separation between the supervisory board and the management board is legally assured as no member of the one board is allowed to be a member of the other at the same time. Theoretically, the German system precludes the power concentration on the CEO-chairman as seen in other countries, thus assuring independent monitoring by the chairman of the supervisory board over the management board. But the reality does not altogether reflect the intention of the legislation. According to an empirical study by Gerum[54] on 62 large firms, this monitoring mechanism functions effectively only in firms whose supervisory board is dominated by one or more blockvote holders. The study shows that in a majority of 64 percent of the sample firms the management board influences the supervisory board. Only in 13 percent of firms does the supervisory board discharge its oversight functions over the management board. In the remaining 23 percent of firms, the supervisory board is strongly involved in the decision making of the management board, a power concentration similar to the Anglo-American, French and Japanese situations. The researcher concludes that this represents 'pathological traits' in the light of the objectives sought by the law[55].

Lack of Neutrality of Outside Directors – USA and Europe

In the United States the board chairman (who is often also the CEO as mentioned already) recommends candidates for outside directors in 81 percent of the 600 firms surveyed by Korn Ferry International. In the UK 80 percent of the non-executive (outside) directors are selected from among the 'old-boy network', reducing their monitoring potential, as reported by Sir Adrian Cadbury[56]. A similar situation is observed in France where new candidates for board membership are recommended by the CEO-chairman in 93.5 percent of the firms controlled by owner-managers, and in 92 percent of firms under managerial control, according to a study by Charreaux and Pitol-Belin[57]. In Germany, no hard data are available, but the preceding findings of Gerum on the dominance of the management board over the supervisory board leads us to infer that in a majority of large firms it is the managers on the management board that effectively determine who will be the members of the supervisory board.

Multiple Directorships – USA and Europe

This is a phenomenon that does not exist in Japan. All the Western countries reviewed here share this convention. In the United States 72 percent of the CEOs of the largest 50 corporations serve on the board of other firms and 50 percent of them have more than 6 outside directorships, according to Bassiry and Denkmejian[58]. In Germany the maximum number of board memberships is set at 10 without counting directorships in subsidiary companies. Bleicher's study of directors[59] shows that 36 percent of his sample assume directorship in more than three corporations. Whenever there is spectacular corporate mismanagement, further reduction in the maximum number of directorships is urged, often to five. In the UK 58 percent of directors assume non-executive directorship positions in other companies and 81 percent of them hold two to four directorships[60]. In France the legal limit is eight directorships plus five at subsidiary firms. Of 13,000 directors, 47 percent have one to 13 outside director positions, two percent have 14 to 50 positions, according to a survey by Bertolus and Morin[61].

The question is to what extent they can be counted on to be an effective monitor and advisor. They surely have enough problems in managing their own company. They do not have in-depth knowledge or information on the business and internal problems of the other companies where they serve as outside directors.

Which System Will Win Out?

The inevitable and tempting question which follows from this kind of international comparison is which system has superiority, if any at all, over the other in the long run in the light of two fundamental criteria: efficiency and equity.

As for efficiency we have limited evidence but one of the first empirical studies revealing a positive correlation between efficiency and the pluralistic concept of the corporation was offered by Kotter and Heskett[62]. They report that firms with cultures that emphasized the importance of all the stakeholders (customers, stockholders, and employees) outperformed by a huge margin firms that did not (see Table 11.3.1). If sufficient similar evidence is accumulated, we may conclude that the pluralistic concept does enhance a firm's efficiency.

The pluralistic concept seems to be more conducive to an equitable distribution of the firm's income, and fairer sharing of risk and

TABLE 11.1
The pluralistic concept may bring better performance – a US study

Based on: John P. Kotter and James L. Heskett *Corporate Culture and Performance*, p. 11 (1992).

11-Year growth	Firms emphasizing value to customers, shareholders & employees	Other firms
	%	%
Revenue	682	166
Workforces	282	36
Stock prices	901	74
Income	756	1

Study carried out between August 1987 and January 1991 with 202 US firms.

power among the stakeholders. This will increase organizational cohesion and survivability, as we have seen in the comparative case studies. Under the monistic concept of the corporation, employees tend to incur a disproportionately higher risk, as their job security is jeopardized in favor of shareholder/manager interests. They are usually the first to bear the brunt of poor decision making by top management, even if they are not responsible for it. This makes it difficult to expect a high commitment from them, under normal conditions or in crisis situations.

Applicability of the Pluralistic Concept

The pluralistic concept of the corporation may find wider applicability in countries outside Japan and may be a more viable and universal way for the modern corporation to promote efficiency and equity. It is not an ideology unique to Japan. An almost identical concept of the corporation was put forward in 1917 in Germany by Walther Rathenau[63] and in the United States by Adolf Berle/Gardiner Means in 1932[64], and by Ralph Cordiner in the 1950s[65].

Walther Rathenau, who was to become Foreign Minister later, succeeded his father as the CEO of the electric engineering firm AEG. In an influential article in 1917 he asserted that 'a big business is not only a product of private interests but it is, individually and collectively, a part of the national economy and of the whole community'[66]. This thesis is believed to have been instrumental in the later development of the concept of 'the firm itself' (*Unternehmen an sich*), which is close to the pluralistic approach. It paved the way for a dilution of shareholder rights, the protection of management positions, the post-World War II co-determination, and the justification of 'hidden reserves' and shares with multiple votes.

Most probably influenced by Rathenau (quoted twice in their seminal work), Berle and Means[67] conclude their book with exactly the same proposition. In the last chapter titled *'The New Concept of the Corporation'*, they suggest:

> neither the claims of ownership nor those of control can stand against the paramount interests of the community. . . . The passive property right (i.e. diffused ownership) . . . must yield before the largest interests of the society. It is conceivable indeed it seems almost essential if the corporate system is to survive that the 'control' of the great corporation should develop into a purely neutral technocracy, balancing a variety of claims by various groups in the community and assigning to each a

portion of the income stream on the basis of the public policy rather than private cupidity.

A similar ideology was espoused by Ralph Cordiner, CEO of General Electric in the 1950s who advocated that top management, as a trustee, was responsible for managing the company 'in the best interest of share-holder, customers, employees, suppliers, and plant community cities'. This concept of the corporation did not last, however, primarily because of the rise of the hostile take-over in the late 1970s, according to Peter Drucker.

Emerging Convergence

The concept of the corporation is firmly rooted in the historic, economic, political and even socio-cultural traditions of the nation. Each approach has its own positive and adverse sides. It would be improbable nor would it be necessary, therefore, that any one concept should drive out another at least in the foreseeable future. Through the cross-fertilization process, nations will be correcting the flaws in their systems, while retaining the core norms. In the process different concepts of the corporation may slowly converge, but certainly not totally. Some signs of such partial convergence are already discernible.

Japan

Japan and Germany are edging towards the Anglo-American model for increased openness and transparency, emphasis of shareholder interest and short-termism. In Japan the traditional emphasis on job security is being eroded and the process seems to be irreversible in the long run for various reasons: firms' tendency to place merit before seniority, perspectives of low growth economy, the changing industrial structure, competitive pressures from the rapidly developing Asian countries, the increasingly detached attitude of young employees to their company, and so on.

Yotaro Kobayashi, Chairman of Fuji Xerox, for instance, made an almost unprecedented declaration for a Japanese executive to the effect that Japanese management giving top priority to employees was no longer tenable. Several companies recently announced their target return on equity to show their emphasis on shareholder wealth. Mitsubishi Corporation has declared that it will raise ROE from currently 0.6 percent to eight percent by the year 2000. Other listed corporations such as Marubeni, Omron, Daikin, etc. are following suit.

The amended Commercial Code came into force on October 1993, albeit under the usual (salutary) pressure from the United States. Every large company is now required to increase the minimum number of statutory auditors from two to three. The newly introduced stockholders' representative action' makes it easier for shareholders to bring lawsuits against company directors as the court fee has been fixed at a flat rate of only ¥8,200 per case, regardless of the size of the claim. The number of shareholders eligible for access to confidential financial documents has been expanded to those with at least three percent ownership, down from the former 10 percent. This revision may be a small step forward but it is still progress.

USA

In the United States, conversely, the traditional restrictions on concentration of funds in a single investment and of board representation at portfolio companies are breaking down. Anti-take-over regulations have been introduced in a number of States, so that the interests of the company, i.e. all stakeholders and particularly employees, are taken into account. Employees are regarded as a major stakeholder and are involved in small group activities and share ownership. Long-term business relations are being introduced notably in the automobile industry between subcontractors and assemblers.

Germany

In Germany legislation against insider trading is finally being passed. The US style audit committee is advocated by senior executives and by scholars as one of the effective remedies to ensure the proper monitoring of the supervisory board. Shareholder activism by Anglo-American institutional shareholders as well as domestic individual shareholders is increasing. In an unprecedented move the CEO and CFO of Metallgesellschaft were simply fired for their responsibility in the alleged mismanagement of oil futures business. Increased reliance on the New York capital markets and the future location of the EU's central bank in Frankfurt am Main will certainly accelerate the Anglo–Americanization process. Disclosure by Daimler-Benz of its hidden assets to conform to the SEC regulations for listing on the New York Stock Exchange is symbolic.

Conclusion

The business organization is one of the few social institutions where the deficit of democracy is pronounced, compared with the national governance system. Lack of consensus as to whose interest the company should be promoting, and insufficient checks and balances among various corporate governance mechanisms are some of the evidence. As Prof. Rappaport[68] of the Northwestern University stresses, corporate govern-ance is 'the last frontier of reform' of the public corporation. This reform is a daunting challenge, but it will determine the economic fate of any industrialized nation in the next century.

Further Readings

Readers interested in delving deeper into the topic of organizational purpose have a richness of sources from which to choose. A good introductory work is the textbook *International Corporate Governance*, by Robert Tricker, which also contains many classic readings and a large number of interesting cases. One of the excellent readings reprinted in Tricker's book is Henry Mintzberg's article 'Who Should Control the Corporation?,' which provides a stimulating insight into the basic questions surrounding the topic of organizational purpose. Another good overview of the issues and literature in the area of corporate govern-ance is presented in the book *Strategic Leadership: Top Executives and Their Effects on Organizations* by Sydney Finkelstein and Donald Hambrick.

Other worthwhile follow-up readings on the topic of corporate governance include the book by Ada Demb and Friedrich Neubauer, *The Corporate Board: Confronting the Paradoxes*, and an excellent compar-ison of five national governance systems given in the book *Keeping Good Company*, by Jonathan Charkham. Recent edited volumes well worth reading are *Capital Markets and Corporate Governance*, by Nicolas Dimsdale and Martha Prevezer, and *Corporate Governance: Economic, Management, and Financial Issues*, by Kevin Keasey, Steve Thompson and Mike Wright.

For further reading on the topic of shareholder value, Alfred Rappaport's book *Creating Shareholder Value* is the obvious place to start. A good follow-up reading is Michael Jensen's article 'Corporate Control and the Politics of Finance.' For a very fundamental point of view, Milton Friedman's classic article 'The Social Responsibility of Business is to Increase Its Profits,' is also highly recommended. For a stinging attack on the stakeholder concept, readers are advised to see 'The Defects of Stakeholder Theory,' by Elaine Sternberg.

For a more positive view of stakeholder theory, Edward Freeman's *Strategic Management: A Stakeholder Approach* is still the book at which to begin. Only recently has stakeholder theory really attracted significant academic attention. Excellent works in this new crop include 'Instru-mental Stakeholder Theory: A Synthesis of Ethics and Economics,' by Thomas Jones, and 'The Stakeholder Theory of the Corporation: Concepts, Evidence, and Implications,' by Thomas Donaldson and Lee Preston.

On the topic of corporate social responsibility, there are a number good books that can be consulted. Archie Carroll's, *Business and Society: Ethics and Stakeholder Management* can be recommended, while the book *International Business and Society*, by Steven Wartick and Donna Wood, has a stronger international perspective. Good articles include 'The Corporate Social Policy Process: Beyond Business Ethics, Corporate Social Responsibility, and Corporate Social Responsiveness,' by Edwin Epstein, and the more academic 'A Stakeholder Framework For Analyzing and Evaluating Corporate Social Performance,' by Max Clarkson.

For an explicit link between strategy and ethics, the book *Corporate Strategy and the Search For Ethics*, by Edward Freeman and Daniel Gilbert, provides a good point of entry. The more recent article 'Strategic Planning As If Ethics Mattered,' by LaRue Hosmer, is also highly recommended. Many books on the general link between ethics and business, such as Thomas Donaldson's *The Ethics of International Business*, deal with major strategy issues as well.

Finally, on the topic of corporate mission a very useful overview of the literature is given in the reader *Mission and Business Philosophy*, edited by Andrew Campbell and Kiran Tawadey. Good follow-up works not in this reader are Derek Abell's book *Defining the Business – The Starting Point of Strategic Planning*, and the article 'Mission Analysis: An Operational Approach,' by Nigel Piercy and Neil Morgan. A interesting book emphasizing the importance of vision is *Built To Last: Successful Habits of Visionary Companies*, by James Collins and Jerry Porras.

Notes

Chapter 1

1. Pettigrew, A., and Whipp, R. (1991) *Managing Change for Competitive Success*, Basil Blackwell, Oxford; Ketchen, D.J., Thomas, J.B. and McDaniel, R.R. (1996) Process, Content and Context: Synergistic Effects on Organizational Performance, *Journal of Management*, Vol. 22, pp. 231–57.
2. Pettigrew, A. (1992) The Character and Significance of Strategy Process Research, *Strategic Management Journal*, Vol. 13, pp. 5–16.
3. Poole, M.S., and Van de Ven, A.H. (1989) Using Paradox to Build Management and Organizational Theories, *Academy of Management Review*, Vol. 14, pp. 562–78; Quinn, R.E., and Cameron, K.S. (1988) *Paradox and Transformation: Toward a Theory of Change in Organization and Management*, Ballinger Publishing, Cambridge, MA.
4. Collins, J.C., and Porras, J.I. (1994) *Built to Last: Successful Habits of Visionary Companies*, Harper Business, New York; Quinn, R.E. (1988) *Beyond Rational Management: Mastering the Paradoxes and Competing Demands of High Performance*, Jossey-Bass, San Francisco.
5. Mason, R.O., and Mitroff, I.I. (1981) *Challenging Strategic Planning Assumptions*, Wiley, New York.
6. Hofstede, G. (1993) Cultural Constraints in Management Theories, *Academy of Management Executive*, Vol. 7, No. 1.
7. Rittel, H. (1972) On the Planning Crisis: Systems Analysis of the 'First and Second Generations', *Bedriftsokonomen* No. 8, pp. 390–6.
8. Emery, F.E., and Trist, E.L. (1965) The Causal Texture of Organizational Environments, *Human Relations*, Vol. 18, pp. 21–32.
9. Schein, E.H. (1985) *Organizational Culture and Leadership*, Jossey-Bass, San Francisco.

Chapter 2

1. Andrews, K. (1987) *The Concept of Corporate Strategy*, Irwin, Homewood. An adapted version of ch. 2 is presented as reading 2.1 in this book.
2. Simon, H.A. (1957) *Models of Man*, John Wiley, New York.
3. Op.cit., note 1.
4. March, J.G., and Simon, H.A. (1993) *Organizations*, 2nd edn, Blackwell, Cambridge, MA.
5. Behling, O., and Eckel, N.L. (1991) Making Sense out of Intuition, *Academy of Management Executive*, vol. 5, pp. 46–54.
6. Von Winterfeldt, D. and Edwards, W. (1986) *Decision Analysis and Behavioral Research*, Cambridge University Press, Cambridge.
7. Langley, A. (1989) In Search of Rationality: The Purposes behind the Use of Formal Analysis in Organizations, *Administrative Science Quarterly*, Vol. 34, pp. 598–631; Langley, A. (1995) Between 'Paralysis by Analysis' and 'Extinction by Instinct', *Sloan Management Review*, Spring, pp. 63–76; Pondy, L.R. (1983) Union of Rationality and Intuition in Management Action, in Srivastva, S. (ed.), *The Executive Mind*, Jossey-Bass, San Francisco; Schoemaker, P.J.H., and Russo, J.E. (1993) A Pyramid of Decision Approaches, *California Management Review*, Vol. 36, Fall.
8. Simon, H.A. (1987) Making Management Decisions: The Role of Intuition and Emotion, *Academy of Management Executive*, Vol. 1, pp. 57–64.
9. Hogarth, R.M. (1980) *Judgement and Choice: The Psychology of Decision*, Wiley, Chichester; Schwenk, C.R. (1984) Cognitive Simplification Processes in Strategic Decision-Making, *Strategic Management Journal*, Vol. 5, pp. 111–28.
10. McCaskey, M.B. (1982) *The Executive Challenge: Managing Change and Ambiguity*, Pitman, Boston.
11. Eden, C. (1989) Using Cognitive Mapping for Strategic Options Development and Analysis (SODA), in Rosenhead, J., (ed.), *Rational Analysis in a Problematic World*, Wiley, London.
12. Baden-Fuller, C.W.F., and Stopford, J.M. (1992) *Rejuvenating the Mature Business*, Routledge, London, pp.13–34; an adapted version of ch. 2 is presented as reading 8.2 in this book; Senge, P.M. (1990) The Leader's New Work: Building Learning Organizations, *Sloan Management Review*, Fall, pp. 7–23.
13. Rittel, H. (1972) On the Planning Crisis: Systems Analysis of the 'First and Second Generations', *Bedriftsokonomen*, Nr. 8, pp. 390–96; Mason, R.O., and Mitroff, I.I. (1981) *Challenging Strategic Planning Assumptions*, Wiley, New York. An adapted version of ch. 1 is presented as reading 1.2 in this book.
14. Simon, H.A. (1972) Theories of Bounded Rationality, in: McGuire, C., and Radner R. (eds), *Decision and Organization*, Amsterdam, pp. 161–76.
15. Kuhn, T.S. (1970) *The Structure of Scientific Revolutions*, University of Chicago Press, Chicago; Johnson, G. (1988) Rethinking Incrementalism, *Strategic Management Journal*, January/February, pp. 75–91.
16. Prahalad, C.K. and Bettis, R.A. (1986) The Dominant Logic: A New

Linkage Between Diversity and Performance, *Strategic Management Journal*, November/December, pp. 485–601.

17. Op. cit., note 10; Weick, K.E., and Bougnon, M.G. (1986) Organizations as Cognitive Maps, in: Sims, H.P. Jr. and Gioia, D.A. (eds), *The Thinking Organization*, Jossey-Bass, San Francisco, pp. 102–35.

18. Noorderhaven, N.G. (1995) *Strategic Decision Making*, Addison-Wesley, Wokingham; Smircich, L., and Stubbart, C. (1985) Strategic Management in an Enacted World, *Academy of Management Review*, Vol. 10, pp. 724–36.

19. De Bono, E. (1970) *Lateral Thinking*, Harper and Rowe, New York.

20. Hurst, D.K., Rush, J.C. and White, R.E. (1989) Top Management Teams and Organizational Renewal, *Strategic Management Journal*, Vol 10, pp. 87–105.

21. Hamel, G. (1996) Strategy as Revolution, *Harvard Business Review*, July–August, pp. 69–82.

22. Kao, J. (1996) *Jamming: The Art and Discipline of Business Creativity*, HarperBusiness, New York.

23. Anderson, J.R. (1983) *The Architecture of Cognition*, Harvard University Press, Cambridge, MA; Schwenk, C.R. (1988) *The Essence of Strategic Decision Making*, Lexington Books, Lexington, MA.

24. Janis, I.L. (1989) *Crucial Decisions: Leadership in Policymaking and Crisis Management*, Free Press, New York.

25. Johnson, G., and Scholes, K. (1993) *Exploring Corporate Strategy: Text and Cases*, 3rd edn, Prentice Hall, Hemel Hempstead.

26. Tversky, A., and Kahneman, D. (1986) Rational Choice and the Framing of Decisions, *Journal of Business*, Vol. 59, No.4, pp. 251–78; Bazerman, M.H. (1990) *Judgment in Managerial Decision Making*, 2nd edn, John Wiley, New York.

27. Isenberg, D.J. (1984) How Senior Managers Think, *Harvard Business Review*, November–December, pp. 81–90; Schoemaker and Russo, op.cit., note 7.

28. Lenz, R.T., and Lyles, M. (1985) Paralysis by Analysis: Is Your Planning System Becoming Too Rational?, *Long Range Planning*, Vol. 18, pp. 64–72; Langley, 1995, op. cit., note 7.

29. Op. cit., note 10.

30. Schwenk, Op. cit., note 9.

31. Weick, K.E. (1979) *The Social Psychology of Organizing*, Random House, New York; Smircich and Stubbart, op. cit., note 18.

32. Dutton, J.E. (1988) Understanding Strategic Agenda Building and its Implications for Managing Change, in Pondy, L.R., R.J. Boland, Jr., and Thomas H. (eds), *Managing Ambiguity and Change*, Wiley, Chichester.

33. Christensen, C.R., Andrews, K.R., Bower, J.L., Hamermesh, R.G., and Porter, M.E. (1982) (1987) *Business Policy: Text and Cases*, 5th and 6th edns, Irwin, Homewood, IL.

34. Ohmae, K. (1982) *The Mind of the Strategist*, McGraw-Hill.

35. Redding, S.G. (1980) Cognition as an Aspect of Culture and its Relationship to Management Processes: An Exploratory View of the Chinese Case, *Journal of Management Studies*, May, pp. 127–48.

36. Kagono, T.I., Nonaka, K., Sakakibira, K. and Okumara, A. (1985) *Strategic vs. Evolutionary Management*, North-Holland, Amsterdam; Keegan, W.J.

(1983) Strategic Market Planning: The Japanese Approach, *International Marketing Review*, Vol. I, pp.5–15.

37. Pascale, R.T. (1984) Perspectives on Strategy: The Real Story Behind Honda's Success, *California Management Review*, Vol. 26, No. 3, pp. 47–72.

38. Nonaka, I., and Johansson, J.K. (1985) Japanese Management: What about 'Hard' Skills?, *Academy of Management Review*, Vol. 10, No. 2, pp. 181–91.

39. Schneider, S.C. (1989) Strategy Formulation: The Impact of National Culture, *Organization Studies*, Vol. 10, pp. 149–68.

Chapter 3

1. Mintzberg, H., and Waters, J.A. (1985) Of Strategies: Deliberate and Emergent, *Strategic Management Journal*, July/September, pp. 257–72.

2. Andrews, K.R., (1987) *The Concept of Corporate Strategy*, Third Edition, Irwin, Homewood, IL. An adapted version of ch. 2 appears as reading 2.1 in this book.

3. Lorange, P. and Vancil, R.F. (1977) *Strategic Planning Systems*, Prentice Hall, Englewood Cliffs; Chakravarthy, B.S., and Lorange, P. (1991) *Managing the Strategy Process: A Framework for a Multibusiness Firm*, Prentice Hall, Englewood Cliffs, NJ. An adapted version of ch. 1 appears as reading 3.1 of this book.

4. Ackoff, R.L. (1980) *Creating the Corporate Future*, Wiley, Chichester.

5. Makridakis, S. (1990) *Forecasting, Planning, and Strategy for the 21st Century*, Free Press, New York. p. 66.

6. Godet, M. (1987) *Scenarios and Strategic Management*, Butterworths, London; Wack, P. (1985a) Scenarios: Uncharted Waters Ahead, *Harvard Business Review*, September/October, pp. 73–89; Wack, P. (1985b) Scenarios: Shooting the Rapids, *Harvard Business Review*, November/December, pp. 139–50; Van der Heijen, K. (1996) *Scenarios: The Art of Strategic Conversation*, Wiley, New York.

7. Wildavsky, A. (1979) *Speaking Truth to Power: The Art and Craft of Policy Analysis*, Little, Brown & Co., Toronto; Mintzberg, H. (1990) The Design School: Reconsidering the Basic Premises of Strategic Management, *Strategic Management Journal*, XI, pp. 171–95.

8. Stacey, R.D. (1993) Strategy as Order Emerging from Chaos, *Long Range Planning*, Vol. 26, No.1, pp. 10–17. This paper appears as reading 9.2 in this book.

9. Pettigrew, A.M. (1977) Strategy Formulation as a Political Process, *International Studies of Management and Organization*, Summer, pp. 47–72; Johnson, G. (1988) Rethinking Incrementalism, *Strategic Management Journal*, January/February, pp. 75–91.

10. Rittel, H.W., and Webber, M.M. (1973) Dilemmas in a General Theory of Planning, *Policy Sciences*, Vol. 4, pp. 155–69.

11. Langley, A. (1995) Between 'Paralysis and Analysis' and 'Extinction by Instinct', *Sloan Management Review*, Spring, pp. 63–76; Lenz, R.T., and

Lyles, M. (1985) Paralysis by Analysis: Is Your Planning System Becoming Too Rational?, *Long Range Planning*, Vol. 18, pp. 64–72.

12. Pascale, R.T. (1984) Perspectives on Strategy: The Real Story Behind Honda's Success, *California Management Review*, Vol. 26, No. 3 (Spring), pp. 47–72.

13. Ghemawat, P. (1991) *Commitment: The Dynamic of Strategy*, Free Press, New York.

14. Evans, J.S. (1991) Strategic Flexibility for High Technology Manoeuvres: A Conceptual Framework, *Journal of Management Studies*, January, pp. 69–89.

15. Burgelman, R.A. (1983) Corporate Entrepreneurship and Strategic Management: Insights from a Process Study, *Management Science*, Vol. 29, No. 12, pp. 1349–64; Burgelman, R.A. (1991) Intraorganizational Ecology of Strategy Making and Organizational Adaptation: Theory and Field Research, *Organization Science*, Vol. 2, pp. 239–62.

16. Pinchot, G., III. (1985) *Intrapreneuring: Why You Don't Have to Leave the Company to Become an Entrepreneur*, Harper & Row, New York; Quinn, J.B. (1985) Managing Innovation: Controlled Chaos, *Harvard Business Review*, May/June, pp. 73–84.

17. Steiner, G.A. (1979) *Strategic Planning: What Every Manager Must Know*, Free Press, New York.

18. Op. cit., note 8.

19. Hedberg, B.L., Nystrom, P.C. and Starbuck, W.H. (1976) Camping on Seesaws: Prescriptions for a Self-Designing Organization, *Administrative Science Quarterly*, Vol. 21, March, pp. 41–65; Nonaka, I. (1988) Creating Organizational Order Out of Chaos: Self-Renewal in Japanese Firms, *California Management Review*, Spring, pp. 57–73.

20. Quinn, J.B. (1980a) Managing Strategic Change, *Sloan Management Review*, Summer, pp. 3–20. This paper appears as reading 3.2 in this book.

21. Mintzberg, H. (1994) The Fall and Rise of Strategic Planning, *Harvard Business Review*, January-February, pp. 107–14.

22. Op. cit., note 2.

23. Hax, A.C., and Maljuf, N.S. (1984) *Strategic Management: An Integrative Approach*, Prentice Hall, Englewood Cliffs.

24. For the entrepreneurial approach see Mintzberg, H. (1978) Patterns in Strategy Formation, *Management Science*, vol. 24, pp. 934–48; Hart, S.L. (1992) An Integrative Framework for Strategy-Making Processes, *Academy of Management Review*, Vol. 17, No. 2, pp. 327–51; discusses the command approach; Shrivastava, P., and Grant, J. (1985) Empirically Derived Models of Strategic Decision-Making Processes, *Strategic Management Journal*, Vol. 6, pp. 97–113; speak of managerial autocracy; while the design approach is covered in Mintzberg, 1990. op. cit., note 7.

25. Lorange, P. (1980) *Corporate Planning: An Executive Viewpoint*, Prentice Hall, Englewood Cliffs; Lorange and Vancil, 1977, op. cit., note 3.

26. Op. cit., note 3.

27. Quinn, J.B. (1980b) *Strategies for Change*, Irwin, Homewood, IL.

28. Steiner, G.A. and Schollhammer, H. (1975) Pitfalls in Multi-National Long-Range Planning, *Long Range Planning*, April, pp. 2–12.

29. Kagono, T., Nonaka, I. Sakakibara, K. and Okumara, A. (1985) *Strategic vs. Evolutionary Management*, North-Holland, Amsterdam.

30. Hayashi, K. (1978) Corporate Planning Practices in Japanese Multinationals, *Academy of Management Journal*, Vol. 21, No. 2, pp. 211–26, p. 221.

31. Ohmae, K. (1982) *The Mind of the Strategist*, McGraw-Hill, New York, p. 225.

32. Gilbert, X., and Lorange, P. (1995) National Approaches to Strategic Management – A Resource-based Perspective, *International Business Review*, Vol. 3, No. 4, pp. 411–23; Mintzberg, H. (1994b) *The Rise and Fall of Strategic Planning*, Prentice-Hall, Englewood Cliffs; Schneider, S.C. (1989) Strategy Formulation: The Impact of National Culture, *Organization Studies*, Vol. 10, No. 2, pp. 149–68.

33. Op. cit., note 31, p. 224.

34. Mintzberg, 1994, op.cit., note 32.

35. Hampden-Turner, C., and Trompenaars, A. (1993) *The Seven Cultures of Capitalism: Value Systems for Creating Wealth in the United States, Japan, Germany, France, Britain, Sweden and the Netherlands*, Doubleday, New York; Lessem, R., and Neubauer, F.F. (1994) *European Management Systems*, McGraw-Hill, London.

36. Mintzberg, H. (1979) *The Structuring of Organizations: A Synthesis of the Research*, Prentice-Hall, Englewood Cliffs.

37. Hofstede, G. (1993) Cultural Constraints in Management Theories, *Academy of Management Executive*, Vol. 7, No. 1. pp. This paper appears as reading 1.2 in this book.

38. Op. cit., note 29; Schneider, 1989, op. cit., note 32.

39. Allaire, Y., and Firsirotu, M. (1990) Strategic Plans as Contracts, *Long Range Planning*, Vol. 23, No. 1, pp. 102–15; Bungay, S., and Goold, M. (1991) Creating a Strategic Control System, *Long Range Planning*, Vol. 24, No. 6, pp. 32–9.

40. Nonaka, I., and Johansson, J.K. (1985) Japanese Management: What about 'Hard' Skills?, *Academy of Management Review*, Vol. 10, No. 2, pp. 181–91.

41. Op. cit., note 4.

42. Trompenaars, A. (1993) *Riding the Waves of Culture: Understanding Cultural Diversity in Business*, The Economist Books, London.

43. Maruyama, M. (1984) Alternative Concepts of Management: Insights from Asia and Africa, *Asia Pacific Journal of Management*, January, pp. 100–11.

44. Op. cit., note 29; Schneider, 1989, op. cit., note 32.

45. Op. cit., note 37.

46. Calori, R., Valla, J.-P. and de Woot, Ph. (1994) Common Characteristics: The Ingredients of European Management, in Calori, R., and de Woot, Ph. (eds), *A European Management Model: Beyond Diversity*, Prentice Hall, Hemel Hempstead; op. cit., note 29.

Chapter 4

1. Miller, D. (1990) *The Icarus Paradox: How Excellent Companies Bring About Their Own Downfall*, Harper Business, New York.
2. March, J.G., and Simon, H.A. (1958) *Organizations*, Wiley, New York; Thompson, J.D. (1967) *Organizations in Action*, McGraw-Hill, New York.
3. Argyris, C. (1990) *Overcoming Organizational Defenses: Facilitating Organizational Learning*, Prentice Hall, Boston; Pondy, L.R., Boland, J.R. and Thomas, H. (1988) (eds), *Managing Ambiguity and Change*, Wiley, New York.
4. Allison, G.T. (1969) Conceptual Models and The Cuban Missile Crisis, *The American Political Science Review*, No.3, September, pp. 689–718; Pettigrew, A.M. (1988) *The Management of Strategic Change*, Basil Blackwell, Oxford.
5. Arthur, W.B. (1996) Increasing Returns and the New World of Business, *Harvard Business Review*, July–August, pp. 100–9; Ghemawat, P. (1991) *Commitment: The Dynamic of Strategy*, Free Press, New York.
6. Greiner, L.E. (1972) Evolution and Revolution as Organizations Grow, *Harvard Business Review*, July/August, pp. 37–46.
7. Gersick, C.J.G. (1991) Revolutionary Change Theories: A Multilevel Exploration of the Punctuated Equilibrium Paradigm, *Academy of Management Review*, Vol. pp. 10–36.
8. Schumpeter, J.A. (1950) *Capitalism, Socialism and Democracy*, 3rd edn, Harper and Brothers, New York.
9. D'Aveni, R. (1994) *Hypercompetition: Managing the Dynamics of Strategic Maneuvering*, Free Press, New York; Hamel, G. (1996) Strategy as Revolution, *Harvard Business Review*, July–August, pp. 69–82.
10. Meyer, A.D. (1982) Adapting to Environmental Jolts, *Administrative Science Quarterly*, Vol. 27, December, pp. 515–37; Meyer, A., Brooks, G. and Goes, J. (1990) Environmental Jolts and Industry Revolutions: Organizational Responses to Discontinuous Change, *Strategic Management Journal*, Vol. 11, pp. 93–110.
11. Johnson, G. (1988) Rethinking Incrementalism, *Strategic Management Journal*, January/February, pp. 75–91; Strebel, P. (1992) *Breakpoints: How Managers Exploit Radical Business Change*, Harvard Business School Press, Boston.
12. Miller, D., and Friesen, P. (1984) *Organizations: A Quantum View*, Prentice Hall, Englewood Cliffs; Tushman, M.L., Newman, W.H. and Romanelli, E. (1986) Convergence and Upheaval: Managing the Unsteady Pace of Organizational Evolution, *California Management Review*, Vol. 29, No. 1, Fall, pp. 29–44.
13. Stacey, R.D. (1993) Strategy as Order Emerging from Chaos, *Long Range Planning*, Vol. 26, No.1, pp. 10–17. This appears as reading 9.2 in this book.
14. Op. cit., note 3; Senge, P.M. (1990) The Leader's New Work: Building Learning Organizations, *Sloan Management Review*, Fall, pp. 7–23.
15. Kagono, T., Nonaka, I. Sakakibara, K. and Okumura, A. (1985) *Strategic vs. Evolutionary Management: A US-Japan Comparison of Strategy and Organiza-*

tion, North Holland, Amsterdam; Nonaka, I. (1988) Creating Organizational Order Out of Chaos: Self-Renewal in Japanese Firms, *California Management Review*, Spring, pp. 9–18.

16. Maidique, M.A. (1980) Entrepreneurs, Champions, and Technological Innovation, *Sloan Management Review*, 1980, pp. 18–31; Day, D.L. (1994) Raising Radicals: Different Processes for Championing Innovative Corporate Ventures, *Organization Science*, Vol. 5, No. 2, pp. 148–72.

17. Waterman, R.H., Peters, T.J., and Phillips, J.R. (1980) Structure is Not Organization, *Business Horizons*, June, pp. 14–26.

18. Mintzberg, H., and Westley, F. (1992) Cycles of Organizational Change, *Strategic Management Journal*, Vol. 13, pp. 39–59.

19. Op. cit., note 18.

20. Hammer, M. (1990) Reengineering Work: Don't Automate, Obliterate, *Harvard Business Review*, July/August, pp. 104–11.

21. Hammer, M., and Champy, J. (1993) *Reengineering the Corporation: A Manifesto for Business Revolution*, HarperCollins, New York.

22. Imai, M. (1986) *Kaizen: The Key to Japan's Competitive Success*, McGraw-Hill, New York.

23. Ouchi, W. (1981) *Theory Z: How American Business Can Meet the Japanese Challenge*, Addison-Wesley, Reading, MA; Pascale, R.T., and Athos, A.G. (1981) *The Art of Japanese Management*, Simon & Schuster, New York; op. cit., note 15.

24. Kagano *et al.*, op. cit., note 15, pp. 89–90.

25. Calori, R., and de Woot, Ph. (eds) (1994) *A European Management Model: Beyond Diversity*, Prentice Hall, Hemel Hempstead; Krueger, W. (1996) Implementation: The Core Task of Change Management, *CEMS Business Review*, pp. 77–96.

26. op. cit., note 23.

27. Kanter, R.M. (1989) *When Giants Learn to Dance*, Simon & Schuster, New York; Mintzberg, H. (1994) *The Rise and Fall of Strategic Planning*, Prentice Hall, Englewood Cliffs.

28. Kagano *et al.*, op. cit., note 15.

29. Nonaka, op. cit., note 15; Stacey, op. cit., note 13.

30. Ouchi and Pascale and Athos, op. cit., note 20.

31. Kagono *et al.*, op. cit., note 15; Calori, R., Valla, J.-P. and de Woot, Ph. (1994) Common Characteristics: The Ingredients of European Management, in Calori, R., and de Woot, Ph. (eds), *A European Management Model: Beyond Diversity*, Prentice Hall, Hemel Hempstead.

32. Kogut, B. (ed.) (1993) *Country Competitiveness: Technology and the Organizing of Work*, Oxford University Press, Oxford, p. 11.

33. Hambrick, D.C., and Mason, P. (1984) Upper Echelons: The Organization as a Reflection of Its Top Managers, *Academy of Management Review*, Vol. 9, pp. 193–206.; Kotter, J.P. (1982) *The General Managers*, Free Press, New York, 1982.

34. Boeker, W. (1992) Power and Managerial Dismissal: Scapegoating at the Top, *Administrative Science Quarterly*, Vol. 27, pp. 538–47; Fredrickson, J.W., Hambrick, D.C. and Baumrin, S. (1988) A Model of CEO Dismissal, *Academy of Management Review*, Vol. 13, pp. 255–70.

Bourgeois, L.J., and Brodwin, D.R. (1983) Putting Your Strategy into Action, *Strategic Management Planning*, March/May.

35. Kagano *et al.*, op. cit., note 15; Hofstede, G. (1993) Cultural Constraints in Management Theories, *Academy of Management Executive*, Vol. 7, No.1. This paper appears as reading 1.2 in this book.

36. Kagano *et al.*, op. cit., note 15; Calori *et al.*, op. cit., note 28.

37. Abegglen, J.C., and Stalk, G. (1985) *Kaisha, The Japanese Corporation*, Basic Books, New York; Pascale and Athos, op. cit., note 23.

Chapter 5

1. Rumelt, R.P. (1980) The Evaluation of Business Strategy, in Glueck, W.F., *Business Policy and Strategic Management*, 3rd edn, McGraw-Hill, New York.

2. Day, G.S. (1990) *Market Driven Strategy, Processes for Creating Value*, The Free Press: New York; Webster, F. (1994) *Market Driven Management: Using the New Marketing Concept to Create a Customer-oriented Company*, John Wiley, New York.

3. Mintzberg, H. (1990) Strategy Formation: Schools of Thought, in Frederickson, J. (ed.), *Perspectives on Strategic Management*, Harper & Row, New York.

4. Porter, M.E. (1980) *Competitive Strategy: Techniques for Analyzing Industries and Competitors*, Free Press, New York; Porter, M.E. (1985) *Competitive Advantage: Creating and Sustaining Superior Performance*, Free Press, New York; reading 5.1 in this book is taken from this work.

5. Buzzell, R.D., and Gale, B.T. (1987) *The PIMS Principles: Linking Strategy to Performance*, Free Press, New York.

6. Prahalad, C.K. and Hamel, G. (1990) The Core Competence of the Corporation, *Harvard Business Review*, May/June, pp. 79–91; this paper appears as reading 6.2 in this book; Sanchez, R., Heene, A. and Thomas, H. (eds) (1996) *Dynamics of Competence-Based Competition*, Elsevier, London.

7. Stalk, G., Evans, P., and Schulman, L.E. (1992) Competing on Capabilities: The New Rules of Corporate Strategy, *Harvard Business Review*, March/April, pp. 57–69; this paper appears as reading 5.2 in this book; Teece, D.J., Pisano, G., and Shuen, A. (1990) *Firm Capabilities, Resources, and the Concept of Strategy: Four Paradigms of Strategic Management*, CCC Working Paper, December.

8. Collis, D.J. and Montgomery, C.A. (1995) Competing on Resources: Strategy in the 1990s, *Harvard Business Review*, July–August, pp. 118–28; Barney, J.B. (1991) Firm Resources and Sustained Competitive Advantage, *Journal of Management*, Vol. 17, No. 1, pp. 99–120.

9. Leonard-Barton, D. (1995) *Wellsprings of Knowledge*, Harvard Business School Press, Boston; op. cit., note 1.

10. Porac, J.F., Thomas, H. and Baden-Fuller, Ch. (1989) 'Competitive Groups

as Cognitive Communities: The Case of Scottish Knitwear Manufacturers,' *Journal of Management Studies*, No. 26, pp. 397–416.

11. Abell, D. (1980) *Defining the Business – The Starting Point of Strategic Planning*, Prentice Hall, Englewood Cliffs, NJ.

12. Aaker, D.A. (1995) *Strategic Market Management*, 4th edn, John Wiley & Sons, New York; Day, G.S. (1994) The Capabilities of Market-Driven Organizations, *Journal of Marketing*, Vol. 58, October, pp. 37–52.

13. Scherer, F.M. (1980) *Industrial Market Structure and Economic Performance*, 2nd Edition, Houghton-Mifflin, Boston; Porter, 1980, op. cit., note 4 and reading 5.1.

14. Penrose, E.T. (1958) *The Theory of the Growth of the Firm*, Wiley, New York, 1958; Wernerfelt, B. (1984) A Resource-Based View of the Firm, *Strategic Management Journal*, April/June, pp. 171–80; Barney, op. cit., note 8.

15. Dierickx, I., and Cool, K. (1989) Asset Stock Accumulation and Sustainability of Competitive Advantage, *Management Science*, December, pp. 1504–11; Itami, H. (1986) *Mobilizing Invisible Assets*, Harvard University Press, Cambridge, MA.

16. Lowendahl, B.R. (1997) *Strategic Management of Professional Business Service Firms*, Copenhagen Business School Press, Copenhagen.

17. Durand, T. (1996) Revisiting Key Dimensions of Competence, Paper presented to the SMS Conference, Phoenix.

18. Op. cit., note 6.

19. Op. cit., note 17.

20. Grant, R.M. (1991) The Resource-Based Theory of Competitive Advantage: Implications for Strategy Formulation, *California Management Review*, Spring, pp. 114–35; Itami, op. cit., note 15.

21. Polanyi, M. (1958) *Personal Knowledge*, University of Chicago Press, Chicago; Nonaka, I. (1991) The Knowledge-Creating Company, *Harvard Business Review*, November–December, pp. 96–104.

22. Nelson, R., and Winter, S. (1982) *An Evolutionary Theory of Economic Change*, Harvard University Press, Cambridge, MA.

23. Porter, 1980, op. cit., note 4.

24. Op. cit., note 4.

25. Op. cit., note 7.

26. Porter, 1980, op. cit., note 4.

Chapter 6

1. Porter, M.E. (1987) From Competitive Advantage to Corporate Strategy, *Harvard Business Review*, May/June, pp. 43–59.

2. Hamel, G., and Prahalad, C.K. (1993) Strategy as Stretch and Leverage, *Harvard Business Review*, March/April, pp. 75–84.

3. Lawrence, P.R., and Lorsch, J.W. (1967) *Organization and Environment*, Harvard University Press, Cambridge, MA; Prahalad, C.K. and Doz, Y. (1987) *The Multinational Mission: Balancing Local Demands and Global Vision*, Free Press, New York.

4. Haspeslagh, P. (1982) Portfolio Planning: Uses and Limits, *Harvard Business Review*, January/February, pp. 58–73.

5. Kaplan, S. (1989) The Effects of Management Buyouts on Operating Performance and Value, *Journal of Financial Economics*, Vol. 24, pp. 217–31; Long, W.F. and Ravenscraft, D.J. (1993) Decade of Debt: Lessons from LBOs in the 1980s, in Blair M.M. (ed.), *The Deal Decade: What Takeovers and Leveraged Buyouts Mean for Corporate Governance*, Brookings Institution, Washington.

6. Anslinger, P.L. and Copeland, T.E. (1996) Growth Through Acquisitions: A Fresh Look, *Harvard Business Review*, January–February, pp. 126–35.

7. Goold, M., and Lansdell, S. (1997) *Survey of Corporate Strategy Objectives, Concepts and Tools*, Ashridge Strategic Management Centre, November.

8. Prahalad, C.K. and Hamel, G. (1990) The Core Competence of the Corporation, *Harvard Business Review*, May/June, pp. 79–91. This paper is presented as reading 6.2 in this book.

9. Op. cit., note 1.

10. Rumelt, R.P. (1974) *Strategy, Structure, and Economic Performance*, Harvard University Press, Cambridge, MA.

11. Prahalad, C.K., and Bettis, R.A. (1986) The Dominant Logic: A New Linkage between Diversity and Performance, *Strategic Management Journal*, November/December, pp. 485–601; Chatterjee, S. (1986) Types of Synergy and Economic Value: The Impact of Acquisitions on Merging and Rival Firms, *Strategic Management Journal*, Vol. 7, pp. 119–39; Ramanujam, V., and Varadarajan, P. (1989) Research on Corporate Diversification: A Synthesis, *Strategic Management Journal*, November/December, pp. 523–51.

12. Nayyar, P.R. (1992) On the measurement of corporate diversification strategy: Evidence from large US service firms, *Strategic Management Journal*, 13 (3), pp. 219–35.

13. Mintzberg, H. (1979) *The Structuring of Organizations: A Synthesis of Research*, Prentice-Hall, Englewood Cliffs; Govindarajan, V. (1988) A Contingency Approach to Strategy Implementation at the Business-Unit Level: Integrating Administrative Mechanisms with Strategy, *Academy of Management Journal*, Vol. 31, pp. 828–53.

14. Campbell, A., and Goold, M. (1988) Adding Value from Corporate Head-quarters, *London Business School Journal*, Summer, pp. 219–40.

15. Henderson, B.D. (1979) *On Corporate Strategy*, Abt Books, Cambridge, MA.

16. Op. cit., note 8.

17. Hamel, G. and Prahalad, C.K. (1994) *Competing for the Future*, Harvard Business School Press, Boston, MA.

18. Campbell, A., Goold, M., and Alexander, M. (1994) *Corporate-Level Strategy: Creating Value in the Multibusiness Company*, John Wiley & Sons, New York. p. 413.

19. Op. cit., note 1.

20. Calori, R. (1994) The Diversity of Management Systems, in Calori, R., and de Woot, Ph. (eds), *A European Management Model: Beyond Diversity*, Prentice-Hall, Hemel Hempstead.

21. Hofstede, G. (1993) Cultural Constraints in Management Theories, *Academy of Management Executive*, Vol. 7, No.1.

Chapter 7

1. Porter, M.E. (1980) *Competitive Strategy: Techniques for Analyzing Industries and Competitors*, Free Press, New York; Porter, M.E. (1985) *Competitive Advantage*, Free Press, New York, reading 5.1 in this book is taken from this work.
2. Hamel, G., Doz, Y.L., and Prahalad, C.K. (1989) Collaborate with Your Competitors-and Win, *Harvard Business Review*, January/February, pp. 133–9. This paper is presented as reading 7.1 in this book.
3. Porter, M.E. (1990) *The Competitive Advantage of Nations*, Macmillan, London.
4. Contractor, F.J., and Lorange, P. (1988) *Cooperative Strategies in International Business*, Lexington Books, Lexington, MA; Piore, M., and Sabel, C.F. (1984) *The Second Industrial Divide*, Basic Books, New York.
5. Best, M.H. (1990) *The New Competition: Institutions of Industrial Restructuring*, Polity, Cambridge; Jarillo, J.C. (1988) On Strategic Networks, *Strategic Management Journal*, Vol. 9, No. 1, pp. 31–41.
6. Williamson, O.E. (1975) *Markets and Hierarchies: Analysis and Antitrust Implications*, Free Press, New York; Williamson, O.E. (1985) *The Economic Institutions of Capitalism*, Free Press, New York.
7. Thorelli, H.B. (1986) Networks: Between Markets and Hierarchies, *Strategic Management Journal*, Vol. 7, No. 1, pp. 37–51; Powell, W. (1990) Neither Market nor Hierarchy: Network Forms of Organization, *Research in Organizational Behavior*, Vol. 12, pp. 295–336.
8. Gerlach, M. (1992) *Alliance Capitalism*, University of California Press, Berkeley, CA.
9. Gomes-Casseres, B. (1994) Group versus Group: How Alliance Networks Compete, *Harvard Business Review*, July/August, pp. 62–74; Weidenbaum, M., and Hughes, S. (1996) *The Bamboo Network: How Expatriate Chinese Entrepreneurs Are Creating a New Economic Superpower in Asia*, Free Press, pp. 23–59.
10. Chandler, A.D. (1990) *Scale and Scope*, Belknop, Cambridge, MA.
11. Adapted from Porter, 1980, op. cit., note 1 and Reve, T. (1990) The Firm as a Nexus of Internal and External Contracts, in Aoki, M., Gustafsson, B., and Williamson, O.E. (eds) *The Firm as a Nexus of Treaties*, Sage, London.
12. Porter, 1985, op. cit., note 1.
13. Harrigan, K.R. (1985) *Strategies for Joint Ventures*, D.C. Heath, Lexington, MA; Mahoney, J.T. (1992) The Choice of Organizational Form: Vertical Financial Ownership versus Other Methods of Vertical Integration, *Strategic Management Journal*, Vol. 13, No. 8, pp. 559–84.
14. Ouchi, W.G. (1980) Markets, Bureaucracies, and Clans, *Administrative Science Quarterly*, Vol. 25, pp. 129–42, p. 130.
15. Williamson, 1985, op. cit., note 6, p. 47.
16. Chesbrough, H.W., and Teece, D.J. (1996) Organizing for Innovation: When is Virtual Virtuous?, *Harvard Business Review*, January–February, pp. 65–73; Quinn, J.B. (1992) *The Intelligent Enterprise: A Knowledge and Service Based Paradigm for Industry*, Free Press, New York.

17. Kanter, R.M. (1994) Collaborative Advantage: The Art of Alliances, *Harvard Business Review*, July/August, pp. 96–108.
18. Kay, J.A. (1993) *Foundations of Corporate Success*, Oxford Universtity Press, Oxford.
19. Op. cit., note 2.
20. Lorenzoni, G., and Baden-Fuller, C. (1995) Creating a Strategic Center to Manage a Web of Partners, *California Management Review*, Vol. 37, Spring, pp. 146–63.
21. Reich, R., and Mankin, E. (1986) Joint Ventures with Japan Give Away Our Future, *Harvard Business Review*, March/April, pp. 78–86.
22. Bleeke, J., and Ernst, D. (1991) The Way to Win in Cross Border Alliances, *Harvard Business Review*, November/December, pp. 127–35.
23. Hamel, G. (1991) Competition for Competence and Inter-Partner Learning Within International Strategic Alliances, *Strategic Mangement Journal*, Vol. 12, Summer Special Issue, pp. 83–103.
24. Badaracco, J.L. (1991) *The Knowledge Link: How Firms Compete Through Strategic Alliances*, Harvard Business School Press, Boston, MA.
25. Prahalad, C.K. and Hamel, G. (1990) The Core Competence of the Corporation, *Harvard Business Review*, May/June, pp. 79–91.
26. Johanson, J., and Mattson, L.G. (1992) Network Position and Strategic Action – An Analytical Framework, in Axelsson, B., and Easton, G. (eds) *Industrial Networks: A New View of Reality*, Routledge, London.
27. Op. cit., note 2.
28. Contractor and Lorange, op. cit., note 4; Kagono, T., Nonaka, I., Sakakibara, K. and Okumara, A. (1985) *Strategic vs. Evolutionary Management*, North-Holland, Amsterdam.
29. Op. cit., note 8.
30. Pascale, R.T., and Athos, A.G. (1981) *The Art of Japanese Management*, Simon & Schuster, New York.
31. Lessem, R., and Neubauer, F.F. (1994) *European Management Systems*, McGraw-Hill, London.
32. Albert, M. (1991) *Capitalisme contre Capitalisme*, Seuil, Paris.
33. Piore and Sabel, op. cit., note 4.
34. Op. cit., note 31.
35. Williamson. 1975, 1985, op. cit., note 6.
36. Op. cit., note 31.
37. Teece, D.J. (1992) Competition, Cooperation, and Innovation: Organizational Arrangements for Regimes of Rapid Technological Progress, *Journal of Economic Behavior and Organization*, Vol. 18, pp. 1–25; Dyer, J.H., and Ouchi, W.G. (1993) Japanese-Style Partnerships: Giving Companies a Competitive Edge, *Sloan Management Review*, Fall, pp. 51–63.
38. Chandler, A.D. (1986) The Evolution of Modern Global Competition, in Porter, M.E. (ed.), *Competition in Global Industries*, Harvard Business School Press, Boston, pp. 405–48; op. cit., note 10.
39. Thurow, L. (1991) *Head to Head*, MIT Press, Cambridge, MA.
40. Op. cit., note 31.
41. Axelrod, R. (1984) *The Evolution of Cooperation*, Basic Books, New York; Teece, op. cit., note 37.

Chapter 8

1. Aldrich, H.E. (1979) *Organizations and Environments*, Prentice Hall, Englewood Cliffs, NJ; Hannan, M.T., and Freeman, J. (1977) The Population Ecology of Organizations, *American Journal of Sociology*, March, pp. 929–64.
2. Nelson, R.R., and Winter, S.G. (1982) *An Evolutionary Theory of Economic Change*, Harvard University Press; Baum, A.C., and Singh, J.V. (1994) (eds), *Evolutionary Dynamics of Organizations*, Oxford University Press, New York.
3. Spender, J.C. (1989) *Industry Recipes – An Enquiry into the Nature and Sources of Managerial Judgment*, Basil Blackwell, New York.
4. Hamel, G. (1996) Strategy as Revolution, *Harvard Business Review*, July/August; Hamel, G., and Prahalad, C.K. (1994) *Competing for the Future*, Harvard Business School Press, Boston.
5. Astley, W.G., and van der Ven, A.H. (1983) Central perspectives and debates in organization theory, *Administrative Science Quarterly*, Vol. 28, pp. 245–73; Hrebiniak, L.G., and Joyce, W.F. (1985) Organizational adaptation: Strategic choice and environmental determinism, *Administrative Science Quarterly*, Vol. 30, pp. 336–49; Wilson, D.C. (1992) *A Strategy of Change*, Routledge, London.
6. Op. cit., note 3.
7. Porter, M.E. (1980) *Competitive Strategy: Techniques for Analyzing Industries and Competitors*, Free Press, New York.
8. Baden-Fuller, C.W.F., and Stopford, J.M. (1992) *Rejuvenating the Mature Business*, Routledge, London, pp. 13–34.
9. Op. cit., note 7.
10. Rumelt, R. (1991) How Much Does Industry Matter?, *Strategic Management Journal*, March, pp. 167–86.
11. Buzzell, R.D., and Gale, B.T. (1987) *The PIMS Principles: Linking Strategy to Performance*, Free Press, New York.
12. Op. cit., note 11.
13. Schmalensee, R. (1985) Do Markets Differ Much?, *American Economic Review*, June, pp. 341–51.
14. Hall, W.K., (1980) Survival Strategies in a Hostile Environment, *Harvard Business Review*, September/October, pp. 75–85.
15. Miller, D., Kets de Vries, M. and Toulouse, J.M. (1982) Top Executive Locus of Control and Its Relationship to Strategy-making Structure and Environment, *Academy of Management Journal*, Vol. 25, pp. 237–53.
16. Hampden-Turner, C., and Trompenaars, A. (1993) *The Seven Cultures of Capitalism: Value Systems for Creating Wealth in the United States, Japan, Germany, France, Britain, Sweden and the Netherlands*, Doubleday, New York; Lessem, R., and Neubauer, F.F. (1994) *European Management Systems*, McGraw-Hill, London.

Chapter 9

1. Hannan, M.T., and Freeman, J. (1977) The Population Ecology of Organizations, *American Journal of Sociology*, March, p. 929–64; Rumelt, R.P. (1995) Inertia and Transformation, in: Montgomery, C.A. (ed.), *Resource-based and Evolutionary Theories of the Firm: Towards a Synthesis*, Kluwer Academic Publishers, Boston, pp. 101–32.
2. Johnson, G. (1988) Rethinking Incrementalism, *Strategic Management Journal*, January/February, pp. 75–91.
3. Bennis, W., and Nanus, B. (1985) *Leaders: The Strategies for Taking Charge*, Harper & Row, New York; Kelley, R.E. (1988) In Praise of Followers, *Harvard Business Review*, November–December.
4. Kotter, J.P. (1990) What Leaders Really Do, *Harvard Business Review*, May–June, pp. 103–11; Nanus, B. (1992) *Visionary Leadership: Creating a Compelling Sense of Direction for Your Organization*, Jossey-Bass, San Francisco.
5. Tichy, N., and Devanna, M. (1987) *The Transformational Leader*, Wiley, New York; Senge, P. (1990) *The Fifth Discipline: The Art and Practice of the Learning Organization*, Doubleday, New York.
6. Finkelstein, S. (1992) Power in Top Management Teams: Dimensions, Measurement, and Validation, *Academy of Management Journal*, Vol. 35, pp. 505–38; Hambrick, D.C., and Mason, P.A. (1984) Upper Echelons: The Organization as a Reflection of Its Top Managers, *Academy of Management Review*, Vol. 9, pp. 193–206.
7. Chandler, A.D. (1962) *Strategy and Structure: Chapters in the History of the American Industrial Enterprise*, MIT Press, Cambridge, MA.
8. Chen, C.C., and Meindl, J.R. (1991) The Construction of Leadership Images in the Popular Press: The Case of Donald Burr and People Express, *Administrative Science Quarterly*, Vol. 36, pp. 521–51; Kets de Vries, M.F.R. (1994) The Leadership Mystique, *Academy of Management Executive*, Vol. 8, pp. 73–92.
9. Meindl, J.R., Ehrlich, S.B. and Dukerich, J.M. (1985) The Romance of Leadership, *Administrative Science Quarterly*, 30, March, pp. 78–102; Pfeffer, J. (1977) The Ambiguity of Leadership, *Academy of Management Review*, Vol. 2, pp. 104–12.
10. Calder, B. (1977) An Attribution Theory of Leadership, in Staw, B., and Salanck, B. (eds.), *New Directions in Organizational Behavior*, St. Clair, Chicago; Sims, H.P., and Lorenzi, P. (1992) *The New Leadership Paradigm: Social Learning and Cognition in Organizations*, Sage, London.
11. Allison, G. (1969) Conceptual Models and The Cuban Missile Crisis, *The American Political Science Review*, No. 3, September, pp. 689–718; Pettigrew, A. (1985) *The Awakening Giant*, Blackwell, Oxford.
12. Weick, K.E. (1979) *The Social Psychology of Organizing*, Random House, New York.
13. Smircich, L., and Stubbart, C. (1985) Strategic Management in an Enacted World, *Academy of Management Review*, Vol. 10, pp. 724–36; op. cit., note 2.
14. Barney, J.B. (1991) Firm Resources and Sustained Competitive Advantage,

Journal of Management, Vol. 17, No. 1, pp. 99–120; Leonard-Barton, D. (1995) *Well-Springs of Knowledge: Building and Sustaining the Sources of Innovation*, Harvard Business School Press, Boston.

15. Pfeffer, J. (1982) *Organizations and Organization Theory*, Pitman, Boston; Leavy, B., and Wilson, D. (1994) *Strategy and Leadership*, Routledge, London.
16. Nelson, R.R., and Winter, S.G. (1982) *An Evolutionary Theory of Economic Change*, Harvard University Press, Reading, MA; Baum, J.A.C., and Singh, J.V. (1994) Organizational Hierarchies and Evolutionary Processes: Some Reflections on a Theory of Organizational Evolution, in Baum, J.A.C., and Singh, J.V. (eds), *Evolutionary Dynamics of Organizations*, Oxford University Press, Oxford.
17. Miller, D., and Friesen, P.H. (1980) Momentum and Revolution in Organizational Adaptation, *Academy of Management Journal*, Vol. 23, pp. 591–614; Tushman, M.L., Newman, W.H., and Romanelli, E. (1986) Convergence and Upheaval: Managing the Unsteady Pace of Organizational Evolution, *California Management Review*, Vol. 29, No. 1, Fall, pp. 29–44.
18. Christensen, C.R., Andrews, K.R., Bower, J.L., Hamermesh, R.G., and Porter, M.E. (1982) (1987) *Business Policy: Text and Cases*, 5th and 6th edns, Irwin, Homewood, IL.
19. Stacey, R.D. (1993) Strategy as Order Emerging from Chaos, *Long Range Planning*, Vol. 26, No.1, pp. 10–17.
20. Kakabadse, A., Myers, A., McMahon, T. and Spony, G. (1995) Top Management Styles in Europe: Implications for Business and Cross-National Teams, *European Business Journal*, Vol. 7, pp. 17–27.
21. Hampden-Turner, C., and Trompenaars, A. (1993) *The Seven Cultures of Capitalism: Value Systems for Creating Wealth in the United States, Japan, Germany, France, Britain, Sweden, and the Netherlands*, Doubleday, New York; Lessem, R., and Neubauer, F.F. (1994) *European Management Systems*, McGraw-Hill, London.
22. Hofstede, G. (1993) Cultural Constraints in Management Theories, *Academy of Management Executive*, Vol. 7, No. 1.

Chapter 10

1. Ohmae, K. (1990) *The Borderless World: Power and Strategy in the Interlinked Economy*, Fontana, London.
2. Bartlett, C.A., and Ghoshal, S. (1995) *Transnational Management: Text, Cases, and Readings in Cross-Border Management*, second edition, R.D. Irwin Inc.
3. Dosi, G., and Kogut, B. (1993) National Specificities and the Context of Change: 'The Co-evolution of Organization and Technology', in Kogut, B. (ed.), *Country Competitiveness: Technology and the Organizing of Work*, Oxford University Press, Oxford.
4. Op. cit., note 2.

5. Hedlund, G. (1986) The Hypermodern MNC – A Heterarchy? *Human Resource Management*, Vol. 25, pp. 9–35.
6. Prahalad, C.K., and Doz, Y. (1987) *The Multinational Mission: Balancing Local Demands and Global Vision*, Free Press, New York; Bartlett, C.A., and Ghoshal, S. (1987) Managing across Borders: New Organizational Responses, *Sloan Management Review*, Fall, pp. 43–53.
7. Porter, M.E. (1990) New Global Strategies for Competitive Advantage, *Planning Review*, May/June, pp. 4–14; Bartlett and Ghoshal, 1987, op. cit., note 6.
8. Kay, J. (1989) Myths and Realities, in Davis, E. *et al.* (eds), *1992, Myths and Realities*, Centre for Business Strategy, London; Krugman, P.R. (1990) *Rethinking International Trade*, MIT Press.
9. McGrew, A.G. *et al.* (eds) (1992) *Global Politics: Globalisation and the Nation-State*, Polity Press, Cambridge; Milner, H. (1988) *Resisting Protectionism: Global Industries and the Politics of International Trade*, Princeton University Press, Princeton; Reich, R. (1991) *The Work of Nations: Preparing Ourselves for 21st Century Capitalism*, Alfred Knopf, New York.
10. Dunning, J. (1986) *Japanese Participation in British Industry: Trojan Horse or Catalyst for Growth?*, Croom Helm, Dover, NH; Kogut, B. (ed.) (1993) *Country Competitiveness: Technology and the Organizing of Work*, Oxford University Press, Oxford.
11. Pitt, M. (1996) IKEA of Sweden: the Global Retailer, in Baden-Fuller, C., and Pitt, M. (eds) *Strategic Innovation*, Routledge, London.
12. Levitt, T. (1983) The Globalization of Markets, *Harvard Business Review*, May/June, pp. 92–102.
13. Douglas, S.P., and Wind, Y. (1987) The Myth of Globalization, *Columbia Journal of World Business*, Winter, pp. 19–29.
14. Calori, R., Valla, J.-P., and de Woot, Ph. (1994) Common Characteristics: The Ingredients of European Management, in Calori, R., and de Woot, Ph. (eds) *A European Management Model*, Prentice Hall, London; Turcq, D. (1994) Is There a US Company Management Style in Europe?, in Calori, R., and de Woot Ph. (eds), *A European Management Model*, Prentice-Hall, London; Yoneyama, E. (1994) Japanese Subsidiaries: Strengths and Weaknesses, in Calori, R., and de Woot Ph. (eds), *A European Management Model*, Prentice-Hall, London.

Chapter 11

1. Rappaport, A. (1986) *Creating Shareholder Value: The New Standard for Business Performance*, The Free Press, New York, p. xiii, reading 11.1 is adapted from ch. 1 of this work.
2. Hart, O.D. (1995) *Firms, Contracts and Financial Structure*, Clarendon Press, Oxford; Rappaport, op. cit., note 1.
3. Charkham, J. (1994) *Keeping Good Company: A Study of Corporate Governance in Five Countries*, Oxford University Press, Oxford; Sykes, A. (1994)

Proposals for Internationally Competitive Corporate Governance in Britain and America, *Corporate Governance*, Vol. 2, No. 4, pp. 187–95.

4. Jensen, M.C., and Meckling, W.H. (1976) Theory of the Firm, Managerial Behavior, Agency Costs, and Ownership Structure, *Journal of Financial Economics*, October, pp. 305–60; Eisenhardt, K.M. (1989) Agency Theory: An Assessment and Review, *Academy of Management Review*, Vol. 14, pp. 57–74.

5. Friedman, M. (1970) The Social Responsibility of Business is to Increase Its Profits, *The New York Times Magazine*, September 13 puts forward the classic argument (Reprinted in Hoffman, W.M., and J.M. Moore (eds), *Business Ethics*, McGraw-Hill, New York, 1990).

6. Berle, A.A., and Means, G.C. (1932) *The Modern Corporation and Private Property*, Transaction Publishers, (reprinted 1991); Freeman, R.E., and Reed, D.L. (1983) Stockholders and Stakeholders: A New Perspective on Corporate Governance, *California Management Review*, Vol. 25, No.3, Spring, pp. 88–106. This article is presented as reading 11.2 in this book.

7. Stone, C.D. (1975) *Where the Law Ends*, Harper & Row, New York.

8. Clarkson, M.B.E. (1995) A Stakeholder Framework For Analyzing and Evaluating Corporate Social Performance, *Academy of Management Review*, Vol. 20, pp. 92–117; Alkhafaji, A.F. (1989) *A Stakeholder Approach to Corporate Governance: Managing a Dynamic Environment*, Quorum Books, Westport, CT.

9. Buono, A.F., and Nichols, L.T. (1985) *Corporate Policy, Values and Social Responsibility*, Praeger, New York; Donaldson, T., and Preston, L.E. (1995) The Stakeholder Theory of the Corporation: Concepts, Evidence, and Implications, *Academy of Management Review*, Vol. 20, pp. 65–91.

10. Jones, T.M. (1995) Instrumental Stakeholder Theory: A Synthesis of Ethics and Economics, *Academy of Management Review*, Vol. 20, pp. 404–37; Solomon, R.C. (1992) *Ethics and Excellence: Cooperation and Integrity in Business*, Oxford University Press, New York.

11. Campbell, A., and Yeung, S. (1991) Creating a Sense of Mission, *Long Range Planning*, August, pp. 10–20; Collins, J.C., and Porras, J. (1994) *Built To Last: Successful Habits of Visionary Companies*, Random House, London.

12. Carroll, A.B. (1993) *Business and Society: Ethics and Stakeholder Management*, 2nd edn, South-Western Publishing, Cincinnati; Langtry, B. (1994) Stakeholders and the Moral Responsibilities of Business, *Business Ethics Quarterly*, Vol. 4, pp. 431–43.

13. Guthrie, J., and Turnbull, S. (1994) Audit Committees: Is There a Role for Corporate Senates and/or Stakeholder Councils?, *Corporate Governance: An International Review*, Vol. 3, pp. 78–89.

14. Bucholz, R.A. (1986) *Business Environment and Public Policy*, Prentice-Hall, Englewood Cliffs; Blair, M. (1995) *Ownership and Control: Rethinking Corporate Governance for the Twenty-First Century*, Brookings Institution, Washington.

15. Epstein, E.M. (1987) The Corporate Social Policy Process: Beyond Business Ethics, Corporate Social Responsibility, and Corporate Social Responsiveness, *California Management Review*, Vol. 29, Spring, pp. 99–114; Wartick, S.L., and Wood, D.J. (1997) *International Business and Society*, Blackwell, Oxford.

16. Cummings, S., and Davies, J. (1994) Mission, Vision, Fusion, *Long Range Planning*, Vol. 27, No. 6, pp. 147–50.
17. McCoy, C.S. (1985) *Management of Values*, Ballinger, Cambridge, MA; Collins and Porras, op. cit., note 11.
18. Falsey, T.A. (1989) *Corporate Philosophies and Mission Statements*, Quorum Books, New York; Hoffman, W.M. (1989) The Cost of a Corporate Conscience, *Business and Society Review*, Spring, pp. 46–7.
19. Abell, D. (1980) *Defining the Business – The Starting Point of Strategic Planning*, Prentice-Hall, Englewood Cliffs; Pearce, J.A. (1982) The Company Mission as a Strategic Tool, *Sloan Management Review*, Spring, pp. 15–24.
20. Bartlett, C.A., and Ghoshal, S. (1994) Changing the Role of Top Management: Beyond Strategy to Purpose, *Harvard Business Review*, November–December, pp. 79–88; Hamel, G., and Prahalad, C.K. (1989) Strategic Intent, *Harvard Business Review*, May/June, pp. 63–77.
21. Op. cit., note 11.
22. David, F.R. (1989) How Companies Define Their Mission, *Long Range Planning*, Vol. 22, No. 1, pp. 90–7; Piercy, N.F., and Morgan, N.A. (1994) Mission Analysis: An Operational Approach, *Journal of General Management*, Vol. 19, No. 3, pp. 1–16.
23. Op. cit., note 16.
24. Collins, J.C., and Porras, J. (1996) Building Your Company's Vision, *Harvard Business Review*, September–October, pp. 65–77; Senge, P.M. (1990) The Leader's New Work: Building Learning Organizations, *Sloan Management Review*, Fall, pp. 7–23.
25. Tricker, R.I. (1994) *International Corporate Governance: Text, Readings and Cases*, Prentice-Hall, Singapore, p. xi.
26. Cochran, Ph.L., and Wartick, S.L. (1994) Corporate Governance – A Review of the Literature, in Tricker, R.I., *International Corporate Governance: Text, Readings and Cases*, Prentice-Hall, Singapore; Keasey, K., Thompson, S. and Wright, M. (eds) (1997) *Corporate Governance: Economic, Management, and Financial Issues*, Oxford University Press, Oxford.
27. Mintzberg, H. (1984) Who Should Control the Corporation?, *California Management Review*, Vol. 27, Fall, pp. 90–115; Demb, A., and Neubauer, F.F. (1992) *The Corporate Board: Confronting the Paradoxes*, Oxford University Press, Oxford.
28. Adapted from op. cit., note 25.
29. Yoshimori, M. (1995) Whose Company Is It? The Concept of the Corporation in Japan and the West, *Long Range Planning*, Vol. 28, pp. 33–45. See also Freeman and Reed, op. cit., note 6.
30. Baysinger, B.D., and Hoskisson, R.E. (1990) The Composition of Boards of Directors and Strategic Control: Effects of Corporate Strategy, *Academy of Management Review*, Vol. 15, pp. 72–81; Donaldson, L., and Davis, J.H. (1995) Boards and Company Performance – Research Challenges the Conventional Wisdom, *Corporate Governance: An International Review*, Vol. 2, pp. 151–60; Zahra, S.A., and Pearce, J.A. (1989) Boards of Directors and Corporate Financial Performance: A Review and Integrative Model, *Journal of Management*, Vol. 15, pp. 291–334.

31. Parkinson, J.E. (1993) *Corporate Power and Responsibility*, Oxford University Press, Oxford; Spencer, A. (1983) *On the Edge of the Organization: The Role of the Outside Director*, Wiley, New York.
32. Op. cit., note 1.
33. Rappaport, A. (1990) The Staying Power of the Public Corporation, *Harvard Business Review*, January–February.
34. Op. cit., note 6.
35. Freeman, R.E. (1984) *Strategic Management: A Stakeholder Approach*, Pitman/Ballinger, Boston.
36. Freeman, R.E., and Gilbert Jr., D.R. (1988) *Corporate Strategy and the Search for Ethics*, Prentice-Hall, Englewood Cliffs; Freeman, R.E., and Liedtka, J. (1991) Corporate Social Responsibility: A Critical Approach, *Business Horizons*, July–August.
37. Op. cit., note 27.
38. Op. cit., note 6.
39. Peters, T.J., and Waterman, R.H. (1982) *In Search of Excellence*, Harper & Row, New York.
40. Treynor, J.L. (1981) The Financial Objective in the Widely Held Corporation, *Financial Analysts Journal*, March–April, pp. 68–71.
41. Op. cit., note 6.
42. Barnard, C. (1938) *The Function of the Executive*, Harvard University Press, Cambridge, MA.
43. Ansoff, I. (1965) *Corporate Strategy*, McGraw-Hill, New York, pp. 33–5.
44. Ackoff, R.L. (1974) *Redesigning the Future*, John Wiley & Sons, New York.
45. Dill, W.R. (1975) Public Participation in Corporate Planning: Strategic Management in a Kibitzer's World, *Long Range Planning*, pp. 57–63.
46. Ackermann, R.W., and Bauer, R.A. (1976) *Corporate Social Performance: The Modern Dilemma*, Reston, Reston, VA.
47. Hayes, R., and Abernathy, W. (1980) Managing Our Way to Economic Decline, *Harvard Business Review*, Vol. 58, No.4, pp. 67–77.
48. Albach, H. (1994) Wertewandel Deutscher Manager, in Albach (Ed.), *Werte und Unternehmensziele im Wandel der Zeit.*
49. Drucker, P.F. (1991) Reckoning with the Pension Fund Revolution, *Harvard Business Review*, March–April, pp. 106–14.
50. Porter, M.E. (1980) *Competitive Strategy: Techniques for Analyzing Industries and Competitors*, Free Press, New York.
51. Suzuki, S., and Wright, R.W. (1985) Financial Structure and Bankruptcy Risk in Japanese Companies, *Journal of International Business Studies*, Spring, pp. 97–110.
52. Abbeglen, J., and Stalk, G. (1985) *Kaisha, the Japanese Corporation*, Basic Books, New York.
53. Rechner, P.L., and Dalton, D.R. (1989) The Impact of CEO as Board Chairperson on Corporate Performance: Evidence vs. Rhetoric, *The Academy of Management Executive*, Vol. III, No.2, pp. 141–3.
54. Gerum, E. (1991) Aufsichtratstypen – Ein Beitrag zur Theorie der Organisation der Unternehmungsführung, *Die Betriebswirtschaft*, No.6.
55. Op. cit., note 54.
56. Cadbury, A. (1990) *The Company Chairman*, Fitzwilliam Publishing, Cambridge.

57. Charreaux, G., and Pitol-Belin, J. (1990) *Le Conseil d'Administration*.
58. Bassiry, G.R., and Denkmejian, H. (1990) The American Corporate Elite: A Profile, *Business Horizons*, May–June.
59. Bleicher, K. (1987) *Der Aufsichtsrat im Wandel*, Verlag Bertelsmann-Stiftung, Guetersloh.
60. Nash, T. (1990) Bit Parts and Board Games, *Director*, October.
61. Bertolus, J., and Morin, F. (1987) Conseil d'Administration, *Science et Vie Économie*, 33, November.
62. Kotter, J.P., and Heskett, J.L. (1992) *Corporate Culture and Performance*.
63. Rathenau, W. (1923) *Vom Aktienwesen, eine geschäftliche Betrachtung*, Fischer, Berlin.
64. Op. cit., note 6.
65. Cordiner, R. (195).
66. Op. cit., note 63.
67. Op. cit., note 6.
68. Op. cit., note 33.

Index